Web Server Programming

Web Server Programming

Neil Gray

University of Wollongong

WILEY

Library of Congress Cataloging-in-Publication Data

Gray, Neil A. B.
    Web server programming / Neil Gray.
       p. cm.
    ISBN 0-470-85097-3 (Paper : alk. paper)
  1. Web servers. 2. Web site development. 3. Internet programming.
I. Title.
    TK5105.888.G719 2003
    005.2'76--dc21

                                          2003006942

British Library Cataloguing in Publication Data

A catalogue record for this book is available from the British Library

ISBN 0 470 85097 3

Typeset in 10/12 pt Times by Ian Kingston Editorial Services, Nottingham, UK

This book is printed on acid-free paper responsibly manufactured from sustainable forestry in which at least two trees are planted for each one used for paper production.

Contents

Preface

This text aims to give you an understanding of the technologies that will be of importance to you if you go on to work in web-application development.

The assumed background for readers of this book is:

- Basic familiarity with the Internet, use of browsers, and an understanding of the role of a web server that returns static and dynamic web pages.

- A working knowledge of HTML.

- An awareness of the role of client-side scripting languages (e.g. JavaScript), though not necessarily programming experience with this technology.

- Programming experience in Java and C++ equivalent to about a one-semester course in each of these languages (C++ is not used to any significant extent in this text; it is employed solely in an example that illustrates the structure of a 'CGI' system prior to the coverage of the more generally useful Perl scripting implementations of CGI).

- Limited acquaintance with ports and sockets for network communications (e.g. completion of an exercise that uses java.net.Socket and java.net.ServerSocket classes).

- Some experience in the use of relational databases and SQL queries.

- At least one previous attempt at using Java's JDBC package to retrieve data from, and modify data in, a simple data table held in a relational database.

There are 11 chapters in this text, as described below.

Chapter 1: Introduction This chapter reviews the basics of web servers and how they handle requests for static and dynamic pages. All this material should already be familiar. HTML, the Common Gateway Interface (CGI) and the HTTP protocol are all briefly described. The chapter includes an example of a C++ CGI program that illustrates the basics of how a client's request is handled. (Appendix A has a brief presentation on HTML and client-side JavaScript.)

Chapter 2: HTTP This chapter goes into the HTTP protocol in more detail. You need some basic understanding of issues such as authorization and content negotiation.

Chapter 3: Apache This chapter introduces the webmaster's responsibilities with regard to the running of a web server. The Apache server is used as the example. You will be responsible for setting up and running such servers. You need to understand how controls can be set on the accessibility of files, and privileges extended to CGI programs.

Chapter 4: IP and DNS   This chapter provides an overview of DNS – Domain Name Services. The DNS system supplies the mapping from the domain names that are acceptable to human users to the IP address numbers that are required by the underlying network protocols. The DNS system is one of the successes of 'open source' software development and also a major example of peer-to-peer computing. The data on machine names and their addresses is simply too large, and too rapidly changing, for management by any central authority. The mapping system relies on the administrators of sub-parts of the total name space to administer their own name servers and to cooperate in supporting the overall naming system. Running your company's DNS system is unlikely to be your first task, but in time you may acquire responsibility for this system, and a basic understanding of DNS is essential for webmasters.

Chapter 5: Perl   This chapter covers the basics of programming in Perl, introduces the database interface module (DBI), and includes some limited examples of Perl as a CGI-scripting language. Though it is still widely deployed, most web sites are moving on from the Perl–CGI scripting technology. However, Perl remains important as a consequence of its original role as an 'extraction and reporting' language. While your site may use other server technologies, you will find yourself relying on Perl for many analysis and reporting tasks.

Chapter 6: PHP4   The PHP system is easy to deploy and PHP scripts are easy to write. This is the technology that you should use when helping an organization first explore the potential of an interactive web site. It is the most appropriate language for implementing most small web-based systems (unless you have a commitment to Microsoft's proprietary ASP scripting technologies). The examples here illustrate solutions to a number of standard problems for web services. They include use of sequences of forms that employ hidden data fields, file upload mechanisms, graphic output pages and use of 'cookies'. (Appendix B has a very brief introduction to Microsoft's ASP scripting technology.)

Chapter 7: Java Servlets   We now switch to Java technologies, looking first at 'servlets'. Realistically, Java systems are more complex to deploy and harder to write than are systems based on technologies like PHP. However, the Java solutions are also inherently better structured and more disciplined. There is a threshold in the scale of a web application; once you cross this threshold, you are better off adopting the Java solutions.

Chapter 8: Java Server Pages   These are not really a technology distinct from servlets. Rather, they illustrate a further refinement and separation of concerns. In a properly implemented Java Server Pages (JSP) system you will find servlets written to handle the basic logic of accepting requests from the clients, 'bean' objects that handle tasks like communicating with databases and implementing business logic, and JSPs that focus on generating the final response page using data passed in beans.

Chapter 9: XML This chapter provides a brief introduction to the eXtensible Markup Language (XML) and related technologies such as XSLT, and then illustrates a few uses, primarily in the context of Java-based web applications. Examples include JSP/XSLT combinations that can generate output either for HTML-based web browsers or for WAP phones using Wireless Markup Language.

Chapter 10: Enterprise Java This chapter provides a brief overview of Enterprise Java, along with an introduction to Enterprise JavaBeans. The aim is simply to give you an understanding of how the EJB technology extends the other Java services covered in earlier chapters, and not to teach you how to program EJBs (for that requires a minimum of a 450 page tutorial in itself). Previous acquaintance with Java RMI or other distributed object technologies will help you understand the EJB approach. (Appendix C has a brief introduction to Microsoft's .NET initiative. At one level, .NET represents a parallel alternative technology to servlets/JSPs/EJBs for large-scale web applications. At a different level, .NET offers a totally new and really rather more coherent model for the relation between browser client and web server components.)

Chapter 11: Future technologies? This chapter covers a recent success story for web support services (Akamai's 'Edge' servers), some speculations on other areas such as peer-to-peer computing and the possibilities for a 'Personal Internet Presence', and comments on the alphabet soup technologies – SOAP, UDDI, WSDL.

The material in this book is all based on 'open source' software that is available for free download via the Internet. You can do all your work on your own Windows 98/2000/XP PC – you would have to download the Windows versions of the Apache and Tomcat servers from http://www.apache.org/, Perl from http://www.activeperl.com/, PHP4 from the Apache site, the Java development kit and some extra javax components from http://java.sun.com/, XML components from the Apache site and J2EE components from Sun. Microsoft's Access database system is quite sufficient to run the examples (via ODBC drivers), but you could download a database such as MySQL. The same sites provide downloadable versions of software suitable for Linux and some Unix platforms.

The majority of the programming examples shown in the text actually use Unix (Solaris) versions of the same software; most of the database examples are based on an Oracle database. There aren't really any major changes needed to the code to adapt the examples to a private Windows system. One of the reasons for using Unix examples is that it allows consideration of the many problems that can arise relating to file permissions and other security controls that apply in a real operating system.

All the web related software systems come with extensive documentation and this text relies on you to supplement the materials given here with information taken from the relevant systems documentation. When you decompress your Apache system, you will find extensive HTML documentation and links to web-based tutorials on how to configure your server. Perl documentation may come as text files for the perldoc reader or as HTML files; in either case, you have dozens of chapters on specific aspects of Perl, all incorporating helpful worked examples. The PHP release comes with a thousand-page manual (as a PDF file); this incorporates a language reference manual and chapters on the functions in the various libraries available for PHP; all sections include illustrative examples. The Java classes for servlets and related components are all documented with the standard Javadoc style documentation. The Apache Tomcat server, used to run servlets, comes with a set of fully configured simple servlet and JSP examples. Sun's EJB kit includes a 450-page tutorial. Because these source materials are inherently available to you, this text leaves out a lot of standard reference material; for example, operator precedence tables for Perl and for PHP are not given – they would simply duplicate information you already have.

Some of the chapters include exercises. These take three forms. 'Practical' exercises involve implementing an actual web-based client–server system; these have quite lengthy specifications and are meant to require 6–18 hours of design, implementation and testing. 'Short answer' questions typify examination questions; they ask for definitions or explanations of concepts covered in the chapter. There are also a few 'exploration' exercises; these are simply suggestions for topics that can be further studied using resources available on the World Wide Web and that are suitable for report-style assignments.

Neil Gray

1

Introduction

This chapter provides a short overview of the basics of web-based services. The web changed from being a purely publishing medium to an interactive e-commerce medium around 1994/1995. The extension of HTML to include support for data-entry forms, extensions to the HTTP protocol to support security and other features, and the introduction of the Common Gateway Interface standards for web server to application communications made it practical to have web-based clients that could submit data for processing by server applications hosted on the web server.

These extensions made business-to-consumer web commerce practical. All consumers could be assumed to have standard web browsers; links between browsers and web servers could be made fairly secure; and web servers had standardized mechanisms for communicating with the applications that could interrogate and update databases, accept orders, report on delivery schedules, and so forth.

The standard web browser could also replace numerous application-specific client programs used for in-house applications in business. Starting in the late 1980s, private in-house client–server applications running on intranets had become popular; the client handled data entry and display and some or all of the business data processing, the other parts of the business processing and the database access were handled on the server. However, there were often problems with these systems; the client programs included 'business rules', but such rules are often subject to change. If the rules were changed, all copies of the client application had to be updated; such updates were often troublesome. In addition, the development team often had to implement multiple versions of the client software to suit different platforms and operating systems. Both problems could be overcome if a system was switched to a web-based architecture. The web-based system would have multiple tiers, with the browser client handling only data entry and display, middleware components handling business rules, and a back-end database for the rest. With business rules implemented in the middleware tier, changes could be more easily incorporated and security on access to the databases could be increased. The use of standard web browsers on the clients removed the need to develop client applications.

With web-based services standardized and entering widespread use, developers could rely on a relatively stable client component and focus attention on the server side. Subsequent developments of server technology have addressed ease of programming, efficiency and sophistication of the server-side environment. There are now a range of server-side technologies, some of which are presented in the rest of this text. To some degree these are competing technologies, but each does have a particular niche area where it is optimal.

The first section in this chapter reviews the basics of client–server programming based on the use of TCP/IP with the Berkeley sockets application programmer interface. These materials are covered in much more detail in Stevens' books *Advanced Programming in the Unix Environment* and *TCP/IP Illustrated*, Vols. 1–3 (Addison-Wesley). Sun's Java tutorial site has simple illustrative Java versions of network programs at http:// java.sun.com/docs/books/tutorial/networking/index.html. The next two sections of this chapter look at web-basics – first delivery of static web resources, and then an overview of technologies such as server-side includes (SSI) and CGI that were the first to support dynamically generated pages. The next section has a brief overview of the HTML used in data entry forms, and of the basic CGI rules; again, supplementary information is available on the web at sites such as http://www.wdvl.com/. CGI programming is then illustrated with a small C++ application (C++ is not commonly used to implement CGI programs; it is used here because most students will have experience in C and C++ and so should be able to read and understand the code). Finally, there is a brief section on the client-side scripting language JavaScript. Good web-based data entry forms should always incorporate JavaScript checking code; its role is simply to verify that all fields have data entered and that the data are not obviously incorrect, and so eliminate wasteful submissions of form data that will be rejected by the server. For simplicity, JavaScript checks are not included in the examples given later in the text, but you should assume that wherever practical the pages would actually include such checking code. JavaScript is another technology documented at http://www.wdvl.com/, and at other sites on the Internet (Appendix A contains a very brief overview of both HTML page layout coding and client-side JavaScript).

1.1 Servers on the Internet

Client–server systems have been operating across networks since the early days of the ARPANET back in the late 1960s. The mechanisms that are used became more or less standardized in the early 1980s. Most of the client–server systems would then have run on variants of the Unix operating system. Network communications standardized on the Internet's Transmission Control Protocol/Internet Protocol suite (TCP/IP). The most popular application programmer interface was the Berkeley 'socket' library. The major servers of the time would have included the file transfer (ftp) server, the telnet server that supported remote log in, mail and news servers, and utility programs such as echo. These servers all involve active clients initiating contact with passive servers. In most cases, the servers are always running as background daemon processes on the machine that is hosting them; the typical server daemon is in a blocked state, waiting for a client to initiate contact and request services.

The Internet Protocol (IP) defines a mechanism for getting packets of data from one machine to another across the Internet. More elaborate protocols are layered over IP. You don't want to send packets between machines; you want to exchange data between particular processes running on these machines. This is handled at the next level in the layered protocol schemes, with protocols such as UDP (User Datagram Protocol) and TCP. Both these protocols define the end points for communications between processes in terms of 'ports'. Ports are operating system resources; at a very simple level, you can view them as having an integer identifier and associated input and output data buffers. A process can claim a port. Server programs use 'well known ports'; they always claim the same port number (e.g. the ftp daemon process that handles file transfers will always claim port 21). Clients that need to use a port only for a short period get an arbitrary port allocated by the operating system. The headers for UDP and TCP packets include the IP addresses of client and server machines, and the port numbers for the client and server processes. The client composes the first packet, inserting the host's IP address once this has been determined, and the 'well known port number' for the desired service; it also inserts its own temporary port number and the IP address of the machine on which it is running. These data allow the server to send response packets that are properly addressed to the client.

The UDP protocol is relatively lightweight. It allows a client to compose a datagram and send this to a server. Usually, a datagram will arrive safely and the server will respond. The programmer has to decide what to do if there is no response, and implement code that will retry a request or abandon the attempted communications. The TCP protocol is much more elaborate. It establishes a reliable bidirectional data stream between client and server. The code in the TCP libraries deals with all the problems of communications; problems such as lost packets, timeouts, repeated packets and flow control requirements. Most client–server systems use TCP layered over IP.

The Berkeley sockets API allows programs to bind 'sockets' to ports. A normal socket is just like a connection to an input/output file that supports standard Unix read-byte and write-byte operations, along with Unix's other more specialized control options. Such data sockets are usually wrapped inside classes that support higher-level I/O operations. A server will use a 'server socket'; this is activated differently than an ordinary data socket. The operating system (OS) deals with the initial input arriving at such sockets, interpreting the data as requests by new clients seeking to establish communication. When a client connects, the OS creates a new data stream socket, and returns this to the server process. The server can then read data from the client and write responses back to the client through this data socket. There can be multiple sockets associated with a single port used by a server process; these would be the 'server socket', and various data stream sockets created for concurrent clients. The OS keeps them separated, using different I/O buffers for each socket.

Client programs have the following idealized structure:

```
Read user input with hostname for server and its well known port number
Convert hostname to IP address
Open a data stream socket connecting to the server (IP, port)
forever
    Read next command as input by user
    Compose request to server
    Write request to data stream socket
    If command was quit then break
    Read response from server
    Display response to client
Close data stream socket
Exit
```

A little crude maybe, but that pseudo-code outline captures the basic structure of telnet clients, ftp clients and even http clients.

There are a variety of server architectures. The simplest is the serial server:

```
Main()
  Create a socket ("server socket")
  Bind server socket to "well known port"
  "Listen" on server socket (activating it so that it can be used for
    client connections)
  forever do
    newDataSocket = accept(server socket, ...)
    handleClient(newDataSocket)
    close newDataSocket

handleClient(datastream)
  forever do
    command = read from datastream
    If(read-error or command==quit) then break
    Process command and generate response
    Write response to datastream
```

An 'accept' system call blocks the server process until a client connects. When the OS has completed the creation of a new TCP connection for the client, it will allow the server process to resume and returns a new data stream socket as the result of the accept call. The server can then handle the client commands, reading client inputs from this data stream socket and writing responses to the socket. When the client is finished, the data stream socket is closed and the server process again makes a blocking 'accept' call to the OS.

Serial servers are rarely used. Their great advantage is that they are very easy to implement, but this is outweighed by their limitation of being able to handle only one client at a time. The OS can queue up other clients who are waiting to connect while a current client is handled, but even with this queuing feature the serial server architecture is not very practical. Generally, you need to be capable of supporting many concurrent clients.

There are now a variety of possible architectures for concurrent servers that can handle multiple clients. One approach uses a single-threaded program that juggles activity on multiple I/O connections. Such servers are relatively efficient; they make light demands on the OS and can handle a reasonable number of clients. Unfortunately, they are rather hard to implement in a correct and robust manner. Threads moved from the exotic to the commonplace in the early 1990s; now thread libraries are standardized. Multithreaded servers are becoming much more common. With this architecture, one thread handles the main 'accept' loop. This thread is normally blocked in the accept system call. When the accept call returns with a new data stream socket, the controlling thread creates a new worker thread that handles communications over this socket. Each individual worker thread can use standard blocking read operations when reading user commands, and standard (potentially blocking) write operations when sending responses. Individual threads can be blocked without disrupting the operation of the overall server process. When a client disconnects, the thread that was used to handle that client may be terminated, or may be pooled and later reused to handle another client.

The original Unix servers were all based on the 'forking server' architecture, and this architecture still remains one of the most common. This architecture involves a 'reception-ist' process that uses the accept system call to handle client connections and a separate server process for each concurrent client. Where a threaded server simply creates a new thread in the server process to handle a new client, a 'forking' server creates a new process (the system call to create a new child process is called fork on Unix, hence the naming 'forking server'). The following pseudo-code provides a crude outline for such a server:

```
Main()
  Create a socket ("server socket")
  Bind server socket to "well known port"
  "Listen" on server socket (activating it so that it can be used for
    client connections)
  forever do
    newDataSocket = accept(server socket, ...)
    fork a new process
    if(this process is the child process) {
      close child's copy of the accept server socket
      handleClient(newDataSocket)
      close newDataSocket
      exit
    }
    else {
      close parent's copy of newDataSocket
    }

handleClient(datastream)
  forever do
    command = read from datastream
    If(read-error or command==quit) then break
    Process command and generate response
    Write response to datastream
```

There are variations on this basic architecture. The Apache server, described in Chapter 3, works with a collection of 'pre-forked' child processes; this arrangement speeds up the handling of clients (the 'fork' operation is relatively slow, taking many milliseconds). It is also possible to use the inetd daemon process to monitor the well known ports for many different servers; when a client connects to a specific port, inetd will launch a new pro-cess running the server program associated with that port. A system's administrator must choose between the use of inetd and a standard 'receptionist' daemon process; the choice is determined by factors such as performance requirements and resource demands.

Each server program has its own command repertoire, or 'application protocol'. This may be quite limited (e.g. telnet only has a couple of simple controls, and a mechanism for putting the client in contact with a Unix login shell on the server). In other cases, such as the 'file transfer protocol' (ftp), there may be many commands. Ftp has commands to login, change directory, list files, and retrieve or submit files. Each ftp command is defined by a keyword and arguments. Each has a number of possible responses defined; a response has a header line with an integer code indicating the success or failure of the command, and then further lines with data.

1.2 Serving static hypertext

Tim Berners-Lee's original 'web' had quite limited objectives. The intent was to make more accessible the various documents being generated at CERN – the European research agency in Geneva that runs the particle accelerators for the physicists studying sub-atomic structure. Like any other large organization, CERN generates numerous reports – management reports, planning reports on proposed future uses of the accelerators, experiment reports, and endless tables of results from experiments. Berners-Lee had been a long-term proponent of hypertext systems, and his vision was to have all these reports linked into a hypertext web, with readers able to navigate via links in the reports. In late 1990 he was given the chance to develop a demonstration system, working with the aid of a vacation student.

The success of Berners-Lee's approach is largely due to its simplicity. There had been earlier attempts at creating hypertext systems, but these had always resulted in complex, proprietary systems. Berners-Lee chose to use plain text documents, annotated with a simple markup language – the language that eventually became the Hypertext Markup Language (HTML). Markup languages of various forms had then been in use for some 15 years; a common use was to annotate plain text by inserting markup tags that conveyed formatting information. Many different word-processing and text-display programs can handle documents in this form. There was an agreed standard for markup languages (SGML – the Standard Generalized Markup Language) that specified how markup tags should be defined and used. Berners-Lee simplified things (a little too much in some places – HTML violates some of the SGML rules for a good markup language). He defined the basic tags that are now familiar to all (even to primary schoolchildren who these days compose web pages). His documents had head and body sections delimited by appropriate tags; formatting tags that allowed section headers of various forms to be specified; and limited paragraph controls, lists, tables, and display controls that change fonts and so forth.

The really smart part was to use markup tags for the hypertext links to related documents. The formats have changed a little, but these 'anchor' tags are familiar to web page authors:

```
<a href=source>Next month's scheduled accelerator downtimes</a>
```

The program that displayed the hypertext (the browser in modern terminology) used some mechanism to highlight the tag and to allow a user to activate this link. Such an action replaced the current document in the browser with the linked document.

The source documents for the other reports could have been on any of the machines in the CERN empire. Consequently, the source references in the hypertext links couldn't simply be file names for local files. They had to identify the source machine as well as the filename. When a link was activated, the browser program would have to connect to a file server program running on the identified machine.

The ftp file transfer protocol has been around since about 1973 (well before TCP/IP and the Internet; it has just evolved as underlying technologies have changed). The ftp protocol allows a client to login, establish a connected session, and then transfer multiple files; it actually makes use of separate control and data transfer connections using two TCP/IP links between client and server. Berners-Lee felt that ftp was too heavyweight a solution. His hypertext users would be reading a report, would get to a link and activate it, and receive a new report that they would read for many minutes before again connecting via another link (possibly a link to a different machine). There was no need for ftp's login sessions, state maintenance and capabilities for transfer of multiple files.

Instead of ftp, Berners-Lee invented a lighter-weight file transfer protocol – the Hypertext Transfer Protocol (HTTP). The HTTP client program would connect to the server machine at the port used by the HTTP server, and submit a simple text message that identified the report file that was required. The HTTP file server was a small program that could be implemented as a forking server (or even as a serial server). It would read the 'get file' request with the specified file and directory pathname, and return the file if it were available. HTTP responses had some similarities to those used in ftp, with a control line with an integer success or failure code, other header data, and then the text of the file appended in the body of the response (actually, ftp sends its content files over a separate TCP/IP link using the main link solely for control information). After serving a single file, the HTTP server process would close the connection (and, in the case of a forking server architecture, the child server process would terminate).

A simple markup language, a simple scheme for identifying resources by machine name and fully qualified file name, and a simple file server: together they constituted the basis for an eminently practical mechanism for supporting a web of hypertext reports. The HTML/HTTP scheme was presented at various conferences in 1991, and the web began its worldwide growth. By early 1993, there were around fifty HTTP web servers on the Internet, and there were about 100 Mbyte per month of HTML network traffic.

In the early days, many different web browsers and web servers competed for adoption. Most incorporated various idiosyncratic features that their authors had added to differentiate their products from those of rivals. The group at the National Center for Supercomputer Applications (NCSA) was one of the more successful. The group at NCSA, with Marc Andreessen (later of Netscape) and others, had the task of developing software for use by clients of the center, clients who used Macintoshes, PCs and various X-enabled Unix systems. The NCSA group developed a new HTTP server and compatible browsers for the different types of client machine and operating system. Extensions were also made to the markup protocol, extensions that allowed embedded images. The prettied up pages with their images greatly increased the popularity of the World Wide Web (WWW), and thousands of copies of the NCSA 'Mosaic' browsers were downloaded. The source code for the NCSA server was in the public domain and started attracting interest (the Apache web server started as a 'patched' version of the NCSA server). By late 1993, there were more than 600 web servers on the Internet and HTML traffic had grown to 200,000 Mbyte per month. Business interest in the WWW was sparked by reports appearing in the *New York Times* and *The Economist*.

Of course, additions like support for images necessitated extensions to the HTTP protocol. If a server could send text or an image (in GIF, JPEG or another image format) as its response, it would have to include some tags in the response header that would tell the browser how to interpret the data in the body of the response. With web servers on the Internet, controls on access to content became appropriate. You might want to publish some documents that were available to all Internet users, others that were available only to users working on machines within your organization, and still other documents that should only be accessed by selected users who could supply some form of name and password identification data. Access controls and authentication mechanisms had to be added to the communications protocol, and implemented in the browser and server programs. The earliest versions of the HTTP protocol were intended simply to download files using the 'get' command; later, a data upload mechanism was added with the 'put' command (like the 'put' command in ftp, this supplies the fully qualified pathname of the file where uploaded data are to be stored). The 'post' command was another addition; here, the named file in the command was a program that would process or store uploaded data. Both 'put' and 'post' commands used data supplied as the body of a request message. The HTTP protocol evolved gradually as such features were incorporated.

1.3   Serving dynamically generated hypertext

A static web is limited; it is just a medium for vanity publishing. Professors can have their research profiles on-line, high-tech savvy individuals can have 'home pages', and companies can have manuals and catalogs online. Anything more useful requires inputs from the client user, inputs that allow the user to identify more precisely the data that are to be displayed.

The first steps beyond the static web involved simple search engines. Some early browsers could display a query page that included a single text input field where a user could type a keyword. The browser would take the word entered and send it back to the server as part of a request. The request was typically composed as a URL specifying the server with a query string appended. The HTTP server might handle the request itself, or might delegate this work to a helper search program. Such simple inputs allowed a server to do things like generate dynamic pages containing links to files that were in some way associated with the keyword that the user had entered.

Another early extension allowed the HTTP web server to perform limited processing of an HTML document before the document was returned to the requesting client. Many sites had found a need for web pages that were built from several source files. In some cases, this was a matter of including the same footer on every page, a footer that included the email address of the webmaster or a company logo. In other cases, there would be a large static page plus a small segment that varied from day to day (for example, a university department might have a page with general notices that included a small segment on 'today's seminar'). Such needs could be handled by having directives in an HTML file directives such as '*include this other file here'*. (For example, the main departmental page, which was rarely edited, would contain an `include` directive referencing a `seminars.html` file that could be changed each day. This `seminars.html` file would contain just the text and formatting tags for a one-paragraph section; it would not be a complete HTML page with head and body sections.) The web server had to read the contents of an HTML file that it was about to return, and then find and process such embedded directives.

This 'server-side include' (SSI) mechanism wasn't limited just to building composite files by including components; there were a number of other options (though they did tend to be rather server-dependent). The more common SSI commands included:

- `config`

Config commands can be used to define the formats used for other SSI commands that do things like print times and dates. They don't result in any text being inserted into the enclosing HTML page.

- `echo`

An echo command can be used to get values of environment variables printed in the page.

- `fsize`

An `fsize` command outputs the size of a specified file (using a `sizefmt` format specification: either a default one, or one set by an earlier `config` command).

- `flastmod`

A `flastmod` command prints the last modification date of the specified file.

- `include`

An `include` command inserts the text of another document or file into the parsed file.

- `exec`

The exec command executes a given shell command or CGI script.

- `cmd *string*`

The server executes the given string using `/bin/sh`.

As an example, a bank or a travel agency could have a large static page that included a small regularly updated section on exchange rates. The main page could be coded as an HTML page with the following section that has embedded SSI commands:

```
<hr>
Exchange rates:
<br>
<size -1>
As of:
<!--#flastmod file="exchange.txt"-->
<size +1>
<br>
<!--#include file="exchange.txt"-->
<hr>
```

This results in a response page displayed on the user's browser that has the exchange rates and a time stamp indicating how recently the rates were updated.

The last two SSI directives, exec and cmd, made use of the fact that on Unix it is very easy to fork a child process, give it some work, and capture its outputs. These commands allowed essentially arbitrary programs to be run as child processes of the web server. These programs could generate dynamic content for pages.

The SSI mechanisms became increasingly elaborate (and increasingly divergent across different implementations of web servers). Some 'extended SSI' implementations allowed for conditional processing with tests on values of environment variables; allowing HTML pages to include server-side code such as the following code that customizes a page according to the location of the client:

```
<!--#if expr="\"$REMOTE_HOST\" = /.*uk/" -->
   <p>Visit our new store in Oxford Street, London.
 <!--#elif expr="\"$REMOTE_HOST\" = /.*au/" -->
   <p>Opening soon in Sydney and Melbourne.
 <!--#else -->
   <p>We have stores in Chicago, Los Angeles, New York, Paris, London, ...
 <!--#endif -->
```

Other extensions included loop constructs, and even mechanisms for submitting SQL queries that were run by databases with the results being embedded in a finalized HTML page. For example, the Jigsaw web server from W3C (late 1990s) could exploit Java's JDBC database package, so allowing code like:

```
<!--#jdbc select="SELECT * FROM top10offers"
   name="result" driver="com.opendb.sql.msql.MsqlDriver"
   url="jdbc:msql://www.xyz.com/top10offers" -->
<!--#jdbc name="result" next="true" -->
<p>Title :
<!--#jdbc name ="result" column="1" -->
cost <!--#jdbc name ="result" column="2" -->
```

SSI mechanisms of various forms are still supported in common web servers. The approach taken with extended-SSI was pursued further, leading to proprietary mechanisms such as the Cold Fusion Markup Language (cfm – lots of server-side features embedded in web documents). Microsoft's Active Server Page scripting technology also stems from the original SSI mechanism.

Although SSI in its various forms could support dynamic pages, the versions available in the mid-1990s were not satisfactory. User input mechanisms were too limited and the facilities offered by different web servers and browsers were too varied. Before industry and commerce could really adopt the web, the mechanisms had to become more standardized. Furthermore, there had to be some security features, such as encryption of client–server communications. Most companies were reluctant to transmit commercial data, and things like credit card numbers, in plain text messages that could get stored in disk buffers, and would travel across network connections that were open to 'sniffer' programs that hackers could deploy to monitor traffic.

The extensions that lead to the modern web came in 1994 with standard 'form' input extensions for the HTML markup language, the standardized Common Gateway Interface (CGI), and the Secure Socket Layer (SSL). These were all combined in the Netscape browser and server available from early 1995.

The SSL is just an extra layer in the protocol stack, coming between the TCP network protocol and the HTTP application protocol levels. With SSL-aware browsers and web servers, there is an extra step taken after a TCP connection is established and before the web server program starts to read client requests. This extra step involves the browser and web server programs negotiating an encryption key that will be used for their data exchanges. The level of encryption is unlikely to deter the NSA, but is quite sufficient to prevent casual hackers from discovering the content of messages (it is easier for hackers to break the security on poorly configured web server machines and download files).

The 'form' extensions to HTML allowed browsers to display pages very much like the input dialog boxes already familiar to Windows and Macintosh users. These pages could contain input text fields, and controls allowing for selection amongst predefined options (radio button controls for sets of mutually exclusive options and checkboxes or menu lists for multiple choice options). An action button in a form allowed the user to submit the entered data for processing on the server. The browser would take the data from the various input fields, encode them for transmission, and return the encoded data to the URL defined as an attribute in the now standardized 'form' tag. The data were returned as a set of *name=value* pairs, with the names taken from the name attributes of the input controls in the form. The pairs are appended to form a string, with an ampersand character used as a separator. (The encoding of data for transmission is not a security encryption; it is simply a letter substitution scheme that avoids potential problems with input values that include characters with special meanings in network protocols, or characters such as newline that would disrupt the structure of an HTTP header. The encoding scheme, x-www-urlencoded, substitutes '+' characters for any spaces in strings, and changes all characters other than alphanumerics into escaped sequences of the form %*xx* with the *xx* hexadecimal digits encoding the character's bit pattern).

CGI's contribution was to standardize the relationship between the web server and a child process forked to handle information entered in a form. The CGI specification defined the data that would get passed to the child process, and the formats for these data. It also defined how the web server would take the output from the child process, add a HTTP header and return these data as the response sent to a client.

With forms allowing substantial user input via browsers, and CGI standards for how to transfer data to and from processing programs, e-commerce became practical. Web browsers provided a universal user interface, allowing developers to focus on the server side.

1.4 Forms and CGI

Forms in web pages group the controls provided for user input. Normally, a data entry page will contain only a single form, but it is possible to have pages with more than one independently handled form. The data that are returned when a form is 'submitted' comprise the information entered into each of the input controls declared within the starting <form ...> and ending </form> tags. A form does not determine the layout of the input controls in the browser window; other HTML tags, such as table tags, can be used to arrange the input controls, along with any associated labels or other surrounding text.

The form tag has a number of attributes; these include:

- action

The action attribute supplies the URL of the program that will process the submitted data.

- method

The method attribute specifies how form data are transferred, either as 'get' or 'post'. With the get method, the *name=value* pairs are appended to the URL as a 'query string'; the post method encloses these data in the body of the HTTP request message.

Generally, the post method is preferred. The data are not as exposed to view, and there is less chance of problems with large inputs (the size of a query string may be limited in some server implementations). The only advantage of the get mechanism is that it does allow a user to 'bookmark' a submission so that the same request can be resubmitted on another occasion. The CGI specifies different ways of transferring 'get' and 'post' data from web server to processing program.

Input controls include:

- Standard 'submit' and 'reset' buttons

```
<input type=submit value="Place order">
<input type=reset>
```

- Checkboxes (non-exclusive choices)

```
Where have you seen details of our special offer?
<input type=checkbox name=source value="Newspaper">
<input type=checkbox name=source value="TV">
<input type=checkbox name=source value="WWW">
```

Each checkbox that is selected will result in another *name=value* pair being sent, e.g. source=TV&source=WWW. The 'checked' attribute can be used to pre-select a checkbox.

- Radio buttons (exclusive choices)

```
<input type=radio name=size value="Regular">
<input type=radio name=size value="Large">
```

As well as being used when submitting data, the name attribute is used by the browser to identify those buttons that form a group. The browser will apply the 'mutual exclusion' rule; when a radio button is selected, the browser deselects any previously selected button in the same group.

- Text (short textual inputs)

```
<input type=text name=email size=30 maxlength=128>
```

The size defines the approximate width (in characters) of the display field in the browser window; the maxlength attribute limits the amount of data that a user can enter.

- Password

```
<input type=password name=passwd size=10 maxlength=8>
```

A password input control simply doesn't echo characters as they are typed. It doesn't apply any encryption, and if the form uses method=get the password appears in the query string of the URL.

- Text area

```
<textarea cols=... rows=... name=...>
text that appears as initial editable content
</textarea>
```

A text area can be used for larger text inputs; it is displayed as a (scrollable) editable region within the browser window. (There are no limits on the amount of input; so it is possible for a user to enter so much data that the maximum length of a query string is exceeded.)

- Menu selection

```
<select>...</select>
```

A select tag set groups multiple option tags. Its own attributes include a name (used to identify the submitted data values), an optional multiple attribute that indicates that multiple selections are permitted, and a size attribute that specifies the number of option choices that should be visible in the browser window. Most browsers display 'selection' input controls as scrolling list boxes.

```
<select name=choice1 size=4 multiple>
  <option selected>string
  ...
  <option>string
</select>
```

Options can have a selected attribute (pre-selects the option), and a value attribute (if provided, this value is used in the *name=value* data sent to the server; otherwise the option string is used as the value). An </option> tag is not required and so is usually omitted.

Many of these controls have additional attributes. For example, there is a tabindex attribute (tabindex=*number*) that can be used to define the order in which input controls are activated if the user navigates among them by using the tab key. As will be discussed briefly in Section 1.6, controls can be associated with 'events' that trigger the invocation of client-side JavaScript code. (There are many HTML tutorials on the web that provide more details about forms; one such site is http://www.wdvl.com/.)

The following pizza order form illustrates a few of these input controls:

```
<form action="http://www.dontdeliverpizzas.com/order.cgi"
  name=pizzaform
  method=POST >
Pizza size<br>
Regular <input type=radio name=p_size value=reg><br>
Family <input type=radio name=p_size value=fam><br>
Popular <input type=radio checked name=p_size value=pop><br>
<p>
Toppings
<select name=tops size=3 multiple>
  <option>Cheese
  <option>Pepperoni
  ...
  <option>Sun dried tomatoes
</select>
Extras
<select name=xtra size=1 multiple>
  <option selected>Coke
  <option>Ice cream
  ...
  <option>Salad
</select>
<hr>
<em>You MUST fill in the following fields:</em>
<p>
Your name
<input type=text size=20 maxlength=50 name=customer >
<p>
Address
<textarea name=address cols=40 rows =3 >
Enter your address here please!
</textarea>
<hr>
<input type=submit value="Place Order">
</form>
```

If this form were submitted, a browser would compose an HTTP post message something like the following, and send this to the default HTTP port (80) at the host machine with domain name http://www.dontdeliverpizzas.com/:

```
POST http://www.dontdeliverpizzas.com/order.cgi HTTP/1.1
```

```
USER-AGENT: ...
ACCEPT: text/plain, text/html
```
Various other header fields as per HTTP/1.1 specification, then a
*   blank line*

```
p_size=fam&tops=Cheese&tops=Sun+dried+tomatoes&xtra=Coke&customer=
Smith&...
```

The web server that receives such a request has to recognize it as a command to run a program, rather than an attempt to retrieve a file. A typical web server is configured to have most CGI programs in a cgi-bin subdirectory in one of the directories associated with the web server; all requests referencing files in this cgi-bin directory are interpreted as commands to run programs. Provided there is some scheme whereby the server can identify them, CGI programs can be located in other directories as well; recognition is often based on something like the use of a file extension such as .cgi. (Chapter 3 contains a few more details, using the Apache web server as an example.) The web server process dealing with the client would fork a new process to handle the request.

When a process forks, the child process starts with a copy of the same code as the parent process; in this case, it would be a copy of the web server program. Of course, the child process has to run a different program, either a CGI program written in C/C++ then compiled and linked to give an executable, or an interpreter for a CGI program written using shell script or Perl script. A process can change the code image that it is running by using the exec system call to load code from a different executable file. (There are a few messy details relating to handling the input/output connections; these have to be dealt with before the exec system call is made. Details are given in Stevens' books.) Like fork, the exec system call is not cheap; there is an additional delay as the disk is accessed and the code is loaded. When the process finally restarts, at the beginning of the main of the newly loaded program, it has to be able to pick up the data with the client's request, and it also has to be able to return its outputs to the web server.

The Common Gateway Interface defined rules for these data transfers between web server and CGI program. Two mechanisms are used; these are 'pipes' connecting the two processes, and environment variables that the web server sets on behalf of the CGI program. A pipe is simply a memory buffer; one process can write to this buffer, and the other process reads from the buffer. A CGI process is always configured so that its stdout (cout) output stream writes to a pipe, with the output data being read from this pipe by the web server process. If a HTTP request is made using the get method, the CGI program will receive all its inputs as values of environment variables. If the request uses the post method, the *name=value* data are transferred via a second pipe joining web server and CGI program. The web server writes all *name=value* data to this pipe; a CGI program is configured so that this pipe connects to its stdin (cin) input stream, allowing it to read the data from its stdin.

Environment variables again take the form of *name=value* pairs. Environment variables are used very extensively in both Unix and Windows operating systems to set parameters such as the directories that are searched for executable files and for library files, the access details for databases, user preferences, and so forth. If you work on a Unix or Linux system, you can use the env shell command to list your default environment (the Windows NT set command works similarly). The login process sets your initial environment. By default, each newly forked process starts with an environment identical to that of its parent. The exec system call used to start a different program has an optional environment argument; this argument is a collection of these name value pairs. Before invoking the exec system call, a process can construct a new environment, one that contains its own environment data along with extra or replacement data. A web server uses this feature to add data to the default environment, data that describe the web server, the current client and the client's request.

The CGI specification defined the data that were to be transferred through environment variables. Some relate to the web server itself; for example:

- SERVER_SOFTWARE

This should identify the server (e.g. Apache, IIS) and its version number.

- SERVER_PORT

The port number used by the server (usually port 80; alternatives include 8080, 8000, and other rarer choices).

These server data are really just for completeness; it is quite unusual for a CGI script or program to need details of the web server that launched it. Another group of environment variables hold data about the client:

- REMOTE_HOST

If the web server is configured to use DNS to lookup hostnames, this will be the hostname of the client's machine.

- REMOTE_ADDR

The value of this environment variable is the IP address of the client's machine.

- REMOTE_IDENT

Usually this variable is not set. It could contain the client's actual login identifier (as used on the client's machine). The client's machine has to be running the identd daemon to provide the information (this process is rarely active), and the web server must be configured to request the information. (Apart from breaching users' privacy, use of the 'identify' feature significantly slows the processing of requests.)

- REMOTE_USER

If a website is password-protected using HTTP authentication, then this variable will be set and will contain the username supplied to the authentication system. (Often this is not the same as the user's personal login identifier.)

- USER_AGENT

This variable contains a string identifying the web browser used to submit the request.

A web server normally logs details of all requests, so most of these data have already been recorded. Most CGI programs and scripts would not make any further use of these data; a few might check the USER_AGENT value so as to generate different responses in styles that are optimal for Netscape or IE browsers.

The environment data characterizing a request will include:

● REQUEST_METHOD

This specifies 'get' or 'post' and is checked by the CGI program so as to determine where the *name=value* data are to be found.

● PATH_INFO

This is the pathname for the CGI program as it appeared in the request. Sometimes extra data are added to the path.

● PATH_TRANSLATED

This is the pathname for CGI program as actually used. A web server can be configured to ignore extra data added to paths, or to change directories specified in the requests to other directories where the files are actually held.

● HTTP_REFERER

If the user submitted the query by clicking on an <a href=...> link, then this variable should have the URL of the page containing that link.

● HTTP_ACCEPT

The value of this variable is a string with details of the MIME types that the user's browser can accept. (This information might be used if the CGI program generated an image as its response rather than a normal web page, and was capable of generating the image in different formats.)

If the form data were 'posted', there would be two more environment variables – CONTENT_LENGTH and CONTENT_TYPE; their values would describe the content in the body of the message (a string, x-www-form-urlencoded, of length ...). The QUERY_STRING environment variable contains any data that are appended, along with a leading '?', to the URL that identified the CGI program. If a form uses the get method, then the query string has all *name=value* data from the form's input fields.

A CGI program can obtain the values of environment variables by using the function char* getenv(char* *env_var_name*) (as defined in C's stdlib library), or the equivalent function for other implementation languages. For example, the following C++ fragment checks details of the server:

```
char *info = getenv("SERVER_SOFTWARE");
cout << "Server is " << info << endl;
info = getenv("SERVER_PORT");
int portnum = atoi(info);
if(portnum != 80) cout << "Using non standard port " << portnum << endl;
```

CGI programs tend to have a fairly regular structure, for they all must perform rather similar processing. The *name=value* data from the form must be extracted; this is pretty standard, with similar code in all programs. It is generally convenient to use a simple struct with fields that correspond to the input fields in the form; the fields in this struct are filled in as the values for the named fields are obtained. (Multi-valued inputs can be mapped onto list fields in this struct, or array fields, or whatever else is convenient.) A rough pseudo-code outline for the typical CGI program is:

```
Output the response's content-type header etc.
Create a struct to hold the request data
Determine whether the request data are in the query-string (get) or
    on stdin (post); read the string
While data remain in string
   Separate out next name=value sub-string
   Split name and value parts of sub-string
   Decode value (reversing space/plus conversion and the
     %xx encoding of special characters)
   Store decoded value in struct field corresponding to name
Process data recorded in the struct
(Update database records)
Generate response using both predefined HTML tags and content text,
    and dynamically generated strings specific to this request
Write response to stdout
```

The first data that a CGI program writes to stdout must be the last lines of the eventual header composed for the HTTP response. These lines are the content type line (e.g. Content-type: text/html) and the blank line that separates the header from the body of the response. If any data are written to stdout ahead of these lines, the web server will have problems and will return an error message to the client. (Beginners writing their first CGI programs often cause difficulties by writing trace messages to stdout, or by having their program crash immediately, resulting in a system message going to stdout.)

1.5 A CGI program and examples

The CGI specification was designed to make it possible to implement CGI programs in essentially any language. A lot of the earliest CGI programs were written in C, but gradually interpreted scripting languages such as Perl became more popular. Many CGI programs were implemented by relatively inexperienced programmers who found the development cycle for an interpretive language somewhat easier than the conventional cycle of edit/compile/re-edit/re-compile/re-edit/.../link/re-edit/re-compile/.../link/and install. Most of the processing in a CGI program tends to be a matter of comparing and combining strings; Perl has inherently better support for such string manipulations than does C/C++. Finally, the Perl DBI module (library) for interfacing to databases was more accessible and easier to use than C/C++ equivalents. Perl is introduced in Chapter 5. This first CGI example uses a little C++ framework.

Since so much of a CGI program is standardized, it is possible to abstract out these standard parts and encode them in an extensible framework. The example framework uses two classes: Token and CGI_Helper. The Token class represents a name/value pair:

```
class Token {
public:
  Token(char *name, char *value);
  ~Token();
  const char *Name();
  const char *Value();
private:
  char *fName;
  char *fValue;
};
```

The CGI_Helper class is a base class that must be subclassed to create an effective CGI program. The CGI_Helper class has no data members of its own; it simply defines the framework functions. There are a few private functions that implement details, such as the %xx to character decoding of strings. The public and protected functions are all defined as virtual, allowing them to be overridden in specialized subclasses.

```
class CGI_Helper {
public:
  CGI_Helper() { }
  virtual ~CGI_Helper() { }
  virtual void HTML_Header(const char* title);
  virtual void HTML_Trailer();
  virtual void Handle_Request();
protected:
  virtual void StartTokens() { }
  virtual void EndTokens() { }
  virtual void Process(char *data);
  virtual void ProcessToken(Token *tok) { }
private:
  int hexvalue(char ch);
  void ReadString(char *str, char*& data, char*endpt);
  Token *GetToken(char*& data);
  void HandleGet();
  void HandlePost();
};
```

A CGI program should create an instance of an effective subclass of CGI_Helper, and then invoke the HTML_Header function to generate page headers, the Handle_Request function to process the *name=value* data, and the HTML_Trailer function to complete the response page. For example:

```
int main()
{
  EchoCGI x;
  x.HTML_Header("Echoing your name value pairs");
  x.Handle_Request();
  x.HTML_Trailer();
  return 0;
}
```

Each of these functions has default definitions that can be overridden by subclasses. The header function outputs the mandatory last two lines of the final HTTP header, and then some standard HTML tags and content text for a page header:

```
void CGI_Helper::HTML_Header(const char* title)
{
  cout << "Content-type: text/html\n\n<html> <head>\n";
  if(title!=NULL) cout << "<title>" << title << "</title>\n";
  cout << "</head>\n<body>\n";
}
```

This function would be overwritten in a subclass that needed to use additional headers (e.g. one that wanted to include 'cookies'), or one that had a more elaborate head section, or some feature such as use of a background image for the body section. The default implementation for the trailer function adds a time stamp at the bottom of a generated page:

```
void CGI_Helper::HTML_Trailer()
{
  cout << "<hr>\n";
  time_t aTime;
  (void) time(&aTime);
  cout << ctime(&aTime);
  cout << "</body>\n</html>\n";
}
```

The Handle_Request member function determines the method used (by picking up the value of the REQUEST_METHOD environment variable) and invokes the appropriate private auxiliary function:

```
void CGI_Helper::Handle_Request()
{
  const char *unknown="Unrecognized request";
  char *request = getenv("REQUEST_METHOD");
  if(request == NULL) {
    cout << unknown << endl;
    return;
```

```
    }
    if(0 == strcmp("POST", request)) HandlePost();
    else
    if(0 == strcmp("GET", request)) HandleGet();
    else cout << unknown << ": " << request << endl;
}
```

These 'handle get' and 'handle post' methods are similar; they read the *name=value* data
from the appropriate source and then invoke the common Process method that handles
these data. The get function is simpler; the data should be available as the value of the
QUERY_STRING environment variable:

```
void CGI_Helper::HandleGet()
{
    // Easy, get the string with all input parameters
    // from an environment string
    char *query = getenv("QUERY_STRING");
    if(query == NULL) return;
    Process(query);
}
```

The post function must allocate a buffer to hold the data (and should free the buffer before
the program terminates); when the inputs are form data in the x-www-form-urlencoded
representation, the environment variable CONTENT_LENGTH should define the buffer size:

```
void CGI_Helper::HandlePost()
{
    char *length = getenv("CONTENT_LENGTH");
    if(length == NULL) return;
    int len = atoi(length);
    if(len == 0) return;
    char *buffer = new char[len+1];
    int i =0;
    for(;i<len;i++) {
        char ch;
        cin.get(ch);
        if(cin.fail()) break;
        buffer[i] = ch;
    }
    buffer[i] = '\0';

    Process(buffer);
    delete [ ] buffer;
}
```

The Process function works through virtual functions that allow customization in subclasses:

```
void CGI_Helper::Process(char *data)
{
  StartTokens();
  while(*data != '\0') {
    Token *tknext = GetToken(data);
    if(tknext == NULL) break;
    ProcessToken(tknext);
    delete tknext;
    }
  EndTokens();
}
```

The GetToken method is a non-virtual function. Its code is defined in the CGI_Helper class; it selects the next *name=value&* sequence from the string that encodes the form data, and creates a new Token object from the data in this substring. The StartTokens, ProcessToken, and EndTokens functions are all virtual, with empty default definitions. These are the functions that need to be provided in effective subclasses of CGI_Helper.

The StartTokens function can output additional HTML tags and static content text, or perform any initialization operations not handled by a constructor. The ProcessToken function is invoked for each name/value pair extracted from the form data; the data in the argument Token would be used to update the data structure with the values.

The EndTokens function is where most of the application-specific work would occur. Typically, this function would use several auxiliary functions. The first would validate the completed struct, composing an error response if some data were unacceptable. If the data were valid, the next auxiliary function would open a file or a connection to a database, and save a record of the submitted data. Finally, other processing functions would be invoked to generate a suitable response for a valid order.

The GetToken function works with a couple of helper functions to perform the selection and decoding of *name=value* pairs:

```
Token *CGI_Helper::GetToken(char*& data)
{
  // looking at data like
  //   customer=John+Smith&phone=02323232323&email=&address=...
  // so should have an = sign, then an & sign (last & is ommitted)
  // would want to build a token name="customer" value="John Smith"

    char *eq_pt = strchr(data,'='); // Find next equals sign
    if(eq_pt == NULL) return NULL;

    int length = (eq_pt - data);
    if(length == 0) return NULL;
```

```
                // have starting point and position of =, ie block of text for
                // the name string, allocate space
                // (possibly pessimistic, if field contains url-encode escapes
                //   it will get shorter)
                  char *name = new char[length + 1];
                  ReadString(name, data, eq_pt);

                  data++;
                  int at_end = 0;
                  char *amp_pt = strchr(data, '&');
                // look for an ampersand to mark end of value
                // (an empty value field, so & as the next character
                // and a missing &, i.e. on last token, are both permitted)
                  if(amp_pt == NULL) { at_end = 1; amp_pt = data+strlen(data); }

                  length = (amp_pt - data);

                  char *value = NULL;
                  if(length != 0) {
                    value = new char[length + 1];
                    ReadString(value, data, amp_pt);
                    }

                  if(!at_end) data++;

                // pass strings to token, it will delete them
                  Token *tk = new Token(name, value);
                  return tk;
                }
```

The ReadString function reverses encoding of names and values (typically, names do not contain special characters, so the decoding is only really necessary for the value fields):

```
void CGI_Helper::ReadString(char *str, char*& data, char *endpt)
{
  int i=0;
  for(;data<endpt;i++) {
    if(*data == '+') { str[i] = ' '; data++; }
    else
    if(*data == '%') {
      data++;
      int h1 = hexvalue(*data);
      data++;
      int h2 = hexvalue(*data);
```

```
        str[i] = (char) (16*h1+h2);
        data++;
        }
     else { str[i] = *data; data++; }
     }
  str[i] = '\0';
}


int CGI_Helper::hexvalue(char ch)
{
  if(isdigit(ch)) return ch - '0';
  ch = tolower(ch);
  return 10 + (ch - 'a');
}
```

The Token class is simply a holder for a couple of strings:

```
Token::Token(char *n, char *v) { fName = n; fValue = v; }
Token::~Token() { delete [] fName; delete [] fValue; }

const char *Token::Name() { return fName; }
const char *Token::Value() { return fValue; }
```

A simple 'Echo Server' can be created by subclassing the CGI_Helper class to create a class that outputs the name/value pairs that it reads:

```
class EchoCGI : public CGI_Helper {
protected:
  virtual void StartTokens() ;
  virtual void ProcessToken(Token *tok);
  virtual void EndTokens();

};
```

In this case, the StartTokens function simply outputs an HTML 'start of list' tag, the ProcessToken function prints a list item with the name and value, and the EndTokens function closes the HTML list:

```
void EchoCGI::StartTokens()
{
  cout << "<ol>" << endl;
}


void EchoCGI::EndTokens()
{
```

```
    cout << "</ol>" << endl;
}

void EchoCGI::ProcessToken(Token *tok)
{
    cout << "<li>" << tok->Name() << "\t: ";
    if(tok->Value() == NULL) cout << "(not specified)";
    else cout << tok->Value();
    cout << endl;
}
```

A more elaborate example is a class to handle a pizza order, as in the earlier form example. This application requires an instance of a simple class to hold the submitted order data, and access to a data file or database. There can be a few configuration problems with database access; typically, a CGI program that uses a database will need to set several extra environment variables (this is illustrated later with the example Perl and PHP CGI programs). In addition, a database account name and password must be encoded in the CGI program. Database access is not illustrated here because of the messy (and database-specific) nature of the low-level C/C++ to database communications code. While the code may be messy, there are no real problems with database access; the database itself handles security, and controls concurrent access attempts by different processes. Code to access files is a little more problematic. The author of the CGI program must deal with concurrency issues, and the overall system must be configured correctly to allow a CGI program to access the files that it needs.

If you have two clients simultaneously contacting your web server, you will end up with two CGI processes trying to update the same file. If they both start to write to the file, their outputs may get interleaved; obviously, this is unacceptable. You have to use schemes that allow a process to claim a file, locking out access by other processes until it is finished with that file. If two CGI programs start 'simultaneously', one will get the lock on the file and proceed; the second will be forced to wait until the first releases the file lock. A file-locking scheme is illustrated in the following code.

File access problems appear on Unix/Linux systems where processes are run with a specific 'user identifier' (user-id), and this user-id determines the files that are accessible. A typical web server is configured to run with the user-id 'nobody'. Child processes inherit the user-id of their parent, so any CGI program started by the web server will also run with the user-id 'nobody'. This can present problems if you want to write your own CGI program and have this program update data files that you have created (because user 'nobody' will not have write access to your files). Your CGI programs can be made 'set user id' programs. Such programs are specially tagged in the Unix/Linux directories; when started, they run under the user-identifier of their owner, and so can access their owner's data files. You may need help from a systems administrator to make your CGI programs run as set-user-id programs.

The actual example has two classes: PizzaCGI and PizzaStruct. The PizzaStruct class has string data members for the data, such as the names of pizza toppings required, extras, delivery data and address. It handles multi-valued inputs, such as the multiple

choices allowed for pizza toppings, by concatenating together the individual strings.
Member functions support operations such as reporting the cost of the order and writing
data to an output stream.

```
class PizzaStruct {
public:
  PizzaStruct();
  ~PizzaStruct();
  void    SetSize(const char* sizeinfo);
  void    AddTopping(const char* toptype);
  ...
  void    Report(ostream& out);
  void    Log(ostream& out);
private:
  double  Cost();
  char*   catenate(const char* old, const char* more);

  int     fSize;
  int     fNumToppings;
  double  fPizzaCost;
  double  fExtrasCost;
  double  fDeliveryCost;
  char*   fTops;
  ...
  char*   fDelivery;;
};

PizzaStruct::PizzaStruct()
{
  fSize = 1; fNumToppings = 0; fExtrasCost = 0.0;
  fTops = fXtras = fDelivery = fCustomer = fAddress =
    fEmail = fPhone = NULL;
}

PizzaStruct::~PizzaStruct()
{
  delete fTops; ... delete fPhone;
}

void PizzaStruct::SetSize(const char* sizeinfo)
{
  fSize = 1;
  if(0 == strcmp(sizeinfo, "fam")) fSize = 2;
  if(0 == strcmp(sizeinfo, "pop")) fSize = 3;
}
```

```
...

void PizzaStruct::AddExtra(const char* extra)
{
  char *temp = catenate(fXtras, extra);
  delete [] fXtras;
  fXtras = temp;

  if(0 == strcmp("Coke",extra)) fExtrasCost += 1.70;
...
  if(0 == strcmp("Salad",extra)) fExtrasCost += 4.50;
}


...

void PizzaStruct::Report(ostream& out)
{
  out << "Your ";
  if(fSize==1) out << "regular ";
  if(fSize==2) out << "Family ";
  if(fSize==3) out << "POPULAR ";
  out << "sized pizza";
  if(fNumToppings>0) out << ", with " << fTops << "," ;
  out << " is now being prepared." << endl;
  out << "Your pizza ";
  if(fXtras != NULL) out << ", and the following extras : "
<< fXtras << "," << endl;
  out << "will be delivered soon by our " << fDelivery <<
" service." << endl;
  out << "The cost will be $" << Cost() <<
". Please have money ready to pay delivery person." << endl;
}

void PizzaStruct::Log(ostream& out)
{
  out << "Customer: " << fCustomer << endl;
...
  out << "Delivery: " << fDelivery << endl;
}
```

The PizzaCGI program owns an output file and its associated file descriptor, a PizzaStruct data member for the data, and a time field; it overrides the three empty virtual functions inherited from the CGI_Helper class – StartTokens, ProcessToken and EndTokens.

```
class PizzaCGI : public CGI_Helper {
public:
  PizzaCGI();
  ~PizzaCGI();
protected:
  virtual void  StartTokens() ;
  virtual void  ProcessToken(Token *tok);
  virtual void  EndTokens();
private:
  fstream       fRecords;
  time_t        fArrivalTime;
  PizzaStruct   fPizza;
  int           fFiledescriptor;
};
```

The CGI program simply creates and uses one of the PizzaCGI objects:

```
int main()
{
  PizzaCGI x;
  x.HTML_Header("Re: Your pizza order");
  x.Handle_Request();
  x.HTML_Trailer();
  return 0;
}
```

The PizzaCGI constructor and destructor handle opening and locking of the file used to log pizza orders, and subsequent unlocking of the file when the program terminates:

```
PizzaCGI::PizzaCGI()
{
  fRecords.open("DataLog",ios::in | ios::out);
  fRecords.seekp(0, ios::end);
  fFiledescriptor = fRecords.rdbuf()->fd();
  lockf(fFiledescriptor, F_LOCK, 0);
}

PizzaCGI::~PizzaCGI()
{
  fRecords.close();
  lockf(fFiledescriptor, F_ULOCK, 0);

}
```

The StartTokens function outputs a little additional HTML for the response page; the EndTokens function deals with the updating of the log file and output of the main part of the response page:

```
void PizzaCGI::StartTokens()
{
    (void) time(&fArrivalTime);
    fRecords << "Order received at " << ctime(&fArrivalTime);
    cout << "<h1>CyberPizza Parlor</h1>";
    cout << "<em>Thank you for your order.</em><br>";
}

void PizzaCGI::EndTokens()
{
    fPizza.Report(cout);
    fPizza.Log(fRecords);
    fRecords << "----" << endl;
}
```

The ProcessToken function uses the token name to determine the appropriate update operation that should be invoked on the PizzaStruct:

```
void PizzaCGI::ProcessToken(Token *tok)
{
    if(0==strcmp(tok->Name(), "phone")) fPizza.SetPhone(tok->Value());
    ...
    if(0==strcmp(tok->Name(), "p_size")) fPizza.SetSize(tok->Value());
}
```

1.6   Client-side scripting

Web browsers run on quite powerful computers; machines capable of doing much more than just paint a screen, process keystrokes, and handle network traffic. Why not offload some work from the server onto the very capable client machine?

There are a few situations where there are real computational tasks that can be done on the client. These situations usually involve simulations coupled with data display: a user controls some simulated world and can change parameters using controls such as scrollbars and checkboxes, and these parameters are input to code that updates the display. Examples include web sites that let you download three-dimensional models of proteins etc., and then view a display in the browser window that shows the protein structure rotating in three dimensions under your control. If you pursue this approach, you get to explore the use of downloadable code such as ActiveX controls and applets.

E-commerce applications have no need for such computational gimmicks. But work can still be done on the client. After it has read the *name=value* data from a form, the next task for the average CGI program is to check the data and, if necessary, to return an error page pointing out mistakes or omissions. This is all rather costly and slow; it is far better if such programmatic checks are done in the client before form data are submitted. (Checks on submitted data must always be included in CGI programs; you can never rely solely on checking performed on the client. Users can disable the script interpreters that run client-side checks; hackers can submit data that purport to come from your checked form, but have been carefully edited to try to confuse your CGI script. Client-side checking is simply an efficiency improvement; it avoids totally wasteful exchanges of obviously invalid inputs.)

Such checks were one of the motivating reasons for allowing client-side scripting code to be included in web pages. Netscape included an interpreter for a scripting language, LiveScript, in the 1995 browser/server release. Web pages could include segments of script code; the interpreter would run these when certain events occurred – events such as the activation of a submit button in a form. The script code could perform basic checks on the data entered in the form. If problems were detected, the script could display an alert box with a warning; the invalid data would not be sent to the server. The user would then be able to re-edit the data and resubmit the form.

This scripting language was renamed JavaScript when the Java craze stated later in 1995. It has been extended and new applications have been found. These days, JavaScript interpreters in browsers run script code to handle more sophisticated kinds of page display, as well as to check form data. Pages can now be multi-layered, allowing for features such as pop-up menus and 'rollover' elements in tables etc. that are associated with different images in different layers. Use of these features can enhance a user's experience of a website, so their use is an important part of commercial web site design; however, such uses are outside the scope of this text.

A form tag can contain an onsubmit attribute whose value identifies a JavaScript function that is to be run. This function returns a boolean value; the submission process takes place only if this value is true.

```
<form action="http://www.pizzas.com/order.cgi" name=pizzaform
  onSubmit= "return confirmPizza(pizzaform)"
  method=POST >
Regular <input type=radio name=p_size value=reg>
...
</form>
```

The JavaScript code for a function like the example confirmPizza function will be declared in the head part of the pizza order page. Functions can be passed arguments such as forms; a form is rather similar to a struct, with named data fields as used in more conventional programming languages. The JavaScript code can access the data entered into selected fields of the struct.

The following fragments illustrate simple checking code:

```
<html><head><title> Pizza CyberParlor</title>
<script language="javascript">
```

```
<!--
function emptyField(textObj)
{
   if(textObj.value.length == 0) return true;
   for(var i=0; i<textObj.value.length;i++) {
      ch = textObj.value.charAt(i);
      if(ch != ' ' && ch != '\t') return false;
      }
   return true;
}
function confirmPizza(formObj)
{
   if(emptyField(formObj.customer) ) {
      alert("You forgot to enter your name");
      return false;
      }
   // Similar checks for address and other fields
   ...

   return true
}

// -->
</script>
</head>
<body><h1>Pizza Order Form</h1>
<p>
<form action="http://www.pizzas.com/order.cgi" name=pizzaform
   onSubmit= "return confirmPizza(pizzaform)" method=POST >
Pizza size<p>
Regular <input type=radio name=p_size value=reg>
...
<p>
Your name
<input type=text size=20 maxlength=50 name=customer>
...
<hr>
<input type=submit value="Place Order">
</form>
<hr>
Have a good day.
</body></html>
```

A user's activation of the 'Place Order' submit button causes a 'submit' event for the form; the onSubmit attribute requires the confirmPizza function to run, passing the function an argument with a reference to the form. The confirmPizza function passes a reference to the 'customer' input field to the auxiliary emptyfield function; there the code checks that the associated data value represents a non-empty string of characters. If the field is in fact empty, the browser displays an alert box. This alert warns the user that additional data must be supplied before the form can be submitted. It isn't much of a check for a valid name, but it is better than submitting a form without any data in the name field. Similar checks would apply to the other text entry fields.

Slightly more extensive scripting code would allow calculation of the cost of a pizza order. This cost could be displayed in an alert box that required the user to confirm submission of the order.

Exercises

Practical

Practical exercises relating to this chapter require a web server and are therefore deferred to Chapter 3. You will require a development environment and a web server for later practical exercises. These are all available for free download from the Internet. The first practical exercise is therefore to obtain the necessary software.

Students running Linux should already possess many of the required components, such as a C++ compiler, a Perl interpreter and the Apache web server. (C++ is only necessary if you want to try out the example C++ code shown in this chapter.) A Java development system (Java System Development Kit Standard Edition) can be downloaded from Sun (http://java.sun.com/). The Tomcat Java-based web server needed for later exercises on servlets and JSPs can be downloaded from the Apache site (http://www.apache.org/), as can the Java libraries needed for handling XML data.

The Java components and the Apache web server have versions that run on Windows (versions 98 and up). Perl and Python for Windows are available from http://www.activestate.com/. Windows users who do not want to deal with the complexities of dual-boot Windows/Linux configurations can still obtain something that is essentially a full Unix development environment (including C++, C, the Postgres database system etc.). The Cygwin system, which is available for free download from http://sources.redhat.com/cygwin/, runs an almost complete Unix environment from within a standard Windows process.

Short answer questions

Some of these questions relate to presumed background knowledge of HTML, browser usage, JavaScript and so forth. Appendix A contains brief coverage of HTML and JavaScript; there is much additional information on the WWW (at sites such as http://www.wdvl.com/).

(1) Explain the following features of a browser: helper applications, plugins, image maps, scripting.

(2) Explain how ports and sockets figure in inter-process communications.

(3) Explain how serial servers, forking servers and threaded servers handle requests from multiple clients.

(4) When and where did the http protocol and HTML language for the Web originate? Why was this hypertext system more successful than earlier attempts?

(5) Explain how HTML forms and CGI programs can be used to submit and process data entered by a user. How do the data entered by the user get delivered to the processing program? How is the program's response returned to the user?

(6) Explain, with brief examples, how client-side JavaScript code can check form-based data entry and enhance HTML's presentation and navigation capabilities.

(7) The attributes of a <form> tag can include method, name, action and onSubmit. Explain the use of each of these attributes.

(8) Explain how 'events' can be coded in HTML tags and used to invoke JavaScript functions.

(9) Explain how the server-side includes (SSI) mechanism can be used to create dynamic pages.

(10) List and explain the usage of the different types of input control that can be incorporated in a standard HTML form.

Explorations

(1) Research the evolution of HTML from Berners-Lee's original version through to HTML 4.0 and XHTML. Write a short report characterizing the major changes in the different versions and explaining the objectives of the XHTML revisions.

(2) Research 'stylesheets' for HTML documents. Write a short report on how stylesheets can enhance the appearance of individual HTML pages and improve consistency in a web site comprised of many pages; illustrate your report with screenshots of a browser displaying pages using various stylesheets.

(3) Research the availability of CGI-related function libraries, and of class libraries for C and C++ programs. Write a short report on the available libraries; illustrate your report with code fragments that show how a C or C++ program may retrieve form data and other server status data.

(4) Research the use of the UDP protocol on the Internet (uses include Massively MultiPlayer Role Playing Games and a number of webcasting mechanisms). Write a report explaining UDP's role.

2

HTTP

The Hypertext Transfer Protocol (HTTP) is now ubiquitous. It is primarily what is says – a hypertext transfer protocol; something that is relatively simple, stateless and generic in character. But because it is deployed so widely, it has been coerced into supporting other uses, such as e-commerce (which is inherently stateful!), naming services, and some forms of remote procedure calls and method invocations on remote objects.

The original version (HTTP/0.9) was a simple protocol for transferring data across the Internet. This was elaborated by the inclusion of features such as support for different defined data types (for example, a server could return a file with a header tag specifying the content as being an image in gif format, jpg format, or whatever). Other extensions supported requests for authorization, caching of copies of data, and so forth. The extended version of the protocol, HTTP/1.0, served for much of the 1990s, but there were always problems with incomplete implementations. Further, the support for caching was limited; there were efficiency problems with HTTP/1.0 requests being limited to the transfer of a single resource; and the HTTP/1.0 standard did not allow for things like 'virtual hosts' (where a single server system presents itself as being a group of distinct servers). These problems necessitated further refinement of the protocol leading to the current version 1.1. The HTTP/1.1 standard has tightened the specification (to avoid problems like those with those *almost but not quite* implementations for HTTP/1.0), expanded the role of caches and proxy servers, and provided more mechanisms for the communicating applications to negotiate details of transfers. With HTTP/1.1, it is possible for the applications to agree to use a connection for a series of requests and responses, or to agree to use a specific form of data compression for a data transfer, or even to swap to using the secure version of the protocol where transfers are encrypted.

Since this book focuses on how servers work in the context of web applications, HTTP forms an essential part of all the technologies that are presented in subsequent chapters. All involve a client using a browser to submit HTTP requests to a server implemented using one of the possible technologies. The different kinds of server handle such requests in different ways, but ultimately all will return an HTTP response with data that are to be displayed by the client's browser. Some of the applications need to use more powerful features of the protocol; for example, several employ HTTP authorization as part of the mechanisms used to restrict access to resources.

The server will generate the data that are returned in response to a client's request. If the same client, or another client, submits a similar request, a new response must be created dynamically. It is rarely appropriate for dynamic response data to be cached.

Consequently, for our applications the caching and proxy features of the HTTP/1.1 protocol are of limited importance. Of course, these capabilities are very important in applications that focus on retrieval of static data.

This chapter provides a brief overview of those aspects of HTTP that will be constantly referenced in the rest of the text. The specification for the protocol is available online (try `ftp://ftp.isi.edu/in-notes/rfc2616.txt` or `http://www.w3.org/Protocols/`). This specification can be consulted for further details; other supplementary are data available at the w3c web site.

2.1   Requests and responses

HTTP/1.1 remains a relatively simple request–response protocol used for communication between an active client and a passive server. The client initiates activities by submitting a request. There are a small number of request types ('Get', 'Post', 'Put', 'Options', ...); most include a resource identifier and supplementary data. Usually, the client submits its request by opening a TCP/IP connection to the actual machine that hosts the server. However, it is possible that a client may open a connection to a proxy machine and send it the request; the proxy machine then acts on behalf of the client, opening a connection to the real server. On the real server, a 'web server' program will read the request. A small fraction of the requests are for information about the capabilities of the web server; the web server responds to these requests itself. Most requests are for 'resources' that exist on the server (a resource might be a data file, or the results from an operation that the server machine can perform).

The web server may respond to a resource request with an initial response message indicating that supplementary data are needed; for example, a name and password might have to be supplied. The client would send such supplementary data over the open TCP/IP link. Once any preliminary negotiations are complete, the web server handles the actual request. The web server may process the request, generating the response data and the response header. Often the web server delegates the handling of the request to a separate process; this separate process will generate a part of the response header and the response data. The output from the separate process gets routed back via the web server that completes the header and sends the HTTP response message back to the client.

In the HTTP/1.0 protocol, the server closes its end of a TCP/IP connection once it has sent its response. This may result in quite inefficient processing of requests. A typical HTML page contains links to images and to stylesheet files. The client browser that parses the HTML will find these links and must download these files before it can display the page to the user. Consequently, the browser must make new connections to the server for each of the files. The opening and closing of a TCP/IP connection has a significant cost and takes time. If each file is transferred through a separately established connection, performance suffers. It is of course possible for a web server to keep open the connection to the client after returning the response to the first request. It can do a blocking read with a timeout on this connection; if no additional request data are received before the timeout occurs, the connection can be closed. If the client browser can handle such an open connection, it can submit a request for an image file or stylesheet file over the same connection. Client and server have to coordinate their activities to make this work. Some HTTP/1.0 implementations supported a Keep-Alive request header; this header was sent if the client was capable of using the open connection. Reuse of a connection is a standard feature in HTTP/1.1; though it is controllable by the participants. A client can specify in a request header that it wishes that its connection be closed after the first response; a server can indicate in a response header that it will be closing the connection once it has completed its current response.

HTTP is basically a simple text protocol. The first line of a request specifies the request method ('Get', 'Post', ...), the 'resource' and the protocol being used (HTTP/1.0 or HTTP/1.1). The next few lines are headers. These lines have a keyword that identifies the type of general header or request header, or entity header, and some data. There will be a blank line following these header data, and then possibly a request body ('entity').

General headers are used to specify properties of the transfer process. One example of a general header is the Connection header, which allows a client to specify that it wants to have its connection closed (Connection: close) as soon as the first response is complete. (Why would you want to do that? It is something messy relating to the use of proxy servers.) The Cache-Control header is a more complex example; a client requesting a resource that might be cached can use a Cache-Control header to specify constraints like the maximum age that it is prepared to accept for that resource. (An example might be a request for the headline page from a news source: you might accept a cached copy of page prepared two hours ago, but you wouldn't want yesterday's headlines.)

Request headers add supplementary information to a request or describe client capabilities. Examples include If-Modified-Since, Range, Accept-Language, Referer, and User-Agent. The header If-Modified-Since can be used with a 'Get' request for a static resource (fixed web page); this can save network traffic if the resource has not been modified as the server sends a short 'not-modified' response instead of a copy of the file. If a resource is large (e.g. a movie clip, audio clip or large image) it may be more convenient for a client to submit requests for successive segments of the data; a Range request allows a client to request a specified byte range from a resource. An Accept-Language header specifies the language preferences that a user has specified in their browser's properties dialog; if the server has a resource available in language variants, it should select the version that best matches the client's requirement. If the client is requesting a resource by activating a hypertext link, the Referer header will contain the URI of the page containing that link. Finally, the User-Agent header will contain a text string identifying the browser that the client is using.

Entity headers define properties of any 'entity' (body of message). An example is the Content-Encoding header; this can be used to specify something like the fact that the body of the message has been compressed using the gzip algorithm. The Content-Length header specifies the size of the message body.

Normally, a request will produce a single response message, but you will get a sequence of request/response, supplementary-request/response exchanges when the client and server have to negotiate some aspect of the transfer (most commonly, the need for password authentication). A response consists of a status line, some number of lines with general headers, response headers, entity headers, a blank separator line, and, where appropriate, a message body that contains the returned data. The status line contains the protocol used, the status code, and an explanatory phrase. The status codes include 200 ('OK' – the resource data are in the message body), 404 ('Not Found' – the requested resource does not exist) and 500 ('Internal Server Error' – your servlet or PHP script has just crashed).

With a few exceptions, responses will include a `Date` header. Other general headers that might occur in a response include `Connection` (the server is signaling its intent to close a connection), `Transfer-Encoding` (for example, used in HTTP/1.1 when the server is unable to determine the response size and is returning it as a series of 'chunks') and `Cache-Control` (the server may add headers that inform intermediate caches as to caching constraints). Specific response headers include `Age`, `Retry-After`, `Server` and `WWW-Authenticate`. An `Age` header would typically appear in a response from a cache; it would give some indication as to how old the returned data are. If the server is returning a 503 'Service Unavailable' response, it can supplement this with a `Retry-After` header that provides some indication of when the service might again be available. The `Server` header identifies the server software. A `WWW-Authenticate` header will appear in a response that a server sends when the client must submit a name and password before access is granted to a resource.

The entity headers in a response with body will include a `Content-Type` header that specifies a mime type for the body (e.g. `Content-Type: text/html`) and a `Content-Length` header (except for the case of 'chunked responses'). Other entity headers for responses may include an `Expires` header for data that have a limited lifetime of validity (e.g. share price quotation), or a `Content-Range` header for a response that contains a subset of the bytes of a resource.

2.1.1   Requests

A request has the form:

```
Request = Request-Line
*(( general-header | request-header| entity-header ) CRLF)
CRLF
[ message-body ]
```

This says that a request is a request line followed by some headers, each on a separate line, followed by a blank line, and an optional message body – CRLF stands for carriage return and line feed, i.e. the character sequence \r\n. The request line specifies the method (request type), the resource and the HTTP version. The resource URI should either be an absolute URI or an absolute path, in which case there should also be a `Host` header, e.g.

```
GET http://www.Our_Shop.com/prices.html HTTP/1.1
```

or

```
GET /prices.html HTTP/1.1
HOST: www.Our_Shop.com
```

This requirement relates to support for 'virtual hosts'. A single server program may be pretending to be the distinct servers for the domains www.Our_Butcher.com, and www.Our_Baker.com; when it gets a request for prices.html it needs to know whether the request is for the butcher's prices or the baker's prices. With the HTTP/1.1 protocol, this information is either in the absolute URI or in the HOST header.

The different request methods are:

- GET

A 'Get' request asks for a resource – either a static resource (fixed web page or image file) or a dynamically generated resource (in which case the URI names the script or program that will generate the resource).

Request headers can change a 'Get' into a conditional get (only get data if modified since ...), or a partial get (get the range of bytes ... to ...). Such supplementary parameters are only appropriate when accessing a static resource.

The URI may have an appended query string. This supplies parameter data for the system that is generating a resource. These data take the form of *name=value* substrings that are separated by ampersand (&) characters. The data in the *name=value* pairs are encoded using the x-www-urlencoded mime type encoding (letters and digits are unmodified, spaces become '+' signs, and other characters are encoded as escaped hexadecimal codes %*xx*).

Browsers allow users to 'bookmark' the URIs used in 'Get' requests – i.e. URIs that include query strings. Such requests can then be easily resubmitted (possibly unintentionally). For this reason, 'Get' requests should not be used for any processing action that could change data on the server. They should be reserved for requests that solicit information. (A user might want to save a 'Get' request to a server that generates dynamic pages. For example, the server might provide a listing of apartments for rent, and the user has saved a request with query string parameters that define the desired suburb and price range. Such a saved 'Get' query could be re-run each day until the user finds an apartment.)

- HEAD

A 'Head' request is similar to a 'Get' except that the data are not included in the response. It is really a request for the headers that would have been associated with the requested data; these headers might include content size or some other information that the client needs to check.

- POST

The 'Post' method allows a client to submit data that are to be processed on the server. The data form the body of the message ('entity'). The URI identifies the processing script or program. Typically, all or part of the submitted data are used to update database tables, or are added to a bulletin board, or are placed in a file.

A response to a POST method is not usually cacheable (this can be overridden by the server). The server will usually acknowledge a change due to a POST request (200 OK, or 204 No data), or may more provide a more explicit acknowledgment (such as 201 Created – if a new file was created – or 202 accepted).

- PUT

The 'Put' method is usually not supported. It allows a client to supply data together with a URI that specifies where these data are to be stored on the server.

The 'Put' method can be used to upload files. However, files are normally 'posted' to a processing program (as multi-part form data); the processing program that handles these posted data can then select where the data are to be saved.

- DELETE

Rarely supported; a 'Delete' request commands the server to delete the resource specified by the URI (you might want to support this method in a specialized context on a local intranet).

- OPTIONS, TRACE and CONNECT

An OPTIONS request solicits information about the server (or, less often, about a resource). A client might use such a request to determine whether a server could switch to secure communications. TRACE requests are for debugging communications (there can be problems if requests must travel via multiple proxy servers etc.). A CONNECT request has a special role related to establishing a secure link through a proxy.

The examples for the web applications will be restricted to 'Get' and 'Post' requests.

2.1.2 Responses

HTTP response messages have the form:

```
Response = Status-Line
*(( general-header | response-header | entity-header ) CRLF)
CRLF
[ message-body ]
```

This says that a response is a status line, followed by some number of headers, a blank line and an optional message body. The status line specifies the HTTP protocol version, status code and phrase.

There are five groups of status codes:

- 1xx

Request received, processing continues.

- 2xx

'Success' (resource retrieved, put, posted etc.).

- 3xx

Further action needed. The 3xx codes are used for situations like a resource being temporarily or permanently moved to a new URI. The response should then include a Location header that contains this URI. Ideally, a browser will interpret this and proceed by submitting a new request to the specified location.

- 4xx

Client error, or request invalid. The 4xx codes are used to specify that a resource is not available, or to indicate that the client has done something wrong, like submitting a request for a non-existent byte range from a resource, or to enforce a requirement like the need to submit name and password data.

- 5xx

Server failure.

The following example of the headers for a HTTP response message is taken from the HTTP/1.1 specification:

```
HTTP/1.1 206 Partial content
Date: Wed, 15 Nov 1995 06:25:24 GMT
Last-Modified: Wed, 15 Nov 1995 04:58:08 GMT
Content-Range: bytes 21010-47021/47022
Content-Length: 26012
Content-Type: image/gif
```

The response codes that are most common for our web applications are:

- 200; OK

Success response code.

- 401; Unauthorized

This is the challenge part of the protocol that allows the user to specify a name and password before access is granted to a controlled resource.

- 500; Internal Server Error

Your server-side script or program has a bug!

2.2 Authorization

On the server side, it is possible to define 'realms' that contain resources for which access restrictions apply. (Almost always, a realm corresponds to a directory and its subdirectories; all files in these directories are subject to the same access restrictions). The restrictions may be based on a client's IP address, on a domain name (this is converted into an IP address when checked), or on a requirement that the user supply a name and password. The server applies any IP (or domain) restrictions as its first step in handling a request. If the client does not satisfy the restrictions, the server will respond with a 'forbidden' message like the following:

```
<HTML><HEAD>
<TITLE>403 Forbidden</TITLE>
</HEAD><BODY>
```

```
<H1>Forbidden</H1>
You don't have permission to access resource
on this server.<P>
<HR>
<ADDRESS>Apache/1.3.17 Server at ... 8080</ADDRESS>
</BODY></HTML>
```

When a client submits a first request for a resource in a password-controlled realm, the server responds with an 'unauthorized' message like the following:

```
HTTP/1.1 401 Authorization Required
Date: Thu, 24 May 2001 08:09:45 GMT
Server: Apache/1.3.17 (Unix)
WWW-Authenticate: Basic realm="Controlled space"
Transfer-Encoding: chunked
Content-Type: text/html; charset=iso-8859-1

1da
<!DOCTYPE HTML PUBLIC "-//IETF//DTD HTML 2.0//EN">
<HTML><HEAD><TITLE>401 Authorization Required</TITLE>
</HEAD><BODY>
<H1>Authorization Required</H1>
This server could not verify that you are authorized to access the docu-
ment requested. Either you supplied the wrong credentials (e.g. bad
password), or Your browser doesn't understand how to supply the creden-
tials required.<P>
<HR><ADDRESS>Apache/1.3.17 Server at ...</ADDRESS>
</BODY></HTML>
```

The server administrator will have chosen the 'realm' name (the name is 'Controlled space' in this example). A client browser will either display the default web page that is included as the body of the message, or handle this challenge properly. The browser should put up a dialog box that identifies the realm and has input fields where the user can enter a username and password. Once these data are entered, they can be sent in an Authorization header of a followup request. The server can then check the name–password combination and return the resource if the password is validated.

Obviously, you would not want to be challenged first for an HTML web page, and then again for every image file or stylesheet file referenced in that page. The client browser solves this by storing the name, password, realm data triple; the browser interprets the realm as the resource path for the first resource requested. It automatically includes the name and password in an Authorization header in every subsequent request for a resource from that realm.

Neither restriction based on IP address nor on HTTP password authentication provides you with much security. Neither is hacker-proof. Further, your data may well end up in temporary cache files on proxy servers and caches somewhere between your client and your server. You should not rely on these technologies when you require real security. They do, however, suffice to prevent most casual browsers from accessing data inappropriately.

2.3 **Negotiated content**

The HTTP/1.1 protocol supports sophisticated mechanisms for clients to specify the desired form of content. In fact, the mechanisms are too sophisticated for most web browsers; only a subset of the content negotiation features gets used regularly.

A client can express preferences using headers like `Accept`, `Accept-Language` and `Accept-Charset`; these should utilize data entered through the browser's preferences dialogs (e.g. IE: Tools/Internet/Languages etc; Netscape: Edit/Preferences/Navigator/Languages). (There is also an `Accept-Encoding` header that is used more or less automatically by the browser to indicate whether it can deal with gzip compressed encoded data or other forms of data encoding). The following examples of `Accept` headers are taken from the HTTP/1.1 specification; they indicate something of the scope for this control mechanism:

```
Accept: audio/*; q=0.2, audio/basic
Accept: text/plain; q=0.5, text/html, text/x-dvi; q=0.8, text/x-c
```

The first example might occur in a request for an audio resource; it specifies that the preferred form would be a resource in audio/basic format (with default 'quality' index 1.0), but any other form would be acceptable (though it would only merit one fifth of the approval of the basic format). The second request might be from a request for a text resource; this client would be happy with either HTML or x-c format data; if these are not available a dvi file would be accepted, and if not that then plain text is OK.

The format of these `Accept` requests has a data type and sub-type (with '*' meaning any subtype), and an optional 'quality' rating. Currently, most browsers do not have mechanisms for entering these quality ratings etc. It would also be unusual for a resource to be available in a large number of formats.

Language and character set controls are more commonly used and are a little better supported in current browsers. An `Accept-Charset` header can specify acceptable character sets; the server might have a document presented in different ways using various character sets to their best effect.

```
Accept-Charset: iso-8859-5, unicode-1-1;q=0.8
```

The `Accept-Language` header is the most frequently used; it allows a client to specify language preferences. Again, using an example from the HTTP/1.1 reference, one could have:

```
Accept-Language: da, en-gb;q=0.8, en;q=0.7
```

Such a header in a request would indicate a preference for a Danish version of the document, with a second preference being English (with British English slightly preferred over other dialects).

Obviously, the server must have multiple copies of resources if it is to honor such requests. There are various possible approaches that can be used by the server to recognize the version of the document most suited to the client. One approach uses language codes as extra file extensions. Thus, you might find a directory with the files index.html.de (German), index.html.fr (French) and index.html.en (English).

2.4   State in a stateless protocol

The original HTTP protocol was intended to be an ultimately low-cost protocol for downloading hypertext files. When HTTP was introduced, ftp (File Transfer Protocol) had been used for over fifteen years. The ftp system is stateful; you login to an ftp site (most ftp sites support guest accounts with no passwords) and you change directory to the directory that you require. The state data that ftp maintains includes your login identifier (and hence the access privileges that you have for files), your current directory, and control settings (e.g. should transfers be binary, or as text with possible format conversions). Your login session allows you to issue commands, such as the commands for changing directories, listing directory contents and starting transfers. When you start a transfer, a second TCP/IP connection is opened for the data transfer; the main connection can still be used to issue control commands. All this state maintenance and control requires a more heavyweight process on the server side and does require multiple connections. The HTTP protocol tried to do without this extra server-side infrastructure; it was at first just a simple protocol for handling 'Get' requests with the minimum of effort by the server.

When you use HTTP to connect to a server, you have an essentially anonymous client which can upload a little data and download one or more files before disconnecting. Apart from entries in its logs, the server has no record of the session. If you connect again, a basic HTTP web server cannot associate your new connection with anything that you did previously. This arrangement is fine so long as you are simply downloading static files or submitting things like simple queries to a search engine that will generate a single dynamic page with the results of your search.

As anyone who has made significant use of a site like Amazon's website, e-commerce web applications involve lots of 'state data'. Amazon's site will recognize regular customers, welcoming them with news on recent publications that might be of interest. It tracks all customers as they browse the site, making up a form of history list of the items they look at and allowing customers to fill a virtual shopping cart with items that they might wish to purchase. If the customer is serious, he or she will proceed to the 'check-out'; regular customers receive express treatment for their credit details and their address details are already known, while casual customers are enabled to enter these data. A shopping visit will typically entail twenty or more independent HTTP sessions, with possibly hundreds of files downloaded. The server has to maintain state information about the client through all of these separate HTTP sessions (the state data include the record of items viewed, the contents of the shopping cart, and the customer identity if a regular customer or if these data have already been entered).

Applications require 'state'; the HTTP protocol does not really support it. In some cases, you can make use of HTTP authorization. Your web resources are placed in a controlled realm and clients must login to gain access. A client login identifier will be included in an `Authorization` header with each subsequent HTTP request, and so can serve as a key for session data maintained on the server. Unfortunately, this mechanism is too restrictive, and also does not scale well into the tens of thousands of users that might be connecting to a commercial site. The result has been a series of 'hacks' that provide other mechanisms for maintaining state data.

Some of these hacks attempt to store the state data on the client, returning all the state information with subsequent pages. Other hacks find some means of storing a key on the client, arranging that the key be returned in each subsequent request. The key identifies client state data saved in the server. These hacks (hidden fields in forms, cookies and URL rewriting) are introduced along with the applications that exploit them. The hacks are language-independent; you will find the same mechanisms used from Perl CGI programs, PHP scripts or Java servlets/JSPs. Two, cookies and URL rewriting, both involve bending the HTTP protocol a little. Cookies use extra headers in the HTTP requests and responses; the HTTP protocol allows for such extensions in principle. The URL rewriting mechanism involves playing with the URL of the resource, inserting extra data in all URLs issued to a client. The issuing server knows how to interpret such extra data if it subsequently receives a request with such a URL.

Exercises

Short answer questions

(1) HTTP/1.1 standardized a number of common additions to the earlier HTTP/1.0 protocol, such as keep-alive, content negotiation, caching control mechanisms, and others. How is performance improved through the use of keep-alive connections from the client browser to the web server? How can the server limit usage of such a connection?

(2) Explain the mechanisms available to support content negotiation.

(3) Given that HTTP is a stateless protocol, explain how the client browser and web server together support a 'logged in' status for access to a controlled realm.

(4) What are the data in HTTP request headers that would enable a web site to track its users and find how the discovered and subsequently navigated through a web site?

(5) Explain how 'get' and 'post' requests package request-specific data that are being sent to a program on the web server.

Explorations

(1) Basic authentication with HTTP is rudimentary: the username and password are essentially transmitted in plain text. Research the more sophisticated alternatives, such as digests and client certificates, and write a short report explaining how these work and what benefits they offer.

(2) The W3C organization, which controls many aspects of the World Wide Web, regards the HTTP/1.1 development as complete. Provision has been made for possible extensions; write a short report on the 'extension framework'.

(3) The W3C site has a code libraries page for HTTP handling that includes an example 'robot'. Robots are programs for building structures that represent parts of a web, or for searching for pages that include keywords. Such programs use HTTP protocols for file access, and have code for finding HTML links in downloaded pages. Some of the main web indices are created through the use of robots. Find out about 'robots' and the rules that should be applied to their operation, and write a report on their implementation and use.

(4) Research the File Transfer Protocol, ftp, and some programs that implement this protocol; find out how much client state they maintain, how they support anonymous and authenticated access, and how they control the use of resources. Write a speculative report on how an Internet-based e-commerce system might have evolved if the stateful ftp protocol had been used as its basis rather than the stateless http protocol.

3

Apache

There is a good chance that sometime in the next few years you will take the role of 'webmaster' for some organization. You will become responsible for configuring the web server; you will have to set limits on how many concurrent clients you wish to support; you may need to place access controls on particular documents; and you may want to log details of your clients. You need to learn how to handle such tasks. An understanding of the workings of a web server also helps you learn how to provide services that go beyond simple page retrieval.

This chapter provides a brief introduction to the Apache server. This is the most common httpd daemon server with a little over 60 per cent of the server market. The Apache server is also incorporated in some commercial servers such as IBM's Websphere product, and one of Oracle's offerings.

Versions of Apache exist for Unix, Linux and Windows. Most of the Unix/Linux implementations will currently use Apache 1.3.27; there will be some movement toward the adoption of Apache 2, which was finalized at the end of 2000. Details of the Apache server (and many related systems) are available from http://www.apache.org/. Supplementary information, news, and some tutorial materials are available at http://www.apachetoday.com/. This book uses Apache 1.3.27 in its examples, so you should install this version.

Your study of the Apache server should involve practical work. Download an appropriate Windows or Linux version of Apache from http://www.apache.org/; install it and run it on your own PC. The installation of the Windows version is trivial – it is a matter of double-clicking the installation .exe or .msi file and then making one change to a configuration file. The Linux/Unix installation is handled through a .configure script that you run, which creates a complex makefile. This makefile must then be used with the make program first to compile and link your Apache, and then to install the Apache executable together with its work files and directories. (Some of the examples in this chapter need to reference the name of the installation directory; these examples assume that your working version of Apache has been installed in /local/apache.)

The Apache web server is modular. There is a core Apache that deals with requests for files. Then there are Apache modules such as those supporting CGI, controls on file access, HTTP content negotiation, and debugging and tracing. Some modules are incorporated by default; other modules are only added if you request them. Finally, there are extension modules such as the modules with Perl and PHP interpreters and the module for Secure Socket Layer SSL communications (these have to be downloaded separately; they are not part of the standard Apache file set). You select the modules that you require, and then you build your Apache server from the parts that you want. (The Windows version of Apache supports dynamic linked libraries; many versions of Unix also have shared object libraries and dynamic linking. If your system does support dynamic linking, you don't have to build a version of Apache with a specific set of modules; you can build a basic version and then later add dynamically linked modules.)

The Apache web server is scalable. You can configure it so that it can run on a typical home/office PC, providing access to a small company's web site. Apache can also be configured to run well on a multi-CPU server PC equipped with fast SCSI disks; such a configuration would suit a service company that provides web services for a limited number of client companies. You can scale Apache up further; one of IBM's server products is basically a large mainframe machine running Apache (it is equivalent to a server farm with hundreds of PC-based web servers). Apache is configured at start up, using data read from a file. The configuration options control aspects such as the number of concurrent clients you need to serve, although (obviously) your server capacity is ultimately determined by hardware – things like the amount of main memory, your network connections, the speed of your disks and your CPUs.

Apache deals with the full HTTP protocol. Thus it can handle content negotiation and authorization. Apache interprets control files that identify those web resources that may only be accessed by those clients who have supplied a correct password. Other elements in this control file supply information needed to resolve content negotiation issues.

This chapter contains brief sections on a number of aspects of the Apache server, explaining some of the responsibilities of the server administrator. These responsibilities include:

- Control of the processes used by the web server.

- Selection of those optional extensions of the core web server that are to be supported.

- Creation of any required security controls on access to specific web resources.

- Logging of usage of a web site.

- Control of mechanisms for the generation of dynamic content.

The final section provides an overview of how you might set up your Apache system and experiment with a few of the controls. This section has some material on the content of the main configuration file for Apache. Your copy of Apache comes with comprehensive HTML documentation (in the /htdocs/manual subdirectory of your installation). This documentation should be consulted for more detail on each of the topics covered in this chapter.

3.1   Apache's processes

The standard version of Apache for Unix/Linux (Version 1.3.27) is a sophisticated version of the forking server 'http daemon' process described in Chapter 1. Apache uses a collection (pool) of 'pre-forked' processes to reduce the time delays and costs that are associated with the creation of new processes. There is a principal process (the 'chief') that monitors the port/socket combination where TCP/IP connection requests are received from clients. This 'chief' process never handles any HTTP requests from the clients; instead it distributes this work to subordinate processes (the 'tribesmen'). Each Apache 'tribesman' acts as a serial server, dealing with one client at a time. When a tribesman process finishes with a client, it returns to the pool managed by the chief. As well as being responsible for the distribution of work, the chief process is also responsible adjusting the number of child (tribesmen) processes. If there are too few tribesmen, clients' requests will be delayed; if there are too many tribesmen, system resources are 'wasted' (the computer may have other work it could do, and such work may be slowed if most of the main memory is allocated to Apache processes).

The Apache process group is started and stopped using scripts supplied as part of the package (the Windows version of Apache is installed with 'start' and 'stop' shortcuts in the Start menu). The first Apache process that is created becomes the chief; it reads the configuration files and forks a number of child processes. These child processes all immediately block at locks controlled by the chief. The chief process and its children share some memory (this is implementation-dependent: it may be a shared file rather than a shared memory segment). This shared memory 'scoreboard' structure holds data that the chief uses to monitor its tribesmen and the lock structures that the chief uses to control operations by tribesmen.

When the chief has created its initial pool of tribesmen, it starts to monitor its socket for the HTTP port (usually port 80), blocking until there is input at this socket. When a client attempts a TCP/IP connection, the socket is activated and the chief process resumes. The chief finds an idle tribesman, and changes the lock status for that tribesman allowing it to resume execution. The chief can then check on its tribe's state. If there are too few idle tribesmen waiting for work, the chief can fork a few more processes; if there are too many idle processes, some can be terminated.

When its lock is released, a tribesman process does an 'accept' on the server socket; this gives it a data socket that can be used to read data sent by a client, and to write data back to that client. The tribesman then reads the HTTP 'Get' or 'Post' request submitted by the client. The tribesman process handles a request for a simple static page, or for a page with dynamic content that will be produced by an internal Apache module ('server-side includes', PHP script etc.). If a request is for a dynamically generated page that has to be produced by a CGI program, the tribesman will have to fork a new process that will run this CGI program. The tribesman will communicate with its CGI process via a 'pipe' (and also via environment variables set prior to the fork operation); data relating to the request are stored in environment variables or are written to the pipe. The response from the CGI program is read from this pipe; this response must start with at least the `Content-Type` HTTP header information. The tribesman process adds a complete HTTP header to this response, and then writes the response on the data socket that connects back to the client.

If the client is using the HTTP/1.0 protocol, the tribesman closes its data socket immediately after writing the response; then it returns itself to the pool of idle processes (by updating the shared scoreboard structure and blocking itself at a lock controlled by the chief). If a request is made using HTTP/1.1, the tribesman will keep the connection open and do a blocking read operation on the data socket. If this attempted read operation is timed out, the process closes the socket and then rejoins the idle pool. If the client does submit another request via the open connection, this can be handled. The procedure can then be repeated for up to a set maximum number of times.

It is fairly common for large C/C++ programs to leak memory a little. Leaks occur when temporary structures, created in the heap, are forgotten and never get deleted. The memory footprint of a process grows slowly when running a leaky program. Apache servers can contain modules from many third-party suppliers, and problems had been observed that were due memory leaks (some operating systems have C libraries that contain leaks). Leaks can now be dealt with automatically. The tribesman processes can be configured so that they will 'commit suicide' after handling a specified number of client connections. The process simply removes its entries from the shared scoreboard and then exits. The chief process can create a fresh process to replace the one that terminated.

These details of process behavior are all controlled via a configuration file, `httpd.conf`, that must be edited by the server's administrator. Entries in the file include the following that control the number of Apache processes:

- `StartServers`

This defines the number of tribesman processes that the chief creates at start-up.

- `MaxClients`

This is an upper limit on the number of processes that you are prepared to run.

- `MinSpareServers`, `MaxSpareServers`

These values control the chief's behavior with regard to idle tribesmen; if there are fewer than `MinSpareServers`, more are created; if there are more than `MaxSpareServers`, some are terminated.

The default values given in the supplied configuration files might suit a small web-hosting company with a multi-CPU PC; you should reduce the values before running an Apache system on an ordinary home/office PC.

A second group of parameters in the configuration file control the behavior of the tribesman processes. These include:

- `Keepalive`

Does this server support HTTP/1.1 'persistent connections' (it should)?

- `MaxKeepAliveRequests`, `KeepAliveTimeout`

These parameters control an individual persistent connection. The client is allowed to submit up to the specified number of requests. The timeout parameter controls how long the tribesman will wait for the next request on the open connection.

- `Timeout`

Another timeout is used in situations where a response is expected from a client. For example, if a user attempts to access a controlled resource, he or she will be prompted to enter a password that must be returned by the browser and checked on the server before the requested data will be sent. A user who does not respond to the prompt should eventually be disconnected.

● `MaxRequestsPerChild`
This is the 'suicide' limit used to avoid problems from leaky code. A child process (tribesman) terminates once it has handled this number of requests.

The Windows version of Apache works slightly differently, requiring just two distinct processes. The first has roughly the same role as that just described for the 'chief' in a Linux/Unix system. Instead of a separate process for each tribesman, Windows Apache just has a thread in a second multi-threaded process. Some of the controls that apply in the Linux/Unix world are irrelevant; for example, the `MaxRequestsPerChild` control does not apply: the threads are not terminated in this way. Similarly, the `MaxClients` control is replaced by a limit on the number of threads.

3.2   Apache's modules

The Apache server has a relatively small core that can handle HTTP 'Get' requests for static pages and modules that provide all the other services of a full HTTP-compliant server. The default configuration for an Apache server incorporates the modules for dynamic pages (CGI and SSI), for controlled access to resources, for content negotiation, and so forth. You can adjust this default configuration to meet your specific needs.

You have essentially total control over the structure of a Linux/Unix version of Apache. You use the 'configure' script to select the modules that you will require; this script builds the makefile that can then be used to create your Apache. The Windows version of Apache has a larger fixed part that incorporates many of the standard modules; the remaining modules are available as dlls. If another module is needed for a Windows version of Apache, you simply un-comment a commented-out `Load-Module` directive in the `httpd.conf` runtime configuration file.

Apache's modules include:

● *Core web server functionality*
  – `mod_cgi`, `mod-env`
    These modules support CGI-style generation of dynamic content.
  – `mod_include`
    This module supports 'server-side includes' that allow the web server itself to create limited forms of dynamic content that are to be inserted into an HTML page prior to its return.
  – `mod_log_config`
    This module handles the basic logs for the server; these record all accesses to web resources and also all errors (such as requests for non-existent files that might indicate bad links in your web site).

- mod_access
  This module allows access to selected web resources to be restricted to clients whose IP addresses satisfy specified constraints.

- mod_auth, mod_auth_db, mod_auth_dbm
  These alternative modules all support access controls that require a client to supply a password before access is granted to specified web resources. They differ with respect to the storage used for the name and password collections.

- mod_mime
  This module determines content type from file extension – so allowing the server to handle a get request for picture.gif by correctly returning a response with the HTTP header content-type=image/gif.

- mod_negotiation
  This module deals with HTTP Accept request headers that specify preferred content type.

- *Server administrator options*
  - mod_status
    This generates an HTML page that displays information about the server; data shown include the number of processes currently handling requests, the number that have finished with their clients but which are still writing log data, and the number of idle processes.

  - mod-info
    This displays a page with details of the configuration options for the server.

Both these displays are of interest only to the administrator of the web server and hackers seeking to disrupt the service. (You use access controls to limit their use to the administrator!)

- *Control of location of resources*
  - mod_userdir
    By default, documents will be taken from the htdocs directory within the Apache system's install directory. Sometimes you may have to allow individual users to have web pages in a subdirectory of their own home directories. This module supports such usage.

  - mod_alias
    This allows you to map pathnames, as specified in <a href= ...> links in web pages (and, consequently, appearing in HTTP get requests), onto different names – the names that actually represent the true file hierarchy. It allows you to conceal the location of resources or simply helps make your site more resilient to change by allowing you to move resources without breaking too many HTML links.

  - mod-rewrite
    This module applies rules for changing request URLs before the server attempts to find the file. There are various uses, but a common one relates to a mechanism for maintaining client session data. The URL rewriting approach to session state mainte-nance involves embedding a client identifier in every URL included as a link in a

page returned to that client. This identifier must then be removed from the URLs used in requests that the client subsequently submits.

- *More exotic modules*
  - mod_imap

    This module supports server-side image-map processing. (Most web pages now rely on browsers to handle image-map interactions at the client side, so you shouldn't really need this.)

  - mod_proxy

    This allows your Apache to act as a proxy server. Other machines on your network may not have direct access to the Internet; all their HTTP requests are instead directed to your proxy server. Your Apache can filter requests by blocking access to named sites, and forwarding other requests to the actual remote server. You can also enable caching; this may be of advantage if you expect many requests for the same resources (e.g. lots of students viewing the same material from a 'Web resources' list).

  - mod_speling (sic)

    Tries to guess what the client meant if there is no resource with the name appearing in the client's request (e.g. guess home.html if the client asked for hme.html).

  - mod_so

    This module is required to support dynamic linking of optional modules.

- *Add-on modules*
  - mod_perl

    Perl is the most popular CGI scripting language; mod_perl improves overall system performance by incorporating a Perl interpreter into the web server, thereby avoiding the need to start and then communicate with a separate CGI process.

  - mod_php

    The interpreter for the PHP scripting language was designed to run within a web server.

  - mod_ssl

    Implements secure socket layer communications.

When choosing modules, you need to take account of issues other than functionality. The more modules that you add, the larger your Apache executable becomes. If the executables grow too large, you risk problems from the operating system starting to swap programs between main memory and secondary storage. Any such swapping will have a major negative impact on performance. Other configuration choices trade functionality against performance or security; for example, while 'server-side includes' (SSI) offer an easy mechanism for adding a limited amount of dynamic content, they are also known to constitute a security risk. Poorly constructed SSI setups have permitted many hacking exploits. You have to decide whether to support SSI.

The modules that you build into your system define its capabilities, but many do not operate automatically. Most of the modules depend on control information in the runtime configuration file. For example, you might add mod_status and mod_info so that you can observe how your Apache system is operating; but your server will not display these performance data until the configuration files are changed. Similarly, you can include mod_access and mod_auth in your Apache, but this in itself will not result in any security restrictions being imposed on your website. You still have to change the runtime configuration file to include sections that identify the controlled resources (e.g. '*all files in directory ...*') and the specific controls that you require (e.g. '*client must be in our company domain*').

3.3 Access controls

There are two quite separate issues relating to access. First, if you are running on a Linux/Unix system, the normal controls on file access apply – your web servers will not be able to serve files that they do not have permission to read. Second, there are the controls that the web server can apply to restrict access by client domain, or in support of HTTP authentication.

On a Linux/Unix system, your Apache will be running with some specified Unix user-identifier; this user-id determines which files can be read. If you launch your own Apache server, it will run with your user-id and will be able to access all your files. (Such a private server cannot use the standard port 80; by default it will use port 8080, although this port number can be changed in the configuration file.) An 'official' Apache web server that runs at port 80 must be launched by the system's administrator (it requires 'root' privilege). Such a server will run with an effective user-id that is chosen by the system's administrator – typically 'www', or 'nobody'. If you are using such a server, you have to have permission to place your web files in the part of the file space that it uses, and you must set the privileges on your files to include global read permission. Many of the mistakes made by beginners involve incorrect Unix access permissions for their files.

The Apache server allows you to provide selective access to resources using restrictions on a client's address, through a requirement for a password, or by a combination of both these methods. Typically, different policies are applied to resources in different directories, but you can have additional global constraints (it is for example possible to specify that clients may never access a file whose name starts with '.ht' – such names are commonly used for Apache password files and some configuration files).

Controls on resources can be defined either in the main httpd.conf runtime configuration file or in .htaccess files located in the directories holding the resources (or holding the subdirectories with resources). Generally, it is best to centralize all controls in the main httpd.conf file. There are two problems with .htaccess files. First, they do add to the work that a web server must perform. If a server is asked for a resource located somewhere in the file space below a point where an .htaccess file might be defined, the server must check the directory, its parent directory, and so on back up the directory path. If an .htaccess file is found, the server must read and apply the restrictions defined in that file. The second problem is that these .htacess files may reduce the security of your web site. This is particularly likely to occur if you allow individual users to maintain files in their private directories and further allow them to specify their own access controls.

Basic controls (which come with mod_access) allow some restrictions based on the IP address or domain name included in the request. The controls allow you to specify that:

- A resource is generally available.

- Access to the resource is prohibited for clients with addresses that fall in a specified range of IP addresses (or a specified domain), but access is permitted from everywhere else.

- Or, more usefully, that access is prohibited except for clients whose IP addresses fall in a specified range or whose domain matches a specified domain.

Controls are defined in the httpd.conf file using Directory, DirectoryMatch or File directives. These directives have the general form:

```
<Directory resource-location>
  control options
</Directory>
```

A Directory directive will have the full pathname of the directory to which the controls apply. A DirectoryMatch, or File directive can use simple regular expressions to identify the resources. The control options include several that are described later; those that relate to access are Order, Allow and Deny.

The Allow option is used to specify the IP range, or domain name, for those clients who are permitted access to a resource. The Deny option identifies those excluded. The Order option specifies how the checks are to apply. If the order is Deny, Allow then the default is that the resource is accessible; the client is checked against the Deny constraint and, if matched, will be blocked unless the client also matches the subsequent more specific Allow constraint. If the order is Allow, Deny then the resource is by default inaccessible; if the client matches the Allow constraint access will be permitted provided the client is not caught by a more closely targeted Deny constraint.

The following examples illustrate constraints applied to the contents of directories (and their subdirectories). The examples assume that your Apache is installed in /local/apache. The first example defines a restricted subdirectory that is only to be accessed by students and others who are logged into the domain bigcampus.edu:

```
<Directory "/local/apache/htdocs/onCampus">
  Order deny, allow
  Deny from all
  Allow from .bigcampus.edu
</Directory>
```

When checking such a constraint, Apache will do a reverse lookup on the IP address of the client to obtain its domain and then check whether this ends with .bigcampus.edu. A second rather similar example would be appropriate if you had a resource that was for some reason not to be available to clients in France:

```
<Directory /local/apache/htdocs/notForTheFrench>
  Order allow, deny
  Allow from all
  Deny from .fr
</Directory>
```

(Such a constraint is not that far-fetched! French courts are trying to enforce French commercial laws on e-commerce transactions made by those residing in France; you might not want to bother with the need to employ French legal representation.)

The standard `httpd.conf` file contains an example of a `File` directive:

```
<Files ~ "^\.ht">
  Order allow, deny
  Deny from all
</Files>
```

This has a regular expression match that defines all files that start with the sequence `.ht`; access to these files is globally prohibited.

Incorporation of any of `mod_auth`, `mod_auth_db` or `mod_auth_dbm` modules into your Apache allows you to utilize HTTP authentication. These modules differ only with respect to how name and password data are stored. The `_db` and `_dbm` modules use various versions of the db/dbm simple database package that is available for Linux/Unix. The basic `mode_auth` module works with text files defining your users and their passwords, and also any user-groups that you wish to have. (The passwords in the password file are held in encrypted form.) The text files are simpler; but if you are likely to have hundreds of users, you should use one of the db packages to avoid performance problems with large text files.

Authentication-based restrictions are typically applied to a directory (and its subdirectories) and are again defined using a `Directory` directive in the `httpd.conf` file. The first time that a client attempts to access a resource in a controlled directory, Apache will respond with a HTTP 401 'authorization required' challenge. This challenge will contain a name (the 'realm' name) that the server administrator has chosen for the collection of resources. The client's browser will handle the challenge by displaying a simple dialog informing the user that a name and password must be provided to access resources in the named 'realm'. Apache keeps the connection open until the client's identification data are returned and can be checked. If the name and password are validated, Apache returns the resource. The client's browser keeps a record of the name, password, realm triple and will automatically handle any subsequent challenges related to other resources in the same realm. Normally, the password is sent encoded as base 64; this is not a cryptographic encoding – it is really just a letter substitution scheme that avoids possible problems from special characters in a password. In principle, a more secure scheme based on the MD5 hashing algorithm can be used to secure passwords; in practice, most browsers do not support this feature (Internet Explorer 5 and above can handle more demanding security controls).

The actual control on a resource may:

- simply require that the user has supplied a valid name-password combination;

- list the names of those users who are permitted access to the resource;

- specify the name of a user-group, as defined in a 'groups' file, whereby all members of the group are permitted to access the resource.

The web server administrator must allocate usernames and passwords and create the files (or db/dbm entries) for the users and groups. There is a utility program, /local/apache/bin/htpasswd, that can be used to create an initial password file or add a user to the password file:

```
#Create the password file in current directory
htpasswd -c .htppasswds firstuser
#add another user
htpasswd .htppasswds anotheruser
```

The htpasswd program prompts for the password that is to be allocated to the user. Group files are simple text files; each line in the file defines a group and its members:

```
BridgePlayers: anne david carol phillip peter jon james
```

The password files should be placed in a directory in the main Apache installation directory.

An example of a Directory directive specifying an authorization control is:

```
<Directory /local/apache/htdocs/notices>
    AuthName "Private Departmental Notices"
    AuthType Basic
    AuthUserFile /local/apache/pwrds/.htpasswds
    AuthGroupFile /local/apache/pwrds/.htgroups
    Require valid-user
</Directory>
```

The AuthName option specifies the name of the realm; the AuthType option will specify 'Basic' (if you are targeting browsers that support the feature, you can specify MD5 encryption of the passwords sent by clients). The AuthUserFile and AuthGroupFile identify the locations of the associated password and group files. The Require valid-user control accepts any user who enters their password correctly. Alternative controls would be Require user carol phillip (list the names of the users who are allowed access to the resource) or Require group BridgePlayers (allow access by all members in BridgePlayers group).

Authorization and IP/domain restrictions can be combined:

```
<Directory /local/apache/htdocs/DevelopMent/hotstuff>
    Order deny, allow
```

```
      Deny from all
      Allow from 130.130
      AuthName ...
      ...
      Require group staff
      Satisfy all
</Directory>
```

This example requires that users be at hosts on the 130.130 network, and that they have established themselves, by entering a name and password, as being a member of the `staff` group. You could use a constraint `Satisfy any`; this would require that either the users were working from the specified domain, or that they had entered a name and password for a `staff` member.

3.4 Logs

Apache expects to maintain logs recording its work. In its standard configuration, Apache records all access attempts by clients and all server-side errors (subject to a minimum severity cutoff that is set by a control parameter). There is further provision for creation of custom logs. For example, you can arrange to log data identifying the browsers used (so, if you really want to know, you can find the proportions of your clients who use Opera, Netscape, IE or another browser). You should plan how to use the data from these logs or turn off as much as possible of the logging. The error logs naturally help you find problems with your site; an analysis of the data in the access logs may help you better organize and market your site.

The logs grow rapidly in size. You should never delete a large log file in the hope that Apache will start a fresh one. Apache keeps track of the file size and will continue to try to write at what it thinks should be the current end of file. There is a little helper program in the /bin directory that allows you to "rotate" log files; existing log files are renamed, and Apache is told to continue writing at the beginnings of the new log files.

An example fragment of an access log is as follows (line breaks have been inserted at convenient points – each entry goes on a single line):

```
130.130.189.103 - - [28/May/2001:14:37:17 +1000]
   "GET /~yz13/links.htm HTTP/1.0" 200 1011
208.219.77.29 - - [28/May/2001:14:37:26 +1000]
   "GET /robots.txt HTTP/1.1" 404 216
130.130.189.103 - - [28/May/2001:14:38:18 +1000]
   "GET /~yz13/image/tb.gif HTTP/1.0" 200 94496
130.130.64.188 - yag [25/May/2001:11:39:49 +1000]
   "GET /controlled/printenv.pl HTTP/1.1" 401 486
```

An access record has:

- The client's IP address.

- A field that could hold the identity (user-id or possibly email address) of the client, but which is usually blank.

- A field that may hold the client's name as in an HTTP authorization header (this will appear if the client has been challenged to enter a name and password required for a particular resource).

- A date and time (and time zone) record.

- A record of the request (get/post/put/.. and resource identifier).

- The HTTP response code.

- The size of the response message.

You can configure your Apache log file specifications so a 'reverse lookup' is done on the client's IP address to get its system's name (hostname and domain); this information can then go in the log file. It is not worth doing this; it slows your web server down. It is more sensible to identify the client machines in a program that analyzes the logs.

You can make your web server attempt to identify each client. There is a server called identd that can be run on a Unix machine. The identd server on a host machine can be asked for the user identifier of a process that is associated with a given TCP/IP port on the same machine. Your web server knows the IP address of the client's host, and knows what port number the client is using; it can package these data in a UDP request that it sends back to the identd port on the client's host. It may get a response with the client's user-id, but it probably won't. This kind of identification is generally considered to be an infringement on the privacy of your clients. Very few Unix machines actually run the identd server, so most identd lookup requests receive no answer. Information can be placed in this logging field in other ways; there are obscure options in some browsers that will result in your client's email address appearing here.

The third field is for a username as entered in an authentication prompt. The date and request fields should be self-explanatory. Hopefully, most of the HTTP response codes will be 200s (successful return of the requested data). A series of 401 responses (the 'authorization required' challenge) followed by requests with different usernames is suggestive of someone trying to guess entries in your password file. Code 404, resource not found, could reflect an error by the client, but the appearance of many 404 responses in the log may indicate the presence of bad HTML links in resources on your site. The response sizes may also signal problems. If the recorded sizes are often less than the actual resource sizes, it means that your clients are breaking connections before downloads are complete – maybe your server is too slow and it is driving clients away.

The first example in the log illustrates a successful request:

```
130.130.189.103 - - [28/May/2001:14:37:17 +1000]
  "GET /~yz13/links.htm HTTP/1.0" 200 1011
```

The client's IP address was 130.130.189.103; the request was for a static HTML file in a user directory. For some reason, this client was still using the old HTTP/1.0 protocol. The client was sent 1011 bytes of data.

The next request is more interesting:

```
208.219.77.29 - - [28/May/2001:14:37:26 +1000]
   "GET /robots.txt HTTP/1.1" 404 216
```

The request was for a `robots.txt` file in the root `htdocs` directory of this server; there was no such file, hence the 404 failure code. A `robots.txt` file is conventionally used to provide information to web spiders – programs that map all resources at a web site, maybe to build indices like those at `excite.com` or to find interesting points for hacker attack. A `robots.txt` file can identify resources that you would prefer not to appear in generated web indices. This record indicated that someone at 208.219.77.29 was running a spider to map the resources on this web server (which was intriguing because this log came from a temporary server running at the non-standard port 2000). A reverse IP lookup identified the source as being someone at `marvin.northernlight.com`. It was not a well-behaved web spider; the rules for web spiders require them to supply the identity (email address) of the person responsible for the spider; this information should have appeared in the second field of the record.

The next request:

```
130.130.189.103 - - [28/May/2001:14:38:18 +1000]
   "GET /~yz13/image/tb.gif HTTP/1.0" 200 94496
```

is a continuation of the first request submitted about a minute earlier. The first request downloaded an HTML page. The page must have had an <img src=...> link. This request is for that image; the request is successful and an approximately 90 kbyte image is downloaded. Because the client's browser is using HTTP/1.0, this request involves a separate TCP/IP connection to the server.

The final request in the group involves a client trying to access a resource in a controlled area. This appears to be a repeat authorization prompt; maybe user 'yag' entered an incorrect password on his or her previous attempt.

It is useful to be able to skim read logs, but they do tend to grow very large and you need auxiliary programs to extract useful data from them. What are the data that might be of interest? The IP addresses of clients sometimes yield useful information; you can convert them to machine names and get the top-level domain associated with each request. Hence you can find something about your clients – how many are in the `.edu` domain, how many are in `.com`, are any from France (`.fr`) – and so forth. You can identify the resources must frequently requested. You can find bad links from the 404 failure responses.

There are a variety of log analysis programs. For example, you could try the Analog system from `http://www.analog.cx/`). This can give you reports with:

- Histograms of traffic (pages and bytes) showing monthly/daily/hourly traffic.

- Summaries on origins of all requests.

- Identities of sites with highest number of requests.
- Result codes.
- Files most requested.

Actually, writing an access log analysis program makes a very good exercise when you are learning Perl. So you are probably better off creating your own Perl program rather than downloading (or paying for) an existing program.

The error log contains reports for all errors of greater than a chosen severity. The control is in a configuration parameter; you can select 'debug', 'info', 'notice', 'warn', 'error', 'crit', 'alert' or 'emerg'. Most sites run at 'warn' level. The log will include entries for missing files, access failures for authorization, problems with file permissions and errors in CGI programs. 'Malformed header' is one of the more common errors in the logs for an Apache system that is being used by people learning to write CGI programs. A 'malformed header' entry means that a CGI program has started a response with text other than the content-type header and following blank line that are required. This is usually the result of the CGI program having inappropriate trace output statements in it, or a CGI program that crashes immediately and causing the generation of some system error message.

Some examples of records from a server's error log are:

```
[Thu May 24 13:27:55 2001] [error] [client 202.129.93.44]
   File does not exist: /packages/csci213-www/documents/ma61
[Thu May 24 14:00:30 2001] [error] [client 130.130.66.60] (13)
   Permission denied: file permissions deny server access:
   /packages/csci213-www/documents/cgi-bin/sp15/ass4/myApplet2.html
...
[Fri May 25 10:31:34 2001] [error] [client 130.130.64.33]
   user Aladdin not found: /controlled/test.html
...
[Sun May 27 20:49:14 2001] [error] [client 130.130.64.1]
   malformed header from script. Bad header=6:
   /packages/csci213-www/documents/cgi-bin/yz13/cgi/cou/counter.cgi
```

More information on the log files is available at http://httpd.apache.org/docs/logs.html.

3.5 Generation of dynamic pages

Most of this text is concerned with elaborate ways of creating dynamic pages through Perl scripts, PHP scripts, Java servlets and Java Server Pages. The basic Apache setup provides support for CGI programs (based on Perl scripts and alternatives), and for the fairly limited 'server-side includes' (SSI) mechanism. The relevant modules (mod_env, mod_cgi and mod_include) are included in the default Apache build.

It is best to limit the number of directories that contain executable code that can generate dynamic pages. The default configuration, as specified in the `httpd.conf` file, permits CGI programs only in the `/local/apache/cgi-bin` directory, and there are no directories that allow for SSI files. These defaults are likely to be too restrictive. If you want to relax the constraints a little, you can add extra `Directory` directives to the main `httpd.conf` file. These extra `Directory` directives must contain control options that permit execution of CGI scripts in a directory or SSI processing of files from a directory.

Server-side includes are flagged by special tags in an HTML file, tags such as:

```
<!--#flastmod ... -->
<!--#include ... --->
<!--#exec ... --->
```

Apache must read the files, check the HTML, and find and process the SSI tags. This adds significantly to the cost of normal retrieval of an HTML file. It is best to use a distinct file extension to flag those files for which SSI processing is required. The conventional extension is `.shtml`; the server has to be configured to handle such files appropriately. The `httpd.conf` configuration file will need to include the directives:

```
AddType text/html .shtml
AddHandler server-parsed .shtml
```

The first directive sets the content type that is to be used in the HTTP header when the texts of the processed files are returned to the client. The second directive enables the actual parsing by the web server.

SSI tags like `flastmod` or `size` are harmless, as is the inclusion of other HTML files via the `include` tag. The execution of code, as allowed by an `exec` tag or by an `include` tag specifying output from a CGI-script, can be risky. The code may be any shell script; if your site is not properly secured, there are ways that hackers can change the script that will be executed from an SSI file. The Apache options that permit the use of SSI do allow you to distinguish between simple uses and uses that involve execution of code. If you want to allow files in a directory to be SSI-parsed, you will need a `Directory` directive that identifies the directory and the level of use that you permit:

```
<Directory /local/apache/htdocs/allow_SSI_here>
  Options +Includes
  ...
</Directory>
```

or

```
<Directory /local/apache/htdocs/allow_SSI_here>
  Options +IncludesNOEXEC
  ...
</Directory>
```

As an example of server-side includes, you could create a simple counter for use in a web page (this script is for Linux or Unix). This would involve a shell script such as the following:

```
Val=`cat counter`
NewVal=`expr $Val + 1`
echo $NewVal > counter
echo $NewVal
```

This code would have to be saved in a file `Count.sh`; the file would have to be made executable, and a file for the counter would have to be created with a data line with the initial value 0. The counter could then be invoked from HTML code in a `.shtml` file as follows:

```
...
<hr>
This page has been accessed
<!--#exec cmd "Count.sh" -->
times.
```

(All the files would need to be in the same directory.)

The `httpd.conf` file contains a `ScriptAlias` directive that identifies the location of your default `cgi-bin` directory. A `ScriptAlias` directive also arranges that Apache will treat all files in the specified directory as executables, so Apache will try to `fork-exec` these files rather than simply return them to the client. If you want CGI programs in other directories, you will need to use a file extension that will identify the CGI programs:

```
AddHandler cgi-script .cgi
```

You might want to use `.cgi` for compiled C/C++ programs and `.pl` for Perl scripts, in which case you could have:

```
AddHandler cgi-script .cgi .pl
```

You will also need `Directory` directives that identify those directories that may contain executable scripts, for example:

```
<Directory /local/apache/htdocs/filesAndCGIs>
  Options +ExecCGI
</Directory>
```

Apache should then run any `.cgi` files in this directory (and `.pl` files if you specified both). There are more details on running CGI programs in `http://httpd.apache.org/docs/howto/cgi.html`.

The web server has to launch a new process for a CGI program (or for an SSI exec tag). The new process is created via `fork` then `exec` calls on Linux/Unix. The new process inherits the same user-id and group-id as the creating process; consequently, it will normally have user-id 'nobody'. Often you will want these processes to run with different user-ids.

One approach, presented briefly in Chapter 1, relies on a set-user-id file system. The Apache system incorporates a safer mechanism via its SUExec extensions. The SUExec mechanism imposes a series of safety checks before it changes the user-id associated with a child CGI process. These checks are intended to prevent anyone from sneakily getting a program to run with user-id = "root", and to avoid running any script or executable that might have been changed by someone other than official owner. You have to be a system's administrator with root access to set up the SUExec extensions. If you run your own Linux system, you could try this as an advanced exercise in Apache administration. The SUExec system is explained more at http://httpd.apache.org/docs/suexec.html.

3.6 Apache: installation and configuration

3.6.1 Basic installation and testing

For Windows users, installation of Apache is trivial. You download your Apache as an compressed executable archive file (from http://httpd.apache.org/). This file can be run; it will create the Apache server and its required files, and add shortcuts to your Start menu. Typically, your Apache will be installed in C:\Program Files\Apache Group\Apache. This directory has subdirectories \bin (executables and scripts), \conf (configuration files), \logs (log files), \cgi-bin (standard directory for your CGI programs) and \htdocs (the standard directory for documents). The htdocs directory should contain several example files, but the cgi-bin directory will probably be empty. You are likely to have to make one change to the \conf\httpd.conf file; this file can be opened with any text editor. The file probably does not have a value specified for the ServerName parameter; you may need to define something like ServerName localhost (or maybe ServerName 127.0.0.1). (If nothing is defined, Apache will try to find a DNS server that can tell it the correct server name based on your machine's IP address and the DNS records; this attempt will fail if you are not linked to a DNS server, so Apache won't start.) After editing httpd.conf, your basic Windows Apache should be ready to run. You can start it from the Start menu, and then start a browser and use this browser to connect to your localhost server.

Linux/Unix users have rather more work to do, but benefit by getting a better understanding of the Apache system. Linux/Unix users will need about 20 Mbyte of disk space for a final Apache deployment directory (/local/apache), and rather more space for a directory where Apache is compiled and linked (/home/me/apache_1.3.27). You download a tar.gzip version of the server (1.3.27 or higher); decompress (gunzip) this archive, and extract the files (tar -xf ...). This process should create a subdirectory apache_1.3.27 in your home directory. This is effectively your master copy. Much of the material from this directory will be duplicated in your final deployment directory.

The apache directory contains bin, cgi-bin, conf, htdocs, icons, logs, src and other subdirectories. The cgi-bin subdirectory contains a few small example programs using shell scripting and Perl. The htdocs directory contains a number of examples, including one used to illustrate content negotiation based on a client's language preferences. It also contains the Apache documentation in the /manual subdirectory.

If you are running your own Linux system, you can install Apache as a standard httpd daemon server that will use port 80. (You have to do the installation when logged in as the system's administrator – root account.) You will need to create user and group accounts for your web server (as described in your Linux manuals); the usernames 'www' or 'nobody' are conventional. The user entry that you create in your /etc/password file should be appropriate for a server – no password (so it is not possible to login on this account), and the shell set to /bin/false. The user and group number that you select have to be specified in the httpd.conf file. If you are only planning to play with Apache for learning purposes, you will find it easier to run Apache under one of your existing user identifiers with the server monitoring port 8080.

The configure script, in /home/me/apache_1.3.27, allows you to define the Apache that you want. The script can be run, from the /home/me/apache_1.3.27 directory, as:

```
./configure --help
```

Running the script with the --help command line parameter results in a listing of all the configuration options. In the disable-module section of this listing there is a table whose contents define the Apache that will be built by default. This table lists all the modules whose code is included in this Apache release and indicates whether they will be incorporated in the built version. The table data should be something like the following:

access=yes	actions=yes	alias=yes
asis=yes	auth=yes	auth_anon=no
auth_db=no	auth_dbm=no	auth_digest=no
autoindex=yes	cern_meta=no	cgi=yes
digest=no	dir=yes	env=yes
example=no	expires=no	headers=no
imap=yes	include=yes	info=no
log_agent=no	log_config=yes	log_referer=no
mime=yes	mime_magic=no	mmap_static=no
negotiation=yes	proxy=no	rewrite=no
setenvif=yes	so=no	speling=no
status=yes	unique_id=no	userdir=yes
usertrack=no	vhost_alias=no	

(Documentation relating to each of these modules is available in the manual subdirectory of your installation, or online at http://httpd.apache.org/docs/mod/.) Modules that are not included by default can be added, and default modules may be dropped.

When you have chosen the modules that you require, you can run the configure script with command line arguments that specify the directory where the working Apache system is to be created and specifying your changes to the default module list. For example, the following command would identify the /local/apache directory as the location where the web server system should be installed, drop support for user directories with web resources, and enable HTTP authorization with the dbm system being used to store username and password data.

```
./configure --prefix=/local/apache \
  --disable-module=userdir \
  --enable-module=auth_dbm
```

(If you were creating an 'official' Apache on Linux, you would define additional options such as the account and group under which the server is to run.) There are many other options that can be used to change things such as the location of the logs directory, or the cache files for a proxy server.

The next two steps are:

```
make
make install
```

The first does all the compilation and linkage of executables; the second copies files and directories into your deployment directory (as specified via the `--prefix` argument for the configure script) which for these examples is `/local/apache`.

The `/local/apache` directory on a Linux/Unix system should contain:

● `bin`

The directory with the httpd executable, support programs like `htpasswd`, and scripts.

● `cgi-bin`

This should contain two demonstration scripts (perl and sh) that echo environment variables (you may find it necessary to change the access permissions for these files before you can run the scripts).

● `htdocs`
  - A welcome page in several European languages.
  - Subdirectory with Apache manual.

● `conf`

Configuration files.

The configuration files include the `httpd.conf` file along with an original unedited distribution version (`http.conf.default`). The `httpd.conf` file has changes such as the inclusion of data defining the actual installation directories, and other adjustments that reflect the options chosen at the configuration stage. While there are many options in the configuration file that you will want to change, the installed system should be capable of being run directly.

The 'out-of-the-box' configured Apache can be run by:

● On Windows: Start/Programs/Apache Web Server/Start Apache

● On Linux/Unix: `/local/apache/bin/apachectl start`

When your Apache has started, you can contact it via a browser aimed at http://localhost or http//localhost:8080.

Apache should display a welcome page. This is actually a demonstration of HTTP content negotiation; there are several versions of the welcome page in different languages. If you exit your browser, restart it and set a language preference and then again contact your Apache, you should be able to get versions of the welcome page in French, Spanish, Italian etc. You should also be able to test run the CGI programs printenv (a Perl script) and test-cgi: http://localhost:8080/cgi-bin/test-cgi (if these demonstration CGI programs don't run, check the access and execution permissions as set in the cgi-bin directory).

On Linux/Unix, you can view the processes that are running using the command ps -ef | fgrep httpd (the ps command gets a listing of all processes, the fgrep filter picks those running the httpd executable). This should show ten processes running Apaches for you (a chief and nine tribesmen). The number is determined by default parameters in the httpd.conf file.

You should shut down your Apache tribe before experimenting with changes to the settings in the httpd.conf file. Your Apache process group can be closed down via the Linux/Unix command /local/apache/bin/apachectl stop, or via the Stop Apache option in the Windows popup menu. On Linux/Unix, it is possible to change the configuration file and get Apache to change over to the new settings without requiring a full shutdown. If you use the apachectl restart command, the Apache chief reads the new options; it terminates all tribesmen and creates new ones that work with the new options (any working tribesmen are allowed to finish their current activities before they are terminated).

3.6.2 The httpd.conf configuration file

An httpd.conf file consists of directives interspersed amongst a lot of explanatory comment. The possible directives are documented at http://httpd.apache.org/docs/mod/directives.html. Some directives are simple one line commands, like the AddHandler directive that notifies Apache that files with a particular extension have to be processed in some special manner (via a 'Handler'):

```
AddHandler cgi-script .cgi
```

Other directives, like the Directory directive, take multiple subdirectives. These directives have a start directive tag, a body and an end directive tag:

```
<Directory "/local/apache/htdocs">
  Options Indexes FollowSymLinks MultiViews
  AllowOverride None
  Order allow, deny
  Allow from all
</Directory>
```

Their effect is to limit the scope of the grouped subdirectives.

You should read through the auto-generated `httpd.conf` file prior to attempting any changes. The first few directives set the global environment for your Apache tribe. The first important directive is the one that specifies the installation directory, e.g.

```
ServerRoot "C:/Program Files/Apache Group/Apache"
```

(Irrespective of platform, Apache code uses "/" as the separator character for directory pathnames.) The installer program will have filled in the value for `ServerRoot`. The next two directives identify files used for housekeeping data – such as the scoreboard file that is employed on systems that don't support shared memory segments. The next few directives set values for controls such as the timeouts on connections, and limits on the number of requests a child process can handle. The Linux/Unix file will have directives that set the limits on the number of server processes, number to create at startup etc.; the Windows configuration file will simply have a limit on the number of threads in the second process (this is effectively the equivalent to the `MaxClients` control). If you will be running your Apache system on a typical home PC (Linux or Windows OSs), you will probably want to reduce the values for all those parameters.

The Linux/Unix file next contains a single example related to the setting up of shared objects – dynamic linking in the Unix world. The corresponding section in the Windows `httpd.conf` file is longer; it has commented out `LoadModule` directives for important optional modules. For example, if you want to support requests concerning the server status, you should uncomment the `LoadModule status_module` directive.

The next group of directives, starting with the `Port 80` directive, set parameters for the Apache chief. If you are setting up a real httpd process on Linux, you may need to change the values in the `User` and `Group` directives, and you will also need to specify your email address in the `ServerAdmin` directive. These directives can be ignored if you are simply running a toy Apache system for learning purposes. If you are setting up a real Apache server, you will also need DNS set up; toy servers can be run with the `ServerName` directive specifying `127.0.0.1` or `localhost`.

The next few directives specify the locations of components like the main directories used for HTML documents and CGI programs. They also set default access permissions that will apply to all directories unless specifically overridden by subsequent directives (as added by you). The main example here is for the `htdocs` directory; this should be something like:

```
<Directory "C:/Program Files/Apache Group/Apache/htdocs">
  Options Indexes FollowSymLinks MultiViews
  AllowOverride None
  Order allow, deny
  Allow from all
</Directory>
```

`Directory`, `File` and `Location` directives group other directives. The `Options` directive allows for the following controls:

- All

Enable all options except MultiViews.

- ExecCGI

Allow execution of CGI scripts in this directory (location).

- Includes, IncludesNoEXEC

Enable processing of server-side includes for appropriate files in this directory.

- Indexes

If user requests a directory, and there is no suitable directory index file (whose name would be defined elsewhere using a DirectoryIndex directive), then a list of files should be returned.

- MultiViews

Enables content negotiation.

- FollowSymLinks, SymLinksIfOwnersMatch

Enable the use of 'links' in a Unix file system.

In this example, the defaults for htdocs and its subdirectories are set to allow clients to view the contents of a directory (as a page with a list of files, or something prettier), enable support for content negotiation, and permit the use of Unix inter-directory links.

The next subdirective, AllowOverride, makes provision for overriding .htaccess files in subdirectories. The options here allow you to specify that nothing be changed (as in the example with AllowOverride None), or that anything be changed (AllowOverride Any). You can be more discriminating and authorize changes on access controls (AllowOverride Limit for IP based controls) or authorization (AllowOverride AuthConfig), as well as more subtle things like specifying that a directory's contents should be handled in different ways with respect to language preferences. You should avoid changes to the AllowOverride setting.

The final options in the example simply specify that by default all the files that you put in your htdocs directory and subdirectories are intended for general web access. These defaults can be replaced by other controls that you specify for particular directories.

The next few elements in the httpd.conf file define options relating to files in user directories, set default values for the names of control and index files, and define the files and formats used for logging. A ScriptAlias directive is then used to define the standard cgi-bin directory, and another Directory directive group sets the access permissions for this directory. The next section of the file contains data used to generate HTML pages with fancy listings of directories (listings that incorporate little GIF images that distinguish subdirectories and different types of files).

The following section of the configuration file has data relating to support for different file types and data used to support content negotiation by natural language type. The first directives are AddEncoding directives; these allow Apache to recognize files with .gz extensions as possibly deserving special handling. The files are returned with special HTTP content-type headers that identify the data as compressed files; some browsers can automatically decompress such files. The next section will have many AddLanguage and

AddCharset directives; these are part of the 'multiview' support for content negotiation. The AddLanguage codes supply language-specific file extensions:

```
AddLanguage da .dk
AddLanguage nl .nl
AddLanguage fr .fr
AddLanguage de .de
```

The same language codes are used by browsers and are specified in the HTTP request header as language preferences. In your browser, you can specify several languages and give them an order of preference.

If, for example, Apache receives a request for the index.html resource in a directory that supports MultiViews (as specified by an Options directive that applies to that directory) and there is no index.html file, it will look for a file index.html.xx where the xx code best matches the language preferences in the request. If you look in your /local/ apache/htdocs directory, you should find a series of such files – index.html.de, index.html.en, index.html.fr, index.html.es – these are the different versions of the Apache welcome page for different European languages. (If you want to have a default file that can be returned when no preferred language version is available, you can have a version index.html.html.)

You can even allow for dialects. Your browser probably has the preference options English-US, and English-United Kingdom (with codes en-us and en-gb). You can add some extra AddLanguage directives that map these dialect preferences to specialized file extensions:

```
AddLanguage en-us .yank
AddLanguage en-gb .limey
```

The next section of the configuration file will have AddType directives for some extra mime types, and then AddHandler directives. The AddHandler directives specify special handling for files with the given extensions. If you included the appropriate modules, your Apache should have built-in handlers for CGI scripts, image map files, parsing of server-side includes, and generating server info and status. If you combine a Perl interpreter or PHP interpreter into your Apache, you will also have handlers for these. The directives in this section of the file include:

```
#AddHandler cgi-script .cgi
#AddType text/html .shtml
#AddHandler server-parsed .shtml
```

You will need to uncomment the first directive if you wish to allow CGI programs in directories other than just the cgi-bin directory. You will need to uncomment the other two directives if you wish to experiment with server-side includes.

The next section of the file will include a Location directive:

```
#<Location /server-status>
# SetHandler server-status
# Order deny, allow
# Deny from all
# Allow from .your_domain.com
#</Location>
```

(There is a similar commented-out server-info section.) These relate to support for the server monitoring facilities that might be needed by a webmaster. When enabled, these are accessed using URLs, e.g. http://localhost:8080/server-status. In this case, the URL does not define a path to a file resource; it is interpreted differently. These Location directives specify how such URL requests should be handled. You should uncomment these directives, and edit the Allow subdirective to reference a domain from where you wish to read the server data.

The final section of the configuration file contains options for Apaches that are acting as proxy servers, and options supporting 'virtual hosts'. If you are able to set up a DNS server, then it is worth playing with the virtual host controls. Virtual hosts allow your Apache to pretend to be several different machines – provided all the machine names are properly registered with the Domain Name Services. This is particularly useful for small Internet Service Providers who host sites for a few customers. Instead of URLs like http://www.small-isp.com.bv/~fashionshop and http://www.small-isp.com.bv/~sportshop, the clients can have URLs like http://www.fashion.com.bv/ and http://www.sportshop.com.bv/. These all map to the same server, but (provided clients are using HTTP/1.1) the server can differentiate between the requests and really make it appear that there are multiple separate servers supporting the different clients. These features are documented at http://httpd.apache.org/docs/vhosts/index.html.

Exercises

Practical

If Apache and Perl are not already installed on your system, download and install these systems. Windows users have the choice of installing the complete Cygwin system or just the Apache for Windows system and ActivePerl. Cygwin gives Windows users a Unix shell and comes complete with versions of Apache and a Perl (http://sources.redhat.com/cygwin/). Apache for Windows and up-to-date Apaches for Linux/Unix can be obtained from the Apache site (http://www.apache.org/). The Windows version of a Perl interpreter recommended for the exercises in Chapter 5 is that available for download from http://www.activeperl.com/. This download is a self-installing archive; by default, it will install a Perl system in C:\Perl.

The following practical configuration exercise requires that you create subdirectories of Apache's htdocs directory with differing permissions. Some directories are to allow CGI scripts or SSI files. Other directories are to allow experimentation with access controls, adding support for server information, and possibly trying to use content negotiation. The exercise involves changing the `httpd.conf` configuration file. Each time you change this file, you should check that your revised version is legal; there is a `configtest` option for the `apachectl` script that verifies your configuration file.

A couple of parts of this exercise may prove impractical in your environment. For example, the testing of IP address-based access restrictions requires that you leave your server running, and connected live to the Internet, while you go and login on some other system from where you can try to submit requests; this may be hard to organize. Another problem might be using server-side includes to execute shell scripts; these will not work in a purely Windows environment.

The examples assume that your Apache root directory is `/local/apache`; you should modify directory names as necessary.

(1) Configure your Apache:

Unix/Linux/Cygwin users should be able to use the `configure` script provided with Apache:

- Use the `--help` option to determine defaults.

- Pick a directory where your installed Apache is to be located.

- Run the `.configure` script giving it arguments identifying the installation directory, enabling support for `server-status` and `server-info` options, and removing one of the lesser used default options, such as `imap`.

- Run `make` and `make install` to build and install your Apache.

Windows Apache users should simply edit the `httpd.conf` file, enabling the load modules for status information etc. (and setting a `ServerName` if this is variable is unset in the file and there is no DNS service available on a local network containing your machine).

(2) Test run your Apache (Unix/Linux/Cygwin installations use the `apachectl` control script, `apachectl -start`; Windows users have an option in the Start menu.

Run a browser pointing at `http://localhost:8080/` (or just `http://localhost/` for a Windows configurations); if 'localhost' does not work, try specifying 127.0.0.1.

By default, your Apache should return a welcome page identifying itself as an Apache server and pointing out that if this page is received it means that the webmaster (you) has not fully configured the web site. (The default setup has the Apache root directory supporting multiviews; if a client browser is configured with language preferences, this welcome page is returned in the closest match available from the set of pages provided by Apache.)

If you don't get a welcome page, go back and repeat stage 1, and do it right.

Note that default welcome pages, such as those provided by Apache and by IIS, have been exploited by hackers. Minor wording changes in the welcome page are sufficient to identify the particular version of the software installed on a server host machine; hacker manuals list the weaknesses of the different versions. Hackers run searches on Google, HotBot, AltaVista etc. looking for sites with these welcome pages (indicating a machine on the Internet that has a web server that has started by default, possibly without the machine's owner even being aware that the server program exists). Once identified, these machines are usurped.

Close down your Apache server.

(3) Remove the Apache-supplied contents of the /local/apache/htdocs directory and all its subdirectories.

Create the following subdirectories in htdocs: *multiv*, *progs*, *over*, *access*.

- multiv

This directory will be used for pages that illustrate support for content negotiation. It will contain multiple copies of the same resource; selections are on the basis of language codes.

- progs

This directory will contain some content files and a CGI program (i.e. a CGI program located in a directory other than the standard cgi-bin).

- over

A Directory directive in your httpd.conf file should permit this directory to have a .htaccess file that will override default access controls and execution options. The directory will contain files that use server-side includes. Access is limited to members of a subgroup of the users that you have defined in a password file.

- access

This directory will contain resources with controlled access based on a combination of IP address and password checking.

(4) Create a subdirectory for password and group files in your /local/apache directory. Use Apache's password utility program to create a password file with names and passwords for half a dozen users. Create a groups file with two groups containing distinct subsets of your users. Password and groups files should have names starting with .ht (so that the httpd.conf file directive denying access applies to these files).

Alternatively, learn how to use the dbm module and the Apache supplied support program that places usernames and passwords in a dbm database.

(5) Create the following content files, form files, and CGI programs:

- Welcome.html in htdocs: this should be a simple 'Welcome to my Apache' page.

- Form and CGI program in htdocs and cgi-bin; install some data entry forms in /local/apache/htdocs and matching CGI programs in /local/apache/cgi-bin.

    Initial example programs should be in C/C++; later examples will use Perl.

    The example C++ code for the 'Echo' and 'Pizza' servers discussed in Chapter 1 is available at the web site associated with this book.

    The little C++ framework that is used in those examples can be used to build new CGI programs. Alternatively, you can obtain the W3C approved C code library from http://www.w3c.org/ and implement a CGI program using this code.

- Multiview documents in /local/apache/htdocs/multiv: a minimum of three documents containing different language variants of related content, together with related image data, should be created in your multiv directory.

  One possible choice is to have an anthem.html that contains a national flag and the national anthem. French, US and German variants would exist as anthem.html.fr, anthem.html.us and anthem.html.de. The ordering of language preferences in a browser will determine which file is returned in response to a request for anthem.html. (You will need to define dialect variations in your browser and in your httpd.conf file if you wish to allow for different countries that share the same base language, e.g. different English speaking countries.)

- CGI form handling code in a document directory htdocs/progs: create a copy of one of your CGI programs in the /local/apache/htdocs/progs directory.

  The httpd.conf file has to have an appropriate Directory directive to allow a CGI program in an htdocs subdirectory. You must follow some standard convention that allows the web server to identify the CGI program files (such as the convention of using names ending in '.cgi'); and you must define the arrangement in the httpd.conf file (see below).

- Using a .htaccess file, group access and server-side includes in /htdocs/over: the htdocs/over directory is to contain a .htaccess file. The .htaccess file is to define access limits and options. Access is to be granted to the document to all members of just one of the user groups that you have defined in your groups file.

  The document is to include server-side include statements such as flastmod and exec. For example, you could have a 'members' page that reported how many times the page has been accessed, and when the previous access occurred. This would use server-side include statements that 'exec' a counter program similar to that described earlier and that used the Unix touch command to change the access date of a file.

- Accessing documents in a controlled directory htdocs/access: this extends access checks to include domain/IP restrictions in addition to password checking; it may be impractical in your environment.

  The htdocs/access directory contains a single HTML document that welcomes those users who have successfully retrieved a controlled resource. The controls specified in the Directory directive limit access to users in a specified domain or to password-checked users in other domains.

(6) Edit your httpd.conf file:

- MinServers, MaxServers, StartServers, MaxClients.
These are too large: you aren't going to get 150 concurrent visitors at your site. reduce MinServers, MaxServers and StartServers to half their current values and allow for 30 clients;

- Change the Directory entry relating to htdocs.
Remove the default that allows for multiview support in all directories and subdirectories.

- Add Directory directives for each of the subdirectories:

- access:
  The contents of this directory are available to clients who can quote any name/password combination from your password file and or are located in a specified domain.

- over:
  The directory is permitted to have a .htacess file. The .htacess file is restricted to containing directives that set access limits and directives that allow it to enable server-side include mechanisms.

- progs:
  The progs directory is permitted to contain CGI programs.

- multi:
  Support for multiviews is enabled in this directory. The directives that will deal with the mapping of languages and English dialects will be added as global directives.

- Mime types section
  Add language entries relating to any dialects of English or any other unusual languages that you support in your multiview documents.

- Enable files ending in .pl or .cgi as cgi-scripts.

- Enable handling of server-parsed html files.

- Permit server-status and server-info requests from your local domain

(7) Check that your edited httpd.conf file is syntactically correct before trying to use it.

(8) If your Apaches are running, try using the restart command to cause them to switch to the control regime defined by your revised httpd.conf file (if they aren't running, just start them as normal).

(9) Try accessing all the resources available via your server. Check the logs (access and error logs) and see if you can identify things like 'page not found', 'authorization challenge' etc.

(10) Use the server info options and compare the information with what you planned when using the .configure script.

(11) Use the server-status option to see how your processes are getting on.

Short answer questions

(1) Explain the following directives from an Apache httpd.conf file:

(a) KeepAlive On
     MaxKeepAliveRequests 100
     KeepAliveTimeout 15

```
(b)  <Files ~ "^\.ht">
         Order allow, deny
         Deny from all
     </Files>

(c)  <Location /server-info>
         SetHandler server-info
         Order deny, allow
         Deny from all
         Allow from .cs.uow.edu.au
     </Location>

(d)  <Directory "/local/Apache/htdocs/Project-X">
         Order deny, allow
         deny from all
         allow from xenon.fbi.gov
         AuthName"X-Files"
         AuthTypeBasic
         AuthUserFile/local/Apache/controls/.htpasswords
         AuthGroupFile /local/Apache/controls/.htgroups
         Require valid-user
         Satisfy all
     </Directory>
```

(2) Explain how a group of Apache httpd processes on Unix (or Linux) work together to handle a stream of client requests.

(3) Explain how the httpd.conf file and .htaccess files are used to configure the environment for an Apache web server.

Explorations

(1) Apache 2.0.4 (or later) is available for download from http://www.apache.org/. Research its process structure and the new features that it offers. Write a short report summarizing its advantages over the 1.3 release.

(2) Apache supports more elaborate access control mechanisms that supplement the usual IP and user/password controls with tests on environment variables. Research how these controls may be used and, if practical, attempt to implement some examples on your Apache system. Write a short report summarizing and illustrating such controls.

(3) Research and write a report on 'virtual hosting'.

(4) Research the problems relating to 'set user id' CGI programs and scripts; identify risks and control mechanisms. Write a short report on these issues.

4

IP and DNS

This chapter contains short presentations on Internet Protocol (IP) addressing and the Domain Name System (DNS). Hopefully, the section on IP addressing is revision of familiar material. The material on DNS is probably new to you.

IP addressing is still mostly based on the IP-v4 protocol. With IPv4, each machine actually connected to the Internet is identified by a 32-bit bit-pattern (IPv6 will increase this to 128 bits). Client machines used for browsers and so forth can have their IP addresses allocated on a per-session basis. Your Internet Service Provider – ISP – probably has a stock of a few thousand IP addresses; your machine is allocated one when you dial in, and this IP address gets reallocated after you disconnect. Sometimes your ISP may even change the IP address that you are using during the course of your session. However, servers obviously require fixed IP addresses – their addresses need to be made known to customers and so cannot be changing all the time.

You would not want to publish an IP address for your server; you want it to have a memorable name that will in itself attract customers – e.g. www.money.com (CNN has that one) or www.sex.com (this has been taken too, as have www.drugs.com and www.rockandroll. com – though its address is suspicious at 1.2.3.4 and it doesn't answer). Your server name has to be registered with the Internet system before clients can use it to reach your services. A server name comprises a machine name and a domain name, and both must be known to other machines on the Internet.

Getting a domain name for your host machine(s) is relatively easy; you just have to pay an organization like Network Solutions (http://www.networksolutions.com/). The rest involves rather more work. Your company is going to have to run programs that support the domain naming system; these programs are going to have to deal with requests for the actual IP addresses of machines in your company's domain. (Actually, it is probably better for a really small company to offload this network administration work to a service company, but eventually a growing company will need to control its own domain). You as an individual are unlikely to become responsible for your company's DNS system for quite a while. But eventually you will get that responsibility (and then you should read the O'Reilly book *DNS and Bind* by Albitz and Liu). Meantime, you do need at least a limited understanding of the mechanisms that do the mapping from domain names to IP addresses.

4.1 IP addresses

The original ARPANET of the late 1960s and early 1970s had a simple addressing scheme for the computers on its wide area network – a one-byte number sufficed as an identifier. In the mid- to late 1970s, local area networks were introduced, exploiting the then new technologies of Token Rings and Ethernet broadcasting. At the same time, interest in the ARPANET grew, with more organizations (universities, government laboratories and some commercial concerns) seeking to connect computers. It became obvious that an expanded version of the ARPANET would be required, and that this network was going to have to deal with organizations that had groups of locally networked computers rather than a single mainframe 1960s-style machine. A changed addressing scheme was required – one that would allow many more machines on the network and which would in some way make allowance for the existence of sub-networks – like the private, local networks that had evolved.

These considerations led to the addressing system adopted for the communications protocols that were devised for the revised ARPANET. The new Internet Protocol system was to be a 'network of networks', or an inter-net. A machine's address was to be composed of a network part and a host part. Three classes of networks were envisaged; in addition, the scheme provided some limited support for multicasting of data and for other future extensions. The different classes of network varied in size. All combinations of network identifier and machine identifier fitted into a 32-bit number; the different classes of network used the bits in different ways. The network class for an address can be determined by examining the first few bits of its address (up to 4 bits). Really, an address is just a 32-bit binary pattern, but such patterns are unsuited for human use. Thus a convention was established where an address was represented a sequence of four decimal numbers, each in the range 0–255, with each number representing one byte of the address. This lead to the now familiar 'dotted decimal' form for IP addresses – e.g. 207.68.172.253 (this is one of Microsoft's computers).

The class A addresses used the first 8 bits of the 32-bit address to identify a network, and the remaining 24 bits of the address were for a machine identifier. The class A group were those where this leading byte represented a number in the inclusive range 1–126; so there were to be at most one hundred and twenty six such networks, each with potentially sixteen million computers. A few of these class A addresses were allocated in the early days of the Internet to organizations such as IBM (which got network 9), AT&T (12), and US defense organizations (MILNET, 26). These class A addresses are distinguished by having a zero-bit as the first bit in the address.

The class B addresses used 16 bits for a network identifier and 16 bits for a machine identifier; this allowed for up to sixty five thousand machines on a network. The first byte in the address for a class B network could have a value in the range 128–191 (decimal values); the second byte could have any value from 0–255. (Class B addresses can be recognized by the first two address bits being 10-binary.) There were something like sixteen thousand such network addresses available. Amongst those allocated in the early days of the Internet were 128.6 which went to Rutgers University, 128.29 for Mitre corporation, 128.232 for the University of Cambridge's Computer Laboratory, and 130.198 for Alcatel.

The class C addresses used 24 bits for the network identifier and only 8 bits for the computer identifier. Class C addresses have a first byte with a value in the range 192–223 (the first three bits are 110-binary). While there were a couple of million such network addresses possible, each of these networks could have at most 254 machines (the machine addresses 0 and 255 are reserved for things like broadcast messages on the network).

Network addresses were allocated by a central Internet authority (which eventually became ICANN – Internet Corporation for Assigned Names and Numbers). Once an organization had a network address, it was responsible for allocating individual machine addresses within its address space.

A two-level system of network and machine identifiers was never very practical. Administering the records of the (60 000+) machines in a Class B network would be quite onerous. Further there were typically complicating factors. An organization might employ multiple technologies – Ethernets, Token Rings or proprietary systems (many of these LAN systems are limited in the number of machines on a particular physical network), or might have its machines distributed over many sites. These complications meant that it was best to break up the address space further. Machine addresses could be administered separately for different physical networks within the organization. Data routing could be made more efficient if the IP routers could take cognizance of different subsets of IP addresses being in different physical networks and relay data only as needed. For these reasons, it became common to 'sub-net' a class A, B or even C network.

Sub-netting is an internal responsibility of the organization. It is achieved by changing how the company's own routers and switches interpret the private 'machine address' part of an IP address. The 24, 16 or 8 bits of address space again get broken up, this time into a 'sub-net' address and a machine address defined relative to its sub-net.

Sub-netting is achieved by the routers using different masks to select bits from an IP address. For example, a standard class B address is composed of 16 bits of network address and 16 bits of machine address. The network part can be identified by an AND operation between the address and the bit pattern 255.255.0.0:

```
10001000.10101010.11110001.01010101 (Address)          136.170.241.85
11111111.11111111.00000000.00000000 (Network mask)     255.255.000.000
-----------------------------------------------------------------
10001000.10101010.00000000.00000000 (Network)          136.170.0.0

10001000.10101010.11110001.01010101 (Address)          136.170.241.85
00000000.00000000.11111111.11111111 (Machine mask)     0.0.255.255
-----------------------------------------------------------------
00000000.00000000.11110000.01010101 (Machine)          0.0.241.85
```

This IP address identifies the machine as number 241.85 within the network 136.170.

The 'network' mask could be made larger; for example, five more bits could be allocated as a sub-net mask:

```
10001000.10101010.11110001.01010101 (Address)          136.170.241.85
11111111.11111111.11111000.00000000 (Net&subnet mask)  255.255.248.000
------------------------------------------------------------------
10001000.10101010.11110000.00000000 (Net&subnet)       136.170.240.0

10001000.10101010.11110001.01010101 (Address)          136.170.240.85
00000000.00000000.00000111.11111111 (Machine mask)     0.0.7.255
------------------------------------------------------------------
00000000.00000000.00000001.01010101 (Machine)          0.0.1.85
```

The machine is now identified as '1.85' within the '30' subnet of the 136.170.0.0 network.

There are restrictive rules on sub-netting. You cannot have machine addresses that are all zero-bits or all one-bits; nor can you have sub-nets that have all zero-bits or all one-bits as their identifiers. These restrictions cut out part of the potential address space. Instead of 32 possible sub-networks being identified by a 5-bit mask, only 30 are allowed. These sub-networks cannot have 2048 machines each, but only 2046. Instead of 65,534 possible machines, a system using a five-bit subnet mask can only have 61,380 machines. If instead you used a three-bit mask, you would have a system that had six subnets, each with up to 8190 machines (for a total of 49140).

The original IP scheme with its class A, B and C addresses, supplemented by sub-netting internal to organizations, worked well from the early 1980s through to the mid-1990s. But a problem then arose – the Internet was growing much faster and it appeared that it might run out of addresses. The class A, B, C scheme does not use the address space very effectively. Very few organizations really require a private address space for sixteen million computers; most can't even make good use of an address space for sixty thousand computers. But the 254 computers of a class C address were often too few, and organizations had to be allocated several class C addresses.

The adoption of IPv6 is seen as the long-term solution to the problems of a limited address space (the address space under IPv6 should allow every human on Earth to own a billion computers all with unique IPv6 addresses). But a reworking of the way that address space is allocated and addresses are interpreted has proven a very effective immediate solution. The scheme – supernetting or Classless Internet Domain Routing (CIDR) – was originally suggested about 1992, and began to be used from around 1994.

Responsibility for address allocation has been devolved down from ICANN to the large Internet Service Providers. The large ISPs are allocated blocks of contiguous IP addresses; a large ISP determines how its chunk of the address space should be partitioned and sold in blocks to smaller ISPs. The smaller ISP will similarly repartition the addresses space and sell on to end customers.

The address partitioning is based on the number of bits allocated to the 'network' part of the address. The old Class A, B and C system had the fixed choices 8, 16 or 24 bits. With CIDR, things are more flexible. For example, suppose that the old Class A network 96 had never been allocated. This address space could be sold to a large ISP. Its potential 16 million IP addresses could be split into 32 blocks that are then on-sold to small ISPs. A bit mask with 13 leading ones identifies the network part for this repartitioned class A address:

```
Network Mask   11111111.11111000.00000000.00000000      255.248.0.0

Addresses      01100000.00000---.--------.--------       96.0.0.0/13
               01100000.00001---.--------.--------       96.8.0.0/13
               01100000.00010---.--------.--------       96.16.0.0/13
```

The small ISP that acquired 96.16.0.0/13 could split this into much smaller blocks. For example, the use of a 20-bit mask for the network part would break up the potential address space into one for many separate networks each capable of holding about four thousand hosts. For example:

```
Network Mask   11111111.11111111.11110000.00000000      255.255.240.0

Addresses      01100000.00000111.0001----.--------       96.7.16.0/20
               01100000.00010011.1001----.--------       96.19.144.0/20
```

A company that rented one of these partitions from the small ISP would be responsible for allocating the four thousand possible IP addresses to its machines. This company might choose to use sub-netting to break this address space into more manageable subnets.

Details of IP addresses are contained in the routing tables used through the Internet. For the imaginary example, most routing tables would need only an entry for 96.0.0.0/8 – all IP packets could be directed to the large ISP that got responsibility the old class A address. This ISP would have a more detailed routing table for the entries 96.0.0.0/13, 96.8.0.0/13 and so forth. These entries would allow the packets to proceed to the smaller ISPs who had purchased subsets of the address space. These ISPs in turn would have still more detailed routing tables enabling the packets to reach the networks managed by the customers who had rented the 4K blocks of addresses.

4.2 IP addresses and names

IP addresses have to be used in packets that are transmitted. But even when converted to dotted decimal form, IP addresses are unsuitable for human consumption. There have to be mechanisms for mapping between IP addresses and memorable names.

ARPANET started with a simple table – after all it had a maximum of some two hundred machines. The table contained entries listing the names and the one byte numbers then used as machine addresses. A program that needed the address of a named server would open the file to read and search the table. The simple table approach was carried forward as ARPANET began its evolution into the Internet, and is still used for some limited purposes. Most computers will have something equivalent to an /etc/hosts file (this is a Unix/Linux file; Windows has a similar file). This will contain the IP addresses and names of the main server machines in a local network; these machines will appear with official names and, possibly, nicknames. An example of a modern version of such a hosts file is:

```
127.0.0.1        localhost         loghost
130.130.68.33    aten.its.uow.edu.au    aten
#
130.130.68.4     draci.its.uow.edu.au   draci
130.130.68.17    kudan.its.uow.edu.au   kudan
130.130.68.29    naga.its.uow.edu.au    naga
130.130.64.1     wraith.cs.uow.edu.au   wraith
130.130.68.64    helios.its.uow.edu.au  helios
```

(The modern versions of the file use the DNS name as the official name.) These files still have a role in the name-to-IP mapping process. Most communications are amongst machines on the same local network; a quick search through such a file will resolve a large proportion of lookup requests.

The initial mechanism for handling name/IP mappings for the whole Internet was based on a similar hosts file. The Internet-wide name/IP mappings were held in a HOSTS.TXT file that was maintained by Stanford Research Institute's Network Information Center (SRI-NIC). SRI-NIC had to be informed whenever an organization added a new machine or removed an existing machine, or in any other way changed IP addresses used within the address space that it had been allocated. SRI-NIC would check for consistencies (all machines in the hosts file had to be given unique names – there weren't any domains back then to help split up the namespace). If the submitted data appeared valid, SRI-NIC would update the main hosts file. Systems administrators for Internetted machines would regularly download the latest hosts file. Resolving the name-to-IP mapping for an Internet host involved a search through a local copy of this reference file.

This scheme proved impractical for the growing Internet. There were several problems. First, the HOSTS.TXT file ceased to be small. Reading and searching through an unordered text file became something of a performance bottleneck as its size grew into the thousands of entries. The size of the file even had direct impact on network performance – there was constant traffic as Internet machines downloaded the latest version from SRI-NIC. There were also problems with validity. Most copies of the file would be out of date. Some entries might refer to IP addresses that had been reallocated; there would be no entries for newer servers in the local copy of the HOSTS.TXT file. Finally, the network traffic load and administrative load on SRI-NIC was becoming too large.

These problems were solved by reflecting them back onto those who were their sources. The problems were all due to organizations increasing the number of machines that they had, changing the names of machines, and changing IP addresses of machines in those parts of the address space that they controlled. The solution was to make each organization look after the name/IP mappings for their own machines (machines in their 'domain' of responsibility).

A machine's name became a composite of a hostname (individual machine name), and a domain name. The domain name was essentially an agreed, standardized name that identifies the organization responsible for inventing the hostname and assigning an IP address to the machine. Name to IP mappings were to be handled by using the domain name to identify the responsible organization and then forwarding a name resolution request to that organization.

Each organization had to run a 'name server' that would handle name lookup requests submitted using a defined protocol. (At least one backup name server was also required in order to keep things running even when a name server machine went down.) Most requests sent to name servers would ask for the IP address of a named host machine that supposedly existed within that organization's 'domain', but some requests would be for the hostname that should be used for a given IP address. The name servers used data files created by the systems administrator for a domain; these files were just slightly more sophisticated versions of a hosts file containing name, IP address and a little additional data for each machine in the domain.

Of course, you have to know the IP address of an organization's name server machine before you can send requests to a name server program running on that machine. This was handled by grouping name servers into a hierarchy. At the very top of the hierarchy, the root, there was to be a name server that had tables that identified the IP addresses for the name servers for each of a small number of 'top-level' groupings or 'domains'. Actually, 13 name server machines shared the task of handling this root table. The IP addresses for these root servers were held in a small, rarely changed data file that could easily be distributed to all sites using the Internet.

An initial set of top-level domains was defined; these included:

- com
Commercial organizations.

- edu
US colleges that had sufficiently distinguished educational programs (i.e. not every US college).

- gov
US federal government organizations.

- mil
US military.

- net
Networking organizations.

- org
Non-commercial organizations and special interest groups.

- int
International organizations.

- arpa
A special 'domain' that has a role in the reverse mapping process – when you have an IP address and want to know the appropriate machine name.

SRI-NIC, and later ICANN, controlled the root servers and the name servers for these top-level domains. A commercial organization seeking to be on the Internet would apply for a domain name within the .com domain. If the application was successful, data on its name server (IP address mainly) would be registered with the .com name server(s). This allowed for domains like ibm.com, hp.com and ford.com. Similarly, the .edu domain included stanford.edu, berkeley.edu and rutgers.edu.

The hierarchical grouping extended to an essentially arbitrary depth (the limit is about 100 levels, though even now it is rare to find a sub-domain that is more than about five levels down). Large organizations could define sub-domains; each sub-domain would have an administrator who would run a name server that handled name–IP lookup requests for machines in that sub-domain. For example, NASA (nasa.gov) has research and construction facilities in Texas, Florida, California and other states in the USA; each of these facilities has its own computer networks. Responsibilities for these networks would be delegated. The name server registered under nasa.gov would not hold data on the names and IP addresses for all of NASA's machines; instead, it would hold the names and IP addresses for the main name servers in sub-domains, such as jpl.nasa.gov, aerospace.nasa.gov, lerc.nasa.gov and ksc.nasa.gov, along with the names and IP addresses of the few machines at NASA head-quarters that were in the nasa.gov domain itself rather than a more specific sub-domain. Ulti-mately, the administrator at nasa.gov is responsible for everything in NASA's domain; but most of the work is delegated. The nasa.gov administrator is immediately responsible only for the data in the tables used by the nasa.gov name servers. These data will include the names and IP addresses of those headquarters machines in nasa.gov and the names and IP addresses of the name servers that are responsible for the delegated sub-domains, such as jpl.nasa.gov. This subset of data is the nasa.gov 'zone' data.

This hierarchical scheme worked, and remains the basis of the current Internet domain naming system. But it did have to be expanded, for it proved too US-centric, and even for this USA it was unsatisfactory. One expansion was to include more than two hundred additional top-level domains – one for each country, along with a few extras for obscure dependencies (e.g. .bv – Bouvet Island, an uninhabited, ice-covered volcanic island nom-inally administered by Norway). The .us domain was introduced to allow US state and local governments and other organizations to have web presences (not allowed under the original scheme because the .gov domain is for the US Federal government, while the .edu domain is only for a subset of the tertiary level US educational system).

Individual countries handle their national domain names in different ways. Some, like the UK and Australia, have sub-domains similar to the original top-level domains. Conse-quently, there are domains like .edu.au, .com.au and .gov.au for educational, commer-cial and government organizations in Australia. Other countries, such as France, have basically a single-level national domain.

There is considerable pressure by organizations to have a second level domain. A domain name like mycompany.com is generally perceived as having a higher status than mycompany.mp.ca.us or mycompany.com.au. This pressure has led to the introduction of addi-tional top-level domains including .biz, and proposed domains such as .mart and .shop.

4.3 Name resolution

This section provides a general explanation of the name resolution process, though in some details it is biased toward the workings of the Berkeley Internet Name Domain program. The general approach and the formats for all messages exchanged are defined by Internet standards; different implementations of the DNS system are interoperable.

The name resolution process starts with some action on a client machine; for example, a user (working at a machine in the bigcampus.edu domain) enters a request to contact www.perl.org. This input could be via a browser, or another similar program. If you looked at the actual code of the client program, you would see that such request is apparently handled by a simple function call: gethostbyname(*string machinename*). Naturally, the reality is a little more complex.

This function call is to a 'stub resolver' – a large amount of library code linked into the client program. The first processing step would typically be to check the given machine name against the names of local machines as defined by an /etc/hosts file. Most requests are apparently for local machines, so these can be quickly resolved. A request for an external machine is recognized and passed to a name server process most likely running on one of the machines in the local network (some part of bigcampus.edu), or on a machine run by the ISP that provides the Internet connection for bigcampus.edu. The client of course must find the IP address of its local name server. Data in the file /etc/resolv.conf should list the IP addresses of several name server programs that could be used; the client code in the stub resolver keeps trying these machines in turn until it establishes contact with one, or has too many failures. Usually there will be no difficulty in establishing contact with a name server process on some local machine; the request for the IP address of www.perl.org can be forwarded to this name server.

This name server process will be handling a variety of tasks. It may be handling external requests for the IP addresses of machines within bigcampus.edu, it may be helping some other domain by doing name-to-IP lookups for that domain as well, and it will be handling name resolution for external machines from the stub resolvers of clients within bigcampus.edu. Name servers do cache the results of recent requests for the IP addresses of external machines, and so will often already have the desired data. But for illustration, we can assume that the Unix system has just been rebooted and the name server process has only just started, and therefore has no cached data. Its first task in this case is to find a name server that deals with the .org domain; this can be handled by an appeal to one of the root servers that handle such requests.

The local name server can obtain the IP addresses of the root servers from a file (administrators of DNS systems may need to update this file every few months, it rarely changes). The local name server will forward the request for www.perl.org to a chosen root server. The root server will not know anything about www.perl.org, but it will be able to return a list of IP addresses of name servers that all have duplicate copies of the data that define the .org zone. The local name server can now cache the data in this list; in future, it will not have to contact the root servers to resolve the address of a machine in the .org domain. (All data exchanged by name servers are stamped with a 'time to live' value; if this is exceeded, the data are flushed from the caches.) Once the local name server knows about name servers for the .org zone, it can select one and send it the request for www.perl.org. The .org name server won't know about www.perl.org, but it will have a record with the IP address of the name servers that handle the perl.org zone; this list gets returned to the local name server, which once again may cache the data. The local name server will again pick a name server that is authoritative for the perl.org zone, and send it the request for the IP address of www.perl.org.

The chosen name server might not itself be in the perl.org domain. A zone like perl.org will usually contain its own primary name server, but there will be secondary name servers (that work with copies of the zone data that they obtain from the primary server). These secondary servers are often in other domains, e.g. it could be machine xxx.ora.com. Irrespective of whether it is a primary or secondary name server, this server should have a record of the IP address of www.perl.org and so can return this value to the local name server. The local name server may again cache this data as well as returning it to the client. If another request for www.perl.org is received before the cached data have expired, the local name server will be able to respond immediately (the response would be tagged as 'non-authoritative' to indicate that it was based on cached data).

Sometimes a client will be attempting to contact a non-existent machine – e.g. ww.perl.org. This would result in an authoritative '*no such machine*' response from the name server that is responsible for the perl.org zone. Negative responses like this also get cached, though only for a short time. This allows a local name server to respond quickly if it knows the request must be invalid.

Most requests to a name server process are these simple '*what is the IP address of ...?*' requests; but there are others such as 'zone transfer' requests, requests for information about a zone, and reverse IP-to-name mapping requests. The primary name server for a zone reads its data from a file created by the systems administrator; secondary name servers get their data from the primary server through requests for the zone data. (Such requests used to be used by hackers to get information about the machines in a company's domain; modern versions of the DNS software limit zone transfer requests to specifically designated secondary name server machines.) Requests for information about a zone are used mainly to get the email address of the administrator. Clients who have problems connecting to servers that are supposed to be available in the zone may need this email address to contact the zone administrator. If a student working from a machine in the bigcampus.edu domain starts hacking other sites, the bigcampus administrator is likely to receive emails with complaints.

A request to turn an IP address, e.g. 128.29.77.133, into a machine name gets converted by the client into a request for information on the 133.77.29.128.in-addr.arpa sub-domain. This gets resolved by requests that find a name server for the arpa zone, then to find a server in the in-addr.arpa zone, then the 128.in-addr.arpa zone, and so forth. The American Registry of Internet Numbers manages these zones. Eventually, the request is identified as being the responsibility of the Mitre organization, which owns the 128.29 network. The request is forwarded to a name server in this zone; this should be able to resolve the query and return the machine identifier mw-77-133.mitre.org.

4.4 BIND

Paul Mockapetris developed the first software implementing the DNS system in 1982 while working for USC. The vast majority of DNS systems currently used employ some version of the Berkeley Internet Name Domain software (BIND). Originally developed at Berkeley (~1984), then at DEC, BIND is now controlled by the Internet Science

Corporation. It has a rather odd version numbering system jumping from version 4.9 to 8, and now 9. Hopefully, most DNS systems are running version 8.2 or 9.2.

On Unix/Linux, BIND is implemented as the named daemon program. If you do become responsible for running a DNS system, your responsibilities will include keeping your copy of named up to date, by downloading the latest updates, and maintaining data in 'zone' files and configuration files for use by the stub resolver and the named process. If you have access to a Unix system on the Internet, it is worth having a look at the files that hold the data for its name server processes (these files should be publicly readable; most will be in the /etc directory).

There are two files used by the stub resolver – /etc/hosts and /etc/resolv.conf. The hosts file simply lists the IP addresses and names of a few heavily used local server machines. The resolv.conf file provides data on the IP addresses of machines that run the named process (the name server) that the stub resolver can call upon; these appear as 'nameserver' entries along with their IP addresses. The file also provides information on how to sort out 'nicknames' for commonly used machines.

Names can be 'absolute' or 'relative'. An absolute name is something like www.perl.org. – note the final '.'. This identifies the machine as host www in the perl sub-domain of the org sub-domain as defined in the root name servers. Relative names don't have a final '.'; it is up to the stub resolver to sort them out; its behavior is controlled by configuration data. If a name does contain any '.' characters it is usually treated as if it were a meant to be an absolute name. Names that have no dots are most often nicknames for commonly used machines; typically, only these are processed further. The resolv.conf file may include a list of domains that can be added to a single element name (or, if desired, to any relative name). For example, suppose there is a cs sub-domain within bigcampus.edu; local servers include balin. cs.bigcampus.edu, dwalin.cs.bigcampus.edu, gandalf.bigcampus.edu and frodo. bigcampus.edu. The resolv.conf file for the cs.bigcampus.edu sub-domain could specify that the 'search' path include cs.bigcampus.edu and bigcampus.edu. A request specifying a server using just using the nickname 'gandalf' would be tried as gandalf.cs.bigcampus.edu and then as gandalf.bigcampus.edu.

The main zone files are simple text files containing records for the various data used in DNS (the format is standardized and the same files could be used by a DNS server other than BIND). Most of the records are simple one-line entries with a record-type identifier and a few data values (comment lines, starting with ';', are permitted in the files). The records include:

- 'Start of Authority'
General data about the zone including the email of the administrator, a version number of the zone file, a default 'time to live' value for IP address values and other data, and other data used by secondary name servers for this zone.

- Name server
These entries identify the name server machines with a primary and at least one secondary name server. Most organizations have collaborative arrangements that lead to additional secondary name servers that run in other networks (a name server can be a primary for one zone and a secondary for several other zones).

● Hosts

There are records that identify the hosts in the zone using their standard names, and other records that allow for alias names for the machines.

It is possible for the DNS entries to have the same name mapped to several different machines. This feature supports a primitive form of load sharing, as illustrated in the example below.

● Mail exchange

The file also contains data that identify the machines that run the mail handling programs for email for addresses within a zone.

The form of these files is illustrated here for the imaginary zone viyce.com (no one has claimed this domain name yet – though 'vice' has been taken) with the C-network 208.209.210 (no-one should be offended, it doesn't exist yet). The administrator for the viyce.com zone can be emailed as mephistopheles@viyce.com. Viyce has the machines gluttony (a.k.a. fatso), wrath, avarice, pride, sloth, lust and envy. Viyce's principal name server is sloth, and gluttony runs a secondary name server; the collaborating firm virtue.com supplies a further secondary name server on their machine prudence. Viyce offers web access to its clients; the web load is distributed over two machines. Two machines, gluttony and wrath, handle mail addressed to users in the viyce domain; gluttony is the preferred mail-handler, wrath is just a backup.

A zone file for this example is:

```
;Start of Authority record identifies:
; main name server, administrator, version number;
; information for 2ndy name servers (how often should they
; refresh their data etc)
; and includes a default time to live for resources:
viyce.com IN SOA sloth.viyce.com mephistopheles.viyce.com (
                666       ; Serial number of zone file
                21600     ; Secondary name servers refresh after 6 hours
                3600      ; 2ndry can contact again after 1 hour if no reply
                604800    ; 2ndry data expire after 1 week if not refreshed
                86400 )   ; Minimum time to live for IPs is 1 day
;
;Name server records
viyce.com.    IN  NS  sloth.viyce.com
viyce.com.    IN  NS  gluttony.viyce.com
;External secondary name server at collaborating site
; viyce.com.  IN  NS  prudence.virtue.com
; better to define this external 2ndry by its IP address ---
viyce.com.    IN  NS  206.206.206.206

; hosts
; these records identify our machines
```

```
        localhost.viyce.com     IN    A      127.0.0.1
        lust.viyce.com.         IN    A      208.209.210.1
        gluttony.viyce.com.     IN    A      208.209.210.2
        wrath.viyce.com.        IN    A      208.209.210.3
        avarice.viyce.com.      IN    A      208.209.210.4
        sloth.viyce.com.        IN    A      208.209.210.5
        pride.viyce.com.        IN    A      208.209.210.6
        envy.viyce.com.         IN    A      208.209.210.7
        ; Round-robin load-sharing of www work across pride and envy
        www.viyce.com.          IN    A    208.209.210.6
        www.viyce.com.          IN    A    208.209.210.7
        ; CNAME records are used for other aliases; they give
        ; the standard name (Canonical NAME) for an alias
        fatso.viyce.com         IN    CNAME gluttony.viyce.com
        ; our mail services:
        viyce.com.    IN MX 10  gluttony.viyce.com.
        viyce.com.    IN MX 20  wrath.viyce.com.
```

The double entry for www.viyce.com is handled by the name server alternating the values used in replies for the IP address of this server; half of the web clients end up using the IP address 208.209.210.6, while the others use 208.209.210.7.

In addition to the main zone file, the DNS administrator would have to create two files containing the data for reverse IP lookups (one of these files is for the special 127.0.0.0/8 local network). The main file for reverse lookups would hold data records like the following:

```
        1.210.209.208.in-addr.arpa. IN PTR lust.viyce.com.
        2.210.209.208.in-addr.arpa. IN PTR sloth.viyce.com.
```

These provide the machine names that match the given IP addresses.

The other configuration file for the named process has a format and content that depends on the version of BIND that is being run. It contains data identifying the zone for which this named process is server (its own zone, and other zones for which it acts as a secondary), data identifying secondary name servers that are permitted to ask for the zone data, and specifications of resource limits (such as the number of open connections permitted).

Exercises

Practical

Practical exercises on configuring a domain name server will not be feasible in most educational institutions. Such exercises would require a subnet of the institution's network that students could take turns at administering (or corrupting). Those with access to a

Unix system can review the local configuration files for their system, and can use the nslookup program (or similar utility) to resolve example names and IP addresses. Another limited practical exercise is to use WWW to explore services offered by companies that help organizations create and manage domains.

Short answer questions

(1) Explain the concept of 'subnetting'.

(2) Define 'domain' and 'zone'.

(3) Explain, by means of an illustrative example, exactly how a domain name is resolved using DNS. You should clarify the role of:

- the client's resolver
- local caching name servers
- root name servers
- authoritative name servers for specific domains.

(4) Explain how 'a nameserver can act as a primary for one zone and a secondary for a number of other zones'.

Explorations

(1) Research the evolution of BIND. Write a short report on its history and outline the directions proposed for future developments.

(2) Research 'Classless Internet Domain Routing'. Write a short report on how machine IP addresses are now allocated and explaining how messages are now routed through the Internet.

5

Perl

Perl predates the Web and its use far transcends its deployment as a convenient language for CGI scripting. Perl is primarily an 'extraction and reporting' language. As such, it should be part of your set of programming tools. While you may want to focus on web applications, you are still going to need to analyze large data sets, such as the log files from your Apache server, and produce reports that abstract the important data. Another reason to learn Perl is to get to use its 'regular expression matcher'; if you haven't previously encountered regular expressions, now is the time to learn.

This chapter starts with a section on Perl's origins, and then a few sections with introductory coverage of the core language. The basic control structures will be familiar to all who have programmed in C or similar languages. Perl has some somewhat unusual data types – lists and hashes. In some respects these are a little like classes: you create lists and hashes; these instances hold data; and there are defined functions that operate on these structures. However, the syntax for code using these basic lists and hashes does not utilize class/object/method conventions. (Perl does have extensions that support real object-oriented-style programming, but these are beyond the scope of this introductory treatment.) Some examples are given to illustrate the use of lists and hashes.

One of Perl's great strengths is its ability to extract sub-strings from text, and to search text to find sub-strings with particular patterns; an example use might be finding links in an HTML document (links are sub-strings that have the general pattern <a href=*something other-stuff> some text* </a>). Perl's 'regular expression' matching functions and operators provide a convenient basis for the construction of such data extraction programs.

Perl has good interfaces to the underlying operating system and file system. Examples in this chapter illustrate how Perl can be used to implement programs that help automate the kinds of task that a system's administrator must perform. Perl has many extension libraries; one, illustrated in this chapter, is the DBI library that allows Perl programs to work with SQL databases. DBI provides elements that will be familiar to those who have worked with Java's JDBC; the names may have changed, but it is again essentially a matter of using `Connection`, `Statement` and `ResultSet` objects.

This chapter ends with some small examples showing Perl used in the context of CGI programming. Simple CGI programs can be written using standard Perl, but there are extension libraries that supply helper objects and functions that may be useful in more demanding applications.

5.1   Perl's origins

Perl's ancestry stems from the tools conventionally employed on Unix systems. Some of these Unix tools data back to the mid-1970s, but still remain in use. The following are among the more important:

- ed (vi) text editor

The ed editor (and its descendants, such as vi) incorporates a regular expression matcher that is used for sophisticated global search and replacement operations.

- sed

sed is a 'script editor'. It can read a control file with ed-style matching and replacement commands, and then apply these commands to input text data file(s).

- awk

awk's role is 'pattern scanning and replacement'. An awk program reads text files line-by-line. Each line is compared with one or more awk patterns; if a line matches a pattern, a particular action is performed. The action might extract data, or simply replace matched text and output the modified line.

- sh

The Unix shell (command interpreter) is itself a powerful tool. sh (or descendants such as bash, ksh csh) allows for looping constructs and command invocations, and of course it supports numerous operations on files and directories. The shell is an infinitely extensible programming language: shell scripts can be saved to files and these files can be marked as 'executable'; these new executables become commands that extend the language.

Generations of Unix programmers have exploited these tools to build complex data processing systems. Shell scripts formed the basic programming skeleton; sophisticated data processing operations were handled through sed and awk scripts. Such script programs are somewhat more limited than C programming, but generally it is quicker to implement a script than to write a new C program for a given task.

Larry Wall, who developed Perl, had grown up with these Unix tools and C programming. He liked the power of C (its high 'manipulexity' rating), and the speed of scripting with sed and awk (their high 'whipitupitude' ratings). What he desired was something that would combine high manipulexity with high whipitupitude; something that, using more conventional programming idioms, could accomplish tasks commonly handled through sed or awk scripts.

Wall composed his new tool from Unix ingredients. From C, he took control structures, I/O libraries and system calls, but left out 'functionitis' and limitations on strings. From sed, he took substitution and translation operations, but left out 'impenetrability' and limitations. awk gave him associations and strings; he went without awk's sloth, and control limitations. From sh he took processes, lists and interpolations, but forsook features like backslashitis, list-string confusions and other limitations. This brew yielded Perl – a Practical Extraction and Reporting Language.

Perl is essentially an interpreted language. The interpreter reads the Perl program (script); checks the syntax, and converts the code into an internal representation that allows faster processing at run time. The converted Perl program is then run. The typical Perl program performs text processing – finding and replacing strings, counting symbols, and so forth. Perl programs will typically perform almost as well as C programs written for the same tasks. Perl's interpreter is in C, and C's stdio I/O libraries are used for reading and writing data. Consequently, the I/O operations of a Perl script are as efficient as those of C programs. Most Perl applications are I/O bound. Any loss in performance from Perl's interpreted data processing code is likely to be small; most of the work will involve I/O operations.

The interpreter defines the core of the Perl language. But this core can be extended through libraries implemented in Perl. Perl is essentially 'open source'. Many extension libraries were contributed as Perl evolved. Contributions were made to organizations like the Comprehensive Perl Archive Network (http://www.cpan.org/) or to the O'Reilly publishing company which hosts www.perl.com. Naturally, every contributor has had his or her own favorite programming idioms and function libraries. All have been incorporated, making the evolved Perl quite an eclectic mix. One of the favorite slogans of the Perl community is 'there is always another way'. If you work through detailed Perl textbooks you will find similar examples coded in widely differing ways.

5.2 Running Perl, and the inevitable 'Hello World' program

First, you need a Perl interpreter. This should be pre-installed on a Unix or Linux system. Typically, the interpreter is in /usr/bin/perl, but on the system I used it was /share/bin/perl. On Unix, you can find your Perl interpreter by using the command which perl. Windows users will have to download a Perl system from the Internet; there is a very good, comprehensive version available free at http://www.activeperl.com/ (ActivePerl is available also in Linux and Solaris variants).

Perl is installed with detailed documentation. The documents include specifications of the core and the various extension libraries; in addition, it contains numerous tutorials and examples. The standard documentation is provided as files for the perldoc viewer; this is a rather limited command line program that allows you to page through a chosen library specification file. The ActivePerl version has the same documentation available as fully interlinked HTML documents; this version of the documentation is much more accessible.

You can explicitly launch the Perl interpreter and require it to read a file with your Perl script:

```
$ perl myperlprog.pl
```

Unix users commonly take advantage of a Unix feature that makes it possible to directly execute scripts in Perl (or sh, or another interpreted language); allowing usage like:

```
$ myperlprog.pl
```

This requires two changes. First, the file must be marked as executable:

```
$ chmod +x myperlprog.pl
```

Second, the file must have a 'magic' first line:

```
#!/usr/bin/perl
```

(The contents of this line are system-dependent. It has to specify the fully qualified pathname to the Perl interpreter; so, on the system that I use, it reads `#!/share/bin/perl`.)

This magic works on Unix because the `exec` system call uses the first two bytes of a file it is loading as a 'magic number' key that specifies how that file is to be handled. The ASCII characters `#!` correspond to the magic number that means that it is a script for an interpreter. The `exec` system call in the Unix OS uses the rest of the input line as the name of the interpreter program and, optionally, as command line arguments for that interpreter. A first line like `#!/usr/bin/perl -w` results in the executable image in `/usr/bin/perl` being loaded, and then started with a command line parameter of '-w'. Windows users will typically have to launch Perl from a command prompt – MS-DOS – window. You will need to have included the directory with your Perl system in your `PATH` variable (the ActivePerl installer has probably done this); you will launch the program by entering something like `perl myperprog.pl`. However, check the Perl system that you do install, as it may allow itself to be launched from the Windows Start menu, or provide some other mechanism.

The inevitable "Hello World" program is:

```
#!/usr/bin/perl
# Inevitable first program (in style of Kernighan and Ritchie)
print "Hello World\n";
```

The final semi-colon is optional. In Perl, a semi-colon is a statement separator, not a statement terminator. Since there is only the one statement, the semi-colon could be dropped. (Perl uses '#' to mark the start of a comment: the comment extends to the end of the line; the `#!` line is just a special comment line.)

5.3 Perl language

Most of the basic control constructs – sequence, selection, iteration, function call, method calls on objects – are similar to their equivalents in C/C++. Inevitably, there are syntactic differences. For example, in Perl a conditional has the form `if(condition) block` instead of `if(condition) statement`; naturally, this leads to lots of errors where experienced C programmers forget to put in the { } braces required for Perl's block construct. Perl does have some novel control structures (for instance, there is a 'back to front' conditional construct – `statement if(condition)`); and there are some odd features like Perl's ability to omit parentheses from a function call statement (well, that feature is in Visual Basic too, but this is not necessarily a commendation).

Perl has its literal constants (numeric values like 12, 1.2e3, 077 – an octal value if it starts with 0; and literal strings like "hello world"). Values are combined using operators; these combinations form expressions. As always, there are precedence rules that define how operators apply (details of all operators and their precedence relationships are covered in the perlop section of the standard Perl documentation). Values from expressions can be tested or assigned to variables. The distinctive features of Perl are first noticeable in its handling of variables, data types and strings.

5.3.1   Scalar variables

Scalar variables hold single values, much like variables of built-in types like int or float in C/C++. One difference is that in Perl, a string is a scalar value. Another difference is that Perl variables do not hold data of a fixed type (this 'typeless-ness' is common to many interpretive languages). A Perl variable can be used to hold a string and then, later, hold a numeric value. (Mostly data values are strings because Perl programs tend to be for text manipulations; numeric data are of course possible. Another type of data, reference values, is not covered in this brief guide). In many situations, automatic type coercions are used; if a variable is used in a context where a numeric value is required, its value will be converted to numeric form; when a string is required then that is how the data are interpreted. Another feature of Perl, and many other interpreted languages, is that variables do not need to be explicitly declared; a declaration is implicit in the first use of a variable. The fact that variables do not need to be declared increases the 'whipitupitude' of Perl code, but it does also increase the risk of errors. There are controls that can be set to make the interpreter require explicit variable declarations.

Variables have names that for the most part follow typical programming conventions – a name starts with a letter, which can be followed by letters, digits and underscore characters (special rules allow other characters in the names of system variables). Perl uses 'type identifiers' to indicate how a variable name is to be interpreted. Scalar type variables must begin with a dollar symbol; later, other Perl data types like lists and hashes will be introduced, and these use other distinguishing symbols to designate the different roles of such variables. The following are valid scalar variable names:

```
$Temp
$inputline
$count
$first_name
$x2
```

Variables can hold numeric values – derived from literal numeric constants, input data or resulting from expressions. The perlnumber section of the documentation contains a little additional information about numeric data. The usual numeric operators are available. The standard binary operators (+, -, *, / and %) are supplemented with an exponentiation operator (**), and Perl has inherited C's ++ and -- increment and decrement operators. Details of all Perl's operators and the precedence relations that exist among them can be obtained using perldoc perlop or following the perlop link in the HTML version of the Perl documentation. The following code fragment illustrates simple use of variables holding numeric data:

```perl
#!/usr/bin/perl
$pi = 3.141593;
$radius = 10.0;
$circumference = 2.0*$pi*$radius;
$area = $pi*$radius**2;
$volume = (4*$pi*$radius**3)/3.0;
print "Radius ", $radius, "\n";
print "Circumference ", $circumference, "\n";
print "Area ", $area, "\n";
print "Volume ", $volume, "\n"
```

Numeric values can be compared using the familiar ==, !=, <, <=, >=, > operators. Perl supports C's +=, -= and related variants on the = assignment operator.

Perl has two slightly different forms of strings – singly quoted strings and doubly quoted strings. There are also many helper functions in the libraries that simplify the declaration of strings containing special characters, such as strings that contain the quote-mark string delimiter characters.

Single quoted strings are literal character sequences that can extend over multiple lines. There are only two special 'escape character sequences': if you want to include a single quote in such a string you must use a preceding backslash character, while two backslashes together appear as a single backslash. The following are valid single quote strings:

```perl
#!/usr/bin/perl
$msg1 = 'Hi mum';
$msg2 = 'Goodbye
  Cruel
    World';
$msg3 = '\tHello World\n';
$msg4 = 'He said "hello world"';
$msg5 = 'Don\'t say "hello world"';
$msg6 = 'Backslashitis,\\, hits again' ;

print $msg1, "\n";
...
print $msg6, "\n"
```

Message $msg2 prints over three lines; $msg3 prints as 'backslash', 't', 'H', ..., 'd', 'backslash', 'n'.

Double quote strings support the same escape character combinations as C. Thus a tab character can be represented as \t, and special characters can be represented by their octal values, such as \017. Perl extends the repertoire of escape characters; extensions include a mechanism for specifying control characters (e.g. \cX is the cntrl-X character) and there is a 'case set' convention. As in C, the backslash character can be used to 'escape' a double quote character, so allowing strings that include double quotes. Unlike C, it is not an error for a string to extend over multiple lines.

Perl double quote strings have the ability to 'interpolate' values from variables. A string can contain the name of a scalar variable (or, as will be illustrated later, the name of a list or a hash); the name is replaced by its stringified value (if it is a string it is copied, if numeric it is converted to a string).

The following examples illustrate doubly quoted strings:

```perl
#!/usr/bin/perl
$who = "mum";
$msg1 = "Hi $who \n"; #interpolation, becomes Hi mum
$msg2 = "Goodbye
\tCruel
\t\tWorld\n";
$amount = 107.23;
$msg3 = "You owe me \$$amount\n";
$msg4 = "He said 'You said \"I've had enough\"'\n";
print $msg1;
...
print $msg4;
```

(Note the \$ escape sequence needed to include a dollar sign in a double quoted string.)

Backslash quoting of " and ' symbols can be tiresome, so there are operators to help build quoted strings: for single quotes, you can use q(...) (or q\...\, q,..., – it is q<*delimiter character*>text<*delimiter character*>), while for double quotes strings you use qq(...) in a similar way. Examples are:

```perl
$num = 5;
$str1 = qq(I'm sorry but here is the ${num}th "Hello World" example\n);
$str2 = q(I'm sorry but here it the ${num}th "Hello World" example\n);
print $str1;
print $str2;
```

String $str1 will be built as a doubly quoted string, so it can interpolate data values. In this example we want the value of $num interpolated in the middle of a string. Here we need to use { } braces around the name part of the scalar reference so that Perl can determine that it is the variable $num and not some variable $numth. String $str2 is a single quoted string; it contains the literal sequence ... the ${num}th "Hello World" ... .

In Perl, there is always another way; and another way of defining a string value for a scalar variable is as a 'here' document (as in some versions of the Unix shell). An example is:

```
$str = <<TEST;
Does this really work?
Ooh. It does.
TEST
```

You can use any name for your 'here string' delimiter (**TEST** in this example).

Perl defines a few operators that work on string data. Strings can be concatenated (this style should be familiar to Java programmers). Perl has a less common string repetition operator. There is a 'concatenating assignment operator' (the string equivalent of a numeric +=). Strings have their own set of comparison operators – eq, ne, lt, le, ge and gt. Examples of string concatenations and repetition are:

```
#!/usr/bin/perl
$msg1 = "Goodbye " . "cruel" . " world" . "\n";
$msg2 = "Stop! " x 5;
$msg2 .= "\n";
print $msg1;
print $msg2;
```

One of Perl's major strengths is its provision of regular expression matching operations. These allow searches for sub-strings and extraction and/or substitution of substrings. Regular expressions are introduced in Section 5.11. A Perl string is a single scalar value, not a C-like char[]. If you need to select specific characters, you must either match against a regular expression, or use the substr(,,) function (substr, which is illustrated later, picks out a sub-string of specified length starting at a specified string position).

Perl has numerous predefined variables that hold string or numeric data. These are documented in the perlvar section of the documentation. For most, you have the choice of using a short cryptic name (often using special characters not normally allowed in names) or a longer 'English' alias. Examples are variables such as $EXECUTABLE_NAME ($^X), $BASETIME ($^T) – the time when the program started – and $PROCESS_ID (or $PID, or $$). The perlvar part of the Perl documentation also contains additional details of the forms allowed for variable names.

5.3.2 Control structures

While it does have its novel features, Perl remains basically a conventional imperative, procedural programming language. The little fragments, as illustrated so far, have each been the bodies of the 'main' functions of simple programs. A 'main()' function is built up from a sequence of statements, supplemented with iterative and selection constructs, and function calls.

The following brief 'main()', consisting of a straightforward sequence of statements, illustrates a point that is worth raising at this stage:

```
#!/usr/bin/perl
$Days = 365;
```

```
$Hours = 24;
$Minutes = 60;
$Sconds = 60;
$Number = $Days * $Hours * $Minutes * $Seconds;
print "There are $Number seconds in a year\n";
```

This little program runs perfectly, producing the result 'There are 0 seconds in a year'. A programmer would probably notice that the output was invalid and look for an error. The error is a consequence of Perl's permissiveness with regard to variable declarations; the programmer has two variables, $Sconds and $Seconds, that are really intended to be one and the same. The variable $Sconds has a value assigned in the fifth line; this variable is not further utilized. In the next line, the $Seconds variable is implicitly declared and its value is used in the calculation expression. Naturally, $Seconds is an uninitialized variable; in a numeric context it has the value zero, while in a string context it is an empty string. By default, Perl does not report errors such as the use of uninitialized variables (after all, the 'whipitupitude' level of the language is increased by the fact that you don't have to initialize variables used for accumulating counts and totals).

In a more complex program, where the outputs are less easy to check, you might miss an error relating to the use of an uninitialized variable. It is always advisable to set the -w 'warning' flag for the Perl interpreter. This can be set on the command line if you are invoking the interpreter explicitly, or can be made a part of the 'hash-bang' line at the start of the program – #!/usr/bin/perl –w.

If run with the warning option enabled, the above program produces the outputs:

```
Name "main::Seconds" used only once: possible typo at Calendar.pl line 7.
Name "main::Sconds" used only once: possible typo at Calendar.pl line 6.
Use of uninitialized value at Calendar.pl line 7.
There are 0 seconds in a year
```

Perl's control structures are documented in the perlsyn section of the documentation. This section of the documentation covers simple and compound statements, iterative constructs, conditionals, substitutes for switch statements, goto constructs and comments.

Perl manages without a switch statement. The if statement has the basic forms:

- if() { ... }
- if() { ... } else { ... }
- if() { ... } elsif { ... } elsif { ... } else { ... }

There is also a 'back-to-front' variant, illustrated in the following fragment:

```
$filecount++ if ("-" eq $tag);
```

Perl's basic iterative structures are a while loop, and a for loop; both are similar, but not identical, to those of C (both require blocks, not simple statements; so once again there is an opportunity for error with C programmers forgetting the { } block delimiters). There are additional iterative constructs for working through lists; these will be presented in Section 5.6. Perl has an until loop; a loop of the form until(condition) block is simply a syntactically sugared variant of a loop like while(!condition) block. The basic for loop has the usual form for(*initialization*; *termination-test*; *loop-action*) block. Perl has constructs equivalent to the break and continue statements used in C's loop constructs; however, in Perl these have different names. In Perl, you use next rather than continue; the statement last replaces C's break.

Perl's while loop has an extra feature – a loop-action component similar to the third element in a for control structure:

```
while (...) { ... } continue { ... }
```

The continue clause is executed for all cycles of the loop, including cases where part of the body is omitted consequent on the use of a next statement:

```
while(condition1) {
    ...
    if(condition2) { next; }
    ...
    if(condition3) { last; }
    ...
}
continue { ... done for next and ordinary loop }
```

The continue clause is optional; most while loops do not use it.

You can of course define your own functions (Perl prefers the older term 'subroutine'). Since core Perl comes with several hundred functions, and many thousands more are available in the contributed libraries, you may find that the function you need has already been written. The next few examples will all use Perl functions from the core or libraries; the mechanisms for defining your own subroutines are introduced in Section 5.7.

A word (alphanumeric sequence) on its own is normally interpreted as a call to a function with that name. So when you forget the $ scalar type tag and write:

```
sum = sum + value;
```

Perl gets all upset with these misplaced function calls to the functions 'sum' and 'value'; typically, the interpreter will mutter something like 'unquoted string "sum" may clash with future reserved word'. Parentheses surrounding the argument list are optional; Perl doesn't mind whether you write:

```
print "Result is ", $result, "\n";
```

or

```
print("Result is ", $result, "\n");
```

Functions can have side effects through access to global variables.

A combination of scalar variables, basic control structures, functions from the library, and a little more on input and output will permit composition of programs similar to those you wrote way back when you took a 'CS1: Introduction to Computing' course.

Perl also supports object-based and object-oriented programming styles. These parts of Perl will not be presented in this brief guide, though we will be using some objects in the sections relating to database access. To invoke a method on an object, first get a value referencing that object, then use the -> method invocation operator. If you are interested in Perl's object features, you can look at the tutorials (perlboot and perltoot) that come with Perl's documentation. There you can learn how to populate a whole farmyard of different animals that respond (by mooing, baaing or neighing) in their own unique fashions.

5.4   Perl core functions

The Perl core defines functions equivalent to the C functions described in the man 2 and man 3 reference sections on Unix. Details of these core functions are available through Perl's perlfunc section of the documentation.

These functions include

- Functions for scalars or strings
chomp, chop, chr, crypt, hex, index, lc, lcfirst, length, oct, ord, pack, q/STRING/, qq/STRING/, reverse, rindex, sprintf, substr, tr///, uc, ucfirst, y///

- Regular expressions and pattern matching
m//, pos, quotemeta, s///, split, study, qr//

- Numeric functions
abs, atan2, cos, exp, hex, int, log, oct, rand, sin, sqrt, srand

- Functions for real @ARRAYs
pop, push, shift, splice, unshift

- Functions for list data
grep, join, map, qw/STRING/, reverse, sort, unpack

- Functions for real %HASHes
delete, each, exists, keys, values

- Input and output functions
binmode, close, closedir, dbmclose, dbmopen, die, eof, fileno, flock, format, getc, print, printf, read, readdir, rewinddir, seek, seekdir, select, syscall, sysread, sysseek, syswrite, tell, telldir, truncate, warn, write

- Functions for fixed length data or records

pack, read, syscall, sysread, syswrite, unpack, vec

- Functions for file handles, files or directories

-X, chdir, chmod, chown, chroot, fcntl, glob, ioctl, link, lstat, mkdir, open, opendir, readlink, rename, rmdir, stat, symlink, umask, unlink, utime

- Functions for processes and process groups

alarm, exec, fork, getpgrp, getppid, getpriority, kill, pipe, qx/STRING/, setpgrp, setpriority, sleep, system, times, wait, waitpid

- Low-level socket functions

accept, bind, connect, getpeername, getsockname, getsockopt, listen, recv, send, setsockopt, shutdown, socket, socketpair

- Fetching user and group info

endgrent, endhostent, endnetent, endpwent, getgrent, getgrgid, getgrnam, getlogin, getpwent, getpwnam, getpwuid, setgrent, setpwent

- Fetching network info

endprotoent, endservent, gethostbyaddr, gethostbyname, gethostent, getnetbyaddr, getnetbyname, getnetent, getprotobyname, getprotobynumber, getprotoent, getservbyname, getservbyport, getservent, sethostent, setnetent, setprotoent, setservent

- Time-related functions

gmtime, localtime, time, times

That was a shortened list; a few segments were culled from the list in the perlfunc documentation.

Perl's basic I/O uses 'filehandles' – these are really just FILE* references as used in C's stdio library. As always, you start with STDIN, STDOUT, and STDERR; you can open additional file handles for input and/or output. There is a special convenience mechanism for opening file(s) listed on the command line. The simplest mechanism for output is to use the print function, as has been illustrated in earlier code fragments. By default, print sends its output to STDOUT. Input is typically handled line-by-line. There is a readline function that is roughly the input line handling function equivalent to the output line handling print, but most Perl code uses the 'diamond' < > operator. Usually, the diamond operator includes a filehandle, e.g. <STDIN> (or <INPUTFILE> if you have assigned a value to INPUTFILE in a call to the open() file-opening function). An empty diamond operator, <>, is associated with an input stream obtained by concatenating together the contents of all the files listed on the command line.

The diamond operator returns the next line from the referenced file:

```
$line = <STDIN>;
```

The entire contents of the input line, including the terminating \n character, are assigned to the scalar variable on the left side of the assignment statement. Very commonly, you want to remove the final \n character; Perl core includes a function, chomp(string), that removes the \n character from the end of the string that it receives as a reference argument. (Actually, it is not the \n character that chomp attacks, it is the value of the variable $INPUT_RECORD_SEPARATOR; usually that will be \n, but where necessary the value can be changed, e.g. on Macintosh systems that use \r.)

The following illustrate basic use of input and continuing use of print style output:

```
#!/share/bin/perl
print "How many hellos do you want?";
$num = <STDIN>;
$str = "Hello World! " x $num;
print $str , " \n";
```

The line input in response to the prompt is read in the $num = <STDIN> line, resulting in a string value in the scalar $num. On the next line, this is used in a construct that requires a numeric value (the repeat factor in the string repetition expression). The input string is automatically coerced to a numeric value (if the input data were not numeric, the resulting value will be zero).

```
#!/share/bin/perl
print "What is your name? ";
$name = <STDIN>;
chomp($name);
print "Hello $name, welcome to Perl\n";
```

Input of the name *Fred* would produce the string 'Fred\n'. This would disrupt output formatting, so here chomp() is used to remove the trailing \n.

5.5 'CS1' revisited: simple Perl programs

These two programs were taken from introductory programming courses and have been reworked to suit the limited amount of Perl covered so far. Both are implemented as single main-line functions with selection and iteration constructs as needed.

5.5.1 Burgers

The following is the (slightly modified) specification for a CS1 program.

The manager of a fast food outlet requires a program to help track sales. The outlet only serves burgers with fries; a burger meal costs $5.95. Customers may order any number of burger meals. The program is to help calculate prices of orders, and is also to keep records of total orders and the largest single order.

The program is to use a simple menu-select style loop with the options:

(1) Place order

(2) Print totals so far

(3) Quit

The order option should result in a prompt for the number of meals required. Any invalid input data (value <=0) are to be discarded; the program is to again prompt the user with the options. Valid input data should result in updates of total sales and, where appropriate, update of the record of the largest order. The program should also respond with an order number and the cost of the order.

The totals option should print details of total sales and largest order.

The quit option terminates the program.

An invalid option selection is reported; then the program repeats the prompt for input.

(*The original specification included a printout showing the exact formats required for inputs and outputs*.)

Obviously, the Perl program requires a while loop containing an if...elsif...else construct.

```perl
#!/share/bin/perl -w
$cost = 5.95;
$orderNum = 0;
$maxorder = 0;
$totalsales = 0;
while(1) {
  print 'Welcome to CS1 Burgers
1. Make an Order
2. Print totals
3. Quit
Enter your choice:';
  $order = <STDIN>;
  if ($order == 1) {
    print "How many meals do you want?";
    $size = <STDIN>;
    if($size <= 0) { next; }
    $orderNum++;
    print "You are customer number : $orderNum\n";
    $ordercost = $cost * $size;
    print "You owe: \$$ordercost\n";
    $maxorder = ($size > $maxorder) ? $size : $maxorder;
    $totalsales += $ordercost;
    }
  elsif($order == 2) {
    print "There were $orderNum customers\n";
```

```
        print "Total amount: \$$totalsales\n";
        print "Maximum number of dishes ordered in a ".
            "single order: $maxorder dishes\n";
        }
    elsif($order == 3) { last; }
    else { print "That was a bad choice. ... Try again"; }
    }
    print "Bye!\n";
```

(Can you remember back to the times when something like this was a hard assignment that took you a week?)

Features to note in the code are:

- A 'forever' while loop; terminated by the last statement in selection option 3.

- The use of a multi-line string definition to simplify the declaration of the prompt string.

- The use of <STDIN> input.

- The automatic coercion of input to a numeric value.

- An if...elsif...else conditional construct (probably intended to be a case statement in the original version of this assignment).

- next and last statements in the body of the loop.

- Proof that Perl has kept C's ternary operator () ?... : ...

- Interpolation of data values into strings.

5.5.2   ls -l

This assignment was actually from a higher-level subject, but it too requires only the most basic of programming structures.

The program is to read data concerning files and directories as obtained from the Unix command ls -l. Input is to be read from STDIN (either pipe from ls -l or redirect from a file produced via ls -l). Example input data are:

```
-r-x--x--x    1 root    bin     20796 Jan 6 2000 acctcom
-r-x--x--x   37 root    bin      5256 Jan 6 2000 adb
lrwxrwxrwx    1 root    root       29 Nov 30 2000 cachefspack ->
                                      ../lib/fs/cachefs/cachefspack
drwxr-xr-x    2 root    bin       512 Jun 10 15:08 sparcv7
```

The program is to process lines relating to simple files and directories; special directory entries, such as links, are to be ignored. The program is to generate an output line for each processed input line. This output line is to rewrite the file permissions in the form of the octal code used for Unix permissions; it is to indicate whether the line relates to a file or directory, and is to print the entry name. When all input lines have been processed, the program is to print counts of the number of files and directories and then terminate. The output for the data shown above should be:

```
511      file     acctom
511      file     adb
755      directory sparcv7
```

The first version of a solution for this assignment is again based on a while loop within which all the processing is performed. The loop reads a line from STDIN, and terminates when an empty line is received (end-of-file condition). The processing depends on the specific characters that are input; Perl's standard substr function is used to select characters from the input line.

```perl
#!/share/bin/perl -w
$files = 0;
$directories = 0;

while($str = <STDIN>) {
  chomp($str);
  $char = substr($str,0,1);
  if ($char eq "-") { $type = "file"; $files++; }
  elsif($char eq 'd') { $type = "directory"; $directories++; }
  else { next; }
  $code1 = 0;
  #compose octal code for owner
  if("r" eq substr($str,1,1)) { $code1 +=4; }
  if("w" eq substr($str,2,1)) { $code1 +=2; }
  if("x" eq substr($str,3,1)) { $code1 +=1; }
  $code2 = 0;
  #compose octal code for group
  if("r" eq substr($str,4,1)) { $code2 +=4; }
  if("w" eq substr($str,5,1)) { $code2 +=2; }
  if("x" eq substr($str,6,1)) { $code2 +=1; }
  $code3 = 0;
  #compose octal code for other
  if("r" eq substr($str,7,1)) { $code3 +=4; }
  if("w" eq substr($str,8,1)) { $code3 +=2; }
  if("x" eq substr($str,9,1)) { $code3 +=1; }
  $code = $code1 . $code2 . $code3;
  # extract file name at end of line

  $name = substr($str, $pos+1);
```

```
        print "${code}\t${type}\t${name}\n";

    }
    print "$files files, and $directories directories\n";
```

The loop `while($str=<STDIN>) { }` reads the next input line and assigns it to the `$str` variable. At end-of-file, `<STDIN>` will return the empty string `""` which is interpreted as false; this terminates the `while` loop.

The `substr()` function supports several usages:

- `substr(str,offset)`

Selects the remainder of the string starting at the characters specified by the offset.

- `substr(str,offset,length)`

Selects a sub-string of specified length, starting at the specified offset.

- `substr(str,offset,length,replacement)`

Replace the sub-string.

An offset can be negative; a negative offset is interpreted as being relative to the end of the string. Most of this program's calls to `substr` are selecting individual characters, so they have specified offsets and unit lengths. The first test determines whether the input data line relates to a directory, a simple file, or some other entry such as a symbolic link. Directories appear in the `ls -l` listing with a 'd' as the first letter; simple files start with a '-' symbol.

This program has rather labored code to build the octal codes for the three permission groups. Explicit tests are made for 'read', 'write' and 'execute' character tags in the input. If a tag is set, the code is incremented by the appropriate amount.

The filename is the last entry on the input line; it will be preceded immediately by a space. The `rindex()` library function finds the last occurrence of a specified sub-string in a string; here it is used to select the last space character (`$pos = rindex($str, " ");`). The name is the sub-string starting at the next character and including all the remainder of the string (`$name = substr($str, $pos+1);`).

In addition to the simple `print` function, Perl programs can also use `printf` from C's `stdio` package. The `printf` function takes a format list argument that permits greater control over output. The simpler `lister.pl` example shown above can be rewritten using a for loop as the basis of a more effective mechanism for computing the access code and `printf` to format the output.

```
    while($str = <STDIN>) {
      chomp($str);
      $char = substr($str,0,1);
      if ($char eq "-") { $type = "file"; $files++; }
      elsif($char eq 'd') { $type = "directory"; $directories++; }
      else { next; }
      $code = 0;
```

```
for($i=1;$i<10;$i++) {
  $code *=2;
  if("-" ne substr($str,$i,1)) { $code++; }
}
$pos = rindex($str, " ");
$name = substr($str, $pos+1);
printf "%o%s" , $code , "\t${type}\t${name}\n";
}
```

In the printf statement, the first argument '%o%s' is the format string; this specifies output of a numeric value in octal, followed by a string. The other arguments are the code, and a string with the type (file or directory) and the entity name. Of course, there is another way of doing it. Since a format string is a doubly quoted Perl string, it can interpolate values. The following variant would be as good:

```
printf "%o\t${type}\t${name}\n " , $code ;
```

5.6   Beyond CS1: lists and arrays

A few more features of Perl must be covered before any more interesting programs can be written. First, we need Perl's 'lists' (or 'arrays'). A Perl list is like a dynamic array class in C++ or Java (e.g. java.util.Vector). Lists do not use Perl's object syntax, but a list is basically an object that owns data and which has an associated group of functions. A Perl list:

- Owns a collection of data elements (usually scalar values, but you can build lists of lists and other more complex structures as explained in the perldsc – 'data structures cookbook' – section of the documentation)

- Does (OK, 'has done to it', as these are not class member functions):
  - Create a list, usually initializing it with a non-empty set of data elements (though empty lists are fine).
  - Add elements 'at front' or 'at end' of the list.
  - Remove elements 'at front' or 'at end' of the lists.
  - Access elements at specific positions (this feature gives it 'array'-like behaviors as well as list behaviors).
  - Return the size of its collection (length of dynamic array).
  - Copy into another array.

Other functions related to lists include functions for sorting lists and for returning copies of lists with the elements in reversed order.

5.6.1   Basics of lists

Lists are designated using the '@' type qualifier. Their names follow the usual conventions – letter followed by alphanumerics (and some other characters in the special names for lists supplied in the Perl core). When forming names, Perl considers the underscore character as a letter. Valid list names are:

```
@mylist
@results
@inputlines
@_data
@list_1
```

Perl maintains distinct 'namespaces' for its different scalar, list and hash data types (and other types like 'file handles'). You can have a scalar $results and a list @results without causing Perl any confusion (though you may upset an inexperienced maintenance programmer who has to look after your code).

List literals are supported:

```
(1, 2, 3)
( "tom", "dick", "harry", "sue")
( $name, $address, $town)
```

List literals are often used to initialize arrays. Another usage has the list literal as an 'lvalue' (something on the left-hand side of an assignment statement). This usage will be illustrated later; it is a convenience feature related to the extraction of specific elements from an existing list. Some examples of list literals being used in list/array creation are:

```
@PlacesIveBeen = (); # I've been nowhere yet - so, an empty list
@GradePts = (45, 50, 65, 75, 85);
@Cities = ( "London", "Paris", "New York", "Rome", "Tokyo", "Sydney");
@people = ( "tom", "dick", "harry", "sue");
@TeenYears = (13 .. 19);
```

The last of these illustrates Perl's '..' range operator. This is a short way of defining the collection as (13, 14, 15, 16, 17, 18, 19). Range operators can be used in 'foreach' iterative constructs – for (1..100); foreach loops are explained later in this section.

Since it is common to need to initialize a list of words, Perl has a helper function qw(). Thus, you could have:

```
@people = qw( tom dick harry sue );
```

The qw() function isn't always appropriate. The following usage:

```
@Cities = qw (London Paris 'New York' Rome Tokyo Sydney);
```

results in a list like:

```
(London, Paris, 'New, York', Rome, Tokyo, Sydney)
```

which is probably not what was intended.

The following code fragment illustrates the creation and use of some lists. The loops illustrate different ways of accessing the list elements:

```
@Cities1 = ("London", "Paris", "New York"); # a list with 3 elements
@Cities2 = qw( Rome 'Los Angeles' "San Francisco"); # 5 elements!
@Cities3 = ("Wagga", "Hay", "Cooma");
#like qq() and q(), qw() allows other delimiters:
@Cities4 = qw\ Thiroul Bellambi Keiraville\;
print "Cities1 :\n";
$size = @Cities1;
for($i=0;$i<$size;$i++) {
  print $Cities1[$i] , "\n";
  }
print "Cities1 :\n";
foreach $city (@Cities2) {
  print $city , "\n";
  }
print "Cities3 :\n";
foreach $i (0 .. $#Cities3) {
  print $Cities3[$i] , "\n";
  }
print "Cities4 :@Cities4\n";
print @Cities4;
```

The line $size = @Cities1; illustrates the use of an array in a 'scalar context'; Perl interprets this as a request for the length of the array; so $size takes the value 3. The first for loop is a conventional counting loop, with the loop index used to index into the @Cities1 collection. Note the usage $Cities[$i]; the data type here is a scalar – we are extracting a single data element from the specified position in the collection.

The second and third for loops are examples of Perl's foreach loop construct. These loops have the form:

```
foreach <variable> (list) block
foreach (list) block
```

(The keyword for may be used instead of foreach, but foreach is more readable.) Usually you want a variable that references the current element from the list, but this is not essential. The first of the foreach loops in the example code simply accesses each of the (five!) elements in $Cities2, printing the name of each in turn. The second is more like a counting for loop; the expression $#Cities3 returns the (scalar) value that is the index of the last element of the list @Cities3. Consequently, this loop is really foreach $i (0, 1, 2) { ... }; this loop again uses array style indexing to extract data elements from the list. Finally, the list $Cities4 is printed twice. The first print statement has the list interpolated into a string; this prints the elements separated by spaces. The final print statement results in a line with all data elements concatenated into one long string (not a particularly useful form of output, just another feature of the Perl system).

Lists can be concatenated together:

```
@Male = qw(Mickey Donald);
@Female = qw(Minnie Daisy);
@DisneyMob = (@Male, @Female, "Pluto");
```

This produces a single-level list (not a Lisp-like list of lists):

```
Mickey, Donald, Minnie, Daisy, Pluto
```

Arrays can be 'sliced' to give subarrays:

```
@line = qw(one two three four);
@firsttwo = @line[0,1];
@line[0,1] = ("five", "six");
```

or can have values pushed and popped:

```
@stack = ();
push(@stack, "one");
push(@stack, "two");
push(@stack, 3, 4);
push(@stack, 5, 6, 7, 8, "nine", 101 );
print @stack, "\n";
$val = pop(@stack);
print "@stack\n";
```

(shift and unshift work in a similar way, operating at the start rather than the end of a list. You can combine pushing and shifting etc. to achieve something like a double-ended queue.)

The reverse function returns a copy of the list with the elements in reverse order. By default, the sort function uses an alphabetic sort, treating all list elements as strings; again it returns a new list.

```
@newRevList = reverse(@aList);
@list1 = qw(This is a test what else Hello World Hi mom etc etc);
# Prints as :
List1: This is a test what else Hello World Hi mom etc etc
# Peform sort, then print sorted list; upper case letters rank
# lower than lower case letters ...
Sorted: Hello Hi This World a else etc etc is mom test what
#Some numeric data
@list2 = ( 100, 26, 3, 49, -11, 3001, 78);
```

```
# Sorted! (Sorted alphabetically)
Sorted:-11 100 26 3 3001 49 78
```

The default sort behavior of alphabetic sorting can be modified; you have to provide your own sort helper subroutine. The helper functions for sorting are a little atypical of user-defined routines, but they are not hard to write. Your routine will be called to return the result of a comparison operation on two elements from the array – these elements will have been placed in the global variables $a and $b prior to the call to your subroutine. (This use of specific global variables is what makes these sort subroutines different from other programmer-defined routines.)

The following code illustrates the definition and use of a sort helper subroutine 'numeric_sort'.

```
#!/share/bin/perl -w
sub numeric_sort {
  if($a < $b) { return -1; }
  elsif($a == $b) { return 0; }
  else { return 1; }
}
@list2 = ( 100, 26, 3, 49, -11, 3001, 78);
@slist2 = sort @list2;
print "List2 @list2\n";
print "Sorted List2 (default sort) @slist2\n";
@nlist2 = sort numeric_sort @list2;
print "Sorted List2 (numeric sort) @nlist2\n";
```

Perl has a special <=> operator for numeric comparisons; using this operator, the numeric sort function could be simplified:

```
sub numeric_sort {
  @a <=> $b
}
```

Perl permits in-line definition of sort helper functions, allowing constructs such as:

```
@nlist2 = sort { $a <=> $b } @list2;
```

5.6.2   Two simple list examples

Many simple databases and spreadsheets have options that let you get a listing of their contents as a text file. Such a file will contain one line for each record; fields in the record will be separated in the file by some delimiter character (usually the tab or colon character). For example, a database that recorded the names, roles, departments, rooms and phone numbers of employees might be dumped to file in a format like the following:

```
J.Smith:Painter:Buildings & Grounds::3456
T.Smythe:Audit clerk:Administration:15.205:3383
A.Solly:Help line:Sales:8.177:4222
```

Perl programs can be very effective for processing such data.

The input lines can be broken into lists of elements. The simplest way is to use Perl's split() function as illustrated in this example, but there are alternative ways involving more complex uses of regular expression matchers. Once the data are in lists, Perl can easily manipulate the records and so produce reports such as reverse telephone directories (mapping phone numbers to people), listing of employees with no specified room number, and so forth.

The following little program (which employs a few Perl 'tricks') generates a report that identifies those employees who have no assigned room:

```
while(<STDIN>) {
  @line= split /:/ ;
  $room = $line[3];
  if(!$room) {
    print $line[0], "\n" ;
    }
}
```

The main 'trick' here is the use of Perl's 'anonymous' variable. The statement while(<STDIN>) clearly reads in the next line of input and tests for an empty line, but it is not explicit as to where that input line is stored. In many places like this, Perl allows the programmer to omit reference to an explicit variable; if the context requires a variable, Perl automatically substitutes the 'anonymous variable' $_. (This feature is a part of the high whipitupitude level of the Perl language: you don't have to define variables whose role is simply to hold data temporarily.) The while statement is really equivalent to while($_ = <STDIN>) { ... }.

The split function is then used to break the input line into separate elements. This function is documented, in the perlfunc section, as one of the regular expression and pattern matching functions. It has the following usages:

```
split /PATTERN/,EXPR,LIMIT
split /PATTERN/,EXPR
split /PATTERN/
```

It splits the string given by EXPR. The PATTERN element is a regular expression specifying the characters that form the element separators; here it is particularly simple: the pattern specifies the colon character used in the example data. The LIMIT element is optional: it allows you to split out the first *n* elements from the expression, ignoring any others. The example code uses the simplest form of split, with merely the specification of the separator pattern. Here split is implicitly operating on the anonymous variable $_ that has just had assigned the value of a string representing the next line of input. The list resulting from the splitting operation is assigned to the list variable @line.

The room was the fourth element of the print lines in the dump file from the database. Array indexing style operations allow this scalar value to be extracted from the list/array @line. If this is 'null' ('undef' or undefined in Perl), the employee's name is printed.

In this example, only one element of the list was required; array-style subscripting is the appropriate way to extract the data. If more of the data were to be processed, then rather than code like the following:

```perl
$name = $line[0];
$role = $line[1];
$department = $line[2];
```

one can use a list literal as an lvalue:

```perl
($name, $role, $department) = @line;
```

This statement copies the first three elements from the list @line into the named scalar variables. It is also possible to select a few elements into scalars, and keep the remaining elements in another array:

```perl
($name, $role, $department, @rest) = @line;
```

Use of list literals would allow the first example program to be simplified to:

```perl
while(<STDIN>) {
    ($name, $role, $department, $room, $phone) = split /:/ ;
    if(!$room) {
        print $name, "\n" ;
    }
}
```

The second example is a program to produce a 'keyword in context' index for a set of film titles. The input data for this program are the film titles; one title per line, with keywords capitalized. Example data could be:

```
The Matrix
The Empire Strikes Back
The Return of the Jedi
Moulin Rouge
Picnic at Hanging Rock
Gone with the Wind
The Vertical Ray of the Sun
Sabrina
The Sound of Music
```

```
Captain Corelli's Mandolin
The African Queen
Casablanca
```

From these data, the program is to produce a permuted keyword in context index of the titles:

```
                 The    African Queen
   The Empire Strikes    Back
                         Captain Corelli's Mandolin
                         Casablanca
             Captain    Corelli's Mandolin
                 The    Empire Strikes Back
                         Gone with the Wind
          Picnic at     Hanging Rock
   The Return of the    Jedi
   Captain Corelli's    Mandolin
                 The    Matrix
                         Moulin Rouge
      The Sound of      Music
                         Picnic at Hanging Rock
        The African     Queen
        The Vertical    Ray of the Sun
                 The    Return of the Jedi
 Picnic at Hanging      Rock
             Moulin     Rouge
                         Sabrina
                 The    Sound of Music
          The Empire    Strikes Back
The Vertical Ray of the Sun
                         The African Queen
                         The Empire Strikes Back
                         The Matrix
                         The Return of the Jedi
                         The Sound of Music
                         The Vertical Ray of the Sun
                 The    Vertical Ray of the Sun
      Gone with the     Wind
```

The program has to loop, reading and processing each line of input (film title). Given a line, the program must find the keywords – these are the words that start with a capital letter. For each keyword, the program must generate a string with the context – separating the words before the keyword from the keyword and remainder of the words in the line. This generated string must be added to a collection. When all data have been read, the collection has to be sorted using a specialized sort helper routine. Finally, the sorted list is printed. (The actual coding could be made more efficient; the mechanisms used have been selected to illustrate a few more of Perl's standard features.) The code (given in full later) has the general structure:

```
@collection = ();
#read loop
while($title = <STDIN>) {
  chomp($title);
  @Title = split / / , $title;
  ...
  foreach $i (0 .. $#Title) {
    $Word = $Title[$i];
    # if keyword, then generate another output line
    # and add to collection
    ...
  }
}
# sort collection using special helper function
@sortcollection = sort by_keystr @collection;
# print the sorted data
foreach $entry (@sortcollection) {
  print $entry;
}
```

Each output line consists in effect of a list of words (the words before the keyword) printed right justified in a fixed width field, a gap of a few spaces, and then the keyword and remaining words printed left justified. These lines have to be sorted using an alphabetic ordering that uses the sub-string starting at the keyword. The keyword starts after column 50, so we require a special sort helper routine that picks out these sub-strings.

The sort routine is similar to the numeric_sort illustrated earlier. It relies on the convention that, before the routine is called, the global variables $a and $b will have been assigned the two data elements (in this case report lines) that must be compared.

```
sub by_keystr {
  my $str1 = substr($a,50);
  my $str2 = substr($b,50);
  if($str1 lt $str2) { return -1; }
  elsif($str1 eq $str2) { return 0; }
  else { return 1; }
}
```

This subroutine requires local variables to store the two sub-strings. Perl permits the declaration of variables whose scope is limited to the body of a function (or, scoped to an inner block in which they are declared). These variables are declared with the keyword my; here the sort helper function has two local variables $str1 and $str2. These contain the sub-strings starting at position 50 from the two generated lines. The lt and eq comparisons done on these strings could be simplified using Perl's cmp operator (it is a string version of the <=> operator mentioned in the context of the numeric sort helper function).

The body of the main while loop works by splitting the input line into a list of words and then processing this list.

```perl
while($title = <STDIN>) {
  chomp($title);
  @Title = split / / , $title;
  ...
  foreach $i (0 .. $#Title) {
  $Word = $Title[$i];
  ... }
}
```

Each word must be tested to determine whether it is a keyword. This can be done using a simple regular expression match. The pattern in this regular expression specifies that there must be an upper-case letter at the beginning of the string held in $Word:

```perl
if($Word =~ /^[A-Z]/) { ... }
```

The =~ operator is Perl's regular expression matching operator; this is used to invoke the comparison of the value of $Word and the /^[A-Z]/ pattern. (Regular expressions are covered in more detail in Section 5.11. Here the ^ symbol signifies that the pattern must be found at the start of the string; the [A-Z] construct specifies the requirement for a single letter taken from the set of all capital letters).

If the current word is classified as a keyword, then the words before it are combined to form the start string, and the keyword and remaining words are combined to form an end string. These strings can then be combined to produce a line for the final output. This is achieved using the sprintf function (the same as that in C's stdio library). The sprintf function creates a string in memory, returning this string as its result. Like printf, sprintf takes a format string and a list of arguments. The output lines shown can be produced using the statement:

```perl
$line = sprintf "%50s %-50s\n", $start, $end;
```

The complete program is:

```perl
#!/usr/bin/perl
sub by_keystr {
  my $str1 = substr($a,50);
  my $str2 = substr($b,50);
  if($str1 lt $str2) { return -1; }
  elsif($str1 eq $str2) { return 0; }
  else { return 1; }
```

```
      }
   @collection = ();
   while($title = <STDIN>) {
      chomp($title);
      @Title = split / / , $title;
      $start = "";
      foreach $i (0 .. $#Title) {
         $Word = $Title[$i];
         if($Word =~ /^[A-Z]/) {
         $end = "";
         for($j=$i;$j<=$#Title;$j++)
            { $end .= $Title[$j] . " "; }
         $line =
            sprintf "%50s %-50s\n", $start, $end;
         push(@collection, $line);
         }
         $start .= $Word . " ";
      }
   }
   @sortcollection = sort by_keystr @collection;
   foreach $entry (@sortcollection) {
      print $entry;
   }
```

In Perl, there is always another way! Another way of building the $end list would use Perl's join function:

```
$end = join ' ' $Title[$i .. $#Title];
```

Perl's join function (documented in perlfunc) has two arguments – an expression and a list. It builds a string by joining the separate strings of the list, and the value of the expression is used as a separator element.

5.7 Subroutines

Perl comes with libraries of several thousand subroutines; often the majority of your work can be done using existing routines. However, you will need to define your own subroutine – if simply to tidy up your code and avoid excessively large main-line programs. Perl routines are defined as:

```
sub name block
```

A routine has a return value; this is either the value of the last statement executed or a value specified in an explicit return statement. Arguments passed to a routine are combined into a single list – @_. Individual arguments may be isolated by indexing into this list, or by using a list literal as an lvalue. As illustrated with the sort helper function in the last section, subroutines can define their own local scope variables. Many more details of subroutines are given in the perlsub section of the documentation.

Parentheses are completely optional in subroutine calls:

```
Process_data($arg1, $arg2, $arg3);
```

is the same as

```
Process_data $arg1, $arg2, $arg3;
```

The 'ls -l' example in Section 5.5.2 had to convert a string such as 'drwxr-x—' into the equivalent octal code; a subroutine to perform this task would simplify the main line code. A definition for such a routine is:

```
sub octal {
    my $str = $_[0];
    my $code = 0;
    for(my $i=1;$i<10;$i++) {
        $code ^=2;
        $code++ if("-" ne substr($str,$i,1));
    }
    return $code;
}
```

This subroutine could be invoked:

```
$str = "-rwxr-x---";
$accesscode = octal $str;
```

For a second example, consider a subroutine to determine whether a particular string is present in a list:

```
member(item,list);
```

As noted above, the arguments for a routine are combined into a single list; they have to be split apart in the routine. The processing involves a foreach loop that checks whether the next list member equals the desired string:

```
sub member {
    my($entry,@list) = @_; # separate the arguments
    foreach $memb (@list) {
        if($memb eq $entry) { return 1; }
    }
```

```
    return 0;
  }
```

Actually, there is another way. There is no need to invent a member subroutine because Perl already possesses a generalized version in its grep routine.

```
grep match_criterion datalist
```

When used in a list context, grep produces a sub-list with references to those members of datalist that satisfy the test. When used in a scalar context, grep returns the number of members of datalist that satisfy requirements

5.8 Hashes

Perl's third main data type is a 'hash'. A hash is essentially an associative array that relates keys to values. An example would be a hash structure that relates the names of suburbs to their postcodes. A reference to a hash uses the % type qualifier on a name; so one could have a hash %postcodes. Hashes are dynamic, just like lists: you can start with an empty hash and add (key/value) pairs.

Typically, most of your code will reference individual elements of a hash rather than the hash structure as a whole. The hash structure itself might be referenced in iterative constructs that loop through all key value pairs. References to elements appear in scalar contexts with a key being used like an 'array subscript' to index into the hash. A hash for a suburb/postcode mapping could be constructed as follows:

```
$postcode{"Wollongong"} = 2500;
$postcode{"Unanderra"} = 2526;
$postcode{"Dapto"} = 2530;
$postcode{"Figtree"} = 2525;
```

The { } characters are used when indexing into a hash. The first statement would have implicitly created the hash %postcode; the subsequent statements add key/value pairs. The contents of the hash could then be printed:

```
while(($suburb,$code) = each(%postcode)) {
  printf "%-20s %s\n" , $suburb, $code;
}
```

Every hash has an implicit iterator associated with it; this can be used via the each function. The each function will return a two-element list with the next key/value pair; after the last pair has been returned, the next call to each will return an empty list; if each is again called, it restarts the iteration at the beginning of the hash. In the example code, each is used to control a loop printing data from the hash. Naturally, given that it is a hash, the elements are returned in an essentially arbitrary order.

Another way of iterating through a hash is to get a list with all the keys by applying the keys function to the hash and using a foreach loop:

```
@keylist = keys(%postcode);
foreach $key (@keylist) {
  print $key, ":\t", $postcode{$key}, "\n";
}
```

If you need only the values from the hash, then you can obtain these by applying the values function to the hash. The delete function can be used to remove an element – delete $postcode{"Dapto"}.

Hashes and lists can be directly inter-converted - @data = %postcode; the resulting list is made up of a sequence of key value pairs. A list with an even number of elements can similarly be converted directly to a hash; the first element is a key, the second is the corresponding value, the third list element is the next key, and so forth. If the reverse function is applied to a hash, you get a hash with the roles of the keys and values interchanged:

```
%pc = reverse %postcode;
while(($k,$v) = each(%pc)) {
  printf "%-20s %s\n" , $k, $v;
}
```

(You can 'lose' elements when reversing a hash; for example, if the original hash listed two suburbs that shared the same postcode – $postcode{"Wollongong"}=2500; $postcode{"Mangerton"} =2500; – then only one record would appear in the reversed hash that would map key 2500 to one or other of the suburbs.)

There are a number of ways to initialize a hash. First, you could explicitly assign values to the elements of the hash:

```
#Amateur Drama's Macbeth production
#cast list
$cast{"First witch"} = "Angie";
$cast{"Second witch"} = "Karen";
$cast{"Third witch"} = "Sonia";
$cast{"Duncan"} = "Peter";
$cast{"Macbeth"} = "Phillip";
$cast{"Lady Macbeth"} = "Joan";
...
$cast{"Gentlewoman 3"} = "Holly";
```

Alternatively, you could create the hash from a list:

```
@cast = ("First witch", "Angie","Second witch", "Karen","Third witch",
"Sonia", "Duncan", "Peter", "Macbeth", "Phillip",...
"Banquo", "John","Lady Macduff", "Lois", "Porter", "Neil", "Lennox",
```

```
"Wang","Angus", "Ian","Seyton", "Jeffrey","Fleance", "Will",
"Donaldbain",
...
..."Gentlewoman 3", "Holly");
%cast = @cast;
```

Lists like that get unreadable, and you are likely to mess up the pairings of keys and values. Hence a third mechanism is available:

```
%cast = ("First witch" => "Angie",
...
"Donaldbain" => "Willy",
"Menteith" => "Tim",
...
"Gentlewoman 3" => "Holly");
```

It is also possible to obtain slices of hashes – one use is illustrated here, where some of the roles in the play are reassigned to different actresses:

```
@cast{"First witch", "Second witch", "Third witch" } =
            ("Gina", "Christine", "Leila" );
```

5.9   An example using a hash and a list

This is a Perl classic: a program that illustrates how Perl is far better suited to text processing tasks than are languages like C, C++ or Java. The program has to count the number of occurrences of all distinct words in a document and then print a sorted list of these counts. For this program, a 'word' is any sequence of alphabetic characters; all non-alphabetic characters are ignored. For counting purposes, words are all converted to lower case (so 'The' and 'the' would be counted as two occurrences of 'the').

The program has to loop, reading lines from STDIN. Each line can be split into words. Each word (after conversion to lower case) serves as a key into a hash; the associated value is the count of occurrences of that word. Once all the input data have been processed, a list of the words (keys of the hash) can be obtained and sorted, and the sorted list used in a foreach loop that prints each word and the associated count.

```
#!/share/bin/perl -w
while($line = <STDIN>) {
  @words = split /[^A-Za-z]/ , $line;
  foreach $word (@words) {
    if($word eq "") next;
    $index = lc $word;
    $counts{$index}++;
  }
```

```
      }
      @sortedkeys = sort keys %counts;
      foreach $key (@sortedkeys) {
        print "$key\t$counts{$key}\n";
      }
```

The split function uses a regular expression that breaks the string held in $line at any non-alphabetic character (the set of all alphabetic characters is specified via the expression A-Za-z; here the ^ symbol implies the complement of that set.) A sequence of letters gets returned as a single element of the resulting list; each non-alphabetic character results in the return of an empty string (so if the input line was "test 123 end" the list would be equivalent to "test", "", "", "", "", "", "end"). Empty words get discarded. The lc function is used to fold each word string to all lower-case characters.

The line $counts{$index}++ is again playing Perl tricks. It uses the value of $index to index into the hash %counts. The first time a word is encountered in the input, there will be no value associated with that entry in the hash – or, rather, the value is Perl's 'undef' value. In a numeric context, such as that implied by the ++ increment operator, the value of 'undef' is zero. So, the first time a word is encountered it gets an entry in the hash %counts with a value 1; this value is incremented on each subsequent occurrence of the same word.

If you wanted the results sorted by frequency, rather than alphabetically, you would simply provide an inline helper sort function:

```
      foreach $key (sort { $counts{$a} <=> $counts{$b} } keys %counts) {
        print "$key\t$counts{$key}\n";
      }
```

The sort function's first argument is the inline code for element comparison, and its second argument is the list of words as obtained by keys %counts. The inline function uses the sort's globals $a and $b as indices into the hash to obtain the count values for the comparison test.

The Perl solution for this problem is of the order of ten lines of simple code. Imagine a Java solution; you would need a class WordCounter, which would employ a java.util.StringTokenizer to cut up an input string obtained via a java.io. BufferedReader. Words would have to be stored in some map structure from the java.util library. The code would be considerably longer and more complex. A C++ programmer would probably be thinking in terms of the STL and map classes. A C programmer would likely start from scratch with int main(int argc, char** argv). Each language has its own strengths. One of Perl's strengths is text processing. All small text processing tasks, like the word counter, are best done in Perl.

5.10 Files and formatting

While STDIN and STDOUT suffice for simple examples, more flexible control of file I/O is necessary. Perl is really using C's stdio library, and it provides all C's open, close, seek, read, write and other functions (along with a large number of functions for manipulating directory entries – e.g. changing a file's access permissions). Perl programs work with encapsulated versions of stdio FILE* file streams. In Perl, these are referenced by 'filehandles'. Conventionally, Perl filehandles are given names composed entirely of capital letters; these names are in their own namespace, separate from the namespaces used for scalars, lists and hashes. (Filehandles do not have a type identifier symbol comparable to the '$' of scalars, '@' of lists, or '%' of hashes.)

An input stream can be opened from a file as follows:

```perl
$file1 = "data.txt";
...
open(MYINPUT1, $file1);
...
while(<MYINPUT1>) {
    # process data from file ...
    ...
}
```

Of course, an attempt to open a file for reading may fail (file not present, file permissions incorrect etc.). The open function returns a boolean result to indicate success or failure. It is advisable to always check such results and terminate if the data are unavailable:

```perl
if(! open(MYINPUT1, $file1)) {
    print "Couldn't open $file1\n";
    exit 1;
}
```

Perl's predefined system variable $! holds the current value of the C errno variable, and so will (usually) contain the system error code recorded for the last system call that failed. If used in a numeric context $! is the code; if used in a string context, it returns a string with a useful error message explaining the error. This can be added to termination messages – print "Couldn't open $file, got error $!\n". An exit statement terminates the program, just as in C; the value in the exit statement is returned to the parent process.

'Print error message and terminate' – this is a sufficiently common idiom that it deserves system support. In Perl, this support is provided by the die function. The check for failure of a file-opening operation would be more typically written as:

```perl
open(MYINPUT1, $file1) || die "Couldn't open $file1, error $!\n";
```

If the message passed to die ends with a \n character, then that is all that is printed. If the error message does not have a terminating \n, Perl will print details of the filename and line number where die was invoked.

Typically, input from files is handled as in previous examples, reading data line by line:

```perl
while(<MYINPUT>) { ... }
```

In Perl, you can read the entire contents of a file in one go, obtaining a list of strings – each representing one line of input:

```
@inputlist = <MYINPUT>;
```

There are other input functions; you can read characters one by one with the getc function, or you can read specified numbers of characters using read.

Output filehandles can be created that allow writing to a file, or appending to an existing file:

```
open(OUTPUT, ">report.txt") || die ...; #new output, or overwrite old
open(ERRORS, ">>errlog.txt") || die ...; #append to file
```

An output filehandle can be used in a print or printf statement:

```
print OUTPUT "Role                    Actor\n";
...
printf OUTPUT "%-20s %s", $key, $val;
```

As Perl evolved, it accepted contributions from all kinds of programmers. My guess is that Cobol programmers contributed the concepts realized through Perl's 'format' mechanisms. Formats constitute an alternative to printf that you can use when you require complicated, fixed layouts for your output reports. Formats are particularly suited to generating line-printer style reports because you can provide supplementary data that are automatically added to the head of each page in the printed report. Some programmers prefer formats because, unlike printf's format strings, they allow you to visualize the way that output will appear.

Formats are directly related to output streams. If you have an output file handle OUTPUT, then you can have a format named OUTPUT. (You could also define an associated OUTPUT_TOP format; this would define a line that is to be printed at top of each page of a printed report sent to output stream OUTPUT.) Formats are essentially 'text templates'. They can contain fixed text, for things like field labels, and fields for printing data. These print fields are represented pictorially:

```
@<<<<       4 character field for left justified text
@|||||||||  8 character center-justified field
@>>>>>>     6 character right justified field
```

Numeric fields that need to have data lined up can be specified using styles such as @####.## – which means a numeric field with total of six digits, two after the decimal point. There are additional formatting capabilities; of course, they are all documented in the standard Perl release documentation (in section perlform).

A format declaration is something like the following:

```
format OUTPUT =
```

```
Picture line
Argument line
Picture line
Argument line
...
.
```

The 'picture lines' contain any fixed text and the field layouts; argument lines specify the variables whose values are to be printed in the fields defined in the preceding picture line. Note that the format declaration must end with a line containing a single '.' character.

The following example of formats is taken from perlform; it illustrates a scheme for a formatted listing of the contents of the /etc/passwd file on a Unix system (in this case, applying the formatting to the default STDOUT stream).

```
# a report on the /etc/passwd file
format STDOUT_TOP =
                        Passwd File
Name                    Login   Office  Uid   Gid Home
----------------------------------------------------------------
.
format STDOUT =
@<<<<<<<<<<<<<<<<< @|||||||| @<<<<<<@>>>> @>>>> @<<<<<<<<<<<<<<<<
$name,                  $login,  $office,$uid,$gid, $home
.
```

These formats are used in the following fragment:

```
open(PASSWD, '/etc/passwd') || die("No password file");
while (<PASSWD>) {
   chomp;
   ($login, $passwd, $uid, $gid, $gcos, $home, $shell) = split(/:/);
   write;
}
```

The various fields of a line of the /etc/passwd file are distributed into the global variables $login etc. The write call (to STDOUT by default) uses the format associated with its file handle – so here use the format that prints the username and other data. (Note that Perl's write is not the same as C's even though the corresponding read functions are similar in the two languages.)

5.11 Regular expression matching

Regular expressions (regexes) define patterns of characters that can be matched with strings. Simple patterns allow you to specify requirements like:

- Match a single character from this group of characters.

- Match one or more characters from this group.

- Match a specified number (within the range ... to ...) of characters.

- Match any character not in this group.

- Match this particular sub-string.

- Match any one of the following set of alternative sub-strings.

- Restrict the match so that it must start at beginning of the string (or end at the end of the string).

You can move on to more complex patterns:

- Find a sequence that starts with characters from this group, then has this character, then has zero of more instances of either of these sub-strings, ..., and finally ends with something that matches this pattern.

- Split out the part of the string that matches this pattern.

- Replace the part of the string that matches this pattern with this replacement text.

Why might you want regexes? Consider an information processing task where you are trying to retrieve documents characterized by particular words; you can add a lot of precision if you can specify constraints like the 'words must be contained in the same sentence' (you could use a pattern specifying something like 'word1, any number of characters except full stop, word2'). Or, as another example, imagine trying to find the targets of all the links in an HTML document. You would need a pattern that specified something that could match an HTML link: <a href="..." and you would want the portion of the matched string starting at the point following the href= and going up to some terminating character. (You would have to specify a clever pattern so as to get around little problems like the parentheses around the target name being optional, and the possibility of some arbitrary numbers of spaces occurring between <a and href tags.)

Perl represents the patterns as strings, usually delimited by the '/' character: /*regular-expression*/. You can use m<*delimiter character*> *regular expression* <*delimiter character*> if you don't want to use the default form for a pattern. The =~ operator is used to effect a pattern match between the string value in a scalar and a regular expression pattern. The result of a pattern match is a success or failure indicator; as a side effect, some variables defined in the Perl core will also be set to hold details of the part of the string that matched. (There is also a 'don't match' operator, !~, which returns true if the string does not match the pattern.) For the most part, regular expressions defined for Perl are similar to those that can be used with the Posix regular expression matching functions that are available in C programming libraries; however, Perl does have a few extensions.

5.11.1 Basics of regex patterns

In the simplest patterns, the body of the pattern consists of the literal sequence of characters you wish to match:

```
/MasterCard/
/Bank Branch Number/
```

Many characters have specialized roles in defining more complex regular expressions; these characters must be 'escaped' if you wish to match a literal string in which they appear: {}[]()^$.|*+?\. Patterns can include the common special characters – \t, etc; the octal escape character sequences are also supported (things like \0172).

The following code is a first example of the pattern match operator; it tests whether a line read from STDIN contains the character sequence Bank Branch:

```
$line = <STDIN>;
if($line =~ /Bank Branch/) { ... }
```

Perl programmers love short cuts, and there is a special convention for testing the anonymous variable $_. You don't need to refer to the variable and you don't need the =~ match operator: you simply use a pattern specification in a conditional. The following might be part of the control loop in a simple 'menu selection' style program (imagine commands like 'Add', 'Multiply', ..., 'Quit'):

```
#read commands entered by user
while(<STDIN>) {
  if( /Quit/ ) { last; }
  elsif( /Add/ ) {
    # perform addition operation ...
    ...
    }
  elsif( /Multiply/ ) {
    ...
    }
  ...
  else { print "Unrecognized command\n"; }
}
```

Users of such a program are liable to enter commands imperfectly, typing things like 'quit', 'QUit' etc. Problems such as this are easily overcome by specifying a case-insensitive match:

```
while(<INPUT>) {
  if( /Quit/i ) { ... }
  ...
}
```

The 'i' appended to the pattern flags the case-insensitive matching option. (The code shown simply tests whether the character sequence q-u-i-t occurs in the input line; the program will happily quit if it reads a line such as 'I don't quite understand'. Later examples will add more precision to the matching process.)

The simplest patterns specify literal strings that must be matched (with the small elaboration of optional case insensitivity). Slightly more complex patterns contain specifications of alternative patterns:

```
/MasterCard|Visa|AmEx/
/(cat's|dog's) (dish|bowl|plate)/
```

The first of these patterns would match any string containing any one of the sub-strings 'MasterCard', 'Visa' or 'AmEx'. The second pattern matches inputs that include 'cat's bowl' or 'dog's plate'. If you are matching a pattern with alternatives, you probably want to know the actual match. After a successful match, the Perl core variable $& is set to the entire string matched; you could use the value of this variable to identify the chosen credit card company.

Literal patterns, even patterns with alternative literal sub-strings, are usually insufficient. Most applications require matches that specify the general form for a pattern, but which allow variation in detail. The character '.' matches any character (if you want to match a literal period character, you need \.). You can define character classes – sets of characters that are equally acceptable. For example, the character class defining vowels is:

```
[aeiou]
```

You can use ranges in these definitions:

```
[0-7]        the octal digits
[0-9a-fA-F]  the hexadecimal digits
```

You can have a 'negated' character class; the characters given in the definition must start with the ^ character. For example, the character class [^0-9] matches anything except a digit. Perl has a number of predefined character classes:

```
\d   digit                      equivalent to [0-9]
\D   negated \d;                 equivalent to [^0-9]
\s   whitespace                  equivalent to [\ \t\r\n\f]
\w   (alphanumeric or _)         equivalent to [0-9a-zA-Z_] "word character"
\W   negated \w                  anything except a "word character"
```

For the most part, you use character classes, or the 'any character' ('.'), in patterns where you want to specify things like 'any number of letters', 'at least one digit', 'a sequence of 12 or more hexadecimal digits' or 'optional double quote character'. Such patterns are built up from a character class definition and a quantifier specifying the number of instances required. The standard quantifiers are:

```
?    Optional tag, pattern to occur 0 or 1 times
*    Possible filler, pattern to occur 0 or more times
+    Required filler, pattern to occur 1 or more times
{n} {n,} {n,m}
     Pattern to occur n times, or more, or the range n to m times
```

Examples of patterns with quantifiers are:

```
/ /+          Requires span of space characters
/0-9/{13,16}  Require 13 to 16 decimal digits (as in credit card number)
(+|-)?[0-9]+\.?[0-9]*
              An optional + or - sign, one or more digits, an optional
              decimal point, optionally more digits - i.e. a signed
              number with an optional fraction part
```

The patterns can be further refined by restrictions specifying where they are acceptable in a string. The simplest restrictions specify that a pattern must start at the beginning of a string or must end at the end of the string. Perl's regex expressions have additional options. Perl defines the concept of a 'word boundary': 'a word boundary (\b) is a spot between two characters that has a \w – word character – on one side of it and a \W on the other side of it'. It is possible to specify that a pattern must occur at a word boundary – forming either the start of a word or the end of a word.

A pattern is restricted to match starting at the beginning of the string if it starts with the ^ character. (Note that the meaning of certain characters varies according to where they are used in a regular expression; if the expression starts with the ^ character, then this must match the start of string, but if the ^ character appears at the start of a character class definition then it implies the complement of the specified character set.) If a pattern ends with a $ character, then this must match the end of the string. Perl's \b (word boundary specifier) can be placed before (or after) a character sequence that must be found at the beginning (or end) of a word – e.g. /\bing/ is a pattern for finding words that start with 'ing'.

Another extra feature in Perl is the ability to substitute the values of variables into a pattern. This allows patterns to depend on data already processed, making them more flexible than they would be if they had to be fully defined in the source text.

More detailed definitions of the forms of patterns are given in the perlre section of the standard Perl documentation. The documentation also includes a detailed tutorial, perlretut, on the use of regular expressions.

The following short program illustrates a simple use of regular expressions. It helps cheats complete crosswords. If you partially solve a crossword, you will be left with unguessed words for which you know a few letters – 'starts with ab, has three more unknown letters, and ends with either t or f depending on the right answer for 13-across'. How to solve this? Easy: search a dictionary for all the words that match the pattern. Most Unix systems contain a small 'dictionary' (about 20 000 words) in the file /usr/dict/words; the words are held one per line and there are no word meanings given – this word list's primary use is for checking spelling. The example program lets the user enter a simple Perl pattern and then matches this with the words in the Unix dictionary file; those words that match the pattern are printed.

```
#!/share/bin/perl
open(INPUT, "/usr/dict/words") || die "I am wordless\n" ;

print "Enter the word pattern that you seek : ";
$wordpat = <STDIN>;
chomp($wordpat);
while(<INPUT>) {
  if( /^$wordpat$/ ) { print $_; }
}
```

The user must enter the pattern, which for the example would be ab...[tf]; the trailing newline character is removed from this input pattern. The loop reads words from the Unix word-list file; each is compared with the pattern. The pattern /^$wordpat$/ specifies that it must match at the start of the line, contain the user-defined input pattern, and end at the end of the line (the crossword solver would not want words that contained the sequence ab...[tf] embedded in the middle of a larger word).

5.11.2 Finding 'what matched?' and other advanced features

Sometimes, all that you need is to know is whether input text matched a pattern. More commonly, you want to further process the specific data that were matched. For example, you hope that data from your web form contain a valid credit card number – a sequence of 13 to 16 digits. You would not simply want to verify the occurrence of this pattern; what you would want to do is to extract the digit sequence that was matched, so that you could apply further verification checks.

Regular expressions allow you to define groups of pattern elements; an overall pattern can, for example, have some literal text, a group with a variable length sequence of characters from some class, more literal text, another grouping with different characters, and so forth. If the pattern is matched, the regular expression matching functions will store details of the overall match and the parts matched to each of the specific groups. These data are stored in global variables defined in the Perl core. The groups of pattern elements, whose matches in the string are required, are placed in parentheses. So, a pattern for extracting a 13–16 digit sub-string from some longer string could be /\D(\d{13,16})\D/; if a string matches this pattern, the variable $1 will hold the digit string.

The following example illustrates the extraction of two fields from an input line. The input line is supposed to be a message that contains a dollar amount. The dollar amount is expected to consist of a dollar sign, some number of digits, an optional decimal point and an optional fraction amount. The pattern used for this match is:

```
/\$([0-9]+)\.?([0-9]*)\D/
```

Its elements are:

```
\$          A literal dollar sign
([0-9]+)    A non-empty sequence of digits forming first group
\.?         An optional decimal point
([0-9]*)    An optional sequence of digits forming second group
\D          Any 'non digit' character
```

The text that matches the first parenthesized subgroup is held in the Perl core variable $1; the text matching the second group of digits would go in $2. Since the second subgroup expression specifies 'zero or more digits', it is possible for $2 to hold an empty string after a successful match. The variables $1, $2 etc. are read-only; data values must be copied from these variables before they can be changed.

```
while(1) {
   print "Enter string : ";
   $str = <STDIN>;
   if($str =~ /Quit/i) { last; }
   if($str =~ /\$([0-9]+)\.?([0-9]*)\D/) {
      if($2) { $cents = $2; }
      else { $cents = 0; }
      print "Dollars $1 and cents $cents\n";
      }
   else { print "Didn't match dollar extractor\n"; }
}
```

Examples of test inputs and *outputs* are:

```
Enter string : This is a test of the $ program.
```
Didn't match dollar extractor
```
Enter string : This program cost $0.
```
Dollars 0 and cents 0
```
Enter string : This program should cost $34.99
```
Dollars 34 and cents 99
```
Enter string : qUIT
```

Often, you need a pattern like:

- Some fixed text;

- A string whose value is arbitrary, but is needed for processing;

- Some more fixed text.

You use .* to match an arbitrary string; so if you were seeking to extract the sub-string between the words 'Fixed' and 'text', you could use the pattern /Fixed(.*)text/:

```
while(1) {
  print "Enter string : ";
  $str = <STDIN>;
  if($str =~ /Quit/i) { last; }
  if($str =~ /Fixed(.*)text/) {
    print "Matched with substring $1\n";
    }
  else { print "Didn't match\n"; }
}
```

Example inputs and outputs:

```
Enter string : Fixed up text on slide.
Matched with substring up
Enter string : Fixed up this text. Now starting to work on other text.
Matched with substring up this text. Now starting to work on other
```

The matching of arbitrary strings can sometimes problematic. The matching algorithm is 'greedy' – it attempts to find the longest string that matches. There are more subtle controls; you can use patterns like .*? which match a minimal string (so in the second of the examples above, you would get the match ' up this ').

Sometimes, there is a need for more complex patterns like:

*fixed_text(**somepattern**)other_stuff**SAMEPATTERN**rest_of_line*

These patterns can be defined through the use of 'back references' in the pattern string. Back references are related to matched sub-strings. When the pattern matcher is checking the pattern, it finds a possible match for the first sub-string (the element '(somepattern)' in the example) and saves this text in the Perl core variable $1. A back reference, in the form \1, that occurs later in the match pattern will be replaced dynamically by this saved partial match. The pattern matcher can then confirm that the same pattern is repeated.

Back references are illustrated in the following code fragments. These fragments might form a part of a Perl script that was to perform an approximate translation of Pascal code to C code. Such a transform cannot be completely automated (the languages do have some fundamental differences, like Pascal's ability to nest procedure declarations); however, large parts of the translation task can be automated.

The simplest transformation operations that you would want are:

```
Count := Count + 1;  =>Count++;
Count:= Count*Mul;   =>Count*=Mul;
Sum := Sum + 17;     =>Sum+=17;
```

For these, you need a pattern that:

- Matches a name (Lvalue); this is to be matched sub-string $1.

- Matches Pascal's := assignment operator.

- Matches another name that is identical to the first thing matched, so you need back reference \1 in the pattern.

- Matches a Pascal +, -, *, / operator; this is to be matched sub-string $2.

- Matches either a number or another name; match sub-string $3.

- Matches Pascal's terminating ';'.

- Allows extra whitespace anywhere.

If an input line matches the pattern, the program can output a revised line that uses C's modifying assignment operators (++, += etc.); inputs that do not match may be output unchanged. A little test framework that illustrates transformations only for '+' and '-' operators is:

```
while(1) {
  print "Enter string : ";
  $str = <STDIN>;
  if($str =~ /Quit/i) { last; }
  if($str A FAIRLY COMPLEX MATCH PATTERN!) {
    # Replace x:=x+1 by x++, similarly x--
    if(($3==1) && ($2 eq "+")) { print "\t$1++;\n"; }
    elsif(($3==1) && ($2 eq "-")) { print "\t$1--;\n"; }
    # Replace x:=x+y by x+=y, similarly for -
    else { print "\t$1 $2= $3;\n"; }
  }
  else { print "$str\n"; }
}
```

The pattern needed here is:

```
/\s*([A-Za-z]\w*) *:= *\1 *(\+|\*|\/|-) *(([0-9]+)|([A-Za-z]\w*)) *;/)
```

The parts are:

- s*   match any number of leading space or tab characters.

- ([A-Za-z]\w*)   match a string that starts with a letter, then has an arbitrary number of letters, digits and underscore characters (should capture valid Pascal variable identifiers). This is matched subgroup $1; its value will be referenced later in the pattern via the back reference \1. Its value can be used in the processing code.

- ' *'   a space with a * quantifier (zero or more); this matches any spaces that appear after the variable name and before the Pascal assignment operator :=.

- :=   the literal string that matches Pascal's assignment operator.

- ' *'   again, make provision for extra spaces.

- \1   the back reference pattern. Needed to establish that it is working on forms like sum:=sum+val;.

- ' *'   the usual provision for extra spaces.

- (\+|*\\/|-)   match a Pascal binary operator. (Characters like '+' have to be 'escaped' because their normal interpretation is as control elements in the pattern definition.)

- ' *'   possible spaces.

- (([0-9]+)|([A-Za-z]\w*))
                 a matched sub-string that is either a sequence of digits – [0-9]+ – or a Pascal variable name.

- ' *'   as usual, spaces.

- ;   Pascal statement separator

Regular expressions for complex pattern matching can become quite large. I have heard, via email, rumors of a 4000 character expression that captures the important elements from email address, making allowance for the majority of variations in the forms of email addresses!

Programs that do elaborate text transforms, like a more ambitious version of the toy 'Pascal to C' converter, typically need to apply many different transformations to the same line of input. For example, a Pascal if ... then needs to be rewritten in C's if(...)... style. If the conditional part of that statement involves a Pascal not operator, it must be rewritten using C's ! operator. Such transformation programs don't simply read a line, apply a transform and output the transformed line. Instead, they are applied successively to the string *in situ*. After each transformation, the updated string is checked against other possible patterns and their replacements.

Perl has a substitution operator that performs these *in situ* transforms of strings. A substitution pattern consists of a regular expression that defines features in the source string and replacement text. The patterns and replacements can incorporate matched sub-strings, so it is possible to extract a variable piece of text embedded in some fixed context and define a replacement in which the variable text is embedded in a slightly changed context.

The imaginary 'Pascal to C transformer' provides another example. One would need to change Pascal's not operator to C's ! operator. The common cases, which would be easy to translate, are:

```
Lvalue := not expression;    =>    lvalue != expression;
if(not expression) then      =>    if(! expression) then
```

The if statement would have to be subjected to further transforms to replace the if...
then form by the equivalent C construct.

A substitution pattern that could make these transformations is:

```
s/(:=|\() *not +/\1 !/;
```

The pattern defines:

- A subgroup that either contains the literal sequence := or a left parenthesis (escaped as
  \( ).

- Optional spaces.

- The literal not.

- One or more spaces.

The replacement is whatever text matched the subgroup (either := or left parenthesis), a
space and C's ! operator.

This substitution pattern would be used in code like the following:

```
while($str=<INPUT>) {
  Chomp($str);
  #apply sequence of transforms to $str
  ...
  #next, deal with Pascal's not operator
  $str =~ s/(:=|\() *not +/\1 !/;
  ...
  print $str, "\n";
}
```

Your first applications of regular expressions will use only the simplest forms of patterns. Your tasks will, after all, be simple things like extracting a dollar amount from some
input text, isolating an IP address from a server log, or identifying which credit card company is preferred. But it is possible, and it is often worthwhile, to try more sophisticated
matches and transforms. You can get many ideas from the Perl perlretut tutorial and
perlre reference documentation.

5.12 Perl and the OS

The Perl core includes essentially all the Unix system calls that are documented in Unix's
man 2 documentation, and also has equivalents for the functions in many of the C libraries

documented in man 3. Perl's functions are documented in the perl func section of the documentation. These functions make it easy for Perl programs to search directories, rename and copy files, launch sub-processes etc. Perl scripts exploiting these functions are often used to automate repetitive tasks for the system's administrator. Here Perl competes with sh itself, and also with Python. Different system administrators will have their own favorite scripting language; I consider Perl superior to sh (in terms of understandability of code) and in practical terms as good as Python.

5.12.1 Manipulating files and directories

Perl's functions for working with directories and files can be illustrated via a short example program for Unix that lists all names in a user-specified directory, identifying those that are directories, those that are links, and those that are simple files. If a directory entry is a simple file, the program attempts to identify whether it is a text file (containing just printable characters). This program uses 'directory handles' and file test operations.

A directory handle provides access to the contents of a directory in much the same way as a file handle provides a means to read data from a file. Directory handles are obtained using the opendir function; the readdir function can then be used to obtain strings corresponding to successive directory entries. (Calls to readdir return the names in the directory, not fully qualified pathnames; the data returned include the entry '.', which referenced the current directory, the entry '..', which references the parent directory, and all 'hidden' files with names starting with '.'.) Like filehandles, directory handles are conventionally given names that use upper-case letters; the names of directory handles exist in another separate namespace maintained by Perl.

Perl has 'file tests' similar to those that exist in the shell. These tests are used as:

```
<test operator> filename
```

Most of the tests return a true/false result. The test operators are:

- -x   is file (or directory) 'executable'?

- -r   is it readable?

- -w   is it writeable?

- -d   is it a directory?

- -l   is it a link?

- -f   just a plain old file maybe?

- -T   is it 'text'?

- -e   does it even exist?

- -s   size in bytes

- -M   days (as real number) since last modified

- ...

The example program has a forever loop in which the user is prompted to enter the (fully qualified) name of a directory on Unix. The program then attempts to read details of the entries in that directory, using the file test operations to compose the required report.

```perl
#!/share/bin/perl

while(1) {
  print "Enter pathname of directory : ";
  $directory = <STDIN>;
  chomp($directory);
  if($directory =~ /^Quit$/i) { last; }
  if(!opendir(DIRHANDLE, $directory) ) {
    print "Couldn't open that directory\n";
    next;
    }
  $directory =~ s#/$##;
  @names = readdir DIRHANDLE;

  foreach $name (@names) {
    if($name =~ /^\.+$/) { next; }
    $fullname = $directory . "/" . $name;
    if( -d $fullname) { print "Subdirectory: $fullname\n"; }
    elsif( -l $fullname) { print "$fullname is a link\n"; }
    else {
      print "$fullname\n";
      if( -x $fullname) { print "\texecutable\n"; }
      if( -T $fullname) {
        $size = -s $fullname;
        print "\tText with $size bytes\n";
        }
      }
    }
  }
}
```

The first argument for opendir is a 'directory handle', this gets set by the opendir function; the second argument is the pathname for the directory. Users vary in how they name directories; most just give the directory name, but some have the habit of adding a trailing '/'; in order to standardize prior to later steps, any trailing '/' character is removed in the pattern substitution step – $directory =~ s#/$##.

The call readdir DIRHANDLE; returns a list with all the entries in the directory accessed via the directory handle. Each element in the list is processed in the following foreach loop. The entries '.' and '..' are ignored – the regular expression specifies a pattern of any number of '.' characters taking up an entire line (from ^ start to $ end). Before the file tests are made, the names of the entries have to be built up to fully specified names incorporating a complete directory path. The fully qualified filenames are obtained by prepending the directory name to the entry name.

The first two tests use the -d and -1 file-test operators to test for a directory and a link respectively (if(-d $fullname) ...). If an entry is a simple file, -x and -T tests can be used to obtain information about it. (Is the executable-bit set? Is it a text file? A file could be both if it is a script.)

The opendir and readdir functions probably represent the easiest way of working with the contents of a directory; but, of course, with Perl there is always another way! Actually, there are two other ways of getting lists of files in directories, and you can use stat function on files to get lots and lots of extraneous information about a file.

An alternative to readdir is the use of shell-style patterns to specify the desired entries in a directory. These shell-style patterns bear a superficial resemblance to regular expressions, but be careful as the meanings of symbols do differ. The shell pattern '*' is used to request every entry in a directory (well, not everything – entry names starting with '.' are excluded): a pattern like '*.pl' means all Perl scripts; while a shell pattern like [AB]*.cc means all cc files whose names start with either A or B. These shell patterns can be used either with the diamond (< >)input file operator or the glob function (see the perlfunc and perlop documentation for more details and subtle differences between these forms of use).

The following is a rewritten version of the last example program. This version uses chdir to change the current working directory to that specified in the input. The shell pattern '*' (all files) is then used with the diamond operator in a foreach loop; this results in the anonymous variable $_ being bound to the names of the successive entries in the current directory; these names are returned as fully qualified pathnames.

```perl
#!/share/bin/perl
while(1) {
  print "Enter pathname of directory : ";
  $directory = <STDIN>;
  chomp($directory);
  if($directory =~ /^Quit$/i) { last; }
  unless(chdir($directory)) {
    print "Couldn't change to that directory\n";
    next;
    }
  foreach (<*>) {
    if( -d ) { print "Subdirectory: $_\n"; }
    elsif( -l ) { print "$_ is a link\n"; }
    else {
      print "$_\n";
      if( -x ) { print "\texecutable\n"; }
      if( -T ) {
        $size = -s;
        print "\tText with $size bytes\n";
        }
```

```
        }
    }
```

The file tests, if(-d)..., and the file size assignment, $size = -s, implicitly reference the anonymous variable $_. Such code is often cutely concise; but remember, code is generally 'wormy' ('write once, read many'). Too many linguistic tricks involving anonymous variables can present major problems to maintenance programmers. So be sparing with your use of Perl tricks.

Perl core has the main file manipulation programs:

- rename

- unlink

- chmod

- mkdir

- rmdir

Most of these functions take a filename argument (either the name of a file in the current working directory, or a fully qualified pathname). All are documented in the perlfunc section of the documentation.

5.12.2 Perl: processes

Since the Perl interpreter is a big C program, it is only natural that Perl programs have access to the C functions in stdlib.h and unistd.h. The following are the most important of the process-related functions:

- system

The system function takes as an argument a string with the command(s) that are to be interpreted by the subordinate shell process that gets launched. This sub-process shares stdin, stdout and stderr with the Perl program that launched it. The parent Perl process waits for the sub-process to terminate. On return, the Perl core variable $? holds information characterizing the sub-process and its termination step (the most useful data is the exit code, which is obtained as $? >> 8).

- fork

This is similar to the fork() function in C. The parent process executes the fork system call, resulting in the creation of an additional child process. Each process resumes executing the same code at the statement following the fork call; the only difference is the value returned from the call. In the parent process, fork returns the process id for the child; the child gets a zero value returned. All this is standard. Perl differs from the standard behavior in that a failure of the fork call (due to too many processes being in existence or some other resource limit) returns undef rather than the conventional negative value.

Programs that use fork can arrange 'parallel' execution – the parent continues processing while the child runs; but more typically, the parent process waits for the child process to terminate. There is the usual requirement that the parent process check the termination status of child processes; if this wait requirement is inconvenient there are workarounds using signals.

● exec

The exec call is standard. It causes the current program image for the process to be replaced by the executable file specified in the call. Other arguments specify the contents of the argv array (the 'command line arguments') and, if desired, the envp environment vector.

You can use the fork-exec calls to manipulate processes; you could even build a network-based server that combined these calls with socket accept calls. Usually, the simpler system call is sufficient for the kinds of tasks that you want a Perl program to offload onto a child process.

Perl has an alternative to the basic system call. This 'backticks' construct is essentially the same as system except that it allows the output from the child process to be captured by the calling program. When a child process is launched (via fork or system), it shares stdin, stdout and stderr with its parent process. As the parent process waits for the child, any output to stdout simply comes back to the terminal controlling the parent Perl process (if parent and child run concurrently, their outputs are intermingled). Sometimes what you want is for the parent Perl process to be able to process the child's outputs.

So you can have a statement in a Perl program like:

```
system("date");
```

This invokes the date operation in shell run for the child process; this prints to the stdout shared with Perl process. Alternatively, you can have:

```
$date=`date`; # backticks around data
$str = "Today is $date\n";
```

This code invokes the date operation in a sub-shell, grabbing the output and, in this case, interpolating it into a string. This is purely as a simple illustration of the mechanism; Perl has its own date access functions if you really want the date. A more realistic use might be in a Perl program organizing a sequence of compilation and linking steps; the output captured from backticks-style system calls could then be information such as error messages from compilation steps.

The following little program illustrates the use of captured data from another system command. Suppose you were the system administrator for some company that had a large number of Sun workstations distributed among various departments. You might be required to produce reports that listed the names and IP addresses of the workstations held by each department, with this report sorted by department. You would have data about your machines in Sun's NIS+ directories (a directory system a bit like LDAP). The data in the NIS+ system include information like canonical (standard) machine name, aliases, IP addresses and so forth; these data can be listed using the shell command `niscat hosts.org_dir`. This command might produce a report like:

```
red.accounting.ourorg.com red.accounting.ourorg.com 209.208.207.1
red.accounting.ourorg.com red 209.208.207.1
blue.accounting.ourog.com blue 209.208.207.2
jabberwok.sales.ourorg.com jaberwork.sales.ourorg.com 209.208.207.46
```

This listing has all the data you need (in this imaginary organization, the canonical names contain the department names); you simply have to extract and report on the specific data relating machines and departments. As shown in this listing, the same machine may appear several times – once for each alias; there will also be extraneous data, such as entries for 'localhost'. The final report should contain only a single entry for each machine, using its canonical name.

So, you write a Perl script that grabs the output from the `niscat` command, extracts data, and prints the sorted data in the format required. The program will need to perform the following steps:

- Capture output from the `niscat` command, getting back essentially a list of lines like those shown above.

- Split each line to get the machine name, alias and IP address.

- Examine the name for machine and department fields (things like 'localhost' will also appear, and should be ignored).

- Store each unique [department, name, IP] combination.

- Finally, print a report of the sorted data.

This program needs a more sophisticated data structure to help identify and then hold those unique [department, name, IP] combinations. Data structures, and 'references', are not part of this introductory Perl component; Perl's basics – scalar, list, hash – can be assembled to create many more complex structures. These are described in the `perldsc` section of the documentation. The `perldsc` reference contains cookbook style examples of lists of lists, lists of hashes, hashes of lists and – what is needed here – a hash of hashes. First, we need a hash indexed by department name. The data stored for each name will be a second hash; this second hash will hold IP address values indexed by machine names. The code here is essentially a copy of the `perdsc` cookbook code illustrating a hash of hashes.

The code starts with a backticks-style system call to get the date, as illustrated above (really, you should use `gmtime` as documented in `perlfunc`). The `foreach` loop works on the list returned by the backticks-style system call that invokes the basic `niscat` report on host machines as listed in the NIS+ data tables – foreach (`niscat hosts.org.dir`). Each line is split at space separators; only the first three elements are required from the line, and these are obtained by assignment to an lvalue list - ($name, $alias, $ip) = split / /. The name string must again be split, at '.' separators, to extract machine name and department name. Finally, these data are inserted into the data structure (note the 'double hash indexing' for the hash of hashes): $machines{$dept}{$machine} = $ip.

```
#!/share/bin/perl

$date = `date`;
$str = "Today is $date";
print $str , "\n";

foreach (`niscat hosts.org_dir`) {
  ($name, $alias, $ip ) = split / /;
  if($name =~ /^(\w+)\.(\w+)/) {
    $machine = $1;
    $dept = $2;
    $machines{$dept}{$machine} = $ip;
  }
}

foreach $dept (keys %machines) {
  print "$dept\n";
  foreach $machine
    (keys %{ $machines{$dept} } ) {
    $ip = $machines{$dept}{$machine};
    printf "\t%-20s\t%16s\n" ,$machine, $ip;
  }
}
```

The second foreach loop simply runs through the keys of the first hash, i.e. the department names. The inner loop picks out the machine names associated with each department and prints machine name and IP address. The expression { $machines{$dept} } selects the hash that is the value associated with the key $dept in the main %machines hash structure.

The final report generated will be in the desired format:

```
accounting
  red     209.208.207.1
  blue    209.208.207.2
  ...
sales
  jabberwok    209.208.207.46
  ...
```

5.12.3 A 'systems programming' example

This slightly larger example illustrates the kind of task that can be automated using Perl scripting for file and process manipulation. The task could also be solved with a shell script or with Python code. Perl is simply versatile; it can handle these systems tasks as well as more complex reporting tasks and CGI scripting.

The actual task is to automate the processing of programming assignments submitted by students just beginning to learn Java. Students submit their work electronically. The existing submission system stores submitted files in a directory hierarchy – there is a level that corresponds to laboratory class and a separate directory is created for each student submission inside this laboratory directory. Tutors who mark the assignments need printouts for the students in their labs. The printout should include a listing of the code, a report on a test compilation, and if compilation is successful a report on a test run. The printouts should be clearly labeled by lab and student identifiers.

A practical system must tolerate common problems. These include incorrect files submitted by students; students who submit files that result in thousands of lines of compilation errors; students who submit files that handle I/O tasks incorrectly (for example the specifications may require that the program read data from a file, but the student submits a program that prompts and waits for input from the keyboard); and there are students who submit programs that produce tens of thousands of lines of output.

A part of the script can be general purpose. The core structure is:

- Get the tutor's name and the laboratory name (these are used to identify the printouts).

- Switch to the correct laboratory directory.

- For each student subdirectory in the laboratoy directory, process submission.

The 'process submission' part would be specific to the requirements of an individual assignment; each assignment differs in the files that it uses and its requirements for input and output. The example program illustrates processing for a case where:

- Students are writing Java.

- File A.java was provided by the lecturer, but was possibly modified by the student.

- File B.java, written by the student, contains the main() for the Java application.

- Other Java files may have been submitted (depending on the student's design for their Java program).

- A README.txt documentation file was supposed to be included.

- The student's Java program requires a single command line parameter and no stdin input when it is run.

- All files were to be submitted as a single 'tarred and gzipped' file A1.tar.gz.

For this example, the processing of a submission involves the following steps:

- Unpack the files.

- If the student included an A.java that is unchanged from that supplied by lecturer, remove it.

- List the README.txt and .java files.

- Copy the default A.class file into the current directory.

- Compile the Java code, limiting output to the last 100 lines of any compilation error report.

- If the program compiled successfully:
  - Run the program with a time limit of 5 seconds to catch those infinite loops.
  - Send the program's output to a temporary file.
  - Print the last 100 lines of the output file resulting from the test run.

- Remove all files created; restore the original tar gzip file.

- Make sure that all error messages (to stderr) are merged with stdout at all stages of processing.

These operations provide lots of illustrations of file manipulations, calls to system to run subtasks, and backticks-style system calls to obtain data from those subtasks. The code is sufficiently complex to justify the use of subroutines.

The example program has the structure:

```
sub processsubmission {
   # Perform successive steps involved in processing one submission
   # This is a lengthy but simple sequence of system calls and
   # file manipulation steps
   ...
}

sub valid {
   # Helper function used to check whether an entry in the "lab"
   # directory corresponds to a student submission - (lab
   # directory is also used to hold control files, data, default
   # class files etc.)
   ...
}

# main line code
# gets input identifying lab class
# change to appropriate directory
# loop:processing entries in that directory.
```

The main line is simple. It checks for the required arguments; changes to the specified directory; uses a system call to invoke the Unix banner command to print a header for the eventual printout; uses opendir and readdir to get the list of directory entries; filters this list to get those entries thought to correspond to directories created for student submissions; and finally loops, processing each separate entry. The output from this program would be directed to a temporary file for later printing. There is one little bit of Perl magic – the opaque statement $| = 1. This sets the current default output stream to 'autoflush' mode, in which buffers are emptied after each output operation. The script is sending output to stdout (by default this would be buffered) and is invoking system calls that also send output to stdout; it would be nice to get the outputs combined in the order they are generated, but buffering may interfere. On some Perl implementations this is handled automatically (buffers are flushed before calls like system); however, not all Perl systems do this, so explicit intervention may be required.

```perl
# Require two command line arguments: tutor name, lab (directory) name

$tutor = $ARGV[0];
$dirname = $ARGV[1];
if(! ((defined $dirname) && (defined $tutor))) {
   print STDERR <<MSG;
Tutor:
This script requires two command line arguments:
1) your name as a banner for printout
2) the directory with the submissions for your lab.
MSG
   exit 1;
}

if(!chdir($dirname)) {
   print STDERR "Couldn't cd to the directory $dirname\n";
   exit 1;
}
$| = 1;
system("banner $tutor");
print "\f";

#Directory should contain subdirectories, one for each student who
#submitted an assignment
#It also contains other files and a 'control' directory used
#by the submission system.

opendir(CWD, ".");
@entries = readdir(CWD);
closedir(CWD);

@entries = sort @entries;

print "Submissions for your lab received from:\n";
```

```
@valid = ();
foreach (@entries) {
  if(valid($_)) {
    print $_, "\n";
    push(@valid, $_);
    }
}

foreach (@valid) {
  printf "\fStart of record for $_\n";
  print STDERR "$_\n";
  chdir($_) || die "Failed to cd into student's subdirectory\n";
  processsubmission;
  chdir("..");
}
```

The short helper function valid is passed the name of a directory entry as obtained by readdir. The directory link entries ('.' and '..') should be ignored, as should the directory control (which is used by the submission system). Some other entries will be for data files etc.; these file entries should be discarded.

```
sub valid {
  $name = $_[0];
  if($name =~ /^\.+$/) { return 0; }
  if($name eq "control") { return 0; }
  if(-d $name) { return 1; }
  return 0;
}
```

The main process submission function involves the following steps:

- Prepare the files.
- Deal with A.java.
- Print required files.
- Try to compile.
- Try to run.
- Tidy remaining files.

The initial steps involve system calls to decompress (gunzip) the file archive and then extract the individual files. Each step involves a system call with the required Unix shell command, and then a check for a returned error code:

```perl
sub processsubmission {
  system("gunzip A1.tar.gz");
  $errcode = $? >> 8;
  if($errcode) {
    print "Corrupted gzip file?\n";
    print STDERR "$_ has corrupt gzip file\n";
    return;
  }
  system("tar -xf A1.tar");
  $errcode = $? >> 8;
  if($errcode) {
    print "Corrupted tar file?\n";
    print STDERR "$_ has corrupt tar file\n";
    return;
  }
  ...
```

Students routinely include extraneous files with their submissions; this script removes any .class files, prints a listing of submitted files for the report, and then deals with the A.java file. The test if(-r "A.java") determines whether this file is present. If this is the same as the original provided by the lecturer, it is not required; if it has been changed, it should be listed and compiled. The Unix diff utility is used to compare the original A.java (held in the parent directory) and that submitted by the student; if the files are identical, the return code from diff is zero. The default A.class file can be copied from the parent directory; if necessary, it will be overwritten with a new version during the compilation step.

```perl
sub processsubmission {
  ...
  ...
  #Remove any .class files
  system("rm -f *.class");
  system("ls -l");
  #has student submitted an A.java
  if(-r "A.java") {
    # if same as that supplied, remove it
    system("diff A.java ../A.java 1>/dev/null 2>/dev/null");
    $code = $? >> 8;
    if($code == 0) {
      system("rm A.java");
      }
  }
  system("cp ../A.class .");
```

The next step is to select all .java and .txt files in the directory and list their contents as part of the report for the tutor. The files are selected using the shell-style pattern *.{java,txt} – any file ending either in '.java' or '.txt'.

```perl
sub processsubmission {
  ...
  ...
  @files = <*.{java,txt}>;
  foreach $file (@files) {
    print "\f$file:\n";
    system("cat $file");
  }
```

Once the files have been listed, an attempt should be made to compile the Java source. The shell command, submitted via the system call, arranges to combine both stdout and stderr output in the same 'compile_errs' file. Some errors result in hundreds of lines of output from the compiler. The compiler will return a non-zero code if there were errors (it is probably a count of the number of errors). If there are errors, the last 100 lines of the error file are printed and the assignment is not run.

```perl
sub processsubmission {
  ...
  ...
  system("javac B.java 2>&1 > compile_errs");
  $compile_error = $? >> 8;
  if($compile_error) {
    system("tail -100 compile_errs");
    print "\fAssignment not run because of compilation errors\n";
  }
  else {
    ...
  }
```

Submissions that compile successfully can be run. Here a sequence of commands is passed via the system call; the first sets a time limit of 5 seconds, the second is the Java run command, and the third is a command to list the last few lines of any output file generated. The Java command combines stdout and stderr streams and maps stdin to /dev/null (so that if a student's Java program attempts to read from stdin it will encounter an effective end of file condition).

```perl
sub processsubmission {
  ...
  ...
  if($compile_error) { ... }
  else {
```

```
    $command = '
ulimit -t 5
java B 17 2>&1 < /dev/null > output
tail -100 output
';
    system($command);
  }
```

The final steps clean out any files that were created and recompress the tar archive file:

```
sub processsubmission {
  ...

  system("rm -f *.java *.class *.txt compile_errs output");
  system("gzip A1.tar");
}
```

This example should serve as a convincing illustration of how Perl scripts can work with the OS.

5.13 Networking

The Perl core does contain a number of the Unix standard network functions such as socket, and gethostbyname. Many of these functions require obscure constants (e.g. integers that represent different protocols) and/or data structures (such as special four-byte packed integers used to hold IP addresses). Use of the network-related functions can be simplified through the help of constants, structures and functions that are defined in Perl's Socket module.

Modules are reviewed briefly in the next section. Essentially, a module typically consists of declarations of extra Perl functions along with some additional variables and constants. A module can be used in much the same way as a C library or a Java package. A Perl program that needs to use components defined in a module can 'use' the module – much like a C program #include-ing a header file, or a Java program importing a package.

The network-related functionality is illustrated here through two little example programs. The first is a really minimal http client; the second illustrates some processing of records from an Apache server's access log.

The http client picks up hostname, and optionally a port number, from the command line. These data are used to build an 'address' structure, this step involves helper functions from the Socket module. Next, a socket connection is opened then set in 'autoflush' mode. The user is prompted for a filename, and this is built into a standard HTTP 'Get' request that is sent via the socket. Finally, the program reads and prints all the lines in the response from the HTTP server.

```perl
#!/share/bin/perl -w

use Socket;

if(@ARGV < 1) {
  print "Invoke with one or two arguments, hostname and optional port\n";
  exit(1);
}

$server = shift @ARGV;
$port = shift @ARGV || 80 ;

$iaddr = inet_aton($server) || die "no host: $server\n";
$paddr = sockaddr_in($port, $iaddr);

$proto = getprotobyname('tcp');
socket(SOCK, PF_INET, SOCK_STREAM, $proto) || die "socket: $!\n";
connect(SOCK, $paddr) || die "connect: $!\n";

select(SOCK);
$|=1;
select(STDOUT);

print "File :";
$input = <STDIN>;
chomp($input);

print SOCK "GET $input HTTP/1.0\n\n";
while($line = <SOCK>) {
  print $line;
}


close(SOCK) || die "close: $!\n";
```

Autoflush mode can only be set on the default output stream. The socket is set in autoflush mode by first making it the default output stream, select(SOCK), then setting autoflush, and finally restoring stdout as the default output. The two command line arguments are obtained by 'shifting' data out of the @ARGV array used for these arguments. This style is really a shell programming idiom, but it is popular among Perl programmers (alternatives include a list literal lvalue, or explicit indexing into the array).

The second example is another 'extraction and reporting' task; the report uses network-related functions to convert an IP address into a hostname. The program is to try to find a list of unique domains for the clients of some web service. The IP addresses of the clients will be converted to hostnames – machine plus domain e.g. 203.132.226.245 P53-max4.wgg.ihug.com.au. The machine name is not important and can be dropped – we are happy with wgg.ihug.com.au. (The code simply drops the first element of a returned host name.) Data on the clients would be available as an Apache access log:

```
210.84.124.193 - - [20/Jun/2001:00:30:50 +1000] "GET /subjects HTTP/1.1"
301 253
203.132.226.245 - - [20/Jun/2001:00:36:22 +1000]
"GET /images/staff.gif HTTP/1.0" 304 —
```

A minimal analyzer would:

- Read the access log.

- Extract the client IP addresses, forming a list of unique IP addresses.

- Look up hostnames corresponding to these IP addresses.

- Strip the machine name to get the domain.

- Form a list of unique domains.

- Print the sorted list.

The inet_aton function can be used to convert a string like 202.132.226.245 into the appropriate 4-byte integer value. This integer IP address can then be looked up using a reverse DNS lookup as performed via the gethostbyaddr function call. (Reverse DNS lookups can be quite slow; this program would run slowly for large files.)

```perl
#!/share/bin/perl
use Socket;

while(<STDIN>) {
  @data = split;
  $callers{$data[0]} = 1;
}

foreach (keys %callers) {
  $addr = inet_aton($_);
  $name = gethostbyaddr($addr, AF_INET);
  if($name eq "") { next; }

  $pos = index($name, ".");
  $name = substr($name,$pos+1);
  $names{$name} = 1;
}
print "Sorting and reporting\n";
foreach (sort (keys %names)) {
  print "$_\n";
```

```
    }
    $val = scalar keys %names;
    print "Our clients were from $val different domains\n";
```

5.14 Modules

Everyone is familiar with the leverage that Java gets from its large collection of packages of useful classes. The Perl community has put in similar effort. There are a huge number of modules available for down load from sites such as http://www.cpan.org/modules/. They include modules with:

- Language extensions and documentation tools

- Experimental thread support

- Utilities (Perl programs for file and directory manipulations)

- Networking support: socket wrappers, ICQ, Gnutella, LDAP, Japper, SMTP, SSL etc.

- Data types and algorithms

- Database interfaces

- User interfaces (TCL/TK, X-windows etc.)

- File utilities

- Text manipulation capabilities

- Natural language helpers (spell check, word stemming, hyphenation etc.)

- XML and XSLT

- Encryption, digests and related security components

- WWW, CGI and HTTP

- MS Windows stuff

- Junk (Am I cruel? It is just I doubt the practical utility of some of the modules, such as that to compute dates using one of the systems proposed for Tokien's fantasy world.)

Modules have to be 'installed' into your Perl environment, usually with the help of a support tool. The ActivePerl system includes a tool called 'PPM'. This tool helps you download files from sites like http://www.cpan.org/ or http://www.activeperl.com/ and then install them in your Perl system.

You should visit the main CPAN site sometime to see the modules available; you will probably find something useful. Our interest in modules is limited to the database support modules and a small subset of the modules that have been developed to support CGI and other web-related activities.

5.15 Databases

5.15.1 Basics

Those who have learned to use JDBC with Java will find Perl's database components quite familiar. Perl's DBI module provides a high-level, uniform mechanism for submitting SQL queries to any database system; the API offered by the DBI module is really very similar to that of JDBC. There is a second lower-level DBD component in Perl; the DBD modules are database-specific drivers. These DBD modules accept requests from the higher level DBI component and translate them and submit them to the actual database system. The code that you write, using DBI, is essentially database-independent. If you need to change the database employed, you simply use a different DBD driver module. (The DBD modules correspond to the drivers installed in a Java system.)

There are DBD modules for most database systems. You can get DBD-Adabas, DBD-Ingres, DBD-Informix, DB-Interbase, DBD-ODBC, DBD-Oracle and so forth. A Unix system will typically have a database installed, and the required DBD module is likely to be in the Perl directories. Linux users may have to install a database like MySQL and then download and install the appropriate DBD module. Windows users often have Microsoft Access installed – this is quite adequate for simple learning examples; if you have Access, you should download and install the DBD ODBC driver. Of course, Windows users can instead install MySQL and its DBD module. (If you are working with ActivePerl, use its PPM tool to fetch and install the required drivers; these are available at the ActivePerl site.)

Fortunately, the average Perl programmer does not have to bother much about the DBD level. There are only two DBD-related programs that you are ever likely to run; both use DBI calls to find information about the DBD drivers and available databases. The first tells you what drivers that are installed on your system:

```
use DBI;
@drivers = DBI->available_drivers;
print "Available drivers : @drivers\n";
```

The second tells you about the databases you can access:

```
use DBI;
print "Enter driver name : ";
$drivername = <STDIN>;
chomp($drivername);
@sources = DBI->data_sources($drivername);
print "sources: @sources\n";
```

This may list many sources. For example, on a Windows machine you use the Control Panel tool ODBC Data Sources to create an ODBC name for each different Access database (or other ODBC-compatible database) that you have created. The source listing will report the names of all these ODBC entries.

Those DBI statements illustrated use of Perl objects. The DBI module defines a DBI object, storing a reference in the module variable DBI. The DBI-> constructs invoke methods of this object. When working with databases, you typically use just this DBI object, 'database handle' objects and 'statement objects'. In all cases, usage is simple; the method invocation operator is applied to the object and the method name.

Typically, you will know the name of the datasource that your program is to use. This name gets coded as a constant string in your program. You use the datasource name when connecting; a successful connect operation returns a database handle (this is similar to Java's java.sql.Connection object). You then use the database handle to prepare an SQL statement for execution and run your query. A query returns an 'object' that can be used to access each row of a response.

Code for connecting to a database will be similar to one of the following:

```
use DBI;
$dbh = DBI->connect("DBI:ODBC:epalfinder");
```

This first example illustrates a connection to an Access database on a Windows 98 machine; the database was associated with an entry named 'epalfinder' in the ODBC data sources table. The next two illustrate connections to an Oracle database; for these it is necessary to specify a database username (HSimpson) and password (Doh). Other database options can be set at this stage, as in the second example which sets the database to auto-commit mode (each database operation is immediately made permanent).

```
$dbh = DBI->connect(
         "dbi:Oracle:CSCI8.CS","HSimpson", "Doh");
#$dbh = DBI->connect("dbi:Oracle:CSCI8.CS",
#        "Hsimpson", "Doh", { AutoCommit => 1} );
```

In Java you would ask a java.sql.Connection object to return a statement object; you would then use this to submit strings with SQL queries. Perl is very similar. You get statement handles from your database handle, and then execute the statement. The code fragment below would attempt to return all data in Table1 of the database referenced by your $dbh handle.

```
$sth = $dbh->prepare("SELECT * FROM Table1");
$sth->execute;
```

You could be more selective:

```
$sth = $dbh->prepare("SELECT * FROM Table1 WHERE GRADE > 3");
$sth->execute;
```

Often you will want queries that depend on data entered by the user. You can employ interpolation when building a query string:

```
print "Enter Grade cutoff : ";
$grade = <STDIN>;
chomp($grade);
$sth = $dbh->prepare("SELECT * FROM Table1 WHERE GRADE > $grade");
...
$sth->execute;
```

Usually it is better to prepare statements with placeholders for arguments, rather than building a specific query each time:

```
# prepare the statement immediately after opening the database connection.
$sth = $dbh->prepare("SELECT * FROM Table1 WHERE GRADE > ? ");
# do other work
...
print "Enter Grade cutoff : ";
$grade = <STDIN>;
chomp($grade);
# invoke the query, with the value of $grade substituted
# for the first (?) placeholder
$sth->execute($grade);
```

The 'prepare' step involves some parsing of the SQL string, and this is relatively costly. So it is more efficient to prepare the statement once, and later bind values to placeholders, rather than create a new SQL query string for each request and then parse that string.

A secondary reason for using prepared statements is that they help avoid messy problems with quoted strings. Suppose you need a query like the following:

```
$sth = $dbh->prepare("SELECT GRADE FROM Table1 WHERE NAME='Smith'");
```

Single string quotes are required around string data in an SQL statement, so you need NAME='Smith'. Usually, the name will be data entered:

```
print "Enter name : ";
$name= <STDIN>;
chomp($name);
$sth = $dbh->prepare("SELECT * FROM Table1 WHERE GRADE > '$name'");
```

The value entered for the name is interpolated into the doubly quoted string with the SQL statement; SQL requires the value to be surrounded by single quote characters. Problems appear with customer names such as O'Brien – the single quote character in the name disrupts the pairing of quotes and results in an error from the SQL system. This problem does not occur if you use '?' placeholders and bind values to the placeholders.

In addition to 'select' statements for data retrieval, you will need 'insert', 'update', and 'delete' statements like the following:

```
$sth = $dbh->prepare("INSERT INTO TABLE1 VALUES (?, ?, ?)");
$sth = $dbh->prepare("UPDATE TABLE SET GRADE= ? WHERE NAME = ?");
$sth = $dbh->prepare("DELETE FROM TABLE1 WHERE NAME='Smith'");
```

If your SQL is faulty, the prepare operation will fail and you get undef as the result:

```
$sth = $dbh->prepare(...);
unless defined $sth die "SQL problem";
```

Correctly formed SQL statements may fail; for example, you will get an SQL error if you attempt to insert a new record with a primary key that fails a uniqueness test. The DBI module variable $DBI::errstr contains an error report if an operation failed. This can be included in any termination message:

```
$sth->execute($data) || die "delete failed because $DBI::errstr";
```

Data retrieved by an SQL select query are accessed via the statement handle; this can be used to retrieve successive rows of the results table:

```
@row = $sth->fetchrow_array;
```

The fetchrow_array method returns undef when have all data have been processed. The typical code pattern for data retrieval is:

```
$sth = $dbh->prepare("select ... = ?");
...
$sth->execute($data1, $data2);
while(@row = $sth->fetchrow_array) {
   ...
}
```

All database handles are closed at program termination. However, you should close database connections as soon as possible:

```
$dbh->close;
```

Database drivers often rely on environment variables. For example, a Unix version of the Oracle driver relies on environment variables to hold information identifying the directories containing Oracle components, version number and related data. You will need to consult your database documentation to find exactly what environment variables must be defined. Usually, you define and 'export' these variables from a '.profile' file (a kind of Unix equivalent to a 'batch' file that is run whenever you log in). If the environment variables are not set correctly, you will not be able to connect to your database.

5.15.2 Database example

This example illustrates basic use of Perl's DBI module. The database contains records of people who wish to participate in an email-based 'pen-pal' service. Subscribers provide their email address, some limited personal information and a set of interests chosen from a predefined set of about 100 possible topics. Searches can be made for other subscribers who share some common interests, and satisfy other constraints.

The database has just one table; the rows characterize subscribers to this 'E-Pal' service. Each subscriber has an email address (assumed for simplicity to fit into a 32 character field); this must be unique, and serves as the primary key. Subscribers normally identify themselves as male or female, but can choose not to specify their gender (in which case they are classified as 'e-persons'). Subscribers can specify restrictions on the type of person with whom they wish to correspond (specifying male, female, e-person or any). For simplicity, a subscriber's interests are represented using five separate integer fields. The table has the following definition:

```
CREATE TABLE EPAL
   (email   varchar(32)      NOT NULL,
    type    varchar(8)       NOT NULL,
    want    varchar(8)       NOT NULL,
    interest1   number(4),
    interest2   number(4),
    interest3   number(4),
    interest4   number(4),
    interest5   number(4),
    CONSTRAINT id_pkey PRIMARY KEY(email),
    CONSTRAINT type_check CHECK (type in ('MALE', 'FEMALE', 'EPERSON')),
    CONSTRAINT want_check CHECK
        (want in ('MALE', 'FEMALE', 'EPERSON', 'ANY'))
);
```

The 'check' constraints are not particularly important and can be omitted if the database that you use does not support such constraints; the program code essentially duplicates these checks.

The example program is a standalone Perl program reading data from the keyboard and working directly with the database. Commands can be given to the program to add records to the database or to perform searches. The code could be adapted to form a CGI script that accepted data entered in HTML forms (the example in the next section illustrates a part of this modified version); this would result in a web-based E-Pal service – something rather more useful than this standalone version.

Very similar input data are required for record addition and searches. Users must enter their own 'type', the 'type' of person with whom they wish to correspond, and must select five interests from the list of predefined interests; if a record is to be added, the input data must also include an email address. The criteria for a successful match in the search are:

- The value for 'type' in the record satisfies the 'want' requirement of a request – with the override that a request 'want=any' matches any value in the type field.

- The 'type' specified in the search request satisfies the 'want' requirement given in the record – again with 'any' being matched by all possible request types.

- The two sets of interests have a non-zero intersection (interests are represented as numbers in the range 1–100; they are not necessarily ordered).

These matching criteria are difficult to express as an SQL selection condition; it is easier for the program to retrieve all records and apply the criteria programmatically.

The overall program structure is:

- Initialization:
  - Create lists and hashes with predefined interests.
  - Open a database connection.
  - Prepare a statement that will be used for insertion.

- DoAdd:
  - Prompt for email, type, wanted type for correspondent and list of interests (each part handled by separate subroutine).
  - Run parameterized insertion request.

- DoSearch:
  - Prompt for type, wanted type and list of interests.
  - Run search request.

- Handle search results:
  - For each retrieved record, match against specified requirements; print emails of those who match.

- Main:
  - Initialize.
  - While not 'quitted':
    - Ask user for add or search request.
    - DoAdd or DoSearch

The program uses a number of global variables, and each subroutine has local variables. The somewhat larger size of the program increases the risk of use of errors resulting from implicit declaration of variables, or the use of uninitialized variables. It is worthwhile changing the mode of the Perl interpreter so that all variables must be declared. Specifying the directive 'use strict' at the start of the program makes this change.

The code should be organized as follows:

- 'uses' directives – setting strict mode and importing modules (in this case, only the DBI module).

```
use strict;
use DBI;
```

- Declaration of program-scope 'my' variables, some initialized at declaration.
- Subroutine definitions.
- Main line code.

The program scope variables and constants are:

```
my $data_source = "dbi:Oracle:CSCI8.CS"; # Use your DB name
my $dbh;
my $searchHandle;
my $insertHandle;
my %interesttable;
# list containing approximately 100 interests
my @interestlist = ( "Abseiling", "Aerobics", ...
   ...
"WebDesign", "WineTasting", "Yoga", "Zen"
);
```

The main line invokes the initialization routine that creates a database connection and sets up table. The main function then has a 'menu-select' loop handling commands entered by the user. The commands handled are 'add', 'search', 'list' (lists contents of interest list) and 'quit'. The code is:

```
initialize;

while(1) {
  my $cmd;
  print "Enter command (add,search, list (interests), quit): ";
  $cmd = <STDIN>;
  if($cmd =~ /quit/i) { last; }
  elsif($cmd =~ /search/i) { doSearch; }
  elsif($cmd =~ /add/i) { doAdd; }
  elsif($cmd =~ /list/i) {
    print "Interest list @interestlist\n"; }
  else { print "Command not recognized\n"; }
}
```

The initialization routine creates a hash that maps interest topic to identifier number. Users must enter their interests and have them checked; here, the hash serves as a faster lookup system than the original list. The other tasks for the initialization routine are opening a database connection and preparation of both a simple SQL selection query and a more elaborate parameterized SQL statement that will be used to enter records. The insert statement requires eight values to be bound – email address, 'type', 'want' and five interest identifiers.

```perl
sub initialize {
  my ($id, $interest);
  $id = 0;
  foreach $interest (@interestlist) {
    $interesttable{$interest} = $id; $id++;
  }
  $dbh = DBI->connect($data_source,
    "HSimpson", "Doh", { AutoCommit => 1})
    || die "Couldn't connect to db\n";
  $searchHandle = $dbh->prepare("SELECT * FROM epal");
  $insertHandle = $dbh->prepare(
    "INSERT INTO epal VALUES ( ?, ?, ?, ?, ?, ?, ?, ? ) ");
}
```

The doAdd function uses three simple helper functions (owntype, wanttype, getinterests) to obtain user input. The getinterests function repeatedly prompts the user until data defining five interests have been entered correctly; it returns a list with the corresponding identifier numbers. Note the call to the execute function; this specifies three explicit arguments and the five-element interest array. This does match the requirements for eight arguments – after all, Perl combines all arguments into a single list anyway, and then splits out the arguments inside the function.

```perl
sub doAdd {
  my ($you, $desire, $email, @interests);
  $you = owntype;
  $desire = wanttype;
  @interests = getinterests;

  print "Your email address : ";
  $email = <STDIN>;
  chomp($email);
  $insertHandle->execute( $email, $you, $desire, @interests)
    || die "Failed to insert record because $DBI::errstr";
}
```

The search function similarly uses the helper functions (owntype, wanttype and getintersts) to obtain data characterising the searcher. It then runs the SQL search query: 'select everything from the epal table'. Each record is read into a list ($searchHandle-> fetchrow_array). The retrieved data are then checked against the request data (some of Perl's unusual 'back-to-front' conditional tests are illustrated in this code).

```perl
sub doSearch {
  my ($you, $desire, @interests, @row);
  my ($theiremail, $theirtype, $theirdesire, @theirinterest);
  my $score;
  $you = owntype;
  $desire = wanttype;
  @interests = getinterests;

  $searchHandle->execute
     || die "Select request failed because $DBI::errstr";

  $score = 0;
  while(@row = $searchHandle->fetchrow_array) {
    ( $theiremail, $theirtype, $theirdesire, @theirinterest)
      = @row;
    # Is record of the type that searcher wants?
    next unless (
    ($desire eq "ANY") || ($desire eq $theirtype));
    # Is searcher of the type that record holder wants?
    next unless (
    ($theirdesire eq "ANY") || ($theirdesire eq $you));
    # Do they have some common interests?
    my @common = (); my $interest;
    foreach $interest (@interests) {
      push(@common, $interest)
        if (grep {$interest == $_ } @theirinterest);
    }
    next if ((scalar @common) == 0);
    $score++;
    print "Contact mail $theiremail:\tCommon interests: ";
    foreach (@common) {
      print "\t$interestlist[$_]";
      }
    print "\n";
  }
  unless ($score > 0) {
    print "Sorry, we currently don't have any contacts for you\n";
  }
}
```

The small helper functions owntype and wanttype repeatedly prompt for input until valid data are entered:

```perl
sub owntype {
my $type;
```

```
            my @allowed;
            while(1) {
              print "Your type : ";
              $type = <STDIN>;
              chomp $type;
              @allowed = qw( MALE FEMALE EPERSON);
              if(grep { /$type/i } @allowed) { last; }
              print "Unrecognized type; allowed values are @allowed\n";
            }
            return uc $type;
            }
```

The getinterests function similarly prompts for interests. Note the use of the exists function used to check whether a topic entered by the user corresponds to an entry in the hash table of interests.

```
sub getinterests {
my @list; my @nlist; my $temp;
while(1) {
  print "Enter five personal interests : ";
  $temp = <STDIN>;
  @list = split /\s/, $temp;
  my $length;
  $length = @list;
  if($length != 5) { print "5 interests required\n"; next; }
  $temp = 1;
  my $item;
  foreach $item (@list) {
    unless (exists $interesttable{$item}) {
      print "Interest $item not recognized\n";
      $temp = 0;
      next;
      }
    push(@nlist, $interesttable{$item});
    }
  if($temp) { last; }
  }
return @nlist;
}
```

5.16 Perl: CGI

Very soon after the widespread adoption of web-based forms and CGI programs, Perl emerged as the favored CGI scripting language. Most of the work in a CGI program consists of extraction of data from text entered in a form page, followed by the generation of large amounts of textual output. This output typically consists of 'template' text with a few embedded, computed values. Such text extraction and generation activities are the natural province of Perl. Further, most CGI programs require some interaction with a database; the DBI module makes this simpler than alternatives like embedded SQL in a C or C++ program.

5.16.1 'Roll your own' CGI code

It is easy to write code that handles simple form-based data entry. The data from a form are available as x-www-urlencoded name=value strings; these can be read either from <STDIN> (if the form uses the post method) or from the environment variable QUERY_STRING (if the form uses the get method). A Perl CGI program to handle form data must:

- Generate the 'content type' part of the standard header for an HTTP response.
- Extract and process the submitted data.
- Generate HTML for response.

Consider for example a web site that advertises toys for children. It would typically have a form used to select between toys for boys and toys for girls. A real web site would use an elaborate graphic page, but the essentials are captured in the following simple text page:

```
<html><head><title>Test page</title></head>
<body>
<form method=post
   action="http://www.kidtoys.com/cgi-bin/form1.cgi">
What are you? <br>
<input type=radio name=sex value=Boy checked>Boy
<input type=radio name=sex value=Girl>Girl
<br>
<input type=submit>
</form></body></html>
```

This form uses the post method, so the submitted data can be read from standard input. The data should consist of a single name=value combination (sex=Boy, sex=Girl); the processing program should handle these, and should also allow for illegal input that does not match any of the expected forms.

A generated response must start with the content type specification. Usually, this will specify text/html (text/plain may sometimes be used); more exotic responses, such as image/gif, are illustrated in Chapter 6: PHP4. The web server that launches the Perl CGI program checks this response header. If the content type is not recognized (or is not followed by a blank line), the web server aborts all processing. The client will receive some error indication and a 'malformed header' entry will appear in the web server's log. (A common error is to have trace statements in the Perl program that start to print data before the header line has been sent.) The first output from a Perl CGI program has to be something like:

```
Content-type: text/html\n\n
```

In the simple case, the input line can be split at the '=' sign so as to extract the value entered in the 'sex' field. This is done in the example code using a simple regular expression that checks for the literal text 'sex=' followed by some number of word characters (Perl's \w character class) and nothing else. Then, a three-way if...elsif...else... construct can generate an appropriate response. These responses can be large chunks of HTML script incorporated as 'here' documents.

```perl
#!/share/bin/perl

print "Content-type: text/html\n\n";

$person= <STDIN>;
chomp($person);
$type = "Hacker";
if($person =~ /sex=(\w*)&*/) {
  $type = $1;
  }
if($type eq "Boy") {
# Generate an HTML response page tailored to boys
# Action-man dolls etc
  print <<BOYS;
<html><head><title>Boys' own page</title><head><body>
  ...
  ...
</body></html>
BOYS
  }
elsif($type eq "Girl") {
# Generate an HTML response page tailored to girls
# Barbie dolls etc
  print <<GIRLS;
<html><head><title>Girls' own page</title><head><body>
  ...
  ...
</body></html>
GIRLS
  }
else {
```

```
  # Invalid input, probably someone trying to hack our site
    print <<HACKER;
<html><head><title>Unrecognized input</title></head>
    ...
</body></html>
HACKER
}
```

Most forms have multiple input fields, and also have free text inputs for data such as names and addresses. The browser will encode the data for each input; spaces are replaced by '+' signs, other non-alphabetic characters are encoded using %<hexdigit><hexdigit> sequences. The '&' character is used as a separator of successive name=value pairs. This encoding of the data must be reversed in the CGI program.

A form for the E-Pal example of the previous section would need:

- Radio button inputs for the Join or Search option ('action' input).

- Radio button clusters for preferences – male, female, e-person, any – ('self' and 'other' inputs).

- A text input for the email address ('email' input).

- A multi-choice selection list for interests ('interests' input).

These inputs would have to be checked to determine whether all data had been entered; then insertion or search requests could be run against a database as illustrated in the previous section.

The following code fragment illustrates the initial handling of data from the form. In this example, the name/value pairs are simply echoed back to the client. The program assumes that the form uses the get method; the processing steps are:

- The QUERY_STRING variable is extracted from the %ENV hash that the Perl core provides to hold environment variables.

- The string is broken into separate into name/value pairs (split using & as the separator).

- The name/value pairs are split into name and value parts (at the = character).

- The x-www-urlencoding of the value part is reversed:
  - Plus to space on value.
  - %xx to character on value.

- Finally, the name/value pairs are echoed.

```
#!/share/bin/perl
print "Content-type: text/html\n\n";

$stuff = $ENV{"QUERY_STRING"};
```

```perl
print "<html><head><title>test</title></head><body>\n";

@splitstuff= split /&/ , $stuff;
print "<ul>";
foreach (@splitstuff) {
  print "<li>";
  ($name, $value) = split /=/;
  # a "global" substitution of + by space.
  $value =~ s/\+/ /g;
  # search for %xx combinations
  # work out replacement character
  # substitute %xx by replacement
  while($value =~ /%([0-9A-Fa-f]{2})/) {
    $old = "%$1";
    $chrcode = "0x$1";
    $chrval = hex $chrcode;
    $symbol = chr $chrval;
    $value =~ s/$old/$symbol/;
  }
  print "$name\t:$value\n";
}

print "</ul>";
print "</body></html>";
```

The string is broken at '&' and then at '=' characters before the value part is decoded. There is always a chance that the user of a browser includes one or other of these characters in the input; this can cause confusion if the entire string is decoded prior to splitting.

A real web-based 'E-Pal' service wouldn't echo the inputs; it would validate the input data and then run 'insert' or 'search' operations on a database, as illustrated in the previous section. There is an extra complication. A CGI program typically runs as user 'www' or 'nobody'; its environment will be inherited from the web server process that launched it. Often you will find that the environment of the web server process does not include the environment variables needed by your database. A CGI program may have to perform some extra initialization steps in which it explicitly adds data to the environment before any calls are made to database drivers etc. The example illustrates something of this extra step.

The main line of the program would involve the following steps:

● Output the http content type header.

● Call an initialization subroutine:
  – Create lists, hash tables with interests (used to check submitted data).
  – Modify environment.
  – Open database connection.
  – Create statement handles.

- Get QUERY_STRING from %ENV;

- Loop extracting and decoding name/value pairs:
  - If name is 'act': record action value.
  - If name is 'self': record requestor value.
  - If name is 'other': record desired value.
  - If name is 'email': record email value.
  - If name is 'interests': add interest value to a list.

- Check that action, own type, other type and interest list have defined values; if not, use a subroutine to print an HTML error page.

- Check that email is defined if action is add.

- Check that values for own type and wanted type are in legal sets (MALE, FEMALE, EPERSON) and (MALE, FEMALE, EPERSON, ANY).

- Check that five interests from the standard list were supplied, and convert from names to numeric values for entry in database.

- If action is add:
  - Execute SQL insert statement with data values from form.
  - Generate a page welcoming latest E-Pal.

- If action is search:
  - Retrieve all records, checking each for suitability.
  - Generate HTML text with details of matches.

The main line code is long and could be further split into subroutines.

The main line starts by outputting partial the http response header, then calls the initialization routine:

```
#!/share/bin/perl
use strict;
use DBI;
# Declare all of the global variables (running with 'strict')
my $dbh;
my $insertHandle;
...
# Define all subroutines
sub initialize { ... }
sub badInterests { ... }
sub checkinterests { ... }
sub checktype { ... }
sub checkwant { ... }
sub badSubmission { ... }
sub badEmail { ... }
sub databaseFailure { ... }
```

```
# start processing by output of partial http header
print "Content-type: text/html\n\n";
initialize;
...
```

With the content type safely set, the program can simply output HTML text. If errors are detected in the inputs, a subroutine can be used to output a predefined error page; typically, one would use here documents to include a block of fixed HTML code. For example, the following routine outputs an error page if there are problems with the set of interests submitted:

```
sub badInterests {
  print <<BAD;
<html><head><title>Please complete interest list</title></head>
<body>
<em>
Sorry but we are unable to handle your request. You must pick
exactly 5 entries from the list of possible interests.
</em>
</body></html>
BAD
}
```

Most of the initialization code is the same as that illustrated in Section 5.15.2. The extra part relates to adding to the environment some information about the database prior to the DBI calls used to create a database connection and initialize statements:

```
sub initialize {
  my ($id, $interest);
  $id = 0;
  foreach $interest (@interestlist) {
    $interesttable{$interest} = $id;
    $id++;
  }
  # Setting Oracle's environment (not all variables essential)
  # Obviously, this environment initialization step is going to
  # depend on your database system --- consult the documentation!

  $ENV{"ORACLE_BASE"} = "/packages/oracle8/u01/app/oracle";
  $ENV{"ORACLE_HOME"} =
    "/packages/oracle8/u01/app/oracle/product/8.1.6";
  $ENV{"ORACLE_SID"} = "csci8";
  $ENV{"TWO_TASK"} = "csci8";
  ...
  $dbh = DBI->connect($data_source,
```

```
        "HSimpson", "Duh", { AutoCommit => 1}) ||
        die "Couldn't connect to db\n";
    $searchHandle = $dbh->prepare("SELECT * FROM epal");;
    $insertHandle = $dbh->prepare(
        "INSERT INTO epal VALUES ( ?, ?, ?, ?, ?, ?, ?, ? ) ");
}
```

With all initialization steps completed, the main-line would continue by picking up the `x-www-urlencoded` data and breaking the string up to derive values for the various input elements:

```
$stuff = $ENV{"QUERY_STRING"};
@splitstuff= split /&/ , $stuff;
foreach (@splitstuff) {
    ($name, $value) = split /=/;
    $value =~ s/\+/ /g;
    while($value =~ /%([0-9A-Fa-f]{2})/) {
        # Code as illustrated above
        ...
    }
    if($name eq "act") { $action = $value; }
    elsif($name eq "self") { $enteredtype = $value; }
    ...
    elsif($name eq "interests") { push(@enteredinterest, $value); }
    else {
    # Some hacker out there. Ignore whatever trash they put in
    }
}
```

The submitted data would then be validated as far as possible:

```
# Check that data was submitted for all essential fields
unless((defined $action) && (defined $enterdesire) &&
    (defined $enteredtype) &&
        ((scalar @enteredinterest) > 0)) {
            badSubmission; exit; }
if($enteredemail eq "") { undef $enteredemail; }
if(($action eq "add") && !(defined $enteredemail)) { badEmail; exit; }

badSubmission unless (checkwant($enterdesire) &&
checktype($enteredtype));

my @numericlist;
@numericlist = checkinterests(@enteredinterest);
```

Finally, the database operations can be invoked and response HTML generated:

```perl
if($action eq "add") {
  $insertHandle->execute( $enteredemail, $enteredtype,
    $enterdesire, @numericlist) ||
      databaseFailure;
  print <<JOIN;
<html><head><title>Thanks for registering with E-Pal</title></head>
<body>
<h1>You are registered</h1>
We hope you find lots of new friends via E-Pal.
</body></html>
JOIN
}
elsif($action eq "search") {
  print "<html><head><title>E-pals for you</title></head><body>";
  my ($score, @row);
  my ($theiremail, $theirtype, $theirdesire, @theirinterest);

  $searchHandle->execute ||
    die "Select request failed because $DBI::errstr";
  $score = 0;
  while(@row = $searchHandle->fetchrow_array) {
    # Code as illustrated earlier
    ...
  }
  unless ($score > 0) {
    print "Sorry, we currently don't have any contacts for you\n";
  }
}
else { badSubmission; }
```

The example code just shown has a few 'die ...' clauses, mostly relating to database problems. If one of these was executed the web client would see a message like 'document contained no data', or maybe an incomplete page. Details of the error would be found in the web server's log file.

5.16.2 Perl: CGI module(s)

Coding your own Perl scripts for CGI was never hard. The code to find parameter values from the form data was a little clumsy, but it was pretty much standardized. Much of the HTML script for a response page would typically be fixed and incorporated as 'here' strings. The Perl code to generate an HTML table containing information abstracted from a database would be straightforward, if a little long-winded.

But everybody was writing Perl CGI scripts, with similar code repeated. Naturally, lots of little components for often-needed HTML fragments were developed; some were submitted to CPAN, and eventually a suite of CGI modules became standardized. These components are also described in the Perl documentation (perldoc CGI etc.).

The main CGI module provides a 'query' object and associated functions for extracting parameter values submitted in forms, functions for formatting standard HTML elements (headers – including cookies, redirection headers and so forth, metadata such as links to stylesheets, HTML links and HTML elements like horizontal rules), and functions that help in the construction of dynamic pages that incorporate elaborate forms. There are extra modules such as one that provides further support for cookies; another is the Carp module, which provides an easy mechanism for inserting message into the web server's log.

The CGI module supports both 'object style' and 'function style' interfaces. In the object style, you obtain a reference to a 'query' object and invoke methods of this object. In the function style, you simply invoke functions defined in the CGI module. Selective imports are possible; these allow the use of particular subsets of the functions defined in the module.

The following simple example makes some basic use of the CGI module to generate process the boys' toys/girls' toys form used earlier. This code uses the function style interface. Functions include param (to pick up the value of a named input field from the form), start_html (sets data that will be included in the head section of the document), h1 (prints an HTML H1 header element containing the specified text) and p (adds a paragraph tag).

```perl
use CGI qw/:standard/;

print header(-type => 'text/html');

$type = param("sex");

if($type eq "Boy") {
  print start_html(
    -title=>'Toys for boys',
    -meta=>{'keywords'=>'Action ...' },
    -BGCOLOR=>'blue');
  print h1("Toys for boys"), p,
    "Just look at our Action Man range ...," ;
  print ul(
    li( {-type=>'disc', ['Mountaineer', 'Scuba diver', ...]})
    );
  ...
  print end_html;
  }
else
if($type eq "Girl") {
  print start_html(
```

```
          -title=>'Toys for girls',
          -meta=>{'keywords'=>'Barbie ...' },
          -BGCOLOR=>'pink');
      print ...
   }
```

If you do use these functions, you embed your HTML strings within Perl function calls. This may make it harder for others to update the HTML later. Sometimes there are advantages in the simpler approach that relies more on blocks of HTML text as 'here' strings.

The documentation for the CGI module should be consulted for more information about the various support functions that are provided.

5.16.3 Security issues and CGI

As illustrated earlier, Perl can launch processes and perform lots of file manipulations. So it is possible for you to attempt quite elaborate tasks involving a CGI program that launches sub-processes that operate on files identified by users, or invokes mail subsystems and so forth. Be cautious. This is the Internet that you are connecting to; out there in cyberspace are individuals who would delight in upsetting your system.

So you have decided to offer a service where you have directories containing files that users might like to view and so have a form where the user can enter a directory name. The CGI program that you use to handle this form lists the contents of the chosen directory and appends another form that allows the user to specify the file they wish to view. The program is something along the following lines:

```
print header(-type => 'text/html');

$dir = param("dirname");
print start_html(-title=>'Directory listing');
print h1("Directory listing for $dir"), p, "Contents of directory:";
print "<pre>";
$command = "ls -l $dir";
$listing = `$command`;
print $listing;
print "</pre>";
# code to generate form for file selection and end page
...
```

What do you suppose happens when a visiting user enters '/htdocs; cat /etc/passwd' in the dirname input field of the first form?

If you are going to run commands that depend on user-supplied data, then you are risking hacker attacks. Really, you should be very wary of any web-accessible service that does anything other than store user inputs for later processing. Hackers can turn even something as innocuous as an email address into a device to obtain data from, or disrupt the workings of, a system if the submitted data are used in a shell command.

If you are determined to use such data, you must write code that carefully teases apart every user input looking for any little hacker-contributed novelties. Only once you have stripped the data down to the character level and reassembled it can you safely use the values in file operations (open, link, rename, ...) or in things like exec commands or system calls.

Perl has a safety feature that helps verify that you have performed checks. You can set the interpreter to work in 'taint' mode (use the -T command line option or the #! line option). In this mode, all input data are treated as tainted – not to be used in OS-related operations. This 'taint' of suspicion propagates from the original data variables to others that are assigned values based on the inputs. The taint must be explicitly removed before you can use the data in an OS related operation. Details about taints, and some related security issues, are covered in the perlsec component of the documentation.

Exercises

Practical

(1) Make sure that your Perl system and its associated documentation are properly installed and that simple 'Hello World' examples run.

Determine what database system you have access to, and if necessary use PPM to go to the Perl home site from where you can download any extra Perl modules that must be installed to allow your Perl programs to work with your database.

(2) Write a Perl program that determines letter frequencies in text files. The program is to:

- Read data from one or more text files whose names are entered on the command line.

- Process each file line by line.

- Convert all alphabetic characters to lower case.

- Extract each character in turn from the line and update a corresponding counter (you may assume that all input files are text files and contain only printable characters).

- When all files have been read, the count data should be sorted.

- The sorted data are to be printed with the highest frequency characters and their counts appearing at the start of the output (for clarity, the output should use the strings 'tab', 'space' and 'newline' rather than these actual characters).

(3) Write a program that will strip all HTML tags from an HTML file, leaving just context text. The program is to:

- Check for two filenames on the command line, terminating if these filenames are not supplied.

- Obtain the names of the input file and the output file by shift operations on @ARGV.

- Confirm that the input file is a text file.

- Read and process the input line by line.

- Change each line by removing all < . . . > sequences using a substitution pattern match (note that an input like '<a href=link>Next</a>' should leave the text 'Next').

- Output the updated text to the output file, omitting any lines that are now blank.

This program will not correctly process HTML tags that are opened on one line and closed on a subsequent line.

(4) Revise the program from Exercise 3 so that it reads the entire input file into memory and processes its contents as a single long string. HTML tags that span multiple lines should now be handled correctly.

(5) Write a program that will use regular expression pattern matching to find all HTML <a href=...> link tags in an input HTML file and will use these data to construct a collection of the names of the different files referenced in links. These filenames are to be printed when the input data have all been processed.

(6) *This example is for implementation on a Unix system where the "finger" command can be used to lookup the name of a user whose login id is known.*
Write a program, StudentList.pl, that is to help administrative staff who have to transcribe students' assignment marks into a University database system. Marks are returned by tutors in files that list student user-ids and marks; for example:

```
aa63    7
am83    7.5
bjr02   8
cjw11   7.5
```

The database system does not display user-ids; instead it lists students by name, ordered by family name.

The finger command can be used to find the name of the person with a given user-id. The following are typical outputs from finger:

```
$ finger bm07
Login name: bm07            In real life: Bradley Milner
Directory: /home/ug/c/bm07  Shell: /share/bin/uow_sh
Never logged in.
$finger rgc01
Login name: rgc01           In real life: Robert George Composti
Directory: /home/ug/u/rgc01 Shell: /share/bin/uow_sh
Never logged in.
```

The StudentList.pl program is to read marks files supplied by tutors, convert user identifiers to names, and list names and marks in the correct order for transcription to the database

For an input file:

```
bm07    8
rgc01   8.5
rvi01   8
```

It should produce the output:

```
Composti          Robert George          8.5
Iyer              Ravichandran V         8
Milner            Bradley                8
```

More specifically, the StudentList.pl program:

- Reads input from a sequence of files listed on the command line.

- File input is read line-by-line.

- Each line consists of a student's user identifier, followed by a tab character or some spaces, and a mark (a number with possibly a fractional part).

- The system finger command is to be used (via 'backticks') to obtain a string containing all the identification data for a user identifier.

- The name data are to be extracted and rearranged.

- A string containing family name, given names and marks, suitably formatted to guarantee alignment, is to be generated.

- The string is added to a collection.

- When all inputs have been read, the collection of strings is to be sorted and the sorted list printed.

You will need to create your own data file with a collection of user ids for some of the users on your Unix system.

Exercises 7–10 use Apache log files as input data. You should try to use log files from a local server. The web site associated with this book does have a couple of compressed files with logs from an Apache system; these files have around twenty thousand records each, which is a reasonable amount of data for analysis.

Apache log files contain data like the following (line breaks have been inserted to fit the data to the page; each record is actually on a single line):

```
203.132.227.144 - - [19/Jun/2001:00:43:46 +1000]
   "GET /current/subject_outlines/ HTTP/1.0" 304 -
203.106.173.151 - - [19/Jun/2001:00:39:57 +1000]
   "POST /cgi-bin/labpref3 HTTP/1.1" 200 563
```

```
203.88.255.122 - - [19/Jun/2001:08:06:03 +1000]
  "GET /subjects/iact417/tut4/g4_2/Image1.jpg HTTP/1.0" 401 397
203.88.255.122 - iact417 [19/Jun/2001:08:06:06 +1000]
  "GET /subjects/iact417/tut4/g4_2/Image1.jpg HTTP/1.0" 200 8408
```

The first element is the client's IP address, the second is almost always just a '-' place holder (it will contain the email address or user identifier in rare cases where the client has chosen to supply this information), the third field will be a user identity if one has been entered in response to an authorization challenge for a controlled realm, the fourth field is a timestamp (date, time, timezone), the fifth field is a quoted string with the 'get', 'post', 'put' or other command (command, resource name, protocol), the fifth field is the HTTP response code, and the final field is the number of bytes of content data contained in the response sent back to the client.

Regular expression matches are required to pick up data such as the protocol level used in a request.

(7) Write a program that reads a log file such as described above and:

- Calculates the percentage of clients who are still submitting requests using the HTTP/1.0 protocol

- Calculates the percentage of requests that were successful (response codes in the 200 region), resulted only in informational responses (response codes in the 300 region), had client errors (response codes in the 400 region) or caused server errors (response codes in the 500 region).

(8) Write a program that will produce a listing of filenames that probably occur as bad links in your web site. This program is to:

- Process only 'get' requests that result in '404 file not found' responses.

- Build a collection of the filenames and counts of the number of requests for each missing file.

- Prints a sorted list of those files and their counts for those files where there are three or more requests; the missing files that are most often requested should be listed first (files with counts of 1 or 2 are usually due to users entering incorrectly spelled filenames).

(9) Write a program that:

- Processes only 'get' requests.

- Ignores requests for image files and icons (files with names ending .ico, .gif, .jpg, .jpeg, .bmp, .png and capitalized variants of these extensions).

- Keeps records of each distinct filename and associated request count.

- When all data have been read, produces a sorted list showing the twenty most frequently requested files and their request counts.

(10) *(This program requires interaction with a Domain Name Server and so can only be done online. Depending on the data files used, it may result in a large number of requests to the DNS system, and so may run slowly.)*

Write a program that

- Constructs a record of all distinct requestor IP addresses and the number of requests they submitted.

- Uses the `gethostbyaddr` function (DNS services invoked) to look up the names corresponding to each distinct address.

- Lists the names of the twenty clients that submit the most requests.

- List counts of total requests from each top-level domain.

Exercises 11 and 12 require a database and use of the DBI module along with the correct database drivers.

(11) Getting the mechanics to work!
Create a database table equivalent to the following SQL table definition (your database system may require the use of some visual editor helper program to 'design' this table, or it may accept the SQL definition).

```
create table demotable (
  id     integer,
  name   varchar(32),
  constraint demotable_pk primary key(id)
);

insert into demotable values ( 1, 'one');
insert into demotable values ( 2, 'two');
insert into demotable values (3, 'three');
```

Write a Perl program that:

- Connects to the database and displays the current contents (submit the query `select * from demotable` and print each row in the result set).

- Allows the user to insert a new record (attempt to pick up error messages if the user violates the primary key constraint).

- Allows the user to modify the name field associated with an existing record.

- Allows the user to identify a record that is to be deleted.

(12) Write a Perl program and define associated database tables for a system that will record member details for a group and allocate unique membership numbers.

The program should be able to:

- List details of all current group members.

- Add a new record with name and address details (fields for family name, given name, middle initial, address, city, zip-code, state); the record's primary key is a membership number that is automatically allocated.

(Automatic allocation of membership number is somewhat database-dependent. For example, Microsoft Access has 'autonumber' fields; an autonumber field will work fine as the primary key and automatically allocated membership number. Oracle has a somewhat more complex 'sequence' construct. One approach that always works is to have a separate table that is used to handle unique number generation for different applications. The rows in this table contain an application name and an integer for the next number that is to be allocated. This table is read using the application name as retrieval key, and then a new number value is written back. The number taken from the numbers table is then used as part of the entry in the membership table. If you want to be really correct, a single database transaction should be used to group operation on both the numbers table and the membership table.)

Exercises 13–15 involve Perl CGI programs. It is easier if students can run their own Apache servers with their Perl programs in their server's cgi-bin *directory, and their HTML pages in its* htdocs *directory. When individual students launch their own Apache servers, the server and the spawned CGI programs all run with the student's user-identifier and so their privileges are those appropriate to students.*

There are quite a number of messy configuration issues to resolve if a single Apache server is to be shared by students. Typically, it is necessary to create individual subdirectories for each student within the htdocs *directory of the shared Apache server; these subdirectories require permissions to hold CGI programs. Often it is necessary to resolve issues of 'set user id' programs, or use of Apache SUExec, so as to arrange that individual students' CGI programs run with their author's access privileges.*

(13) Getting the mechanics to work!
Write a Perl CGI 'hello world' program.

The implementation should involve a static HTML page, a Perl CGI program and a dynamically generated response page.

The static HTML page displays a simple form that has an 'Enter your name here' input text box, and a submit button. Submission invokes a Perl program that generates a well-formatted HTML response page, containing a 'Hello ...' greeting that echoes the name that was input in the form. The response page should also include a date stamp showing the time and date as recorded on the server host machine.

(14) Getting the mechanics to work II: adding the backend database.
Write a Perl CGI database access system. The system is to allow viewing and updating of a simple data table, such as the demotable defined in Exercise 11.

The implementation should involve a static HTML page, a Perl CGI program, a database, and a dynamically generated response page.

The static HTML page displays a simple form that allows the user to select listing, updating, deletion and insertion operations on the (number, name) demotable defined above. A radio button group can be used to define the required operation; input text fields will be needed for number and name (their values will only be used in a subset of the operations); and, of course, there will be a submit button. Submission invokes a Perl program that generates a well-formatted HTML response page containing a report appropriate to the operation selected – either listing of all entries in a table, or a success or failure message for the operations that modify the table.

(Depending on how the OS and database environments are set up, it may be necessary for the CGI program to explicitly define some environment variables that control database access. Details depend on the local system configuration.)

(15) Write a Perl CGI program that handles membership applications for some group. The system will involve two static HTML pages, a couple of Perl CGI programs that generate dynamic response pages, and the same membership database as used in Exercise 12.

The first HTML page and CGI program should handle new applications. The form page should have input fields for member details (name, address). The CGI program adds a new record to the members data table and returns a 'Welcome new member' page that informs the new member of their allocated membership number.

The second HTML page and CGI program are for the group administrator. This form page should allow the administrator to view, update and delete records. The program should perform the required database operations and report on their outcome via the dynamically generated response page.

Deploy the programs on your Apache server so that the membership application component is generally accessible while the administrator control component is within a 'controlled realm' so that usage is subject to name/password checks.

Short answer questions

(1) Compose a pattern that will extract a (4-digit) phone number and an optional fax number from listings that include lines like:

```
Phone: 6744      Fax: none
Phone: 5433      Fax:
Phone: 5344      Fax: +61 2 42345678
```

(2) Here is a short Perl program that can be used to test whether one has come up with the required regular expression to perform some matching and extraction task:

```
#!/share/bin/perl

#define the pattern in a doubly quoted string
$pat = ...;
```

```
print "Target pattern is $pat \n";
#let user enter data to test the pattern
while(<STDIN>) {
  if( /$pat/ ) {
    print "\tInput matched\n";
#uncomment if checking for a subexpression
#   print "\t\tFirst subexpression matched was $1\n";
  }
}
```

For example, the pattern definition $pat = "^a.*z\$" would allow the program to match all input lines with first letter 'a' and last letter 'z'.

Explain, with help of examples, the input data that are being tested for by the patterns with following definitions (where appropriate, identify matched sub-expressions):

```
$pat = "=[0-9A-Fa-f]{32}\\s";
$pat = "^[^:]+:([^:]+):";
$pat = "(\\d\\d):(\\d\\d):";
$pat = "\\W(thread|p_thread|pthread)\\W";
```

(Note that these patterns are being defined as doubly quoted strings, so 'extra' back-slash characters are required as shown.)

Explorations

(1) Pick an application area, such as encryption, XML parsing, support for Simple Object Access Protocol (SOAP), CGI/HTML processing or similar; then go to http:// www.cpan.org/ (home to Perl modules) and find out about Perl support in your chosen area. Download some representative modules and run small examples using them. Write a report on the potential for using Perl in the chosen area; illustrate your report with fragments from your test examples.

6

PHP4

PHP4 is another of the open source quick hacks that grew explosively and became a fairly well-established industry. It is essentially the open source competitor for Microsoft's proprietary Active Server Page technology. The PHP4 system is simple to deploy (it integrates best with Apache, but can work with other web servers), and PHP4 scripting code is easy to write (it is probably the easiest to use of all the server-side technologies). It has grown into one of the most widely used server-side technologies. It is mainly deployed for small web sites – small companies, sites belonging to individuals and so forth – but there are some major commercial users.

This chapter starts with brief sections on the origins of PHP and on its syntax. A series of simple examples are then used to illustrate its application. More advanced examples follow that illustrate common web needs such as multi-page forms, file uploads, database access and graphical response pages. (I prefer PHP over all other alternatives when it comes to generating response pages that include graphical images that are based on user-submitted data.) The final section looks at different ways in which an application can maintain state information about clients in the stateless world of WWW and HTTP.

6.1 PHP4's origins

Rasmus Lerdorf wrote the first version of PHP to manage his home page; hence the original PHP name, an acronym for *Personal Home Pages*. Lerdorf's original 1994 implementation involved a group of Perl scripts; this system was expanded with a 'Form Interpreter' component to produce PHP/FI 2.0. In 1997, Zeev Suraski and Andi Gurmans constructed a parser for this steadily evolving scripting language, which led to the PHP3.0 implementation that was the first version to establish a really significant user population. The current version, PHP4, has tidied up the language, improved the implementation and incorporated as standard many features that were only available as contributed add-on libraries in the earlier PHP3.

Why did PHP emerge and why did it grow? It faced established competitors. When the Common Gateway Interface (CGI) protocols were established, NCSA supplied function libraries for C/C++ that handled common tasks like the extraction of name/value pairs from a browser-supplied query string. Perl had proved popular, and many libraries were emerging to support Perl-based CGI systems.

Lerdorf provides his own explanation for PHP's popularity via a small example in which he compares the programs that are needed to echo 'name' and 'age' data as entered in a simple HTML form. His first version illustrates how he would write a C version:

```
#include <stdio.h>
#include <stdlib.h>
#include <ctype.h>
#include <string.h>

#define ishex(x) (((x) >= '0' && (x) <= '9') || \
            ((x) >= 'a' && (x) <= 'f') || \
            ((x) >= 'A' && (x) <= 'F'))

int htoi(char *s) {
  int    value;   char    c;
  c = s[0];
  if(isupper(c)) c = tolower(c);
  value=(c >= '0' && c <= '9' ? c - '0' : c - 'a' + 10) * 16;
  c = s[1];
  if(isupper(c)) c = tolower(c);
  value += c >= '0' && c <= '9' ? c - '0' : c - 'a' + 10;
  return(value);
}

void main(int argc, char *argv[]) {
  char *params, *data, *dest, *s, *tmp;
  char *name, *age;
  puts("Content-type: text/html\r\n");
  puts("<html><header><title>Form Example</title></header>");
  puts("<body><h1>Welcome</h1>");
  data = getenv("QUERY_STRING");
  if(data) {
    params = data; dest = data;
    /*
    In situ replacement of x-www-urlencoded string with
    decoded version.
    */
    while(*data) {
      /* Plus to space */
      if(*data=='+') *dest=' ';
      else if(*data == '%' && ishex(*(data+1))
        && ishex(*(data+2))) {
          /* Hex combination to character */
          *dest = (char) htoi(data + 1);
          data+=2;
```

```
        }
      else *dest = *data; /*copy ordinary characters */
      data++; dest++;
    }
    *dest = '\0';
    s = strtok(params,"&");
    do {
      tmp = strchr(s,'=');
      if(tmp) {
        *tmp = '\0';
        if(!strcmp(s,"name")) name = tmp+1;
        else if(!strcmp(s,"age")) age = tmp+1;
      }
    } while(s=strtok(NULL,"&"));
    printf("Hi %s, you are %s years old\n", name,age);
  }
  puts("</body></html>");
}
```

The joys of C hacking revealed! The code has multi-line macros, explicit pointer dereferencing, overwriting of a string *in situ* with replacement operations performed character by character, use of C's somewhat opaque string tokenizer, and string search and comparison functions. While experienced C programmers can produce such code swiftly and correctly, most coders are somewhat error-prone when writing code of this nature. Such code can also be problematic to maintain; imagine what could happen when a non-programming, creative designer decides to change the HTML parts to pretty up the response page.

Perl is a substantial improvement:

```
use CGI qw(:standard);
print header;
print start_html('Form Example'),
  h1('Welcome');
if(param()) {
  print "Hi ",em(param('name')),
  "You are ",em(param('age')),
  " years old";
}
print end_html;
```

But Perl is still 'programming' with fragments of embedded HTML.

Lerdorf's PHP version gets straight to the point. All that is needed is some HTML with a little data captured from the submitted form:

```
<html><header>
<title>Form Example</title>
```

```
</header>
<body><h1>Welcome</h1>
<?if($name):?>
Hi <?echo $name?>,
you are <?echo $age?> years old
<?endif?>
</body></html>
```

The PHP solution is based on code embedded in HTML (rather than HTML embedded in code as in Perl and C) using PHP constructs explicitly tailored to the handling of WWW data. Code is minimized; often it can be expressed entirely in terms of small code fragments embedded in the HTML. The example code also uses a feature that can permit fields in a form to automatically become named PHP variables in a program that must process the form's data.

One factor contributing to PHP's growth has been the ease of coding, as illustrated in the example above. Another factor is the relative efficiency of the PHP system. You can run a PHP interpreter as a CGI program (you can even build a standalone version that can be used as a script interpreter, comparable to the Perl and Python interpreters, and so use PHP as your main Unix/Linux scripting language). But typically PHP is integrated directly into the web server. The most common variant of the PHP interpreter is a module integrated into an Apache web server (there are also ISAPI and NSAPI modules for the IIS and Netscape iPlanet servers, and there is support for other less common systems). Integration saves the cost of the separate CGI process launch and results in higher performance.

PHP is growing. The site http://www.php.net/ has summary data from surveys conducted by Netcraft and other web analysis companies; these data show the recent growth. Between January 2000 and September 2001, PHP grew in usage from about 400,000 of the IP addresses surveyed to over one million; in terms of domains, the growth was from approximately 1.2 million to around 7 million. Other surveys (from SecuritySpace) show that by September 2001 about 44 per cent of all Apache sites were running with the PHP module installed (compared with only about 5 per cent using the Jserv extension that supports some versions of the Java servlet technologies).

As an 'open source' project, PHP accepts contributions from enthusiasts and has naturally acquired a library of add-on components, just like those that have been contributed to CPAN to enhance Perl. The libraries include:

- GD graphics: the GD library makes it particularly easy to generate purely graphic dynamic response pages or to generate graphic images that are embedded in more elaborate response pages.

- LDAP, SNMP, IMAP, FTP components: these support use of common protocols for file transfer, mail, network management and so forth.

- An XML parser.

- PDF generation and FDF (PDF forms).

- zlib (compressed I/O).

- SWF (Flash).

- MCRYPT.

- Database drivers (Traditionally, PHP uses database-specific interfaces. These can allow for some optimizations that exploit features of specific database implementations. A database neutral interface, comparable to Java's JDBC or Perl's DBI, is becoming available.)

The PHP distribution includes a thousand page manual. This covers installation, basics of PHP programming, core functions and the libraries; most sections include worked examples. Integration with an Apache server on Windows is simple; all you need do is uncomment some lines in the Apache `httpd.conf` file and copy a couple of '.dll' files from the PHP release directory. Slightly more work is required for Unix or Linux; you must change your Apache '.configure' options and build a new version of the server.

6.2 PHP language

A recipe for PHP:

- Take a firm base of C (control structures, operators, and so forth).

- Leaven with a little mixing of C++ and Java (limited support for classes).

- Generously top with fragments of Perl (Perl's influence appears through features like the form of simple variables, a degree of 'typelessness', strings that interpolate values of variables, and associative arrays that map keys to values).

- Add some unique WWW flavorings.

6.2.1 Simple variables and data types

Since PHP originally derives from some CGI-style Perl scripts, it is unsurprising that PHP variables are in many ways like those in Perl. Details of variables are covered more fully in Chapter 7 of the PHP 4.0 manual. Variable identifiers start with the '$' character and have name strings composed of alphanumeric characters. Simple variables hold a single value (string, numeric, boolean). PHP has arrays that are similar to Perl's associative arrays; there is no distinct array type with different '@' or '%' type identifier, just the [] subscripting operator applied to a variable name. Variables can have quasi-global or local scope; PHP is unusual in that, by default, functions create 'holes' in the scope of global variables (this will be illustrated later).

As a typical interpreted language, PHP does not require explicit variable declarations; variables come into existence when used. Variable types are not defined; the same variable may at different stages of a program's execution hold string, numeric or boolean data. Automatic type conversions are applied in appropriate contexts; string data are converted to numeric form if the value is required in an expression involving numeric operators. Numerics can be integer- or real-valued. As in Perl, there are distinct types of string variables – single and double quoted variants. The boolean type has the predefined constants TRUE and FALSE (there are some other predefined constants – details are given in Chapter 8 of the PHP distribution manual). Some examples of variables:

```
$seven = 7;
$sevenandahalf = 7.5;
$largernumber = 7.5e33;
$ok = true;
$str1 = "This is a string\n\tas you can see.";
$str2 =
  "Double quote strings have escape combinations like \\, \$, \r, \013";
$str3 = 'Single quoted strings only handle \\ and \' escape sequences';
```

As in Perl, you can initialize a string with a 'here' document.

```
$str = <<<END
Multi-line chunks of text suit
'here documents'.
END;
```

Note that the syntax for 'here' strings differs from that of Perl.
  As in Perl, you can interpolate the value of a variable into a string:

```
$postage = 2.50 + $weight*6.0;
...
$message = "Postage comes to \$ $postage \n";
```

Arrays can be created by explicitly setting each array element value:

```
$a[0] = "Hi";
$a[1] = "mom";
$b["one"] = 1;
```

An existing array can be extended with new elements that are added at the end:

```
$a[] = "hello"; // equivalent to $a[2] == "hello"
$a[] = "world"; // and $a[3] == "world"
```

An alternative approach uses the array function; this style is reminiscent of the initialization of a Perl hash:

```
$a = array(
"author" => "Horstmann",
```

```
                "title" => "Core Java",
                "cost" => 34.95",
                "stars" => "****",
                );
```

The PHP interpreter has a large number of predefined variables that are available to any script that it runs. These variables do depend on your system configuration. The phpinfo() function can be used to get a printout of the variables that are defined in your system. The following may be included:

- SERVER_NAME: the name server host under which the current script is executing.

- SERVER_SOFTWARE: server identification string.

- SERVER_PROTOCOL: name and revision of the information protocol via which the page was requested; e.g. 'HTTP/1.0'.

- REQUEST_METHOD – 'GET', 'HEAD', 'POST', 'PUT'.

- QUERY_STRING: the query string, if any, via which the page was accessed.

- HTTP_COOKIE_VARS: an associative array of variables passed to the current script via HTTP cookies.

- HTTP_GET_VARS: an associative array of variables passed to the current script via the HTTP GET method.

- HTTP_POST_VARS: an associative array of variables passed to the current script via the HTTP POST method.

- Also, all the general environment variables of the process running the web server.

When a form is submitted to a PHP script, the form's variables are made available to the script by PHP. The exact mechanism depends on the configuration options used when setting up the PHP module for the web server. The forms variables (its named input fields etc.) may be defined, automatically, as global variables; alternatively they may be accessible via the global array $HTTP_POST_VARS (or $HTTP_GET_VARS). For example, the following form defines an input field username:

```
<form action="identify.php" method="post">
Name:
<input type="text" name="username">
<br><input type="submit"></form>
```

The value entered in this input field will be available to a PHP script either as the value of $username or as $HTTP_POST_VARS['username']. (Lerdorf's example in the previous section relies on automatic declaration of form variables as globals.)

System behavior in this regard is controlled by the configuration variable register_globals. If this is true, then form variables are defined. This is dangerous. Your

PHP program may need to use values of its environment variables – things like PATH, LD_LIBRARY_PATH or SHELL. Suppose your form, with variables Name, Age and Sex, uses the GET method; you would expect to receive data in a request like identify. php?Name=Hacker&Age=16&Sex=Male and want the variables $Name etc. defined. What you will receive is often going to be something more like identify.php?Name=Hacker& Age=16& PATH=%2fusr%2fbin&...&... with your visitor hoping that you will overwrite your $PATH variable.

Variables are 'declared' simply by usage; their scope runs from the point of declaration to the end of the declaring function or program. This can cause behavior that is initially unintuitive to C programmers, as in the following:

```
$count = 0; // global variable
function foo() {
   ...
   $count++; // Er, no, not that global $count,
            // a local implicitly declared variable
   ...
}
```

If you want to use a global variable within a function, *then say so*:

```
$count = 0; // global variable
function foo() {
  global $count;
  ...
  $count++;
  ...
}
```

Function scope variables are 'automatics' stored on the stack and are lost on exit from the function. The 'static' qualifier can be used with local variables of the function – the same semantics as C/C++:

```
function foo() {
  static $a = 0; // Initialization performed just once
  ...
  $a++; // Incremented value will remain for next call
  ...
}
```

Sometimes you may need to query the type of the data held in a variable, or force conversion to a specified type. The type of a data value can be tested using predicates like is_long(...) or is_double(...) (these functions are detailed in Chapter LXIII of the PHP manual). PHP also has gettype() and settype() functions, and type casting constructs:

```
$val = 9.87654;
print gettype($val); // should say double
settype($val,integer);
print $val; // should print 9
```

The settype function changes the value of the variable to which it is applied. If you simply needed the integer part of the value, you could have used a type cast: $ival = (integer) $val.

6.2.2 Operators

PHP uses the operators from the C language, supplemented with few Perl-inspired additions. There are:

- The usual arithmetic and related operators:
  - +, -, /, * and %
  - The assignment operator = and the usual variants: +=, -= etc.
  - ++, -- (pre and post versions as in C/C++/Java).
  - Comparison operators: ==, !=, >=, <=, > and <.
  - Bitwise operators for integers: |, &, ^, ~, >> and <<

- C's ternary conditional operator ?::

  ```
  $max = ($max > $val) ? $max : $val;
  ```

- Logical operators: ||, && and !.
- Perl-like string operators:
  - . (concatenate) and .= (concatenating assignment).
  - == (we have to use functions like strncasecmp() to do other string comparisons).
- Perl's backticks 'Execution operator':

  ```
  $output = `cat /etc/passwd`;
  echo "<pre>$output</pre>";
  ```

There are the usual rules for operator precedence – multiplication (*) binds more strongly than addition (+). As always, it is best to use parentheses to clarify the structure of complex expressions rather than rely on uncertain remembrance of precedence relations. The PHP reference manual includes a short chapter that has lists of all the operators and precedence tables.

6.2.3 Program structure and flow control

Fundamentally, PHP is just another interpreted, imperative procedural language. A basic script has 'includes' for any function libraries that are not automatically loaded, then global variable 'declarations' and initializations, function definitions and a sequence of statements that are executed in order. Most scripts form parts of web pages with the script code interspersed with blocks of HTML text. The PHP code is bracketed within a <? start tag and a ?> end tag; these tags separate the code from HTML tags and content text, allowing a page with PHP code to be processed easily by an HTML-aware editor.

The basic 'sequence of statements' structure of an imperative language is supplemented with the usual selection and iteration constructs, along with function calls and method calls applied to objects. The selection statements are:

- A C-like `if` statement (unlike Perl, you are not forced to have blocks):
  - `if(...)` statement
  - `if (...)` block

- `if ... else` structure and `if ... elseif ... elseif ... else` structure:
  - `if(...) ... else ... ;`
  - `if(...) ... elseif(...) ... else ...;`
Note how this differs from Perl in the spelling of `elseif`.

The selection statements have an alternate syntactic form, motivated by the frequent need to intermix bits of PHP code and bits of plain HTML text. This alternate form uses `if(): ... else:` and a final `endif` terminator for the construct:

```
<h2>Some interesting links for you:</h2><ul>
<? if($sex=="male") : ?>
<li><a href=http://www.porn.com>Beauty</a>
<li><a href=http://www.beer.com>Food and drink</a>
<li><a href=http://www.footy.com>Culture</a>
<? else: ?>
<li><a href=http://www.makeup.com>Beauty</a>
<li><a href=http://www.health-foods.com>Food and drink</a>
<li><a href=http://www.ballet.com>Culture</a>
<? endif; ?>
</ul>
```

PHP does have a switch statement:

```
switch ($i) {
case 0:
  ...
  break;
case 1:
  ...
  break;
case 2:
  ...
  break;
}
```

PHP supplements the usual C-style iterative constructs:

- while(...) ...
- do ... while (...)
- for(initialize; test; increments) ...

with a Perl-like foreach structure. Two forms of this foreach structure are shown in the following code fragments:

```
<?
$names = array ("tom", "dick", "harry", "sue" );
foreach($names as $name) {
  print "$name<br>";
}

$roles = array (
  "tom" => "Project Lead",
  "dick" => "Chief Programmer",
  "harry" => "Graphic Designer",
  "sue" => "DB guru"
);
foreach($roles as $name=>$role) {
  print "$name\t$role<br>";
}
?>
```

PHP uses C's break and continue statements rather than the Perl last and next statements.

6.2.4 Functions

There are thousands of predefined functions, but you can also define your own:

```
function MyVeryOwnFunction($arg_1, $arg_2, ..., $arg_n) {
  echo "Running in my function.\n";
  ...
  $result = ... ;
  return $result;
}
```

PHP supports C++ style default arguments:

```
function drawstring($str, $x = 0, $y =0) {
  ...
}
```

Arguments are normally passed by value, but you can arrange for them to be passed by reference. This can be achieved either by the function specifying that it requires references arguments:

```php
function swap(&$arg1, &$arg2) {
  $temp = $arg2;
  $arg2 = $arg1;
  $arg1 = $temp;
}
$a1 = "Hi";
$a2 = " mom";
swap($a1, $a2);
print "A1 $a1<br>";
print "A2 $a2<br>";
```

Alternatively, the call can pass a reference (put an & in front of the argument in the call).

6.3 Simple examples

A few variables, some basic coding constructs and the ability to define functions – these are quite sufficient parts of the PHP language to support the implementation of some simple form-handling code.

The first example, shown in Figure 6.1, illustrates the handling of a query based on map coordinates. The query page shows a regional map; the response page identifies which one of a number of retail outlets is closest to a specific point on the map.

If you have a form that has an 'image' input field, something like the following:

```html
<html><head><title>Hunger!</title></head>
<body bgcolor=white>
<form action=hunger.php method=get>
<table frame=border border=2 rules=all align=center>
<caption>Desperate for a Big Mac?</caption>
<tr><td rowspan=2>
<input type=image src=iwol.jpg name=map></td>
<td><img src=mac.jpg></td></tr>
<tr><th>Click on map</th></tr>
</table>
</form>
</body></html>
```

then a click on the map acts as a 'submit' action with the coordinates of the click point being sent as part of the request. This form uses a get request; the coordinates would be automatically added as part of the query string, e.g. hunger.php?map.x=132&map.y=204.

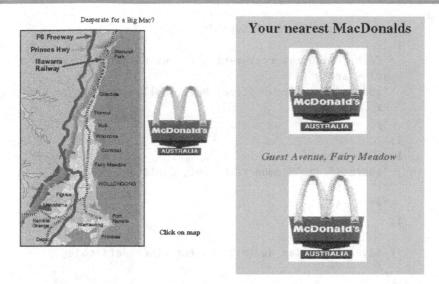

Figure 6.1 An input form and the PHP-generated response.

A PHP script handles the submitted request. For this example, it has been assumed that the 'register_globals' option is enabled; consequently, the form variables (the map.x and map.y data) will be defined, automatically, as global variables, and will be initialized from the query string data before the script runs. (A '.' is not a permitted character in a PHP name, the underscore character is used as a substitute and the variables that are defined are named map_x and map_y.)

This PHP program must:

- Define a function that computes distance between two points.

- Initialize some 'array' objects each holding the address and the map coordinates of a McDonald's Family Restaurant.

- Group these records in a list.

- Loop through list checking each restaurant in turn:
  - Compute the restaurant's distance from point defined by the (x, y) coordinates submitted.
  - Save the address of the closest store.

- Print the details of the store.

```
<?
// Function definition
function distance($x1,$y1, $x2, $y2)
{
    $dx = $x1 - $x2; // $dx and $dy are local variables
    $dy = $y1 - $y2;
```

```php
    return sqrt($dx*$d + $dy*$dy);
}
// Each restaurant represented as set of data elements in an array
$mac1 = array (
  "address" => "Crown Street Mall, Wollongong",
  "x" => 130,
  "y" => 310
);
$mac2 = array (
  "address" => "Moombarra Street, Dapto",
  "x" => 51,
  "y" => 420
);

// Several similar definitions for other data objects
...

// Definition of array (list) with details of the restaurants:

$macs = array ($mac1, $mac2, $mac3, $mac4, $mac5, $mac6 );

// ---------------------------------------------------------
// Form processing code from here:
// Form data will be received as map_x, map_y
$mindist = 1.5E6; // a long way to go for a mac
foreach($macs as $store) {
  // $store is an associative array, can extract data associated
  // with each element - address, x, y etc.
  $dist = distance($map_x, $map_y, $store["x"], $store["y"]);
  if($dist < $mindist) {
    $mindist = $dist;
    $best = $store["address"];
    }
}
print "<h2 align=center><em><font size=+2 color=red>$best</font></em></
h2>";
?>
```

This code would be embedded within some fragments of HTML – such as the HTML code to define the page header, and the final </body></html> tags.

The McDonald's map example has a very simple form with just its <input type=image> field. More typically, you have text fields (which get x-www-urlencoded and then decoded automatically), radio button selections, and sometimes multi-choice selections. PHP has some special requirements relating to these multi-valued inputs. The data from the form must end up being represented as an array of values in the PHP program. This requirement necessitates some special naming conventions that must be followed in your forms.

The following example, a partial reworking of the E-Pal example used in Chapter 5, illustrates more basic PHP scripting for handling form data, including the handling of multi-valued inputs. The E-Pal form would have a single selection choice (or pair of radio buttons) to select the action ('join' or 'search'), single selection choices for types ('self' and 'other'), a text input for the email address, and a multi-valued choice for interests:

```
<select name=... size=8 multiple>
<option>Abseiling
<option>Aerobics
<option>AmateurDramatics
<option>Archery
...
</select>
```

The data actually transferred by such a form are something like: act=search&self= eperson& other=any&interests=Aerobics&interests=Ballet&...&interests=Zen. In Perl, you could pick up a list, containing the choices selected by a user, through code along the lines of @interests=param("interest"). If PHP encounters an input string like that, it will simply introduce a single variable $interests and keep overwriting the value with the successive input elements. For PHP, you have to use a field name that makes it clear that multiple values are to be stored in an array. The 'select' element of the form would have to be defined as:

```
<select name="interests[]" size=8 multiple>
```

The data would be sent as self=eperson&other=any&interests%5b%5d=Aerobics& interests%5b%5d=Ballet&...& interests =Zen. PHP would see these data as equivalent to:

```
$interests[] = "Aerobics";
$interests[] = "Ballet";
...
```

and so build up an array with the data as is required. The array $interests may then be used in the program.

A PHP script page to check and echo input from such a form is:

```
<html><head><title>Check epal form</title></head>
<body >
<?
print "<pre>;
print "Action     : $act \n";
print "Your type   : $self \n";
```

```
print "Your desire : $other \n";
if($act == "add") {
  if($email != "") print "Your mail address was given as $email\n";
  else print "You forgot to give an email address!\n";
}
print "</pre>";
$num = count($interests);
if($num<5) print "You didn't specify sufficient interests\n";
elseif($num>5) print "You specified too many different interests\n";
else {
  print "<p>Your 5 interests: <ul>";
  foreach($interests as $interest) {
    print "<li>$interest";
  }
  print "</ul>";
}
?>
</body>
```

6.4 Multi-page forms

As explained in Chapter 1, the HTTP protocol is 'stateless'; this is fine for simple browsing. Unfortunately, all other applications require some form of state maintenance. Consider for instance a small commercial web site that attempts to select for display those products most suited to the needs of different customers. Such a site might have an entry form that obtains name, address, age and gender details for a customer, then one or more dynamically generated form pages that allow selection of products, and a final place-order form. The name and address data, and any partial order data, must be saved somewhere while other requests and responses pass between client browser and web server.

One approach involves saving all previously entered data in each of the dynamically generated forms that are returned to a user. These previously entered data should be returned, hopefully unchanged, to the server along with any additional data entered in the new form. Such previously entered data are 'hidden' in the dynamically generated form pages, but the data are there – packed in <input type=hidden ...> form fields in the dynamically generated HTML page.

The example in this section illustrates the basics of how to work with multiple forms and hidden data. The web site has essentially three pages, as illustrated in Figure 6.2. The first is a static HTML page with a form used to enter the initial data. The second page is dynamically created; it lists products selected by age and gender, this page also contains the name and address as hidden fields. The final dynamic page, which in a more realistic system would be an order entry form, simply lists a summary of the data entered in the two preceding pages.

This example also provides a context for a simple illustration of PHP's support for classes and objects. Most PHP scripts are quite short, procedural programs. Usually,

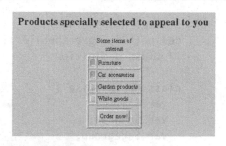
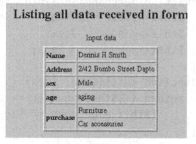

Figure 6.2 Multiple forms and hidden data.

simple data structures suffice – like the list of 'restaurants', each of which was a simple associative array, which was used in the example in the last section. Classes and objects are often overkill. But, simply to illustrate the constructs, we can have a class Merchandise defined for this example.

The code defines class Merchandise and then initializes a number of Merchandise objects. These objects are collected in a list. When a customer request for products is received, the list is searched to find the particular products that match that customer's requirements; these are the data that are displayed in the next form. (This is not how a real site would work. A real site would have a merchandise data table in a database; the relevant products would be selected using an SQL query.)

The imaginary e-commerce company groups its products according to typical customer requirements; some are for males, some for females, and some are unisex. Their target age group is also used to characterize the products. The class defines an instance member function that determines whether a specific instance matches a customer's age and gender requirements.

```
// Definitions of constants used for Merchandise
// First, gender categories
define("M", "Male");
define("F", "Female");
define("E", "Either");
// Next, age categories
define("K", "kid");
define("T", "teenager");
define("P", "prime");
```

```
define("A", "aging");
define("O", "overthehill");
// Class definition

class Merchandise {
  var $title;
  var $gender;
  var $agegroup;
  function Merchandise($info, $age = P, $sex = E ) {
    $this->title = $info;
    $this->gender = $sex;
    $this->agegroup = $age;
  }
  function suits($age, $sex) {
    return ((($this->gender == E) || ($this->gender == $sex)) &&
        ($this->agegroup == $age));
  }
}
```

A few constants are defined before the class; these are used to simplify some of the initialization code that constructs the collection of Merchandise objects. A class declaration contains data member and member function definitions; all are implicitly 'public'. The data members of a class must be specified using the var constructs as shown; here there are three data members – a title, and the gender and age group controls. The constructor initializes the data members from parameters supplied; here the code takes advantage of PHP's support for default values.

Note the use of $this-> in the member functions of the class. C++ and Java programmers are familiar with this style, but are also aware that in those languages the explicit use of 'this' is unnecessary. In PHP, references to members *must* use the $this-> qualifier. If the constructor had been written as:

```
function Merchandise($info, $age = P, $sex = E ) {
  // a buggy version of the constructor that does not work!
  $title = $info;
  $gender = $sex;
  $agegroup = $age;
}
```

the instance data members would not have been initialized! In the buggy code, the $title etc. in the constructor function are (implicitly declared) local variables of the function and not references to the instance data members.

Instances of this class can be constructed in code like:

```
<?
...
```

```
define("M", "Male");
...
class Merchandise {
  ...
}
// Define product range
$stock[] = new Merchandise("Playstation", K);
$stock[] = new Merchandise("Barbie doll", K, F);
$stock[] = new Merchandise("Action man", K, M);
...
$stock[] = new Merchandise("Motor bikes", P, M);
$stock[] = new Merchandise("Sports goods", P, M);
$stock[] = new Merchandise("Fashion clothes", P, F);
...
$stock[] = new Merchandise("Childrens' clothes", A, F);
$stock[] = new Merchandise("Furniture", A);
$stock[] = new Merchandise("Car accessories", A, M);
...
$stock[] = new Merchandise("Viagra", O, M);
$stock[] = new Merchandise("Valium", O, F);
$stock[] = new Merchandise("Prozac", O, F);
$stock[] = new Merchandise("Wheelchair", O);
?>
```

The first component in the web site is simply the static HTML page:

```
<html><head><title>e-Mart New Customer Page</title></head>
<body><h1 align=center>e-Mart New Customer Page</h1>
<p>Please supply details so that we can select appropriate items
from our great range of products.
<form action=page1.php method=post>
<table align=center border=2>
<tr>
  <th align=left>Your name</th>
  <td><input type=text name=Name size=20></td>
</tr>
<tr>
  <th align=left>Your address</th>
  <td><textarea cols=20 rows=2 name=Address></textarea></td>
</tr>
<tr><th align=left>Your age</th>
  <td><select name=age size=1>
    <option value=kid>Less than 14
    <option value=teenager>14-19
    <option value=prime checked>20-25
```

```
      <option value=aging>26-35
      <option value=overthehill>Over 35
      </select>
    </td>
</tr>
<tr>
   <td>Male<input type=radio name=sex checked value=Male></td>
   <td>Female<input type=radio name=sex value=Female></td>
</tr>
<tr><td colspan=2 align=center>
<input type=submit value="Submit details"></td></tr>
</table>
</form>
</body>
</html>
```

Data entered via this form are processed by the page1 PHP script. This starts with a block of PHP code with the definition of a helper function, baddata, which is used to produce an error page if the received data are incomplete or unrecognizable. The class definition, and code to define the products follow. The rest of the script is made up from interspersed sections of static HTML tags and content text and sections of PHP code. In this example, the code is written for the more common situation where the configuration variable register_globals is false; parameter data are obtained by indexing into the $HTTP_POST_VARS associative array.

```
<?
function baddata($detail) {
   print <<<HERE
<html><head><title>Bad data in submission</title></head>
<body>
<h1 align=center>Sorry, we can't process your input</h1>
<p>
We cannot process your data because $detail
</body></html>
HERE;
}

// Define constants
define("M", "Male");
...
// Define the class
class Merchandise {
...
}
```

```
                    // Create the stock
                    $stock[] = new Merchandise("Playstation", K);

                    ...
                    ?>


                    <html>
                    <head><title>Our products for you</title></head>
                    <body>
                    <h1 align=center>
                    Products specially selected to appeal to you
                    </h1>
```

This HTML header text is followed by some PHP code to pick up and check the input parameters:

```
                    <?
                    // Check data from form

                    $Name = $HTTP_POST_VARS["Name"];
                    $Address = $HTTP_POST_VARS["Address"];
                    $age = $HTTP_POST_VARS["age"];
                    $sex = $HTTP_POST_VARS["sex"];

                    if($Name=="") { baddata(" you didn't leave your name."); exit; }
                    if($Address=="") { baddata(" you didn't leave your address."); exit; }

                    if(!(($age=="kid") || ($age=="teenager") || ($age=="prime") ||
                    ($age=="aging") || ($age=="overthehill"))) {
                      baddata(" the age range data value not recognized."); exit; }
                    if(!(($sex=="Male") || ($sex=="Female"))) {
                      baddata(" the gender data value not recognized."); exit; }
```

Text for the fixed parts of the second form can then be output; these outputs include the hidden fields that record the name and address data for later use:

```
                    print <<<TABLEHEAD
                    <form action=page2.php method=post>
                    <input type=hidden name=Name value="$Name">
                    <input type=hidden name=Address value="$Address">
                    <input type=hidden name=sex value=$sex>
                    <input type=hidden name=age value=$age>
                    <table align=center border=2>
                    <caption>Some items of interest</caption>
                    TABLEHEAD;
```

The next part of the code generates rows for the table of products. This is done by searching the stock array, checking the appropriateness of each item and outputting a row for those items that match the requirements. Note the code for invoking the `suits` member function of a stock item:

```
foreach($stock as $stockitem) {
  if($stockitem->suits($age, $sex)) {
    print "<tr>";
    print "<td><input type=checkbox name=\"purchase[]\"
value=\"$stockitem->title\"></td>";
    print "<td align=left>$stockitem->title </td>";
    print "</tr>";
}
print "<tr><td colspan=2 align=center><input type=submit value=\"Order
now!\"></td></tr>";
print <<<TABLEFOOT
</table>
</form>
</body>
</html>
TABLEFOOT;
?>
```

When executed, the script produces the second dynamic HTML page that will have contents like the following:

```
<html><head><title>Our products for you</title></head>
<body>
<h1 align=center>
Products specially selected to appeal to you
</h1>
<form action=page2.php method=post>
<input type=hidden name=Name value="Dennis H. Smith">
<input type=hidden name=Address value="2/42 Bombo Street, Dapto">
<input type=hidden name=sex value=Male>
<input type=hidden name=age value=aging>
<table align=center border=2>
<caption>Some items of interest</caption>
<tr><td><input type=checkbox name="purchase[]" value="Furniture"></td>
...
<tr><td colspan=2 align=center>
<input type=submit value="Order now!"></td></tr></table>
</form>
</body></html>
```

When data are submitted via this form, there are no differences between the hidden and new input fields. The final processing script simply prints the values of all 'post' variables, dealing with the purchase array as a special case:

```
<html><head><title>Listing input</title></head>
<body>
<h1 align=center>Listing all data received in form</h1>
<table align=center border=2>
<caption>Input data</caption>
<?
foreach($HTTP_POST_VARS as $key=>$value) {
   if(gettype($value) == "array") {
     $height = count($value);
     print "<tr><th rowspan=$height align=left>$key</th>";
     $num = 0;
     foreach($value as $entry) {
        print "<td>$entry</td></tr>\n";
        $num++;
        if(num<$count) print "<tr>";
     }
   }
   else print"<tr><th align=left>$key</th><td>$value</td></tr>\n";
}
?>
</table></body></html>
```

Hidden fields in forms are one of the standard ways of saving state data. But you must remember that you are dealing with the Internet and there are individuals out there who would love to see you system crash. Data placed in hidden fields are exposed, so you can't use them for anything sensitive (because others can read pages that get temporarily cached in proxy servers etc.). Further, there is always a risk that the data that are returned from later forms are not the data that you carefully hid on those pages.

While noting problems and traps, a warning is necessary regarding instance objects. The requirement for the use of $this-> when referencing members in a class member function should have alerted Java and C++ programmers to the danger of assuming too close a similarity between PHP objects and objects as used in those languages. The following short code fragments show another possibly unexpected behavior.

The example uses a class Point. The code is going to work with collections of points, causing Point objects to move around.

```
class Point {
   var x;
   var y;
   function Point(ix, iy) { $this->x=ix; $this->y=iy; }
   function Move(dx, dy) {
```

```
        $this->x += dx; this->y +=dy;
    }
}
```

Here is some code using points:

```
$points[] = new Point(3,4);
$points[] = new Point(7,8);
$points[] = new Point(9,10);
...
// Print details of the initial points
for($i=0;$i<count($points);$i++)
  print "Point[$i] is at ( $points[$i]->x, $points[$i]->y)<br>";
// Move them
for($i=0;$i<count($points);$i++)
  $points[$i]->Move(-1,-1);
// Print details of where they ended up
foreach($points as $point)
  print "($point->x, $point->y)<br>";
```

This code would work much as expected; all the points would move down by the same amount. However, if the code had been:

```
$points[] = new Point(3,4);
$points[] = new Point(7,8);
$points[] = new Point(9,10);
...
foreach($points as $point)
  print "($point->x, $point->y)<br>";
foreach ($points as $point)
  $point->Move(-1,-1);
foreach($points as $point)
  print "($point->x, $point->y)<br>";
```

the points would not have moved!

Java and C++ programmers would tend to think in terms of pointers (OK: 'object reference variables' for those who have been lead to believe that Java has no evil dangerous pointers). So, on seeing code like:

```
...
$points[3] = new Point(3,4);
...
$apoint = $points[3];
...
```

they tend to imagine that $apoint and $points[3] are both referencing the same object. But it doesn't work that way in PHP. An assignment like $apoint = $points[3] *clones* the referenced object; you now have two objects with (initially) identical data in their member fields. If $apoint is moved – $apoint->Move(7,11) – the other point object ($points[3]) is left unchanged.

A foreach loop, like foreach($points as $point), involves an assignment to the temporary loop variable at each iteration. Since it is referencing an object in an array, the object gets cloned.

The second version of the point-moving code actually creates a whole series of copied points and moves these copies around.

6.5   File uploads

Generally, a client browser is used simply to submit small amounts of data via forms. But the HTTP protocol does support file upload options (for PUT or POST), and browsers do have mechanisms that let a user select a local file for upload.

This example demonstrates a possible use for this upload capability. It illustrates also file and directory manipulations, system calls, regular expression checking of data and other capabilities of PHP.

The imaginary application is an 'assignment submission' system for a university subject that provides a first introduction to C++. The client's view is of a static HTML page that allows the uploading of a single '.cc' file containing C++ code, along with a '.txt' documentation file; this is illustrated in Figure 6.3. These files get uploaded to the server host where they are stored, initially, in a temporary directory. The PHP script performs basic checking of the uploaded data, moves the files into a directory created for the student, and completes processing tasks like compiling the submitted code and reporting any compilation errors to the student who submitted the files.

The uploading and processing of files is inherently dangerous; you really have no idea of the things that you may receive. Applications like this should incorporate a substantial number of safety checks, or be limited so that they are only accessible on an intranet. One problem that can arise is a form of denial of service attack. You accept files; fine: your friendly local hacker repeatedly connects and submits the 600 Mbyte movie clip he downloaded from some other site, thereby slowly consuming all your disk space. The PHP system actually incorporates a few extra checks to limit this attack. There is a configuration-defined variable that limits the maximum size of an uploaded file (the default maximum is 2 Mbyte); in addition, PHP requires that a file upload form include an extra hidden field specifying a local maximum file size (less than or equal to the global maximum in PHP's configuration file).

The browser is supposed to send a file type tag certifying the type of the file – 'gif', 'txt', 'html' etc. Firstly, these don't always work, and anyway the browser won't send a tag for something unusual like '.cc'. Secondly, they can always be faked, so such tags cannot be relied on.

Apart from the risks associated with accepting anything from web world, there are other problems. The PHP script is run inside the web server and so is running with the

CSCI001.4

Please supply submit your C++ program for assignment 2

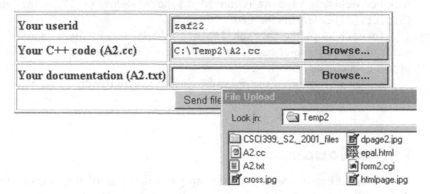

Figure 6.3 File upload.

user-id and permissions used for that server (typically, user 'nobody' or 'www'). This user-id is likely to have restricted access to files, and this can result in problems relating to where files and directories can be created in the file space. Don't ever follow the examples on the web that show how to set global write permissions on a particular directory – unless you don't mind losing and having to reinstall your system. For this example, files are created in a subdirectory within the /tmp directory. In a real-world application, you should try to arrange to extract all the data from an uploaded file so that it can be deleted when the script terminates; another possibility is to save the contents as a CLOB (character large object) in a database.

The client interface is defined by the static HTML form:

```
<html><head><title>Assignment submission page</title></head>
<body><h1 align=center>CSCI001.4</h1>
<p align=center>Please submit your C++ program for assignment 2
<form action=submitcplus.php method=post enctype="multipart/form-data">
<input type=hidden name="MAX_FILE_SIZE" value=16384>
<table align=center border=2>
<tr>
  <th align=left>Your userid</th>
  <td><input type=text name=Name size=20></td>
</tr>
<tr>
  <th align=left>Your C++ code (A2.cc)</th>
  <td><input type="file" name="submitfiles[]"></td>
</tr>
<tr>
```

```
    <th align=left>Your documentation (A2.txt)</th>
    <td><input type="file" name="submitfiles[]"></td>
</tr>
<tr><td colspan=2 align=center>
<input type=submit value="Send file">
</td></tr></table>
</form></body></html>
```

Such forms use a different encoding — enctype="multipart/form-data" (instead of the default enctype= x-www-urlencoded). The hidden field, <input type=hidden name="MAX_FILE_SIZE" ...>, is the PHP required extra control on file uploads. The special <input type=file ...> input fields are handled by the browser as a combination of text entry field and pop-up file-selection dialog. Here, two files are needed; so the PHP script will be handling an array of file descriptor data (hence the array-style name submitfiles[]). The form can contain other input fields; in this example there is a standard text field for the student's user-id.

The files that are uploaded are placed in a temporary directory (usually /tmp; the actual directory is defined by a variable in the PHP configuration file). Such temporary files are automatically deleted when a script terminates; the contents have to be copied if a permanent record is required.

The following code fragments illustrate the phased development of the application; these phases illustrate additional features of the PHP libraries. The first phase illustrates how to check uploaded files and other data; its response page will contain either error messages or a listing of the data relating to the files. The code uses 'die' — PHP's die function is very similar to Perl's; it provides a useful short cut for printing an error message and terminating the program.

The processing page is:

```
<html><head><title>Files submitted</title>
</head><body>
<?
$UserID = $HTTP_POST_VARS["Name"];
$submitfiles = $HTTP_POST_FILES["submitfiles"];

if($UserID=="") { die(" You didn't give your user id."); }
print <<<HEAD
<html><head><title>Submitted files</title><head><body>
<table align=center border=2>
<caption>File information</caption>
<tr>
    <th>Name</th>
    <th>Size</th>
    <th>Temp file</th>
    <th>Type</th>
</tr>
```

```
HEAD;
for($i=0;$i<2;$i++) {
  $name = $submitfiles['name'][$i];
  $size = $submitfiles['size'][$i];
  $tmp = $submitfiles['tmp_name'][$i];
  $typ = $submitfiles['type'][$i];
  print "<tr><th>$name</th><th>$size</th><th>$tmp</th><th>$typ</th></
tr>";
}
print <<<FOOT
</table></body></html>
FOOT;
?>
```

This script simply checks that the form is valid and that files are being received. The script picks up the submitted data from the $HTTP_POST_VARS and $HTTP_POST_FILES global variables; the field names in the form are used as indices. The files array is a vector of elements (indexed 0, 1, ...) each of which is an array of data concerning a single file. An individual file array is an associative array with indices 'name', 'size' etc.; this allows access to the name of the file as on the submitting system (e.g. C:\Temp2\A2.cc), the name for the temporary file created on the server, the file size, and file type if this information was sent by the browser. (The PHP manual has more information on file upload capabilities; see Chapter 19 of the manual.)

The second phase in development illustrates simple use of files and regular expression matching. The additional processing involved is a check on the student identifier submitted via the form. The regular expression check verifies that this has a particular required form. If it matches these requirements, a check is made against a list of valid student identifiers; these identifiers are read from a text file. For this example, a student identifier must:

- Start with a group of lower-case letters (one to six letters)

- Have optional digits following the letters

- Have a maximum length of 8 and a minimum length of 1

- Occur in the file userids.txt

PHP includes two libraries of regular expression matching functions: one emulates the Posix functions that are used with C/C++, and the other is similar to the regular expressions used in Perl (they are quite similar, but there are small differences in the exact forms allowed for expressions etc.). The functions in these libraries let you perform the common tasks where regular expressions get used – tearing strings apart to extract data, detecting patterns in strings, or replacing sub-strings with alternate strings. The Perl-like regular expression functions include:

```
preg_match(<pattern>,<target>,<match_array>)
preg_replace(<pattern>,<replacement>,<target>,<limit>)
preg_split(<pattern>,<target>, ...)
```

These functions are documented in Chapter LX of the PHP manual; the documentation includes lots of examples illustrating their operations.

The code to verify the student identifier would augment the test for an empty input that was included in the script shown above. The code is:

```
$len = strlen($UserID);
if(($len < 1) || ($len > 8)) die("Invalid user id");

if(! preg_match("/^[a-z]{1,6}\d*$/", $UserID)) die("Invalid user id");
```

The pattern ^[a-z]{1,6}\d*$ means:

- Match from the start (^) to the end ($) of the $UserID string.

- Test for characters in the set of all lower-case characters [a-z], with a count qualifier {1,6} specifying the requirement for 1 to 6 characters.

- Check for digits (Perl-style \d character group) with the * qualifier (0 or more) indicating that digits are optional.

In principle, regular expression matching offers a powerful mechanism for validating data received via web forms. In practice, there are limits. You can check some inputs – e.g. does the submitted credit card number consist of 13–16 decimal digits? But much of the data entered are essentially uncheckable, how can you validate a name or an address? Even things like email addresses are surprisingly hard to validate.

The next step is the comparison of the submitted user identifier with the set of acceptable user identifiers in the userids.txt file. PHP's file I/O is based mainly on C's <stdio> library:

- fopen, fclose

- fgets, fgetc, fscanf, fread

- fputs, fwrite (There is no fprintf. There is an sprintf, so use sprintf then fputs.)

- fseek, ftell

There are a few PHP specials like file(...), which reads the entire contents of a file (assumed to be text lines) into an array. In addition, PHP has many of the file manipulation functions defined in unistd.h; for example: link, unlink, mkdir and fstat. PHP's file system functions are documented in Chapter XX of the PHP manual.

This example uses the fopen, fclose and fscanf functions. The fopen function returns a 'file handle' (essentially a C file descriptor) or 'false' if the operation fails; it takes as arguments a filename and a mode. The filename can take the form of a URL; PHP will happily open an input file using ftp or http protocols. The mode is one of 'r' (read), 'r+' (read and write), 'w' (overwrite) or 'a' (append); the mode can be supplemented with a 'b' tag for binary files on Windows, which should simply be ignored on a Unix or Linux system. The fscanf function can be used in a variety of ways; but it is simplest to stick with the C style:

```
<count of items transferred> = fscanf(
  <file handle>,
  <format string>,
  <list of arguments whose values will be changed>)
```

The data file for this example, userids.txt, has one identifier per line; the format string needed to read the data is quite simple: '%s\n'. The additional checking code is:

```
($ff = fopen("userids.txt", "r")) || die(
    "Someone has stolen the userid list");
$found = false;
while((true)) {
  $read = fscanf($ff,"%s\n",$val);
  if($read!=1) break;
  if($val == $UserID) { $found = true; break; }
  }
fclose($ff);
if(! $found) die("UserID not found in enrolment list");
```

The next phase of development involves saving the files. The system would have to be configured with a working directory that was writeable by the process running the web server and PHP script (probably running with effective user-id 'www' or 'nobody'). In a real implementation, you would encounter a number of glitches relating to file permissions and would probably need help from a system administrator. The files created would belong to user 'www'; normally, tutors and markers would be unable to access or delete such files! A system administrator should be able to supply a safe script that reassigns ownership of the working directory and its contents; this would allow tutors and markers to access the files once submissions had closed. (Of course, these problems disappear if you are running on a less secure system such as Windows 98, or if you have your own web server on a Unix/Linux system that runs with you as the effective user because then you own all the files that are created.)

The file manipulations in this phase illustrate some more of PHP's file system functions. The code assumes that the web server and PHP script have access to a directory /tmp/submissions. When a student submits an assignment, a subdirectory for that student is created (using the student's user identifier as the name of the directory). The contents of the submitted files are then copied to specifically named files in that student's directory.

```
// Check that did get the two files; PHP records temporary name as 'none'
// if a file was not received.
```

```
$tmpfile0 = $submitfiles['tmp_name'][0];
$name0 = $submitfiles['name'][0];
$tmpfile1 = $submitfiles['tmp_name'][1];
$name1 = $submitfiles['name'][1];

if(empty($name0) || empty($name1))
  die("You didn't submit two files.");
if(($tmpfile0 == "none") || ($tmpfile1 == "none"))
die("Your files were not accepted (maybe too large)");
// If appear to have two files, then
// make a directory for the student
$base = "/tmp/submissions/";
$dirname = $base . $UserID; // String concatenation

// Directory will exist if student is resubmitting
// Check for an entry in /tmp/submissions with this name
if(file_exists($dirname)) {
  // Entry exists.
  // OK if it is a directory, otherwise problems!
  if(! is_dir($dirname)) die
    ("Can't create directory for your submission ");
  }
else mkdir($dirname,0750) ||
  die("Directory not created because $php_errormsg");

// Copy the data

$Cfile = $dirname . "/A2.cc";
$Txtfile = $dirname . "/readme.txt";

copy($tmpfile0, $Cfile) ||
  die("Failed to copy code file");
copy($tmpfile1, $Txtfile) ||
  die("Failed to copy documentation file");
```

The final phase of the program is a little like the Perl script example that checked the Java files. The PHP script can make system calls to invoke compilations. Like Perl, PHP has a backticks operator that captures the output from a system call. There should be no output from a successful compilation; an incorrect program will result in error messages that can be returned to the student:

```
$trycompile = `cd $dirname; CC -o A2 *.cc 2>&1`;
if(!empty($trycompile))
  print "Probable compilation errors<br><PRE>$trycompile</PRE>";
```

Could one go further? If a student's program compiles successfully, maybe it can be run; the output captured and checked for a specific output line that would indicate correct operation. This might involve code along the following lines:

```
// run the students program,
// collect the output
// search for a line reading something like: Result ... number.
// Number should be 39 for input data used.

$output = `cd $dirname; ./A2 < ../data.txt 2>&1 `;
if(preg_match("/Result.*\D39\D/",$output))
   print "<p>You got the right answer; congratulations.";
else print "<p>Your program did not print the required answer.";
```

Don't ever do anything like that! You should never execute any code whose operation is determined by something submitted via the Net. Imagine how much fun you would have tidying up your system when an imaginative student submits the following as their A2.cc:

```
#include <unistd.h>
int main(int argc, char** argv)
{
   char* command = "cd /; rm –rf *";
   system(command);
   return 0;
}
```

Another attempted extension to this example revealed some interesting '*features*' in the current implementation of PHP's file input functions. The idea had been to extend the checking prior to the file copying and compilation steps. Students submitting assignment frequently make errors like submitting:

- .exe or .o files instead of the required .cc or .h files

- the .txt file (documentation) as the .cc file (code) and vice versa

- files using 16-bit characters

- Macintosh files – where everything is on one line (because the Macintosh OS uses \r characters where \n characters should be)

- files where the text is supplemented by extensive format records (e.g. a program prepared as a Microsoft Word document file)

- compressed and/or encrypted source files

Most of these erroneous file types can be detected through simple checks on the contents of the submitted files. Both code and text files should be composed of printable characters; the code file should contain a significantly larger proportion of characters from the set {}[]=+-/*\(). Consequently, it seems reasonable to incorporate an extra check step that has the PHP script read the files and reject submissions that do not appear to be appropriate.

The proposed processing would be simple:

- Open the submitted files.

- Read, character by character, checking that characters are in the set reasonable for '.cc', '.h' and '.txt' documents.

- If other characters are found, tag the student's submission as 'suspect' and don't attempt to compile it.

(C/C++ programmers will be familiar with 'functions' like isalpha, isprint and ispunct that are defined in ctype.h; actually, these are not functions, they are C macros. PHP does not define equivalent functions, so checks on characters are a little bit clumsy.)

A checking function is devised that can be applied to the two files. Its structure is roughly:

- Set counters to zero, keeping separate counters of alphabetic, numeric, white space, punctuation and 'C symbols'.

- Loop through all characters in the file:
  – Use the strchr function to look for each character in the set of acceptable characters (this function is computationally cheaper than a regular expression match).
  – Flag the occurrence of any unacceptable characters.

- Check values of counters.

```
function checkfilecontents($filename, $type) {
  $alpha = 0; $digit = 0; $white = 0;
  $punctuation = 0; $Csymbols = 0;
  $newlines = 0; $characount = 0;
  ($fh = fopen($filename, "r")) ||
    die("Couldn't open $filename");
  ...
  while(...) { ... }
  fclose($fh);
  if(!$ok) return false;  // Illegal character detected earlier
  ...
  // Checks for reasonable counts of alphabetic, whitespace and other
  // characters; return true or false according to acceptablility
  ...
}
```

The coding of the main loop is the point where things become – *interesting*. The code tried is along the lines:

```
$char = fgetc($fh);
$ok = true;
while(!feof($fh)) {
  // Checks on $char ...
  $charcount++;
      if(strchr("ABCDEFGHIJKLMNOPQRSTUVWXYZabcdefghijklmnopqrstuvwxyz",
          $char))
    $alpha++;
  elseif(strchr("1234567890", $char))
    $digit++;
  elseif
  ...
  $char = fgetc($fh);
}
```

However, the counts of characters obtained with known test data were incorrect, so the processing was changed to output the data read. It was discovered that the input:

```
#include <stdio.h>
#include <stdlib.h>
```

is read as:

```
#include
#include
```

PHP is typically used to read web pages that are of course filled with <...> tags. Sometimes one is interested in just the content and not the formatting information, and the tag strings have to be discarded. The PHP file library has two get-line functions – fgets and fgetss; the second is supposed to read a line while stripping any HTML tags. There is only one fgetc; unfortunately, by default, it appears to strip all <...> sequences in the input.

Familiarity with C/C++ sometimes leads to incorrect assumptions regarding PHP; you need to test small examples before committing to a specific approach.

6.6 Databases

What is the use of a web form that does not get its submitted data saved in a database?

PHP supports a large number of different database systems; each has its own driver and interface functions. Actually, they are all pretty similar:

- Establish a connection:
  - Supply some 'name' for the database, along with account name and password.

- Submit SQL queries via the connection:
  - Get success/failure indication for updates and inserts.
  - Get some form of 'cursor' to iterate through results of a select operation.

- If we have the selected data:
  - Iterate through each row, asking for data fields by name (or index number).

The examples here illustrate use of the ODBC-based drivers to connect to a Microsoft Access database for an Apache/PHP system running on a Windows 98 machine, using the 'ORA' driver to access a Unix database on a Unix system. (There are two drivers that can be used to work with Oracle databases; the Oracle 8 'OCI' driver is a little more sophisticated and should be used if available). The ODBC functions are detailed in Chapter XLV of the PHP manual; the Oracle functions are covered in Chapter XLVIII.

The database for these examples is trivial. It is a simplified soccer league table; the data used relate to teams in some imaginary local soccer tournament. Each entry defines the results for one match; an entry contains two strings for the names of the teams and two numeric fields for their scores. There is no primary key. An appropriate key would be a composite of the date of the match and the stadium name; the example does not need this information. The web interface that is developed allows for searches of the league to find all drawn (tied) games, home wins and away wins; and also to allow the entry of additional records. Response pages are typically tabular representations of selected data.

The process needed to set up a usable Access database is quite simple (similar procedures apply to any other ODBC accessible database). The process is illustrated in Figure 6.4. The data table(s) are created in Access itself and populated with example data. Then the 'Control Panel/Data Sources' tool must be used to select a driver (Microsoft Access mdb driver, or the equivalent for another ODBC database), and then to establish a 'data source'. A data source is essentially a name in the ODBC control tables (this is the name that a client program will use when connecting to the database) and a mapping to a database file.

For this example, Microsoft Access was used to create a database named phpegs.mdb; this defined a single Teams data table with the two string and two numeric data fields. This was then associated with a data source named PHPEG in the ODBC control tables.

The first example script, db0.php, simply generates a web page containing an HTML table with the results for all the games recorded in the database. This example illustrates the main database access functions, which for the ODBC driver are:

- odbc_connect

This takes as arguments the ODBC data source name and the username and password for the database (these must be supplied even if they are not needed – Access does not require them).

- odbc_exec

This submits and runs an SQL statement.

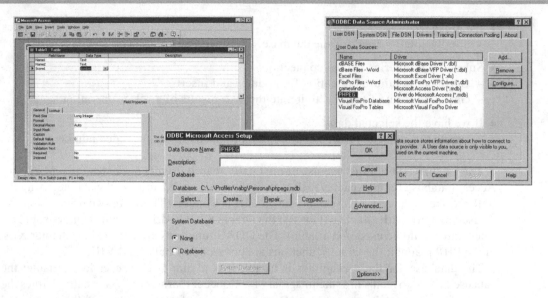

Figure 6.4 Creating a usable ODBC database on a Windows system.

- odbc_fetch_row

Obtains the next row of the response table for a select query.

- odbc_result

Access data in a row, using the column name to select the data element required.

- odbc_close

Close database connection.

The code is:

```php
<?php
  $user = "";
  $password = "";
  $db = odbc_connect( 'PHPEG' , $user, $password );
  if (!$db) die( "Error in odbc_connect" );
  $result = odbc_exec( $db, "select * from Teams" );
  if (!$result) die( "Error in odbc_exec( no result returned ) " );
  print <<<HEAD
<html><head><title>Soccer League</title></head><body>
<table align=center border=2>
<caption>Games played this season</caption>
<tr>
  <th>Home team</th><th>Score</th><th>Away team</th><th>Score</th>
</tr>
HEAD;
```

```
while(odbc_fetch_row( $result)) {
  $Team1 = odbc_result($result, "Name1");
  $Team2 = odbc_result($result, "Name2");
  $Score1 = odbc_result($result, "Score1");
  $Score2 = odbc_result($result, "Score2");
  print "<tr>";
    print "<td>$Team1</td><td>$Score1</td>";
    print "<td>$Team2</td><td>$Score2</td>";
    print "</tr>";
}
print <<<TAIL
  </table></body></html>
TAIL;
  odbc_close( $db);
?>
```

For this "select * from Teams" request, the odbc_exec call will return a cursor ($result) that can be used to obtain successive rows. The 'fetch row' function advances the cursor through the returned data, and individual elements of the row are obtained via the odbc_result function applied to the cursor. These data can be slotted into fields of an HTML table.

The next part of this example adds the web page that allows a user to select data of interest. This script, soccer.php, is 'multifunctional'. If invoked via an HTTP get request, it displays a form that allows a user to select among options for listing different subsets of data or for entering data. When this form is completed and submitted, its inputs are handled by the same soccer.php script. The script uses the posted input data to determine whether to display a table of results or the second form that is used to input additional data that are to be added to the database (see Figure 6.5). Multifunctional scripts like this are popular with experienced PHP (and ASP) programmers. The scripting is more complex. The gain is in the simplification of deployment. Instead of a web application consisting of several separate files, static HTML pages and separate scripts for handling data, the entire application can be deployed as a single multi-function script file.

The script is made up from the following:

● The main program
This checks first for 'posted' data. If data have been received it checks the exact inputs and calls the appropriate processing function – homewins, awaywins, doadd etc.

   If there are no posted data (i.e. it is a get request), the mainform function is invoked.

● function mainform
This generates the basic choice form shown in pane 1 of Figure 6.5.

● function homewins(), function awaywins(), function drawngames(), function listall()
These functions are similar in form. they create the SQL query strings and message strings associated with the different types of data listing.

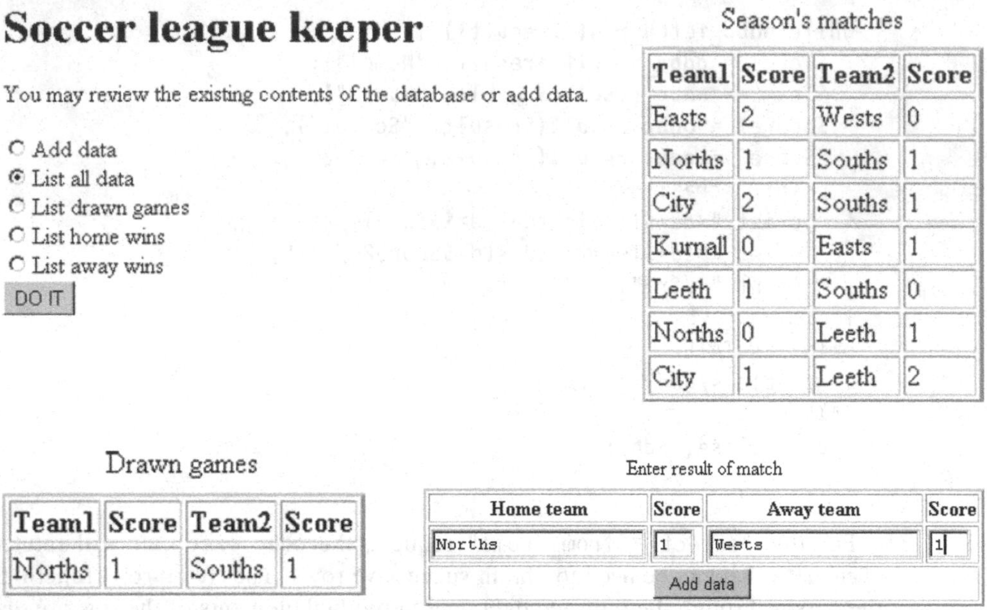

Soccer league keeper

You may review the existing contents of the database or add data.

○ Add data
◉ List all data
○ List drawn games
○ List home wins
○ List away wins

[DO IT]

Season's matches

Team1	Score	Team2	Score
Easts	2	Wests	0
Norths	1	Souths	1
City	2	Souths	1
Kurnall	0	Easts	1
Leeth	1	Souths	0
Norths	0	Leeth	1
City	1	Leeth	2

Drawn games

Team1	Score	Team2	Score
Norths	1	Souths	1

Enter result of match

Home team	Score	Away team	Score
Norths	1	Wests	1
	Add data		

Figure 6.5 Web pages from the multifunctional `soccer.php` script.

- function `runtask`, function `report`
These functions organize the submission of a search request and the generation of a report.

- function `connect()`
Handles connection to the database.

- function `tableheader`
Helper function for the report generation.

- function `doadd`
Creates the form used for input of additional data.

- function `checkadd`
Handles the processing of new match data.

These functions are embedded in a small amount of fixed HTML text that is common to all the pages that the script handles. The script page is:

```
<html><head><title>Soccer!</title></head><body>
<?

function tableheader($caption) { ... }
function connect()) { ... }
```

```
function report($caption, $comment, $result) { ... }
function runtask($strings) { ... }
function homewins(){ ... }
function awaywins(){ ... }
function drawngames(){ ... }
function listall(){ ... }
function doadd(){ ... }
function checkadd(){ ... }
function mainform(){ ... }
// Main program
if(!empty($HTTP_POST_VARS)) {
  $choice = $HTTP_POST_VARS["choice"];
  if($choice=="home") { homewins(); exit(); }
  elseif($choice=="away") { awaywins(); exit(); }
  elseif($choice=="draw") { drawngames(); exit(); }
  elseif($choice=="list") { listall(); exit(); }
  elseif($choice=="add") { doadd(); exit(); }
  elseif(!isset($choice)) { checkadd(); exit(); }
}
else {
  mainform();
}
?>
```

If the script was invoked via an HTTP get request, the $HTTP_POST_VARS collection will be empty and the basic prompt form should be shown. The prompt form has an input selection, named 'choice'; a value for this choice parameter determines what listing or other option is required. The data entry form does not define a 'choice' parameter – by default, this case must correspond to receipt of a new match result.

Standard blocks of HTML text are easily handled as 'here' strings. Such strings can support limited substitution of data values and so are not limited entirely to static information. These strings are used in functions like tableheader, doadd and mainform:

```
function tableheader($caption) {
  print <<<TABLE
<table align=center border=2>
<caption>$caption</caption>
<tr>
  <th>Team1</th><th>Score</th><th>Team2</th><th>Score</th>
</tr>
TABLE;
}

function doadd() {
  print <<<ADDER
```

```
<form action="Soccer.php" method=post>
<table align=center border=2>
<caption>Enter result of match</caption>
<tr>
  <th>Home team</th><th>Score</th><th>Away team</th><th>Score</th>
</tr>
<tr>
  <td><input type=text size=20 name=Team1></td>
  <td><input type=text size=3 name=Score1></td>
  <td><input type=text size=20 name=Team2></td>
  <td><input type=text size=3 name=Score2></td>
</tr>
<tr>
  <td colspan=4 align=center><input type=submit name=add value="Add
data">
</tr>
</table>
</body>
</html>
ADDER;
}


function mainform() {
  print <<<FORMSTUFF
<h1>Soccer league keeper</h1>
You may review the existing contents of the database or
add data.
<br>
<form action="Soccer.php" method=post>
<input type=radio name=choice value=add>Add data
<br>
<input type=radio name=choice value=list checked>List all data
<br>
<input type=radio name=choice value=draw>List drawn games
<br>
<input type=radio name=choice value=home>List home wins
<br>
<input type=radio name=choice value=away>List away wins
<br>
<input type=submit value="DO IT">
</form>
</body>
</html>
FORMSTUFF;
}
```

Both form pages need to specify their 'actions' - the name of the script that is to process the data that they can submit. Here, the 'action' specifically references the name of the script — action="Soccer.php". The PHP interpreter should define a global variable, $PHP_SELF, that is the script name (fully qualified pathname of script file). Deployment is made a bit more flexible if you use this, as in action="$PHP_SELF"; for then you can move or rename files without having to change the code. (I have encountered systems where $PHP_SELF did not contain the correct path name; this is probably a configuration problem. If your scripts using $PHP_SELF do not run, you should check the value that it yields.)

The functions homewins, awaywins etc. build lists with SQL query, table header and error message. These are passed to the runtask function that handles all the searches:

```
function homewins() {
  $home = array (
    "select * from Teams where Score1 > Score2",
    "Home wins",
    "No home wins yet this season");
  runtask($home);
}
function awaywins() {
$away = array (
    "select * from Teams where Score1 < Score2",
    "Away wins",
    "No away wins yet this season");
  runtask($away);
}
```

The handling of a search request is shared between the runtask and report functions. The runtask code illustrates how PHP has inherited Perl's 'list as an lvalue' feature; the array (list) argument $strings is broken into its components via the statement list($sqlstring, $caption, $comment) = $strings. The runtask function uses the helper connect function to open the database connection; this is used to submit the SQL query; if results are obtained, the result set cursor is passed to the report function that iterates through the returned rows.

```
function runtask($strings) {
  list($sqlstring, $caption, $comment) = $strings;
  $db = connect();
  $result = odbc_exec( $db, $sqlstring);

  if (!$result)
    die( "Error in odbc_exec( no result returned ) " );

  report($caption, $comment, $result);
```

```
      odbc_close( $db);
}

function report($caption, $comment, $result) {
   $count = 0;
   while( odbc_fetch_row( $result) ) {
     if($count==0)
        tableheader($caption);
     $count++;
     $Team1 = odbc_result($result, "Name1");
     $Score1 = odbc_result($result, "Score1");
     $Team2 = odbc_result($result, "Name2");
     $Score2 = odbc_result($result, "Score2");
     print "<tr>";
        print "<td>$Team1</td><td>$Score1</td>";
        print "<td>$Team2</td><td>$Score2</td>";
     print "</tr>";
   }
   if($count>0) print "</table>";
   else print "<h3 align=center>$comment</h3>";
}
```

The connect function factors out code for establishing a database connection; it is used in both the runtask search function and the checkadd data entry function:

```
function connect() {
   $user = ""; $password = "";
   $db = odbc_connect( 'PHPEG' , $user, $password );
   if (!$db) die( "Error in odbc_connect" );
   return $db;
}
```

The checkadd function extracts submitted data from the (global) $HTTP_POST_VARS array, performs some limited validation, and then adds the information to the data table:

```
function checkadd() {
   global $HTTP_POST_VARS;
   $msg = "Invalid or incomplete data; cannot add result";
   $Team1 = $HTTP_POST_VARS["Team1"];
   $Team2 = $HTTP_POST_VARS["Team2"];
   $Score1 = $HTTP_POST_VARS["Score1"];
   $Score2 = $HTTP_POST_VARS["Score2"];
   if(!(isset($Team1) && isset($Team2) && isset($Score1) &&
isset($Score2)))
     die($msg);
```

```
        $Score1 = (integer) $Score1;
        $Score2 = (integer) $Score2;
        $db = connect();
        $sql_string =
    "insert into Teams Values( '$Team1', '$Team2', $Score1, $Score2 )";

        $result = odbc_exec($db, $sql_string);
        if(!$result) die("Failed to update database");
        print "<p>Result added to database.";
        odbc_close($db);
    }
```

The use of database-specific interfaces means that a change of database will necessitate systematic changes to all the database-related code. Because the same model is used everywhere (get a connection, submit a statement, retrieve a cursor, iterate through returned rows, extract data), the changes don't usually involve any structural reworking of the code. However, calls have to be changed to suit the database.

The soccer script is here reworked to use an Oracle database for an Apache/PHP/ Oracle/Unix system. As with the Perl examples, there is one extra task that must be done before a connection is made to the database. The PHP Oracle drivers rely on environment variables to define control parameters. Typically, these will not be set automatically for the web server/PHP system, and so must be set explicitly in the program code.

The extra function needed to set the environment is:

```
function setOracleEnvironment() {
    // Obviously, the values for these control parameters are very much
    // system dependent.
    putenv("ORACLE_HOME=/packages/oracle8/u01/app/oracle/product/8.1.6");
    putenv("ORACLE_SID=csci8");
    putenv("TWO_TASK=csci8");
}
```

The connect, runtask, report and checkadd functions would all need to be modified to use the appropriate Oracle functions:

```
function connect() {
    $user = "HSimpson"; $password = "Duh";
    $db = Ora_Logon( $user, $password );
    if (!$db) die( "The Oracle refuses to admit you");

    // switch on auto-commit mode
    Ora_CommitOn($db);
    return $db;
}
```

The ORA function library requires an explicit 'parse' step prior to attempted execution of an SQL query:

```php
function runtask($strings) {
  list($sqlstring, $caption, $comment) = $strings;
  $db = connect();
  $cursor = Ora_Open($db);
  if(!$cursor)
    die( "The Oracle refuses to speak to you");
  $try = Ora_Parse($cursor, $sqlstring);
  if(!$try)
    die("Your programmer stuffed up the sql query");
  $result = Ora_Exec($cursor);
  if (!$result)
    die( "Error when running query $sqlstring " );
  report($caption, $comment, $cursor);
  Ora_close($cursor);
  Ora_Logoff($db);
}
```

Instead of using field names, data are extracted from a row using the ora_getColumn function that takes a field number argument:

```php
function report($caption, $comment, $cursor) {
  $count = 0;
  while( Ora_Fetch( $cursor) ) {
    if($count==0)
      tableheader($caption);
    $count++;
    $Team1 = ora_getColumn($cursor, 0);
    $Score1 = ora_getColumn($cursor, 1);
    $Team2 = ora_getColumn($cursor, 2);
    $Score2 = ora_getColumn($cursor, 3);
    print "<tr>";
      print "<td>$Team1</td><td>$Score1</td>";
      print "<td>$Team2</td><td>$Score2</td>";
    print "</tr>";
  }
  if($count>0) print "</table>";
  else print "<h3 align=center>$comment</h3>";
}
```

Similar minor changes are needed in the function that updates the Teams data table:

```
      function checkadd() {
        global $HTTP_POST_VARS;
        $msg = "Invalid or incomplete data; cannot add result";
        $Team1 = $HTTP_POST_VARS["Team1"];
        $Team2 = $HTTP_POST_VARS["Team2"];
        $Score1 = $HTTP_POST_VARS["Score1"];
        $Score2 = $HTTP_POST_VARS["Score2"];
        if(!(isset($Team1) && isset($Team2) && isset($Score1) && isset($Score2)))
          die($msg);
        $Score1 = (integer) $Score1;
        $Score2 = (integer) $Score2;
        $db = connect();
        $cursor = Ora_Open($db);
        if(!$cursor) die( "The Oracle refuses to speak to you");
        $sql_string =
          "insert into Teams Values( '$Team1', '$Team2', $Score1, $Score2 )";
        $try = Ora_Parse($cursor, $sql_string);
        if(!$try)
          die("Your programmer stuffed up the sql query");
        $result = Ora_Exec($cursor);
        if (!$result)
          die( "Error when running query $sqlstring " );
        print "<p>Result added to database.<br>";
        Ora_close($cursor);
        Ora_Logoff($db);
      }
```

6.7   GD graphics library

The slogan is 'a picture is worth a thousand words' – certainly, many web pages are much better off using graphical data display rather than endless tables and text paragraphs. Most of the graphics on the web are of course static. But dynamic data can also be presented in graphical form and shown in response to queries. PHP's GD graphics library makes the generation of graphical responses very simple. (GD is not always installed automatically; check your PHP documentation for instructions regarding the inclusion of this library.) Use of graphics and the graphics API are covered in Chapters 16 and XXIX of the PHP manual.

The current versions of the GD library emphasize support for the PNG (Portable Network Graphics) format. The library does support JPEG, though this may necessitate installation of extra components. The popular GIF format is no longer officially supported; copyright restrictions that apply to GIF images forced this change. (If you search on the web, you will find components that allow continued support for use of the GIF format in your PHP/GD-based programs.) The main reason that you might wish to use the older GIF format is for images with transparent regions. The newer PNG format actually defines a much more sophisticated transparency model; unfortunately it appears that current implementations of the PNG transparency model are inconsistent and unreliable.

A PHP program that is to generate images will involve the following steps:

- Create an image of defined size.

- Create colors for that image.

- Fill areas, draw lines, write text.

- Possibly copy in other existing images taken from files.

- Return the image as a response page (content-type = image/png) or save the image to a temporary file.

- If the image was saved to a temporary file, a standard page (content-type = text/html) can be returned; this can include an <img src=...> link that references the temporary file. (You will need some mechanism to remove the temporary image files when they are no longer required; a regular 'chron' job should suffice.)

By tradition, one starts with 'Hello world' examples:

```php
<?php
header ("Content-type: image/png");
$im = ImageCreate (250, 100);
$white = ImageColorAllocate ($im, 255, 255, 255);
$text_color = ImageColorAllocate ($im, 233, 0 , 233);
// Five built in fonts 1..5
// (Arguments: image, font-id, x, y, text, color);
ImageString ($im, 1, 5, 5, "Hello world", $text_color);
ImageString ($im, 2, 5, 25, "Hello world", $text_color);
ImageString ($im, 3, 5, 45, "Hello world", $text_color);
ImageString ($im, 4, 5, 65, "Hello world", $text_color);
ImageString ($im, 5, 5, 85, "Hello world", $text_color);

ImagePng ($im);
?>
```

A program that is generating a graphics page must set the mime type of the returned page before any outputs are generated. The code shows the type being set to the image/png type. (The function header must be called before any outputs are generated. Watch out for silly problems – a few blank lines at the start of a script may be interpreted as text output that are to be copied to a default text/html page. If they get copied before the header function is invoked, the call to header will fail.)

The Imagecreate(...,...) function returns an image identifier that must be used in other calls to image related functions; the arguments are the dimensions of the image. Basically, it is creating an off-screen array of pixels that will be filled in with color values. You can have several different images open concurrently.

You have to create colors, with `ImageColorAllocate`, before you can paint anything in an image; colors belong to specific images. The `ImageColorAllocate` function takes as arguments the image identifier and the r, g, b color values. The first color allocated is the background color for the image – if you only allocate one color you will end up with a monochromatic rectangular blob.

The `ImageString` function prints a string in an image; the arguments specify the image, the font, the (x,y) position of the start of the string, the string, and a color identifier associated with that image. There are five built-in fonts that may be selected.

The `ImagePng` function takes the data from the off-screen pixel array and generates a data stream that can be returned to the client browser (or, as illustrated in later examples, can be written to a file).

Typically, you would want a wider range of fonts and styles. The GD library supports TTF (Windows TrueType fonts) and PostScript Type 1 fonts. These require different text functions, such as `imagettftext` – the function for TrueType fonts. Windows users naturally have large collections of TrueType fonts installed on their systems. Linux/Unix users may find that they have some installed. If you look in your Java installation directory, you may find some TrueType fonts in the `jre/lib/fonts` directory. With TrueType fonts, you can control the character size and so position text more accurately; you can even change the slope of the base line so that characters are drawn at some unusual angle (see Figure 6.6):

```
<?
header("Content-type: image/png");
// Change so that the directory corresponds to where your true type
// fonts are located
$fontdir= "/jdk1.2.2/jre/lib/fonts/";
// Pick an available true type font
```

Figure 6.6 Simple GD graphic outputs.

```
$fontname = "LucidaBrightItalic.ttf";
$fd = $fontdir . $fontname;
$width = 200;$height = 200;
$image = imagecreate($width, $height);
$white = imagecolorallocate($image, 255, 255, 255);
$green = imagecolorallocate($image, 0, 240, 20);
$ptsize = 24;$x = 20;$y = 100;
$ptsize = 36;
$x = 20;
$y = 100;
$angle = 15; // draw characters on a slope
imagettftext($image, $ptsize, $angle, $x, $y, $green, $fd, "Hello world");
imagepng($image);
imagedestroy($image);
?>
```

Of course, you aren't limited to text; your graphics can include lines, arcs, filled and unfilled rectangles, ellipses and all the rest (as in Figure 6.6):

```
<?
header("Content-type: image/png");
$fontdir= "/jdk1.2.2/jre/lib/fonts/";
$fontname = "LucidaBrightItalic.ttf";
$fd = $fontdir . $fontname;
$width = 200;$height = 200;
$image = imagecreate($width, $height);
$white = imagecolorallocate($image, 255, 255, 255);
...
$something = imagecolorallocate($image, 123, 201, 177);
$ptsize = 36;$x = 20;$y = 50;$angle = -2;
imagettftext($image, $ptsize, $angle, 20, 110, $green, $fd,
  "Not just text");
// image arc, centre, width, height, start/end angles
imagearc($image, 40, 20, 70, 30, 115, 225, $orange);
imagefilledrectangle($image, 300, 300, 400, 325, $purple);
imageline($image, 0,200,100,0, $something);
imageline($image, 100, 0, 200, 200, $something);
imagestringup($image, 3, 400, 400, "Look Ma! No hands", $something);

imagepng($image);
imagedestroy($image);
?>
```

(The imagedestroy function disposes of off-screen pixel arrays. It is a good idea to get rid of images as soon as possible; they should be destroyed when your script terminates, but you can explicitly destroy them earlier.)

Instead of returning an image as the response to a request, you can generate the image, save it in a temporary file, and return a normal HTML web page that has <img src=...> links referencing your temporary file. You will have to arrange for regular purging of the file system that you use for temporary image files (a chron job running a few times a day should suffice). It is advisable to add extra header data to the response that indicate that the page should not be cached (if it is cached, it may be reused at some time after the deletion of the image it references). Figure 6.7 illustrates the output page from the following code which creates an HTML page with a couple of links to the same generated image.

```php
<?
// don't set the response type to image, accept text/html default
// header("Content-type: image/png");
// maybe set an expiry date to discourage caching etc.
header ("Expires: Fri, 1 Jan 1999 00:00:01 GMT");
// Code for image as before
...
...
imagestringup($image, 3, 400, 400, "Look Ma! No hands", $something);
...
// arguments to tempnam may not be utilized, see documentation
$tempfilename = tempnam("./tmpimages/", "picy");
imagepng($image, $tempfilename );
imagedestroy($image);
?>
<html><head><title>Pictures</title></head>
<body><h1>Here are my scribbles</h1>
<p>
<img src="<? print $tempfilename?>" width=100 height=67
align=right>First copy
<br><hr>
```

Here are my scribbles

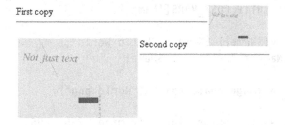

Figure 6.7   Generated HTML page with links to generated images.

```
<p>
<img src="<? print $tempfilename?>" width=200 height=133 align=left>
Second copy
<hr></body></html>
```

All the examples so far are static images that don't depend on inputs. For dynamic images, you simply need a better script! You aren't limited to composing a picture from scratch either. You can build an image that is a collage of existing images with additional new data superimposed. This allows for a slightly more interesting 'Hello World' – as illustrated in Figure 6.8. This 'Hello World' uses a static HTML form page:

```
<html><head><title>Hello</title></head>
<body>
<form action=helloworld.php method=post>
<table align=center border=2>
<tr>
  <th>What is your name?</th>
  <td><input type=text name=Name size=20 maxlength=20></td>
</tr>
<tr>
  <td colspan=2 align=center><input type=submit value="Hello World"></
td>
</tr>
</table></body></html>
```

Generation of the response involves initialization of a new image with an existing image taken from a file, and overwriting with a text string based on the inputs received:

```
<?
header("Expires: Mon, 26 Jul 1997 05:00:00 GMT", "Content-type:
  image/png");

$fontdir= "/jdk1.2.2/jre/lib/fonts/";
$fontname = "LucidaBrightItalic.ttf";
$fd = $fontdir . $fontname;

$Name = $HTTP_POST_VARS['Name'];

if(empty($Name)) $Name = "Hello World";
else $Name = "Hello " . $Name;

$image = imagecreatefromPNG("World.png");

$white = imagecolorAllocate($image, 255, 255, 255);
$black = imagecolorAllocate($image, 0, 0, 0);
```

Figure 6.8 A dynamic 'Hello World'.

```
$centreX = 300; $centreY = 64;
$ptsize = 12; $angle = 0;
$dimensions =
  imagettfbbox ($ptsize, $angle, $fd, $Name);

$width = $dimensions[2] - $dimensions[0];
$height = $dimensions[1] - $dimensions[7];
$width = $dimensions[2] - $dimensions[0];
$height = $dimensions[1] - $dimensions[7];

$x = $centreX - ($width / 2);
$y = $centreY + ($height / 2);

imagettftext($image, $ptsize, $angle, $x, $y, $black, $fd, $Name);
  ImagePng($image);
?>
```

Real-world use of graphics will be for histograms and trend charts – things like plotting the price of some share over the last 30 days of trading, or the tally of votes in some ongoing election. The final graphics example illustrates such a dynamically generated histogram. The example was inspired by those 'Big Brother' and 'Survivor' shows that were briefly popular on television. Some of those shows had associated web sites that allowed viewers to vote for the contestant that they wished to have thrown out of the contest. My site allowed students to vote faculty out of our school – see Figure 6.9.

The voting form is a static HTML page. The 'contestants' were all represented in a table – the table elements were either <input type=image ..> submit buttons, or conventional <input type=submit ...> buttons (for those faculty for whom there was no suitable picture). A vote could be cast by simply clicking on an entry in this table. The name of the

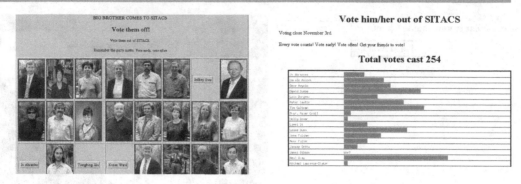

Figure 6.9 'Big Brother' voting form and dynamic histogram response page.

submit button was transferred (if an image button was used, the name would have ignorable (*x,y*) coordinate data appended). The processing involved the following steps:

- Receive name of contestant from form.
- Find in database, update record.
- Get all records for database.
- Construct histogram from record data.
- Output to temporary file.
- Construct response page that includes the histogram.

The structure of the static HTML page is:

```
<html><head><title>Big Brother </title>
</head><body><p align=center><font size=+2>
BIG BROTHER
</font><br><br><h1 align=center>Vote them off!</h1>
<p align=center>Vote them out of SITACS.
<p align=center>Remember the party motto: <em>Vote
early, vote often</em><br>
```

```
<form action=bigbrother.php method=post>
<table border=2 align=center>
<tr>
<td>
<input type=image src=images/DOE_JOHN.jpg name=JD width=100 height=150>
</td>
<td>
<input type=image src=images/CROFT_LARRA.jpg name=LC width=100 height=150>
</td>
```

```
                 ...
                 <td>
                 <input type=submit name=DS value="Dennis Smith">
                 </td>
                 </tr></table></form></body></html>
```

The script page is:

```
<html><head><title>Another vote</title></head>
<body>
<h1 align=center>Vote him/her out of SITACS</h1>
<p>Voting close November 3rd.
<p>Every vote counts! Vote early! Vote often! Get your friends to vote!
<?
// Identifiers for histogram
$names = array (
"DS" => "A/Prof. Dennis Smith",
"LA" => "Prof. Larra Croft",
...
);

function connect() { ... }
function update($person, $db) { ... }
function getdata($db) { ... }
function makeImage($data) { ... }

// Main line of script
$db = connect();
foreach($HTTP_POST_VARS as $key=>$val) {
  if(preg_match("/_[xy]$/", $key))
    { $temp = explode("_", $key); $identifier = $temp[0]; }
  else $identifier = $key;
}

if(isset($identifier)) update($identifier, $db);
$voterecord = getdata($db);

odbc_close($db);
makeImage($voterecord);

print "<br><br><h1 align=center>Your vote may make the difference</h1>";
print "<p align=center><em>Vote again soon!</em>"

?>
</body></html>
```

The connect function establishes a connection with a database; here, use of an ODBC Access database is again illustrated:

```
function connect() {
  $user = ""; $password = "";
  $db = odbc_connect( 'PHPEG' , $user, $password );
  if (!$db) die( "Error in odbc_connect" );
  return $db;
}
```

The code checking the data from $HTTP_POST_VARS finds the name associated with the selected input (stripping away any _x or _y from an image name). If a name is found, the update function is invoked:

```
function update($person, $db) {
  $result = odbc_exec( $db,
    "update BigBrother set Votes=Votes+1 where Name='$person'" );
  if (!$result) die( "Error in odbc_exec( update failed ? ) " );

  odbc_free_result($result);
}
```

The getdata function builds an array containing the full names and votes for each of the 'contestants':

```
function getdata($db) {
  $result = odbc_exec( $db, "select * from BigBrother");

  if (!$result)
    die( "Error in odbc_exec( no result returned ) " );

  $data = array();
  while( odbc_fetch_row( $result) ) {
    $Name = odbc_result($result, "Name");
    $Votes = odbc_result($result, "Votes");
    $data[$Name] = $Votes;
  }
  odbc_free_result($result);
  return $data;
}
```

The data in the array are then used to plot the histogram. The code is straightforward; it is a little lengthy because of the possible need to scale the data so that the histogram columns can be displayed in their entirety:

```
function makeImage($data)
{
  global $names;
  $num = count($data);
  $total = 0;
  $max = 0;
  foreach($data as $key=>$value) {
    $total += $value;
    $max = ($value > $max) ? $value : max;
  }

  print "<h1 align=center>Total votes cast $total</h1>";

  $imagewidth = 800;
  $imageheight = 20*$num;
  $w = (integer) $imagewidth * 0.9;
  $h = (integer) $imageheight * 0.9;

  $tempfile = "/tmp/afile" . $total . ".png";
  print "<p align=center>";
  print "<img src=\"$tempfile\" width=$w height=$h border=2>";
  // Create the image and allocate colors
  $image = ImageCreate ($imagewidth, $imageheight);

  $white = ImageColorAllocate ($image, 255, 255, 255);
  $text_color = ImageColorAllocate ($image, 233, 0 , 233);
  $fill_color = ImageColorAllocate($image, 255, 50, 50);
  $black = ImageColorAllocate($image,0,0,0);
  // Draw frame and row lines for the histogram
  ImageLine($image, 0, 0, 0, $imageheight, $black);
  ImageLine($image, 0, $imageheight-2,
    $imagewdith-1, $imageheight-2, $black);
  ImageLine($image, 0, 0, $imagewidth, 0, $black);
  ImageLine($image, $imagewidth-1, 0, $imagewidth-1, $imageheight,
    $black);

  // Set coordinates for initial for initial row
  // Set scaling factor for column length
  $x1 = 5; $x2 = 200;
  $y = 18;
  if($max<50) $max = 50;
  // Loop through "contestants" outputting full name
  // and column proportional to their votes
  foreach($data as $key=>$value) {
    $fullname = $names[$key];
```

```
    ImageString ($image, 2, $x1, $y-10, $fullname, $text_color);
    if($value==0)
      ImageString($image, 2, $x2, $y-10, "Who?", $text_color);
    else {
      $scaled = ($value*600)/$max;
      $scaled = (integer) $scaled;
      imagefilledrectangle($image, $x2, $y-12,
        $x2+$scaled, $y+2, $fill_color);
      }
    ImageLine($image, 0, $y+4, $imagewidth, $y+4, $black);
    $y+=20;
  }
  // Save the image to file
  imagepng($image,$tempfile);
  imagedestroy($image);
}
```

6.8 State

Section 6.4 contained an example illustrating how the hiding of previously submitted data in subsequently generated dynamic form pages can preserve client state. That scheme works in part, but it is only really useful if you are working through a fixed sequence of forms, all of which must be completed in a specific order. There are many other situations where it is useful to maintain some representation of client state, even though the client is going to be moving around, following different links to various parts of your web site. Consider for instance a web site where you want to include advertisements in the banner portion of the pages that you return, most of these pages being essentially static information. Your client will be following arbitrary links amongst your pages, but you would still like to save 'client state' – if simply something like a record of the advertisements that the client has already seen, so that you can show other products. But you don't have any forms, and there are no form submission actions that you could rely on to return hidden field data.

'Persistent state client side cookies' are the basis of an alternative mechanism for preserving state. 'Cookies' are:

- Small blocks of data created in the server
- Sent to the client in the HTTP header portion of a response
- Saved by the client's browser
- Returned to your server in the HTTP header portion of subsequent requests

The rules for cookies permit a server to create up to twenty distinct cookies associated with a particular resource, with each individual cookie having up to 4 kbyte of data. Each cookie can have:

- Data:

The data take the form of name/value pair(s).

- An expiry date:

This can be a date in the past, meaning that the cookie should be deleted immediately from the browser's records; the current date, meaning that the cookie is to be deleted when the client terminates execution of the browser program; or a date in the future (supposedly not more than one year into the future), which means that the browser should keep the cookie for future reference.

- A domain:

This should identify the domain where the cookie originated. For example, the cookie might specify `bigcompany.com`. Such a cookie can be returned to any machine in that domain, e.g. `www1.bigcompany.com` or `www2.bigcompany.com`.

- Optional path data:

The site for `bigcompany.com` might include separate file hierarchies for the 'marketing' and 'manufacturing' divisions; both might use cookies to record data about their clients. In such a situation, it might be worth setting 'path' controls so that cookies set by scripts in the 'marketing' hierarchy are only returned when the client submits GET/POST requests for other marketing resources.

Cookies are used in two main ways. A cookie can be a data carrier. A script that has extracted data can store these in a cookie that gets returned with a response page. The cookie data are returned in the next request; they can be picked up by the next script and processed. This approach is similar to using hidden fields to hold previously submitted data. The second style of use has the cookie merely as an identifier; all application data are stored on the server. The identifier's value – a carefully constructed string with a randomized component – is allocated by the first processing script and returned as a cookie with the script's response page. This identifier cookie now labels your client. It can serve as a primary key for database records, or as a part of a file identifier. The identifier is returned to your server each time the client makes a new request. Processing scripts that extract data from later submissions can associate these data with the identifier in the returned cookie. Data can be added to database tables or files (or, in some situations, can be saved in memory records managed by the web server). Obviously, the identifier style is safer (data are not repeatedly transferred over the net, so there is less risk of exposure, and data are not returned to clients, so reducing the potential for adjustment of values by hackers). However, as illustrated by the first of our two cookie examples, there are situations where the cookie as a data carrier is quite adequate.

The first cookie example involves a company that wants to advertise its wares on the main welcome page of its web site. This main page is composed as a frameset; one frame has contents generated by a little PHP script that selects a product to advertise. Each time a customer returns to this main page, he or she should see a different product advertised in the advertisement frame. The frameset for the main page is:

```
<html><head><title>Portal</title></head>
<frameset cols="240,*">
<frame src="advert.php">
<frame src="mainframe.html" scrolling="auto">
</frameset>
</html>
```

with the `advert.php` script being used to generate the contents of the frame in the left column.

The example code is considerably simplified – products are defined as records in an array rather than being read from disk, and they are advertised in sequence (working cyclically once a customer has seen already products once), so the last advertisement number is the only data that has to be stored. This information is saved as a cookie – 'timtam=*number*'. If the advertisements were shown in a more randomized order, you could have a cookie value as a string like *number#number#number*, with the numbers identifying those advertisements already shown. The record of advertisements seen is to last about a week, so the cookie will be set with a specified expiry date. The starting point in the collection of products is picked randomly for new clients.

The script `advert.php` is:

```
<?
// Define data for products, in a real system would read
// this information from a database.
$products = array(
  array (name=>"chair",
    src=>"images/chair.jpg",
    description=>"Ergonomic chair"),
  ...
);

// Processing code starts here:
$numproducts = count($products);
srand((double)microtime()*100000);
$choice = 0;
// Did the client return our "timtam" cookie?
// If it was returned, client has already seen some adverts.
// so take the next in sequence.
// If the cookie was not returned, this is a new client, pick
// randomly a starting advert.

$mycookie = $HTTP_COOKIE_VARS["timtam"];
if(!isset($mycookie)) {
  $choice = rand(0, $numproducts);
}
else {
```

```
    $choice = $mycookie;
    $choice++;
    if($choice==$numproducts) $choice=0;
}

// set the cookie for next time
$howlong = 7 * 24 * 3600;
setcookie("timtam",$choice, time() + $howlong);

$item = $products[$choice];
$description = $item["description"];
$source = $item["src"];
// Generate HTML page that will be placed in the
// advert frame of the frameset.
print <<<HERE
<html><head></head><body bgcolor=#dddddd>
<h1>Buy now</h1>
<p>See our detailed product catalog for wonderful
items such as these!
<h2>$description</h2>
<img src=$source>
<br>
<a href=catalog.html target=CATALOG>Our catalog</a>
</body></html>
HERE;
?>
```

The setcookie function must be called before any call to header or any output of text. Its arguments are: name, value, expiry time, optional path, optional domain, and 'requires secure connection' (you can limit cookies so they are only set if using a SSL network connection). The expiry time can be set by adding an offset to the current time – here the offset represents one week into the future (+ 7 * 24 * 3600 seconds). If the domain argument is not given, the hostname is used.

It would not matter if this cookie was viewed inappropriately – so if the last advertisement seen was #27, do what you like with that information. Nor would it matter if a hacker changed the value, they would simply change the sequence in which they saw the products. But more generally, it is dangerous to store data on the client. You should never store a value that you have computed from input data that have been discarded, and you should always validate any returned values before using them in later scripts.

The second example uses a cookie to store only a session key. Data relating to a client's session are held in the server; in this example, the data are held in a file whose name matches the session key. The example is a trivialized shopping site where the data that are to be stored are the contents of a 'shopping cart'.

Apparently, there are hackers with nothing better to do than try usurping shopping sessions at small web sites. They do this by guessing the sequence used to generate session keys and creating their own cookie with a session key that they have guessed as being that in use by some other customer. If they guess correctly, they can confuse the server by joining an ongoing session and changing the contents of the shopping cart (imagine the fun that you can have doing things like changing some child's order for *Harry Potter and the Chamber of Secrets* into an order for Proust's *Remembrance of Times Past*). To prevent this, the mechanism used to generate session keys has to incorporate a significant random element. There are now various standard key-generation mechanisms; these should be used in preference to *ad hoc* schemes.

The example is a site for acme.com.bv – an imaginary company that sells computers, office furniture and computer books. Acme's web-site comprises the following PHP scripts and static pages:

- Welcome.php
This is the entry point to the site with links to the main product pages; it also allocates the session key.

- Furniture.php, Books.php, Computer.php
These pages are simple form pages used to order products; in the example, it is all hard-coded; a real system would generate these pages from data in a database.

- Purchases.php
Records an order submitted from one of the form pages; the order is appended to the session file. (Orders cannot be rescinded.) Provides links back to other order forms or on to the checkout processing stage.

- Checkout.php
Essentially just a form requesting the name and address of the customer.

- Final.php
This script simply lists the data submitted; a real script would add the order to a table in a database.

- getwithit.html
Most of the scripts incorporate a check for the cookie set on the Welcome page. If the cookie is not set, then either the client is running with cookies disabled in their browser or they have managed to jump past the welcome page. This static page asks for cookies to be enabled and provides a link to the welcome page.

- Session file
This is a text file generated to hold records of all orders submitted via the forms pages.

(Some of these scripts are not shown below; those omitted are essentially trivial and are left as 'an exercise for the reader'.) Several of the scripts require the same code fragments – specifically the code that checks for the presence of a cookie and diverts the user to the getwithit.html page if no cookie is found. PHP supports a form of file includes; the required code fragment can be included in all pages that need it.

The Welcome.php script is little more than a static page with links to the main shopping pages. The scripting code that it contains is that needed to allocate a session identifier. The mechanism used is that recommended in the PHP manual – basically you generate a random number based on the current time, but this is not in itself sufficiently secure, so you use the MD5 hashing algorithm to mix up the bits of this random string. This approach is standard; it is considered to produce keys that are sufficiently opaque as to deter the average hacker. The code for this script is:

```php
<?
$existingSession=$HTTP_COOKIE_VARS["SessionData"];
if(!isset($existingSession)){
   srand((double)microtime()*100000);
   $token = md5(uniqid(rand()));
   setcookie("SessionData",$token,0);
}
?>
<html><head><title>Welcome to our world</title></head>
<body bgcolor=white><h1>Welcome</h1>
We always like customers. Bring your friends along.
<p>Our departments:
<ul>
<li><a href=furniture.php>Furniture</a>
<li><a href=computers.php>Computers</a>
<li><a href=books.php>Books</a>
</ul></body></html>
```

The cookie is set as a 'session cookie' (timeout of zero); it will disappear from the client's browser when the browser is terminated. (The name 'SessionData' might seem rather unsafe – likely to clash with the same name used by another site. But there is actually no problem; the browser identifies the cookies by the domain as well as the name. So, acme.com.bv will only receive SessionData cookies that it has set itself.)

The code fragment that checks for the cookie can be held in a separate file – chkrdir.inc:

```php
<?
$existingSession=$HTTP_COOKIE_VARS["SessionData"];
if(!isset($existingSession)){
   header("Location: getwithit.html");
   exit();
}
?>
```

If the cookie is not found, this sends an HTTP-style redirection order back to the client's browser. This response has just header data, the important part being the 'Location' directive that tells the browser what page it really is to fetch. The file getwithit.html is a static text page; the contents explain how a cookie is a harmless session tag, suggest that the user enable cookies, and provide a link back to the Welcome page. Other scripts in this web should all start by including this chkrdir.inc fragment. (You don't have to use the suffix '.inc – include file. If you do use it, you should be aware that if someone can guess the names of your .inc files then they can download your code – by default, both web server and browser will treat these as text files. You might want to add a security control to your httpd.conf file that prohibits client access to all .inc files.)

The scripts that generate the forms for purchasing goods are simplified versions of those needed in a real site – the form is really just a static HTML table. This form can be submitted; submission invokes the purchase.php script. Alternatively, the user may chose to follow a link to a different order form or the checkout desk. These forms all allow multiple items to be purchased, so the input field associated with purchases is an array; the values for individual inputs are unique identifiers such as ISBNs for books and product codes for the furniture.php page.

```
<?
include("chkrdir.inc");
?>
<html><head><title>Books</title>
</head><body bgcolor=white>
<h1 align=center>Buy a book</h1>
<form action=purchase.php method=post>
<table align=center border=2>
<caption>Available books</caption>
<tr>
  <td>
  <input type=checkbox name="books[]" value=ISBN:078972310>
  </td>
  <td>
  Don't Make Me Think! S. Krug, R. Black; This is the book
  you need if you want to design great web pages.
  </td>
  <td>
  $24
  </td>
</tr>
  // and a few more books
  ...
<tr>
  <td align=center colspan=3>
  <input type=submit value="Buy Books">
  </td>
</tr></table></form><br><hr><ul>
<li><a href=furniture.php>Furniture</a>
<li><a href=computers.php>Computers</a>
<li><a href=checkout.php>Checkout</a>
</ul></body></html>
```

The purchases.php script must start by confirming the presence of the SessionData cookie; if the cookie is found, the checking code saves the value – the session identifier – in a global PHP variable. The purchases script next checks for posted order data – computers, books or furniture, depending on the form page used to submit the data. If data are received, they will be as an array of product codes. The script appends these to a file. The file is named from the session identifier; it is opened in append mode (which creates the file if it does not already exist). The data values (product codes) are urlencoded before being written (substitution of space by +; other non-alphabetic characters by %xx escapes). This is not essential in this example, but sometimes helps, as session data might include multi-line text inputs from an HTTP form's text-area. If the data are urlencoded they can be more easily written and read as single one-line transfers.

```php
<?
include("chkrdir.inc");
// chkrdir.inc will either
// set global variable $existingSession to our sessionkey
// or, if no session key found, redirect the user.
function recordorder($item) {
  global $fp;
  $coded = urlencode($item) . "\n";
  fwrite($fp,$coded);
}
function process($data) {
  if(!isset($data)) return;
  if(!is_array($data)) return;
  if(empty($data)) return;
  foreach($data as $val)
    recordorder($val);
}


$computers = $HTTP_POST_VARS["computers"];
$books = $HTTP_POST_VARS["books"];
$furniture = $HTTP_POST_VARS["furniture"];
// Create file name based on session, open in append mode
$filename = "./orders/" . $existingSession;
$fp = fopen($filename, "a");
// Process any data received from a form
process($computers);
process($books);
process($furniture);
fclose($fp);
?>
<html><head><title>Continue shopping or checkout</title></head>
<body bgcolor=white><h2>Order recorded</h2><p>
You may continue shopping or proceed to checkout.
```

```
<ul>
<li><a href="computers.php">Computers</a>
...
<li><a href="checkout.php">Checkout</a>
</ul><hr>
<p>Want to work for us?
<p><a href=jobs.html>Visit our vacancies page</a>
</body></html>
```

A fairly high proportion of visitors to commercial web sites start filling a shopping basket with speculative purchases but never proceed to final checkout. The result is a lot of abandoned session files. If you are running a site like this, you will need a regular chron job that sweeps through your orders directory deleting all files that haven't been used for six hours or so.

Cookies are the most convenient of the mechanisms for preserving client state. Unfortunately, they cannot be relied on. The user of a browser can at any time choose to delete all existing cookies. Many users run their browsers with support for cookies disabled (estimates of cookie-less customers go as high as 20 per cent). Commercial sites that wish to handle cookie-less customers require an alternative approach to saving state.

You cannot use hidden fields in forms because these are not sufficiently flexible. You cannot place cookies on the client browser, because your client is paranoid. But somehow, you must place at least a session key in the response pages that you send, and have some reliable mechanism for getting the browser to return this session key.

What data always pass back and forth between client and web server? Really, the only data that are always passed are the URLs for the pages in your <a href=...> links and <form action=... > tags. If you are going to hide a session key somewhere, it is going to have to be inside these URLs. This is the basis of the 'URL rewriting' scheme for maintaining client state. URL rewriting is a relatively tedious operation; you must change every link that occurs anywhere in a page that you return to a client. Each URL is modified by the inclusion of the session key.

With URL rewriting, client state is again preserved on the server host, either in database tables or session files. The session key relates the client to the saved data. This key is just an alphanumeric string like the value for a SessionData cookie. The string gets embedded in the URLs. There are a variety of ways that you can do this embedding; it depends on how you intend to remove the session key when processing a request returned by the client.

The simplest approach is to append the session key as a query string to every URL. So where your original page was:

```
<ul>
<li><a href="computers.php">Computers</a>
...
<li><a href="checkout.php">Checkout</a>
</ul><hr>
```

you will need something like:

```
$tag = "?SessionData=" . $token;
...
?>
<html><head>...</head>
<body>
...
<ul>
<li><a href=computers.php<? print $tag ?> >Computers</a>
<li><a href=books.php<? print $tag ?> >Books</a>
<li><a href=furniture.php<? print $tag ?> >Furniture</a>
<br>
<li><a href=checkout.php<? print $tag ?> >Checkout</a>
</ul>
```

which will produce an HTML link like:

```
<li><a href=computers.php?SessionData=b492ea45b089c1143754180d7107291c>
Computers</a>
```

The browser would record this information in the 'query string' (you can have a query string even when you are 'posting' data) from where it could be accessed by your program:

```
<?
unset($token);

$qstr=$HTTP_SERVER_VARS['QUERY_STRING'];
if(preg_match(
  "/SessionData=([0123456789abcdef]{32})/",$qstr,$matches)) {
  $token = $matches[1];
}
if(!isset($token)){
  srand((double)microtime()*100000);
  $token = md5(uniqid(rand()));
}
$tag = "?SessionData=" . $token;
...
```

The code is using a Perl-style regular expression match on the query string. The expression specifies a sequence of exactly 32 hexadecimal digits following the string SessionData=; these are in parenthesized match group. (The preg_match function stores details of its matches in the $matches array: match[0] holds the entire string matched, match[1] holds the first selected component, etc.)

The query string is really intended for other uses. The session identifier can be embedded at other points in the URL, but this requires special action by the web server. You can, for example, have something like the following in your script file:

```
http://www.acme.com.bv/<? print $tag >/books.php
```

The session identifier tag now appears as part of the path name for a resource. You can configure an Apache server with the mod-rewrite module and provide rules for processing the file path names that occur in requests. A rule could specify that the server discard a 32 hex-digit sequence that occurs as the top-level directory in a pathname. Your processing script can still pick up the key because it can obtain the unedited version of the pathname from the web server.

You can do your session management using files and either cookies or URL rewriting (or both). However, if your needs are standard, then you can use PHP's session library functions. These functions handle all the basic tasks that have been illustrated in this section.

Exercises

Practical

These exercises require that PHP be deployed as part of an Apache server system. As with the Perl exercises, configuration is a lot easier if students can run their own Apache servers rather than try to deploy their PHP applications onto a single shared Apache server. For most institutions, the best approach would probably be to install Apache on Windows machines and then add PHP (the PHP download gives instructions on the small changes needed to the httpd.conf file for Windows). An Access database on Windows is quite adequate for learning exercises.

(1) Create a PHP program:

```
<?php
phpinfo();
?>
```

and install it in your web directory as info.php. Try invoking it via your browser (http://localhost:portifnot80/pathname/info.php).

It should respond with a well-formatted HTML page that details the control settings for, and optional libraries that are linked with, your PHP.

(If it doesn't, keep hacking at the httpd.conf file until you have correctly set the elements that allow PHP scripts to be recognized and interpreted!)

(2) Implement the soccer league example using the database system available to you; use whatever database specific interface is appropriate.

If your PHP installation includes the newer database-independent module, re-implement the programs using this module. (In subsequent exercises, use whichever proved easier to use of the database-specific or the database-independent modules.)

(3) If you require something more elaborate than HTTP authorization, you can implement your own PHP scripting code that controls user access to data.

Implement a PHP script that validates whether a user has access to a resource or should be denied. The script should:

- Apply a test on the IP address of a would-be client. The client's IP address must match a regular expression pattern that determines acceptable addresses (e.g. use a pattern that corresponds to the network part of your own domain). If the client's address does not match, the script should use the PHP header() function to return a 'Forbidden' response.

- Check for values for $PHP_AUTH_USER and $PHP_AUTH_PW. If these are not set, the script is to use the header() function to return an 'Authorization required' response (invent some arbitrary name for the 'controlled realm').

- If $PHP_AUTH_USER and $PHP_AUTH_PW are set, they are to be validated against data in a simple array of name/password pairs defined in the script. If the submitted data don't match an entry in this table, an 'Authorization required' response should be sent again. If the data do match, a welcome page should be sent (the contents of this welcome page are the only data that are controlled by the login mechanism in this example).

Chapter 17 of the PHP manual contains some examples relating to PHP scripted control of the HTTP authorization mechanism/

Exercises 4–8 use a simple database that records marks for students enrolled in a course. The main database has a single table 'MarksFile'. The data in this MarksFile table are:

- *A student identifer (9 characters)*

- *A password (up to 16 characters)*

- *A tutorial group number*

- *Five numeric fields that represent marks obtained in five assessable components of some course. (An entry of –1 indicates that no work has yet been submitted by a student for a particular assessable component.)*

The following SQL fragment illustrates a way to define and populate the table.

```
CREATE TABLE MarksFile
        (identifier      CHAR(9) NOT NULL,
        password         VARCHAR(16) NOT NULL,
        tutorialgroup    number(4),
        mark1            number(4),
        mark2            number(4),
```

```
         mark3            number(4),
         mark4            number(4),
         mark5            number(4),
         CONSTRAINT identifier_pkey PRIMARY KEY(identifier)
);

INSERT INTO MarksFile VALUES
   ('u98765432', 'r6Yj*8', 1, 6, 5, 7, -1, -1 );
INSERT INTO MarksFile VALUES
('u98445662', 'tE38-hhhg', 2, 5, 9, 6, 15, -1 );
```

This table should be defined along with at least thirty invented records for students divided amongst at least two tutorial groups.

In this example, the database contains the actual passwords; this is done to make it slightly easier to set up. You can easily implement a more realistic version where the databases holds encrypted passwords. The PHP library includes Unix's standard crypt *function; this can be used to encrypt passwords when creating entries in the database. The password submitted in a form is also encrypted and the two encrypted strings are compared.*

(**3**) Write a system that allows students to retrieve their personal data from this table. The system is to comprise a static HTML web page and an accompanying PHP script that handles data posted from that page. The page has an input text field for the student identifier and an input password field for the password. The PHP script retrieves the MarksFile record associated with the identifier, returning an error page if the password submitted from the HTML form does not match that in the database. If the password is matched, the PHP script prints a table showing the marks for those assessment items for which the student has submitted work.

(**4**) Write a similar system that allows a student to enter a request for a histogram showing the distribution of marks that have been recorded for submissions for a chosen assessment item. The HTML form should have fields for name, password and assessment number. The response page is either a pure graphic page (type image/png) that shows a histogram like that illustrated in Figure 6.10, or a text page reporting that too few students have

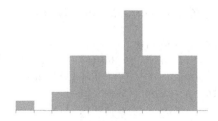

Results for class in assignment 2

Figure 6.10

results recorded (don't draw histograms if there are fewer than five actual marks recorded for the assessable item).

(**6**) Write a PHP script that:

- Handles a get request by displaying a form that allows the user to request either retrieval of individual marks from the MarksFile table, or the display of a class histogram.

- Handles a put request by generating the appropriate form of HTML page;

- Uses authentication code adapted from the earlier exercise. When the PHP script starts, it must check for values in the variables for $PHP_AUTH_USER and $PHP_AUTH_PW; if these are not set it is to respond with a header() response that initiates the HTTP authorization challenge. If the data are set, the identifier/password combination should be checked against data in the MarksFile table.

Check that your system allows a user to request marks and several histograms while only supplying their user-identifier and password on the first request.

(**7**) Create an additional table for the student marks system that contains identifiers, passwords and tutorial class for tutors (each tutor associated with one tutorial class). Create a system that has PHP mediated HTTP authentication (checking that it can only be used by a tutor who supplies his or her password). A get request should result in a form that has submit options that will allow the tutor to see either a list of the identifiers of the students in the tutorial group for which he or she is responsible, or a page that shows marks for a chosen assessment item. These requests are 'posted' to the same PHP script. A response page that shows a list of student identifiers uses just a simple HTML <ul>...</ul> list. The response page showing marks for an assessment item should include two histograms; the first shows the overall class results, the second shows the marks distribution for the tutor's own class.

(**8**) Provide an additional option for the tutor that allows input of marks for a chosen assessment item. The tutor is to use an HTML form to select the assessment item and submit a request. This requests results in the return of a dynamically generated HTML form page with an input text field for each student in the tutor's class. These input text fields are individually named using the student identifiers, and will contain as initial values the marks as currently recorded in the MarksFile table. The tutor can change the data in any number of input fields and submit this HTML form. This second submission will be handled by another PHP script; this script will update all marks for the tutorial group students in the chosen assessment item. The response from this script is an HTML page that lists student identifiers and associated marks as now recorded in the MarksFile table.

(**9**) PHP scripting (or ASP scripting) is the appropriate technology for all those small web sites for small companies, special interest groups, parent–teacher groups and similar. As an example, consider the requirements of the 'Kiddies Kare Kooperative' (sic!).

'Kiddies Kare' is a 'cooperative' that enables young couples to share baby care resources. The cooperative has a collection of items that can be borrowed for periods from

1 month to 1 year. It keeps its records in a database with two main tables and one auxiliary table. The main tables are the 'members' table:

```
create table coopMembers (
        id              integer,
        name            varchar(32) not null,
        password........varchar(16) not null,
        address         varchar(64) not null,
        memblevel       integer,
        constraint coopmemb_pk primary key(id)
);
```

used to keep records on members (the level attribute is explained below); and the 'items' table:

```
create table coopItems (
        id              integer,
        description     varchar(64) not null,
        c_id            integer,
        due             date,
        constraint coopitem_pk primary key(id),
        constraint coop_cid_fk foreign key(c_id) references
            coopMembers(id)
);
```

that records details of items in the cooperative's loan collection. (The c_id field is null if the item is in stock and available for loan, otherwise it holds the membership number of the member who has already borrowed the item. The due date field is only meaningful if the c_id field is not null; it then represents the date by which the item should be returned by the member who has it.)

The extra table is used when allocating new membership numbers or new item numbers:

```
create table uniqueIDS (
  name varchar(16),
  value integer
);
```

The table has two entries – Items and Members – whose values are the most recently issued unique identifiers for loan items and membership numbers respectively.

The coop has three levels of membership:

• Ordinary members, who borrow items and search the database by keyword (e.g. a search for toy will return details of all items that contain the string toy in their descriptions).

- Administrators, who can add loan item records and record returns (and can also search for or borrow items).

- Senior administrators, who have the additional options of adding new member records and new loan item records.

The cooperative members don't like the interface for the current database system and want a web-based interface. The following specification is provided:

The system is to be accessed via a web page (or group of web pages) that allow submission of data for processing by a single PHP script. The PHP script is to use authentication controls so that it is only available to members; for technical reasons, it is not possible to have the web server perform the authentication; authentication must be handled in the PHP script. Names and passwords entered in the HTTP authentication dialog on the browser must match records in the database. The web page (or pages) has a set of data entry forms that can be used to:

- *Request a search*. This form has a single text input field and a form submission button; the data entered in the input field are interpreted as a keyword, and the response is a table that lists the item identifier, description and status of all items where the description contains the specified keyword. The status data in the report should indicate whether that item is available for loan, or they should show the date when an item already on loan is due to be returned to the cooperative.

- *Borrow an item*. This form has a text input field for the item number, a single selection choice with options 1, 3, 6 and 12 months (default of 3 months), and a form submission button; the script should check that the specified item number is valid, returning an error page for invalid data. If the number is valid, the script should check whether the item is available for loan; if the item is already loaned, the script should return an error page reporting when the item should become available (the script should also check whether the member submitting the request is the one who currently has the loaned item, and point out this detail if it applies). If the request can be satisfied, the script determines the due date for the loan (adding the loan period to the current date). It then updates the coopItems table, inserting the membership number of the member who has borrowed the item and the due date for return. The response page notes the loan of the item, giving its number, its description and the due date for return.

- *Return an item*. This form has a text input field for the item number and a form submission button; the script again starts by checking whether the item number is valid, returning a suitable error response page if the item number is invalid or is not currently recorded as being on loan. If the data are valid, the coopItems table is updated.

- *Register an item*. This form has a text input field and a form submission button. The script checks that the member using the form has the right to add items to the database (an error response is generated if this is not permitted). The script gets a new item number from the uniqueIDs table (updating that table) and creates a new record in the coopItems table. (Strictly, those two operations form a single transaction and should be done under transactional control. However, this refinement can reasonably be ignored in the current context.) A response page is generated that reports the newly assigned item number.

- *Register a new member.* This form has text input fields for member name and address, a single selection choice (or radio button set) offering ordinary, administrator and senior administrator membership levels, and a form submission button. The script checks that the member using the form has the right to add members to the database (an error response is generated if this is not permitted). The script gets a new member number from the uniqueIDs table (updating that table) and creates a new record in the coopMembers table. A response page is generated that reports the newly assigned member number.

Implement a version of the system required by this child-care cooperative.

(10) *The following exercise allows for more explorations with graphics and also file uploads.*
Implement a PHP script system that provides a service similar to the 'Oscarize Me' service (Figure 6.11).

The 'Oscarize Me' service has a collection of images of male and female stars being awarded Oscars; associated with each of these images are record structures that define coordinates that frame the head of the awardee.

Clients submit an image, preferably a photo of their face with a transparent background (defined using a PNG editing tool). The client's image file is uploaded and scaled so that it can be superimposed on the image of the chosen film star. The program returns a page displaying the composite image.

Have you ever wanted to be awarded an Oscar

Figure 6.11

(11) *The following exercise allows for exploration with of state maintenance using cookies.*

Implement a version of the 'Pelmanism' card game as a PHP web-based application. The application is to use a single PHP script and no static HTML pages. There script can generate a 'new game' page, a 'continuing game' page or a 'game over, do you want to play again' page.

Games are played one move at a time. A game can be played for a few moves, and then be suspended and resumed days later.

In the Pelmanism card game you start with a shuffled deck of cards, all but one face down. In each move, you turn one card face up; if it matches the card previously face up, you have won the pair and either leave them both face up or remove them from the playing area. If the cards don't match; the previous face up card is turned face down. The game relies on memory. Initially you must turn cards over at random, but gradually you get to remember where you have seen a particular card previously, and so can find the pairs. The idea is to find all pairs with the minimum of moves.

This version should use a decorative card deck consisting of 24 face cards, with two of each in the deck (you can select the images of face cards, I used my colleagues' photos from their web pages; your local faculty probably provides a similar set of photos). The cards are displayed on a 6 × 8 grid; all but one of the cards start face down (the back of the card cards should show an image such as your college's logo).

The array of cards is displayed in a table within an HTML form (Figure 6.12); the table holds a 6 × 8 set of image submission buttons (`<input type=image src=...name=... width=... height=...>`). It is similar to the 'BigBrother.html' example. The 'name' of an image button is a string that specifies its position in the grid.

When a card is clicked (i.e. when a particular image submission button is activated), the form data are submitted for processing by the PHP script. The submitted data identify the name of the button used, and hence the grid position clicked by the user. The script checks

Continuing

A game of SITACS Happy Family

You have made 57 guesses, and found 9 pairs so far.

Figure 6.12

whether the card at the selected grid position matches that previously displayed. If they match, both get turned up, otherwise the new card becomes the face up card with the previous card turned face down. The script records the number of moves made.

Obviously, this involves 'session based state data'. Each game is different. The cards start in a random arrangement. Multiple concurrent players each play their own games. Each player has made a different number of moves. In each game, different pairs have been found and are face up.

The state of a game can be represented as structure with a move count, an identifier of the current face-up unmatched card, and a set of 48 tokens that represent the images at each grid position and whether they are face up or face down. This information can easily be serialized into some string format.

The system is to use cookies for state maintenance. You can have the cookie contain an encrypted version of the serialized string that represents the game state (liable to be hacked), or use an MD5 hashed random token that also acts as the name of a file where the data are saved. The following outline of your script assumes that you are using a file to maintain state and that the cookie's value is simply used as a filename.

Your PHP script, named Pelmanism.php, should:

- Start by checking for an identification cookie. If none is received with the request, the script generates a suitably randomized identifier and adds a cookie for this identifier to the header with an expiry data some three to five days hence.

- Checks for the existence of a file, in the /tmp directory, with a name that matches the random identifier.
  - If this file does not exist, it is created with data for a new game. A new game has the set of 24 pairs of cards randomly allocated to positions in the grid. No pairs have been matched. One randomly chosen card is face up. A 'New Game' response page is generated showing the initial configuration. The game's starting state is saved to the newly created file. The script terminates.
  - If the file does exist, the game state is restored. The HTTP_POST_VARS data are examined to find an identifier for the button used. The script code then checks whether the card at the selected position matches the current face-up unmatched card.
  - If the cards match, and this is the 24th pair found, the game has been completed. The existing data file for the game associated with the session identifier is deleted. A 'game over' page is generated; this contains a link that allows a new game to be started. The script terminates.
  - If the selected card matched the previous selection, but fewer than 24 pairs have been found, the script updates the number of pairs found and arranges that the matched pair be displayed face up. If the cards were not matched, the record of the last selected card is updated. A new response page is generated. The updated state of the game is saved. The script terminates.
  - If no valid data were received for the card selection, it is a wasted move. The script just updates the count of moves, and redisplays the same card tableau as before. This situation will occur when a player returns to the game after abandoning play for a while, or if the player clicks an already face-up card.

(12) The examples in the text show how cookies can be used to hold state data in the client's browser, and how to use cookies (or URL rewriting) to store a session key on the client that permits access to state data held on the server.

The PHP libraries include some additional session support functions (Chapter LXV of the PHP manual). These use the cookie and URL-rewriting mechanisms to handle client session keys. The functions provide a somewhat higher level, richer interface for the application programmer.

Rework the text examples to utilize the standard PHP session-handling functions.

Short answer questions

(1) Explain how each of the following approaches can be used to maintain state for a web application:

- Hidden fields in forms.

- HTTP authorization (or equivalent login system).

- Cookies.

- URL rewriting.

(2) Outline the steps required to generate a complex HTML response page that includes bar charts and other pictures that have been dynamically generated from data entered in a form.

(3) Summarize the risks involved with file uploads and some of the mechanisms that may be used to minimize these risks.

(4) How might you implement user authentication and authorization mechanisms that go beyond those supplied in the HTTP protocol?

(5) Explain how PHP-style scripting is superior to CGI mechanisms for most simple web applications.

(6) In PHP 3, form variables were automatically introduced into global scope. As normally configured, a PHP 4 system allows such variables to be accessed only via the global array $HTTP_POST_VARS (or $HTTP_GET_VARS for forms using method=get). Why was this change made?

Explorations

(1) 'The future of PHP'. Research and report on this topic.

(2) 'PHP usage in the current Web'. Research and report on this topic.

7

Java Servlets

This chapter introduces 'servlets'. Servlets form the basis of Java web server technologies. You can write your own servlets to handle web requests, or you can use Java Server Pages that are converted automatically into servlets.

These servlet examples begin the move to more elaborate web sites. Simple web applications require little more than a static HTML form data entry page, and a script to process the submitted data. But as you move to more ambitious services you start to require a more effective architecture for your 'web applications'. A web application typically has several different programs that combine to handle different aspects of a problem; some might handle requests from clients, while others are used by administrators. These applications need to be deployed as a group along with necessary static HTML pages and image files. The applications may need to exchange data. There may be special security requirements that limit the use of particular functions to particular classes of users. The servlet technology provides a good basis for building such more elaborate web applications.

This chapter starts with a general overview of servlets. The next section uses a simple example to illustrate how servlets are built and deployed. This is followed by a slightly more detailed overview of the Java class libraries from which servlets are constructed. The remaining sections in the chapter use more elaborate examples to illustrate the construction of web applications and the use of additional features such as security constraints that accord different capabilities to different classes of user.

7.1 Servlet overview

Servlets (server-side applications) were conceived as a Java-based alternative to CGI scripting. Basically, a servlet was to be an instance of a class that could handle HTTP 'get' and 'post' requests. A web server that supported servlets was to be similar to Apache combined with mod-Perl or mod-PHP. The standard web server would handle requests for static pages and images; when it encountered a request for a dynamic page, it would pass that request to an interpreter that would process the request and generate the response. Now, the interpreter was to be a Java Virtual Machine (JVM) running a servlet.

In practice, there are a variety of different configurations for servlet-based systems. Some are themselves Java programs. These 'standalone servlet containers' combine a very basic HTTP server with a system that loads and runs Java code used to generate dynamic pages. Other 'in-process servlet containers' are really just like Apache with mod-PHP; an existing web server is extended with a module that holds a JVM and related servlet container components. Servlet programs are run in this environment. Finally, there are 'out of process servlet containers'. These are intended for higher demand sites. A standard web server, such as Apache, handles static pages and requests that still involve alternative technologies like Perl-CGI scripts. Other processes run servlet containers; these processes are pre-allocated, possibly running on different machines so as to provide a form of load sharing across machines. The web server has a small module that selects those requests that involve servlets; this module farms these requests out to the servlet containers.

You can pay for a servlet container. If you pay the right supplier, you will get a higher performance system. Alternatively, you can use Tomcat, from apache.org, for free. Tomcat is the 'reference' implementation for Java servlets (and the related JSP technology). Tomcat can be run as a standalone servlet container; as well as hosting servlets for dynamic pages, it will handle requests for text, HTML, GIF and other static files. Alternatively, you can configure a combination of Apache and Tomcat(s) to set up an 'out-of-process servlet container' system. Apache will apply all the proper configuration rules controlling access to data, and handle static pages, server-side includes and the rest; servlet requests are routed via an Apache module through to a Tomcat.

When learning about servlets, it is simplest to set up Tomcat as a standalone server. This is a really easy installation task – run an unmodified script on Unix/Linux, or simply double click a self-load executable on Windows. Your Tomcat server will handle HTTP requests at port 8080 (this can be changed if really necessary; it is controlled by a parameter in a configuration file). Your Tomcat will serve files from a subdirectory of its own installation directory

When you first start learning about servlets, you will be impressed (probably unfavorably) by the complexity of the overall system. You have to distribute files in subdirectories with specified hierarchical structures and names, and you have to write deployment descriptions that are sometimes as long and complex as the servlet code for generating your dynamic pages. There are reasons for this complexity.

With servlets, you begin to think in terms of 'web applications'. It is no longer a matter of a couple of static HTML pages, one form page, and a little script that generates a dynamic response page. The scale of the endeavor has changed. An application that justifies the use of the Java-based technologies will involve many separate servlets for generating different dynamic pages, along with static HTML pages, images and so forth. These servlets may need to work together fairly closely, sharing information that relates to the application as a whole. If you want to move your application to another host, you must move all the files and reconstruct your system so that the reinstalled files have similar relationships.

If you look at the htdocs and cgi-bin directories of your Apache server, you will probably find your directories are as messy as mine were. I found a large number of files – .html, .pl, .php, images – with no coherent organization. I had to read the contents to discover what tasks they related to; I had no easy way of identifying the groups of files that made up any one application. With servlets, it is quite different. The webapps directory of your servlet container system will contain a set of '.war' files. These are really Java '.jar' files – compressed archives containing multiple files within a defined subdirectory structure. Generally, when a servlet container starts up it will expand these archive files, creating subdirectories for each application. Each .war file is a complete application. It contains all the static HTML pages and Java Server Page script pages in a top-level directory; associated images would go in a subdirectory. Another subdirectory holds a file with deployment description details, a subdirectory for any special Java packages (libraries) that are required, and a further subdirectory with the .class files (and optionally the .java source files) for the servlet application code. The deployment description file can contain initialization data (e.g. username and password for a database – avoiding the need for this to be coded in the program), and security controls (these provide for automatic linking with the HTTP authentication system for getting usernames and passwords). When you move an application to a different host, you simply copy the .war file and maybe edit some parameters in the deployment description file. I suppose you could be equally disciplined in your deployment of PHP or Perl technologies, but you probably won't be. With the Java technologies, you have no choice. You must follow a disciplined approach to deployment.

As well as enforcing a more disciplined approach to deployment, the Java systems provide good support for more sophisticated and demanding server-side applications. Enthusiasts for Perl and PHP will protest that their systems are equally sophisticated, and that they have libraries that allow server-side programs to use network connections, persistent database connections and so forth. The Java systems do tend to be more comprehensive. For example, it is easy to build a web application where servlets share access to memory-based data structures, and where pools of persistent database connections can be managed. Or, as another example, you could have a servlet that used a socket connection to communicate with a C program that manages some analog-to-digital input – so allowing you to have dynamic web pages that display real-world data.

Further, the object-oriented style of Java encourages more coherent program structures. With a real servlet-based application, you will typically see the 'servlet object' performing a relatively limited controlling role. Objects that are instances of other classes are used to perform application-specific business tasks. Business rules, which may need to be changed, are built into these support classes. These classes may be usable in many applications – offline Java applications as well as online, servlet-style web applications.

If you want a few static web pages, a couple of forms and some simple database records, then the Java systems are overkill. If you are more ambitious, servlets and related technologies become relevant.

7.2 A first servlet example

The servlet container/servlet system is an object-oriented framework application. Sun's programmers (who supplied the initial structure for what is now Apache Tomcat) have already coded all the main behaviors. A program, written by the Sun developers, instantiates various Sun-defined classes to create the objects that form the 'servlet container'. Control is passed to one of these objects; this reads the deployment files for all the entries in the associated webapps directory and builds tables identifying the servlets that it can run. The container then waits to handle incoming HTTP get and post requests.

When the first HTTP get or post request is received for a particular servlet, the container object identifies the class needed, creates an instance of that class, and initializes it; information about the class and initialization data are obtained from the tables built earlier. The container then creates input and output streams so that the new servlet can read request data and write response data. Then the 'service' method of the servlet is invoked to handle the request. When the servlet finishes handling its client's request, the input and output streams are closed by the container. The servlet itself is normally kept around, waiting for the next request. The container can destroy servlet objects; this rarely utilized option is there to allow the reclamation of underutilized resource in a busy container that hosts many different servlets.

When your server starts to get busy, you will have many concurrent get and post requests. The servlet container has no problems with this, as it is multi-threaded: each client is associated with a separate thread and separate input and output streams. The container handles thread management issues; it may create and destroy threads, or it may use a pool of reusable threads. But you only have one servlet object. Servlets should be 'thread-safe' – which means that generally neither instance data members nor static class members should be present. Sometimes, it is appropriate for a servlet to have instance data or class data; but in those cases, mutex locks must be explicitly used in the servlet code to restrict access so that the shared data are used by one thread at a time.

Sun's programmers have written the thread management code. They have also written all the framework code to create and destroy servlets and manage I/O connections. So where do you come in?

You have to define a concrete servlet class that implements behaviors that are left abstract in the servlet classes defined in Sun's framework. Sun's framework includes the definitions of a servlet class hierarchy:

- Servlet (interface)
This defines essential functionality: `init`, `destroy`, `get-config-info`, `service`.

- Generic servlet (abstract)
This class adds logging, parameters, context, and other features.

- HttpServlet (abstract)
Still an abstract class, the `HttpServlet` class has an effective `service` method. This function uses data defining the HTTP request, and dispatches the request to the appropriate 'get', 'put', 'post' or 'delete' method.

Your servlet class should extend the `HttpServlet` abstract class and provide an effective implementation of at least one of `doGet`, `doPost` or the other action methods required by the `HttpServlet.service` method. You need define only one of these methods; Sun's framework code will generate an error response if your servlet is invoked using an HTTP request that you do not support.

Sun's framework uses 'request' and 'response' wrapper classes for the HTTP input and output streams. Instances of these classes are created by the framework code and passed to the `HttpServlet.service` function, and thence to the `doGet` or `doPost` method that the servlet programmer defines. Typically, the response from a servlet is a dynamically generated HTML page; such a page can be written easily by getting a `PrintWriter` object associated with the servlet response and using normal `java.io` output functions. The servlet programmer can read the HTTP standard input stream or query string. Form data can be split into name/value pairs, and any `x-www-urlencoding` can be reversed. But all this work is standard, independent of any application. So, this functionality is built into Sun's `HttpServletRequest` class. In most cases, servlet programmers simply use `HttpServletRequest.getParameter` operations to pick up values entered in forms.

The first example illustrates a simple servlet that handles data entry from a form. The form uses an HTTP get request; it has one data input field. The servlet has a doGet function. This function reads and processes the input from the form. The input is supposed to be a positive number; the servlet returns the square root of that number.

7.2.1 Form and servlet code

The form is defined as a static HTML page:

```
<html><head><title>Form Data Entry Page</title></head>
<body>
<h1 align=center >Fill in some data</h1>
<p>The demo servlet works out square roots, so feed it a number.
<p>
<form method=get action="/demo/sqrtservlet">
  <input type=text name=number>
  <input type=submit>
</form>
</body></html>
```

The servlet class, `SqrtServlet`, is defined as an extension of Sun's `HttpServlet` class:

```
import java.io.*;
import java.util.*;
import javax.servlet.*;
import javax.servlet.http.*;
public class SqrtServlet extends HttpServlet {
  public void doGet (HttpServletRequest request,
    HttpServletResponse response) throws ServletException, IOException
  {
    ...
  }
}
```

The doGet function must extract the string entered in the form's 'number' input field and then try to convert this string to a numeric value. If the string does not represent a number, or if it corresponds to a negative number, the servlet should generate a response page with an error message. If the input data are valid, then they are processed and a results page is generated.

```java
public void doGet (HttpServletRequest request,
  HttpServletResponse response) throws ServletException, IOException
{
  response.setContentType("text.html)
  // Pick up PrintWriter output stream for response
  PrintWriter out = response.getWriter();
  // Generate standard HTML header etc
  out.println("<html>" +
    "<head><title> Square roots </title></head>" );
  out.println("<body >" );

// Pick up name=value bindings for data from form, only
// the one parameter here
String data = request.getParameter("number");
double value = 0;
  // Does string represent a number?
  try { value = Double.parseDouble(data); }
  catch(Exception e) {
    // Error response, non-numeric input
    out.println("<p>Need NUMERIC data.");
    out.println("</body></html>");
    return;
  }
  // Must be non-negative
  if(value<0.0) {
    out.println("You are living in an imaginary world");
    out.println("</body></html>");
    return;
  }
  // Data are valid, process and respond
  value = Math.sqrt(value);
  out.println("Your square root value is " + value);
  out.println("</body></html>");
}
```

The class HttpServletRequest supports a number of functions for getting parameter values with form data. The example code uses the basic getParameter(*name*) function that returns the value (as a String) for the parameter (or null if the parameter is not defined). Multi-valued parameters, such an HTML 'selection' that supports multiple choices, can be obtained using the getParameterValues method; this returns a String[] with the choices as selected in the form. The response object can be asked to return a reference to an associated PrintWriter, as was done in this code, where PrintWriter out was set to allow responses to be written. Response information can be simply written to this stream.

7.2.2 Installation, Compilation, Deployment

The coding for the static web page and the servlet are easy. But before you can run the example, you have to install Tomcat and create appropriate deployment directories.

You should download a version of Tomcat from http://jakarta.apache.org/ tomcat/; typically, the distribution version will come as a gzip compressed tar archive file (or zip archive for a Windows version). The archive should be decompressed to create a Tomcat directory hierarchy at a suitable point in your file system. (Some later examples need to refer to the directory names; in these examples the name 'tomcat' will be used as if it were the full path name of the installation directory). The tomcat directory will be created with the following subdirectories (may differ depending on the version of Tomcat):

- bin

This contains scripts to run Tomcat.

- common/lib

This contains 'jar' archives with the class files for javax.servlet; you will need to include this directory in the classpath that you use when compiling your servlets (more details later). You may need to ass jar files with your database drivers to this directory.

- src

This contains the interface definitions for javax servlet classes.

- conf

This contains configuration files; occasionally it is necessary to change some of the default configuration parameters.

- webapps

This contains the 'web applications'; when first installed, there are a number of examples provided by programmers at Apache. You create your own application subdirectories within this directory.

- docs

This contains HTML documentation concerning the Tomcat system.

- work

This directory (created when needed) is used by the Tomcat system. Its main purpose is to hold temporary files and generated servlets for applications using Java Server Page technology.

The webapps subdirectory will contain

- ROOT

This is the default directory used by the Tomcat system. It contains an index.html with links to information about Tomcat and links to the Apache examples

- examples

This contains examples from apache.org that illustrate aspects of servlets and JSP web applications.

These webapps components will be present initially as .war (web application archive) files; they are expanded to directory hierarchies when the Tomcat server is first run.

It is easiest if you run your own Tomcat server, rather than attempting to learn servlet technology using a server that is also used by other people. There are no problems running Tomcat on an individual Linux, Unix or Windows workstation. If you must use a time-shared Unix system to run individual copies of Tomcat, then there will have to be some scheme for allocating different port numbers to the Tomcats used by different students. Two port numbers must be changed in the tomcat/conf/server.xml configuration file (the 'Connectors' section at the end of the file). Use of a single shared Tomcat system leads to other problems, such as problems over file permissions and with the server itself (sometimes, the server will have to be restarted after a new web application is installed in the webapps directory; this is very inconvenient when many students must share a single server).

When running your own Tomcat server, you will use a Linux/Unix terminal session (or an MS-DOS Command Prompt window on Windows) to control the server. This session is used to issue the commands that start and stop the server. You should check your Tomcat documentation for current settings; usually you need to set some environment variables and then invoke 'start' and 'stop' scripts that launch the server or shut it down. On Unix, you could use something like the following script fragment:

```
# Change to the tomcat directory - substitute full path name for tomcat
cd tomcat
# Define environment variables that specify directory locations
TOMCAT_HOME=`pwd`; export TOMCAT_HOME
# Substitute the correct path for your JDK java system:
JAVA_HOME=/packages/java/jdk/1.4.01; export JAVA_HOME
# Start the server
./bin/startup.sh
```

You should close down your Tomcat when it is no longer needed (./bin/shutdown.sh); if you simply logoff, it may continue running as a background process holding on to port 8080. (Any trace output written by your code, via System.out.println, will be found in Tomcat's log/catalina.out log file.)

The Tomcat server takes a couple of minutes to start up. After this time, you should use a browser to access it at http://localhost:8080. (Sometimes the DNS tables or hosts file may be set up incorrectly and 'localhost' is not defined; if it does not work, try the full hostname of your workstation or the explicit IP address 127.0.0.1. If nothing works, contact your local friendly system administrator.) If Tomcat has been installed correctly, you should be able to explore Apache's documentation for Tomcat and the example servlets from Apache. When you have finished exploration, close your browser and shut down the Tomcat server.

Strictly, an application should be deployed as a .war file. However, Tomcat (and most other servlet containers) allow developers to create the directory structures that are implicit in the .war file and install components directly in these directories. You will need to create a demo directory inside tomcat/webapps; then inside this demo directory, create a file 'formpage.html' with the static HTML web page listed above.

The main directory associated with a web application, tomcat/webapps/demo in this example, must contain a WEB-INF subdirectory. This WEB-INF subdirectory holds:

- web.xml

This file contains a specification of deployment parameters for the web application.

- lib

This optional subdirectory contains any special libraries that may be needed. These libraries will be Java archive files (.jar files). Later examples, such as those in Chapter 9, will illustrate cases where extra libraries are needed. The simple examples do not require extra libraries (except possibly database driver jar files).

- .classes

This subdirectory should contain the .class files for the servlet(s) and helper classes that are defined for a specific web application. The .java source files can be included but are not required. (During development, you would normally include the .java source files; when the application was completed, you would move the source to some other location.)

For this example, you need to create the directories tomcat/webapps/demo/WEB-INF and tomcat/webapps/demo/WEB-INF/classes.

The Java code shown earlier should be created as tomcat/webapps/demo/WEB-INF/ classes/SqrtServlet.java. The javax.servlet classes are not part of the standard Java development libraries, so naive attempts to compile the SqrtServlet.java code will fail. The required javax class definitions are available as the servlet.jar file included in the lib directory of the Tomcat installation. This file must be added to your classpath prior to an attempt at compiling the servlet code. On Unix:

```
# Change to servlet directory
cd tomcat/webapps/demo/WEB-INF/classes
# Add the javax libraries to the class path,
# libraries are in common/lib subdirectory of tomcat directory
# 4 levels up
ls ../../../../common/lib
#Should show a set of jar files including servlet.jar
echo $CLASSPATH
# That shows what you usually have
CLASSPATH=../../../../common/lib/servlet.jar:$CLASSPATH
# That added the servlet stuff to the libraries that are normally used

# Try compilation
javac SqrtServlet.java
```

Finally, you must create the file tomcat/webapps/demo/WEB-INF/web.xml. This should contain the following deployment description:

```
<?xml version="1.0" encoding="ISO-8859-1"?>
<!DOCTYPE web-app
PUBLIC "-//Sun Microsystems, Inc.//DTD Web Application 2.2//EN"
"http://java.sun.com/j2ee/dtds/web-app_2_2.dtd">
<web-app>
  <servlet>
    <servlet-name>myservlet</servlet-name>
    <servlet-class>SqrtServlet</servlet-class>
  </servlet>
  <servlet-mapping>
    <servlet-name>myservlet</servlet-name>
    <url-pattern>/sqrtservlet</url-pattern>
  </servlet-mapping>
</web-app>
```

The first line (<?xml ... ?>) simply identifies this as an XML document. The 'document type' on the following lines provides a reference to the specification for Web Application documents. The application specific data are between the <web-app> start tag and the </web-app> end tag.

In this case, the application data are limited to identification data. The first component, the data in the <servlet> ... </servlet> tag, relate a 'servlet name' to the implementation class. The 'servlet name' is used by the container to identify the servlet (its 'registered name'); the 'servlet class' identifies the Java class that this servlet instantiates. The servlet mapping data relate the servlet's registered name to the (partial) URL(s) that will be used to access it.

A servlet can be associated with more than one URL. In addition to the URL sqrtservlet, it could have a (partial) URL like surprise.html. Such a URL can be useful if a web site had a page that was originally a static HTML page but which evolved into a dynamic servlet generated page; the URL-mapping scheme would allow the old name to be retained, so avoiding the problems with broken links.

After creating all the directories and files, and after having successfully compiled the servlet code, you should restart your Tomcat. Your new web-based 'square-root service' should be available at http://localhost:8080/demo/FormPage.html. Hopefully, it will work.

7.2.3   web.xml deployment files

Really, the web.xml document is fulfilling the same role as a host of environment variables; you could compare it to:

```
SERVLET_NAME=MyServlet; export SERVLET_NAME
SERVLET_CLASS=SqrtServlet; export SERVLET_CLASS
```

But obviously something like the web.xml file is much more convenient. All necessary 'environment' data are packaged together. Later examples will illustrate the use of elements in the XML file that correspond to command line initialization arguments.

A 'web.xml' file can be thought of as being a kind of elaborate data structure – a structure that contains fields. Each field holds either environment data, or initialization data either for the servlet object or for the container that is to run the servlet. Many of these fields will contain lists of substructures, with each substructure itself being constructed from fields and lists. Some of fields in these structures may relate to optional features; these can be empty. If no data are provided, the servlet system works with default values for the corresponding control elements.

Most web applications involve more than one servlet. Consequently, the typical web.xml file packages environment data and initialization data for several different servlets. Such a file will contain a sequence of subsections:

- Servlet(s)

Name, description, class file, initialization parameters (name, value, and description), special load options, 'security roles' and other data.

- Servlet mappings

Servlet name/URL pairs (it is quite acceptable for the same servlet to be registered under different names).

- Security constraints

Details of the servlets to which constraints apply and identification of user groups who have access.

- Controls relating to logging-in for access to restricted servlets.

The web application DOCTYPE file contains a definition of the overall document structure, and the form of each of these subsections. (They are supposed to appear in the order specified in the document type definition file. All servlets should be defined before the servlet mappings; servlet mappings come before security constraints and so forth. The Tomcat component that processes these web.xml files is fairly tolerant of minor errors – it will simply print warnings as it starts up.)

Sun could have chosen to define a structure for these data – something like a CORBA IDL struct or COM structure, or even a Java class. A GUI-based helper program would have been used to enter data to produce a binary file that was loaded and processed by the servlet container. The XML style was chosen because of its greater flexibility. A web.xml file is simply a structured text file with essentially self-describing data. If Sun decides to add new features in the next release of the servlet definition, their controls will appear as extra self-describing text elements in updated web.xml files, and as a new part in the standard document type definition. Current containers, based on the previous definition, will simply ignore any new data that relate to unimplemented extensions.

7.3 Sun's servlet-related classes

Sun's servlet code (as implemented in the GenericServlet and HttpServlet classes) defines the basic life cycle methods along with methods that can be used to obtain information about the servlet, the overall web application (context) and the container. The life cycle of a servlet involves creation, initialization, multiple uses via its service method, and final destruction.

The container creates a servlet when the first request is received for that servlet. (There is a 'load on startup' configuration option that can be used to require the container to instantiate a servlet immediately on server start up. Servlet instantiation can take several seconds, so sometimes it is worth pre-loading servlets to avoid irritating their first users!) After instantiating a new servlet, the container calls its init method. The GenericServlet class defines an empty, no operation init method. You will often want to override this and provide an effective initialization function. The tasks performed in an init function are things like getting parameters and creating instance resources.

For example, it is sometimes appropriate for a (lightly used) servlet to own a connection to a database. This connection would be opened in the init function, closed in the destroy function, and be used (subject to a mutex lock) in some function called from the servlet's doGet or doPost action functions. You might want to have the name and password for the database provided as parameters (rather than have them encoded as strings in the Java source files). Initialization parameters can be part of a web.xml file:

```
<servlet>
  <servlet-name>ServletA</servlet-name>
  <servlet-class>ExampleServlet</servlet-class>
  <init-param>
    <param-name>DBUser</para-name>
    <param-value>HSimpson</param-name>
  </init-param>
  <init-param>
    <param-name>DBPassword</para-name>
    <param-value>Duh</param-name>
  </init-param>
  <load-on-startup/>
</servlet>
```

An initialization function that creates a database connection using the specified name and password obtained from initialization data would be something like the following:

```
...
import java.sql.*;
import javax.servlet.*;
import javax.servlet.http.*;
public class ExampleServlet extends HttpServlet {
  // Some constants
  private static final String dbDriverName = "...";
  private static final String dbURL = "...";
  // The database connection - implicitly shared by
  // concurrent clients (so use own locks!)
```

```
    private Connection theDBConnection;

public void init() throws ServletException{
    // Code to pick up initialization data
    String userName = getInitParameter("DBUser");
    String userPassword = getInitParameter("DBPassword");
    try {
    Class.forName (dbDriverName);
      theDBConnection = DriverManager.getConnection(
        dbURL,
        userName, userPassword);
    }
    catch(Exception e) {
    // Maybe print some trace statements
    // then throw a ServletException
    ...
    }
}
```

Another thing that you might want to do in an init method is allocate a worker thread. Such a thread should not continuously compute – that would drain resources from the servlet container. A suitable use would be something like a thread that worked with a Socket connection to another process that provides some regularly updated data – e.g. a stock price ticker. The extra thread could handle input from that socket and abstract data for a servlet that, on request, displays graphs of recent changes in stock prices.

A destroy method complements an init method. If the init method claims resources, these should be released in the destroy method:

```
public void destroy() {
  if(theDBConnection != null) {
    try {
      theDBConnection.close();
    } catch(Exception e) { }
  }
}
```

If you do create extra threads in an init method, you must remember to stop them in your destroy method. A servlet's destroy method will be called when the server closes down (assuming it is closed down properly) or when a busy container needs to reclaim resources from an idle servlet.

Most of the work of a servlet is done as a result of calls to its service method. You can override the service function itself; but, typically, for a servlet derived from the HttpServlet class you just define one or both of the doGet or doPost methods. Some servlets simply generate dynamic pages in response to HTTP-get requests; these implement only doGet. Other servlets handle input from forms and have only a doPost function.

A very common idiom is for a servlet to use its doGet function to generate a form, and use its doPost function to handle data submitted via that form.

If you have instance data defined for your servlet, you must take account of the multi-threaded nature of a servlet container. One option is to define your servlet class with a restriction that the container limits usage of such a servlet to one thread at a time:

```
public class The_IHateThreads_Servlet extends HttpServlet
   implements SingleThreadModel {
...
}
```

The container treats such a servlet as if it had redefined all its methods as synchronized. The usual way, though, is simply to apply mutex locks (Java synchronization) to just those small code fragments that actually involve use of the instance data (or class data):

```
public class ExampleServlet extends HttpServlet {
...
private Connection theDBConnection;

private void doUpdate(String ID, String Address)
   throws SQLException {
// Client has submitted form that changed contact
// address data for account "ID"
String sqlQuery = "update accounts set Address=? where ID=?";
...
// Claim exclusive use of database connection
synchronized(theDBConnection) {
   PreparedStatement pstmt =
      theDBConnection..prepareStatement(sqlQuery);
   pstmt.setString(1, Address);
   pstmt.setString(2, ID);
   pstmt.executeUpdate();
   ...
   }
...
}
```

If you have instance data like individual int counters, then you will have to use an extra instance data member, of class Object, to provide a mutex lock that you can use when altering the int data member.

There is a ServletConfig object associated with each servlet. Strictly, it is this object that owns data like initialization parameters and a servlet's registered name (the getInitParameter method in the GenericServlet class is simply a convenient short cut – it invokes the real access function in the associated ServletConfig object).

Another important helper object is the ServletContext. There is a ServletContext object for each separate web application (webapps .war file or expanded webapps subdirectory). All the servlets and JSPs that are defined in a web application share the same context object. A servlet can obtain a reference to its ServletContext through the GenericServlet.getServletContext method.

The ServletContext object provides access to information like the server software identifier, and has some utility methods such as one that can identify the MIME type for a file. The context object also supports some rather specialized 'resource' functions which help with file access; it is possible to have a servlet running in a distributed environment where it does not have direct access to all its data files and so cannot simply use standard java.io file manipulations. But a ServletContext's most important role is to help organize communication among the different servlets that make up a web application. Later examples illustrate how a ServletContext can act as a holder of shared data – data that all the servlets in an application may need to read, and one or more may need to update (it may be much more efficient to place such data in the care of the ServletContext instead of having the equivalent data in database tables).

The class javax.servlet.http.HttpServletRequest acts as a wrapper for the HTTP request data. The class defines a large number of methods that can be used to access specific parts of the request data. These access method include:

- Methods returning general data about the request (standard HTTP information):
  - String getRemoteAddr
  - String getRemoteHost
  - String getRemoteUser – relies on use of HTTP authentication
  - String getMethod
  - int getServerPort
  - String getServerName

- Methods returning data that form part of the HTTP request header:
  - Enumeration getHeaderNames
  - String getHeader(String name)
    Ask for any specific HTTP header: e.g. CHARSET ACCEPT
  - Locale getLocale
    Packaged version of Accept-Language header data
  - String getAuthType
    Returns information about form of HTTP authentication (if any) used – BASIC, FORM etc.
  - Cookie[] getCookies
    Returns array with all cookies that arrived with HTTP header. A Cookie object holds a name/value pair along with supplementary data such as domain, path and maximum age in seconds.

- Methods relating to request data:
  - Enumeration getParameterNames
  - String getParameter(String name)
  - String[] getParameterValues(String name)

- String getQueryString
- int getContentLength
- String getContentType
- ServletInputStream getInputStream
  Provides an input stream for reading binary data (e.g. upload of an image)
- BufferedReader getReader
  Provides a reader for text input.

- Methods for passing data between servlets:
  - Object getAttribute(java.lang.String name)
  - void setAttribute(java.lang.String name, java.lang.Object o)

- Method relating to session support:
  - Session getSession()

A servlet should either use the parameter access function (getParameter, getParameter Names, getParameterValues) or the input streams. If you try to mix styles, you will fail.

The typical servlet reads its parameter data and generates a response. But there are other possibilities. These alternatives involve things like forwarding of a partially processed request to another servlet or JSP, or redirection of an entire request to some other resource (static web page or a different servlet). With redirection, the client browser receives an HTTP 'resource moved' response with the identity of the revised location; the browser re-submits the request using the revised URL.

The forwarding of requests is common in servlet–JSP combinations. The servlet will handle the actual HTTP request. This will usually involve extraction of data from a database. The servlet will package the retrieved data as an instance of a simple data carrier class (a 'bean'). This bean can be attached to the request as an extra named attribute. The request can then be forwarded to a JSP where the final response, based on data in the bean, is created.

```
public void doGet (HttpServletRequest request,
HttpServletResponse response) throws ServletException, IOException
{
String myData = request.getParameter("data");
  // Code invoking a work on a database that produces
  // response data packaged in a MyBean object
  MyBean theDBInfo = doWhatever(myData);

  // Attach the bean to the request as a named attribute
request.setAttribute("theData", theDBInfo);
// Get helper object that can forward the request (and
// bean) to next servlet or JSP (defined by a name
// string - jspReportPage)
  RequestDispatcher dispatch =
    request.getRequestDispatcher(jspReportPage);
  // Forward the request
```

```
    dispatch.forward(request, response);
}
```

Examples using forwarding are illustrated in Chapter 8.

If a servlet encounters some problem – bad input data, some mishap with the database – it is going to have to return an error page rather than a dynamic response page. Quite often, the contents of the error page are fixed (just a prettied-up version of a message like '*Sorry, the database is unavailable. Please try later.*'). It is always best to minimize the amount of HTML tags and content text buried in a servlet, so rather than have the error messages handled by the servlet you could simply redirect the request to a static web page:

```
if(dbConnection==null) {
    response.sendRedirect("/demo/NoDB.html");
    return;
}
```

As well as the redirect message (which is sent as a HTTP response with a header section and no content), the HttpServletResponse object can be used to send other header data. Content is added after all headers have been sent; it is written to a stream obtained from the response object (either a binary stream or a PrintWriter text stream). All header data must be sent prior to any content data. The content output is actually buffered; this allows a servlet to generate some content before it finalizes all the header data. If the content buffer is filled, or is explicitly flushed, then headers are sent (if no header data are defined, the system provides a simple header specifying the content type as text/plain). An exception is thrown if a servlet attempts to add data to the header after sending some content data.

The HttpServletResponse class defines (or inherits) a large number of methods including:

- Methods relating to content output streams and buffering:
  - void setBufferSize(int size)
    You can set the buffer size if for some reason the defaults are inappropriate.
  - void flushBuffer
    Forces any content in the buffer to be written to the client.
  - boolean isCommitted
    Returns a boolean indicating whether the response has been 'committed' (i.e. header data have already been finalized and returned to web server and maybe thence to client).
  - ServletOutputStream getOutputStream
    Get OutputStream suitable for binary data.
  - java.io.PrintWriter getWriter
    Get PrintWriter to send textual response.

- Methods for setting header data:
  - void setContentType(java.lang.String type)
    Use to set any content type other than the default text/plain.

- void setContentLength(int len)
- void setLocale(java.util.Locale loc)
  Sets headers such as charset and language
- void addCookie(Cookie cookie)
- void addDateHeader(java.lang.String name, long date)
- void addHeader(java.lang.String name, java.lang.String value)
- void sendError(int sc)
- void sendError(int sc, java.lang.String msg)
- void setStatus(int sc)
  The HttpServletResponse class defines a series of constants (SC_OK, SC_CREATED etc.) that correspond to the standard HTTP response codes.

In addition, there are helper methods like encodeURL(String). The encodeURL method is used if it is necessary to use the URL rewriting approach for maintaining session state (as explained later).

7.4   Web application example: 'Membership'

This web application comprises a servlet, a helper class, static HTML pages and a stylesheet. It provides an illustration of how application-specific issues can be moved into helper classes, leaving the servlet primarily as a control element. Helper classes are often reusable in other Java applications. It is best to minimize the amount of HTML tags and content text that are embedded in Java servlet code; the use of stylesheets can help, as can the use of static pages wherever possible.

   The actual example involves handling of a form that obtains details from an applicant seeking to become a member of a special interest group. Data from the form are processed by the servlet; if the data are incomplete, the servlet prompts for re-submission of input. If the data pass some cursory validation tests, they are recorded in a new member record and a membership number is allocated. The response page that is generated is a simple welcome page, reporting the new member's membership number and providing links to pages with more information about the interest group.

   The application comprises the following:

- InfoPage.html
A static web page with the form for data entry (as an alternative, you could generate this in a doGet method of the servlet).

- NoDB.html
Displayed if encounter errors relating to access to the database ('*Database problems ... please try later*').

- ThisWeek.html, NewMembers.html, ...
Place holders for information pages that would exist in a real version of the application.

- `mystyle.css`

A simple stylesheet used to illustrate the principle of having stylesheets to help reduce HTML coding in the servlet.

- `web.xml`

The inevitable deployment file (still quite a simple one).

- `InfoServlet.java`

This servlet has a doPost function to handle input from the form. It manages a database connection; returns either a success response, or an error page, or a partially filled in form for completion (sent if the data that were initially submitted were incomplete).

- `SubscriberRecord.java`

A 'bean' – a class holding a collection of data fields with 'get' and 'set' access and mutator methods. A SubscriberRecord object is also responsible for getting itself saved to a database table or restored from a table.

- Members and memnum

Two tables in a relational database.

The SubscriberRecord class is the token 'reusable' part of the code. It could be used in other applications, for instance an application that acquired demographic statistics of the members – average age, proportion of males and females etc.

The database usage in this example is simple. The main table, members, records details of members; the only operation on this table is an 'insert' of new data. The table fields are:

- Integer identifier

This identifier (membership number) serves as a primary key.

- Given name, family name, email

Each of these is a varchar(32) text field.

- Sex

varchar(10) (could have database-enforced constraints to verify that only allowed inputs were 'male' or 'female', but these were not specified in the database; instead the checks are done in the code).

- Age

Number(4) (the code applies checks for acceptable inputs).

The second table, memnum, is used to provide unique membership numbers. Many databases support some form of 'auto-increment' number; the database can be asked for the current value, and the value is then automatically incremented. However, this is not a universal feature of databases, and even where it is available there are implementation-specific aspects. So here the task is handled manually. Since lots of applications require sequential numbers – membership numbers, order numbers, transaction identifier numbers etc. – the approach is generalized. The memnum table is intended for general use; it has two fields, the first being an application identifier (a string, field 'fortable') and the second being the numeric value representing the current number. The pseudo-code for getting a number allocated is:

```
select number from memnum where fortable=...;
newval = number+1;
update memnum set number=newval where fortable=...;
```

Ideally, there should be no gaps in the sequence of membership numbers. This means that the processes of allocating a new number and creating a new record in the membership table should form a single atomic step. So in this example, there will be explicit controls on the transaction (Java's JDBC defaults to committing each individual database operation as it is performed).

A memnum data table will have to be created and initialized with one entry (fortable="members", number=0) before the example can be run.

The static HTML infopage uses a form with a tabular layout of input fields for given and family names, age and email address, and a single option selection for sex:

```
<html><head><title>New Subscriber</title></head>
<body bgcolor=white>
<h1 align=center>
Please supply some details for our records.
</h1>
<p>
<form method=post action="/demo/subscriber">
<table align=center border=2>
<caption>Subscriber details</caption>
<tr>
  <th>Given name</th>
  <td><input type=text size=20 maxsize=30 name=GivenName></td>
</tr>
<tr>
  <th>Family name</th>
  <td><input type=text size=20 maxsize=30 name=FamilyName></td>
</tr>
<tr>
  <th>Age (must exceed 17)</th>
  <td><input type=text size=4 maxsize=4 name=Age></td>
</tr>
<tr>
  <th>Sex</th>
  <td>
    <select name=Sex size=1>
      <option selected>Male
      <option>Female
    </select>
```

```
        </td>
     </tr>
     <tr>
       <th>Email</th>
    <td><input type=text size=20 maxsize=30 name=Email></td>
     </tr>
     <tr>
       <td colspan=2 align=center>
       <input type=submit>
       </td>
     </tr>
     </table></form>
     </body></html>
```

The other static HTML pages are all simple.

The servlet redirects a request to the NoDB.html page if there are any database-related problems. If the data entered in the form are incomplete, or fail simple validation tests, the servlet responds with a page that lists details of the data that were not acceptable and a version of the same data entry form with acceptable data pre-loaded into the fields. If the submitted data pass the simple validation tests, the servlet generates a dynamic welcome page.

The page used for unacceptable data has to highlight information, so it needs a variety of HTML tags for setting colors and styles etc. A stylesheet can help in that it can define things like a background and special paragraph styles. If a stylesheet is used, the HTML code in the programs is limited to a single tag identifying the paragraph style to be used, instead of having several tags. The use of a stylesheet also makes it easier for a web designer to update the overall appearance of a page or an entire site. This example uses the illustrative stylesheet:

```
BODY {
background-color: #FFFFFF;
background-image: none;
color: #000000
}
P.Subject1 {
font-size:24pt;
font-family: Arial, Helvetica, Sans-Serif;
text-weight:bold;
color:#ff0000;
text-align:center
}
P.Warn {
font-size:20pt;
font-family: Arial, Helvetica, Sans-Serif;
text-weight:bold;
```

```
color:#ff0000;
text-align:center
}
```

The servlet has the normal methods for a form-handling servlet – init, doPost and destroy. The doPost method utilizes a group of private helper methods. The init method is used to create a database connection; this is released in the destroy method. A servlet to handle membership applications is unlikely to encounter heavy demand; consequently a single database connection is quite adequate. In the very rare circumstances where two or more users attempt to join simultaneously, they will suffer a one or two second delays as their attempts to access the database are serialized by a mutex lock controlling the connection. The use of a persistent database connection allows for faster execution than a system that opened the connection for the duration of each individual request; and provided you are not too limited in the total number of open connections, the use of a persistent connection is going to put less demand on your database system.

The servlet code outline is:

```
import java.io.*;
import java.util.*;
import java.sql.*;
import javax.servlet.*;
import javax.servlet.http.*;

public class InfoServlet extends HttpServlet {
  // Substitute correct data for your database system!
  private static final String userName = "HSimpson";
  private static final String userPassword = "Doh";
  private static final String dbDriverName =
      "oracle.jdbc.driver.OracleDriver";
  private static final String dbURL =
      "jdbc:oracle:thin:@myhost:1521:csci8";
  private Connection dbConnection;

  public void init() {
    try {
      Class.forName (dbDriverName);
      dbConnection = DriverManager.getConnection(
        dbURL,
        userName, userPassword);
      // Change the default auto commit style connection
      // Need to control transaction limits
      dbConnection.setAutoCommit(false);
    }
    catch(Exception e) { }
  }
```

```
      public void destroy() {
        if(dbConnection != null) {
          try {
            dbConnection.close();
          }
          catch(Exception e) { }
        }
      }

      private void sendRetryResponse(HttpServletResponse response,
        SubscriberRecord aRecord)
        throws ServletException, IOException
      {
        // Compose page with error report and new version of form
        ...
      }


      private void sendWelcome(HttpServletResponse response,
        int membernum, String name)
        throws ServletException, IOException
      {
        // Compose page with welcome
      }

      public void doPost (HttpServletRequest request,
        HttpServletResponse response)
        throws ServletException, IOException
      {
        // Process form data and select response
        ...
      }
    }
```

In its doPost method, the servlet creates a SubscriberRecord object and loads it with the data obtained from the form. The SubscriberRecord class implements the limited data integrity checks used in this example. The servlet can ask if the data appear acceptable; all elements will have had to pass their integrity checks for the SubscriberRecord to respond affirmatively. Based on the response, the servlet can use one or other of its response generation functions:

```
public void doPost (HttpServletRequest request,
  HttpServletResponse response) throws ServletException, IOException
{
  // If init step failed, dbConnection is null.
  // Redirect client to the apology page
  if(dbConnection==null) {
```

```
        response.sendRedirect("/demo/NoDB.html");
        return;
        }


    // Create a subscriber record (bean), and set its fields
    // to hold the data supplied by the form
    SubscriberRecord aRecord = new SubscriberRecord();
    aRecord.setGivenName(request.getParameter("GivenName"));
    aRecord.setFamilyName(request.getParameter("FamilyName"));
    aRecord.setAge(request.getParameter("Age"));
    aRecord.setSex(request.getParameter("Sex"));
    aRecord.setEmail(request.getParameter("Email"));

    // Were data acceptable? If not, ask user to re-enter data!
    if(!aRecord.isValid()) {
        sendRetryResponse(response, aRecord);
        return;
        }

    // Try insert into database, if get any failure will receive
    // a -1 response, else get newly allocated membership number
    int membernum = aRecord.createInDatabase(dbConnection);

    if(membernum<1) {
        // Once again, if have database problems, send client
        // to apology page.
        response.sendRedirect("/demo/NoDB.html");
        return;
        }

    // Everything appears to have worked! Welcome the new member.
    sendWelcome(response, membernum, request.getParameter("GivenName"));
    }
```

Ideally, a doPost method should have a simple control flow to determine the form of a response. The generation of the response content should be handled by auxiliary helper functions. Detailed processing of submitted data should either be handled by instances of application specific helper classes, or be located in auxiliary helper functions.

It is worth looking at the helper SubscriberRecord class before examining the code that generates the response pages. A SubscriberRecord is basically a little struct that holds a subscriber's name, age and other data. It has accessor (get) and mutator (set) functions for each data member. It has functions to load and store its data in a database table. The 'set' functions implement the limited data integrity checks – names not too long or too short, an age that is an integer and is in the accepted range 18–99. If data are not acceptable, the corresponding data member is set to null (or zero for the age member).

```java
import java.sql.*;
public class SubscriberRecord {
  // Constants defining acceptable properties of data
  private static final int NAMELENGTH = 30;
  private static final int MINAGE =18;
  private static final int MAXAGE = 99;
  // Data members, matching both form fields and relational
  // database fields
  private String  givenName;
  private String  familyName;
  private String  eMail;
  private int     age;
  private String  sex;
  private int     id;
  public boolean isValid() {
    return
      (givenName != null) &&
        (familyName != null) &&
          (eMail != null) &&
            (sex != null) &&
              ((age>=MINAGE) && (age <= MAXAGE));
  }

  // Similar get and set methods for all String data members
  public String getGivenName() { return givenName; }
  public void setGivenName(String aName) {
    givenName = null;
    if(aName == null) return;
    int len = aName.length();
    if((len<1) || (len > NAMELENGTH)) return;
    givenName = aName;
  }

  public String getFamilyName() { ... }
  public void setFamilyName(String aName) { ... }

  public String getEmail() { ... }
  public void setEmail(String aName) { ... }

  public String getSex() { return sex; }
  public void setSex(String gender) {
    sex = null;
    // Tests work even if gender is null!
    if("Male".equals(gender)) sex = gender;
    else
```

```
      if("Female".equals(gender)) sex = gender;
    }

    public int getAge() { return age; }
    public void setAge(String ageStr) {
      age = 0;
      try {
        int val = Integer.parseInt(ageStr);
        if((val>=MINAGE) && (val <=MAXAGE))
          age = val;
      }
      catch(Exception e) { }
    }

    public boolean loadFromDatabase(int idNumber, Connection db) {
      // Not used in this example; turns up in later example
...
    }

    public int createInDatabase( Connection db) {
      // Create a new record in members table with a membership
      // number obtained from the memnum table
...
    }
}
```

The createInDatabase method has a large try-catch block around all its database code; within this there is a synchronized block so that only a single thread may use the connection. The first part of the code deals with the update of the membership number record; the second part deals with the creation of a new member record. The database connection had auto-commit disabled in the init method; consequently, the first database operation acts as an implicit start transaction, and there is an explicit commit (end transaction) after all operations are performed.

```
    public int createInDatabase( Connection db) {
      int idnumber = -1;
      try {
        synchronized(db) {
          // First, get a new membership number.
          Statement stmt = db.createStatement ();
          String request =
            "select number from memnum where fortable='members'";
          ResultSet rset = stmt.executeQuery(request);
          int value = 0;
          // Should get a result! If not, database is corrupted!
```

```
          if(rset.next()) {
            value = rset.getInt("number");
          }
          else {
            stmt.close();
            return -1;
          }
          value++;
          // Write back updated value
          request = "update memnum set number=" +
              value +
              " where fortable='members'";
          stmt.executeUpdate(request);
          stmt.close();
          // Deal with membership record
          PreparedStatement pstmt = db.prepareStatement(
            "insert into members values( ?, ?, ?, ?, ?, ?)");

          pstmt.setInt(1, value);
          pstmt.setString(2, givenName);
          pstmt.setString(3, familyName);
          pstmt.setString(4, eMail);
          pstmt.setString(5, sex);
          pstmt.setInt(6, age);
          pstmt.executeUpdate();
          idnumber = value;
          db.commit();
        }
      }
      catch (Exception e) {
        db.rollback();
        System.out.println("Exception " + e);
      }
      return idnumber;
    }
```

If the SubscriberRecord is both valid and successfully saved in the database, the servlet should generate a welcome page incorporating the name and membership number of the new member:

```
public class InfoServlet extends HttpServlet {

    ...
    private void sendWelcome(HttpServletResponse response,
      int membernum, String name)
```

```java
        throws ServletException, IOException
{
    response.setContentType("text/html");
    PrintWriter out = response.getWriter();
    out.println("<html>" +
    "<head><title>Welcome " +
        name +
        "</title></head>" );
    out.println("<body bgcolor=white>");
    out.println("<h1 align=center>Welcome</h1>");
    out.println("<font size=+2 color=blue><p align=center>");
    // Small touch of 'personalization' of response!
    out.println(name +
        " : your membership number is " +
        membernum);
    out.println("</font>");
    out.println("<p>Hello " + name);
    out.println("<p>Glad to have you in our group.");
    out.println("Please record your membership number.");
    out.println("<br><h2>Links to useful information<ul>");
    out.println("<li><a href=/demo/NewMembers.html>"+
        "Information for new members</a>");
    out.println("<li><a href=/demo/ThisWeek.html>" +
        "Chat sessions for this week</a>");
    out.println("</ul></body></html>");
}

    ...

}
```

The page generated for erroneous or incomplete input is a bit more complex; it is here that
illustrative use is made of the stylesheet to slightly reduce the number of HTML tags needed.
This response page tries to comply with the rules for good netiquette. Error pages for forms
should indicate what was wrong, should allow entry of missing/incorrect data, should not
require any correct data to be re-entered, and should allow the user to change any previously
entered data. The generated form is initialized with all data that were thought to be valid.
Details of valid and invalid data are obtained from the partly filled in SubscriberRecord.

```java
private void sendRetryResponse(HttpServletResponse response,
    SubscriberRecord aRecord) throws ServletException, IOException
{

    String tempStr = null;
    PrintWriter out = response.getWriter();
    // Output HTML tags for start of page, including link to style
```

```
// sheet; note the need to escape some quotes (need to write a
// string that contains double quote characters)
out.println("<html>" +
  "<head><title>Please re-enter data</title>" +
  "<link rel=stylesheet types=\"text/css\" href=\"mystyle.css\"" +
  "</head>" );
out.println("<h1>You need to resubmit your form</h1>");
// Make use of defined styles
out.println("<p class=Subject1>" +
  "Some of the data that you sent were incomplete or invalid");
out.println("<hr><font color=red><ul><p class=warn>");

// Code that prints a warning for each data element that failed
// validation
if(aRecord.getGivenName() == null)
  out.println("You didn't supply your 'Given name'");

// Similar code checking and reporting any errors in age, email
// or other data fields
...

out.println("</ul></font><hr>");

// Code to generate a form with data filled in wherever possible.
// Start with fixed form HTML tags.
out.println("<p><form method=post action=\"/demo/subscriber\">");
out.println("<table align=center border=2>");
out.println("<caption>Subscriber details</caption>");

// Generate table row with input field for Given Name
out.println("<tr><th>Given name</th>");
out.println("<td><input type=text size=20 maxsize=30");
// If name was entered previously, define it as value of input field
// (it will appear in field when form displays on client browser)
tempStr = aRecord.getGivenName();
if(tempStr != null)
  out.println("value=\"" + tempStr +"\" ");
out.println(" name=GivenName></td></tr>");

// Now get similar code for the other input fields
out.println("<tr><th>Family name</th>");
...
out.println(" name=FamilyName></td></tr>");

out.println("<tr><th>Age (must exceed 17)</th>");
```

```
...
out.println(" name=Age></td></tr>");

out.println("<tr><th>Sex</th>");
out.println("<td><select name=Sex size=1>");
tempStr = aRecord.getSex();
if("Female".equals(tempStr))
  out.println("<option>Male<option selected>Female");
else
  out.println("<option selected>Male<option>Female");
out.println("</select></td></tr>");

out.println("<tr><th>E-mail</th>");
...
out.println(" name=Email></td></tr>");

out.println("<tr><td colspan=2 align=center>");
out.println("<input type=submit>");
out.println("</td></tr></table></form>");


}
```

The partially filled data entry form has to have any seemingly valid data included as value attributes in the input text tags:

```
<input type=text name=GivenName value=??? size=20 maxsize=30>
```

Names can include spaces or strange characters – e.g. O'Toole or Van Gogh. Consequently, it is necessary to put the name within double quotes:

```
<input ... value="Van Gogh" size=20 ... >
```

rather than

```
<input ... value=Van Gogh size=20 ... >
```

It is possible that your helpful user has included double quote characters in the input. If you really want to be safe you should use java.net.URLEncoder.encode() to convert the initializing values to x-www-urlencoded form prior to including them in the returned page.

This web application must still be deployed. It can go in the same tomcat/webapps/demo folder as the square root server. The static HTML files and the stylesheet file would go in the demo folder. The SubscriberRecord.java and InfoServlet.java file would go in the tomcat/webapps/demo/WEB-INF/classes folder. The Java sources would have to be compiled, again taking care to set the classpath to include the servlet.jar file when compiling the servlet code. The database tables would have to be created with a suitable database tool, and an initial entry would have to be created in the memnum table (fortable=members, number=0). Finally, a composite web.xml file would have to be created for the two tomcat/webapps/demo servlets:

```xml
<?xml version="1.0" encoding="ISO-8859-1"?>
<!DOCTYPE web-app
    PUBLIC "-//Sun Microsystems, Inc.//DTD Web Application 2.2//EN"
    "http://java.sun.com/j2ee/dtds/web-app_2_2.dtd">
<web-app>
  <servlet>
    <servlet-name>myservlet</servlet-name>
    <servlet-class>SqrtServlet</servlet-class>
  </servlet>
  <servlet>
    <servlet-name>infoservlet</servlet-name>
    <servlet-class>InfoServlet</servlet-class>
  </servlet>
  <servlet-mapping>
    <servlet-name>myservlet</servlet-name>
    <url-pattern>/sqrtservlet</url-pattern>
  </servlet-mapping>
  <servlet-mapping>
    <servlet-name>infoservlet</servlet-name>
    <url-pattern>/subscriber</url-pattern>
  </servlet-mapping>
</web-app>
```

This web.xml file (placed in tomcat/webapps/demo/WEB-INF) is still quite simple; it just has to identify the two servlets and the URLs that are used to access them.

When all the parts have been installed, the application should run and provide a web service that allows users to join a user group (presumably one for those interested in finding square roots).

Web applications are supposed to be delivered in .war files for easy deployment on other systems. If you are taking a university course using these Java technologies, you will probably be required to submit any web applications that you develop as .war files. You can create a .war file for this application by the following steps (described for Unix; similar steps apply in a Windows environment):

- Change to your tomcat/webapps/demo directory (cd tomcat/webapps/demo).

- Use the jar utility (the Java archiver, which should be in the /bin directory of your JDK system) to create a .war file containing all the HTML files, stylesheet files, and the entire contents of the WEB-INF subdirectory:

```
jar -cf demo.war WEB-INF *.html *.css
```

- Move the resulting .war file to a safe location (this is the file that you might have to submit for an assignment).

- Change directory out of the demo directory, then delete the tomcat/webapps/demo directory and all its contents (rm -rf tomcat/webapps/demo).

- Place the demo.war file back into tomcat/webapps.

Try restarting your Tomcat server; the demo subdirectory should be recreated automatically and the applications should again be available.

7.5 Client state and sessions

It is the same old HTTP protocol underneath. So, servlets face a familiar problem – the protocol is stateless, but the majority of applications require maintenance of state data. The same old hacks must be employed:

- Hidden fields in forms
- HTTP authentication
- Cookies
- URL rewriting

Hidden fields can be used in a servlet-based system in a manner identical to that illustrated with PHP scripts. Servlet-1 would process input from a static form (Form1.html) and generate a dynamic Form2 with the data from Form1 held as hidden fields in the displayed form. Servlet-2 would process the inputs from Form2 and reprocess the inputs originating from Form1. The encoding of the hidden fields would be very similar to that just illustrated with the InfoServlet's 'data re-input' form. This mechanism is viable provided that the application does involve simply a sequence of forms that must be completed in order; but it is rarely preferable – there are too many risks associated with exposure of data to inappropriate inspection and modification.

If you can make your users 'log in' by providing a username and password for HTTP authentication, then you have 'state'. The browser saves the data triple (name, password, URL for the protected 'realm'); the name and password are resubmitted with subsequent requests to the same realm. Your servlet can check the identity of the client submitting a request (HTTPServletRequest. getRemoteUser()). The user's identity can serve as a primary key for database records, so allowing you to maintain the client's state in a server-side database. A servlet can handle HTTP authentication in its own code; if a request arrives with an undefined remote user, the servlet can generate a response with simply a header specifying the need for HTTP style authentication. More typically, a servlet requiring a 'log in' step would use the security controls that are provided as part of the servlet environment and are specified in the web.xml deployment file (use of deployment security is illustrated later). Names and passwords are satisfactory if you have a fixed clientèle for your application – a set of persons to whom you can pre-allocate usernames and passwords. The approach obviously does not suit the typical shopping site accessible to all in cyberspace. (The passwords are also not that secure; risks should be assessed carefully before deploying this approach in a serious application.)

The typical shopping site must rely on cookies or URL rewriting. Cookies are preferred, but given the number of users who disable cookies you may need to rely on URL rewriting, or use both. As discussed in the context of PHP scripting, you can use cookies to hold data or use them simply to hold an identification key for state data held on the server. Cookies should only hold non-critical data: things like the PHP example with a cookie that held details of 'advertisements already seen'. Critical data should not travel repeatedly between client and server and should not be exposed to possible tampering; consequently, most sites will use a cookie that is simply a session key.

The `javax.servlet.http` package defines a `Cookie` class. Cookies are created with a name/value pair. (The value string assigned to a cookie should not contain any characters like newlines, ampersands, question marks, whitespace etc. If you really need such characters in your cookies, then encode with `java.net.URLEncoder` before setting the value, and decode with `java.net.URLDecoder` after extracting a value.) The `Cookie` class has a number of accessor and mutator methods that include:

- `String getName()`
Returns the name of a cookie.

- `String getValue(); void setValue(String newValue)`
Return the current and assign a new value to a cookie.

- `String getDomain(); void setDomain(String pattern)`
Returns/sets the domain name specified for a cookie.

- `String getPath(); void setPath(String uri)`
Returns/sets the path associated with a cookie (so that it is only returned to a subset of the servlets on the server).

- `int getMaxAge(); void setMaxAge(int expiry)`
Returns/sets the maximum age in seconds associated with a cookie (by default, cookies are created as 'transient' with a maximum age of –1; these cookies are automatically deleted from the client when the browser terminates).

As noted earlier, the `javax.servlet.http.HttpServletRequest` class has a `Cookie[]` `getCookies` method to retrieve any returned cookies. The `HttpServletResponse` class has `addCookie` and `setCookie` methods to put cookies in the header portion of a response.

You can create your own session management code based directly on cookies. The code would be analogous to that illustrated for PHP scripting. All the servlets in an application would have to incorporate the same code fragment. This code would check 'get' and 'post' requests for a returned session identification cookie; if a cookie was not found, the code would generate a suitably randomized session identifier, and add it as a cookie to the response header. The session identifier would serve as a primary key for database records.

Of course, you have to allow for clients who disable cookies. You can try insisting that your clients use cookies (if a servlet fails to find a cookie when one was expected, you redirect the client to a static HTML page informing the client that cookies must be enabled). Alternatively, you also support URL rewriting. As in PHP, the URL rewriting approach relies on systematic changes to all links in a returned page. Each link must be rewritten to include your session identifier as a query string (or something similar).

You can build it all for yourself – session key generation, cookie handling code, URL rewriting of HTML links, and a database with the session key as a primary key for records. If you need to perform some very elaborate processing, or need something unusual with your state data, then you might wish to have such detailed control. But most applications do essentially the same session maintenance operations. The 'standard' code for session maintenance is supplied as part of the `javax.servlet.http` package in the form of the `HttpSession` class.

You gain in two ways if you use the `javax.servlet.http.HttpSession` class. First, the `HttpSession` class has methods that implement most of the detailed coding (you still have to take account of the need for possible URL rewriting). Second, a `HttpSession` object is memory resident and its life cycle is managed by the container. It is much more efficient to hold session data in memory rather than access a database (or data file) at each step. If you are managing your own session and a client starts a session but never completes it, you are typically left with orphaned files or database records that need to be removed by some support process. With `HttpSession` objects, the container handles this tidying up. One of the configuration parameters for a web application is a 'session timeout'; the container notes the use of all `HttpSession` objects and will automatically dispose of any that have not been used for a period greater than this session timeout (by default, the timeout is typically 30 minutes).

A servlet can explicitly request creation of a session object, or can ask for a reference to an existing session object; these requests are handled partly by the `HttpServletRequest` and partly by the container. If a servlet requests a session object, one gets created and a cookie with its session identifier is returned in the next response to the client (the client will be asked for permission to set a cookie `JSESSIONID=...`). While cookies are pre-ferred, the system must also deal with URL rewriting. A servlet that uses sessions must employ a helper method in the `HttpServletResponse` class to rewrite all links in the page that it generates. The servlet that actually creates a session will in fact return both a cookie with the session identifier, and a page with the session identifier inserted into to all links (e.g. Tomcat will return a page with HTML tags with like `<form action="/demo2/ servlet2;jsessionid=d341..." ...>`). If a client subsequently returns a JSESSIONID cookie along with a request, or if it requests a resource with a session identifier appended to the resource name, the container will find the corresponding session object and asso-ciate it with the `HttpRequest` that it prepares for the servlet that must handle the client's new request. After the first return of a session identifier, the container knows whether the client supports cookies. If the client is not supporting cookies, the container will not bother to include cookies in subsequent headers and will instead rely on the URL encoding of the session. If the client does support cookies, the `HttpServletResponse` object will treat any subsequent requests to encode links as 'no-ops'.

The `HttpServletRequest` class has the session-related methods:

- `HttpSession getSession()`

Returns a session for this request, creating one if none exists.

- `HttpSession getSession(boolean create)`

If there is a session object associated with the request, it is returned. Otherwise, depending on the value of the `create` argument, either a session object is created or a null is returned.

- `public boolean isRequestedSessionIdFromCookie(); public boolean isRequested SessionIdFromURL()`

These functions let the servlet programmer determine whether cookies or rewritten URLs are being used (rare for a servlet programmer to really need to know this).

The main session-related method in the `HttpServletResponse` class is encode `URL(String aLinkUrl)`. This function appends the session identifier of the current session to the given URL if this is necessary (either we know that the client does not support cookies or we do not yet know the client's behavior).

A session object is a carrier for your application specific state data. It owns a collection object that can hold name/value attribute pairs. You add your data with a `setAttribute` method, and later retrieve data with a `getAttribute` method. Other access methods include one to return the session identifier, one to get a list of all attribute names, and one reporting the time the session was last used.

The following example, illustrating the use of sessions, is essentially a reprise of the PHP shopping cart example. The site has dynamic form pages for selling books, furniture and computers, a purchase page, and a checkout page. All are dynamic; each page corresponds to a servlet. The example also illustrates a customized 'log in' system; sometimes the HTTP authentication system is inappropriate and you will wish to handle 'log ins' for yourself; this code illustrates one approach. The shopping site has become a 'members only' site controlled by a servlet that gets a user to enter a name and user identifier (using the same database and `SubscriberRecord` as in the earlier example). The `LoginServlet` that handles these inputs is the one that creates the session object used by the other servlets in the group; if another servlet encounters a request without an associated session, it redirects the client back to the original login page.

This web application comprises:

- Static HTML pages:
  - `Login.html`
    A simple form with input fields for name and membership number.
  - `NoDB.html`
    Apology page displayed if have problems with database access.
  - `NonMember.html`
    Page displayed if submitted username/membership number combination appears invalid

- Servlets:
  - `LoginServlet`
    This has a `doPost` function to handle data from the `Login.html` form. If login is

successful, it creates the session object that will hold the shared data for the other servlets (primarily, the PurchaseServlet and the CheckoutServlet). The shared data represents the site's 'shopping cart' – here just use a java.util.Vector to hold the product identifier strings.

- BooksServlet, ComputerServlet, FurnitureServlet
  Like the PHP scripts in the PHP version, these servlets are essentially identical. Each has a doGet function that generates a form listing some items that can be purchased. The data in the forms is hard coded where a real implementation would generate the forms using data taken from a database.
- PurchaseServlet
  Handles input from the forms generated by the above servlets; identifiers of selected items are added to the 'shopping cart' vector held by the session object.
- CheckoutServlet
  Simply lists the contents of the shopping cart.

- Auxiliary classes
  - SubscriberRecord
    This is the same class as in the earlier 'membership' example.

- Database
  - Members
    This example uses the members table from the 'membership' example.

- Web.xml
  As usual, there is a deployment file for the application.

A simple vector of strings is an adequate representation of a 'shopping cart' and its contents. Sun's own servlet tutorial site includes the 'Duke's Book Store' example; this has a more functional shopping cart class as well as a 'shopping item' class.

The initial login page is:

```
<html><head><title>On-line Discount Store</title></head>
<body bgcolor=white>
<h1 align=center>Members' Discount Store</h1>
<h2>This is a "members only" discount store</h2>
<hr>
Please supply your name and membership number.
<table align=center border=2>
<form action=/demo2/login method=post>
<tr>
  <th>Given name</th>
  <td><input type=text name=GivenName size=20 maxsize=30></td>
</tr>
<tr>
  <th>Membership #</th>
  <td><input type=text name=Identifier size=6 maxsize=6></td>
```

```
    </tr>
    <tr>
     <td colspan=2 align=center><input type=Submit value=Login>
    </tr>
   </form>
   </table>
   </body></html>
```

The LoginServlet checks data from this form data against data in the members data table from the membership example. It owns a database connection providing access to this table and makes use of the SubscriberRecord class. Its init, and destroy methods handle creation and removal of the database connection; their code is similar to that illustrated earlier. If the user submits a valid username and identifier, the doPost function creates a session object, and uses a helper function to generate a welcome page with links to the shopping servlets. The session key is encoded in the generated links.

```java
import java.io.*;
import java.util.*;
import java.sql.*;
import javax.servlet.*;
import javax.servlet.http.*;

public class LoginServlet extends HttpServlet {
  private static final String userName = "HSimpson";
  ...
  private Connection dbConnection;

  public void init() {
    // Similar to "membership" example
    ...
  }

  public void destroy() { ... }

  public void doPost (HttpServletRequest request,
    HttpServletResponse response) throws ServletException, IOException
  {
    // Check that did get database connection
    if(dbConnection==null) {
      response.sendRedirect("/demo2/NoDB.html");
      return;
    }
    // Pick up form inputs
    String identifier = request.getParameter("Identifier");
    int id = 0;
```

```java
try {
  id = Integer.parseInt(identifier);
}
catch(Exception e) { }
String givenName = request.getParameter("GivenName");

// Create a subscriber record, get it to try to load
// data associated with specified membership number
// (returns false if no such record)
SubscriberRecord aRecord = new SubscriberRecord();

boolean idOK = aRecord.loadFromDatabase(id, dbConnection);

// Validate that record existed and name matches that entered
// If fail, redirect user
if(!idOK || (!givenName.equals(aRecord.getGivenName()))) {
  response.sendRedirect("/demo2/NonMember.html");
  return;
}

// It is ok, create a session object, and welcome user
HttpSession current = request.getSession(true);
sendWelcome(response);
}

private void sendWelcome(HttpServletResponse response)
  throws ServletException, IOException
{
  response.setContentType("text/html");
  // Mostly just static text for welcome page with links
  // Note encodeURL() calls - add session identifier to link
  String deptcode = null;
  PrintWriter out = response.getWriter();
  out.println("<html>" +
  "<head><title>Welcome </title></head>" );
  out.println("<body bgcolor=white><h1>Welcome</h1>");
  out.println("<p>Our departments:<ul>");

  out.print("<li><a href=\"");
  deptcode = response.encodeURL("/demo2/Furniture");
  out.print(deptcode);
  out.println("\">Furniture</a>");

  // Similar links put in for other departments (books,
  // computers)
```

```
    ...
    out.println("</ul></body></html>");
  }
}
```

The BooksServlet, ComputerServlet and FurnitureServlet all implement just a doGet method that generates a form page (when a user clicks an <a href=...> link in a page, the browser sends an HTTP 'get' request for that page). The first step in these doGet methods is a check whether the session object exists (ask for existing object, specifying that none be created); if the session is not defined, then the client is redirected to the login page. All links in generated HTML must continue to be encoded – just in case the user has cookies disabled.

```java
import java.io.*;
import java.util.*;
import javax.servlet.*;
import javax.servlet.http.*;

public class FurnitureServlet extends HttpServlet {

  public void doGet (HttpServletRequest request,
    HttpServletResponse response) throws ServletException, IOException
  {
    // Check for session
    HttpSession current = request.getSession(false);

    if(current==null) {
      // User has tried to skip the login, redirect.
      response.sendRedirect("/demo2/Login.html");
      return;
    }
    // Display HTML form
    sendForm(response);
  }

  private void sendForm(HttpServletResponse response)
    throws ServletException, IOException
  {
    response.setContentType("text/html");
    // The usual, lots of output statements building
    // up an HTML page (it will be easier in JSP)
    String strcode = null;
    String deptcode = null;
    PrintWriter out = response.getWriter();
```

```
out.println("<html><head><title>Furniture</title>");
out.println("</head><body bgcolor=white>");
out.println("<h1 align=center>Buy Furnishings</h1>");
// Where we do have a link, must "encode" it to include
// the session (if needed)
strcode = response.encodeURL("/demo2/Purchase");
out.print("<form action=");
out.print("\"" + strcode + "\"");
out.println(" method=post>");
out.println("<table align=center border=2>");
out.println("<caption>Furniture</caption>");
// Now get lots of rows with checkboxes etc
out.println("<tr>");
  out.println("<td>");
  out.println("<input type=checkbox name=buys ");
  out.println("value=KCHR>");
  out.println("</td>");
  out.println("<td>Ergonomic posture chair.");
  out.println("</td>");
  out.println("<td>");
  out.println("$99");
  out.println("</td>");
out.println("</tr>");
// More of the same
...
...
out.println("<tr>");
  out.println("<td align=center colspan=3>");
  out.println("<input type=submit value=\"Buy Furniture\">");
  out.println("</td>");
out.println("</tr>");
out.println("</table>");
out.println("</form>");
out.println("<br>");
out.println("<hr>");
out.println("<ul>");
// All links must get session encoding ...
deptcode = response.encodeURL("/demo2/Books");
out.print("<li><a href=\"");
out.print(deptcode);
out.println("\">Books</a>");
...

strcode = response.encodeURL("/demo2/Checkout");
out.print("<li><a href=\"");
```

```
      out.print(strcode);
      out.println("\">Checkout</a>");
      out.println("</ul>");
      out.println("</body>");
      out.println("</html>");

   }
}
```

The `PurchaseServlet` has a `doPost` function that uses private auxiliary functions to handle submitted data and the generation of the next page; this page has an acknowledgment of the order and links back to the input selection pages and also on to the final checkout page. The `processOrder` method extracts form data and adds them to the collection owned by the session object.

```
import java.io.*;
import java.util.*;
import javax.servlet.*;
import javax.servlet.http.*;

public class PurchaseServlet extends HttpServlet {

   public void doPost (HttpServletRequest request,
      HttpServletResponse response) throws ServletException, IOException
   {
      // Get existing session object.
      HttpSession current = request.getSession(false);
      if(current==null) {
         response.sendRedirect("/demo2/Login.html");
         return;
      }

      processOrderItems(current, request);

      sendPage(response);
   }

   private void processOrderItems(HttpSession current,
      HttpServletRequest request) throws ServletException
   {
      // Get the "shoppingcart" attribute associated with the session
      Vector v = (Vector) current.getAttribute("shoppingcart");
      // If none exists, this is the first order for this session;
      // create a Vector (the cart)
      if(v==null) v = new Vector();
```

```
    // All inputs will be listed under "buys" (common name for
    // the checkboxes); pick up the entire set with a
    // getParametervalues operation
    String[] items = request.getParameterValues("buys");
    if(items!=null) {
      // Add to the vector
      int len = items.length;
      for(int i=0;i<len;i++)
        v.addElement(items[i]);
      // Vector (new or updated) put back into possession of session
      current.setAttribute("shoppingcart ", v);
    }
  }

  private void sendPage(HttpServletResponse response)
    throws ServletException, IOException
  {
    response.setContentType("text/html");
    // The usual, generate an HTML page with any links encoded
    String strcode = null;
    String deptcode = null;
    PrintWriter out = response.getWriter();

    out.println("<html><head><title>");
    out.println("Continue shopping or checkout</title>");
    out.println("</head><body bgcolor=white>");
    out.println("<h2>Order recorded</h2>");
    out.println("<p>Continue shopping or proceed to checkout.");

    out.println("<ul>");
    deptcode = response.encodeURL("/demo2/Books");
    out.print("<li><a href=\"");
    out.print(deptcode);
    out.println("\">Books</a>");

    ...

    out.print("<li><a href=\"");
    out.print(strcode);
    out.println("\">Checkout</a>");
    out.println("</ul>");
    out.println("</body>");
    out.println("</html>");

  }
}
```

The CheckoutServlet gets invoked when the client follows one of the links in either a products form page or the response page produced by the PurchaseServlet. Its doGet method uses private helper functions to produce a display of the contents of the 'shopping cart' vector.

```java
// The usual imports
...

public class CheckoutServlet extends HttpServlet {

  public void doGet (HttpServletRequest request,
    HttpServletResponse response) throws ServletException, IOException
  {
    HttpSession current = request.getSession(false);
    if(current==null) {
      response.sendRedirect("/demo2/Login.html");
      return;
    }

    listOrderItems(current, response);
  }

  private void listOrderItems(HttpSession current,
    HttpServletResponse response) throws ServletException, IOException
  {
    response.setContentType("text/html");
    PrintWriter out = response.getWriter();
    out.println("<html><head><title>Your order ...</title>");
    out.println("</head><body bgcolor=white>");

    Vector v = (Vector) current.getAttribute("shoppingcart");
    if(v!=null) {
      out.println("<h2>Items in your cart</h2>");
      out.println("<ul>");
      Enumeration e = v.elements();
      while(e.hasMoreElements()) {
        String str = (String) e.nextElement();
        out.print("<li>");
        out.println(str);
      }
      out.println("</ul>");
    }
    else out.println("The shopping cart was empty");
    out.println("</body>");
    out.println("</html>");
  }
}
```

The LoginServlet made use of a SubscriberRecord's ability to load itself from the members data table:

```java
import java.sql.*;

public class SubscriberRecord {
  // As shown for the "members" example


  ...

  public boolean loadFromDatabase(int idNumber, Connection db) {
    // Try to load data for record with key idNumber
    // Clear private data members
    givenName = null;
    familyName = null;
    eMail = null;
    sex = null;
    age = 0;
    id = 0;
    try {
      // Claim exclusive use of database
      synchronized(db) {
        Statement stmt = db.createStatement ();
        String request =
          "select * from members " +
          "where membernumber=" + idNumber;
        // Run the query, if get a result copy data
        ResultSet rset = stmt.executeQuery(request);
        if(rset.next()) {
          givenName = rset.getString("GIVENNAME");
          familyName = rset.getString("FAMILYNAME");
          eMail = rset.getString("EMAIL");
          sex = rset.getString("SEX");
          age = rset.getInt("AGE");
          id = idNumber;
          stmt.close();
          }
        else stmt.close();
        // Database in mode where require explicit commits
        db.commit();
      }
    }
    catch (Exception e) {
      return false;
    }
```

```
        // Return success/failure result
        return id==idNumber;
    }


}
```

The deployment file continues to be quite simple. It identifies the servlets and the URLs that are used when accessing them:

```
<web-app>
  <servlet>
    <servlet-name>loginservlet</servlet-name>
    <servlet-class>LoginServlet</servlet-class>
  </servlet>

  <servlet>
    <servlet-name>booksservlet</servlet-name>
    <servlet-class>BooksServlet</servlet-class>
  </servlet>

  ...

  <servlet-mapping>
    <servlet-name>loginservlet</servlet-name>
    <url-pattern>/login</url-pattern>
  </servlet-mapping>

  <servlet-mapping>
    <servlet-name>booksservlet</servlet-name>
    <url-pattern>/Books</url-pattern>
  </servlet-mapping>

  ...
</web-app>
```

This servlet version has two advantages over the PHP script version of the same site. First, when properly deployed in would be packaged as a single .war file that contains all static pages and the WEB-INF subdirectory with the deployment file and its directory of .class files. This packaging makes the application simpler to move and re-deploy. Second, the memory resident session object is a more efficient representation of the state data than the file that is used with PHP; and, further, the container takes responsibility for any abandoned sessions.

7.6 Images

The PHP 'Big Brother' voting example illustrated how images are often the best way of presenting response data. While the PHP image libraries do seem a little easier to use than their Java counterparts, it is possible for a servlet to return a GIF image (or other format image). Generation of images requires the use of classes that are not in the standard Java libraries. Standard Java awt code can create an image, but the image must be encoded in GIF or JPG format before it can be returned to a client. Image encoders are available from Sun (in the package `com.sun.image.codec.jpeg`) or from `http://www.acme.com/`. The `acme.com` web site has links to a useful library of Java components that includes a GIF encoder.

A servlet can generate an image file as a response by:

- Using the `ServletOutputStream` associated with the response rather than the usual `PrintWriter`. A `ServletOutputStream` supports output of binary data.

- Setting the content-type of the response to `image/gif` (or `image/jpg` as appropriate).

- Using an instance of Java's `BufferedImage` class.

- Getting the associated `Graphics` object.

- Using this `Graphics` object to perform `java.awt` drawing operations.

- Encoding the resulting image.

(You may have problems running graphics examples on a shared Unix server with Xlib graphics; these are essentially configuration problems. At some points, the Java awt code seeks information about the graphics devices available. If none are defined, the image is not generated. The Xlib graphics library relies on an environment variable, `DISPLAY`, referencing an X-server. You should seek help from your system administrator regarding the setting of this environment variable. Java 1.4 awt has some extra functionionality aimed at avoiding such problems.)

The example generates a fixed image purportedly illustrating a histogram of utility usage; its output is illustrated in Figure 7.1. The image is GIF-encoded, using the package `Acme.JPM.Encoders` from `http://www.acme.com/`. The Acme package should be downloaded and installed in the `.classes` directory where the servlet is defined (the package is quite large; you can save space by extracting just the GIF encoder and its support classes and changing the import statements in the example code).

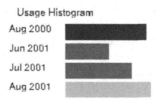

Figure 7.1 A simple graphic image response page from a servlet.

The servlet code is:

```
import java.io.*;
import java.util.*;
import javax.servlet.*;
import javax.servlet.http.*;
import java.awt.*;
import java.awt.image.*;
import Acme.JPM.Encoders.GifEncoder;

public class HistogramServlet extends HttpServlet {

  public void doGet (HttpServletRequest request,
    HttpServletResponse response) throws ServletException, IOException
{
    Graphics g = null;
    try{
      // Pick up output stream for binary data
      ServletOutputStream out = response.getOutputStream();
      // Set the header type to say that we are returning an
      // image (gif encoded)
      response.setContentType("image/gif");
      // Create work space for building image in memory
      BufferedImage bi = new BufferedImage(
        400,600, BufferedImage.TYPE_4BYTE_ABGR);
      // Get the Graphics object that can be used to "draw"
      // in workspace image
      g = bi.getGraphics();
      // Draw ...
      g.setColor(Color.white);
      g.fillRect(0,0,400,600);
      g.setColor(Color.black);
      g.drawString("Usage Histogram", 20,20);

      g.setColor(Color.black);
      g.drawString("Aug 2000", 10, 40);
      g.setColor(Color.blue);
      g.fillRect(80, 30, 100, 20);

      ....
      // When image is complete, get an encoder,
      // In this case, the Acme gif encoder
      // Arguments are image and stream to which will
      // write encoded version
      GifEncoder encoder = new GifEncoder(bi, out);
```

```
        // encode and send to client
        encoder.encode();
    }
    finally {
        // Always remember to tidy up after using a Graphics
        // object.
        if(g!=null) g.dispose();
    }
  }
}
```

7.7 Security features

Servlet containers incorporate security controls that are a limited extension and refinement of HTTP authentication. Restrictions can be placed on servlets; only logged in users can access restricted servlets. The restriction system can even differentiate among different servlet methods – some users might be able to use both get and post (read and update) methods of a servlet, while others might be restricted to get (read) access to the same servlet. Security restrictions are primarily a deployment issue. A servlet can be written and then deployed in different environments with or without security restrictions. However, if a servlet is designed for use with security restrictions, its code can obtain details of the permissions pertaining to the current client; these details are obtained from the servlet container. This allows a servlet to generate dynamic pages with content specifically selected for different classes of users.

Restrictions are not defined for individual users; instead they apply to 'roles' that users may fill. Really, 'roles' are simply the same as user groups in HTTP authentication. In HTTP authentication, users can have individual names and passwords in the password file, while a group file contains a list of 'groups' and the user-identifiers of the members of each group. With servlets, 'roles' replace 'groups'. The password files contain entries for each user; the entries comprise username, password and a list of the roles permitted to that user.

The deployment specification, the web.xml file, contains any restrictions on access to servlets. The restrictions are composed of the following elements:

● Security constraints:
These identify the restricted servlets and methods. Servlets are restricted to users who are acting in specified roles.

● Login configuration:
This element defines how the login process is handled. The choices include use of the normal HTTP authentication dialog, a customized version of the standard dialog, and more elaborate schemes using digests or client authentication certificates.

● Security roles:
These elements simply list the role names that are referenced in the security constraints and in the associated password files.

Browser support for digests and client certificates is limited; usually, the login constraints for servlets are either 'basic' (use the default browser support for HTTP authentication) or 'form' (use a customized version of the HTTP authentication). The form style is preferred because it allows for a site-specific login page that can provide help information along with input fields for a user's name and password.

The example for this section illustrates:

- Form authentication

- Using roles to adapt behavior of servlets

- Using shared data held in an attribute of the servlet's context

The example is a web application that records the times that employees spend on different tasks and calculates pay. The application comprises a number of servlets and associated static HTML pages. There are three classes (roles) of user: 'boss', 'manager' and 'worker'. The application has a simple database with three tables: one table records details of work times (employee identifier, hours, task), another records employee/manager relations (managers can inspect their employees' records), and the third table contains pay rates for different types of task. The servlets are:

- `Hours` servlet

- `Rates` servlet

- `ShowRecord` servlet

Employees in all roles can use the `Hours` servlet; however, its detailed behavior is role-dependent. The `doGet` method displays a form that can be used to enter the hours worked and task type. The task type is chosen from a dynamically generated option list – while there are some overlaps, the types of tasks performed by workers, managers and the boss do vary. The `doPost` method is common to all users; it adds a work record to the work data table.

The `ShowRecord` servlet is similar in that it can be used by all employees, but its behavior is again role-dependent. Employees in the worker role can use this servlet to obtain a display of their own individual records. Managers can see their own records or the records of any employee that they manage. A worker is immediately shown their personal data; a manager is presented with a form in which the name of an employee can be entered. When this name is returned to the servlet, that employee's record will be displayed (if the manager is permitted to see the data).

Only an employee in the boss role can use the final servlet: `Rates`. This servlet can be used to add new task types or change the pay rates associated with existing task types.

In total, the application comprises:

- Static HTML pages:
  - Login page
    Customized login page for entry of name and password (see Figure 7.3 on p. 310).

- Error page
  Users are redirected to this page if the entered name/password combination is invalid.
- Bad data
  Used to display error messages for erroneous inputs.
- No DB
  Used to display error messages if any database operation fails.
- No access
  Error report page for an attempt to view records without authority.

- Servlets and support classes:
  - `RateChangeServlet` – insert or update records in rates data table; also updates an in-memory copy.
  - `WorkerServlet` – record hours worked and task.
  - `CheckRecords` servlet – inspect records of self or subordinate.
  - `DBInfo`
    Helper class for establishing connection with database.
  - `RatesRecord`
    An object that contains an in-memory representation of data held in the main rates data table; held as an attribute of the context and available to all servlets in this application.

- Data tables (illustrated in Figure 7.2):
  - Work
    Fields: name and activity as varchar, hours as double. This holds records of the time an employee spent on a task of a specified type.
  - Manages
    Fields: Employee and manager (both varchar). This holds records identifying employees and their immediate manager.
  - Rates
    Fields: task (varchar) and rate (double). This holds the defined task types and corresponding pay rates.

- Deployment controls
  - `Web.xml`
    'Web app' deployment file with security controls.
  - `tomcat/conf/users.xml`
    File in main Tomcat configuration directory that must be updated with names, passwords and roles of the users of the web application.

There should be a `tomcat-users.xml` file in the `tomcat/conf` directory. The default file contains three records used in the Apache supplied example illustrating security constraints on servlets. Additional entries must be created in this file for user accounts invented for this web application. Each entry consists of a single XML 'user' tag with attributes that define a username, a password and a list of roles permitted to that user. The role names allocated must correspond to those that are defined later in the `web.xml`

Manages

Employee	Manager
Anne	Claire
Susan	Claire
David	Claire
Martin	Samuel
Leila	Samuel
Keith	Samuel
Claire	Colin

Rates

Activity	Rate
Thinking	1.5
Designing	2.5
Documenting	2.5
Coding	4.5
Testing	5
Debugging	7.5
Meetings	20
Sales presentations	30
Customer contact	35
Conference	100
Business lunch	120
Golf	145
Client entertainment	180

Work table

Name	Activity	Hours
Anne	documenting	2
Colin	business lunch	4
Anne	coding	6
Claire	meetings	4
David	coding	2
Anne	thinking	3
Leila	documenting	4
Leila	coding	6
Leila	testing	3

Figure 7.2 Illustrative tables for the time management web application.

deployment file. The updated version of the `tomcat-users.xml` file as used for this example is:

```
<tomcat-users>
  <user name="tomcat" password="tomcat" roles="tomcat" />
  ...
  <user name="Anne" password="7ftGvqm" roles="worker" />
  <user name="Claire" password="Erialc" roles="manager,worker" />
  <user name="Leila" password="s8hhgv45pn" roles="worker" />
  ...
  <user name="Colin" password="Password" roles="boss,manager,worker" />
</tomcat-users>
```

Enter your name and password

Name:	
Password:	
OK	

Figure 7.3 A simple customized form for HTTP authentication.

The default browser-supplied dialog used for HTTP authentication is rarely appropriate. Most companies will wish to customize their login page. The servlet container supports such customization; the customized login page must simply use specified names for fields and return the inputs for processing by a specified action element. The following login form produces the simple login page illustrated in Figure 7.3.

```
<HTML><TITLE>Acme Record's Login</TITLE>
<BODY>
<FORM METHOD=POST ACTION=j_security_check>
<table align=center border=2>
<caption>Enter your name and password</caption>
<TR>
  <TD ALIGN=right><B>Name:</B></TD>
  <TD><INPUT TYPE=TEXT NAME="j_username" VALUE="" SIZE=15></TD>
</TR>
<TR>
  <TD ALIGN=RIGHT><B>Password:</B></TD>
  <TD><INPUT TYPE=PASSWORD NAME="j_password" VALUE="" SIZE=15></TD>
</TR>
<TR>
  <TD COLSPAN=2 Align=CENTER><INPUT TYPE=submit VALUE=" OK "></TD>
</TR>
</TABLE>
</FORM></BODY></HTML>
```

The required names for inputs and form action are highlighted (the names j_security_check etc. reference standard parts of the servlet container). The login page, and an error page that is displayed if the name and password do not match an entry in the tomcat-users.xml file, must be named in the web.xml file. The typical error page informs users that they have entered invalid data, and provides a link that takes them back to the login page.

In this example, each servlet manages a private connection to the database. As usual, a lock controls a connection so that only one thread can use a connection. These servlets all perform their database activities in private auxiliary functions called from their doGet or doPost methods; these auxiliary functions are defined as synchronized – so applying a lock to the entire function that accessed the database.

The DBInfo class is a simple helper class used by the servlets when they need to open database connections. Its real role is to serve as a single point where details like drivers, passwords etc. have to be defined.

```java
import java.sql.*;

public class DBInfo {
  // Substitute appropriate values for your database and drivers
  public static final String userName = "HSimpson";
  public static final String userPassword = "Duh";
  private static final String dbDriverName =
      "sun.jdbc.odbc.JdbcOdbcDriver";
  private static final String dbURL =
      "jdbc:odbc:Acme";
  public static final Connection connectToDatabase() {
    Connection dbConnection = null;
    try {
      Class.forName (dbDriverName);
      dbConnection = DriverManager.getConnection(
        dbURL,
        userName, userPassword);

    }
    catch(Exception e) { }
    return dbConnection;
  }
}
```

The rates data are relatively heavily used. Each request to record work needs to access the rates data (the choices of task type appropriate to show to different employee roles are based on pay rate). The display of work done by an employee also needs to compute overall pay and must access the rate data. This usage makes worthwhile the use of an in-memory copy of the rates data.

The class RatesRecord is instantiated to provide an in-memory version of the rates data. It owns a Hashtable that maps String task names to Double values that hold pay rates. Its constructor loads the necessary data from the corresponding table in the database.

```java
import java.util.*;
import java.sql.*;

public class RatesRecord {
  private Hashtable rates = new Hashtable();

  public Enumeration keys() { return rates.keys(); }
```

```
      public double getRate(String task) {
        double rate = 0.0;
        try {
          Double data = (Double) rates.get(task);
          rate = data.doubleValue();
        }
        catch (Exception e) { }
        return rate;
      }

      public RatesRecord() {
        loadTable();
      }

      private void loadTable() {
        Connection db = DBInfo.connectToDatabase();
        if(db != null) {
         try {
          Statement stmt =
            db.createStatement ();
          String request =
              "select * from rates";
          ResultSet rset = stmt.executeQuery(request);

          while(rset.next()) {
            String key = rset.getString("ACTIVITY");
            double val = rset.getDouble("RATE");
            Double dval = new Double(val);
            rates.put(key,dval);
          }
          stmt.close();
          db.close();
         }
         catch(Exception e) { }
        }
      }
    }
```

A RatesRecord object is placed in the ServletContext as its RatesTable attribute.
Each servlet in this web application accesses the same ServletContext; if it needs the pay
rates data, a servlet asks for this RatesTable attribute. If this attribute is null, the
requesting servlet instantiates a RatesRecord and places it in the ServletContext; the
new RatesRecord loads the most recent data from the database. Once loaded, the record is
available for subsequent use by the same servlet, or any other servlet in the application.

The RateChangeServlet implements both doGet and doPost methods. Its doGet method creates a simple form that the boss can use to enter task names and pay rates. The doPost method handles input with a new task and rate, or input with a new rate for an existing task. The servlet owns a database connection, used to update the rates table; this is obtained, using the helper DBInfo class, in the init function and released in the destroy function. There is only one boss, so mutex locks did not appear necessary for this database connection!

```java
import java.io.*;
import java.util.*;
import javax.servlet.*;
import javax.servlet.http.*;
import java.sql.*;
import java.security.*;

public class RateChangeServlet extends HttpServlet {

    private Connection dbConnection;
    public void init() {
      dbConnection = DBInfo.connectToDatabase();
    }

    public void destroy() {
      if(dbConnection != null) {
        try {
          dbConnection.close();
        }
        catch(Exception e) { }
      }
    }

    private boolean updateActivity(String activity, double newRate)
    {
      // Update database
      ...
    }

    private boolean addActivity(String activity, double rate)
    {
      // Insert new record into database
      ...
    }

    public void doPost (HttpServletRequest request,
HttpServletResponse response) throws ServletException, IOException
```

```
   {
    ...
   }

   public void doGet (HttpServletRequest request,
HttpServletResponse response) throws ServletException, IOException
   {
    ...
   }
 }
```

The page generated by the doGet function is fixed; it could equally well have been handled as a static HTML page.

```
public void doGet (HttpServletRequest request,
  HttpServletResponse response) throws ServletException, IOException
{
  response.setContentType("text/html");
  PrintWriter out = response.getWriter();
  out.println("<html><head><title>Change hourly rate</title></head>" );
  out.println("<body bgcolor=white>" );
  out.println("<form action=\"/combo/Rates\" method=post>");
  out.println("<table align=center border=2>");
  out.println("<tr><th>Activity</th><td>");
  out.println("<input type=text name=Activity size=20 maxsize=32>");
  out.println("</td></tr>");
  out.println("<tr><th>Hourly rate ($)</th>");
  out.println("<td><input type=text name=Rate size=5 maxsize=5></td>");
  out.println("</tr>");
  out.println("<tr>");
  out.println("<td colspan=2 align=center>");
  out.println("<input type=Submit value=\"Submit Change\">");
  out.println("</tr></table>");
  out.println("</form></body></html>");
}
```

The doPost method must check the input data; if either input is missing, or the rate data cannot be interpreted as a numeric value, the user is redirected to an error report page. The existing rates record is checked to determine whether the data relate to a new type of task or represent a change to an existing pay rate; appropriate auxiliary functions are called to perform the database insert or database update operation that is required. The response page merely acknowledges the update. The code destroys any existing RatesRecord in the ServletContext; the next servlet to need rates data will load a new version with the updated information.

```
public void doPost (HttpServletRequest request,
```

```java
        HttpServletResponse response) throws ServletException, IOException
{
  // Pick up form data
  String activity = request.getParameter("Activity");
  String rate = request.getParameter("Rate");
  // Perform limited validation of submitted data
  if((activity==null) || (rate==null) ||
      (activity.equals("")) || (rate.equals(""))) {
    response.sendRedirect("/combo/BadData.html");
    return;
  }
  double drate = 0.0;
  try {
    drate = Double.parseDouble(rate);
  }
  catch(Exception e) {
    response.sendRedirect("/combo/BadData.html");
    return;
  }
  // Need to check against existing records; obtain
  // the RatesTable from the shared ServletContext
  ServletContext ctx = getServletContext();
  RatesRecord rates = (RatesRecord) ctx.getAttribute("RatesTable");
  if(rates==null) {
    // Must be first user, create a record to hold data
    // as already in database
    rates = new RatesRecord();
    ctx.setAttribute("RatesTable", rates);
  }
  // Get existing rate; if 0, it's a new record
  double dcurrent = rates.getRate(activity);
  boolean ok = true;
  // Invoke insert or update operation on database
  if(dcurrent==0.0)
    ok = addActivity(activity, drate);
  else
  if(dcurrent != drate)
    ok = updateActivity(activity, drate);

  // Remove rates table from context - that will force next servlet
  // to load an updated copy
  ctx.removeAttribute("RatesTable");
  // Warn user if there were database problems
  if(!ok) {
    response.sendRedirect("/combo/NoDB.html");
```

```
        return;
    }
    response.setContentType("text/html");
    // Report that all is well
    PrintWriter out = response.getWriter();
    out.println("<html><head><title>Change recorded</title></head>");
    out.println("<body bgcolor=white>");
    out.println("<h2>Update performed</h2>");
    out.println("<p>The table of hourly pay rates has been updated");
    out.println("</body></html>");
}
```

The auxiliary addActivity and updateActivity methods perform straightforward database operations (these methods could be made synchronized if there was a possibility of concurrent use).

```
private boolean updateActivity(String activity, double newRate)
{
  try {
    Statement stmt = dbConnection.createStatement ();
    String insertcommand =
      "update rates set rate = " +
      newRate +
      " where activity='" + activity + "'";
    stmt.executeUpdate(insertcommand);
    stmt.close();
  }
  catch(Exception e) { return false; }
  return true;
}

private boolean addActivity(String activity, double rate)
{
  try {
    Statement stmt = dbConnection.createStatement ();
    String insertcommand =
      "insert into rates values (";
    insertcommand = insertcommand + "'" + activity + "', ";
    insertcommand = insertcommand + rate + ")";
    stmt.executeUpdate(insertcommand);
    stmt.close();
  }
  catch(Exception e) { return false; }
  return true;
}
```

The WorkerServlet has the same overall structure – init and destroy methods for managing a database connection, a doGet function that generates a form, and a doPost function that, with the help of auxiliary functions, handles input from the form. The behavior is slightly more interesting as the content of the form now depends on the role taken by the client.

```java
import java.io.*;
import java.util.*;
import javax.servlet.*;
import javax.servlet.http.*;
import java.sql.*;
import java.security.*;

public class WorkerServlet extends HttpServlet {
  private Connection dbConnection;
  public void init() { ... }
  public void destroy() { ... }

  synchronized private boolean recordWork(
    String name, String activity, double hours)
  {
    // Update Work data table
    ...
  }

  public void doPost (HttpServletRequest request,
    HttpServletResponse response) throws ServletException, IOException
  {
    ...
  }

  private void showOptions(HttpServletRequest req, PrintWriter out)
  {
    // Generate the options for a select box.
    // Options are task names from rates table; the choice
    // of tasks is role dependent.
    ...
  }

  public void doGet (HttpServletRequest request,
    HttpServletResponse response) throws ServletException, IOException
  {
    response.setContentType("text/html");
    PrintWriter out = response.getWriter();
    out.println("<html><head><title>Record Work</title></head>" );
```

```
        out.println("<body bgcolor=white>" );
        out.println("<form action=\"/combo/Hours\" method=post>");
        out.println("<table align=center border=2>");
        out.println("<tr><th>Hours worked</th><td>");
        out.println("<input type=text name=Hours size=5 maxsize=5>");
        out.println("</td></tr>");
        out.println("<tr><th>Activity</th>");
        out.println("<td><select name=Activity size=1>");
        showOptions(request, out);
        out.println("</select></td></tr>");
        out.println("<tr>");
        out.println("<td colspan=2 align=center>");
        out.println("<input type=Submit value=\"Submit Record\">");
        out.println("</tr></table>");
        out.println("</form></body></html>");
    }
}
```

The data entry form has a field for input of hours worked, and a selection that displays a list of options for task types. These options are created in the auxiliary showOption method. This obtains information about the user's role from the HttpServletRequest object and details of pay rates from the RatesRecord in the ServletContext (creating this RatesRecord if none exists). The options are selected based on a combination of role and rate data.

```
private void showOptions(HttpServletRequest req, PrintWriter out)
{
  // Get pay rate data from RatesRecord in ServletContext
  ServletContext ctx = getServletContext();
  RatesRecord rates = (RatesRecord) ctx.getAttribute("RatesTable");
  if(rates==null) {
    // Create if first user
    rates = new RatesRecord();
    ctx.setAttribute("RatesTable", rates);
  }
  double low = 0.0;
  double high = Double.MAX_VALUE;
  // Will list options for all tasks in pay low to high, setting
  // these limits according to role of user.
  // (Could make limit values into initialization parameters, this
  // would ease task of dealing with effects of rate changes)
  if(req.isUserInRole("boss"))
    low = 25.0;
  else
  if(req.isUserInRole("manager")) {
    low = 5.0;
```

```
    high = 30.0;
  }
  else high = 5;
  // Read rate data from RatesRecord, generate option lines
  // as needed.
  Enumeration activities = rates.keys();
  while(activities.hasMoreElements()) {
    String activity = (String) activities.nextElement();
    double dval =rates.getRate(activity);
    if((dval<low) || (dval>high)) continue;
    out.print("<option ");
    out.print("value=\"" + activity +"\">");
    out.println(activity);
  }
}
```

The doPost method has the usual structure – read the submitted data, validate (redirecting the user to the error page if the data are invalid), using an auxiliary function to handle database operations, and finally generating a response page. The submitted form data have to be supplemented with the user identity, as recorded when the user logged in to this protected servlet.

```
public void doPost (HttpServletRequest request,
  HttpServletResponse response) throws ServletException, IOException
{
  // Read, validate inputs - redirect user if have problems
  String activity = request.getParameter("Activity");
  String time = request.getParameter("Hours");
  if((activity==null) || (time==null) ||
      (activity.equals("")) || (time.equals(""))) {
    response.sendRedirect("/combo/BadData.html");
    return;
  }
  double dtime = 0.0;
  try {
    dtime = Double.parseDouble(time);
  }
  catch(Exception e) {
    response.sendRedirect("/combo/BadData.html");
    return;
  }
  // Pick up name of user
  String name = request.getRemoteUser();
  if(!recordWork(name, activity, dtime)) {
    response.sendRedirect("/combo/NoDB.html");
```

```
    return;
    }
// All went well, report success
response.setContentType("text/html");
PrintWriter out = response.getWriter();
out.println("<html><head><title>Work recorded</title></head>");
out.println("<body bgcolor=white>");
out.print(name +" spent " + dtime + " hourse working on " +
  activity);
out.println("</body></html>");
}
```

The example code gets the username via the getRemoteUser() method of the request object. This approach is semi-obsolescent; the preferred interface is now the HttpServletRequest. getUserPrincipal() method. However, in some tests run with this example, getUserPrincipal returned incorrect data (the call occasionally returned the identity of the previous user, rather than the current user). This bug may have been fixed in the version of the Tomcat system that you use, allowing you to change the code to use the preferred interface.

The recordWork method, synchronized to prevent use by multiple threads, does a simple update of the work data table:

```
synchronized private boolean recordWork(
  String name, String activity, double hours)
{
  try {
    Statement stmt = dbConnection.createStatement ();
    String insertcommand =
      "insert into Work values (";
    insertcommand = insertcommand + "'" + name + "', ";
    insertcommand = insertcommand + "'" + activity + "', ";
    insertcommand = insertcommand + hours + ")";
    stmt.executeUpdate(insertcommand);
    stmt.close();
  }
  catch(Exception e) { return false; }
  return true;
}
```

The final servlet in the group, the CheckServlet, again exhibits role dependent behavior. Its doGet method will invoke an auxiliary reporting routine for a client who is in the worker role; if the client is a manager, the doGet function displays a form for entry of an employee name. This servlet once again has a database connection, created in the init method and cleared up in the destroy method; this is used to read data from the work and manager tables. The servlet again needs to identify the remote user both when generating a report for a worker and when checking manager/employee relationships. The RatesTable held by the ServletContext is accessed when generating reports.

```java
import java.io.*;
... // The usual imports

public class CheckRecords extends HttpServlet {
  private Connection dbConnection;
  public void init() { ... }
  public void destroy() { ... }

  public void doGet (HttpServletRequest request,
    HttpServletResponse response) throws ServletException, IOException
  {
    if(request.isUserInRole("manager"))
      generatePrompt(response);
    else
      generateReport(request.getRemoteUser(), response);

  }

  public void doPost (HttpServletRequest request,
    HttpServletResponse response) throws ServletException, IOException
  {
    ...
  }

  private void generatePrompt(HttpServletResponse response)
    throws ServletException, IOException
  {
    // Send HTML form for entry of employee name
    ...
  }

  synchronized public void generateReport(String name,
    HttpServletResponse response) throws ServletException, IOException
  {
    // Select, then print details, of all records in the Work
    // table relating to specified name
    ...
  }

  synchronized private String getManager(String person)
  {
    // Accesses Manager table to find manager for
```

```
        // specified employee
        ...
    }

}
```

The form page for entry of an employee's name is fixed; an alternative way of getting this to the client would have been redirection to a static HTML page.

```
private void generatePrompt(HttpServletResponse response)
    throws ServletException, IOException
{
    response.setContentType("text/html");
    PrintWriter out = response.getWriter();
    out.println("<html><head><title>Check records</title></head>" );
    out.println("<body bgcolor=white>" );
    out.println("<form action=\"/combo/ShowRecord\" method=post>");
    out.println("<table align=center border=2>");
    out.println("<tr><th>Employee's name</th>");
    out.println("<td><input type=text name=ENAME size=20 maxsize=32>
        </td>");
    out.println("</tr>");
    out.println("<td colspan=2 align=center>");
    out.println("<input type=Submit value=\"Submit Request\">");
    out.println("</tr></table>");
    out.println("</form></body></html>");
}
```

The doPost function must confirm that it received a name as input, redirecting the user if there was no data. A work report can be generated if the entered employee name is the same as the username (it is a manager reading his or her own work records). In other cases, the servlet must first confirm that the user really is a manager and then determine whether he/she manages the named employee.

```
public void doPost (HttpServletRequest request,
    HttpServletResponse response) throws ServletException, IOException
{
    String person = request.getParameter("ENAME");
    if((person==null) || (person.equals(""))) {
        response.sendRedirect("/combo/BadData.html");
        return;
    }
    String client = request.getRemoteUser();
    if(client.equals(person)) {
        // Manager reads own records
        generateReport(client,response);
```

```
        return;
    }
    // Confirm that user is a manager (if not, send them an access
    // denied error page)
    if(!request.isUserInRole("manager")) {
      response.sendRedirect("/combo/NoAccess.html");
      return;
    }

    // Find manager of employee named in form
    String mm = getManager(person);
    // Is the user that manager?
    if(!client.equals(mm)) {
      // No, and since managers can't look at other records of
      // employees they don't manage must deny access
      response.sendRedirect("/combo/NoAccess.html");
      return;
    }
    // All is well, generate work report
    generateReport(person,response);
}
```

The getManager function involves a simple database query:

```
synchronized private String getManager(String person)
{
  String manager=null;
  try {
    Statement stmt = dbConnection.createStatement ();
    String selectcommand =
      "Select * from Manages where EMPLOYEE='" + person + "'";
    ResultSet rset = stmt.executeQuery(selectcommand );
    if(rset.next()) {
      manager = rset.getString("Manager");
    }
    stmt.close();
  }
  catch(Exception e) { }
  return manager;
}
```

The synchronization lock prevents multiple threads trying to use the database connection simultaneously.

The reporting function generates the final response page with the list of recorded work items from the works table and an estimate of pay now due. Synchronization is again used to limit access to one thread at a time. The calculation of total pay requires access to the RatesRecord held by the ServletContext. The body of the function is a big try-catch block; any errors involving the database result in the client being diverted to the standard apology page.

```java
synchronized public void generateReport(String name,
  HttpServletResponse response) throws ServletException, IOException
{
  try {
    response.setContentType("text/html");
    // Generate header for work report response page
    PrintWriter out = response.getWriter();
    out.println("<html><head><title>Check records</title></head>" );
    out.println("<body bgcolor=white>" );
    out.println("<h1 align=center>Records for " + name + "</h1><p>");
    int count = 0;
    double total= 0.0;
    // Pick up record with details of pay rates
    ServletContext ctx = getServletContext();
    RatesRecord rates = (RatesRecord) ctx.getAttribute("RatesTable");
    if(rates==null) {
      rates = new RatesRecord();
      ctx.setAttribute("RatesTable", rates);
    }

    Statement stmt = dbConnection.createStatement ();
    String selectsql =
      "Select * from Work where NAME='" + name + "'";

    ResultSet rset = stmt.executeQuery(selectsql);
    // Generate a table with work records (there may be none)
    while(rset.next()) {
      if(count==0) {
        // Output table header on first time
        out.println("<table align=center border=2>");
        out.println("<caption>Recorded work</caption>");
        out.println("<tr><th align=center>Activity</th>");
        out.println("<th align=center>Hours</th>");
        out.println("<th align=center>Amount</th>");
        out.println("</tr>");
      }
      count++;
      // Grab data from result set
      String key = rset.getString("activity");
      double val = rset.getDouble("hours");
```

```
                  // Lookup rate in RatesTable
                  double rate = rates.getRate(key);
                  double amount = val*rate;
                  // Output line of HTML table
                  out.println("<tr><td align=right>"+ key + "</td>");
                  out.println("<td align=right>"+val+"</td>");
                  out.println("<td align=right>$"+amount+"</td>");
                  out.println("</tr>");

                  total+=amount;
              }
              stmt.close();
              // Final outputs, total earnings ...
              if(count==0) out.println("No work records available");
              else out.println("</table><p>Total earnings $"+total);
              out.println("</body></html>");
          }
        catch(Exception e) {
          response.sendRedirect("/combo/NoDB.html");
          }
      }
```

The web.xml file is a little more complex in this case. As usual, the file must define the servlets and their URLs; in this example, the class names, registered servlet names and URLs all happen to be distinct. The additional security control data consists of a 'security constraint' section for each controlled servlet (actually, each URL – so you could have different security constraints applying to the same servlet that depend on how the name under which it is accessed), a single login record, and a set of role names corresponding to the worker, manager and boss roles. The login record specifies the mechanism (BASIC for using HTTP default authentication, FORM if using the custom version); if the FORM style is specified, the login record must also identify the form page and the error page. 'Security role' records simply name the roles.

```
    <web-app>
      <servlet>
        <servlet-name>
          HoursServlet
        </servlet-name>
        <servlet-class>
          WorkerServlet
        </servlet-class>
      </servlet>

      <servlet>
        <servlet-name>
```

```
      RatesServlet
    </servlet-name>
    <servlet-class>
      RateChangeServlet
    </servlet-class>
  </servlet>

  ...

  <servlet-mapping>
    <servlet-name>
      HoursServlet
    </servlet-name>
    <url-pattern>
      Hours
    </url-pattern>
  </servlet-mapping>

  <security-constraint>
    Constraint data for /ShowRecord URL
    ...
  </security-constraint>

  <security-constraint>
    Constraint data for /Rates URL
    ...
  </security-constraint>

  <security-constraint>
    Constraint data for /Hours URL
    ...
  </security-constraint>

  <login-config>
    <auth-method>
      FORM
    </auth-method>
    <form-login-config>
      <form-login-page>
        /loginpage.html
      </form-login-page>
      <form-error-page>
        /errorpage.html
      </form-error-page>
    </form-login-config>
  </login-config>
```

```
        <security-role>
          <role-name>
            worker
          </role-name>
        </security-role>
        <security-role>
          <role-name>
            manager
          </role-name>
        </security-role>
        <security-role>
          <role-name>
            boss
          </role-name>
        </security-role>

    </web-app>
```

A security constraint consists of one (or more) 'web resource collection' and an associated 'authorization constraint'. A web resource collection is basically a set of URLs and a list of HTTP methods; it must also contain a name (which does not serve any real purpose except maybe to help document things). An authorization constraint is basically a set of role names. The entry for the Rates service, which can only be utilized by clients in the boss role, is:

```
<security-constraint>
  <web-resource-collection>
    <web-resource-name>
      AcmeCompany
    </web-resource-name>
    <url-pattern>
      /Rates
    </url-pattern>
    <http-method>
      GET
    </http-method>
    <http-method>
      POST
    </http-method>
  </web-resource-collection>
  <auth-constraint>
    <role-name>
      boss
    </role-name>
  </auth-constraint>
</security-constraint>
```

The other two services have similar security constraint records, except that they specify the worker role in their authorization constraints.

Exercises

Practical

These exercises require a servlet engine. The Apache Tomcat engine, run in standalone mode, is probably the most suitable. This is available as a compressed (Windows .exe or .zip, or Unix/Linux tar-gzip) file for download from http://jakarta.apache.org/tomcat/. The file can be decompressed and will install a version of Tomcat on your machine. The system includes extensive documentation and examples. Applications should be prepared in some private directory and copied into Tomcat's webapps directory when ready; apart from installing your applications, the only other changes that you may need to make are to files in Tomcat's .config directory. This directory holds the usernames and passwords file, and other control files.

It is preferable to have each student run his or her own Tomcat server. If students are using a single time-shared system, a scheme will be required so that each uses a different port number for the server (rather than have conflicts over the single 8080 port).

If you are using a database driver other than Sun's jdbc.odbc driver, you must install a jar file with driver classes. It is simplest if you place this in the common/lib directory of your Tomcat system. (With Oracle for example, you would take a copy of Oracle's classes12.zip file that is used to distribute the drivers and place a copy, named oracle.jar, in the common/lib directory.)

The exercises suggested for PHP can of course be re-implemented using servlets.

(1) Tomcat installation
This exercise simply checks out your Tomcat, using the 'square root servlet' example from the chapter. Some details of the instructions (like fragments of shell script) pertain to Unix/Linux, but it is quite easy to adapt the exercise to a Windows environment (using batch files and a command prompt window).

(a) Decompress the downloaded file (here assumed to be jakarta-tomcat-4.1.18.tar.gz).

```
gunzip jakarta-tomcat-4.1.18.tar.gz
tar -xf jakarta-tomcat-4.1.18.tar
```

(b) Rename its directory (this step is not necessary if you like typing long names).

```
mv jakarta-tomcat-3.3.1 tom
```

(c) Change to your tom directory and create an executable file with contents something like the following:

```
TOMCAT_HOME=`pwd`; export TOMCAT_HOME
```

```
JAVA_HOME=/packages/java/jdk/1.4.1; export JAVA_HOME
./bin/startup.sh
echo "REMEMBER TO PUT OUT YOUR TOMCAT BEFORE YOU GO TO BED"
```

Save this as waketom; make it executable (chmod +x).

(d) Now wake your tomcat:

```
waketom
```

(Keep this terminal session or 'command prompt' window separate so that you can continue to control your tomcat server.)

(e) Start a browser; visit your favorite pages, then go to

```
http://localhost:8080
```

Your tomcat should respond (don't go directly to your tomcat pages; the tomcat server is pretty slow starting up!).

(f) On first acquaintance, follow link to servlet examples supplied by apache.org. Explore these examples and also the links to the documentation on the servlet classes.

(g) In another terminal window, cd to your tom/webapps directory, and make a demo subdirectory. In demo create a WEB-INF subdirectory, and in WEB-INF create a classes subdirectory.

(h) In tom/demo create a file formpage.html with content similar to the chapter example (shown here for convenience):

```
<html>
<head><title>Form Data Entry Page</title></head>
<body bgcolor=white>
<hr>
<h1 align=center >
Fill in some data
</h1>
<p>
The demo servlet works out square roots, so feed it a number.
<p>
<form method=get action="/demo/sqrtservlet">
<input type=text name=number>
<input type=submit>
</form>
</body>
</html>
```

and chmod this file to allow global read permission.

(i) Try to view your page from you web browser:

```
http://localhost:8080/demo/formpage.html
```

It appears that this file isn't there. This is because Tomcat looks at its `web-apps` directory on start up, and only deals out stuff that was there when it started.

Put your tomcat to rest (in the window where you started tomcat, do `bin/shutdown.sh`).

Wake a new tomcat (keep this terminal session separate so that you can continue to control your tomcat).

Try viewing your page; it should be there this time.

(j) In `tom/demo/WEB-INF` create a file `web.xml` with content such as:

```xml
<?xml version="1.0" encoding="ISO-8859-1"?>
<!DOCTYPE web-app
PUBLIC "-//Sun Microsystems, Inc.//DTD Web Application 2.2//EN"
"http://java.sun.com/j2ee/dtds/web-app_2_2.dtd">
<web-app>
  <servlet>
    <servlet-name>servlet2</servlet-name>
    <servlet-class>SqrtServlet</servlet-class>
  </servlet>
  <servlet-mapping>
    <servlet-name>servlet2</servlet-name>
    <url-pattern>/sqrtservlet</url-pattern>
  </servlet-mapping>
</web-app>
```

(k) In `tom331/demo/WEB-INF/classes` create a file `SqrtServlet.java` with content like:

```java
import java.io.*;
import java.util.*;
import javax.servlet.*;
import javax.servlet.http.*;
public class SqrtServlet extends HttpServlet {
public void doGet (HttpServletRequest request,
HttpServletResponse response)
throws ServletException, IOException
{
response.setContentType("text/html");
PrintWriter out = response.getWriter();
    out.println("<html>" +
      "<head><title> Square roots </title></head>" );
    out.println("<body >" );
    String data = request.getParameter("number");
    double value = 0;
```

```
        try {
          value = Double.parseDouble(data);
        }
        catch(Exception e) {
          out.println("<p>Need NUMERIC data.");
          out.println("</body></html>");
          return;
        }
        if(value<0.0) {
          out.println("You are living in an imaginary world");
          out.println("</body></html>");
          return;
        }
        value = Math.sqrt(value);
        out.println("Your square root value is " + value);
        out.println("</body></html>");
      }
    }
```

(l) Compile your SqrtServlet.java file. There is a small problem here; you need javax.servlet and javax.servlet.http. These packages are not included in the standard Java release, so you have to modify your classpath so that it includes the necessary files.

The files that you want are in a .jar archive in your tom/lib. You can devise a scheme for setting the classpath using the absolute pathname of this lib directory, or you can use a scheme that defines the file location relative to the .classes directory where your application code is located. The following illustrates a mechanism using relative pathnames:

```
#.classes is below WebInf, which is below demo, which is below webapps
#which is below Tomcat's main install directory that contains
#the common/lib subdirectory; so go up 4-levels than down into lib
ls ../../../../common/lib
#That should have listed a set of jar files including servlet.jar
echo $CLASSPATH
#That shows what you usually have
CLASSPATH=../../../../common/lib/servlet.jar:$CLASSPATH
#That added the servlet stuff to the libraries that you use
```

Now you can try

```
javac SqrtServlet.java
```

It should compile without errors.

(m) Try entering a number in the form that is still in your browser window from step (i). It won't work: it says there is no demo/servlet2. Remember, Tomcat works with the stuff that was there when it woke up. Your servlet wasn't there then.

Put down the tomcat. Reincarnate it.

(n) When your server is ready, again try to access formpage.html and use this form to submit a request for the servlet to find the square root of a number. You should get a meaningful response.

The main example for this chapter is a slightly larger exercise involving a number of separate servlets, some session data and some application data, some database tables, and some static HTML pages that together make up a 'web application'. Naturally, the exercise involves database access and security roles for users.

(2) The JavaJunk shop

This is another little web-fronted shop that allows users to place orders, and that keeps records of its activities in tables in a database. This particular web shop sells gift items with the Java logo to the insanely rich with no better use for their money. The product range is defined by data in a database table; details of available products and prices are presented via a servlet-generated form. Clients can place orders; these orders are recorded in a Session attribute (memory-resident) data structure. Administrators may monitor activities and perform tasks such as defining a temporary discount on a range of products, or requiring that warehouse records data be extracted from sales records and saved in another database table.

The web application implementing the shop has:

- A database table with data on its products:

```
create table JavaProducts (
   id             varchar(16),
   description    varchar(64) not null,
   price          number(8,2),
   constraint     jp_pk primary key(id)
);
```

- Another database table that is used to record sales.

Sales records define the total number of items and total value of sales for each different distinct product sold on a given day (or part of a day).

Discounts may have been applied for part of a sales period, so the value of the sales may be less than that expected based on the list price for the items.

Normally, sales records are added on a daily basis, but can be processed more often.

These records contain date, product code, number and value; one of your servlets creates these records.

- A static 'login' HTML page and a static 'error on login' HTML page. These are the only static HTML pages used in this application (some of the servlets are registered with names like 'xxx.html' and so may appear to clients as if they were HTML pages).

- Servlets used by customers.

- Servlets used by administrative staff of the shop.

- Some 'application' data shared by all the servlets in the web application (these data represent the records in the JavaProducts data table, supplemented with additional data such as temporary discounts that can be used to promote sales of specific items).

- Session data that hold information supplied by customers.

Customer view

A customer should use the URL http://*hostname:port*/JavaShop.html. The servlet generated response page is an order form for the various products available from the JavaJunk store. This form should appear something like the following example:

Welcome to the Java Store

Our current product range

Description	Unit cost	Number required	Comments
Java Logo Laptop Briefcase	$59.95	0	Buy me!
Java Logo Leather Jacket	$300.00	1	Buy me!
Sun Logo Cross Morph Pen	$54.95	0	Discounted by 10%
Java Logo Rubber Coaster Mug	$14.95	0	Buy me!
Sun Logo Latte Mug	$8.95	0	Discounted by 5%
Sun Logo Denim Shirt	$42.95	0	Buy me!
Java Logo Bean Bag Chair	$72.00	0	Buy me!
Java Logo T-Shirt	$15.95	0	Buy me!
Duke Puppet	$6.60	4	Buy me!
Java Logo Sandwich Cap	$12.95	0	Buy me!

For each product a description is shown, together with a price, an entry field that allows the customer to specify the number of units required for that item, and a comment field that will contain promotional information such as current discount rates.

The form also includes a submit button.

The data submitted in the form are checked by the receiving servlet. If all product counts are zero (or are invalid, e.g. given as negative amounts), the original order form is redisplayed. If at least one item has been ordered, a second form page is displayed that allows the customer to enter name and address data. This second form page should appear similar to the following example:

Complete Order

Please enter your details

Your name	nabg
Your address	Sitacs

Complete Order

When this form is submitted, the customer receives a final page with details of the order placed:

Checkout from the Java Store

The results

Customer name :	nabg
Customer address :	Sitaos
1 of Java Logo Leather Jacket @ $300.00	$300.00
2 of Duke Puppet @ $6.60	$13.20
Total cost	$313.20

Administrators' view

Those administrating the JavaJunk shopping site must have usernames and passwords defined in Tomcat's control file, and must be capable of acting in the role 'Admin'.

The initial page returned to an administrator client displays a form that allows an administrator to select processing options (which are handled by one or more servlets):

- *View products*: submission of a 'view products' request results in a simple page with a tabular view of product codes, product descriptions, prices, and comment fields.

- *Change discount*: this option results in a form where the administrator can enter a product code and discount percentage.

- *View orders*: this results in a page with a tabular view of the orders that have been placed since the last database update.

- *Save orders*: this selection should result in a simple page acknowledging that the database records have been saved.

The discount percentage rates that an administrator may enter must be positive non-zero integral values less than or equal to 25. A request to change the discount percentage rate is checked; a simple error response page is returned if either the product code is invalid or the requested discount rate is unacceptable. If the rate change is accepted, a response page is generated confirming the change; this page contains product code, description and the previous discount rate if this was non-zero.

A listing of orders will show the item code, number of items ordered, and customer details; it should appear something like the figure at the top of the page opposite.

When the administrator chooses to save data, these data records are coalesced and the details with product codes, total number sold, total value of sales and a date are saved as new records in the database. For example, if different customers have ordered 1, 3, 6, 2 and 1 instances of the Duke puppet, then a single record is added to the database specifying the code for the puppet, the total of 13 sold, the total sales price and the date.

The memory-based records of sales are cleared once the records have been written to the database. (Details of customers are not saved in this exercise.)

All response pages for administrators' option requests will contain a link that returns the administrator to the initial choice page.

Java Store : Current Orders

Item code	Number required	Sale value	Customer details
JWear0023	1	$300.00	Charles Mason; 3 Cliff Road, Town
JGift0005	1	$49.46	Charles Mason; 3 Cliff Road, Town
JWear0017	1	$42.95	Charles Mason; 3 Cliff Road, Town
JGift0010	1	$59.95	Dianna Moors; 3 Station Road, Town
JWear0033	1	$204.25	Dianna Moors; 3 Station Road, Town
JGift0005	3	$148.36	Dennis Smith; 24 Bomba Street, Town.
JGift0001	6	$39.60	Dennis Smith; 24 Bomba Street, Town.
JGift0001	2	$13.20	Marilyn Armstrong,;
JWear0023	1	$300.00	Thomas Hook; 4 Canal Road, Town.
JGift0004	6	$89.70	Thomas Hook; 4 Canal Road, Town.
JWear0014	1	$12.95	Jane Mowa; 2/17 Church Street, Town
JGift0022	1	$54.95	Jane Mowa; 2/17 Church Street, Town
JWear0016	1	$15.95	Kazimir Otthot; 7 Lourdes Lane, Town
JWear0033	1	$204.25	Kazimir Otthot; 7 Lourdes Lane, Town
JGift0003	2	$17.00	Chemya Valdens; 6 Harbor Drive, Town
JGift0001	2	$13.20	Chemya Valdens; 6 Harbor Drive, Town

Application and session data

The application data consist of an object that owns a collection of product details, and an object that owns a collection with details of recent orders.

The object that owns the product details is created by the first servlet that needs it. It creates the initial product details objects by loading data from the database. The product details objects contain all the information in the JavaProducts table together with an extra field for a discount rate. The collection object and the individual product details objects are used extensively by all servlets.

The records of items that have been ordered are held in another collection object belonging to the application as a whole. This gets created by the first servlet that needs it.

These collection objects are not simply instances of java.util Collection classes; they are instances of application specific classes with defined behaviors. They use java.util collections. Their member functions manage the collection, provide access to product details objects etc.

Customer usage of the system is session-based. The system will place a session identification cookie on the client browser (optionally, you can also write the code for the URL rewriting scheme that supports clients who refuse cookies). A session object is used to hold details of the products ordered while the system is obtaining name and address data from the customer.

Database

The database has just the two tables, one of which you must define. You should add appropriate constraints so that the database itself does some validation.

Database connections are open only for short times. At startup, a database connection is opened, the product data are loaded, and the connection is closed. Each time an administrator saves the current memory records, a database connection should be opened, used to write all the new data records, and then be closed.

Servlets and 'beans'

You must create the appropriate servlets and all the extra beans and other helper classes required by the application. You must compose the web.xml deployment file with the necessary security constraints defined.

'Get' methods of servlets create the HTML pages with the forms; 'post' methods of the servlets handle input data and generate response pages (which may be forms that are posted to other servlets).

.war file

When your application is working, you are to package it as a deployable .war file: JavaJunk.war. (Use the jar archive tool: simply name the output file as a .war file instead of the normal .jar type.)

Short answer questions

(1) Explain how 'user roles' can be defined and used to restrict access to servlets and servlet methods, or can change the operation of those methods.

(2) A web application comprising several servlets and, possibly, JSPs can arrange for data to be kept in memory and shared among all components. How?

(3) As well as accessing shared web application data as described in your answer to the last question, a servlet can obtain input from initialization parameters, data submitted via 'get' or 'post' HTTP requests, and from other servlets that have performed preprocessing steps. Explain each of these mechanisms.

Explorations

(1) Tomcat is the 'reference' implementation of a servlet engine and is readily available and easy to install. However, there are several other servlet engines available, each claiming particular advantages. Research the claimed merits and market shares of these different engines, and write a short report that provides a comparative evaluation of the products.

(2) The latest specification for servlets has enhanced support for 'filters' that can be used to modify requests and responses. Research these filters and write a short report on their role and their use.

8

JSP: Java Server Pages

Java Server Pages (JSPs) are an extension to Java servlet technology; behind the scenes, JSPs are actually servlets. The difference is one of style; servlets are characteristically 'programs', while JSPs are closer to 'markup' documents. A JSP can deal with all aspects of request processing and response generation; but more typically, these activities are distributed over different server-side components with the JSP part focusing on the generation of a response page once the necessary data have been obtained. Thus, JSPs really represent a move toward 'separation of responsibilities'. A web application will often comprise servlets that organize overall control flow, helper classes ('beans') that incorporate application logic, and JSPs that create response pages.

JSPs will contain 'code'. They may resemble PHP scripts with 'Java scriptlet' code fragments embedded among HTML tags and content text. However, they can (and usually do) take an alternative form that uses specialized markup tags. These special tags act as parameterized templates from which a support system can generate actual code. The tag-based style is more attuned to the procedures that must be used to produce attractive, elaborate web pages.

This chapter starts with a general overview of JSPs. The next two sections use simple illustrative examples to convey general ideas of JSP structures. The various elements that are possible in a JSP are then reviewed. The next section offers a more realistic example that combines servlets for control, helper ('bean') classes for application logic, and JSPs for display. The final section provides an introduction to the mechanisms that underlie the 'tag' style of JSP programming.

8.1 JSP overview

Sun had expected that servlets would replace CGI and become the dominant server-side technology. This just did not happen. CGI–Perl combinations continued in wide-scale use; where this technology was replaced the move was usually to Microsoft's Active Server Page (ASP) technology or to PHP. Although limited to the Microsoft IIS server, use of ASP grew rapidly. PHP came from nowhere and easily outgrew servlets in number of sites, if not importance of sites.

One advantage of both ASP and PHP is that, if done well, these technologies can largely separate logic coding and HTML display coding. The servlet style, with HTML tags and content embedded in code e.g. `out.println( "<body bgcolor=#3333ff ...><h1>...</h1>...")`, greatly limits the ability of a 'web designer' to adapt and change page layouts.

The use of stylesheets can give the web designer some limited control over the appearance of pages; but really, those long functions with their numerous `out.println(...)` statements just don't seem the right way to handle generation of the actual response page.

Sun introduced Java Server Pages as a response to this partial failure of servlet technology. A JSP is an HTML document with embedded 'directives', 'actions' and 'scriptlets'. An interpreter, in the web server, processes JSPs before they are returned to the client. This processing of a JSP yields a final, pure HTML document for display by the client browser. 'Directives' in the original JSP provide control information for the system that interprets the JSPs. 'Actions' and 'scriptlets' are essentially code; they define how data can be processed, ultimately to yield dynamically generated strings that get embedded in the final HTML text. Actions resemble HTML tags with many attributes. They are tiny parameterized code templates; the attributes used in an action tag are slotted into predefined Java statements. Scriptlets are comment-like tags enclosing Java statements (they look rather like JavaScript tags that contain code that is to be interpreted on the client browser).

JSP is a servlet-based technology. A JSP is actually 'compiled' into a servlet before it is used. The HTML tags and content text from the page get buried in `out.write(...)` statements in the automatically generated servlet. The actions and scriptlets expand into Java code that is embedded within the automatically generated code produced by this 'compilation' process. But this code-like nature of a JSP is not apparent in its source text. A JSP appears to be an HTML document, devoted to defining layout and content text, with just a few unusual tags appearing among the normal HTML tags. A web designer can use any of the popular web page editing tools to manipulate JSPs; working with the editing tools, a designer can produce visually impressive pages. One of the main aims of the JSP technology is this improved support for these data presentation aspects.

You can work entirely using JSPs. Your creative artist builds the basic JSP in a web page editor. Your programmer adds the action tags and scriptlet code tags to generate the dynamic content. Your creative artist can re-edit and refine the page, without damaging the embedded code. The resulting page can then be interpreted. Such a page can do anything that a standard servlet can do: grab form data from parameters, process these data, access databases and produce tabular reports.

A secondary aim of the JSP technology is the partial automation of source code creation. You don't write a complete servlet; you simply insert a few scriptlets among your HTML tags and the system does the majority of the coding. When a JSP is first used, the server (Tomcat or equivalent) passes the JSP file to a subordinate process that expands the JSP file into a definition of a servlet (as a `.java` source file), and then compiles this servlet. The new servlet is then loaded into the servlet container and used to service the client's request.

Simple JSPs can be complete in themselves – HTML tags, content text and little fragments of code in either action tag or scriptlet form. But of course, when the tasks that must be performed grow more complex, the code elements tend to expand and may dominate the page text. Just as with servlets, where ideally the servlet delegates work to helper classes, it is best to keep the JSP simple by delegating work to helper objects. For example, consider a JSP that must accept data from a form, verify the data, transfer the data to a database table, and finally generate an acknowledgment. Such a JSP would normally employ an instance of a helper class. The code in the JSP would create this helper object, transfer the form data into data members of the helper object, ask the helper object to perform the necessary interactions with the database, and finally ask the helper object for some strings with the data that are to form the response.

The use of instances of arbitrary helper classes by a JSP will tend to limit the JSP system's ability to auto-generate code. However, JSPs use instances of helper classes in a small number of quite stereotyped ways. It is possible to take advantage of this stereotyped usage and design helper classes so that the JSP system can continue to generate much of the code. Most of a JSP's use of a helper object involves putting data into the object (setting its data members), or extracting data from the object (getting its data members). If helper classes follow the rules for 'JavaBeans', then their mutator (set) methods, and accessor (get) methods will have standardized names and argument lists. The system that is used to auto-generate code can use Java reflection to obtain details of the methods of a helper class and, provided the naming conventions are followed, can generate much of the code interactions between the JSP component and its helper objects.

While you can work purely with JSP and helper 'bean' classes, it is often better to combine servlets written by professional programmers with JSPs composed by web designers. Typically, data entered in a form must pass through a series of validation steps, then some decision logic must be applied to determine the exact processing required. The actual processing may be elaborate, involving database access, iteration through retrieved records, and so forth. Often, a lot of code is needed for these decision processes. Such code fits better in a conventional programming structure, like servlet classes and helper classes, rather than in action tags and code fragments scattered inside some HTML document.

A servlet can be written to receive the client's request and sort out how it is to be handled. The servlet can create instances of helper bean classes that actually perform the business logic and get to hold the resulting data. Once the processing is complete, you will end up with some beans, instances of simple data carrying classes, whose contents needs to be shown in a response page. The servlet can forward the beans to a JSP component. The JSP component can then obtain data from the beans and embed these data in an elaborate, visually pleasing page.

Since JSPs are really servlets, they must run in a servlet container. Tomcat is again the most appropriate container, at least while learning the technology. The deployment of JSPs on Tomcat is similar to the deployment of servlets (maybe just a little bit simpler). A complete JSP web application, e.g. `jspdemo`, will normally comprise some JSPs, static HTML pages, and possibly supporting servlet and bean classes. Such an application should be packaged as a `jspdemo.war` file and installed in the `webapps` directory of your Tomcat server. When developing a new web application, it is again more convenient to work with the expanded directory form, and so use a `webapps/jspdemo` directory. This directory would hold the JSPs and static HTML pages; it would normally have a `WEB-INF` subdirectory containing a `web.xml` deployment file, libraries and a classes subdirectory for any supporting servlets and bean classes (servlets generated from the JSPs are created in subdirectories of the `tomcat/work` directory). If you are using helper bean classes and/ or supporting servlets, you must compile these Java files before you attempt to use any JSP that depends on them. Really simple JSP systems sometimes manage without the `WEB-INF` subdirectory and its contents.

There are a couple of minor things to note before using JSPs with Tomcat. First, you must remember that a lot of work has to be done the first time a JSP is used by a client; the system must generate a new servlet, compile the new servlet, and load the servlet and supporting bean classes into the servlet container. This takes time; your computer has not died, it is just busy. Once the servlet is loaded into the container, the performance becomes somewhat more acceptable. Second, the tomcat/work directory needs to be manually cleaned out on a regular basis; it contains a detailed history of all your failed and forgotten JSPs and their corresponding servlets.

8.2   The 'Guru' – a JSP example

'Hello World' programs are too hackneyed! This first JSP example is a kind of 'fortune cookie' program – clients can request advice from the 'Guru' who will reply with a randomly chosen statement of advice, or a comment on the ways of the world. The Guru system is comprised of a JSP, Advice.jsp, and a helper Guru class. The JSP uses scriptlet style code to create a Guru and ask its advice. The example relies on default parameters applying to JSPs, and so hides quite a number of details that will have to be exposed in later more realistic examples. Unfortunately, some coding details vary with the version of Tomcat that is utilized. The code shown first is for a Tomcat 1.3 system. Tomcat 1.4 introduces a couple of complications, as explained later.

The example should be constructed in a jspdemo subdirectory of your tomcat/webapps directory. This directory will be used to hold the Advice.jsp file, and a WEB-INF subdirectory. The WEB-INF subdirectory has a classes subdirectory; the Guru.java file is installed in this classes subdirectory. This simple example does not require a web.xml deployment file.

8.2.1   The scriptlet Guru

The Advice.jsp file contains the following:

```
<html><head><title>The Guru</title></head>
<body bgcolor=white>
<h1 align=center><font color=red>
Today's advice from the Guru
</font></h1>
<% Guru theGuru = new Guru(); %>
<p>
<%= theGuru.enlightenMe() %>
</body></html>
```

The two highlighted lines are embedded scriptlet code. The first creates an instance of the Guru class; the second invokes the enlightenMe method of the new Guru object. The first scriptlet results in code in the generated servlet but nothing in the final resulting HTML page. The second scriptlet (actually, an 'expression'), within the <%= ... %> tags, is to return a string – the resulting string is embedded in the final HTML page.

The Guru class has the definition:

```
import java.util.Random;
public class Guru {
  private static Random rr;
  private static final String[ ] Sayings = {
    "Women like silent men. They think they're listening.",
    "When a man brings his wife flowers for no reason, there's a reason.",
    ...
    "Rich bachelors should be heavily taxed. It is not fair that " +
    "some men should be happier than others."
  };
  public String enlightenMe() {
    int select = rr.nextInt(Sayings.length);
    return Sayings[select];
  }
  {
    rr = new Random();
  }
}
```

The Guru class owns a random number generator. This is used to select an entry from a collection of aphorisms (contributed by Oscar Wilde and others). The enlightenMe method returns the next randomly chosen saying.

After you have installed and test run your version of the Guru service (http://localhost:8080/jspdemo/Advice.jsp), you will be able to find the generated servlet in your tomcat/work directory. The code will be similar to that shown below. The generated servlet will have a complex name incorporating the name of the JSP. This servlet is a subclass of org.apache.jasper.runtime.HttpJspBase which itself is a subclass of the normal HttpServlet class. The class may have a static initializer block and a couple of other methods defined, but its main method is a _jspService method that gets invoked instead of the normal HttpServlet's service method. This _jspService method contains standard template code, along with out.write statements for the JSP's HTML and content text, and inserts of code fragments for any action tags or scriptlets.

```
import javax.servlet.*;
import javax.servlet.http.*;
import javax.servlet.jsp.*;
import javax.servlet.jsp.tagext.*;
import java.io.PrintWriter;
import java.io.IOException;
import java.io.FileInputStream;
import java.io.ObjectInputStream;
import java.util.Vector;
import org.apache.jasper.runtime.*;
```

```
import java.beans.*;
import org.apache.jasper.JasperException;
public class _0002fAdvice_0002ejspAdvice_jsp_0 extends HttpJspBase {
  static { }
  public _0002fAdvice_0002ejspAdvice_jsp_0( ) { }
  private static boolean _jspx_inited = false;
  public final void _jspx_init() throws JasperException { }
  public void _jspService(HttpServletRequest request,
    HttpServletResponse response)
      throws IOException, ServletException
  {
    ...
  }
}
```

A _jspService method is basically a big try–catch block; the code to generate the response page is inside the body of the try:

```
public void _jspService(HttpServletRequest request,H
  HttpServletResponse response) throws ...
{
  JspFactory _jspxFactory = null; PageContext pageContext = null;
  HttpSession session = null;
  ServletContext application = null; ServletConfig config = null;
  JspWriter out = null; Object page = this; String _value = null;
  try {
    ...
  } catch (Exception ex) {
    if (out.getBufferSize() != 0) out.clearBuffer();
    pageContext.handlePageException(ex);
  } finally {
    out.flush();
    _jspxFactory.releasePageContext(pageContext);
  }
}
```

The body of the try block starts with a lot of initialization statements that get references to the ServletContext and ServletConfig objects, set to the response type to text/html etc:

```
if (_jspx_inited == false) { _jspx_init(); _jspx_inited = true; }
_jspxFactory = JspFactory.getDefaultFactory();
response.setContentType("text/html;charset=8859_1");
pageContext = _jspxFactory.getPageContext(this, request, response,
    "", true, 8192, true);
application = pageContext.getServletContext();
```

```
config = pageContext.getServletConfig();
session = pageContext.getSession();
out = pageContext.getOut();
```

Eventually, you will find the statements generated from the JSP. Each is tagged with a comment that identifies the source page, line and column numbers of the text that was translated to produce a specific Java statement.

```
// HTML // begin [file="/.../webapps/jspdemo/
Advice.jsp";from=(0,0);to=(4,0)]
out.write("<html><head><title>Test JSP</title></head>\r\n<body
bgcolor=white>\r\n<h1 align=center><font color=red>Today's advice from
the Guru</font></h1>\r\n\r\n");
// end
// begin [file...from=(4,2);to=(4,30)]
Guru theGuru = new Guru();
// end
// HTML // begin ...
out.write("\r\n<p>\r\n");
// end, begin etc.
out.print( theGuru.enlightenMe() );
// etc.
out.write("\r\n</body>\r\n</html>\r\n");
```

As explained earlier, HTML tags and content text are simply embedded in out.write or out.print statements; ordinary scriptlet code is copied unchanged; expressions using the <%= ... %> tags are converted into calls to out.print. (Java programmers often feel that a tag like <%= theGuru.englightenMe() %> should be written as <%= theGuru.englightenMe(); %>, i.e. as a complete Java statement. This is wrong. When the text gets embedded in an out.print(...), a statement with a terminating semicolon will cause a syntax error.)

Tomcat 1.4 has made things slightly more complex. The generated servlet class is now declared as being a part of the org.apache.jsp package. This has the side effect of preventing the use of classes that are not themselves parts of packages – like a simple Guru class defined in the WEB-INF/classes subdirectory. With Tomcat 1.4, the Guru class must be defined as part of a package, e.g. package/mystuff, and be located in directory WEB-INF/classes/mystuff. Further, the Advice.jsp page must explicitly import the class using a directive of the form <%@ page import="mystuff.Guru" %> at the start of the page. (This change in Tomcat 1.4 will break numerous examples in web tutorials and textbooks; but the fix isn't hard if you know what to do.)

8.2.2 The tagged Guru

A small modification to the Guru class would allow the JSP code to use action tags rather than scriptlet code. The revised JSP is:

```
<html><head><title>The Guru</title></head>
<body bgcolor=white>
<h1 align=center><font color=red>
Today's advice from the Guru
</font></h1>
<p>
<jsp:useBean id="theGuru" class="Guru" />
<jsp:getProperty name="theGuru" property="enlightenment" />
</body></html>
```

Action tags are grouped in tag libraries. The 'jsp' tag library is an intrinsic part of the JSP system; other tag libraries can be added if desired. Each tag in a tag library is associated with a parameterized code template; the attributes associated with the tag in the JSP get slotted into this code template. Here, two jsp tags are used. The first tag, the jsp:useBean tag, creates an object; attributes like those shown can name the object (giving an identifier for use in scriptlet code) and specify its class (there is also a scope attribute, its use will be illustrated in later examples). The second tag, jsp:getProperty, is associated with code that uses an accessor function to read data from an object (and, if necessary, invokes a toString method on the returned data element). The attributes for the getProperty tag are the name of the object and the name of the required property. (Note how the attributes' names exhibit slight inconsistencies – 'id' versus 'name'.)

Use of the jsp:getProperty tag requires that the class of the helper object (class Guru) have an interface that complies with the JavaBeans coding conventions. Accessor functions should have names of the form getX(), here getEnlightenment(). The jsp:getProperty tag uses the matching name *enlightenment* (note the case variations – the tag wants a lower-case name, whereas the method must have get followed by the name with an upper-case first character – *Enlightenment*).

The revised ('beanified'?) Guru class is:

```
package mystuff
public class Guru {
  private static Random rr;
  private static final String[ ] Sayings = {
    ...
  };
  public String getEnlightenment() {
    int select = rr.nextInt(Sayings.length);
    return Sayings[select];
  }
  {
    rr = new Random();
  }
}
```

The difference between the two versions may seem trivial at this stage. However, there are advantages in the second form with its reliance on XML-like tags rather than scriptlet code.

The action tag style results in pages that are simpler in structure. 'Code' using action tag templates is less likely to be damaged by a web designer editing the page than would be code that uses scriptlets. These differences should become more apparent with later examples.

8.3 Membership example

This example reworks part of the 'Membership' example from Section 7.4. This JSP version is mainly to illustrate communication between a JSP and a 'beanified' SubscriberRecord object, and also communication amongst JSPs. As before, the membership example has a form filled by applicants seeking membership of an interest group. Data from the form are transferred to a SubscriberRecord object; this can save its contents to a newly created database record, returning a membership number. The response page prints an acknowledgment along with the allocated membership number.

A slightly modified version of the original InfoPage.html form is as follows:

```
<html><head><title>New Subscriber</title></head>
<body bgcolor=white>
<h1 align=center>
Please supply some details for our records.
</h1>
<p>
<form method=post action="/jspdemo/Subscriber.jsp">
<table align=center border=2>
<caption>Subscriber details</caption>
<tr>
  <th>Given name</th>
  <td><input type=text size=20 maxsize=30 name=givenName></td>
</tr>
<tr>
  <th>Family name</th>
  <td><input type=text size=20 maxsize=30 name=familyName></td>
</tr>
  <%-- Continuing much as before --%>
  ...
<tr>
  <td colspan=2 align=center>
  <input type=submit>
  </td>
</tr>
</table></form>
</body></html>
```

The obvious change is to make the action attribute of the 'form' tag reference the JSP rather than the servlet. However, you must also take care of the form's field names. They must comply with capitalization conventions used in the jsp tag library and the beans. For

example, the rules would require a form field 'sex', a property name 'sex' in a
jsp:getProperty tag, and an access function getSex() in the corresponding bean class.

The Subscriber class from Chapter 7 basically complies with the naming conventions
for a bean class, though as will be explained below there are problems with the existing
'Age' methods:

```
package membership
public class SubscriberRecord {
  private String    GivenName;
  ...
  public boolean isValid() { ... }
  public String getGivenName() { return GivenName; }
  public void setGivenName(String aName) { ... }
  public String getFamilyName() { return FamilyName; }
  public void setFamilyName(String aName) { ... }
  public String getEmail() { return Email; }
  public void setEmail(String aName) { ... }
  public String getSex() { return Sex; }
  public void setSex(String gender) { ... }
  public int getAge() { return Age; }
  public void setAge(String AgeStr) { ... }
  // createInDatabase method - some changes from earlier version
  ...
}
```

A first version of the Subscriber.jsp page illustrates solely the transfer of data into an
instance of a SubscriberRecord and retrieval of these same data:

```
<%@ page language="java" contentType="text/html" session="false" %>
<jsp:useBean scope="request" id="userInfo"
    class="membership.SubscriberRecord">
  <jsp:setProperty name="userInfo" property="*" />
</jsp:useBean>
<html><head><title>OK</title></head><body>
<ul>
<li>
<jsp:getProperty name="userInfo" property="givenName" />
<li>
<jsp:getProperty name="userInfo" property="familyName" />
<li>
<jsp:getProperty name="userInfo" property="age" />
<li>
<jsp:getProperty name="userInfo" property="sex" />
<li>
<jsp:getProperty name="userInfo" property="email" />
</ul></body></html>
```

The first line in this page is a directive. The values of attributes in a directive like this determine details of the initialization and other code in the generated servlet.

```
<%@ page language="java" contentType="text/html" session="false" %>
```

This directive specifies that the 'scripting language' used in the page is Java (this is the default, and it is the only scripting language supported by most JSP systems), and that the response type of the generated page is text/html (again this is the default). The final attribute in this directive switches off 'sessions'. The default for a JSP is for the generated servlet to ask for a current session, creating one if necessary; this then results in the client being prompted to accept a cookie when a response page is returned. Many simple applications can manage without sessions because they have no state data to maintain. The session feature should be turned off when not required.

The next page element is a jsp:useBean tag; this one has a start tag, body and end tag, with the body containing some code to be executed immediately after the SubscriberRecord object is created:

```
<jsp:useBean scope="request" id="userInfo"
    class="membership.SubscriberRecord">
  <jsp:setProperty name="userInfo" property="*" />
</jsp:useBean>
```

The attributes in the jsp:useBean start tag identify the class (SubscriberRecord) and provide an object identifier (userInfo). In this case, the scope attribute is also set. The scope attribute determines exactly how the code in the resulting servlet will create the SubscriberRecord object.

The servlet code generated for a jsp:useBean tag can make a new object:

- An attribute of the HttpRequest object (scope="request").

- An attribute of the Session object (scope="session").

- An attribute of the ServletContext object (scope="application").

- A 'local variable' in the _jspService method (this is the default, but can be specified explicitly as scope="page"). (Actually, it is bit more complex than that. There is actually a local variable in the generated _jspService function, with the name specified by the id attribute, which does get used to reference the created object. However, the actual object is created and placed in a collection owned by the generated servlet; it can be retrieved by name from this collection. This usage makes the generated code more uniform; all references to beans tend to be in the form 'get attribute ... of page/servlet-context/session/request'.)

Here, the scope is set to request; page scope would suffice for the first version of this JSP, but the example is extended later to show how the request, and attached attribute data, can be passed among JSPs.

The body of the jsp:useBean tag in this page contains a jsp:setProperty tag that will expand into code that copies all the input form data to the corresponding fields in the new SubscriberRecord object:

```
<jsp:setProperty name="userInfo" property="*" />
```

The jsp:setProperty tag can be used to set a specific property, e.g. <jsp:setProperty name="userInfo" property="familyName" ... />. Other attributes for this tag can be used to define the source for the data; the source defaults to a request parameter (request.getParameter("familyName")). The property="*" feature is a short cut for the very common case where you want to transfer all form data into the corresponding data members of a bean. The tag gets expanded into Java code that gets an Enumeration with the names of the parameters, then loops making getParameter calls on the request object to get the data, and setX(...) calls on the bean to set corresponding fields. The code uses Java reflection to identify and then perform the actual method calls on the bean.

If you try running this JSP example, you should find that the SubscriberRecord's age member remains unset, irrespective of the data you enter in the age field in the form. All the other fields should work, however. This problem is related to the function signatures:

- public int getAge() { return Age; }
- public void setAge(String AgeStr) { ... }

The code generation system that creates the servlet uses the signature of the 'get' method to guide its operation. Since the get function has the form int getAge(), the code is set to use a function with the signature void setAge(int). This function is not defined in the SubscriberRecord class, so the Age data member is not set. (There is no error report; the age data are simply ignored.)

You could try redefining the age methods in the SubscriberRecord class:

```
public void setAge(int val) {
  if((val>=MINAGE) && (val <=MAXAGE))
     Age = val;
  }
public int getAge() { return Age; }
```

The generated code for the servlet would now get a String via request.getParameter("age"), convert this to an integer using Integer.parseInt(...) and invoke the void setAge(int) method.

Unfortunately, invalid data in the form (like 'old' in the age field) now cause a NumberFormatError exception to be thrown in the servlet code. The response page shows merely a stack trace. A better solution might be the following redefinition of the functions:

```
public String getAge() {
  if(Age==0) return null;
  else return Integer.toString( Age);
```

```
  }
  public void setAge(String AgeStr) {
    Age = 0;
    try {
      int val = Integer.parseInt(AgeStr);
      if((val>=MINAGE) && (val <=MAXAGE))
        Age = val;
    } catch(Exception e) { }
  }
```

This applies generally; you should make all get/set methods for beans work with String data.

Exceptions in a generated servlet do result in unattractive response pages with stack traces. These should not be shown to clients. The JSP system has a mechanism that allows you to specify that if an exception occurs the client should be redirected to an apology page. This feature requires an additional directive at the start of your JSP where you name the helper JSP that will deal with the reporting of exceptions:

```
<%@page isErrorPage="false" errorPage="exceptions.jsp" %>
```

A special directive is used to flag an exception handling JSP. The page can use scriptlet code to obtain details of the exception (forwarded from the failing servlet). A simple version is as follows:

```
<%@page isErrorPage="true" %>
<html><head><title>Errors!</title></head>
<body bgcolor=red>
<h1 align=center>Run time errors</h1>
<p>The program hit a problem and an exception was thrown.
<p>Tell the programmer that the exception was
<%= exception.toString() %>
</body></html>
```

The next step in developing the 'Membership' application involves checking the validity of the entered data and either forwarding the user to an error page or proceeding to create a new database record. This portion of the example illustrates basic communication between JSPs.

The code in the JSP now becomes a mix of scriptlets and actions. It is difficult to avoid scriptlet code at places where it is necessary to make conditional tests, or where you need iterative constructs. The revised Subscriber.jsp page is now:

```
<%@ page language="java" contentType="text/html" session="false" %>
<jsp:useBean scope="request" id="userInfo"
    class="membership.SubscriberRecord">
  <jsp:setProperty name="userInfo" property="*" />
</jsp:useBean>
```

```
<% if(! userInfo.isValid()) { %>
  <jsp:forward page="badInput.jsp" />
<% } %>
<% if(userInfo.createInDatabase() < 1) { %>
  <jsp:forward page="NoDB.html" />
<% } %>

<html><head><title>Thank you for registering</title></head><body>
<h1>Thank you</h1>
<p>Your membership number is
<jsp:getProperty name="userInfo" property="id" />
</body></html>
```

The code to create a SubscriberRecord and set its data members from the data in the form is the same as before. Once the record is set, it can be asked whether it is valid:

```
<% if(! userInfo.isValid()) { %>
```

This scriptlet fragment starts a block in the generated servlet. Sometimes, the contents of the block are all defined in terms of Java code; in such cases, the entire block is defined within <% start and %> end tags. However, it is quite common for the block to define HTML tags and content text that are to be conditionally output. Sometimes, as in this example, the body of the block can be defined using action tags. Here, we get the jsp library tag that can forward a request (and attached attributes) to another JSP (or servlet, or even static HMTL page):

```
<jsp:forward page="badInput.jsp" />
```

Finally, the Java code block that was opened with the <% if(!userInfo.isValid()) { %> scriptlet must be closed, so we get the next scriptlet element:

```
<% } %>
```

The next processing step asks the SubscriberRecord object to save its data in a database and return either a valid membership number or, if the database operations failed, a failure indicator. If there was a failure, the user is redirected to a static HTML page with an apology. This processing is again handled through a combination of a scriptlet, an action tag and a final scriptlet:

```
<% if(userInfo.createInDatabase() < 1) { %>
  <jsp:forward page="NoDB.html" />
<% } %>
```

If all went well, the JSP can output some HTML text containing the new member's membership number:

```
<html><head><title>Thank you for registering</title></head><body>
<h1>Thank you</h1>
<p>Your membership number is
<jsp:getProperty name="userInfo" property="id" />
</body></html>
```

The other JSP, for reporting errors in the data entry form, is as follows:

```
<%@ page language="java" contentType="text/html" session="false" %>
<jsp:useBean scope="request" id="userInfo"
    class="membership.SubscriberRecord" />
<html><head><title>Bad data</title>
</head><body>
<% if(userInfo.getGivenName()==null) { %>
   You forgot to enter your given name.
<% } %>
<%--...Similar code for other data elements --%>
...
<% if(userInfo.getAge()==null) { %>
   You forgot to enter your age, or the value was invalid.
<% } %>
</body></html>
```

This page is more limited than the servlet version in Chapter 7, in that it reports errors in the entered data but does not generate a new, partly initialized form for re-input of data. The servlet generated for this page will find a `SubscriberRecord` as the `userInfo` attribute attached to the incoming `HttpServletRequest`; it does not create a new object. Here the scriptlet code does illustrate conditional inclusion of content text:

```
<% if(userInfo.getGivenName()==null) { %>
   You forgot to enter your given name.
<% } %>
```

The message warning of a missing name is only printed if this data element is unset in the `SubscriberRecord`.

The database related code of the `SubscriberRecord` class had to be modified slightly to make it suitable for this simple JSP system. The servlet example in Chapter 7 had a database connection that belonged to the servlet and which was passed to a `SubscriberRecord` that had to save or load its state. It is possible to use the same approach for JSPs; it would involve:

- Declaring an instance data member to hold a reference to the connection

- Providing an 'initialization' function for the JSP; this function would open the connection.

- Passing the database connection as an argument in scriptlet code that invokes database operations.

- Providing a 'destroy' function in the JSP to close the connection.

Special 'declaration' scriptlets are needed to define the data member and extra member functions; there is a limited example in the next section showing these declarations.

However, it was simpler in this case to let the SubscriberRecord open its own connection to a database when it needed it. This approach might be too costly in a system that handled many registrations, but it is not a problem if the registration rate is only a few per hour. The code to open and close the database connection was added to the createInDatabase method of the SubscriberRecord class.

8.4 JSP: page contents

The Guru and Membership examples should have conveyed the general form of simple JSP applications. It is now necessary to review in more detail the various elements that can appear in a JSP. These are:

- Directives

- Action elements

- Scripting elements

- Template text

Directives provide control information to the component that generates the servlet from the JSP. Data that may have to be provided include:

- Page attributes
  - Is a session to be used for state maintenance?
  - How are output data buffered?
  - Is there a page that can be invoked if an exception occurs?
  - Does the scriptlet code have any dependencies on particular Java packages, e.g. java.sql?

- Includes
  - These allow a page to include fragments of prepared text from other files.

- Taglib
  - Taglib directives identify libraries containing custom action elements that supplement the standard jsp tags.

Action elements are the XML-like tags that can appear in a page. There is a standard set of action elements (the jsp tag library). These jsp actions include common operations on beans (use, get property, set property), some operations for communication with other JSPs or servlets (forwarding a request, including some output from another servlet), and a few miscellaneous things like help for setting up an applet that is to appear in a response page. You are not limited to using only the standard JSP tags. There are other tag libraries available from Apache, and also from O'Reilly publishers. You can even define your own tag libraries and employ your own action tags.

Scripting elements include:

- Standard scriptlets – blocks of Java code.

- Expressions – code returning strings that are to appear in the final HTML page.

- Declarations – definitions of instance data members and member functions for the generated servlet.

Standard scriptlets have the form:

```
<%
some Java code
%>
```

The code is copied unchanged into the generated servlet. It can include variable declarations; any variables are defined as local to the _jspService method. Their scope is from the point of declaration to the end of the enclosing block (this would usually be the try ...catch ... block where output is generated, but could be an inner block).

Expressions have the form:

```
<%= Java expression %>
```

An expression gets translated into code of the form out.print(*Java expression*) in the generated servlet.

Declarations allow you to define extra instance (and even class) data members and additional methods for the generated servlet. A typical use would be defining a database connection and related initialization and destroy functions for a JSP-servlet that was to manage a connection (as illustrated with some of the servlets shown in Chapter 7). Such usage would require something like the following:

```
<%!
  java.sql.Connection dbConnection;
  public void jspInit() {
    /* connect to database */
    ...
  }
  public void jspDestroy() {
    /* close that connection */
    ...
  }
%>
```

Declarations use the special <%! ... %> delimiters. (The initialization and destruction methods that you can override are called jspInit and jspDestroy.)

All the standard HTML and content text fragments in the JSP are referred to as 'template text'. These text fragments are simply packed into a large number of output statements in the generated _jspService function.

```
out.write(bit more html);
out.write( bit more content text);
...
```

8.4.1 JSP directives

Directives have the form:

```
<%@ directivetype attr1="value1" attr2="value2" ... %>
```

The directive types are include, taglib and page.

An include directive has a single attribute: a filename; it is used to merge files prior to the conversion to servlet form. For example, if you wanted the same block of HTML tags and content text in every page in some group, you could define this standard text as an include file and use include directives in all the JSPs.

A taglib directive allows you to use an additional tag library to supplement the standard jsp tags. A taglib has two attributes: prefix and uri. The prefix specifies the first part of a tag name (like the jsp part of the tag names jsp:useBean, jsp:setProperty). The uri is a cross reference to an entry in the web.xml file; this file will contain a specification of the source containing the tag library code and templates. A JSP can contain multiple taglib directives.

The page directive is the most commonly used and has the largest number of possible attributes. Typically, multiple page directives are used rather than a single directive with a host of attributes. Attributes for a page directive include

- language
Defaults to Java, and for most systems there is only Java; some JSP implementations allow JavaScript code fragments instead.

- extends
You can define your own servlet base class, a refinement of HttpJspPage; but it would be unusual to want to do this.

- info
Text describing your JSP (for use in sophisticated development environment that has some GUI-based builder program for creating JSPs).

- isThreadSafe (true/false)
Set to false if you really want a 'single thread model' servlet (defaults to true – i.e. thread safe).

- `isErrorPage` (true/false)

An error page has an `Exception` object defined; typically, the script in an error page reports errors as encoded in this object. This attribute defaults to false; most JSPs are not error pages.

- `contentType`

Used to set content type (defaults to `text/html`).

- `import`

Reference java package used in scriptlet code within the JSP (e.g. `import="java.sql.*, java.util.*"`).

- `session` (true/false)

Default is JSPs are parts of a session, with a cookie used to carry a session identifier. This is often unnecessary, so disable sessions when appropriate.

- `errorPage`

This tag is used to specify the URL of a JSP error page that will handle exceptions thrown in the servlet code generated from this page. You should define this if you want exceptions in the servlet to result in the client being redirected to an apology page.

- `autoflush` (true/false)

This is another control that is rarely used. Normally, when a servlet fills its output buffer, this buffer is flushed. But you can set it up so that filling of the buffer is treated as an error that will result in an exception being thrown. The default is `true` – buffers get flushed and can be refilled with additional data.

- `buffer`

This option allows you to set the size of the output buffer used by the servlet (e.g. `buffer="16kb"`).

8.4.2   jsp: tag library

The more important action tags in the `jsp` tag library are:

- `useBean`
- `getProperty`
- `setProperty`
- `forward`
- `include`

A `useBean` directive will appear as `<jsp:useBean ... />` or `<jsp:useBean ...> ...` *body* `... </jsp:useBean>`. If present, the body code is used to initialize a bean; it can take the form of scriptlet code of action tags. The main attributes in the `useBean` tag are:

- `class`

This is a string with the fully qualified name (packages etc.) for the bean class.

- `id`

Variable name for the object that is being created (for use in scriptlet code etc.).

- `scope`

One of `page`, `request`, `session` or `application` (defaults to page). Use `application` (`ServletContext`) scope for data that are shared by all JSPs and servlets in a web application; use `request` scope if it may be necessary to pass data to, or receive data from, another JSP or servlet; and use `session` scope for data that belong to a stateful session that is being maintained for a client.

The code generated for a `useBean` action tag checks for an instance of the specified class, with the given identifier, in the specified scope. So for example, if the scope is 'application', the code will check whether the `ServletContext` has an attribute with the required name and class; if the scope were `session`, the code would check for a session attribute. If the required object does not exist, it is created and associated with the specified scope. When JSPs are used to produce final output from data prepared by a servlet, they will typically pick up beans in `request` scope.

The `getProperty` tag has two attributes – `name` and `property`. A `setProperty` tag has the same two attributes, and in addition may have either a `param` attribute or a `value` attribute. If neither `param` nor `value` is specified, the generated code is of the form `request.getParameter(name)`; if param is given, then its value is used instead of the name in the `request.getParameter` call. Alternatively, you can use the `value` attribute, and this can specify any arbitrary data source – a constant, or the result of a Java expression. For example, you could have something like `<jsp:setProperty name="theData" property="day" value="<% new java.util.Date() %>" />`.

The `forward` and `include` tags both take a single page attribute; its value is the URI for the resource to which the request is being transferred. If the `forward` tag is used, then any partial generated response is discarded, and the request (along with any beans attached as attributes) is forwarded to the specified resource. If the `include` tag is used, the output buffers with partial results are flushed (so sending headers and committing the response) and the request is passed to the other resource (servlet or JSP). When the other resource finishes, the current JSP should resume its processing of the request.

8.5 Servlet, bean and JSP examples

Servlets and JSPs are now both reasonably mature technologies, having been around for about five years. Developers have experimented with different ways of using and combining these technologies. The preferred strategy for Java server-side applications is now to limit the code in a JSP to that required for the display of dynamic data, to have control code in a pre-processing servlet, and to have application specific business logic in helper bean classes. Further, as far as practical, action tags are preferred over scriptlet coding within the JSP component. The example for this section illustrates the construction of a web application with this preferred form. (It is a very small example, but it does resemble real applications; you have to use your imagination to scale it up and see how the suggested problems and solutions might work for real.) The example is developed in stages; it starts with a JSP and bean solution, where the JSPs contain a relatively large amount of scriptlet control code. The servlet is then added to take over the control functions, allowing some simplification of the JSP code. Finally, various substitutions of action tags for scriptlet code are explored.

The example is a reworking of the soccer league example that was used in Section 6.6 to illustrate how PHP could work with a database. The database has a single table with the results of games in some imaginary soccer league. Each record has four fields – the two teams and the two scores. In this version the system supports just the queries – list all matches, list drawn (tied) matches, list away wins and list home wins.

The first version of the application has the following components:

- `Soccer.html`

This is a simple static page that allows the user to request a search for results of interest.

- `Soccer.jsp`

Supposedly a highly graphic, attractive page that presents the results of a search.

- Beans (and other support classes) in package `soccer`:
  - `SoccerSearchBean`

    An instance of this class handles the actual search request, submitting an SQL query and processing the result set. Results are returned as a collection of `SoccerGame` objects.
  - `SoccerGame`

    This is a simple bean that has data members corresponding to the four data elements in each row of the Soccer table.
  - `DBInfo`

    A helper class used to create a database connection; holds data such as database URL, driver name, and username and password.

- Database

This holds a single table, Teams, containing the records for matches.

The application is deployed in `tomcat/webapps/jspeg`, with a `WEB-INF` subdirectory that initially contains only a `classes/soccer` subdirectory to hold the three support Java classes.

The JSP:

- Gets the query type from the submitted form data.

- Creates a bean to organize the search and sets a field identifying the search type.

- Requests that the bean perform the search.

- Retrieves an iterator with the search results.

- Uses the iterator to generate rows for an HTML table.

The `Soccer.html` page has a series of `<a href ... >` links for the different search options. These embody query strings with the search code. The JSP will pick up the data as the value of the `searchType` request parameter.

```
<html><head><title>Soccer searcher</title></head>
<body bgcolor=white>
<h1 align=center>
Search the little soccer league table
</h1>
<ul>
<li><a href="http://localhost:8080/jspeg/Soccer.jsp?searchType=all">
List all games</a >
...
<li><a href="http://localhost:8080/jspeg/Soccer.jsp?searchType=away">
List away wins</a>
</ul>
</body>
</html>
```

The DBInfo class is essentially the same as that illustrated in Section 6.6. It provides a connectToDatabase method that returns a connection to the database identified by a URL string defined as a constant in the DBInfo class.

The SoccerGame class is not a true bean (it has no setX() mutator methods). It is really just a holder for the two String and two int data elements that hold details of a game. It does have a set of getX() accessor methods, and it also has a method for copying data from a ResultSet object into its data members.

```
package soccer;
import java.sql.*;

public class SoccerGame {
  private String    team1;
  private String    team2;
  private int       score1;
  private int       score2;

  public String getTeam1() { return team1; }
  public String getTeam2() { return team2; }
  public String getScore1() { return Integer.toString(score1); }
  public String getScore2() { return Integer.toString(score2); }

  public void loadFromResultSet(ResultSet rset) throws SQLException
  {
    team1 = rset.getString("TEAM1");
    team2 = rset.getString("TEAM2");
    score1 = rset.getInt("SCORE1");
    score2 = rset.getInt("SCORE2");
  }
}
```

A SoccerSearchBean:

- Owns:
  - A string data member to hold the type of the search.
  - A vector to hold a collection of retrieved SoccerGame objects.
  - Some string constants for SQL queries.

- Does:
  - Allows setting of search type.
  - Perform search, collecting results in memory.
  - Reports on number of items found for search.
  - Returns an iterator allowing access to retrieved items.

```java
package soccer;
import java.sql.*;
import java.util.*;
public class SoccerSearchBean {
  private static final String allstr =
    "select * from TEAMS";
  private static final String drawstr =
    "select * from TEAMS where SCORE1=SCORE2";
  // Similar SQL queries for home wins and for away wins
  ...
  private String searchType;
  private Vector results;
  public void setSearchType(String typ)
  {
    searchType = typ;
  }

  public Iterator games() {
    if(results!=null)
      return results.iterator();
    else
      return null;
  }

  public int numGames() {
    if(results!=null)
      return results.size();
    else
      return 0;
  }

  public void doSearch()
  {
```

```
        results = new Vector();
        try {
          Connection db = DBInfo.connectToDatabase();
          Statement stmt = db.createStatement();
          String request = allstr;
          if("drawn".equals(searchType))
            request = drawstr;
          else
            // Similar code to select query string
            // for other options
          ...

          ResultSet rset = stmt.executeQuery(request);
          while(rset.next()) {
            SoccerGame sg = new SoccerGame();
            sg.loadFromResultSet(rset);
            results.addElement(sg);
          }
          rset.close();
          stmt.close();
          db.close();
          }
        catch(Exception e) { ... }
      }
  }
```

The JSP supposedly embodies 'pretties' – artwork, advertisements, links to related pages, some client-side JavaScript code for rollovers, pop-ups and other entertainments. These elements are left to creative web designers. Here, the focus is on the JSP scripting. The Soccer.jsp file contains:

```
<%@ page import="java.util.*" %>
<%@ page import="soccer.*" %>
<html><head><title>Soccer League Results</title></head>
<body bgcolor=white>
<!--
Imagine that this is page contains lots of HTML directives to build a
really pretty page. A page with a tiled picture background (soccer balls
ad infinitum); assorted advertisements strategically placed. All created
by some creative artist utilizing an interactive editing program.

Embedded in amongst that auto-generated HTML will be a
few fragments of JSP scripting: actions, scriptlets, etc.
-->

<h1 align=center><font color=red>Little league soccer results</font></h1>
```

```
<p>
<jsp:useBean id="theLeague" class="soccer.SoccerSearchBean" />
<jsp:setProperty name="theLeague" property="searchType" />
<%
    theLeague.doSearch();
%>
<%  if(theLeague.numGames()==0) { %>
    <p>There haven't been any such games yet. But the season
    is young; come back again soon.
<%
    }
    else {
%>
    <table align=center border=2>
    <caption>Results</caption>
    <tr>
        <th align=center>Home Team</th>
        <th align=center>Away Team</th>
        <th align=right>Home Team Score</th>
        <th align=right>Away Team Score</th>
    </tr>

<%
    Iterator it = theLeague.games();
    while(it.hasNext()) {
      SoccerGame sg = (SoccerGame) it.next();
%>
      <tr>
        <td><%= sg.getTeam1() %></td>
        <td><%= sg.getTeam2() %></td>
        <td><%= sg.getScore1() %></td>
        <td><%= sg.getScore2() %></td>
      </tr>
<%
    }
%>
    </table>
<%
    }
%>
</body></html>
```

The JSP starts with a page directive with an import attribute. The scriptlet code is going to be using a java.util.Iterator. This dependence on the java.util package must be specified:

```
<%@ page import="java.util.*" %>
```

The page starts with a fairly typical set of tags, specifying a bean that is to be used and copying form data into the new bean (you can put the setProperty action in the body of the useBean action, or have it as a separate entity – it really makes no difference):

```
<jsp:useBean id="theLeague" class="soccer.SoccerSearchBean" />
<jsp:setProperty name="theLeague" property="searchType" />
```

Scriptlet code is then used to invoke the search operation:

```
<%
  theLeague.doSearch();
%>
```

Next, there is the large conditional construct: if (theLeague.numGames()==0) {...} else { ... }. The then clause in this conditional involves simple output of fixed HTML tags and content text. The else clause is more elaborate; here the table of results must be formatted. This involves some template text and the iterative loop that generates rows for the HTML table.

```
<%-- Scriptlet code for the loop control statement --%>
<%
    Iterator it = theLeague.games();
    while(it.hasNext()) {
      SoccerGame sg = (SoccerGame) it.next();
%>
  <%-- Loop body is mix of template text and embedded expressions. --%>
    <tr>
      <td><%= sg.getTeam1() %></td>
      <td><%= sg.getTeam2() %></td>
      <td><%= sg.getScore1() %></td>
      <td><%= sg.getScore2() %></td>
    </tr>
<%-- Scriptlet code closing the block opened in the while statement --%>
<%
    }
%>
```

The embedded scriptlet coding is not too overwhelming. But even in this simple case there are constructs like:

```
<%
    }
%>
```

```
        </table>
    <%
    }
    %>
```

The first scriptlet here is closing the `while` block; then there is a fragment of conditionally included template text (the `</table>` tag); and finally, a second scriptlet fragment closes the block opened in the `else` clause above. Such code is obviously fragile. A non-programming web designer who is improving this page is quite likely to move or remove one of those scriptlet tags, resulting in code that will not compile.

Really, the application involves a request for a search that results in one of two different responses. If there are results that match the search query, e.g. the client requested 'away wins' and there have been some away wins, their details should be listed in a well-presented table. If there are no results, a different response should be generated. This is basically the approach taken in the next version of this web application. A pre-processing servlet is used to handle the initial request. It creates and runs the `SoccerSearchBean`. The servlet then transfers control to one or other of two different JSPs to generate appropriate responses.

The components in the revised version are:

- `Soccer.html`

The `<a href=...>` links now reference the servlet's URL, as specified in a `web.xml` deployment file.

- `MatchReport.jsp`, `NoResult.jsp`

These separate JSP components present the different styles of response for the different search outcomes.

- `web.xml`

A `web.xml` deployment file is required in any more sophisticated JSP system – either one using specialized libraries, or as here working with a servlet.

- `PreprocessServlet.java`

This servlet has the control logic that runs the request and forwards results to the appropriate JSP display component. (Code goes in the `WEB-INF/classes` directory.)

- `SoccerGame.java`, `SoccerSearchBean.java` and `DBInfo.java`

These helper classes are unchanged; they are in the `WEB-INF/classes/soccer` directory.

The deployment file, `web.xml`, is once again a simple one. It defines the servlet and the URL that will be used to reference it in the `Soccer.html` page:

```
<web-app>
  <servlet>
    <servlet-name>SoccerServlet</servlet-name>
    <servlet-class>PreprocessServlet</servlet-class>
  </servlet>
```

```
    <servlet-mapping>
      <servlet-name>SoccerServlet</servlet-name>
      <url-pattern>/SoccerInfo</url-pattern>
    </servlet-mapping>
  </web-app>
```

In this example, the role of the PreprocessServlet is simply to handle HTTP get requests. It could have been given responsibility for a persistent database connection; but this responsibility has been left in the SoccerSearchBean. The doGet function creates a SoccerSearchBean, sets its search type from the request parameter data and invokes its doSearch method. Depending on the results of the search, the doGet function uses one or other of the private auxiliary methods, doSuccess or doSearchFail, to deal with forwarding of the request to the appropriate JSP for final prettying up.

```java
// The usual Servlet imports ... and
import soccer.*;

public class PreprocessServlet extends HttpServlet {
  // Constant strings;
  // The first few are different forms of failure message that can be
  // forwarded to a JSP that reports failed searches
  private static final String
    allstr = "We couldn't show you any results, the season hasn't started!";
  private static final String
    drawstr = "There haven't been any drawn games yet this season.";
  private static final String
    homestr = "There haven't been any home wins yet this season.";
  private static final String
    awaystr = "There haven't been any away wins yet this season.";
  // These strings define the URLs for the JSPs that pretty
  // up the final response.
  private static final String jspFailPage = "NoResult.jsp";
  private static final String jspReportPage = "MatchReport.jsp";

  public void doGet (HttpServletRequest request,
    HttpServletResponse response) throws ServletException, IOException
  {
    // Get form data from request
    String search = request.getParameter("searchType");
    // Create and initialize the bean
    SoccerSearchBean ssb = new SoccerSearchBean();
    ssb.setSearchType(search);
    // Run the search
    ssb.doSearch();
    // Select appropriate reporting stage
```

```java
            if(ssb.numGames()==0)
               doSearchFail(search, request, response);
            else
               doSuccess(ssb, request, response);
        }

        private void doSearchFail(String search,
            HttpServletRequest request, HttpServletResponse response)
               throws ServletException, IOException
        {
            // A failure results in a explanatory message being
            // forwarded along with the request to the "No Result" JSP

            // Pick the appropriate message string
            String reason = allstr;
            if("drawn".equals(search))
              reason = drawstr;
            else
            if("home".equals(search))
              reason = homestr;
            else
            if("away".equals(search))
              reason = awaystr;
            // Add message as attribute of request
            request.setAttribute("Message", reason);
            // Prepare to forward
            RequestDispatcher dispatch =
               request.getRequestDispatcher(jspFailPage);
            // Forward request and error message
            dispatch.forward(request, response);
        }


        private void doSuccess(SoccerSearchBean ssb,
            HttpServletRequest request, HttpServletResponse response)
               throws ServletException, IOException
        {
            // The SoccerSearchBean has a vector of results for display
            // to the client. Add this bean as an attribute of the request,
            // and forward to the "Match Result" JSP
            request.setAttribute("theLeague", ssb);

            RequestDispatcher dispatch =
               request.getRequestDispatcher(jspReportPage);

            dispatch.forward(request, response);
```

```
    }
  }
```

The data placed as attributes of the request (the String with a message, or the SoccerSearchBean) will be available to the JSP components as request-scope beans.

The NoResult.jsp has to embed an error message into an 'interesting' response page. The interesting features can be left to a web designer. The minimal code for this JSP is:

```
<%--
Imagine this to be a page filled with graphic pretties, along with the
small amount of dynamic content as shown! --%>
<html><head><title>Soccer League Results</title></head>
<body bgcolor=white>
<h1 align=center><font color=red>No Results</font></h1>
<p>
<jsp:useBean scope="request" id="Message" class="String" />
<p>
<%= Message %>
</body></html>
```

MatchReport.jsp has to format a table with the results of interest. It can obtain the SoccerSeachBean from the request and get the Iterator from the bean. Then it can have scriptlet code again to handle generation of the table rows:

```
<%-- The usual apology - "this is really a pretty page with lots of
HTML" --%>
<%@ page import="java.util.*" %>
<%@ page import="soccer" %>
<html><head><title>Soccer League Results</title></head>
<body bgcolor=white>
<h1 align=center><font color=red>Search Results</font></h1>
<p>
<%-- Pick up SoccerSearchBean with the data --%>
<jsp:useBean scope="request" id="theLeague"
    class="soccer.SoccerSearchBean" />
<table align=center border=2>
<caption>Results</caption>
<tr>
  <th align=center>Home Team</th>
  <th align=center>Away Team</th>
  <th align=right>Home Team Score</th>
  <th align=right>Away Team Score</th>
</tr>
<%-- Get Iterator from bean, use it to control while loop --%>
<%
```

```
    Iterator it = theLeague.games();
    while(it.hasNext()) {
      SoccerGame sg = (SoccerGame) it.next();
%>
  <%-- Body of while loop, --%>
  <%-- Once again a mix of template text and expressions --%>
  <tr>
    <td><%= sg.getTeam1() %></td>
    <td><%= sg.getTeam2() %></td>
    <td><%= sg.getScore1() %></td>
    <td><%= sg.getScore2() %></td>
  </tr>
<%-- Scriptlet tag closing the block started at while --%>
<%
    }
%>
</table></body></html>
```

These changes have improved the JSPs. These now focus solely on presentation; there is no application logic and no complex nested conditional code. But there is still scriptlet code for the loop and expressions for accessing data held in SoccerGame objects.

You might have expected jsp:getProperty action tags to be used instead of the expression, i.e. something like

```
<jsp:getProperty name="sg" property="team1" />
```

rather than

```
<$%= sg.getTeam1() %>
```

However, you cannot use jsp:getProperty tags on arbitrary scriptlet variables because of the way the action tags are translated. An action like <jsp:getProperty name="x" property="y" /> does not translate to the Java code x.getY(). Instead, the code is something along the following lines:

- Look up something called x in the 'page context' and find out what it is.

- Use reflection to find whether it has a getY() function.

- Build a Method object that will call this getY() on the appropriate x object.

- Run the Method object.

If you want to use the action tag style on an ordinary scriptlet variable, you must first 'promote' the variable – making its name and class known to the PageContext object that manages page context data. This can be done as follows:

```
<%
  Iterator it = theLeague.games();
  while(it.hasNext()) {
    SoccerGame sg = (SoccerGame) it.next();
    pageContext.setAttribute("sg",sg,PageContext.PAGE_SCOPE);
%>
    <tr><td>
      <jsp:getProperty name="sg" property="team1" />
    </td>
```

The `PageContext.setAttribute` method takes as arguments the identifier that will be used to name the object in `getProperty` and `setProperty` actions, a reference to the actual object, and the scope in which it is to be registered. (You can register variables in session scope, request scope or application scope.) Once registered, the script variables can be used in action tags.

If you limit yourself to the standard `jsp` tag library, you cannot further simplify the code. The JSP still has to have that scriptlet code for the iterative construct:

```
<%
  Iterator it = theLeague.games();
  while(it.hasNext()) {
    SoccerGame sg = (SoccerGame) it.next();
    pageContext.setAttribute("sg",sg,PageContext.PAGE_SCOPE);
%>
<tr>
  ...
  <jsp:getProperty name="sg" property="score2" />
  </td>
</tr>
<% } %>
```

But there is no need to limit yourself to the `jsp` tag library. There are other libraries that are more versatile.

8.6 Tag libraries

The iterative loop in the example from the last section can be defined using action tags. For example, using the tag libraries from Apache, you could have:

```
<logic:iterate id="sg" collection="<%= theLeague.games() %>" >
  <tr>
    <td><bean:write name="sg" property="team1" /></td>
    <td><bean:write name="sg" property="team2" /></td>
    <td><bean:write name="sg" property="score1" /></td>
```

```
        <td><bean:write name="sg" property="score2" /></td>
    </tr>
</logic:iterate>
```

The action tag style suits JSPs. The clear matching 'begin' and 'end' XML style tags are probably understood by the web designer's web page editing tool; they may even be vaguely understood by the web designer. Code implemented using tags is far less likely to be broken when page layouts are adjusted.

The logic:iterate tag comes from the Apache 'struts' tag library. Struts is comprised of several subsections. There is the 'beans' tag library, which contains utility components such as the bean:write tag used in the code fragment above. The 'html' tags provide an alternative approach to the composition of HTML forms. The 'template' tags assist in the transfer of data among JSPs. The 'logic' tags, of which logic:iterate is the pre-eminent example, allow you to avoid most scriptlet coding.

The Apache struts library is rather sophisticated, so it is worth looking first at a simple example that illustrates the definition and use of a customized action tag.

8.6.1 Defining a simple customized action tag

Action tags are defined as Java classes. These classes extend base classes that are defined in the javax.servlet.jsp.tagext package provided by Sun. When an action tag is used in a JSP, the JSP to servlet translation replaces the tag with expanded template code. This code will instantiate an instance of the tag class, initialize it and invoke various operations on the new 'action tag' object.

Tags are used in JSPs in one or other of the following styles. The first style simply invokes the action, applying it to data supplied as attributes:

```
<lib:tag attribute="..." attribute="..." />
```

The second style includes a 'body' between a start and an end tag:

```
<lib:tag attribute="..." ... >
    Some other stuff ...
</lib:tag>
```

Both get translated into code in the servlet along the lines of the following pseudo-code:

```
Create an instance of the action tag class
Perform operations to set attributes, add to page context etc.
Invoke the 'doStartTag' operation of the action tag object
...
// More stuff here relating to any 'body'
...
Invoke the 'doEndTag' operation of the action tag object
Release the action tag object
```

There are two kinds of tag, based either on the `TagSupport` class or on the `BodyTagSupport` class. The code expansion of the simpler kind of tag, based on the `TagSupport` class, is:

```
Create instance of the action tag class
Invoke operations to set attributes, page context, etc.
if(actionTagObject.doStartTag()== EVAL_BODY) {
  // Code obtained by translation of body (if any body is present)
  ...
  }
if(!actionTagObject.doEndTag==EVAL_PAGE) {
  Abort processing of rest of this page
  }
Release
```

The doStartTag operation can output some HTML content and perform other operations; it returns an `int` that indicates whether the content of any body part is to be included in the generated page (thus you can build simple conditional constructs from `TagSupport` objects). The doEndTag operation can generate additional HTML page output; its other role is to check for any failure conditions that might indicate that further processing of the page was to be abandoned.

The BodyTagSupport base class is designed for more complex cases. It has additional methods: `setBodyContent`, `doInitBody` and `doAfterBody`. The doInitBody method can be used to introduce control variables, such as loop counters, and perform other initialization tasks. The doAfterBody method returns either the result `EVAL_BODY_TAG` or `SKIP_BODY`; if it returns `EVAL_BODY_TAG`, the body of the action construct is re-evaluated – this is the basis for constructing loops. The most elaborate feature of the BodyTagSupport class is its buffering of any output produced during the evaluation of the body. A BodyContent object collects any HTML and content text written by the body. These data are then available for further editing in the doEndTag method, or are used for final output. This rather complex mechanism allows for tags that filter output in various ways. This feature is used in sophisticated tag libraries such as the `xsl` tags used to convert XML to HTML.

The following example defines a simple action tag for date stamping an HTML document. This tag, `mytag:DateStamper`, is an example of a class that extends the `TagSupport` class. It takes a single attribute and produces a couple of lines of output; for example, the following line in a JSP:

```
<mytag:DateStamper comment="This is a Test" />
```

could result in the following output in the HTML page:

```
<hr>
This page, entitled This is a Test, was generated on Mon Dec 10
11:55:37 GMT+11:00 2001.
<br>
```

(The date shown would be the date on which the example was run.)

The DateStamper class extends javax.servvlet.jsp.tagext.TagSupport. It defines a setComment method that will be used to set the value of its comment attribute, and a doEndTag method that outputs the generated text to the HTML page.

```java
package mine;
import java.util.*;
import java.io.*;
import javax.servlet.jsp.*;
import javax.servlet.jsp.tagext.*;
public class DateStamper extends TagSupport
{
  protected String comment = null;
  public String getComment() {
    return comment;
  }
  public void setComment(String cm) {
    comment = cm;
  }
  public int doEndTag() {
    try {
      String datestr = (new Date()).toString();
      pageContext.getOut().println(
        "<hr>This page entitled, " +
        comment
        + ", was printed on " +
        datestr +
        "<br>");
    }
    catch(Exception e) { }
    return EVAL_PAGE;
  }
}
```

An action tag object like this gets its (buffered) output stream from its PageContext (a reference to this PageContext is set in one of the initialization methods). The class is defined as part of a package (the mine package). It is the only class in this package. The .class files for a tag library are normally supplied as a Java archive containing all the classes in a package; for this example, it would be a mine.jar archive file.

The deployment of a tag library can be more involved than its coding. A JSP must first specify that it wants to use tags from the mytag tag library; this is done via a taglib directive that specifies the prefix, mytag, and a URI. Depending on its form, this URI can be complete or may be interpreted relative to data provided in a deployment web.xml file. The web-app specification in the web.xml file must specify the location of an XML document, the 'tag library descriptor', which contains data describing the tags in the tag library. Normally, this file would be placed in a tlds subdirectory of the web application's WEB-INF directory. The code (.class files) for the tag library classes themselves must be in the CLASSPATH when compiling the servlet that is obtained from the JSP.

An example could use something like the following JSP that specifies the tag library, and uses a mytag:DateStamper action:

```
<%@ taglib uri="/mytaglib" prefix="mytag" %>
<html><head><title>My Tag Test</title></head>
<body bgcolor=white>
<h1 align=center>Test Document</h1>
<p>
Hello Work, Hi Mom, and other standard greetings.
<mytag:DateStamper comment="My Tag Test" />
</body></html>
```

This JSP would be deployed as part of a web application; this would require a WEB-INF subdirectory containing the web.xml deployment file and other data. In this case, the web.xml data have to define only the tag library; this is done using a taglib tag that has taglib-uri and taglib-location nested tags. The taglib-uri entry matches the uri used in the JSP; its location tag identifies the mytaglib.tld file.

```
<?xml version="1.0" encoding="UTF-8"?>
<!DOCTYPE web-app PUBLIC '-//Sun Microsystems, Inc.//DTD Web Application
2.2//EN' 'http://java.sun.com/j2ee/dtds/web-app_2.2.dtd'>
<web-app>
  <taglib>
    <taglib-uri>
      /mytaglib
    </taglib-uri>
    <taglib-location>
      /WEB-INF/tlds/mytaglib.tld
    </taglib-location>
  </taglib>
</web-app>
```

A taglib description document contains details of all the tags in a library; in this case there is only the one tag – the DateStamper tag. Each tag has to have defined its name (DateStamper) and its class (mine.DateStamper), along with restrictions on any 'body' that may be used with the tag, and details of the attributes. The DateStamper tag should not be used with a body; so its bodycontent is defined as empty. The tag requires a single attribute named comment.

```
<?xml version="1.0" encoding="ISO-8859-1" ?>
<!DOCTYPE taglib
PUBLIC "-//Sun Microsystems, Inc.//DTD JSP Tag Library 1.1//EN"
```

```
                "http://java.sun.com/j2ee/dtds/web-jsptaglibrary_1_1.dtd">
                <taglib>
                  <tlibversion>1.0</tlibversion>
                  <jspversion>1.1</jspversion>
                  <shortname>mytag</shortname>
                  <tag>
                    <name>DateStamper</name>
                    <tagclass>mine.DateStamper</tagclass>
                    <bodycontent>empty</bodycontent>
                    <attribute>
                      <name>comment</name>
                      <required>true</required>
                    </attribute>
                  </tag>
                </taglib>
```

Typically, a Java archive file containing the mine package would be located in the WEB-INF/lib directory of the web application. In a simple case such as this, it is sufficient to copy DateStamper.class file into the WEB-INF/classes directory.

8.6.2   Using tag libraries

While you can define your own action tags, this is a fairly arcane area for development work. Mostly, you can use tags from the existing libraries, such as Apache's struts or Taglib tag libraries.

The Taglib library contains tags for manipulating things like java.util.Date objects, java.sql Statement and Connection objects, for handling email and so forth. The struts library has subsections like its HTML section, its beans section and its logic section.

The struts HTML tags can be used to help construct HTML forms and other portions of HTML documents. For example, instead of the JSP containing standard HTML tags and contents like

```
<a href="/vallink.jsp?name=newValues">Display of values</a>
```

You could use the HTML action tag set and have the following:

```
<html:link page="/vallink.jsp" name="newValues">
Display of values
</html:link>
```

This tag set includes tags for creating buttons, checkboxes, textareas and other components of forms. Each action tag takes a host of both required and optional arguments.

In the typical case, you would not want to use the HTML tags because they make the directives for content layout more 'programmatic' and less amenable to the visual editors that will be favored by your web designer. However, these tags might be useful if you have a fairly complex system that has some programmed element that generates the source code for the JSPs that you intend to use.

The bean group of the struts taglib tags is really a reworking and extension of the original jsp tags. It replaces the jsp:useBean, jsp:getProperty, and jsp:setProperty tags with a larger and more versatile set of actions. The new actions include 'cookie', 'define', 'header', and 'parameter' that support the creation of new scripting variables that are initialized with values taken from different sources. The 'write' action renders the value of a specified data element as a String.

The struts logic tag library includes actions for manipulating sub-strings, for value comparison, for forwarding and redirecting requests, and for handling iterative constructs. Each of these action tags takes a number of required and optional attributes. For example, the iterate tag has attributes that include:

- collection, name and property

These attributes define different ways of specifying the collection that is to be used. The collection can be specified directly using the name attribute. If the name and property are used together, the collection will be obtained by invoking a 'get property' action on the named object. The value of a collection attribute is an arbitrary runtime expression that defines the collection that will be traversed by the iterative process. The collection can be an array of Java objects, an Enumeration, an Iterator, a Map or another collection class.

- id

This names the page scope bean that will hold the current element of the collection.

- indexID

This optional attribute names a JSP bean that contains the current index into the collection.

A JSP that uses struts will need to include taglib directives for the taglib descriptor files:

```
<%@ page import="java.util.*" %>
<%@ page import="soccer.*" %>
  <%@ taglib uri="/WEB-INF/struts-bean.tld" prefix="bean" %>
  <%@ taglib uri="/WEB-INF/struts-logic.tld" prefix="logic" %>
<html><head><title>Soccer League Results</title></head>
<body bgcolor=white><h1 align=center><font color=red>Search Results
</font></h1><p>
<jsp:useBean scope="request" id="theLeague"
  class="soccer.SoccerSearchBean" />
<table align=center border=2>
...
<logic:iterate id="sg" collection="<%= theLeague.games() %>" >
  <tr>
    <td><bean:write name="sg" property="team1" /></td>
    <td><bean:write name="sg" property="team2" /></td>
    <td><bean:write name="sg" property="score1" /></td>
    <td><bean:write name="sg" property="score2" /></td>
```

```
        </tr>
    </logic:iterate>
</table></body></html>
```

The example uses actions from both the struts-logic and struts-bean libraries and so has two taglib directives. These explicitly reference the location of the corresponding tld files, so there is no need for an additional web.xml deployment file with mapping data.

The tag library descriptor files, struts-bean.tld and struts-logic.tld, would have to be copied from the struts main directory into the WEB-INF directory for the application. The struts.jar file would have to be copied into a WEB-INF/lib directory.

The struts libraries are available in source form. If you really do need to learn how to write code for the more complex types of tag, you can study the code for classes like the iterate tag class.

Exercises

Practical

The exercise continues with use of the Apache Tomcat engine employed in the exercises for Chapter 7. There are a couple of additional servlet/JSP exercises at the end of Chapter 9; those exercises combine servlet/JSP technologies with the use of XML and other markup languages.

(1) This exercise involves creating a servlet/JSP web application with two versions of the JSP components; one version of the JSPs should use scriptlet coding, while the other should use tag libraries (a third variant is examined in one of the XML exercises in Chapter 9).

The exercise involves a departmental 'Workflow' system used by 'staff', 'supervisor' and 'accountant' users. Staff users can submit funding requests (travel, equipment, personal expenses etc.), and can later review the status of their requests. The requests are saved as database records. Supervisors can review all requests that have been submitted by staff members and which have been neither approved nor rejected. Supervisors can choose to approve or reject selected requests. Accountants can review requests that have supervisor approval but which have not had funding checks. An accountant's approval or rejection of a request terminates the flow. All details of requests, both approved and rejected, are stored permanently in the database.

This toy version of a Workflow system has two tables in its database. One table is used simply as a source of unique identifiers (if your database can supply unique record identifiers, use these in preference to identifiers supplied from this secondary table). The main table defines a record with:

- an identifier (supplied by the database system itself, or created using an auxiliary table as illustrated in earlier examples)

- an integer status field, (0=rejected, 1=submitted waiting approval, 2=approved by supervisor waiting accountant, 3=processed by accountant)

- a string naming the requestor

- a string with details of the request

- the date that the request was submitted

- a string naming the supervisor who processed the request

- an integer for supervisor decision (0 reject, 1 approve)

- a string for supervisor's comment

- the date of the supervisor's review

- a string naming the accountant who processed the request

- an integer for the accountant's decision (0 reject, 1 approve)

- a string for the accountant's comment

- the date of the accountant's review

You will need to define this main table and supply some initial data records; other records can be added via the web application that you develop. You will also need to add a number of users to your Tomcat users–password–role file. Most of your users should be in role 'staff'; there should be a couple of users in each of the 'supervisor' and 'accountant' roles. The roles are mutually exclusive.

These Workflow record data are accessed via a security controlled web application that comprises three servlets, a few static HTML pages, some bean classes and some JSPs. The web application uses servlets mainly for control, beans for application logic and JSPs for display. The servlets load data into beans that are attached to requests forwarded to JSPs. Servlets determine a user's role and modify their responses appropriately.

Users initiate processing by entering a URL for one of the servlets (Servlet1 in the description below) in their browser's 'address' field, thereby causing a 'get' operation on that servlet. The servlet/bean/JSP response creates a page that shows retrieved data, and which also includes a data entry form used to submit subsequent requests to other servlets.

The servlets

- *Servlet1*

This entry point servlet creates the data that are to be displayed in a JSP-generated page that will be returned the client browser. Data retrieved from the database are held in a Records object ('bean') that owns a collection of RequestData objects ('beans'). These RequestData objects contain copies of data records retrieved from the database.

This servlet has a doGet method that checks the *role* of the user, handling 'staff', 'supervisor' and 'accountant' users in distinct ways. With 'staff' users, it directs a Records object to load all records submitted by the staff member, whose identity can be obtained from the login data associated with the controlled web application. For supervisors, it directs the Records object to load all records that have been submitted but which have not yet been assessed (records with status=1). For accountants, it directs the Records object to load all records that have been approved by a supervisor but which have not yet been reviewed by an accountant (records with status=2).

The user's role is also used when forwarding the request, and appended Records object, to a JSP. Two JSPs are used. The first JSP is for staff users; the second is for supervisors and accountants. Details of the JSPs are given below.

● *Servlet2*

This servlet handles the submission of new requests from staff users. It creates an additional record in the database, and then displays a simple acknowledgment page. The submitted request contains only the staff member's description of the item sought (this should include the cost, though this is not checked by the application). Servlet2 obtains the staff member's name from the login record, and date and time data from the operating system. The other data in the created database record take default values or nulls.

● *Servlet3*

This servlet handles the submission of 'approval/reject' inputs from supervisors and accountants. It updates the appropriate record in the database and displays a simple acknowledgment page.

'bean' classes

● *Records*

This owns the collection of RequestData objects (use any java.util collection that seems appropriate). It should have two methods that load appropriate data from the database; one takes a staff member's name as an argument, the other takes a status value as an argument. These methods submit appropriately parameterized SQL queries to the database and fill the collection with RequestData objects that are created to hold the information returned in the rows of the result set for the query.

Other methods of the Records class will include accessor functions for the collection (or maybe for an Iterator associated with the collection).

● *RequestData*

This class defines a holder for strings, integers and dates. You will need to invoke access methods from scriptlet JSP code and from tag library-based JSP code.

static HTML pages

Static HTML pages will be needed for the login and for error reports etc.

JSPs

● *Requestor.jsp*

This JSP displays a table with details of requests submitted by the staff member who invoked it. The table should show for each request: request number, status, description and date submitted. If a supervisor has reviewed the request, the table should also identify the supervisor, his or her decision, the comment and the review date. If an accountant has also reviewed the request, the table should again show the relevant review data.

The form for entering additional funding requests appears below this table. This form has a single text input field, 'Description', used to enter details of the staff member's latest request, along with a submit button. Figure 8.1 illustrates a possible appearance for a page generated by this JSP.

Accountant	Approval	Comment	Date
Sandra	true	OK	2002–02–06

Request #	Status	Description	Date
14	Implemented	$891 for part SS024–x3	2002–01–30

Supervisor	Approval	Comment	Date
Carmen	true	OK	2002–02–04

Accountant	Approval	Comment	Date
Sandra	true	OK	2002–02–06

Request #	Status	Description	Date
19	Approved by supervisor	$1900 for lazerout	2002–02–20

Supervisor	Approval	Comment	Date
Carmen	true	OK	2002–02–28

Request #	Status	Description	Date
21	Approved by supervisor	$1000 for copy of Office–2100	2002–02–22

Supervisor	Approval	Comment	Date
Carmen	true	OK	2002–02–28

New request

Description	I

Make Request

Figure 8.1

- *Reviewer.jsp*

Both supervisors and accountants can use this JSP. It should display a table with details of those requests that are waiting review, and a form that allows the supervisor or accountant to take action on a selected request. The table should show for each request: request number, requestor name, description and date submitted. If a supervisor has reviewed the request, the table should also identify the supervisor, the decision, the comment and the review date.

The form for entering decision data appears below this table. This form has three input controls; the first is a text input field used to enter the identifier number of the request; the second consists of a pair of radio button controls with values 'Approve' and 'Reject'; and the final control is a text input field 'reason' used to enter a comment. Figure 8.2 illustrates a possible appearance for a page generated by this JSP.

- JSP versions

You should create the same two JSPs using scriptlet and tag technologies.

- Requestor1.jsp/Reviewer1.jsp

These JSPs pick up an Iterator from the request. Scriptlet (Java) code embedded in the mainly HTML code of the JSP should arrange to process each item accessed via

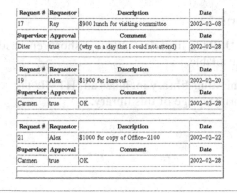

Figure 8.2

the iterator. The "RequestData" object obtained at each cycle of the iterative loop can be accessed to retrieve the data needed for the table.

– `Requestor2.jsp/Reviewer2.jsp`

These pages are similar to those in version 1; however, `logic:iterate` and `logic:present` tags from the struts logic library are used instead of scriptlet code for control, and `bean:write` tags are used instead of scriptlet code to get data values for printing in the table. Your `WEB-INF` directory will need to contain a copy of the `struts.jar` library file and the tag library descriptors for the `struts-logic` and `struts-bean` libraries. The JSPs will need appropriate directives specifying the use of these extra tag libraries.

Short answer questions

(1) Explain how servlets and JSPs can:

- Share 'application' data

- Maintain 'session' data

- Augment 'request' data and then pass the modified request to other servlets/JSPs

(2) Explain the 'JSP Model 2 or MVC' architecture for a web application.

(3) Why are action tags preferable to scriptlet coding for JSPs?

(4) Explain how Java reflection mechanisms and 'bean' coding conventions make it possible for bean manipulation code to be generated automatically.

Explorations

(1) Research 'JSP tag libraries'. Write a short report identifying the major tag libraries that are now available.

(2) The Apache struts library includes an 'HTML' tag section. Identify and write a report on the appropriate usage of this library.

9

XML

This chapter has first an introductory overview of XML (eXtensible Markup Language) and a few of its applications, and then an example showing how XML (along with associated technologies such as the stylesheet language) can be used to organize the display of data. The next section has a brief foray into Wireless Markup Language (WML) and its applications. Finally, there is an introduction to XML parsing.

9.1 XML overview

XML: another story of success beyond all expectation! The eXtensible Markup Language was to be '*a simple, very flexible text format derived from the Standard Generalized Markup Language*'; one that was designed to '*meet the challenge of large-scale electronic publishing*'. The applications envisaged for XML included:

- The definition of industry-specific protocols for the exchange of data, with an emphasis on the data of electronic commerce.

- The provision of sophisticated stylesheet mechanisms that would allow users to display data in chosen formats.

- Support for metadata – data *about* information – that would help people find information and help information producers and consumers find each other

The original proposed application of XML for defining industry-specific protocols for data interchange has proven successful. Numerous industries have agreed on standards for XML documents that should be used for business intercommunication. XML for data interchange is not limited to commercial applications. Scientists want to exchange data – on astronomical observations, protein sequences, chemical reactions and so forth. As the use of XML for data interchange has grown, numerous other data exchange applications have been found in areas including education, arts and entertainment, news services, and multimedia. Each such use is described via a document type definition that specifies the data elements that will appear in the XML documents. There are semi-official standards for these XML-based systems; they can obtain endorsement from W3C (the organization that defines standards for the Web). The site http://www.xml.org/ contains details of recently approved standards.

As well as succeeding in these areas, numerous less obvious applications of XML have emerged. The web.xml files, as used in the last two chapters, constitute one such application; these XML files have proven to be a fine replacement for older schemes for defining environment data and initialization data. (Microsoft's .NET system uses similar files to specify its deployment.) XML turns up again with 'Ant'. Ant – another project from apache.org – is a program build-tool primarily for Java applications; it is a platform-independent build-tool comparable to Unix's make tool or the batch file build facilities in Windows. Ant works from program structure definitions encoded in XML files. A quite different use is in the Simple Object Access Protocol (SOAP); here XML documents are used as part of the infrastructure supporting a form of Remote Procedure Call (where an object in one program utilizes the services of an object in some other program most likely running on a different machine). SOAP is an attempt to finesse all the interprocess communication protocols used in Java-RMI, CORBA etc.; SOAP codes its messages as little XML documents.

The varied applications of XML are outside the scope of this text. This chapter provides only a brief introduction to XML and related technologies and then illustrates a few uses, primarily in the context of Java-based web applications.

XML is, primarily, *a method for putting structured data in a text file*. The data can be anything – data records retrieved from some database table, environment and initialization data for a program, chemical reaction mechanisms, astronomical tables, mathematical formulae, insurance claim forms, instructions for deploying a software package, or anything else you want. Most often the data are fairly mundane; they are the data that you would get by doing a join on a group of relational tables. So they might be customer identification data (number, name, address, phone, optionally a fax number, email address), or order data (book ISBN, quantity, unit price).

Generally, an XML text file has a defined structure. This structure is normally defined in a separate file, though the structure definition can be included as a kind of header for the data in the XML data file itself. The 'document type descriptor', in this supplementary file, can specify the 'elements' that must be described in the data file. For each element, it gives details of required and optional sub-elements; this scheme extends to an arbitrary degree of nesting. For each sub-element, the document type description defines the data fields, along with some information about the values permitted in these fields.

So what is so great about a text data file and a supplementary data description file?

One of the slogans promoting XML suggests an answer – 'Portable Data'. The XML data file and the related structure description file supply the data that you require, making you independent of the original data source. The data source supplies these documents. You use them as you wish to:

- Display the data.
- Perform further processing on the data.

A data display example could, for instance, involve data from a database containing the names, phone numbers and email addresses of your friends. You might wish to display such data in pretty HTML tables for your web browser; you might also wish to have much simpler Wireless Markup Language (WML) tables for display on your WAP phone. You could write two separate data access systems, but you could use a single access program that returned the data as an XML file, and have two different display components that format these data as desired.

As an illustration of a 'processing' application, consider a database of books. There are many ways that you might want to process the information in such a database: find all the books mentioning a particular word in their title, find books by a given author, find the average cost of a book, find the books still on back order etc. If you were offering this as a service via a web interface, you would have to support many different searches against your database. It might be simpler to offer a single service – '*download an XML file with the book data*'. Users could then write their own little programs to scramble through the resulting text file, extracting the specific data that they require.

If you have exclusive use of a data source, you are usually better off writing programs that extract and manipulate the data directly. The conventional approach interrogates a database using specific queries that extract only the data that are required; these data are immediately available for processing by the same program. The more costly XML route involves the following steps:

- Interrogation of the data source with a general query.

- Creation of a verbose XML text document containing all the data in the result set.

- Transfer of the text file to a client, or to a separate process, for further processing.

- Re-analysis of the contents of the text file.

- Extraction of the subset of data that are really required.

- Processing of the selected subset data.

- Generation of output.

The extra costs arise from the need to generate and transfer the large intermediary text files, and through the repeated parsing of the same data.

You would want to avoid those costs if you have exclusive use of the data; but if you are sharing data, the XML route is preferable. It is more flexible, and often more secure. The flexibility comes from the fact that you do not have to predefine the uses of the data and support these different uses at the data source. The source simply delivers a copy of the data; the client uses the copied data as desired. The security advantage comes from the narrowing of the interface that is presented by the data source. If you try to support multiple uses at the data source, you typically start by defining a Java remote interface or a CORBA IDL interface, or some remote interfaces for EJB objects. Specialized server programs implementing these interfaces have to be written for the different applications. Then you must deploy these servers with access control lists, roles etc. to try to limit who does what to your database. If data can be modified in the database, you must have security analyses of each of the data modification functions, and lots of code segments, in different programs, that check submitted data. If you follow the XML route, you have at most two functions to support – '*download the XML data file*' and '*upload an XML update file*'. Uploaded data can be thoroughly checked before they ever get near the database.

9.2   XML and friends

XML is just one of a group of interrelated technologies. The group includes:

- DTD: the Document Type Definition system used to specify the structure of an XML document.

- XSL: the eXtensible Stylesheet Language that can be used to define rules for transforming an XML document into another format (such as HTML, WML or Adobe PDF).

- XQL: a 'query language' designed to allow representation of queries that are to be run against relational databases.

- XPATH: a mechanism for locating/identifying specific elements within an XML document.

- Schema: a newer, more sophisticated document definition system that will eventually replace DTD.

- SAX: an application programmer interface that defines methods useful for programs that need to read XML documents and perform simple data extraction tasks.

- DOM: another application programmer interface that defines more elaborate mechanisms that allow a program to construct and manipulate a data structure that represents the structure and holds the content data extracted from an XML document.

A 'marked up' document consists of content text (data) embedded within 'tags' that convey metadata – information about how to display or interpret the subsequent section of content text. HTML should be a familiar example of a markup language (although it is a bit sloppy and does not obey all the rules for a good markup language). HTML has a predefined set of tags that convey information about how a web browser should display the content text. Tags can be used in a number of ways

- *<tag>body text</tag>*
For example: `<bold>Buy now!</bold>`
   (HTML is sloppy in that it tolerates missing end tags; for example, most HTML lists appear like `<ul><li>...<li>...<li>...</ul>`, with none of the list-item `<li>` tags ever being properly closed by a matching `</li>`.)

- *<tag with values for required and optional attributes>body text</tag>*
For example: `<th colspan=4 align=center>Seasonal costs</th>`

- *<tag with values for required and optional attributes>*
For example: `<input type=submit onfocus="...">`
   (Here again, HTML is sloppy. There is nothing to indicate an end for the `input` tag.)

XML is a more disciplined markup language. It is a language that allows the definition of a custom set of tags. An XML document will again consist of text (data) embedded within tags (along with optional 'processing instructions', and possibly a `DOCTYPE` declaration –

both are described later). Tags can have required and optional attributes. Attribute values must appear in quotes (double quotes are preferred). The document can contain many nested elements (*start-tag*, *body*, *end-tag*), with any attributes required for an element appearing in its start tag. A tag that merely requires attributes has to be self-closing, so an XML version of the input tag example would have to be `<input type="submit" onfocus="..." />`.

An XML document is 'well formed' if all tags are properly closed, and the elements (tags and content data) are correctly nested. Elements are nested when a start tag is followed by another start tag, body, end tag combination that comes before the element's own matching end tag. For example, in the following fragment, the `servlet-name` and `servlet-class` elements along with their data are both properly nested within the servlet element:

```
<servlet>
  <servlet-name>
    RatesServlet
  </servlet-name>
  <servlet-class>
    RateChangeServlet
  </servlet-class>
</servlet>
```

The following fragments are badly formed XML documents:

```
<servlet>
  <servlet-name>
    RatesServlet
  <servlet-class>
  </servlet-name>
    RateChangeServlet
  </servlet-class>
</servlet>

<servlet>
  <servlet-name>
    HoursServlet
  <servlet-class>
    WorkerServlet
  </servlet-class>
</servlet>
```

The first fails because of incorrect nesting of tags, while the second fails because of the missing end tag for the servlet name.

The requirement for correct nesting of elements implies that well-formed documents have implicit tree-like structures. There is a root-element – the first tag that is opened (e.g. the `web-app` element in a `web.xml` file). Elements nested within this correspond to first-level nodes within the tree. Further nesting of elements leads to sub-branches. Data appear at the leaves of the tree. Many of the processing functions that are applied to XML documents incorporate basic tree-traversal algorithms such as those studied in data structures courses.

The 'well-formed' requirement represents a very weak constraint on the contents of an XML document (though it is a constraint that is violated by most HTML pages). A stronger constraint on the content of an XML document is a requirement that it is 'valid' – that is, its use of tags complies with rules specified in an accompanying Document Type Definition.

Validity checks are not necessary for all XML documents. A `tomcat-users.xml` file with its names, passwords and roles must be a well-formed XML document, but there is no document type definition for this file, and there are no checks done on its structure:

```
<tomcat-users>
  <user name="tomcat" password="tomcat" roles="tomcat" />
  <user name="role1" password="tomcat" roles="role1,worker" />
  <user name="John" password="LOS1z3" roles="worker " />
  ...
  <user name="Colin" password="Password" roles="boss,manager,worker" />
</tomcat-users>
```

However, most XML documents have associated document type definitions, and are required to be compliant with their definitions.

A Document Type Definition (DTD) can specify the permitted elements; their structural relationships (e.g. '*a servlet-name element can only be used within the body of a servlet element*'); and their attributes. A DTD can specify constraints like the following:

- Element X is composed of:
  – Exactly one Y1
  – One or more Y2s
  – Optionally a Y3
  – Any number of Y4s
  – And either a Y5 or a Y6

- Element Y1 is composed of a Z1 or a Z2.

- Element Z1 is a text string.

DTDs are written using simple forms of regular expressions. The following is part of the DTD that defines the correct form for `web.xml` files as used for servlets:

```
<!ELEMENT web-app (icon?, display-name?, description?, distributable?,
  context-param*, servlet*, servlet-mapping*, session-config?,
  mime-mapping*, ..., security-role*, ...)>
<!ELEMENT icon (small-icon?|large-icon?)>
<!ELEMENT small-icon (#PCDATA)>
```

```
...
<!ELEMENT param-name (#PCDATA)>
...
<!ELEMENT servlet (icon?, servlet-name, display-name?, description?,
  (servlet-class|jsp-file), init-param*, load-on-startup?,
  security-role-ref*)>
<!ELEMENT servlet-name (#PCDATA)>
...
<!ELEMENT init-param (param-name, param-value, description?)>
...
```

This particular DTD defines only tags and their structural relations; it does not mention any attributes.

The ELEMENT servlet part states that the body of a servlet tag can contain:

- An optional icon element ('?' used to indicate 0 or 1 as in regular expressions)

- A servlet-name element

- An optional display-name element

- An optional description element

- Either a servlet-class element or a jsp-file element (regular expression with '|' operator)

- Zero or more init-param elements ('*' used to indicate 0–*n* as in regular expressions)

- An optional load-on-startup element

- Zero or more security-role-ref elements

Similarly, it specifies that an init-param contains a param-name element, a param-value element and an optional description; both the param-name and param-value consist of text data (#PCDATA – parsed character data). In all cases, the specified elements must appear in the order shown in the DTD.

A complete web.xml document such as would have to be validated against this DTD is:

```
<?xml version="1.0" encoding="ISO-8859-1"?>
<!DOCTYPE web-app
  PUBLIC "-//Sun Microsystems, Inc.//DTD Web Application 2.2//EN"
  "http://java.sun.com/j2ee/dtds/web-app_2_2.dtd">
<web-app>
  <servlet>
    <servlet-name>servlet1</servlet-name>
    <servlet-class>GreetingsServlet</servlet-class>
  </servlet>
  <servlet-mapping>
```

```
        <servlet-name>servlet1</servlet-name>
        <url-pattern>/servlet1</url-pattern>
    </servlet-mapping>
</web-app>
```

The first line, `<?xml ... ?>` is a 'processing instruction'. These are similar to directives in JSPs; they provide information to an interpreter that is processing the XML file. This instruction defines the dialect of XML that is used in the document. The next entry, `<!DOCTYPE ... >`, specifies the DTD that contains the rules for a valid web-app document. A DOCTYPE declaration names the document type, in this case a 'web-app', and provides a URI for the DTD file. If the DTD represents an official standard, the URI can be specified as PUBLIC and will reference a URI on the web. If the DTD is a little home-brew affair, the URI would be specified as SYSTEM and would identify a file in the local system. You can have both – it means that there is an official public standard and that you have a copy in your local file system.

The web-app DTD, as shown in part above, contained only ELEMENT definitions as used to specify structural relations. More typically, a DTD will be made up from ELEMENT definitions, ATTLIST attribute definitions and ENTITY references.

Element definitions can take a variety of forms:

- `<!ELEMENT TagOnly EMPTY>`

For example: `<!ELEMENT distributable EMPTY>`

This form specifies that a *TagOnly* element, such as the 'distributable' element defined in the web-app DTD, is simply to appear (or not appear as the case may be) in an XML file (if it appears it may have some attributes). It should not be used with a body part. An entry in an XML file for this element would appear like `<distributable />`.

- `<!ELEMENT TypicalInfoField (#PCDATA)>`

For example: `<!ELEMENT param-name (#PCDATA) >`

This form defines an element whose value is 'parsed character data' – really a string. An entry in an XML file for this element would appear like `<param-name>DBUser</parma-name>`.

- `<!ELEMENT StructuralElement ([Nested Element], [Nested Element], ... ) >`

For example: `<!ELEMENT context-param (param-name, param-value, description?>)`

This form defines the real structure of an XML document by specifying how elements are composed of nested sub-elements.

The rules for defining nested elements within a structural element are similar to simple regular expressions. The following symbols may be appended to the names of nested sub-elements:

- ?   Tag for optional sub-element

- *   Tag for $(0..n)$ repeatable optional sub-element

- + Tag for (1..*n*) repeatable required sub-element
- | Used to specify alternatives

As well as defining the structural relations among elements, and thereby the permitted nesting of tags in a compatible XML document, the DTD should specify the attributes that are permitted in the tags and should indicate whether or not these are required or optional. Constraints specifying attributes take the form:

```
<!ATLIST element
  attribute-name type modifier
  ...
>
```

The attribute names are arbitrary. Types can include CDATA (which means that the element value must be a character string), or an enumeration of constants, or may be entity references (the type of the data being defined by the referenced entity). Modifiers can be default values, or the #IMPLIED tag (which really means that the attribute is optional), or be #REQUIRED which just specifies that some value must be provided if the tag appears in an XML document. The DTD for JSPs (http://java.sun.com/dtd/jspxml.dtd) contains examples defining attributes for various elements. For example:

```
<!ELEMENT jsp:directive.include EMPTY>
<!ATTLIST jsp:directive.include
  file %URI; #REQUIRED
>
```

These lines mean that a jsp include directive in a JSP should have no body; if it appears, a jsp:include tag must have a file attribute whose value is the URI of the file that is to be included (earlier in the jspwxml.dtd file, there is an entity declaration that says that a %URI is made up of character data). A similar use of attributes appears for the jsp page directive:

```
<!ELEMENT jsp:directive.page EMPTY>
<!ATTLIST jsp:directive.page
  language    CDATA      "java"
  extends     %ClassName; #IMPLIED
  contentType %Content;   "text/html; ISO-8859-1"
  import      CDATA      #IMPLIED
  session     %Bool;     "true"
  buffer      CDATA      "8kb"
  autoFlush   %Bool;     "true"
  isThreadSafe %Bool;    "true"
  info        CDATA      #IMPLIED
  errorPage   %URL;      #IMPLIED
  isErrorPage %Bool;     "false"
>
```

This states that a jsp page directive should have a language attribute, whose value will be a name; if the attribute is not present, the default value java should be used. Default values are provided for the other required attributes that define properties like the content type of the returned document. The extends, import, info and errorPage attributes are optional.

Entity references are mainly used to insert either small pieces of fixed text or the contents of complete files into an XML file. For example, given the following entity definitions in a DTD:

```
<!ELEMENT CNOTICE (#PCDATA)>
<!ENTITY MyShortNotice "Copyright by me">
<!ENTITY MyLONGNotice PUBLIC "http://me.org/legal/copyright.xml" >
```

you could use the following entity reference in an XML document:

```
<CNOTICE>&MyShortNotice</CNOTICE>
```

and in effect substitute in the short version of the copyright notice.

The jspxml.dtd used entities to define commonly used value patterns for its attributes:

```
<!ENTITY % ClassName "CDATA">
<!ENTITY % Bool "(true|false|yes|no)">
```

DTDs are usually defined separately in their own files. But you can have a DOCTYPE declaration that contains the element definitions etc. as a kind of 'here' document. Such a declaration can go at the start of an XML file. The following example (from http://www.vervet.com/) is supposed to define an appropriate structure for a newspaper article. It would appear at the start of each XML file that used this definition:

```
<!DOCTYPE NEWSPAPER [
<!ELEMENT NEWSPAPER (ARTICLE+)>
<!ELEMENT ARTICLE (HEADLINE, BYLINE, LEAD, BODY, NOTES)>
<!ELEMENT HEADLINE (#PCDATA)>
<!ELEMENT BYLINE (#PCDATA)>
<!ELEMENT LEAD (#PCDATA)>
<!ELEMENT BODY (#PCDATA)>
<!ELEMENT NOTES (#PCDATA)>
<!ATTLIST ARTICLE AUTHOR CDATA #REQUIRED>
<!ATTLIST ARTICLE EDITOR CDATA #IMPLIED>
<!ATTLIST ARTICLE DATE CDATA #IMPLIED>
<!ATTLIST ARTICLE EDITION CDATA #IMPLIED>
<!ENTITY NEWSPAPER "Vervet Logic Times">
<!ENTITY PUBLISHER "Vervet Logic Press">
<!ENTITY COPYRIGHT "Copyright 1998 Vervet Logic Press">
]>
```

DTD documents are not themselves defined using XML style tags; they have their own distinct structural rules. They also have limitations. You can specify requirements like 'optional element', 'occurs zero or more times' and 'should contain text data', but you cannot specify requirement like 'sub-element that should appear exactly three times' or 'must be a string of hexadecimal digits'. The newer 'Schemas' provide greater flexibility and are themselves well-formed XML documents. Currently, DTDs are the dominant technology for defining the structure of valid XML documents, but this will change with a move to the use of Schemas.

9.3   XSL, XSLT and XML display

The eXtensible Stylesheet Language (XSL) can be used to implement 'programs' that specify how to transform an XML document into some changed form. The changed form might be an XML document based on a different DTD, or an HTML document, or a PDF file. These "programs" incorporate structure-matching rules that identify the elements of an XML document that are to be processed, and quasi-procedural style code to define the actual transformations applied to the selected data. The code can be quite sophisticated; incorporating features like the ability to sort extracted data prior to its insertion into a new document.

An XSL 'program' file is, naturally, an XML document with its own DTD. This DTD defines the forms of the various matching rules that you can use. XSL documents have the basic structure:

```
<?xml version="1.0"?>
<xsl:stylesheet xmlns:xsl="http://www.w3.org/1999/XSL/Transform"
version="1.0">

...

</xsl:stylesheet>
```

An XSL Transform (XSLT) system takes the rules from an XSL stylesheet and applies them to the contents of given XML documents. An XSLT incorporates an interpreter for the xsl stylesheet rule tags. Microsoft's IE browser incorporates such an XSL processor. IE can download an XML file, identify the required XSL stylesheet from a link in the XML file, download this stylesheet, and apply the transforms to the contents of the XML file to display the data. This in-built capability makes IE an attractive environment for experimenting with XML/XSL combinations. (As so often with Microsoft products, IE's XSL interpreter is not quite compatible with the standards. It is also designed to support and encourage the use of various Microsoft-specific extensions.)

Most of the examples used in this section and the next relate to the display of data from the soccer match database that was used earlier in both PHP and JSP examples. The following illustrates a well-formed XML data file that contains information extracted from that database:

```
<?xml version="1.0" encoding="ISO8859-1" ?>
<SOCCER>
<GAME day="04-09-00">
<HOME>Norths</HOME>
<AWAY>Souths</AWAY>
<SCORE1>1</SCORE1>
<SCORE2>2</SCORE2>
</GAME>
<GAME day="04-09-00">
<HOME>East</HOME>
<AWAY>Wests</AWAY>
<SCORE1>2</SCORE1>
<SCORE2>1</SCORE2>
</GAME>
</SOCCER>
```

If IE is used to display a file, it will make a reasonable attempt at indicating the inherently tree-structured nature of the contents of the document. IE's basic output is illustrated in Figure 9.1.

The data in this document should really be displayed in tabular form within a standard web page display. This requires a stylesheet – XSL 'program'. This will have to specify that some standard HTML be used to perform tasks like putting a title on the page and setting up the structure of an HTML table with its column headers. Next, there will need to be some code that specifies how each GAME element in the XML document be processed to yield data that will form the content of a single row of this table. Finally, the standard HTML tags that close a table and complete the page will have to be output.

An XSL program to accomplish these tasks is:

```
<xsl:stylesheet xmlns:xsl="http://www.w3.org/TR/WD-xsl">
  <xsl:template match="/">
```

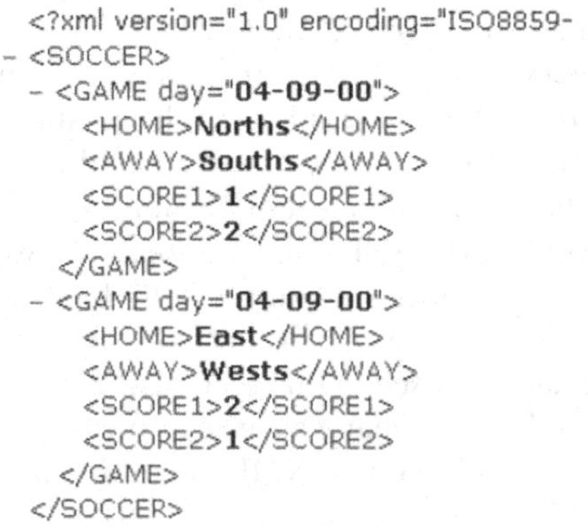

```
<?xml version="1.0" encoding="ISO8859-
- <SOCCER>
  - <GAME day="04-09-00">
      <HOME>Norths</HOME>
      <AWAY>Souths</AWAY>
      <SCORE1>1</SCORE1>
      <SCORE2>2</SCORE2>
    </GAME>
  - <GAME day="04-09-00">
      <HOME>East</HOME>
      <AWAY>Wests</AWAY>
      <SCORE1>2</SCORE1>
      <SCORE2>1</SCORE2>
    </GAME>
  </SOCCER>
```

Figure 9.1 Internet Explorer displaying the structure of an XML document.

```
<html> <body>
<table border="2" bgcolor="blue" align="center">
<tr>
  <th>Home team</th><th>Away team</th>
  <th>Home score</th><th>Away score</th>
  <th>Date</th>
</tr>
<xsl:for-each select="SOCCER/GAME">
  <tr>
    <td><xsl:value-of select="HOME"/></td>
    <td><xsl:value-of select="AWAY"/></td>
    <td><xsl:value-of select="SCORE1"/></td>
    <td><xsl:value-of select="SCORE2"/></td>
    <td><xsl:value-of select="@day"/></td>
  </tr>
</xsl:for-each>
</table>
</body></html>
</xsl:template>
</xsl:stylesheet>
```

The XML document has to be changed to include a link to the XSL stylesheet:

```
<?xml version="1.0" encoding="ISO8859-1" ?>
<?xml-stylesheet type="text/xsl" href="Soccer.xsl"?>
<SOCCER>
<GAME day="04-09-00">
...
</GAME>
...
</SOCCER>
```

When given this combination of XML data file and XSL program file, IE produces a display like that shown in Figure 9.2.

The example XSL program has the basic structure:

Home team	Away team	Home score	Away score	Date
Norths	Souths	1	2	04-09-00
East	Wests	2	1	04-09-00

Figure 9.2 Internet Explorer displaying the same data as processed using an XSL program.

```
<xsl:stylesheet xmlns:xsl="http://www.w3.org/TR/WD-xsl">
  <xsl:template match="/">
    <!-- Code defining processing and fixed content for output -->
    <html> <body>
    ...
    <xsl:for-each select="SOCCER/GAME">
      ...
    </xsl:for-each>
    </table></body></html>
  </xsl:template>
</xsl:stylesheet>
```

The xsl:stylesheet element encloses 'template match' element(s). A template match element has an attribute that identifies those elements of an XML file that are to be processed; the body of a template match element can contain text that is to be output whenever such an element is found, and also code for extracting data from the XML element. Here only one template match element is used. It specifies its matching target as '/' – i.e. the root element (just as '/' on Unix means the root element of the file hierarchy). (Using '/' works with IE's XSL interpreter, but does not work with all XSL interpreters; more typically, the tag for the root element would have to be specified – match="SOCCER".)

When a match is found, the body of an xsl:template is processed. Here, the body consists of some HTML tags. These are copied to the output (the buffer where the HTML page is being assembled). These HTML tags provide the header for the table with the column captions etc.

The next element in the stylesheet is the xsl:foreach construct. This takes a select argument that specifies the elements of the XML document that it is to match. This argument is an XPATH expression; it is very similar in structure to a partial directory path for a Unix file hierarchy. Here the pattern specifies that all GAME elements within the SOCCER context are to be processed:

```
<xsl:for-each select="SOCCER/GAME">
  <tr>
    <td><xsl:value-of select="HOME"/></td>
    <td><xsl:value-of select="AWAY"/></td>
    <td><xsl:value-of select="SCORE1"/></td>
    <td><xsl:value-of select="SCORE2"/></td>
    <td><xsl:value-of select="@day"/></td>
  </tr>
</xsl:for-each>
```

The processing applied to each GAME element involves extraction of data using the xsl:value-of operations. Those with a form like <xsl:value-of select="HOME"> are to get the character data associated with an element (the HOME element) nested within the current element (i.e. the current SOCCER/GAME element). The final example, <xsl:value-of select="@day">, is to get the value of the day attribute of the current SOCCER/GAME element.

Once extracted, the selected data are embedded among the HTML tags that define the content of a row in an HTML table.

A slightly more elaborate version of the same XSL program is:

```
<?xml version='1.0'?>
<xsl:stylesheet xmlns:xsl="http://www.w3.org/TR/WD-xsl">

<xsl:template match="/">
  <html><body>
  <table border="2" align="center">
  <caption>Draw Soccer Matches</caption>
  <tr>
  <th>Home team</th>
  <th>Away team</th>
  <th>Home score</th>
  <th>Away score</th>
  <th>Date</th>
  </tr>
  <xsl:for-each select="SOCCER/GAME[SCORE1 = SCORE2]">
    <tr>
      <td><xsl:value-of select="HOME"/></td>
      <td><xsl:value-of select="AWAY"/></td>
      <td><xsl:value-of select="SCORE1"/></td>
      <td><xsl:value-of select="SCORE2"/></td>
      <td><xsl:value-of select="@day"/></td>
    </tr>
  </xsl:for-each>
  </table>
  <br /> <br /><hr />
  <table border="2" align="center">
  <caption>Home Wins</caption>
  <tr>
    <th>Home team</th>
    ...
    <th>Date</th>
    </tr>
  <xsl:for-each select="SOCCER/GAME[SCORE1 &gt; SCORE2]">
    <tr>
      <td><xsl:value-of select="HOME"/></td>
      ...
    </tr>
  </xsl:for-each>
  </table><br /> <br /><hr />
  <table border="2" align="center">
  <caption>Away Wins</caption>
```

```
<tr>...</tr>
<xsl:for-each select="SOCCER/GAME[SCORE1 &lt; SCORE2]">
  <tr>
    <td><xsl:value-of select="HOME"/></td>
    ...
  </tr>
</xsl:for-each>
</table><br /> <br /><hr />
</body></html>
</xsl:template>
</xsl:stylesheet>
```

Figure 9.3 illustrates the IE display when this XSL program was used to format data for a slightly more comprehensive XML listing of soccer match results. The code defined within the template match now has three loops, each for processing different subsets of the match data. The first processes drawn games, the second deals with the home wins, and the third displays away wins. These different subsets are specified using more complex XPATH expressions. The basic path – SOCCER/GAME – is supplemented by a test on the values of elements within the current SOCCER/GAME element. The drawn matches are those with equal scores – [SCORE1 = SCORE2], home wins have [SCORE1 > SCORE2] (you

Home wins

Home team	Away team	Home score	Away score	Date
East	Wests	2	1	04-09-00
Eagles	Steelers	2	1	04-09-00
City	Wests	2	1	11-09-00
East	Norths	3	1	11-09-00
City	Rovers	2	0	11-09-00

Away wins

Home team	Away team	Home score	Away score	Date
Norths	Souths	1	2	04-09-00

Drawn games

Home team	Away team	Home score	Away score	Date
City	United	0	0	04-09-00
Rovers	Forest	1	1	04-09-00

Figure 9.3 Data display from a more elaborate XSL program.

have to use > because the '>' symbol is, of course, serving a specialized role as a tag-closing character). Another point to note is that all the HTML tags that are included in the XSL document must comply with the need for 'well-formedness' – so they must all be closed. This requirement accounts for the slightly odd-looking tags <br /> and <hr />.

This example illustrates how you can avoid the need for specialized processing at the data source. Previously, as in the PHP and JSP examples, listings of drawn games, away wins etc. had to be produced by specialized processing at the data source. Now the source can simply dump all data – the results of all soccer games – as an XML file. The data selection can be handled within the formatting and display component.

There are a number of tutorials on XSL available on the web; the sites include http://www.nwalsh.com/docs/tutorials/xsl/xsl/frames.html and http://www.xml101.com/xsl/default.asp/. The XSL 'programming' constructs include:

- 'Function definitions': an xsl:template has a role analogous to a function; it specifies how a particular type of element in the XML file should be processed. The element type is defined by the XPATH expression given in the template. There are mechanisms defined for applying all templates (there is a fairly involved priority scheme that determines which template to process first when there are several that could be run because data elements are present that satisfy their XPATH requirements). There are also mechanisms for explicitly invoking a specific template.

Simple examples have a single template that matches the root element of the XML document. This is a bit like beginner Pascal and C programming examples, where everything is in a single main() function.

- Loop construct: the xsl:for-each element acts very much like a Perl/PHP foreach statement acting on a list; the list of data elements processed is determined by the select attribute of an xsl:for-each tag.

- Conditional constructs: these include an xsl:if and and xsl:choose that, together with xsl:when and xsl:otherwise components, makes a form of case statement.

- Built-in sorting capability: this is provided via the xsl:sort element and also by order attributes in selection clauses used in constructs like xsl:for-each.

- Data access: the xsl:value-of construct is used to get values from nested elements or from attributes of the current element in the XML file.

There are a few more exotic xsl operators that are occasionally required.

Some of xsl's sorting abilities are illustrated in the following example. The data file comes from the Apache toolset for working with XML; this is an XML file with information about birds:

```
<?xml version="1.0" encoding="UTF-8"?>
<?xml-stylesheet type="text/xsl" href="birds.xsl"?>
<Class>
  <Order Name="TINAMIFORMES">
```

```
    <Family Name="TINAMIDAE">
      <Species Scientific_Name="Tinamus major">
      Great Tinamou.</Species>
      <Species Scientific_Name="Nothocercus">
      Highland Tinamou.</Species>
      ...
    </Family>
  </Order>
  <Order Name="GAVIIFORMES">
    <Family Name="GAVIIDAE">
    ...
```

The following XSL program produces an HTML page with these data shown in tabular form. The 'program' is again written like a single main() function (with a template that matches the root element – Class). This outputs the HTML page headers; then in the loop

```
<xsl:for-each select="Class/Order" order-by="+ @Name" >
```

it works through each of the 'Orders' of birds, displaying tabular data for that order. The Order elements in the XML file are in an arbitrary sequence. The report is required to display the tables for the different Orders in ascending sequence by Name – so the GAVIIFORMES data should appear before the TINAMIFORMES. This sorting requirement is specified through the order-by attribute in the xsl:for-each tag; an order-by attribute specifies ascending order ('+') or descending order ('-') and identifies the data element or attribute used.

```
<?xml version='1.0'?><xsl:stylesheet xmlns:xsl="http://www.w3.org/TR/WD-
xsl">
<xsl:template match="/">
  <html><head><title>Apache's Birds</title></head> <body>
    <xsl:for-each select="Class/Order" order-by="+ @Name" >
    <h1><xsl:value-of select="@Name" /></h1>
    <xsl:for-each select="Family" order-by="- @Name" >
    <table><tr><th>Scientific Name</th><th>Common Name</th></tr>
      <xsl:for-each select="Species">
        <tr><td><xsl:value-of select="@Scientific_Name" /></td>
        <td><xsl:value-of select ="." /></td></tr>
      </xsl:for-each>
      </table>
    </xsl:for-each>
    <br /><br /><hr />
    </xsl:for-each>
  </body> </html>
</xsl:template>
</xsl:stylesheet>
```

Each Order consists of several Families, and a Family comprises many species. The report separates the sections for different orders by horizontal rules. Each Order has separate tables for each Family, with a table containing the scientific and common names for the species in that family. The tables generated for the Families are shown in reverse order of Family name (<xsl:for-each select="Family" order-by="- @Name" >). Each table row contains the scientific name of the species as given by the Scientific_Name attribute of a Species element; the common name is the value of that element (current element has an XPATH '.' – just like the current directory when traversing a Unix file hierarchy):

```
<tr><td><xsl:value-of select="@Scientific_Name" /></td>
<td><xsl:value-of select ="." /></td></tr>
```

For an example using conditionals, consider a program that produces a table of book records that highlights those 'on special'. The example book data are illustrated in the following XML file:

```
<CATALOG>
  <BOOK>
  <TITLE>Java and XML</TITLE>
      <AUTHOR>B. McLaughlin</ AUTHOR >
      <PUBLISHER>USA</PUBLISHER>
      <COMPANY>O'Reilly</COMPANY>
    <LISTPRICE>39.95</LISTPRICE>
    <OURPRICE>31.95</OURPRICE>
    ...
  </BOOK>
  <BOOK>
  ...
  </BOOK>
  ...
</CATALOG>
```

Books are 'on special' if OUR_PRICE is less than LIST_PRICE. Part of an XSL program for displaying these data in an HTML table could be:

```
<table border="2" align="center">
<tr>
  <th>Title</th><th>Author</th><th>Comment</th>
</tr>
<xsl:for-each select="CATALOG/BOOK">
  <tr>
    <td><xsl:value-of select="TITLE"/></td>
    <td><xsl:value-of select="AUTHOR"/></td>
    <xsl:if match=".[OURPRICE &lt; LISTPRICE]">
      <td>On special</td>
```

```
    </xsl:if>
  </tr>
</xsl:for-each>
</table>
```

These examples illustrate a small part of the power of XSL. It makes practical the use of 'Portable data' – XML files with raw data that are to be subject to further selection. With IE, one can simply dump the XML data onto the client browser, which, with the aid of a downloaded XSL program, does the final processing for selection and display of the data. However, one cannot in general rely on the client doing the XSL transforms – it is not a standard feature of all browsers and is too resource-intensive for something like a PDA-based browser or a WAP-phone browser. Usually, the XML data are transformed on the web server immediately prior to transmission back to the client.

The site `http://www.xml101.com/xsl/default.asp` contains examples that illustrate how server-side processing can be done, using VBScript and a `Microsoft.XMLDOM` object on a Microsoft IIS server. For an Apache server, one of the easier ways of processing XML is to use Java Server Pages. Apache has developed an `xsl` tag library for use with the JSP technology.

A first illustrative JSP version of the soccer example involves:

- A JSP with the XML data already embedded in the text of the page.

- An XSL program in a separate file.

- The Apache XSL-related tag class libraries and their associated taglib descriptors installed in the `WEB-INF` subdirectory for the application.

The example JSP is:

```
<%@ page language="java" contentType="text/html" %>
<%@ taglib uri="/xsltaglib" prefix="xsl" %>
<html><head><title>Soccer Games</title></head><body bgcolor="white">
<xsl:apply xsl="Soccer1.xsl">
<?xml version="1.0" encoding="ISO-8859-1"?>
  <SOCCER>
    <GAME day="04-09-00">
      <HOME>Norths</HOME>
      <AWAY>Souths</AWAY>
      <SCORE1>1</SCORE1>
      <SCORE2>2</SCORE2>
    </GAME>
  ...
  </SOCCER>
</xsl:apply>
</body></html>
```

The `taglib` directive specifies use of the `xsl` tags; the `uri` is a partial reference that is resolved relative to data in the `web.xml` deployment file. The `xsl:apply` tag identifies the source file with the XSL transforms and has a body that 'contains' the XML that is to be transformed. In this first example, the body of this tag is the actual XML data; later this will be changed to be an action tag that will retrieve the XML from an appropriate source.

The XSL program for displaying the soccer results in a tabular form is a slightly modified version of that shown earlier. The version for IE and the version for JSP require different references for the standard XSL documents. Another change is that the Java version has to specify the main template as having a match on the SOCCER tag rather than the document root.

```
<?xml version='1.0'?>
<xsl:stylesheet version="1.0"
  xmlns:xsl="http://www.w3.org/1999/XSL/Transform">
<xsl:template match="SOCCER">
  <table border="2" align="center">
  <caption>Draw Soccer Matches</caption>
  <tr>
    <th>Home team</th>
    ...
    <th>Date</th>
  </tr>
  <xsl:for-each select="GAME[SCORE1 = SCORE2]">
  <tr>
    <td><xsl:value-of select="HOME"/></td>
    ...
  </tr>
  </xsl:for-each>
  </table><br /> <br /><hr />
  <table border="2" align="center">
  <caption>Home winds</caption>
  <tr>
    <th>Home team</th>
    ...
    <th>Date</th>
  </tr>

  <xsl:for-each select="GAME[SCORE1 &gt; SCORE2]">
    ...
  </xsl:for-each>
  ...
</xsl:template>
</xsl:stylesheet>
```

The deployment of this example would require a WEB-INF directory with a lib subdirectory holding the xalan.jar, xerces.jar and xsl.jar files downloaded from Apache's XML site; a tlds subdirectory holding the xsl.tld file also from Apache; and finally a web.xml file. The web.xml file would be:

```
<?xml version="1.0" encoding="UTF-8" ?>
<!DOCTYPE web-app ... >
<web-app>
  <taglib>
    <taglib-uri>/xsltaglib</taglib-uri>
    <taglib-location>/WEB-INF/tlds/xsl.tld</taglib-location>
  </taglib>
</web-app>
```

Of course, it is atypical to have the data defined as XML source embedded in the JSP itself. Typically, the data are created by a servlet, a bean or an EJB accessing a database; these data are then held in a bean that gets passed to the JSP for final output. This bean has some accessor method that returns a string with the XML data. Just for this demonstration, one could have a bean holding the predefined data that are returned, as an XML string, through a getResults method:

```
public class SoccerBean {
  public String getResults() {
    StringBuffer buf = new StringBuffer();
    buf.append("<SOCCER>");
    buf.append("<GAME>");
    ...
    return buf.toString();
  }
}
```

The Soccer.jsp page, as modified to use this bean, is:

```
<%@ page language="java" contentType="text/html" %>
<%@ taglib uri="/xsltaglib" prefix="xsl" %>
<html><head><title>Soccer Games</title></head>
<body bgcolor="white">
<xsl:apply xsl="Soccer1.xsl">
<?xml version="1.0" encoding="ISO-8859-1"?>
  <jsp:useBean id="infoBean" class="SoccerBean" />
  <jsp:getProperty name="infoBean" property="results" />
</xsl:apply>
</body>
</html>
```

The `jsp:useBean` action creates an instance of the `SoccerBean` class. The `jsp:getProperty` action gets a string with the XML. This XML string is the body for the `xsl:apply` tag and is therefore the data processed by the `Soccer1.xsl` program.

A different display of the same soccer results data could be obtained by changing the XSL program file that is invoked by this JSP. The JSP/XSL system is not limited to generating HTML outputs. If a different XSL program is used, one can obtain a different form of output. One possibility would be WML (Wireless Markup Language) as used on WAP phones. Generating WML documents and making them available through WAP phones would maybe entertain soccer fanatics, letting them check the league results on their phones as they travel home from a match.

9.4 XML and XSL generating WML

Currently, WAP phones appear to be a technology-based solution seeking a good problem. The phone companies are hoping that a 'killer' application will eventually appear that will result in customers spending much more time (and money) on their phones. In the meantime, there are a number of small web-based interactive applications. The Wireless Markup Language (WML) supports a limited version of form-style data entry; the data are sent to the web server and there can be handled just like input from HTML forms as displayed by a conventional browser. Responses can be prepared and returned to the phones. (Your web server must support the `wml` mime type and send all WML documents with an HTTP header specifying `contentType="text/vnd.wap.wml"`. If the `wml` mime type is not defined in its configuration tables, your server is liable to change the HTTP `content-type` to `text/plain`. WAP phones do not appreciate plain text responses.)

Obviously, the small display screen available on phones is a limitation. The typical screen can display four or five lines of about twenty characters, possibly with some limited scrolling ability that allows a few more lines to be viewed. The memory available on a WAP device is also restricted. These limitations necessitate a different model for documents. HTML pages are often tens of thousands, even hundreds of thousands of bytes in size; they can have essentially arbitrarily large display areas; they can incorporate framesets, multiple layers and elaborate graphic elements. None of these things is possible for WML documents.

WML documents do not use HTML's page model. Instead, they are based around the idea of a 'card deck'. A WML document, as sent to a WAP device, consists of one or more 'cards'. Each individual card contains data that can be displayed within the confines of a small phone screen. A card deck will incorporate some mechanism for moving between cards (a little bit like intra-page links within an HTML document). The total size of a card deck will be limited to a few thousand bytes.

A WML card deck document contains:

- WML markup tags; these include structural tags that define the cards, formatting tags for content layout and style, navigation tags (intra-deck links to other cards, inter-document links to other resources), and tags defining input fields for forms.

- Content text.

- Sometimes, simple, small pictures encoded in .wbmp format.

- Possibly a small amount of WMLScript. WMLScript has a role equivalent to JavaScript in an HTML web page; the client browser executes the scripted code.

The WML markup language is based on XML and consequently is not as sloppy as HTML. All tags must be properly closed; a WML document must be a 'well-formed' XML document. (WML browsers are typically very fussy, and will gag on something as trivial as an extra new-line character before the <wml> tag.)

There are a number of WML tutorials on the Net; one is at http:// www.w3schools.com/wap/default.asp. The following notes just outline a few key points. A WML document is an XML document, normally starting with a <?xml ...?> processing instruction, and a DOCTYPE declaration. The root element for the document is bounded by a <wml> start tag and </wml> end tag. This will contain one or more <card>...</card> elements. The <card> tag has a number of attributes, including id and title; these both take string arguments. The id attribute serves a role analogous to an <a name=...> anchor tag in an HTML document; it identifies a specific section of the document, enabling intra-document jumps. The value of the title attribute should be shown at the top of the phone screen whenever the card is displayed.

Within a card, one can have content text formatted within <p>...</p> paragraph tags. The text can have line breaks (
 tag), and style tags: italic (<i>...</i>), bold (...), underline (<u>...</u>) and font size changes (<big>...</big>, <small>...</small>). You have no guarantees as to whether these different styles will all appear distinct on current WAP devices. There is a <table> tag with a columns attribute; a number of table row elements (<tr>...</tr>) can be nested within a <table>...</table> tag pair; and each row can enclose a number of table data elements (<td>...</td>). However, given the limited screen width, it is difficult to have meaningful tables.

Links can be created using <a href="...">...</a> tags. WML has an alternative slightly more elaborate link mechanism using an anchor tag that encloses either a go or prev tag. A go tag has an attribute identifying a destination (another document, or another card in the current deck – e.g. <go href="Date.jsp"> or <go href="#Card3">); a prev tag (<prev/>) returns to the previous displayed card.

A simple WML site will consist of some static WML pages and some JSPs that generate dynamic WML pages. For example, the following three files make up a simple 'date' application:

- Demo1.wml
A simple static WML page with a link to a JSP.

- Date.jsp
A simple JSP that generates dynamic content (it outputs the current date).

- web.xml
The web.xml file contains the mime type definition for WML; this is needed to make sure that the Tomcat server will return the response with the correct HTTP headers.

These files would have to be deployed in your tomcat/webapps directory (the static .wml file and the JSP could go in tomcat/webapps/xmlex, with the web.xml file in a WEB-INF subdirectory).

The static WML file is:

```
<?xml version="1.0"?>
<!DOCTYPE wml PUBLIC "-//WAPFORUM//DTD WML 1.1//EN"
"http://www.wapforum.org/DTD/wml_1.1.xml">
<wml>
  <card id="Demo1" title="Demo1/Card1">
    <p>
      <a href="Date.jsp">Tell me the date</a>
    </p>
  </card>
</wml>
```

This will display the title and link text on the WAP phone screen, along with a GO... tag that is mapped to one of the phone's buttons.

The JSP is a really a WML document (instead of an HTML document) that contains a scriptlet:

```
<%@ page language="java" contentType="text/vnd.wap.wml" %>
<?xml version="1.0"?>
<!DOCTYPE wml PUBLIC "-//WAPFORUM//DTD WML 1.1//EN" "http://
www.wapforum.org/DTD/wml_1.1.xml">
<wml>
  <card title="The date">
    <p>The date is <b>
    <%= (new java.util.Date()).toString() %>
    </b></p>
  </card>
</wml>
```

The web.xml file has the declaration of the wml mime type:

```
<?xml version="1.0" encoding="UTF-8"?>
<!DOCTYPE web-app PUBLIC '-//Sun Microsystems, Inc.//DTD Web Application
2.2//EN' 'http://java.sun.com/j2ee/dtds/web-app_2.2.dtd'>
<web-app>
  <mime-mapping>
    <extension>
      wml
    </extension>
    <mime-type>
      text/vnd.wap.wml
```

```
        </mime-type>
      </mime-mapping>
    </web-app>
```

Of course, you need a WAP-enabled phone to test the new 'date' service running on your Tomcat server. WAP phone *emulators* are cheaper than phones (and also make it easier to get screenshots). There are a number of emulators available for free download (there used to be several listed in the appropriate section of Yahoo's Computers & Internet information pages; phone companies like Nokia have emulators available at their sites). Figure 9.4 illustrates a display from the M3Gate emulator, available from http:// www.m3gate.com/; this emulator is a relatively stable Windows application that runs in association with IE. (Emulators come in many forms: helper applications for a browser, applets, even versions implemented entirely in JavaScript. However, many of the downloadable emulators are unreliable, with problems like crashes, freezes or failing to interpret WML correctly. You will probably need to experiment with more than one before you find something that suits your system and style of use.)

The motivation for looking at WML was supposedly the need to display the soccer results on a WAP phone, so this application had better form the next example. The small screen of a phone cannot display the same amounts of data as were displayed in the HTML league listings shown in Figure 9.3. The data will need to be spread over a number of cards, with a first card providing links to the cards displaying details of draws, home wins and away wins.

Figure 9.4 A WAP-phone emulator displaying the contents of a static WML page.

This application simply reworks the version at the end of the previous section. The JSP uses an XSL formatting program, together with the xsl taglib library, to format some XML (it is the same page as before; it simply references a different XSL file). A SoccerBean object provides the data as a String representation of an XML document. The new page differs from the previous one really only in the name of the XSL program file:

The XSL program that formats the data for a WAP phone is as follows:

```
<?xml version='1.0'?>
<xsl:stylesheet version="1.0" xmlns:xsl="http://www.w3.org/1999/XSL/
Transform">
<xsl:output doctype-public="-//WAPFORUM//DTD WML 1.1//EN" doctype-
system="http://www.wapforum.org/DTD/wml_1.1.xml"/>
<xsl:template match="SOCCER">
<wml>
<card id="Results" title="Match Results" >
  <p>
  <anchor>Drawn games<go href="#Draws"/></anchor><br/>
  <anchor>Home wins<go href="#Homes"/></anchor><br/>
  <anchor>Away wins<go href="#Aways"/></anchor><br/>
  </p>
</card>
<card id="Draws" title="Drawn Games">
  <xsl:for-each select="GAME[SCORE1 = SCORE2]">
     <p><xsl:value-of select="HOME"/>-
     <xsl:value-of select="AWAY"/>:
     <xsl:value-of select="SCORE1"/>-
     <xsl:value-of select="SCORE2"/></p>
  </xsl:for-each>
  <p><anchor>All matches<prev/></anchor></p>
</card>
<card id="Homes" title="Home wins">
  <xsl:for-each select="GAME[SCORE1 &gt; SCORE2]">
     <p><xsl:value-of select="HOME"/>-
     <xsl:value-of select="AWAY"/>:
     <xsl:value-of select="SCORE1"/>-
     <xsl:value-of select="SCORE2"/></p>
  </xsl:for-each>
  <p><anchor>All matches<prev/></anchor></p>
</card>
<card id="Aways" title="Away wins">
  <xsl:for-each select="GAME[SCORE1 &lt; SCORE2]">
     <p><xsl:value-of select="HOME"/>-
     <xsl:value-of select="AWAY"/>:
     <xsl:value-of select="SCORE1"/>-
```

```
        <xsl:value-of select="SCORE2"/></p>
    </xsl:for-each>
    <p><anchor>All matches<prev/></anchor></p>
</card>
</wml>
</xsl:template>
</xsl:stylesheet>
```

It matches the SOCCER element in the XML, and outputs static WML tags and content text that define a first card with links to the other cards in the deck:

```
<anchor>Drawn games<go href="#Draws"/></anchor><br/>
```

This anchor link provides an intra-deck jump (it could have been written as `<a href="#Draws">Drawn games</a>`). Each of the other cards displays a chosen subset of the data; the subset is selected according to the XPATH specification in the xsl:for-each tag:

```
<xsl:for-each select="GAME[SCORE1 &gt; SCORE2]">
    <p><xsl:value-of select="HOME"/>-
    <xsl:value-of select="AWAY"/>:
    <xsl:value-of select="SCORE1"/>-
    <xsl:value-of select="SCORE2"/></p>
</xsl:for-each>
```

The selected data are output as the contents of a paragraph. A tabular format could have been used instead; the code would be along the following lines:

```
<card id="Draws" title="Drawn Games">
  <p>
  <table columns="4">
  <xsl:for-each select="GAME[SCORE1 = SCORE2]">
    <tr>
      <td><xsl:value-of select="HOME"/></td>
      <td><xsl:value-of select="AWAY"/></td>
      <td><xsl:value-of select="SCORE1"/></td>
      <td><xsl:value-of select="SCORE2"/></td>
    </tr>
  </xsl:for-each>
  </table>
  <anchor>All matches<prev/></anchor></p>
</card>
```

Each card ends with a link back to the first page.

The WAP and HTTP versions of this JSP/XSL combination illustrate how the same data can be displayed in different ways according to the needs of the client. In principle, it is possible to use a single JSP that can generate whichever output is appropriate. The JSP can use scriptlet code to obtain information about the protocol used for a request and so select the content-type of the response and the stylesheet program that should be used to generate the response. This would involve scriptlet code along the following lines:

```
<%
    String styleSheet=null;
    if(request.getProtocol().indexOf("WAP") != -1) {
      styleSheet = "Soccer1w.xsl";
      response.setContentType("text/vnd.wap.wml");
    }
    else {
styleSheet = "Soccer.xsl"; response.setContentType("text/html");
    }
%>
...
<xsl:apply xsl="<%= styleSheet %>" ...>
...
```

Of course, this does not work when using WAP phone emulators because these use the HTTP protocol. (You can fake things if you want to test a JSP that is supposed to generate different responses. You simply add an extra parameter to the 'get' request – this parameter defining the kind of output you require.)

The power of the web comes from interactivity. More sophisticated WML examples use a request card deck (defined either as a static WML document or as a dynamically generated WML document) and a JSP that can generate a dynamic response. WML has number input elements that are similar to those used in HTML pages. There is a `select` element (supporting single or multiple selections):

```
<p>What do you think is best?
  <select name="Items" title="Vices?">
    <option value="Sex">Sex</option>
    <option value="Drugs">Drugs</option>
    <option value="RocknRoll">Rock and Roll</option>
  </select>
</p>
```

(The select tag has a `multiple` attribute that should be set to true if multiple selections can be made.) The appearance of the select element will vary with the WAP phone or phone emulator. You might get the above WML data displayed with the prompt followed by a selection table; alternatively, one screen will display the prompt ('What do you think is best?'), the current choice, and an 'Options' button, while a second screen shows the table of options.

There is an input element:

```
<p> UserName:
<input type="text" name="user"/>
</p>
```

This might display as UserName : [<name, if data already entered>] with an 'Edit' button that changes the display to one where characters can be entered (data entry is SMS-style multi-keying on real phones, emulators let you use the keyboard); alternatively, the display might show the UserName label beside an data entry box. WML has a fieldset element that can be used to group a number of input elements.

The following little application illustrates the use of these input elements. It is the beginnings of a pizza order system. It uses an order card deck (static WML document) and a JSP that simply confirms the data that were submitted. The static WML document has three cards. The first solicits the size of pizza required. The second is used to get the user's selection of toppings (multiple choices from a given selection). The last card is used for entry of username and address, and also for submission of the combined data for processing on the server. The cards are linked via do action buttons.

```
<?xml version="1.0"?>
<!DOCTYPE wml PUBLIC "-//WAPFORUM//DTD WML 1.1//EN"
"http://www.wapforum.org/DTD/wml_1.1.xml">
<wml>
  <card id="Size" title="Pizza size">
  ...
  </card>
  <card id="Tops" title="Toppings">
  ...
  </card>
  <card id="Customer" title="Info">
  ...
  </card>
</wml>
```

The pizza size card has a single choice selection. The <do type="accept" ...> tag results in an action button, linked to one of the phone buttons, that allows the user to move to the card for selecting pizza toppings.

```
<card id="Size" title="Pizza size">
  <do type="accept" label="Select toppings">
    <go href="#Tops" />
  </do>
  <p>Pizza size
    <select name="PSize" title="Pizza">
      <option value="Regular">Regular</option>
```

```
            <option value="Large">Large</option>
            <option value="Family">Family</option>
        </select>
    </p>
</card>
```

The 'toppings' card has a similar link allowing movement to the final card, and a multiple choice selection:

```
<card id="Tops" title="Toppings">
    <do type="accept" label="Delivery">
        <go href="#Customer" />
    </do>
    <p>
    <select name="Tops" multiple="true">
        <option value="Cheese">Extra cheese</option>
        <option value="Tomato">Tomato</option>
        <option value="Pepperoni">Pepperoni</option>
    </select>
    </p>
</card>
```

The final 'Info' card has a fieldset with two text inputs for the client's name and address data. It also has a more complex do action element that arranges for data to be submitted.

```
<card id="Customer" title="Info">
    <do type="accept" label="Submit">
        ...
    </do>
    <p>
        <fieldset title="Info">
            Name: <input name="Name" type="text"/><br/>
            Address: <input name="Address" type="text"/>
        </fieldset>
    </p>
</card>
```

The form submission step must identify those data elements that are to be sent in the request to the server as name/value pairs. It must also specify whether a 'get' or 'post' style request is to be used. The variables are the names of the input elements, like the text strings for name and address or the selection elements.

```
<do type="accept" label="Submit">
    <go href="form3.jsp" method="post">
```

```
      <postfield name="CustomerName" value="$(Name)"/>
      <postfield name="Address" value="$(Address)"/>
      <postfield name="Size" value="$(PSize)"/>
      <postfield name="Toppings" value="$(Tops)"/>
    </go>
  </do>
```

The go element has attributes that identify the processing program and the data transfer method. The body of the go element can contain postfield tags. These take attributes that specify the name value pairs for the request data. The values are taken from the variables that hold the data obtained in the various input elements of the card deck. Thus, in this example, the CustomerName parameter sent with the request will hold the value input in the text input field called Name. The Toppings parameter contains a set of comma-separated values for the options selected in the Tops select element.

The JSP program for this example merely lists the inputs. The page imports the java.util library because its scriptlet code uses an Enumeration. It generates a card deck with a single card that lists the parameter data on separate lines:

```
<?xml version="1.0"?>
<!DOCTYPE wml PUBLIC "-//WAPFORUM//DTD WML 1.1//EN" "http://
www.wapforum.org/DTD/wml_1.1.xml">
<%@ page contentType="text/vnd.wap.wml" %>
<%@ page import="java.util.*" %>
<wml>
  <card id="Response" title="Data echo" >
  <p>Data entered<br/>
<%
  Enumeration names = request.getParameterNames();
  while(names.hasMoreElements()) {
    String aName = (String) names.nextElement();
    String[] values = request.getParameterValues(aName);
    for(int i=0;i<values.length;i++)
      out.println(aName + "=" + values[i] + "<br/>");
    }
%>
</p>
</card>
</wml>
```

9.5 Simple API for XML

The previous sections illustrated methods for selection and display of data from an XML file. The other intended use of XML 'portable data' was for the client to process the data. The basic assumption behind the processing uses is that the client has the DTD describing the structure of an XML file, and that there is agreement as to the meaning of the data held in the different elements of such an XML document. Since the client can understand the structure of the document, and knows the significance of each element, the client can find whatever data are desired. Ultimately, the client will want the content text and attribute name/value pairs that are associated with specific elements in the document. The client's real processing work will involve the manipulation of these data.

However, the processing of an XML document does require the completion of a large number of routine housekeeping tasks such as the following:

- Reading the raw text data as a character stream

- Recognition of the tags and extraction of the text that represent a tag and its attributes.

- Separation of a tag's attribute string into name/value pairs.

- Isolation of the content text in the body of a tag.

But these 'parsing' tasks are all routine; they are done in essentially the same way in all applications that process XML files. Consequently, these parsing tasks can be separated out into a standard parser component that can be implemented as a set of procedural library functions or as the instance of some class.

There are a couple of different approaches for combining standard parsing code and application-specific processing code. One approach has the 'parser' build a tree structure that represents the content of the original document. This tree will have nodes corresponding to each element in the document; attached to these nodes will be lists of attributes, and where appropriate text data from the body of an element. When the parser has finished building this structure, application-specific code can traverse the resulting tree structure to find and process those nodes with required data. An alternative somewhat simpler approach has the parser 'call back' to the client code every time it completes the extraction of an element's tag and its attributes, or when it has isolated the content text in the body of an element. The client code that uses such a parser provides it with a link to a set of content handling functions, or a content handling object that implements a set of data handling methods. Whenever the parser has a complete data element ready for processing, it uses these links to call the appropriate method.

For example, if the parser were processing a web.xml file such as:

```
<web-app>
  <servlet>
    <servlet-name>servlet1</servlet-name>
    <servlet-class>GreetingsServlet</servlet-class>
  </servlet>
  <servlet-mapping>
    <servlet-name>servlet1</servlet-name>
    <url-pattern>/servlet1</url-pattern>
  </servlet-mapping>
</web-app>
```

its approach would be:

XML document element	Call back request
(about to open input)	*Get ready to process data*
`<web-app>`	*Do something with a web-app tag with no attributes.*
`<servlet>`	*Do something with a servlet tag with no attributes.*
`<servlet-name>`	*Do something with a servlet-name tag with no attributes.*
`servlet1`	*Do something with the content-text "servlet1".*
`</servlet-name>`	*Processing of the servlet-name tag is finished, tidy up.*
`...`	
`</web-app>`	*Processing of the web-app tag is finished, tidy up.*
End of file	*We have finished; close up.*

The application-specific processing code has to be written to take action for those elements and content text sections that are of value. The application code can discard data relating to elements that are of no interest.

The approach just outlined is that used by parsers built to support the Simple API for XML (SAX). There are many implementations of SAX parsers in a whole variety of languages. The most convenient one for use with Java is probably the xerces system from Apache. This is available for download from `http://xml.apache.org/xerces2-j/index.html`. The file `xerces.jar` must be included in the CLASSPATH of a Java program that needs to used this parser

A Java program using the `org.apache.xerces.parsers.SAXParser` parser will:

- Define a concrete class that extends the `ContentHandler` class; the methods defined for this class embody the application-specific code for handling the tags and character data.

- Have a `main()` that:
  - Creates a `SAXParser` object and an `Application-ContentHandler` object.
  - Links the `SAXParser` to its content handler.
  - Links the parser to an input stream from where it can read the XML document.
  - Gets the parser to process the file.

The example XML document for this section contains a listing of the contents of a database about Java books:

```
<LIST>
  <BOOK rank="1">
    <ISBN code="0130894680"/>
    <TITLE>Core Java 2, Volume 1: Fundamentals 5/e</TITLE>
    <AUTHORS>Cay S. Horstmann, Gary Cornell</AUTHORS>
    <FORMAT>(Paperback)</FORMAT>
    <STARS>4.5</STARS>
    <SHIPS>1</SHIPS>
    <LISTPRICE>44.99</LISTPRICE>
```

```
            <OURPRICE>31.49</OURPRICE>
            <SAVE>13.50</SAVE>
        </BOOK>
        <BOOK>
        ...
```

(Amazon kindly provided accurate data about Java books! A search for Java books at Amazon was returned as an HTML page; the source for this page was saved. The resulting file was edited into XML format, partly manually and partly through use of a Perl script.)

The first task for this example is simply to find:

- The cost of the least expensive book

- The cost of the most expensive book

- The average cost of a Java book

The 'content handler' for this program needs to pick out the OurPrice elements from the input stream; the next piece of content text should then represent a price that should be processed. All other elements and content text in the input stream should be ignored. The content handler will need data elements representing minimum and maximum prices found so far, an element in which to accumulate the total cost, and a counter for records processed. When the entire data file has been parsed, the content handler can be asked to compute the average book cost and print all its data.

A content handler should implement the methods:

- void startDocument
This method is called at the beginning of a document; it should create storage structures, initialize data etc.

- void endDocument
This method is called at the end of a document; it should tidy up, maybe release resources, and possibly prepare data for final stage analysis or output.

- void startElement(String namespaceURI, String localName, String qName, Attributes atts)
This method is called whenever the parser has a start tag. The name arguments identify the tag (the arguments used depend on options controlling the parser; you can get just the tag name in the qName argument, or you can get you can get a more elaborate path name). The most common processing action is to set a data member to hold the value of the tag name.

- void characters(char[] ch, int start, int length)
This method is called whenever the parser finds some content text; the argument with the character array holds the text. Typically, the saved value of the 'element' name is used to resolve how this text should be processed.

- void endElement(String namespaceURI, String localName, String qName)
This method is called when the parser has an end tag.

The actual concrete class will normally extend org.xml.sax.helpers.Default Handler. This class provides default (do nothing) implementations for unused functions (in the example, these include startDocument and endDocument). The DefaultHandler class also implements a number of other interfaces, such as an error handler interface. The class for the example is:

```java
public class Prices extends DefaultHandler {
  // currentElement - establishes context for the processing of
  // character data; set in startElement
  private String currentElement;
  // Application data for book prices
  private float minPrice;
  private float maxPrice;
  private float averagePrice;
  private int count;
  private java.util.Stack callStack;
  public Prices()
  {
    // Initialize - a bit redundant in this example; but
    // needed in more realistic situations
    currentElement = null;
    minPrice = Float.MAX_VALUE;
    maxPrice = (float) 0.0;
    averagePrice = (float) 0.0;
    count = 0;
    callStack = new java.util.Stack();
  }

  public void startElement (String uri, String local,
    String qName, Attributes atts) throws SAXException
  {
    callStack.push(currentElement);
    // Identify element being processed
    currentElement=qName;
  }

  public void endElement(String namespaceURI, String localName,
    String qName) throws SAXException
  {
    currentElement= (String) callStack.pop();
  }

  public void characters(char[] ch,
    int start, int length) throws SAXException
  {
```

```
      // Context dependent processing - here, process character
      // data for OURPRICE elements
      if("OURPRICE".equals(currentElement))
        processOurPrice(new String(ch, start, length));
    }

    private void processOurPrice(String str)
    {
      // Parse the price string (ignore bad data)
      // Update pricing records
      try {
        float cost = Float.parseFloat(str);
        minPrice = (minPrice < cost) ? minPrice : cost;
        maxPrice = (maxPrice > cost) ? maxPrice : cost;
        averagePrice += cost;
        count++;
      }
      catch(Exception e) { }
    }

    public void reportResults()
    {
      // Application specific reporting function
      if(count==0) {
        System.out.println("There are no results to report");
        }
      else {
        averagePrice = averagePrice/((float)count);
        System.out.println("Minimum price $"+minPrice);
        System.out.println("Maximum price $"+maxPrice);
        System.out.println("Average price $"
                              +averagePrice);
      }
    }
```

The complete program is:

```
import org.apache.xerces.parsers.SAXParser;
import org.xml.sax.Attributes;
import org.xml.sax.helpers.DefaultHandler;
import org.xml.sax.SAXParseException;
import org.xml.sax.SAXException;
import java.io.IOException;

public class Prices extends DefaultHandler {
```

```
      // Data members and member functions as shown above...
      public static void main (String[] args) {
      if(args.length != 1) {
         System.out.println("Need name of file to process!");
         System.exit(1);
      }
       String fileName = args[0];
       // Create the content handler object
       Prices pd = new Prices();
       // Create the parser, then link to content handler
       SAXParser parser = new SAXParser();
       parser.setContentHandler(pd);
       try {
          // Parser the XML file, data captured by content
          // handler as parsing progresses
          parser.parse(fileName);}}
      catch (SAXException e) { System.err.println (e); }
      catch (IOException e) { System.err.println (e); }
      // Report on captured data
      pd.reportResults();
   }
}
```

As a slightly more elaborate example based on the same data, consider a program that is
to construct a collection holding data on the 'good' Java books (where 'good' is defined as
being awarded four or more stars by Amazon's customers). The program will have to construct a collection of record structures that hold the data for each book; the class book is
defined for this purpose:

```
class book {
   private String  title;
   private String  authors;
   private float   cost;
   private float   stars;
   public void setTitle(String str) { title = str; }
   public void setAuthors(String str) { authors = str; }
   public void setCost(String cst) {
      try {
         cost = Float.parseFloat(cst);
      }
      catch(Exception e) { }
   }
   public void setStars(String strs) {
      try {
         stars = Float.parseFloat(strs);
```

```
      }
      catch(Exception e) { }
   }
   public float getStars() { return stars; }

   public String toString() {
      StringBuffer buf = new StringBuffer();
      buf.append(title);
      buf.append("; ");
      buf.append(authors);
      buf.append("; $");
      buf.append(Float.toString(cost));
      buf.append("; ");
      buf.append(Float.toString(stars));
      buf.append("*");
      return buf.toString();
   }
}
```

The content handler, class Books, will have to:

- Create a java.util.Vector to store the collection of good Java books; this can be done in its startDocument method.

- A new book object will have to be created for each BOOK element in the XML file; this can be done in the startElement method if the element is a BOOK.

- Fill the book object with the authors, title, cost and ratings data when these elements are read. This will be done in a characters method, with context data defining the current element being used to identify the field to which the characters relate.

- Either add a highly rated book to the growing collection, or discard a book if its rating is insufficient. This can be done in the endElement method when this is called with the context for a BOOK.

The example program is:

```
import org.apache.xerces.parsers.SAXParser;
import org.xml.sax.Attributes;
import org.xml.sax.helpers.DefaultHandler;
import org.xml.sax.SAXParseException;
import org.xml.sax.SAXException;
import java.io.IOException;
import java.util.*;

class book {
```

```java
    // Definition as shown above
    ...
}

public class Books extends DefaultHandler {
  // Need data members for the book collection, the current
  //   book being worked on when parsing the file, and the
  //   current XML element being processed
  private Vector    myBooks;
  private book      currentbook;
  private String    currentElement;
  Stack             callStack;

  public void startDocument()throws SAXException
  {
    // Create the collection object
    myBooks = new Vector();
    callStack = new Stack();
  }

  public void endDocument()throws SAXException
  {
    // Print the report on good books
    System.out.println("Good Java Books");
    Enumeration e = myBooks.elements();
    while(e.hasMoreElements())
      System.out.println(e.nextElement());
  }

  public void startElement (String uri, String local,
    String qName, Attributes atts) throws SAXException
  {
    callStack.push(currentElement);
    // Create new book whenever appropriate
    // and record current context
    if("BOOK".equals(qName)) {
      currentbook = new book();
      }
    currentElement=qName;
  }

  public void endElement(String namespaceURI, String localName,
    String qName) throws SAXException
  {
    // If completing work on a BOOK element, check the data that
```

```java
                // were recorded in current book object. If it is a
                // "good" book, add it to the collection; otherwise forget it.
                if("BOOK".equals(qName)) {
                    if(currentbook.getStars()>=4.0)
                        myBooks.addElement(currentbook);
                    currentbook=null;
                }
                currentElement= (String) callStack.pop();
            }

        public void characters(char[] ch,
            int start, int length) throws SAXException
        {
            // Record those data elements that are of interest
            // placing data in current (book) object.
            String str = new String(ch, start, length);
            if("AUTHORS".equals(currentElement))
                currentbook.setAuthors(str);
            else if("OURPRICE".equals(currentElement))
                currentbook.setCost(str);
            else if("STARS".equals(currentElement))
                currentbook.setStars(str);
            else if("TITLE".equals(currentElement))
                currentbook.setTitle(str);
        }

        public static void main (String[] args) {
            if(args.length != 1) {
                System.out.println("Need name of file to process!");
                System.exit(1);
            }
            String fileName = args[0];
            // Create content handler, create parser, link them
            Books bks = new Books();
            SAXParser parser = new SAXParser();
            parser.setContentHandler(bks);
            try {
                // Process the XML document
                parser.parse(fileName);
            }
            catch (SAXException e) { System.err.println (e); }
            catch (IOException e) { System.err.println (e); }
        }
    }
```

Processing with the aid of a SAX-parser suits most simple applications. But sometimes it is necessary to make many passes through the complete document structure to collect all the data that are needed. The use of XSLT to generate HTML or WML is an example. The 'Soccer league' listings required repeated traversals of the league data – first to find and list the drawn games, then again for the away wins, and finally for the home wins. An XSL transform system works by building a tree-like data structure for the matched element for a template (in the example, it was the root SOCCER element); the code within a template can then traverse this tree and find the sub-elements of interest. XSL is a special case, but there are many general applications that do require more detailed analyses of the data. These applications suit general-purpose parsers that are more sophisticated than the SAX parsers.

9.6 DOM – the Document Object Model

The Document Object Model (DOM) started out with an idea for a method for organizing data in web pages. The aim was to take the web beyond mere browsing, and support more sophisticated data retrieval. The data in pages were to be structured and described using tags with defined semantics. This would allow search programs (web spiders and similar systems) that could work much more effectively because they would 'understand' the contents of the documents that they encountered. DOM has evolved. It is now predominantly an approach for representing and manipulating structured data – XML data.

The DOM defines a tree-structured representation for the contents of an XML document. The DOM application programmer interface defines functions that can be used to search this tree, extracting required data. There are many implementations of the DOM API. With Java, you use a standard DOM parser (e.g. an instance of org.apache.xerces.parsers.DOMParser) to validate XML documents and build DOM models of their contents. A DOM model is represented as an instance of a class implementing org.w3c.dom.Document. This Document class inherits and defines numerous methods for searching for data elements, for modifying data elements, and for manipulating the links in the DOM tree structure itself.

The use of DOM for processing an XML file is significantly more costly than a SAX-based approach. The parsing is a little more elaborate, but the main cost increases relate to data storage. (A DOM parser may employ a SAX parser to do part of its work; some of the errors that can be thrown by the parser are actually instances of SAX error classes.) The parser builds rather elaborate tree structures, with many different kinds of tree node and numerous links among these nodes. The DOM API, which specifies the functions used to access and manipulate a document tree structure, is somewhat complex.

However, the overall program structure is just as simple as SAX. A DOM-based program will have a main() that:

- Instantiates a DOM parser.
- Links the parser to the data source with the XML file.
- Sets parsing options (e.g. validating or non-validating; when in validating mode, the parser must be able to access the DTD file for the XML document that it is processing).

- If validating, links the parser to an 'error handling' object – this gets called when the parser encounters a problem with the XML file. The error handler may print warning messages or terminate processing.

- Gets the parser to run.

- Retrieves the resulting Document object.

The rest is application-specific!

The remaining code in the program will involve different traversals of the Document to obtain data.

The following example reworks the 'books' problem just explored using SAX. The DOM version will use an instance of Apache's DOMParser class to build a Document object with all the information in the book's XML file (the example also includes a DTD for this XML document and optionally requires that the parser validate the file). When the Document has been created, two traversals are performed. The first gathers the data needed for determining the price ranges of Java books; the second identifies and prints data on the books with a four-star or higher rating. Both traversals use one of the simpler Document accessor methods – getElementsByTagName. This is used to find the BOOK elements in the structure; then other accessors – getFirstChild, getNodeValue – are used to obtain data like the book titles.

The program structure is:

```java
// Imports of all the xml stuff and the dom definitions
// (all the classes are in the xerces.jar file; this must be in the
// CLASSPATH to compile and run the program)
import org.apache.xerces.parsers.DOMParser;
import org.xml.sax.ErrorHandler;
import org.w3c.dom.*;
import org.w3c.dom.traversal.*;
import org.xml.sax.SAXException;
import org.xml.sax.SAXParseException;
import org.xml.sax.SAXNotRecognizedException;
import org.xml.sax.SAXNotSupportedException;
import java.io.IOException;

class errs implements ErrorHandler {
    // A Dom parser requires an error handling assistant that implements
    // the ErrorHandler interface.
    ...
}


public class DOMAnalyzer{

    public static void main (String[] args) {
        // Pick up arguments with name of XML file (arg[0]) and
```

```
      // optional arg[1] that can specify need to validate
      // against DTD
      ...
      // Create parser, set options
      DOMParser doma = new DOMParser();
      ...

      try {
        // Parsing
        doma.parse(fileName);
      }
      catch (...) {
        // Deal with various possible exceptions
        ...
      }

      try {
        // Document traversal part.
        // First, get the document tree structure
        Document domTree = doma.getDocument();
        // Get a list of nodes for books
        ...
      }
    }
    catch(Exception e) {
      System.err.println(e);
    }
  }
}
```

Class errs simply implements the methods void warning (SAXParseException e), void error (SAXParseException e) and void fatalError (SAXParseException e). All print details from their exception arguments; the fatalError method terminates the program with a call to System.exit.

In more detail, the code to create and initialize the parser is as follows:

```
if(args.length<1) {
  System.out.println("You forgot to name the XML data file");
  System.exit(1);
  }
String fileName = args[0];
boolean doValidate = false;
if(args.length>1) {
  if("true".equals(args[1])) doValidate = true;
}
```

```
DOMParser doma = new DOMParser();

if(doValidate) {
   // Set validation feature,
   try {
      doma.setFeature (
        "http://xml.org/sax/features/validation", true);
   }
   catch (SAXNotRecognizedException e) { System.err.println (e); }
   catch (SAXNotSupportedException e) { System.err.println (e); }

   doma.setErrorHandler (new errs());
}
```

The actual parsing step may throw SAX exceptions or I/O exceptions:

```
try { doma.parse(fileName); }
catch (SAXException e) { System.err.println (e); System.exit(1); }
catch (IOException e) { System.err.println (e); System.exit(1); }
catch (IOException e) { System.err.println (e);
```

The Document.getElementsbyTagName method does a pre-order traversal of the tree structure and returns a list (NodeList) with all the Element objects. Here it is used to get a list of node structures that represent the BOOK elements in the XML document. Each of these Element nodes has a link to a list of child nodes; this contains the components that represent the XML attributes and nested elements.

```
try {
   // Pick up reference to Document
   Document domTree = doma.getDocument();
   // Ask Document to do pre-order traversal that builds a list
   // with containing references to the Element nodes that represent
   // BOOK elements in the XML file
   NodeList bookNodes =
      domTree.getElementsByTagName("BOOK");
   ...
}
```

This list of 'book nodes' can then be processed to extract the price data. The list is accessed via a function that returns a requested element (identified by index number). This Element should represent a BOOK; it will itself be a tree structure with the tree containing nodes for nested elements like the TITLE, AUTHOR, LISTPRICE and other data elements in the XML file. The price analysis requires the OURPRICE data; these data are found via another getElementsByTagName request. This function returns a list of elements; there should be only one entry in the returned list. This entry is again a little tree structure; it should hold a single child element that has a value that represents the character data that appeared in the XML file's <OURPRICE>...</OURPRICE> element. The access code picks up the first element of the list (item(0) applied to list returned by the 'get elements by tags' method), finds its child node (getFirstChild), and obtains the String value (getNodeValue). This String can be converted to a numeric value and used to update the price data. The code for this section is:

```
...
NodeList bookNodes =
  domTree.getElementsByTagName("BOOK");

float minprice = Float.MAX_VALUE;
float maxprice = (float) 0.0;
int count = 0;
float average = (float) 0.0;
for(int i=0;i<bookNodes.getLength();i++) {
  // This Node list should hold Element nodes, so typecast down
  Element bNode = (Element) bookNodes.item(i);
  // It is a "BOOK node" - a tree with child nodes that represent
  // nested elements for TITLE, LISTPRICE, OURPRICE etc.
  // Search for the sub-tree related to an OURPRICE nested element
  // Pick up list, grab first element; it is the first (only!)
  // OURPRICE element; it is a structure with a sub-tree for nested
  // data (like the actual price data)
  Node priceNode = bNode.getElementsByTagName("OURPRICE").item(0);
  // Get down into priceNode structure to find nested element with
  // characters data from XML file
  String price = priceNode.getFirstChild().getNodeValue();
  // Process numeric value (all this code is deep within
  // a big try catch block - this will catch errors if get
  // non-numerics in price field of XML document)
  float aprice = Float.parseFloat(price);
  minprice = (minprice < aprice) ? minprice : aprice;
  maxprice = (maxprice > aprice) ? maxprice : aprice;
  average += aprice;
  count++;
}
System.out.println("Price report - ");
System.out.println("Minimum price $" + minprice);
...
```

A second traversal of the list of BOOK elements may then be made. The code finds the nested element that represents the star rating for a book (there is the possibility that the book is unrated). If the rating is adequate, the other data are extracted from the BOOK element's sub-tree, and are printed.

```
System.out.println("The popular Java books:");
for(int i=0;i<bookNodes.getLength();i++) {
  Element bNode = (Element) bookNodes.item(i);
  NodeList temp = bNode.getElementsByTagName("STARS");
  if(temp.getLength()==0)continue; // A book without a star rating
  Node starsNode = temp.item(0);
  String starCode = starsNode.getFirstChild().getNodeValue();
  float stars = Float.parseFloat(starCode);
  if(stars<4.0) continue;

  Node titleNode = bNode.getElementsByTagName("TITLE").item(0);
  System.out.print(titleNode.getFirstChild().getNodeValue());

  Node authorsNode = bNode.getElementsByTagName("AUTHORS").item(0);
  System.out.println("; " + authorsNode.getFirstChild().getNodeValue());

}
```

If the XML document was to be checked for validity, a file with a DTD would have to be created; and a link to this DTD file would have to be set in the XML document file. The XML file would get a DOCTYPE link:

```
<?xml version="1.0" encoding="UTF-8"?>
<!DOCTYPE LIST SYSTEM "books.dtd">
<LIST>
  <BOOK rank="1">
  ...
  </BOOK>
  ...
</LIST>
```

The books.dtd file could contain the following:

```
<!-- DTD for Books -->
<!ELEMENT LIST (BOOK)+>
<!ELEMENT BOOK (ISBN, TITLE, AUTHORS, FORMAT?, STARS?, SHIPS?,
LISTPRICE?, OURPRICE, SAVE?, USEDPRICE? )>
<!ATTLIST BOOK rank CDATA #REQUIRED>
<!ELEMENT ISBN (#PCDATA)>
<!ATTLIST ISBN code CDATA #REQUIRED>
<!ELEMENT TITLE (#PCDATA)>
<!ELEMENT AUTHORS (#PCDATA)>
<!ELEMENT FORMAT (#PCDATA)>
<!ELEMENT STARS (#PCDATA)>
<!ELEMENT SHIPS (#PCDATA)>
```

```
<!ELEMENT LISTPRICE (#PCDATA)>
<!ELEMENT OURPRICE (#PCDATA)>
<!ELEMENT SAVE (#PCDATA)>
<!ELEMENT USEDPRICE (#PCDATA)>
```

Exercises

Practical

The servlet/JSP/XML exercises continue use of the Apache Tomcat engine as employed in the exercise for Chapters 7 and 8. Use the M3Gate phone emulator from http:// www.m3gate.com/; you can obtain alternative emulators from companies such as Nokia (see also the explorations exercise below).

The XML parser exercises can be done with the xerces parser downloaded from http:/ /xml.apache.org/xerces2-j/index.html. Copy xerces.jar into the directory where you are developing an application and then specify a classpath like classpath=.:./ xerces.jar.

(1) Implement a third version of the JSPs needed in the example web application from the exercise at the end of Chapter 8. This version is to have a modified Records class with an extra method that returns a java.lang.String that is an XML dump of the data in all the RequestData objects in its collection. The JSPs are to use XSL stylesheets to generate the required web pages with the data listings and the forms. These XML/XSL-based JSPs are simple: invoke XSLT processor using an XSL script (request.xsl, review.xsl) applied to data obtained via the 'get xml data' method of the Records bean that is passed from servlet to JSP.

The real code is in the two .xsl stylesheet files that you must create.

Your WEB-INF directory will need to contains a tld subdirectory with the xsl.tld file, and a lib subdirectory with components like xerces.jar and xsl.jar. The JSPs will need directives like <%@ taglib uri="/xsltaglib" prefix="xsl" %>.

(2) Implement a more complete version of the 'pizza order' example application that allows WAP-equipped customers to submit orders for customized pizzas via the web phones.

(3) Build an application that combines:

- Static form pages.

- A control servlet.

- A bean that loads its data from database tables and which provides access to its data through a function that returns an XML document.

- A JSP that creates a response through the use of an XSL stylesheet that formats data from an XML document.

- XSL stylesheets for generating both HTML and WML documents.

The system is to allow students to obtain lecture details for chosen subjects. Queries may be submitted either via forms displayed on a web browser, or via a form displayed on a WAP-enabled phone. The system will respond with data for the subjects; the WAP-based display will, naturally, show only a subset of the data shown via a browser.

The system should have the following components:

- Query.html, Query.wml

These are static form entry pages for HTTP and WAP browsers. The form allows a user to select a discipline (from among a set of options in a select entry field), and a session of interest (again, picking an option – Autumn, Spring, Summer, Annual – from the options of a select). A discipline is something like Mathematics, IT, Computer Science, Biology, ...; details of all subjects in that discipline should be retrieved. The form also includes a 'Style' parameter (as a hidden field in the HTML form, and as an extra postfield in the WML form); this parameter is included so that the JSP can select the appropriate document encoding and XSL stylesheet.

- NoData.html, NoData.wml

These are static pages that are returned if there are no data that satisfy a user's request.

- LectureServlet

This has a doPost() method that handles data from either the WML or HTML forms. The servlet should own a connection to a database (opened in its init() function and closed in its destroy() function). The doPost function extracts the discipline and session parameters and uses these to initialize an 'InfoBean'. The InfoBean is to search for data on all subjects in the chosen discipline and session. The servlet should check whether any subject details were retrieved (e.g. a request for a Summer session Maths subject might fail to find any). If no subjects were found, the servlet should use response redirection to an appropriate error page (NoData.html or NoData.wml). If the InfoBean found some subjects matching the chosen combination of discipline and session, the servlet will add the bean to the request as an extra attribute and forward the request to the JSP for final processing.

- Database

The database has three tables. The first table lists all subject codes for each discipline: e.g. Mathematics/MATH101, Mathematics/MATH102, Biology/BIOL235.

The second table contains data for a subject. The subject code acts as a primary key; other data include subject title, lecturer, session of offer, photo of lecturer (as a string field with the filename of the image; this file name can be placed as an <img ...> link in a returned HTML page), and a brief description of the subject contents.

The third table contains lecture times. Each row has a subject code, a time string (contains day and time), a location string (lecture theater) and duration (hours of lecture).

You will need to invent data to populate your tables. You need sufficient data so that there are subjects defined in at least two disciplines; one discipline has more than one subject in at least spring and autumn sessions, and these subjects have one or more lecture times allocated. (About 20 rows of data are needed in your three tables.)

- InfoBean

An InfoBean is created by the servlet, is used to retrieve data, and is passed to the JSP. The JSP will get its data from the InfoBean as an XML string. The InfoBean will retrieve data by using the 'discipline' information to obtain a list of subject codes from the first table, retrieving each subject record from the second table and checking the session of offer, creating a 'Subject' record for each subject offered in the desired discipline and session, and finally retrieving lecture times for the subject. (Several of these operations can be combined through the use of a more elaborate SQL query.) The bean will store these data in a vector. A getResults() function will create a string with its results represented in the form of an XML document with a DTD something like the following (there is no need to actually define a DTD and verify the documents):

```
<!ELEMENT RESULTS (SUBJECT)+>
<!ELEMENT SUBJECT (CODE, LECTURER, TITLE, PHOTO, ABSTRACT, LECTURE+)>
<!ELEMENT CODE (#PCDATA)>
<!ELEMENT TITLE (#PCDATA)>
<!ELEMENT LECTURERE (#PCDATA)>
<!ELEMENT PHOTO (#PCDATA)>
<!ELEMENT ABSTRACT (#PCDATA)>
<!ELEMENT LECTURE (TIME, LOCATION, DURATION)>
<!ELEMENT TIME (#PCDATA)>
<!ELEMENT LOCATION (#PCDATA)>
<!ELEMENT DURATION (#PCDATA)>
```

- Java Server Page

This will be a simple JSP that extracts the Style parameter from the request and uses this to set the document type and select a stylesheet. It will then use XSL and the chosen stylesheet to format data obtained from the InfoBean that is passed as an attachment in the request context.

- WMLConvert.xsl, HTMLConvert.xsl

These stylesheets contain XSL code for formatting data in the XML document from the InfoBean.

The HTML stylesheet will generate a page that starts with a contents section that is a list of intra-page links to sections for each subject. Each subject will have all data shown, with lecture times shown in a table.

The WML stylesheet will generate a first card with a list of links to cards generated for each subject. Each subject card will show the subject title and lecture times.

The following XML parsing exercises require an XML data file containing a reasonable amount of data (several hundred data items). This data file purportedly contains records of usage of resources at a web site (with the original data coming from an Apache log file). You can write a Java or Perl program to generate a suitable data file containing invented records. (If you did the Perl exercises that created a database of records from Apache log files, you could rework that program to generate a database with the required data, and then have a simple Perl or Java program that dumps the database contents as an XML file.

Some databases have an XML output feature that can generate such XML dumps automatically.)

The XML file consists of a resourcelist *element with several hundred* resource *elements. Each* resource *is characterized by a* name *(supposedly the path name of a resource on the local web server) and two counts (*campus *and* remote*) that record the number of requests for the resource from within the host domain and from sites external to the host domain. A resource also has a category attribute that distinguishes text files (*.html*,* .txt*,* .pdt*), images (*.gif*,* .png*), CGI programs/scripts, JSPs etc.*

The following fragment illustrates the form of this XML document:

```
<resourcelist>
  <resource category="text">
    <name>/subjects/index.html</name>
    <campus>65</campus>
    <remote>52</remote>
  </resource>
  <resource category="image">
    <name>/people/jkjones/jkj.jpg </name>
    <campus>22</campus>
    <remote>14</remote>
  </resource>
  ...
  <resource category="cgi">
    <name>/cgi-bin/tutorials.cgi </name>
    <campus>24</campus>
    <remote>0</remote>
  </resource>
  ...
</resourcelist>
```

Two data analyses are to be performed. These are two be implemented as two SAX parser programs and then re-implemented using a DOM parser to create at tree representation of the data that can then be traversed twice to extract the different information required.

(4) Statistics

This SAX program, or DOM program subtask, is to process the data in the XML file and extract the following information for both 'text' and 'image' data categories:

- Minimum usage
- Maximum usage
- Average usage
- Standard deviation in usage data

Separate statistical records are to be prepared for on 'campus' and 'remote' usage.

When all the data have been processed, the program is to produce a report similar to the following:

```
Accesses to Text data
--------------------------------
On campus use:
Minimum usage       : 1
Maximum usage       : 448
Average usage       : 87
Standard deviation  : 114.56

Remote use:
Minimum usage       : 1
Maximum usage       : 2544
Average usage       : 166
Standard deviation  : 417.21

Accesses to Image data
--------------------------------
similar style of report
```

(5) Usage analysis

This program is to produce a report that identifies:

- The text file most frequently used from on campus.

- The text file most frequently used from off campus.

- a list of all text files that are used significantly more frequently from off campus than from on campus (include files where more than 65 per cent of the total usage is from off campus); the listed data should show filename and on-campus and off-campus usage counts.

Short answer questions

(1) Explain the different approaches used by SAX and DOM parsers for XML documents.

(2) Explain the structure of each 'Element' defined in the following DTD and the resulting structure for a valid XML fragment.

```
<!ELEMENT security-constraint (web-resource-collection+,
  auth-constraint?, user-data-constraint?)>
<!ELEMENT web-resource-collection (web-resource-name, description?,
  url-pattern*, http-method*)>
<!ELEMENT web-resource-name (#PCDATA)>
```

Explorations

(1) Research and report on the existing services that deliver WWW-related content through to WAP phones.

(2) The phone companies are suffering; their stock prices have slumped because they have spent too much on the purchase of radio spectrum slots for future generation phone services. They cry out for a killer application that will induce millions of customers to substantially increase their mobile phone usage (and expenditure).

Get some ideas by researching the proposals that have already been made for services delivered via WAP phones, come up with the killer application, and write a draft proposal that will attract start-up funding for your application.

(3) Pick a business domain (finance, real estate, health care etc.) and research and report on the extent to which there has been agreement for standard XML documents for data interchange.

(4) The original WAP/WML specifications make no provision for anything like 'cookies' thus limiting the range of applications to those that don't require stateful sessions.

There are proposals for adding equivalent mechanisms. Research these proposals and report on likely WAP extensions that will help support stateful sessions.

(5) Research and write a short report on the different phone emulators that are available for testing WML applications.

(6) Applications of XML include all kinds of mundane things, like defining software configurations, describing program structures, encoding remote procedure calls, representing dumps of database tables and defining EDI formats. Get onto the WWW and discover and report on some of the more unexpected and esoteric applications of XML.

(7) Research and report on the advantages of 'schemas' (as compared to older DTDs).

(8) Research and report on the merits of the different XML parser implementations for Java (xerces is not the only parser library).

(9) Many database systems now incorporate mechanisms for dumping the contents of tables, or the results of queries, as XML documents. Research and write a report on the extent of XML support in the database that you use (if it does not have XML support, pick something like SQLServer or Oracle).

10
Enterprise Java

This chapter provides an introduction to Enterprise Java technologies. These technologies (and the somewhat comparable .NET technologies from Microsoft, see Appendix C) are aimed at applications that are far more demanding than the simple 'web site with order form'-style applications reviewed in earlier chapters. These technologies support component-based approaches to the design, implementation and deployment of enterprise level applications; applications that typically involving inter-working of objects in different processes on different machines, and updates of multiple databases. The goal is to simplify the construction of distributed transactional applications, reducing development times and costs.

Enterprise Java comprises a number of separate but interrelated Java technologies. You are somewhat familiar with four of them: Java Database Connectivity JDBC, Java Servlets, Java Server Pages, and Java-XML. Other Enterprise technologies include:

- JavaMail

- Java IDL and related support for CORBA – Common Object Request Broker Architecture

- Enterprise JavaBeans (EJB)

- Java Messaging Services

- Java Transactions

- Java API for XML Processing

- Java Naming and Directory Interface (JNDI)

The JavaMail API provides programmers with a convenient interface to the mail services supported by the operating system. It could be used in, for example, an application that relies on email services to acknowledge orders submitted via the web and then to provide updates on the progress of the order.

EJB and CORBA are both distributed object technologies. These technologies are used to build multi-tier client server systems. A typical three-tier system would have a Java client application, a middleware component that would either be a CORBA application or an EJB application, and a back-end database. Web-based clients would typically form part of a four-tier system. The browser-based client would work with a web server that would most likely use servlets. This web server would then work with the CORBA or EJB engine; once again, there would be back-end database(s). Programs built using these technologies involve communications among objects instantiated in different processes (it is similar to, though generally a little more complex than, Java RMI which you may have encountered previously). Ultimately, client and server objects communicate via messages transferred over TCP/IP networks. A major aim of the distributed object technologies is the concealment of this network layer. A client program (a Java client application, or a servlet in a web server) will make use of instances of proxy (stub) classes that have interfaces that mimic those of the real server classes as instantiated in the EJB or CORBA engine. When an operation is invoked on a proxy, this object packages the request and uses low-level library components to transmit it to the server process. There the request is read, analyzed to identify the server object required, and converted into an invocation of the appropriate server operation. The server-side infrastructure code takes result data, packages them for transmission and sends them back to the client process. There the returned data are picked up by the proxy, allowing it to sustain the illusion that it did the work and is returning a result. Invocations on remote objects are synchronous; the client thread that invokes an operation on a proxy is blocked until the response is received.

Java Messaging services support a different, asynchronous model for client–server relations among objects. Sometimes, it is more convenient for a client to package a request, and submit this package to a queuing system. Server processes will extract requests from this message queue, perform the work required, and queue responses. At some later time, a client will retrieve the response to its request. The EJB system has recently been extended so that it can be integrated with Messaging-style services.

With JDBC, you can control the transactional character of operations that use a particular database connection. In more complex cases, transactions may involve multiple databases; such situations require more elaborate control mechanisms. The Java Transaction API provides a high-level interface to services implemented using Java Transaction Services. The JTS layer is modeled on, and can interoperate with CORBA transaction systems.

The Java API for XML Processing (JAXP) is a second-generation version of Java classes for XML and is intended by Sun to become the standard for Java applications. It incorporates both SAX and DOM parsers, and also incorporates support for XSL stylesheet processing.

The JNDI naming and directory components provide a uniform interface to many different 'naming services', so simplifying the tasks of the developer. Naming services that are used by programs include DNS; COSNaming (a naming service used to obtain references to CORBA objects); the Lightweight Directory Access Protocol (LDAP), which is a widely used directory service applied to things such maintaining lists of employees (an employee might have a name comprising person name, employment unit and department name); and NIS+, a naming service used on groups of Sun Solaris machines that enables the sharing of files and user accounts across those machines. All these services support some form of compound name; they vary in the nature of the components in the name and the rules for name construction. The JNDI interfaces try to conceal such differences of detail.

If you are implementing a medium sized web-based application in Java, you should find that JDBC, servlets, JSP and a little XML to be quite sufficient. You move into the other areas of Enterprise Java only when attempting something much more ambitious. The scale of the endeavor is obviously vast. EJBs are the next Enterprise technology with which you might work. The introductory tutorial manual for EJBs has over 450 pages. This tutorial must be supplemented with reference manuals detailing the class interfaces and manuals explaining the use of necessary support tools. Most of the other Enterprise technologies are of comparable complexity.

This chapter provides a brief introduction to EJB technology. The EJB development kit is available as a download from Sun (at `http://java.sun.com/j2ee/download.html`; see also `http://java.sun.com/products/`). The download package includes archives with the class files, interfaces, class documentation, support tools, a tutorial and examples. It is intended for Solaris and Windows NT-based operating systems; it may work on Windows 98 and similar systems, but is not officially supported on these systems. Part of the content of this chapter is a commentary on the examples in this EJB tutorial. The examples in the tutorial form a sequence illustrating various facets of EJB structure and deployment, but really only the last of the examples (the transactional bank) illustrates an appropriate use of the technology.

10.1 EJB background

10.1.1 Smart beans in smarter containers

The Java examples in the last few chapters have illustrated an increasing 'separation of concerns'. A servlet's task becomes primarily a limited technical one, dealing first with the receipt of a request, then with delegation of work to 'beans' that perform business-oriented and database-related tasks, and finally transfer of responsibility for the generation of the response to a JSP. Some beans have the business logic; it is here that you get the rules that determine what operations should be performed. Other beans are more concerned with the transfer of data to and from tables in databases, using database connections to run SQL operations. The database connections will be managed by something – maybe the servlet, maybe the beans themselves. A Java Server Page becomes primarily responsible for the display of the data that are to be shown to the client. A JSP may obtain its data directly from beans that it receives from a servlet, or it may use XML helper classes to format XML data returned by beans.

Servlet and JSP both run within a 'container' (along with any 'data beans' and 'business beans' that the servlets create). The container handles instantiation of server objects (servlets and JSPs); it also supports mechanisms that help servlets and JSPs collaborate; and it can help the servlets maintain session state. An entire servlet–JSP system is deployed in accordance with instructions in a `.war` file; this file can contain declarative constraints that specify security restrictions on the use of different servlet methods, along with initialization data for parameters such as database identifiers and passwords.

This implementation style can be pursued further. The container part can be made more sophisticated. For example, maybe the container should become responsible for the database connections. There would be two possible gains from such an allocation of responsibility. First, it would lead to more uniform design of different applications developed for a company. All applications would rely on the container for their database connections; rather than the current situation where typically some applications have servlet-managed database connections, while other applications accord this responsibility to beans. Secondly, allocation of such responsibility to the container should allow for the use of standardized code that applies more sophisticated mechanisms for connection pooling.

Additional 'standard' code might be incorporated into the container. For example, data beans are essentially in-memory representations of rows in database tables that are created by loading data from the database; their accessor methods provide read access to the data, while their mutator methods involve database updates. A lot of the code for using such data beans is essentially standard; some of this code can be incorporated into the container system, while other parts of the code might be capable of being created using systems for automatic code generation.

The 'declarative deployment' approach is also open to extension. For example, many applications involve transactional updates on multiple data beans. The code needed to support transactions can again be largely standardized. If the transactional code can be built into the container, individual business beans would not need to reimplement it. Instead, the business beans could have declarative descriptors attached; these would identify those operations that were transactional in nature, and maybe give further details such as the required level of transaction isolation.

Such more sophisticated containers do exist. They are 'Enterprise JavaBean' containers. Rather than servlets and JSPs, they hold Enterprise JavaBeans (EJBs). EJBs can be viewed as sophisticated versions of the little data beans and business beans that are used by servlets and JSPs. EJBs are intended to be reusable components that can be incorporated into many different applications. An EJB container uses a deployment descriptor file in much the same way that a servlet container, such as Tomcat, uses a `.war` file. The deployment descriptor file for an EJB container specifies the EJBs that it can run, and the databases that it uses. Each individual EJB specification in this deployment file can contain supplementary data on access controls, as in servlets, and now transactional controls as well.

Often, a system will be deployed with a web container that continues to hold servlets and JSPs, and an EJB container that holds the EJBs. Code in the servlet running in the web container must invoke operations of beans hosted in the EJB container. In simple test configurations, a single process may incorporate both containers. In more realistic deployments, one process runs the web container (e.g. Tomcat); while another process, probably on a different machine, runs the EJB container. The separation of web server and application server may permit additional security controls; a first firewall can be used to protect the web server, and an additional firewall can protect the application server. This increased protection is sometimes a motivating factor for the choice of EJB style rather than simpler servlet-and-bean style implementations. If you are using Java application clients, rather than web browser clients, then code in the client application must invoke operations of EJBs held in an EJB container run by some other process, again typically running on another machine.

10.1.2 Distributed objects

Although it is helpful to view EJBs as more sophisticated versions of the little helper bean classes used with servlets, and to treat an EJB container as a more powerful version of a servlet container like Tomcat, the EJB systems actually originated elsewhere. They are really the product of experience obtained with CORBA systems.

CORBA remains the premier distributed object technology system. CORBA's strengths include its ability to support systems where client and server are implemented in different languages, and its comprehensive set of 'services' that extend the basic distributed object model. CORBA developments are of particular importance in organizations that have substantial legacy code (existing applications in Cobol, C, C++, Ada etc. that still constitute major parts of the company's IT infrastructure). CORBA components can be used to build object-style interfaces to such applications. New client applications, using Java-based graphic interfaces, are enabled to work with these CORBA objects and thus exploit all the company's existing IT systems. However, CORBA programming is challenging. A lot of the code in a CORBA program, particularly code for the server side, has to focus on 'housekeeping' – managing the life cycles of the various server objects that are created and used. Particular patterns of object use do frequently reappear in different CORBA applications, but each time, similar complex code must be used to implement these patterns.

The EJB approach exploits the regular coding patterns that are found in distributed object systems. An EJB container incorporates much of the same low-level code that would exist in a CORBA server (in fact, it may be the same code; some EJB vendors have built their products on top of existing CORBA servers). However, the EJB container extends the basic network-related code with additional code that supports certain common uses of server-side objects. For example, server-side programs frequently need data bean objects – things that represent the information in a row of a relational table. A CORBA programmer must wrestle with issues like the need to have a subordinate 'Portable Object Adapter' that implements a suitable 'servant management' policy, and must select among different policies such as the use of 'servant activators', 'servant locators' or a 'default servant'. The EJB developers finessed all of this. Noting that these data beans were one of the most common uses of objects created on the server, they built in support for such objects. The EJB term for data beans is 'Entity beans'. EJB containers take responsibility for managing the life cycle of Entity beans. An EJB container keeps Entity beans in memory. If memory gets short and an Entity bean appears inactive, the container can get rid of it and still reinstate it if it is again needed. None of this life cycle management need concern the application programmer, who can instead devote more time to application specific issues.

Other common patterns in distributed computing involve various forms of 'session objects' for clients. A client connects to the server and is allocated a session object that it uses to submit requests; these requests may involve operations on many different server-side data objects. Sometimes, the requests that can be made to a session object are all independent; the session object is not changed in anyway, it simply acts as an intermediary. Many different clients can use the same object. In other cases, the server-side object stores data on behalf of the client, so each client must work with a separate instance of the class. Once again, a CORBA programmer implementing such systems must worry about servant retention ('servant' is CORBA-speak for a server-side object), servant activation, and so forth. The EJB designers again selected the most common patterns of usage and built in support for 'Session Beans' (with stateless and stateful variants). Once again, the EJB container framework code gets the major part of the responsibility for life cycle management.

The 'factory object' design pattern frequently appears in distributed computing. The server hosts a single 'well-known' object (its name might be published through something like the rmiregistry for an RMI server, or a COSNaming name server for CORBA). This object typically has two methods – 'create a new *XX* object with identifier...' and 'find or reinstantiate the existing *XX* object with identifier...'; thus, it acts as a 'factory' for *XX* objects. The EJB developers picked on this mechanism as essentially the only one whereby clients could contact objects in a server, and again provided additional support code in the EJB container.

EJB is restrictive: you must use factory objects to create and access other objects; you can have only two kinds of Session bean and these must obey various usage constraints; Entity beans have specified restrictions and requirements. Server-side objects in CORBA can be far more varied and sophisticated, but are harder to program. EJB sacrifices versatility, but provides more support for the most common uses of distributed objects.

Distributed object technologies like Java RMI and CORBA always have support components. These include compilers and code generators, the runtime 'object request broker' (ORB) components for client and for server, and naming services that help a client find a named server object. Java RMI's rmic is an example of a code generator; rmic takes information on a server class and generates the corresponding proxy class that will be used by clients. Name servers include Java RMI's rmiregistry, and CORBA COSNaming name servers. An EJB system is similar is similar to these other technologies. It is actually a bit more automated. Developers do not explicitly compile client stubs (as they would do for RMI); instead, the code generation and compilation processes are invoked automatically as an EJB program is assembled. The EJB container has all the server-side ORB components; clients work with a few objects from `javax.rmi` and `javax.naming` packages along with application specific stub classes. A naming service is built into the EJB container (this naming service is for the 'factory' objects that clients must contact before they can work with session or entity beans).

For all its automation, an EJB system remains a distributed technology. Your coding style must change to reflect this. When you implement a servlet with a few helper beans, you are thinking about a single application built from a few classes that you largely define for yourself. When you develop with EJB, you have two applications – client and server, and often two separate development groups. Development of the EJB-based server application involves designing session beans and entity beans that are based on fairly complex classes defined in the EJB framework, and writing the code for a few of their methods while leaving others to an automatic code generation system. The client part may be a servlet, or a separate Java application. It has to contain code for establishing network connections, creating proxy objects and invoking operations via proxies.

Your code changes in other ways as well. For example, if you use a simple data bean to represent a 'customer' in a servlet, you will probably implement fine-grained accessor and mutator methods such as get/set-Name, get/set-Address, get/set-CustomerID, and so forth. Since the servlet and data bean would both be in the same address space, these are all simple method calls. In an EJB implementation, your client (servlet or application) would have a 'Customer Proxy' object while the actual Customer Entity Bean would exist in the separate address space of the EJB container. Each method invocation on the Customer involves network communications, and a quite substantial amount of work by the EJB container. Fine-grained access to individual data elements becomes inappropriate because of these overheads. Instead, you must implement a much coarser-grained interface, using methods such as 'get data' and 'set data' in your customer class. These methods would involve the transfer of an instance of a subsidiary data struct (a simple class with public data members for all the different data fields in a customer object).

You must design your classes in accord with coding conventions for the EJB framework. This naturally includes provision of effective methods for abstract functions inherited from framework base classes. In addition, there are many naming conventions that must be complied with; a lot of the support code gets generated automatically and the code-generators depend on your following the naming conventions.

Finally, there are some unusual aspects to the way that server interfaces are defined in EJB. Typically, as in RMI and CORBA, a server 'interface' is defined; this lists the public methods of the server class giving details of return and argument types and so forth. A server class will implement this interface, as will the automatically generated client proxy (stub) class. Such inheritable interfaces are not used in EJB. The creators of the EJB system chose instead to rely rather heavily on Java reflection. With Java reflection, the runtime system builds Method objects that have data elements that identify the object that is to perform the work, the member function of that object that is to be used, and the argument data. Extensive runtime checks can be performed to verify that correct versions are being used and that all data are of appropriate types. A side effect of this use of reflection is the oddity in the way that the interfaces are defined. Typically, you declare the classes for the client and for the actual implementation quite separately. The client class declarations are used in the system that auto-generates client proxy classes (and some helper classes used in the server process). Class declarations for the client classes and actual implementation class must of course match with respect to the defined public methods of the server (because otherwise the system will not be able to create appropriate Method objects).

10.2 EJB basics

10.2.1 Servers, containers and beans

An EJB server will run as a process on your server machine. It will host various 'containers'. Containers can be web containers (for servlets), or EJB containers that hold enterprise beans. Larger scale applications typically involve multiple EJB servers with one or more hosting web containers, and several others holding EJB containers. The beans used in a single application may exist in different EJB containers. Communications between client proxies and beans, and inter-communications among beans, normally involve network message traffic; a call from a session bean to an entity bean will go down through an elaborate protocol stack to the TCP/IP level, and then come back up through the same protocol stack. The EJB-2 specifications allow for some optimizations of communications among beans that are by design going to be instantiated in the same container.

The current version of Enterprise Java defines three kinds of Enterprise Bean:

- Session beans – used to perform tasks for clients.

- Entity beans – represent a 'business entity', most often a block of data taken from a row in a relational table.

- Message beans – these allow an EJB server to act as a server for asynchronous message style client–server systems.

Message beans are somewhat specialized; many EJB servers do not yet incorporate support for them.

Session beans should seem familiar to those who have worked with Java RMI or another comparable distributed object systems. They have a set of public methods that represent services that are offered to clients. Although the EJB system explicitly supports stateful and stateless sessions, there is only one SessionBean class defined by the EJB framework. The two types tend to have somewhat different application-specific member functions, and do have to be handled differently by the container. Data in the deployment file identify whether a particular SessionBean subclass should be handled as a stateful or stateless bean.

A *stateless* session bean will offer one or more procedural-style services. A good use of such a bean would be to support database queries, where the various queries involve tasks like performing joins on database tables, or the retrieval/update of related data taken from more than one database. Such a session bean will return any results as records (instances of some simple 'struct' like class) held in a Java collection object. A client will establish contact with such a session bean, submit a request with parameters that identify the records that are to be retrieved, and receive the results. A stateless session bean will forget all about its current client on completion of an invoked method. (You can make an analogy between a stateless session bean and a HTTP server.) Typically, an EJB container will create a few instances of each stateless session bean class when it starts, and have these ready to receive client requests. (An EJB server is multi-threaded, but it will not allow beans to be used by more than one thread simultaneously; hence the need to have multiple instances of a stateless bean.) All stateless session beans are identical; a client that submits several successive requests may have each request handled by a different stateless session bean (you could make another analogy between a pool of stateless session beans and a pool of Apache tribesmen). Stateless session beans can have data members, but these are only for things like database connections supplied by the EJB container, or read-only reference data, or for temporary data used while processing an individual request.

A *stateful* session bean performs a sequence of tasks on behalf of a specific client. It has to be created with an identity (e.g. the name of the client). Operations on a stateful bean will return results to the client, and may also change instance variables in the bean itself. Subsequent operations may combine parameter data with data from these instance variables. (You can make an analogy between a stateful session bean and an ftp server. Each client who uses ftp gets a separate process that holds data, such as the client's login identity, the current working directly, and the transfer mode for files. 'Change directory' operations define the context for subsequent operations like directory listings and transfer requests.) A popular example use of a stateful session bean is a web 'Shopping Cart'; such a bean could have a `Vector` holding records with item-identifier and quantity members for each item picked by the client. The state data members in a bean are application specific, but all must be instances of `java.io.Serializable` types or simple built in types (e.g. `String`, `int`, `int[]`, `Integer`, ...). A busy EJB server may have to transfer little used stateful session beans to secondary file storage; a bean that has been removed from memory gets recreated when its client next makes contact.

Entity beans represent persistent data. In principle, an entity bean can represent data that are stored in a file, in an object database, in a hierarchical database, or in a relational database; overwhelmingly, they are used with relational databases. Each bean has an identity element – equivalent to a primary key for a database. (Often, this primary key is an instance of `java.lang.String` or `java.lang.Long` classes, but you can define a more specialized primary key class. Commercial Enterprise Java development environments incorporate various 'wizards' that help manage the definition and use of such auxiliary classes.)

There are two types of entity bean: beans that manage their own transfers to/from persistent storage (Bean Managed Persistence – BMP), and beans that rely on the container to manage transfers (Container Managed Persistence – CMP). In the case of BMP beans, the developer writes code that obtains a JDBC database connection from the container and uses this to perform SQL operations; the bean class includes declarations for the persistent data members. With CMP beans, most of the database access code is generated automatically; the developer supplies a declarative bean descriptor that identifies the required persistent data elements and, in some cases, must also provide some database operation statements in an EJB-specific dialect of SQL (these statements are also stored in the bean's declarative descriptor). A programmer-defined CMP bean class is actually abstract; the system defines a concrete subclass. A CMP bean class does not define data members equivalent to its declared persistent data members; instead it has get/set access functions (virtual data members). The automatic code generation system creates a concrete subclass with the data members and transfer functions that use a database connection to run SQL operations.

An entity bean must be created the first time it is ever used; creation of the bean inherently involves creation of an entry in the database. This entry is associated with the bean's identity – primary key. Subsequently, an entity bean is 'found'; it is recreated from data in the database. A 'remove' operation on a bean must also entail deletion of the database record.

A container may recycle the entity beans that it actually creates in memory; recyclable beans reduce the work that must be done by the storage manager. An entity bean has a data member for its primary key; setting this data member establishes the identity of the bean. When the primary key member has been set, the bean can be told to reload its other data members. Typically, a container will pre-allocate a number of entity beans from each entity class that it manages; these pre-allocated beans don't have any initial identity – their keys are unset. When a specific bean is needed, a pooled bean is used and given an identity. If a client discards a bean, the container can make sure that the database copy is updated, and then return the bean to its pre-allocated pool.

10.2.2 The life of a bean

The container manages the life cycle of all beans. Thus, for a stateful session bean, the container will have to create a bean initialized with a client-supplied identity, allow the client to use the bean, possibly transfer the bean to secondary storage ('passivate' the bean), activate (restore) a saved bean, and finally remove the bean. For an entity bean, the container must take a pooled bean, give it an identity, and get it to reload its other data; at various subsequent times, the container must ensure that bean and database versions are kept consistent.

The life cycle management code is standard and incorporated into the container, but life cycle operations do impinge on application-specific code. For example, a stateful session bean may have acquired a database connection; this connection is not going to be of much use if the bean has got itself transferred to secondary storage. A session bean should release any such connection before it is 'passivated' and reacquire a new connection when subsequently activated. Such application-specific needs are handled through 'hook functions'. These 'hook' member functions are defined as abstract life cycle-related functions in the base classes such as `javax.ejb.SessionBean` and `javax.ejb.EntityBean`. There are several such functions, for there are many places where it might be necessary to perform some application-specific processing before or after the container invokes one of the life cycle methods. All these functions must be given definitions in the bean classes, though very often they are empty definitions (e.g. `void ejbPassivate() { }`).

10.2.3 Classes and interfaces

When you define an Enterprise bean, you have to define three classes and interfaces. The first class is the real bean class itself; this class will be a subclass of `javax.ejb.SessionBean` or `javax.ejb.EntityBean`. The second interface, which extends `javax.ejb.EJBObject` (which itself extends `java.rmi.Remote`), is the remote interface for the service. This must define public functions with signatures identical to the application-specific functions defined for the enterprise bean. The EJB system will generate a concrete class that implements this remote interface. This class is the proxy class that is actually instantiated in a client.

The third interface that you must define is the interface for the 'factory' that is used to find or to create enterprise beans on behalf of the client. The EJB system generates more than one class implementing this interface; there is the real factory class used in the EJB container, and a proxy class that allows the client to communicate with the factory. Although the term 'factory' has been widely used for years, the EJB developers picked a different name for their interface. In EJB terms, this is the 'Home' interface; it extends `javax.ejb.EJBHome`.

A Home interface for a session bean will be simple, involving just one or more 'create' methods (there are a few other methods declared in the parent EJBHome class, e.g. `remove`). A stateless session bean requires only a single, no-argument 'create' method. Stateful session beans need create methods with arguments that supply an identity and, possibly, other initial state data. The corresponding enterprise bean must define matching functions that can be used to pass these initializing data to the bean; these must be named 'ejbCreate' and have argument lists that match the create functions in the Home interface.

The Home interfaces for Entity beans are more complex. Usually they will define 'create' methods, though occasionally this is not necessary (it is possible that entries in the database are created only by existing legacy applications). In addition to any 'create' methods, these Entity bean Home interfaces also define 'find' methods. One obvious method is 'find by primary key'; this is used to recreate an entity bean whose key is known. For both 'create' and 'find by primary key' methods, a Home interface returns a reference to an instance of the application specific subclass of EJBObject.

However, the 'finder' mechanism is more general than this. As in all database-related work, it is often necessary to obtain collections of all records that satisfy constraints on the values of data members. Such extra 'find' methods are commonly included in the Home interfaces for entity beans and implemented in the Entity bean class itself (the Entity bean class must define an ejbFind*XX* method for each find*XX* method defined in the Home interface). For example, with a 'Customer' entity bean, as well as the standard findByPrimaryKey(String customerID) method, you might want a method like findByCustomerName(String Name); this would retrieve data on all customers whose names matched the given name string. Such methods naturally return collections; they are collections of EJBObjects (i.e. client stub objects). (Actually, it is a bit more complex than that. The implementation of an ejbFind... method in the Entity bean class will return either a primary key object or a collection of primary key objects. The container then changes this into a remote object reference, or collection of remote object references, and returns these data to the client. Since the system is based on Java RMI, the support code in the server returns these references packaged in serialized instances of the client-side stub objects.)

Entity beans do have to have associated 'remote' and 'home' interfaces (a bean can only be contacted via a remote proxy created by a factory object that implements the 'home' interface). This allows client code (in a servlet or a Java application) to obtain a reference to an entity bean, and then use this to invoke operations on the database through that bean. Such usage is dubious. It results in client code incorporating the business rules that determine permitted operations on databases and so forth. Generally, it is better for such rules to be implemented via code in reusable session beans. A client application or servlet works with a session bean (in a client–server relationship); the session bean acts as an intermediary, working with the entity beans (again in a client–server relationship, with the session bean as client and the entity beans as servers). The session bean must still utilize the 'home' interface of the entity bean class to obtain proxies for the entity beans that it needs. This arrangement allows session and entity beans to run in different containers. However, there are obviously significant costs in using this general mechanism when session and entity beans are actually instantiated in the same container. The EJB Version 2 implementation defines the classes javax.ejb.LocalObject and javax.ejb.LocalHome; when you plan for objects that are always going to be created in the same container, you can use these classes as the base classes instead of EJBObject and EJBHome. Apart from this use of different base classes, your program structure does not need to change much. Of course, the 'proxy' classes created with these local interfaces are normal Java classes and their method calls are normal Java calls, thereby avoiding the network-related overheads of remote interfaces. (You do need to remember that there are changes to how arguments are passed. Client (session bean) and server (entity bean) parts now work with the same parameter objects, instead of the server getting a separate copy. The server may change these argument objects and any such changes will affect the client. This does not happen with remote interfaces.)

10.2.4 EJB clients and EJB deployment

When you have implemented your Enterprise bean classes, and created the associated remote and home interfaces for each class, you must still write your client code. Simple client applications resemble clients for RMI systems. They start with a standard sequence of code used to establish contact with the server (in the case of a servlet client, this would best be done in the servlet's init method). Where an RMI client will typically be trying to create a proxy for some object identified in the rmiregistry, an EJB client will be trying to get a proxy for a Home object in the EJB container. If the connection attempt is successful, the client will then use this initial Home proxy object to submit a 'create' or 'find' request for the actual session or entity bean with which it wishes to work. This operation will again result in a proxy object that the client may then use. As in RMI programs, the rest of the code seems straightforward; the client uses the proxy as if it were any other local object, invoking methods and receiving results. The code must arrange to catch RemoteExceptions, and, as with RMI, all arguments used in method invocations must be serializable with the server working with a copy of the data passed.

Finally, you must assemble and deploy your system. This step is a little bit like the processes of writing a web.xml deployment file, and then building a .war file for a completed servlet/JSP application; though inevitably it is more complex.

Sun's view of the future has development teams that include individuals with specialized skills such as 'web component creator', 'enterprise bean author', 'client application author', 'application assembler' and 'application deployer/administrator'. You have some experience with the role of 'web component creator', having created web applications with static HTML files, JSPs, web.xml deployment files and servlets. Apart from writing the code for the enterprise beans, an 'enterprise bean author' must also compose a deployment XML file. This file, ejb-jar.xml, is considerably more complex than the web.xml files and is never composed by hand; instead, the developer will use some GUI-based 'wizard' that steps through the creation process (Sun's kit includes the deploytool program that incorporates an Enterprise Bean Wizard). This wizard allows the developer to select the class files that make up a bean (remote and home interfaces, and the enterprise bean itself), and then specify deployment details such as whether the bean is a session bean or an entity bean.

The role of 'client application author' would probably suit someone with prior experience with Java RMI; the general programming style is similar. The 'application assembler' takes .jar files with the enterprise bean components and client application components, and .war files with servlet/JSP client applications, and assembles these into an 'Enterprise Archive' (.ear file). This archive again incorporates a fairly complex deployment XML file that is created with the help of a wizard tool. Among other data, this deployment file contains name mappings that relate the 'server names' used in clients (servlet/application) to the enterprise bean that provides the services. Finally, the 'application deployer/administrator' is responsible for running the EJB server (this is the j2ee program in Sun's kit), and for adding .ear files to the server's repertoire.

10.3 Session bean examples

Sun's kit includes tutorial examples illustrating stateless and stateful session beans. These examples are intended only to illustrate the structure and use of such beans; neither example represents an appropriate use of EJB technology.

10.3.1 Stateless server

The first example is a stateless session bean that handles currency conversion. (The most appropriate technology for such an application would probably be a little PHP script accessing a database table with current conversion rates.) For simplicity, the example converter has just two methods implementing specific conversions (dollars to yen, yen to euro) using fictitious exchange rates defined as constants. The Converter Bean example comprises:

- `Converter.java`
The file for the remote interface declaration (the two conversion functions).

- `ConverterHome.java`
The file with the Home interface; as always for stateless session beans, this is very simple, defining solely a no-argument create method that returns a Converter object.

- `ConverterBean.java`
This file has the code implementing the stateless session bean.

- `ConverterClient.java`
This contains a simple client application that tests the bean.

- `index.jsp`
This (rather oddly named) file contains a JSP with a large chunk of scriptlet code that invokes operations on a Converter.

Both the interfaces are simple (lots of import statements are required, see the example files):

```
public interface Converter extends EJBObject {
    public double dollarToYen(double dollars) throws RemoteException;
    public double yenToEuro(double yen) throws RemoteException;
}

public interface ConverterHome extends EJBHome {
    Converter create() throws RemoteException, CreateException;
}
```

They are both defining `java.rmi.Remote` interfaces (EJB is based on Java RMI, though with a wire protocol based on CORBA's IIOP – Internet Inter-ORB Protocol). Consequently, every method may throw `java.rmi.RemoteExceptions`. It is standard for the creation functions for all enterprise beans to throw `javax.ejb.CreateExceptions`. While it is unlikely that an attempt to create a session bean would fail, you would certainly get a create exception if you attempted to create an entity bean with an identifier identical to that of an existing bean (leading to a non-unique primary key in the corresponding database table).

The enterprise bean is:

```
public class ConverterBean implements SessionBean {
  // Constructor and life-cycle methods
  ...
  // Application specific server methods, signatures
  // to match methods in "remote" interface
  ...
}
```

Session beans are required to have a no argument constructor (public ConverterBean() {}) and must provide effective implementations for the life cycle methods declared in the SessionBean class. It is common for most or all these methods to get null definitions; they are after all just hook functions, included to allow for special cases where some particular action is needed before or after the container forces some major life cycle change on the bean.

```
public void ejbCreate() {}
public void ejbRemove() {}
public void ejbActivate() {}
public void ejbPassivate() {}
```

There is one more inherited method that must be defined, setSessionContext(SessionContext sc). The container calls setSessionContext just after it creates the bean, and before it calls the ejbCreate initialization function. The argument is a reference to an object that can supply information such as details of a client's identity (if using some security controls) or the state of any current transaction. A bean can have a SessionContext instance member that is used to save a reference to this context; the setSessionContext method sets this member for later use. Like most session beans, this bean does not have any need to access the context and so this method is empty:

```
public void setSessionContext(SessionContext sc) {}
```

The application-specific member functions are trivial, e.g.:

```
public double dollarToYen(double dollars) { return dollars * 121.6000; }
```

The client application program is:

```
public class ConverterClient {
  public static void main(String[] args) {
```

```
        try {
            // Use naming service to obtain reference to Home (factory)
            // object associated with ConverterBean class
            ...
            // Use "home" object (proxy) to create a session bean in EJB
            // EJB server, and return reference for proxy
            ...
            // Invoke operations on bean via proxy
            ...
        }
        catch (Exception ex) {
            // Report any exceptions
            ...
        }
    }
}
```

EJB clients use JNDI naming services to contact the name server that is built into a container. An InitialContext object is created and then used to lookup a named resource:

```
Context initial = new InitialContext();
Object objref = initial.lookup("java:comp/env/ejb/SimpleConverter");
```

The naming service in the server has a structure equivalent to a file hierarchy, with an 'environment' section that has subsections for EJBs, and for database sources etc. The 'JNDI name' used by the client application will correspond to an entry in the ejb section. This SimpleConverter entry is created when the application is deployed and the name mapping data are in one of the XML deployment files. This lookup step is generally similar to that in an RMI program (e.g. CalculatorFactory theWorks = (CalculatorFactory) Naming.lookup("rmi://cs.bigcampus.edu:13456/Calc"). The RMI Naming.lookup operation uses a URL that identifies the host machine and port used by the required rmiregistry program; and then has a simple object name. The JNDI-based version defines the source machine and port for the naming server from system parameters (taken from a properties file, or as command line environment variables, or set in code). In this example, it is relying on defaults with the EJB server running on the local host using standard ports.

The Object reference returned from the lookup operation must be cast to the appropriate type. Ordinary Java casts cannot be used here; instead, a 'narrowing' operation is done, as in CORBA:

```
ConverterHome home = (ConverterHome)
PortableRemoteObject.narrow(objref, ConverterHome.class);
```

(This narrowing operation performs further runtime checks that verify that objects are indeed of the appropriate type.)

Once a reference to the Home (factory) object has been obtained, it can be used to create a currency converter object:

```
Converter currencyConverter = home.create();
```

Finally, the conversion operations may be performed using this converter:

```
double amount = currencyConverter.dollarToYen(100.00);
System.out.println(String.valueOf(amount));
```

The web-based client uses a JSP; this JSP is run in a web container hosted in the j2ee engine alongside the EJB container. The JSP displays a form, and possibly some output text showing the results for any previous operation. The form allows the user to enter the amount of money that is to be converted. Scriptlet code is used for the interactions with the EJB system. The JSP starts with a page directive that imports the various Java packages required, then has a declaration section for some of the scriptlet code, and finally some HTML tags, content text and scriptlet expressions:

```
<%@ page import="Converter,ConverterHome,javax.ejb.*, javax.naming.*,
javax.rmi.PortableRemoteObject, java.rmi.RemoteException" %>
<%!
  // Declare instances variables and member functions for
  // servlet generated from this page
  ...
%>
<html><head><title>Converter</title></head>
<h1><b><center>Converter</center></b></h1>
<hr>
<p>Enter an amount to convert:</p>
<form method="get">
<input type="text" name="amount" size="25">
<br>
<p>
<input type="submit" value="Submit">
<input type="reset" value="Reset">
</form>
<%
  String amount = request.getParameter("amount");
  if ( amount != null && amount.length() > 0 ) {
    Double d = new Double (amount);
%>
<p>
<%= amount %> dollars are <%= converter.dollarToYen(d.doubleValue()) %>
Yen.
<p>
```

```
<%= amount %> Yen are <%= converter.yenToEuro(d.doubleValue()) %> Euro.
<%
}
%>
</body></html>
```

The scriptlet code includes a large declaration section with an instance variable to hold a reference to the converter and a jspInit method that establishes the connection. The code for this jspInit method is similar to the code in the application client (Sun's developers chose to have the JSP and the application client use different names for the service, and use this feature to illustrate further use of the JNDI naming services). The declarative section of the scriptlet code is:

```
private Converter converter = null;
public void jspInit() {
  try {
    InitialContext ic = new InitialContext();
    Object objRef = ic.lookup("java:comp/env/ejb/TheConverter");
    ConverterHome home = (ConverterHome)
      PortableRemoteObject.narrow(objRef, ConverterHome.class);
    converter = home.create();
  }
  // several catch clauses for different possible exceptions
  ...
}

public void jspDestroy() { converter = null; }
```

Sun's tutorial contains several pages of detailed instructions that explain the steps needed to assemble and deploy this EJB application and its clients. The archive files and the XML deployment files that get created are not intended for human consumption. However, their structure and content for this simple example are reasonably revealing and may help you obtain a better understanding of the deployment process. (The structures for the archive files, and the forms for the XML files, are largely standardized. An application built for one EJB implementation is supposed to be easily transferred to another. However, a particular EJB system may create the odd specialized XML file with deployment data that are specific to its EJB server.)

The 'Enterprise Archive' (.ear) file created for this example contains the following files and directories:

```
ejb-jar-ic.jar
war-ic.war
app-client-ic.jar
META-INF/MANIFEST.MF
META-INF/application.xml
META-INF/sun-j2ee-ri.xml
```

One .jarhave to be installed on a client machine that runs the application client; the other .jar file contains resources used by the EJB server that will host this bean. The .war file contains the resources that are needed by the web server that hosts servlets and JSPs.

The application.xml file describes the module structure; in this case, there are three modules (server, client and web client):

```
<application>
  <display-name>ConverterApp</display-name>
  <description>Converter demo</description>
  <module>
    <ejb>ejb-jar-ic.jar</ejb>
  </module>
  <module>
    <java>app-client-ic.jar</java>
  </module>
  <module>
    <web>
    <web-uri>war-ic.war</web-uri>
    <context-root>converter</context-root>
    </web>
  </module>
</application>
```

The other XML resource file is a J2EE implementation-specific file. It contains data such as mapping of resource names used in clients to JNDI names as used in the name server component of the EJB server.

The main ejb-jar-ic.jar file contains the .class files for the ConverterBean and its associated home and remote interfaces, and the ejb-jar.xml deployment file. It is this ejb-jar.xml file that contains all the information that the container needs to operate with a particular enterprise bean. The file for this example is:

```
<ejb-jar>
  <display-name>ConverterJAR</display-name>
  <enterprise-beans>
    <session>
      <display-name>ConverterEJB</display-name>
      <ejb-name>ConverterEJB</ejb-name>
      <home>ConverterHome</home>
      <remote>Converter</remote>
      <ejb-class>ConverterBean</ejb-class>
      <session-type>Stateless</session-type>
      <transaction-type>Bean</transaction-type>
      <security-identity>
        <description></description>
        <use-caller-identity></use-caller-identity>
```

```
        </security-identity>
      </session>
    </enterprise-beans>
  </ejb-jar>
```

This deployment file declares only the single session bean. The data identify the reference name for the bean, its implementation classes and its session type. Here, the bean is defined as a stateless session bean; this information will be used at run time to determine the life cycle methods that should be called and the approach to be taken regarding the creation of beans (in this case, pre-allocate a pool of stateless session beans and never bother with passivation/activation). The file contains entries for transaction controls and security controls; here, these entries are essentially empty: there are no controls.

10.3.2 Stateful server

Sun's second session bean example is a variation on the ubiquitous shopping cart for a bookstore site. (Again, it isn't intended to illustrate a good use of EJB, merely to illustrate the form of the classes. Sun has a better shopping cart in the 'Duke's bookstore' servlet example.) The only features of interest are the various 'create' methods in the home interfaces (and corresponding 'ejbCreate' methods in the session bean class), the return data types for one of the cart's methods (it illustrates a bean returning collections of data, in this case a collection of Strings), the state data (identifier data for the bean, and a Vector to store books), and some minor details of the XML deployment file (like the tag identifying it as a stateful bean).

The home and remote interfaces for the cart are:

```
public interface CartHome extends EJBHome {
  Cart create(String person)
    throws RemoteException, CreateException;
  Cart create(String person, String id)
    throws RemoteException, CreateException;
}


public interface Cart extends EJBObject {
  public void addBook(String title) throws RemoteException;
  public void removeBook(String title)
    throws BookException, RemoteException;
  public Vector getContents() throws RemoteException;
}
```

Sun uses an auxiliary BookException class to illustrate how a bean can throw an application-specific exception.

The CartBean class defines instance data members and the two ejbCreate methods that match the create methods in the home interface. These methods will throw create exceptions if given unacceptable data:

```java
public class CartBean implements SessionBean {
  String customerName;
  String customerId;
  Vector contents;

  // ejbCreate (initialize) methods
  public void ejbCreate(String person) throws CreateException {
    if (person == null) {
      throw new CreateException("Null person not allowed.");
    }
    else customerName = person;
    customerId = "0";
    contents = new Vector();
  }
  public void ejbCreate(String person, String id) throws CreateException {
    if (person == null) {
      throw new CreateException("Null person not allowed.");
    }
    else customerName = person;
    // Code to check validity of id argument
    ...
    contents = new Vector();
  }

  // Business methods
  public void addBook(String title) { contents.addElement(title); }
  public void removeBook(String title) throws BookException {
    boolean result = contents.removeElement(title);
    if (result == false) {
      throw new BookException(title + " not in cart.");
    }
  }
  public Vector getContents() { return contents; }

  // Life cycle methods
  ...
}
```

The life cycle methods would again all be empty because this bean does not require any special actions on life cycle changes. You can put tracers in life cycle methods (or any methods); these can help debugging. It is a bit like putting tracers in your servlets; there the messages appeared in the window for the terminal session controlling the Tomcat server (or were sent to a log file). With EJBs, trace messages will appear in a window associated with the EJB server.

```
public void ejbPassivate() {
   System.out.println("Pasivating cart for " + customerName);
}
```

(You will find it hard to provoke your j2ee server into passivating a bean when running toy examples that are this small.)

Sun's development kit comes with pre-built versions of these examples as well as source. The pre-built ejb-jar.xml file contains a couple of interesting features:

```
<ejb-jar>
  <enterprise-beans>
    <session>
      <display-name>CartEJB</display-name>
      <ejb-name>CartEJB</ejb-name>
      <home>CartHome</home>
      <remote>Cart</remote>
      <ejb-class>CartBean</ejb-class>
      <session-type>Stateful</session-type>
      <transaction-type>
        Container</transaction-type>
      <security-identity>
         ...
      </security-identity>
    </session>
  </enterprise-beans>
  <assembly-descriptor>
    <method-permission>
      <unchecked />
      <method>
        <ejb-name>CartEJB</ejb-name>
        <method-intf>
          Remote</method-intf>
        <method-name>
          getContents</method-name>
        <method-params />
      </method>
      ...
    </method-permission>
    ...
    <container-transaction>
      <method>
        <ejb-name>CartEJB</ejb-name>
        <method-intf>Remote</method-intf>
        <method-name>getContents</method-name>
        <method-params />
```

```
          </method>
          <trans-attribute>
            Required
          </trans-attribute>
        </container-transaction>
        ...
      </assembly-descriptor>
   </ejb-jar>
```

In addition to the enterprise bean section, where this bean is duly marked as stateful, the file now contains an assembly descriptor section. This has data on all methods; these data describe restriction and transactional controls. In this case, all the data are simply default values. In real-world applications, these elements play an important role in defining controls that the container will place on the use of these beans.

10.4 An Entity bean

Bank account examples must be the 'Hello World' programs for distributed systems; they appear with every introductory presentation of technologies like RMI, CORBA, EJB and SOAP. Sun's tutorial keeps in fashion, using a bank account as its first illustration of an entity bean.

These beans represent rows from a database table defined as follows:

```
CREATE TABLE savingsaccount
(
  id VARCHAR(3)
    CONSTRAINT pk_savingsaccount PRIMARY KEY,
  firstname VARCHAR(24),
  lastname VARCHAR(24),
  balance DECIMAL(10,2)
);
```

Access to these beans is obtained via a SavingsAccountHome interface; this naturally supplements a 'create' operation with some 'find' operations:

```
public interface SavingsAccountHome extends EJBHome {
  public SavingsAccount create(
    String id, String firstName,
    String lastName,
    double balance)
      throws RemoteException, CreateException;
  public SavingsAccount findByPrimaryKey(String id)
      throws FinderException, RemoteException;
  public Collection findByLastName(String lastName)
```

```
      throws FinderException, RemoteException;
   public Collection findInRange(double low, double high)
      throws FinderException, RemoteException;
}
```

The findByPrimaryKey method recreates a bean that represents a specified account; the other two 'find' methods return collections (accounts where a surname matches, accounts with a balance in a specified range). These 'find' method all have the potential of throwing FinderExceptions (e.g. an invalid account identifier supplied to findByPrimaryKey).

A client can deposit and withdraw funds, and review other properties of an account; these operations are defined through the remote interface:

```
public interface SavingsAccount extends EJBObject {
   public void debit(double amount)
      throws InsufficientBalanceException, RemoteException;
   public void credit(double amount)
      throws RemoteException;
   public String getFirstName()
      throws RemoteException;
   public String getLastName()
      throws RemoteException;
   public double getBalance()
      throws RemoteException;
}
```

This interface exhibits a rather fine-grained structure. Sun simply wanted to illustrate several access functions. As noted earlier, a real entity bean would typically provide a coarser-grained mechanism for reading all account data in a single operation, so as to cut down on the overheads associated with multiple remote accesses.

The demonstration client application that Sun provides is pretty much as you would expect. JNDI naming services are used to establish a connection, via a proxy, to a Home implementation object in the server; the local Home proxy is then used to perform actions such as account creation, retrieval of an existing account identified by its identifier (findByPrimaryKey) and retrieval of collections of accounts (findByLastName). The account objects (proxies) obtained via these operations are then used to invoke operations on the entity beans and thence on rows in the underlying database.

```
public static void main(String[] args) {
   try {
      Context initial = new InitialContext();
      Object objref = initial.lookup("java:comp/env/ejb/
         SimpleSavingsAccount");
      SavingsAccountHome home =
         (SavingsAccountHome)PortableRemoteObject.narrow(objref,
            SavingsAccountHome.class);
```

```
        SavingsAccount duke = home.create("123", "Duke", "Earl", 0.00);
        duke.credit(88.50);
        ...
        duke.remove();


        ...

        SavingsAccount jones = home.findByPrimaryKey("836");
        jones.debit(2.00);


        ...

        Collection c = home.findByLastName("Smith");
        Iterator i=c.iterator();

        while (i.hasNext()) {
          SavingsAccount account = (SavingsAccount)i.next();
          String id = (String)account.getPrimaryKey();
          double amount = account.getBalance();
          System.out.println(id + ": " + String.valueOf(amount));
        }

        ...


      }
    catch (InsufficientBalanceException ex) { ... }
    catch (Exception ex) { ... }
  }
```

The example code creates an account for Java's Duke mascot, but also 'removes' this account bean, so deleting the entry from the database. The finder methods provide access to pre-existing accounts.

The SavingsAccountBean has to implement standard life cycle methods, create and finder methods that match those declared in the Home interface, and business methods that match those declared in the remote interface. This is a 'Bean-Managed Persistence' example, so the class has to handle its own relations with the underlying database tables. For this, it needs a database connection and has to submit SQL requests via this connection. The database functions are mainly implemented as private auxiliary methods. The Java file for the class must obviously import the sql packages. The javax.naming package is also required; beans use the JNDI naming service when establishing contact with their databases.

```
public class SavingsAccountBean implements EntityBean {
  // Instance data members
  // Life cycle methods
```

```
    // Create and find methods for Home interface
    // Business methods (Remote interface)
    // Auxiliary functions for accessing the database
}
```

Since this is a BMP Entity bean, it must define instance data members that correspond to the fields in the database record:

```
private String id;
private String firstName;
private String lastName;
private double balance;
```

It also requires a database connection, and a reference to its `EntityContext`. (If an Entity bean is activated, it has to ask the context for its primary key; it will be activated if it is being 'found' rather than being 'created'.)

```
private EntityContext context;
private Connection con;
```

The life cycle methods include activation and passivation (use a pooled bean to represent a row that already exists in the database, finish with entity bean and recycle it), load and store (make bean and data table consistent), remove (delete database row) and set/unset entity context.

```
public void ejbActivate() {
  // (context data member set in setEntityContext, called earlier)
  id = (String)context.getPrimaryKey();
}

public void ejbPassivate() { id = null; }

public void ejbLoad() {
  try {
    loadRow();// Work done in auxiliary private method
  }
  catch (Exception ex) {
    throw new EJBException("ejbLoad: " + ex.getMessage());
  }
}

public void ejbStore() {
  try { storeRow(); }
  catch (Exception ex) { ... }
}
```

```
public void ejbRemove() {
  try { deleteRow(id); }
  catch (Exception ex) { ... );
}
```

The set and unset entity context methods are also used to establish and destroy a database connection. (The setEntityContext method is called when an Entity bean is created by the container and placed in the bean pool; unsetEntityContext is called when a bean is finally destroyed. If the setEntityContext method is used to establish a connection, then the bean always has a database connection ready.) The real work for creating the database connection is done in a private auxiliary member function shown later.

```
public void setEntityContext(EntityContext context) {
  this.context = context;
  try { makeConnection(); }
  catch (Exception ex) { ... }
}

public void unsetEntityContext() {
  try { con.close(); }
  catch (SQLException ex) { ... }
}
```

The SavingsAccountBean class has to define an ejbCreate method that matches the create method in the Home class. Each ejbCreate method must have an accompanying ejbPostCreate method with the same argument list:

```
public String ejbCreate(String id, String firstName,
  String lastName, double balance) throws CreateException {

  if (balance < 0.00) {
    throw new CreateException ("Negative initial balance.");
  }

  try { insertRow(id, firstName, lastName, balance); }
  catch (Exception ex) { ... }

  this.id = id;
  this.firstName = firstName;
  this.lastName = lastName;
  this.balance = balance;

  return id;
}
```

```
public void ejbPostCreate(String id, String firstName,
  String lastName, double balance) { }
```

A create method for an Entity bean must insert a row into a database table; here, this is done in the auxiliary insertRow method. It must also initialize data members for the bean. The return value is the primary key value that identifies the new bean and table row (in this example, the primary key is an instance of java.lang.String, but it could be a programmer defined key type). The container gets this key, uses it to help build a remote reference for this bean object, and returns the remote reference to the client that invoked the create method. In the client, the remote reference is used to initialize a proxy.

'Post create' methods are often empty (but they must still be defined). 'Post create' is just another hook function that allows for special processing steps that are occasionally required.

'Finder' methods may seem a little odd, particularly the ones used to obtain collections of entity beans (e.g. all accounts for customers named 'Smith'). They are 'instance' methods of the entity bean class. The home-implementation object (or other container object) that is dealing with a 'find' request grabs an unused entity bean, and invokes the find method on this bean. A class member function might have been more natural because it is not really a case of asking a specific instance of the class to do something that relates to its own state. However, the use of static class methods would have necessitated a class data member with a connection to a database, and synchronization controls on this connection; so, the instance method was adopted.

```
public String ejbFindByPrimaryKey(String primaryKey) throws
FinderException {
  boolean result;
  try {
    result = selectByPrimaryKey(primaryKey);
  } catch (Exception ex) { ... }
  if (result)
    return primaryKey;
  else
    throw new ObjectNotFoundException(primaryKey + " not found.");
}

public Collection ejbFindByLastName(String lastName)throws
    FinderException {
  Collection result;
  try {
    result = selectByLastName(lastName);
  }
  catch (Exception ex) { ... }
  return result;
}
```

The business methods, which match the methods declared in the remote interface, are all quite simple:

```
public void debit(double amount) throws InsufficientBalanceException {
  if (balance - amount < 0)
    throw new InsufficientBalanceException();
  balance -= amount;
}

public void credit(double amount) { balance += amount; }

public String getFirstName() { return firstName; }
```

Note that the mutator methods, debit and credit, do not explicitly involve calls to database functions. The mechanisms for keeping the Entity bean and the corresponding row in the database mutually consistent are considered later.

The makeConnection method, invoked from setEntityContext, uses JNDI to obtain a datasource associated with its specified dbName:

```
private String dbName = "java:comp/env/jdbc/SavingsAccountDB";

private void makeConnection() throws NamingException, SQLException {
  InitialContext ic = new InitialContext();
  DataSource ds = (DataSource) ic.lookup(dbName);
  con = ds.getConnection();
}
```

The JNDI structure in the EJB server has a jdbc 'subdirectory' that holds configuration data relating to databases (comparable to the ejb subdirectory that contains details of the beans themselves). An entry in one of the XML deployment files is used to set a reference to the appropriate database in the SavingsAccountDB entry. A DataSource is a class that manages database connections; typically using a pool of pre-allocated connections to its database ('closing' a connection returned by a DataSource simply returns it to the DataSource for closure or reallocation).

The four basic database operations – insertRow, deleteRow, loadRow and storeRow – all have the expected SQL operations performed using prepared statements associated with the database connection:

```
private void insertRow (String id, String firstName, String lastName,
    double balance) throws SQLException {
  String insertStatement =
    "insert into savingsaccount values ( ? , ? , ? , ? )";
  PreparedStatement prepStmt =
    con.prepareStatement(insertStatement);
  prepStmt.setString(1, id); ... prepStmt.setDouble(4, balance);
```

```
    prepStmt.executeUpdate();
    prepStmt.close();
}
```

Much of the potential benefit of prepared statements, as opposed to simple statements, is lost when they are created and destroyed like this; they work best if they are prepared once and are reused many times. In principle you could recode the example to create the prepared statements immediately after the database connection is obtained. However, the statements do have the secondary benefit of avoiding problems relating to inappropriately quoted strings, such as those that can arise when you have to insert strings that contain quote characters, for example a name like O'Brien, into a quoted SQL string.

```
private void deleteRow(String id) throws SQLException {
    String deleteStatement =
        "delete from savingsaccount where id = ? ";
    PreparedStatement prepStmt =
        con.prepareStatement(deleteStatement);
    prepStmt.setString(1, id);
    prepStmt.executeUpdate();
    prepStmt.close();
}
```

The loadRow method obviously has to run a select query specifying the record with the required primary key, and then copy data from the result set into the data members of the bean:

```
private void loadRow() throws SQLException {
    String selectStatement =
        "select firstname, lastname, balance " +
        "from savingsaccount where id = ? ";
    PreparedStatement prepStmt =
        con.prepareStatement(selectStatement);
    prepStmt.setString(1, this.id);

    ResultSet rs = prepStmt.executeQuery();
    if (rs.next()) {
        this.firstName = rs.getString(1);
        this.lastName = rs.getString(2);
        this.balance = rs.getDouble(3);
        prepStmt.close();
    }
    else {
        prepStmt.close();
        throw new NoSuchEntityException(id +" not found in database.");
    }
}
```

The storeRow method runs an SQL update that replaces each field with data taken from the bean:

```
private void storeRow() throws SQLException {
  String updateStatement =
    "update savingsaccount set firstname = ? ," +
    "lastname = ? , balance = ? " +
    "where id = ?";
  PreparedStatement prepStmt =
    con.prepareStatement(updateStatement);
  prepStmt.setString(1, firstName); ... prepStmt.setString(4, id);
  int rowCount = prepStmt.executeUpdate();
  prepStmt.close();

  if (rowCount == 0)
    throw new EJBException("Storing row for " + id + " failed.");
}
```

The 'find' functions have some interesting features. First, there is the function that is used when finding a entity bean with a known identifier:

```
private boolean selectByPrimaryKey(String primaryKey) throws
    SQLException {
  String selectStatement =
    "select id from savingsaccount where id = ? ";
  PreparedStatement prepStmt =
    con.prepareStatement(selectStatement);
  prepStmt.setString(1, primaryKey);

  ResultSet rs = prepStmt.executeQuery();
  boolean result = rs.next();
  prepStmt.close();
  return result;
}
```

Essentially, this runs a query of the form 'is there a record with this identifier'; if the returned result set is non-empty, the record must exist.

The selectByLastName method builds a collection containing the primary keys of all records where the names match the given name (in this case, it is a collection of java.lang.Strings, as here the primary key is of type String). Again, the method has to run an SQL 'select' query, taking the identifiers from the result set obtained for the matching rows in the data table:

```
private Collection selectByLastName(String lastName) throws SQLException
{
```

```
String selectStatement =
    "select id from savingsaccount where lastname = ? ";
PreparedStatement prepStmt =
    con.prepareStatement(selectStatement);
prepStmt.setString(1, lastName);
ResultSet rs = prepStmt.executeQuery();
ArrayList a = new ArrayList();

while (rs.next()) {
  String id = rs.getString(1);
  a.add(id);
}

prepStmt.close();
return a;
}
```

The overall behavior of a request to find an entity with a given key is approximately:

Client invokes findByPrimary key method of its Home proxy
"Home implementation" object in server grabs an unused
  SavingsAccountBean and invokes ejbFindByPrimaryKey on this bean;
Bean invokes its own selectByPrimary key method, and confirms that key
  is valid, Bean returns the primary key to "Home Implementation" object
"Home Implementation" object (or other object in container) grabs
  another pooled SavingsAccountBean and activates it giving it the
  primary key as its identifier;
"Home Implementation" object (or other object in container) constructs a
  remote reference for this bean;
Remote identifier returned to client, local SavingsAccount proxy
  object constructed around remote reference
Client attempts to invoke a method of its new SavingsAccount proxy,
  request transmitted through to EJB-server/container;
Container invokes ejbLoad on the appropriate SavingsAccountBean
SavingsAccountBean runs another SQL query against database, this time
  retrieving all the data row of table.
Container invokes business method of bean on behalf of client.

Two separate queries have had to be run against the database before the bean can be used; the first checking the primary key, the second loading the rest of data when these are actually required.

The mechanisms invoked for the 'find collection' methods are similar. First a database query is run to retrieve simply the primary keys associated with the records that will be required. These primary keys are used to initialize a set of entity beans; remote references to these beans are returned to the client and used in the construction of proxies. As the client uses each entity bean in turn (e.g. when iterating through the collection and printing data), another SQL select statement must be run against the database to retrieve the other data members of the required entity. So, if there are 50 accounts with the last name 'Smith', there will be more than 50 SQL select queries run against the database.

Sun's tutorial files include a pre-built copy of the savings account application, with its XML deployment files. These contain a few interesting elements. The `ejb-jar.xml` file contains the data that define the bean; first there is the `<enterprise-beans>` element containing the bean declaration. This identifies the bean as an entity bean, identifies its classes, establishes it as responsible for its own persistent storages (it's a BMP bean), identifies the kind of primary key it uses (`String`), and finally has some resource mapping data that relate its 'jdbc/SavingsAccountDB' reference to a class that can handle access:

```
<ejb-jar>
  <display-name>SavingsAccountJAR</display-name>
  <enterprise-beans>
    <entity>
      <display-name>SavingsAccountEJB</display-name>
      <ejb-name>SavingsAccountEJB</ejb-name>
      <home>SavingsAccountHome</home>
      <remote>SavingsAccount</remote>
      <ejb-class>SavingsAccountBean</ejb-class>
      <persistence-type>Bean</persistence-type>
      <prim-key-class>java.lang.String</prim-key-class>
      <reentrant>False</reentrant>
      <security-identity>
        <description></description>
        <use-caller-identity></use-caller-identity>
      </security-identity>
      <resource-ref>
        <res-ref-name>jdbc/SavingsAccountDB</res-ref-name>
        <res-type>javax.sql.DataSource</res-type>
        <res-auth>Container</res-auth>
        <res-sharing-scope>Shareable</res-sharing-scope>
      </resource-ref>
    </entity>
  </enterprise-beans>
```

The next section of the file has the `<assembly-descriptor>`. This contains a `<method-permission>` element defining access controls for each method of the Savings AccountBean. These permissions are generally similar to the role-based controls used with the simpler servlets; here, there are no restrictions applied to the methods listed. The entries also give full details of the individual methods – their arguments and whether they are part of the home or the remote interfaces.

```
<assembly-descriptor>
  <method-permission>
    <unchecked />
    <method>
      <ejb-name>SavingsAccountEJB</ejb-name>
      <method-intf>Remote</method-intf>
      <method-name>getFirstName</method-name>
      <method-params />
    </method>
    ...
    <method>
      <ejb-name>SavingsAccountEJB</ejb-name>
      <method-intf>Home</method-intf>
      <method-name>create</method-name>
      <method-params>
        <method-param>java.lang.String</method-param>
        <method-param>java.lang.String</method-param>
        <method-param>java.lang.String</method-param>
        <method-param>double</method-param>
      </method-params>
    </method>
    ...
  </method-permission>
```

The next section of the file defines transactional controls on methods.

```
<container-transaction>
  <method>
    <ejb-name>SavingsAccountEJB</ejb-name>
    <method-intf>Remote</method-intf>
    <method-name>debit</method-name>
    <method-params>
      <method-param>double</method-param>
    </method-params>
  </method>
  <trans-attribute>Required</trans-attribute>
</container-transaction>
<container-transaction>
  <method>
    <ejb-name>SavingsAccountEJB</ejb-name>
    <method-intf>Home</method-intf>
    <method-name>findByLastName</method-name>
    <method-params>
      <method-param>java.lang.String</method-param>
    </method-params>
```

```
      </method>
      <trans-attribute>Required</trans-attribute>
    </container-transaction>
    <container-transaction>
      <method>
        <ejb-name>SavingsAccountEJB</ejb-name>
          <method-intf>Remote</method-intf>
          <method-name>getBalance</method-name>
          <method-params />
        </method>
        <trans-attribute>Required</trans-attribute>
      </container-transaction>
      ...
    </assembly-descriptor>
  </ejb-jar>
```

Here, the container has responsibility for transaction management, and in all cases transactional control is required.

The mechanism for transactional control of a business method is roughly as follows:

```
Client invokes business operation on proxy, request conveyed to
   container on the server;
Container marks start of transaction
Container guarantees that bean is in a valid state consistent with data
   table by invoking ejbLoad on bean;
Bean runs an SQL select query on database (database informed that
   request part of a transaction), all bean data are loaded;
Container invokes business method of bean;
Container guarantees that data table is consistent with possibly changed
   bean state by invoking ejbStore on bean;
Bean runs an SQL update operation on database, saving all bean data;
Container marks end of transaction, notifying the database that it
   should commit
Response data returned to client;
```

(Some EJB implementations have non-standard extensions that allow business functions to be marked as accessor or mutator; this information, added to the deployment descriptor, allows the container to miss out the store operation in the case of accessor methods where the bean would not have been changed). Databases handle transactional operations in different ways. Some databases lock data records that have been touched, keeping the locks until the transaction commits; others let operations proceed until the commit step, and then check time stamps on data that will reveal any interference from other transactions (in these cases, a 'non-serializable' or similar exception gets thrown). The locks used, or accesses still permitted to other transactions, depend on the transaction isolation level used by the database. This often defaults to 'read-committed', but many business operations require the more stringent 'serializable' isolation level. A bean can change the isolation level used for its transaction when it first acquires a connection to the database (`con.setTransactionIsolation(TRANSACTION_SERIALIZABLE);`)

It is this container-managed transaction control that makes the simple `debit` and `credit` methods of the `SavingsAccountBean` actually work correctly. The situations can be quite complex. Different clients may be working with different copies of a `SavingsAccountBean` for the same account, copies that have been created in different EJB containers. Without the synchronization with the database, and the associated transactional locks or serializability checks, it would be easy for one of the clients to end up with stale data in its bean. With the transaction control, the beans are always updated before client access, and the database is updated after client access to the bean. (Of course, this is fairly heavy going for an operation such as `credit`, and even more heavy going for something like `getBalance`.)

Entity beans are supposed to improve the efficiency of program developers. A developer doesn't need to bother with transactional details; the container handles these. A developer doesn't have to include access control code to check on the identity of a user; standard access control code is built into the container.

Other extensions to entity beans may further enhance the productivity of developers. These extensions include support for handling relations among entities, and in the case of CMP beans there is the feature of automatic generation of most of the database access code. Relations among entity beans deal with things like an 'order' entity and its associated 'items' (items might be represented as entity beans, but a simpler class would possibly suffice). The order would have data members such as order-identifier, customer name and address; these would correspond to fields in an order table. The items would have item codes and quantities; again these would map to fields in an item table. The order entity bean would probably own a collection of items (implemented as an `ArrayList` or something similar). The database representation of this relationship would mostly likely be achieved by the item table having a foreign key field for the identifier of the order of which an item is a part. When an order bean is reinstantiated, all its associated items should also be recreated. There are coding styles proposed for implementing relations in BMP beans; CMP beans can use declarative descriptions of such relationships, and sort things out for themselves through the automatically generated code. Relations and CMP styles are illustrated by other examples in Sun's tutorial.

While these features for the standardization of processing and the automation of coding are helpful, they do come at a cost. The generalized mechanisms used with entity beans tend to hammer the database, requiring many more accesses than would more naïve coding in helper beans that are hard-coded to run within a servlet container. A developer creating such a helper bean would probably implement something like the credit operation via an SQL update statement such as '*update savingsaccount set balance = balance + ? where id =?*'. This operation would be less costly than the EJB's transactional group of operations: reload bean, change field, update entire row. Similarly, a task such as finding the full names, account identifiers and balances of all accounts for clients called 'Smith' would probably be done using a single SQL query of the form '*select * from savingsaccount where lastname=?*', and then a processing step where the result set was accessed to build a collection of simple structs holding the required data. Again, this would involve less database-related activity than the EJB mechanisms of building a collection of entity objects, then accessing these (under transactional controls) to retrieve the various data elements required.

10.5 Real-world EJB

Sun's last example is too large and elaborate for the code to be covered here in detail; in any case, it is the structure that matters more, for this example illustrates EJBs as they should be. Once again, it is a banking example.

There is a back-end database with a number of tables:

- Customer table (customer number, name, address etc.).

- Account table (account number, type, balance, limits etc.).

- A table effectively listing the accounts that can be used by each customer (customers may use multiple accounts, some accounts are shared by many customers).

- Tables used to supply unique identifier numbers for new accounts or for new customers.

- A transaction table (An unfortunate coincidence of names – this has nothing to do with database transactions. This auditing record has time-stamped details of the debit and credit actions performed on accounts.).

(Tables such as 'customer', 'account' and 'transaction' represent real business entities and get mapped to entity beans; tables with auxiliary data, such as (customer-number, account-number) pairs or counters, are accessed directly.)

There are two types of client. One is a Java client application supposedly for in-house use by the banking staff. The others are web clients (JSPs); these are for customers to use to perform banking operations via the Internet.

Of course, there are beans – session beans that encode the banking rules and work on behalf of the clients and entity beans that represent rows from the tables. The entity beans (and database tables) are not exposed to the clients; session beans act as intermediaries in all requests. Simple struct-like helper classes are used where appropriate. Thus, there is an 'account details' class (identifier, balance, list containing the identifiers of customers who can use the account); clients can obtain a complete 'account details' object instead of making multiple remote requests for individual data elements.

These applications utilize security controls. Two groups of user are distinguished – *BankCustomer* and *BankAdmin*. Individual users must have a predefined username associated with one or other group, and must 'login' providing their name and password. New customer accounts can only be created by users in the *BankAdmin* group; only those in the *BankCustomer* role can get to read details from the transactions table. The systems administrator must create the user accounts in a file belonging to the EJB server (much like the task of creating accounts in the tomcat-users.xml file). Web clients use standard HTTP authentication methods, as illustrated earlier for simple servlets and JSPs. Name and password data can be added to the system properties (java.util.Properties collection) in a

Java client application; if the appropriate properties are set prior to a JNDI
InitialContext() call, they are checked when the next lookup request is made. (There
are small differences here among EJB implementations; for example, Sun's j2ee system
uses the properties j2eelogin.name and j2eelogin.password; other implementations
have their own variants). The actual name and password data can be provided as environment variables specified on the command line when a Java client is started; otherwise, the
client runtime may prompt the user for these data.

The architecture for the web components is complex. Sun has chosen to illustrate
numerous other potentially interesting features of JSPs and servlets along with the essential web-EJB features. Thus the web clients (and the Java application as well) support
internationalization with multilingual versions. The JSPs exploit their own unique tag
library, as well as using some tags from the struts library. The response pages are formed
in accord with templates that create a response combining the outputs of multiple JSPs;
this template-based scheme illustrates a rather elaborate mechanism for achieving a standardized 'look and feel' for a set of pages. All web-requested actions are routed via a
single dispatcher servlet that uses parameter data to distinguish the various requests. The
proxies for the home factory objects for the three session beans are maintained in an application scope variable that is an instance of a bean manager class. The client application is
a relatively simple GUI-based program, using the 'swing' components to construct an
interface that allows bank administrators to create customers and accounts and so forth.
Like the web components, the client application is somewhat over engineered.

The entity beans – AccountBean, CustomerBean and TxBean – are for the most part
straightforward, being slightly more sophisticated versions of the SavingsAccountBean.
They use a different approach to managing their database connection; instead of maintaining a connection for their entire lifetime, these beans 'open and close' a new connection for each operation performed on their data tables. The other major difference from the
SavingsAccountBean is their support for coarse-grained access functions – using
"getDetails" methods that return little structs rather than have accessors for all the individual data members. (Some data members do have separate accessors, e.g. an account's
balance member has an accessor because this value needs to be checked in banking operations such as the withdraw operation in the banking-transaction controller.) The
AccountDetails and AccountBean classes are representative. The AccountDetails class
is a Serializable class, with data members for the banking information and get/set
methods (it has to be a Serializable, as it is used as a result of remote calls):

```
public class AccountDetails implements java.io.Serializable {

    private String accountId;
    private String type;
    ...
    private ArrayList customerIds;

    public AccountDetails(String accountId, String type,
    ..., ArrayList customerIds) {
    this.accountId = accountId; ...; this.customerIds = customerIds; }
```

```
        public String getAccountId() { return accountId; }

        ...

        public ArrayList getCustomerIds() { return customerIds; }

        public void setType(String type) { this.type = type; }

        ...
    }
```

The AccountBean class has a few business methods such as its getDetails method and get-/set Balance methods, the usual life cycle methods, and a couple of 'finder' methods, including one that searches the (customer-number, account-number) table and builds a collection of all accounts associated with a specified customer.

```
public class AccountBean implements EntityBean {

    private String accountId;
    private String type;
    ...

    private EntityContext context;
    private Connection con;

    public AccountDetails getDetails() {
        // Account data from accounts table already in data members
        // but need to get list of all customers from table with
        // customer-ids and account ids
        try { loadCustomerIds(); }
        catch (Exception ex) { ... }

        return new AccountDetails(accountId, type, description, balance,
            creditLine, beginBalance, beginBalanceTimeStamp,
            customerIds);
    }

    public double getBalance() { return balance; }

    ...

    public void setBalance(double balance) { this.balance = balance; }

    ...
```

```
    public String ejbCreate(String accountId, String type,
        String description, ... ArrayList customerIds)
            throws CreateException, MissingPrimaryKeyException {

        if ((accountId == null) || (accountId.trim().length() == 0))
            throw new MissingPrimaryKeyException ("ejbCreate: ...");

        this.accountId = accountId; ...; this.customerIds = customerIds;

        try { insertRow(); }
        catch (Exception ex) { ... }

        return accountId;
    }
    ...
}
```

The database connection is obtained (via JNDI lookup of a datasource) for each operation:

```
private void makeConnection() {
    try {
        InitialContext ic = new InitialContext();
        DataSource ds =
            (DataSource) ic.lookup(CodedNames.BANK_DATABASE);
        con = ds.getConnection();
    }
    catch (Exception ex) { ... }
}

private void releaseConnection() {
    try { con.close(); }
    catch (SQLException ex) { ... }
}
```

The basic loadAccount method, invoked from ejbLoad, is similar to the loadRow method of the SavingsAccountBean:

```
private void loadAccount() throws SQLException {
    makeConnection();
    String selectStatement =
        "select type, description, balance, credit_line, " +
        "begin_balance, begin_balance_time_stamp " +
        "from account where account_id = ? ";
    PreparedStatement prepStmt = con.prepareStatement(selectStatement);
```

```
    prepStmt.setString(1, accountId);

    ResultSet rs = prepStmt.executeQuery();

    if (rs.next()) {
      type = rs.getString(1);
      ...
      beginBalanceTimeStamp = rs.getDate(6);
      prepStmt.close();
    releaseConnection();
    }
    else {
      prepStmt.close(); releaseConnection();
      throw new NoSuchEntityException(
        accountId + " not found in database.");
    }
  }
}
```

Data for the customers who can use an account is obtained from the customer/account cross-reference table:

```
private void loadCustomerIds() throws SQLException {
  makeConnection();
  String selectStatement =
    "select customer_id " +
    "from customer_account_xref where account_id = ? ";
  PreparedStatement prepStmt = con.prepareStatement(selectStatement);

  prepStmt.setString(1, accountId);
  ResultSet rs = prepStmt.executeQuery();
  customerIds.clear();

  while (rs.next()) {
    customerIds.add(rs.getString(1));
  }
  prepStmt.close();
  releaseConnection();
}
```

This cross-reference table is also used in the selectByCustomerId method that implements the ejbFindByCustomerId finder method; this creates a collection of all accounts accessible by a specified customer:

```
private Collection selectByCustomerId(String customerId) throws
SQLException {
```

```
      makeConnection();
      String selectStatement =
        "select account_id " +
        "from customer_account_xref " +
        "where customer_id = ? ";
      PreparedStatement prepStmt = con.prepareStatement(selectStatement);
      prepStmt.setString(1, customerId);

      ResultSet rs = prepStmt.executeQuery();
      ArrayList a = new ArrayList();

      while (rs.next()) {
        a.add(rs.getString(1));
      }

      prepStmt.close();
      releaseConnection();
      return a;
    }
```

The CustomerControllerBean is fairly representative of the three session beans used in this example. The main new features of interest are how a session bean works with entity beans, and how sometimes it may directly access data tables on its own behalf. The stateful or stateless nature of these session beans is handled somewhat oddly in the examples. The ejb-jar.xml files provided with the example have these classes deployed as stateful beans; however, the create methods defined in their home interfaces do not provide for identifier arguments. Their remote methods define services that are essentially stateless, as arguments supply all required information. There are some data members in each of these classes that are quasi-state; for example the CustomerControllerBean keeps a reference to the last Customer used in operations such as getDetails and avoids performing a new find operation if the next request relates to the same Customer.

The home and remote interfaces for the controller are:

```
public interface CustomerControllerHome extends EJBHome {
  CustomerController create() throws RemoteException, CreateException;

}
public interface CustomerController extends EJBObject {
  publicString createCustomer (String lastName,
    String firstName, String middleInitial, String street,
    String city, String state, String zip, String phone,
    String email) throws RemoteException;

  public void removeCustomer(String customerId)
    throws RemoteException, CustomerNotFoundException;
```

```
public ArrayList getCustomersOfAccount(String accountId)
   throws RemoteException, CustomerNotFoundException;

public CustomerDetails getDetails(String customerId)
   throws RemoteException, CustomerNotFoundException;

public ArrayList getCustomersOfLastName(String lastName)
   throws RemoteException;

public void setName(String lastName, String firstName,
   String middleInitial, String customerId)
      throws RemoteException, CustomerNotFoundException;

public void setAddress(String street, String city,
   String state, String zip, String phone, String email,
   String customerId)
      throws RemoteException, CustomerNotFoundException;

}
```

The CustomerControllerBean has some data members, business methods that match the remote interface, a create method, EJB life cycle methods, and a few private auxiliary functions for database operations.

```
public class CustomerControllerBean implements SessionBean {
   // Data members
   // "Remote" business methods
   // EJB stuff
   // Database auxiliary methods
}
```

The data members include a reference to a Home object for Customer beans; this controller is going to be using lots of customer entity beans, and the only allowed mechanism is to use a home interface to obtain a proxy implement the Customer remote interface. There is also a Connection data member; once again this is a temporary, every database operation 'opens and closes' the database connection. The other two members relate to the last Customer object processed.

```
private String customerId;
private CustomerHome customerHome;
private Customer customer;
private Connection con;
```

The customerHome reference is set when the controller bean is created in the ejbCreate method (the EJBGetter helper class is merely a collection of static functions that do JNDI style lookups on resources):

```
      public void ejbCreate() {
        try {
          customerHome = EJBGetter.getCustomerHome();
// really, that is
// InitialContext initial = new InitialContext();
// Object objref initial.lookup(CodedNames.CUSTOMER_EJBHOME);
// return (CustomerHome)
//     PortableRemoteObject.narrow(objref, CustomerHome.class);
        }
        catch (Exception ex) { ... }

      customer = null;
      customerId = null;
    }
```

The other life cycle functions are all null:

```
public CustomerControllerBean() {}
public void ejbRemove() {}
public void ejbActivate() {}
public void ejbPassivate() {}
public void setSessionContext(SessionContext sc) {}
```

The class has private makeConnection and releaseConnection members to open and close the con database connection as needed; they are very similar to the corresponding functions illustrated for the AccountBean class shown above. The customerId and Customer data members are set in a private auxiliary function, customerExists, that gets called from all methods that implement actions on individual customer records:

```
private boolean customerExists(String customerId) {
  if (customerId.equals(this.customerId) == false) {
    try {
      customer = customerHome.findByPrimaryKey(customerId);
      this.customerId = customerId;
    }
    catch (Exception ex) { return false; }
  }
  return true;
}
```

A reference to the required Customer (remote proxy) is obtained using the findByPrimaryKey finder method of the home interface using the home proxy created in ejbCreate.

The methods setName and setAddress operate on existing customer records:

```java
public void setName(String lastName, String firstName,
   String middleInitial, String customerId)
     throws CustomerNotFoundException {

   if (lastName == null)
     throw new IllegalArgumentException("null lastName");
   // Similar checks on other arguments
   ...
   // Get remote proxy for the required customer
   if (customerExists(customerId) == false)
     throw new CustomerNotFoundException(customerId);
   // Invoke change operations via the proxy
   try {
     customer.setLastName(lastName);
     customer.setFirstName(firstName);
     customer.setMiddleInitial(middleInitial);
   }
   catch (Exception ex) { ... }
 }
```

Creation of a new customer record requires that the controller session bean first work
with the database (via a little helper class) to obtain a new unique customer identifier, and
then use the CustomerHome interface to create the new database record and corresponding
entity bean:

```java
public  String createCustomer (String lastName,
        String firstName, String middleInitial, String street,
        String city, String state, String zip, String phone,
        String email) {

   if (lastName == null)
     throw new IllegalArgumentException("null lastName");
   // Additional data validation steps
   ...

   try {
     makeConnection();
     customerId = DBHelper.getNextCustomerId(con);
     // DBHelper just obtains current id value from table
     // and increments the table's value ready for next time.
     customer = customerHome.create(customerId,
       lastName, firstName, middleInitial, street,
       city, state, zip, phone, email);
     releaseConnection();
   }
```

```
      catch (Exception ex) { ... }

      return customerId;
   }
```

The removeCustomer method involves the controller bean in getting a reference for a Customer with the given identifier, running an SQL update of the form 'delete from customer_account_xref where customer_id= ?', and finally a remove operation on the Customer proxy (which will lead to the corresponding entity bean performing the deletion in the customer table).

The controller bean can also return collections of CustomerDetails objects, as in its getCustomersOfAccount method. This uses the findByAccountId method in the CustomerHome interface to obtain a collection of customers sharing an account, and then invokes the getDetails method on each Customer remote proxy in the collection.

```
   public ArrayList getCustomersOfAccount(String accountId)
      throws RemoteException, CustomerNotFoundException {

      Collection customerIds;

      if (accountId == null)
         throw new IllegalArgumentException("null accountId");

      try {
         customerIds = customerHome.findByAccountId(accountId);
         if (customerIds.isEmpty())
            throw new CustomerNotFoundException();
      }
      catch (FinderException fx)
         throw new CustomerNotFoundException();

      ArrayList customerList = new ArrayList();
      Iterator i = customerIds.iterator();

      while (i.hasNext()) {
         Customer customer = (Customer)i.next();
         CustomerDetails customerDetail = customer.getDetails();
         customerList.add(customerDetail);
      }
      return customerList;
   }
```

The clients obtain references to the session beans via the home interfaces. In the Java client application, contact with the EJB components is the responsibility of a DataModel object; its constructor obtains the home references:

```
// Private EJB variables
private static CustomerController customer;
private static AccountController account;
...
public  DataModel(BankAdmin frame, ResourceBundle messages) {
        this.frame = frame;
        this.messages = messages;

   // Look up and create CustomerController bean
   try {
     CustomerControllerHome customerControllerHome =
       EJBGetter.getCustomerControllerHome();
     // Helper EJBGetter class does JNDI lookup operation,
     // type cast etc
     customer = customerControllerHome.create();
   }
   catch (Exception NamingException) { ... }
   ...
}
```

Once it has a home reference, the Java client can create new customers:

```
if(currentFunction == 1) { //Add new customer information
  try {
    custID = customer.createCustomer(last, first, mid, str, cty, st,
      zp, tel, mail);
    return 0;
  } catch (RemoteException ex) { ... }
}
```

or get details of existing customers:

```
protected void searchByLastName(String returned) {
  try {
    ArrayList list = customer.getCustomersOfLastName(returned);
    if(!list.isEmpty()){
      String custID =
        ((CustomerDetails)list.get(0)).getCustomerId();
      JOptionPane.showMessageDialog(frame, custID,
        "Customer ID is:", JOptionPane.PLAIN_MESSAGE);
    } else {
      frame.messlab.setText(returned + " " +
        messages.getString("NotFoundException"));
    }
  }
}
```

```
  catch (RemoteException ex) { frame.messlab.setText("RemoteException"); }
}
```

The JSP clients use an application scope instance of a `BeanManager` that is created with proxies for the session beans:

```
public class BeanManager {
  private CustomerController custctl;
  private AccountController acctctl;
  private TxController txctl;

  public BeanManager() {
    try {
      CustomerControllerHome home =
        EJBGetter.getCustomerControllerHome();
      custctl = home.create();
    }
    catch (RemoteException ex) { ... }
    catch (CreateException ex) { ... }
    catch (NamingException ex) { ... }

    try {
      AccountControllerHome home =
        EJBGetter.getAccountControllerHome();
      ...
    }
    catch (...) { ...}
    ...
  }

  public CustomerController getCustomerController() {return custctl; }

  ...
}
```

The proxies for the session beans can then be used in scriptlet code in the JSPs, as in the following fragment from the 'transfer funds' JSP that has to list the accounts available to a customer:

```
<jsp:useBean id="beanManager" class="com.sun.ebank.web.BeanManager"
  scope="application"/>
<jsp:useBean id="transferBean" class="com.sun.ebank.web.TransferBean"
scope="request"/>
<%
  ArrayList accounts =
```

```
      beanManager.getAccountController().getAccountsOfCustomer(
        request.getUserPrincipal().getName());
    ResourceBundle messages =
      (ResourceBundle)session.getAttribute("messages");%>
  <center>
  <table border=0 cellpadding=2 cellspacing=0 width=500>
    <tr>
    ...
    </tr>
    <logic:iterate collection="<%= accounts %>" id="ad"
      type="com.sun.ebank.util.AccountDetails">
      <tr>
        <td><jsp:getProperty name="ad" property="description"/></td>
        ...
      </tr>
    </logic:iterate>
  </table>
  ...
```

The scriptlet code gets the remote proxy for the account controller session bean from the beanManager object and uses this to invoke the getAccountsOfCustomer method from which it obtains a collection of AccountDetails object. These details are then shown in a table generated using logic:iterate tags from the struts library.

The deployment files for these EJBs now include specific access controls as well as elements previously illustrated. The customer-ejb XML file contains details of both the controller session bean and the entity bean (both need resource references related to their JNDI requests for database connections, and the controller bean also has ejb references related to its requests to get Home interfaces).

```
  <ejb-jar>
    <description>no description</description>
    <display-name>CustomerJAR</display-name>
    <enterprise-beans>
      <session>
        <description>no description</description>
        <display-name>CustomerControllerEJB</display-name>
        <ejb-name>CustomerControllerEJB</ejb-name>
        <home>CustomerControllerHome</home>
        <remote>CustomerController</remote>
        <ejb-class>CustomerControllerBean</ejb-class>
        <session-type>Stateful</session-type>
        <transaction-type>Container</transaction-type>
        ...
        <resource-ref>
          <res-ref-name>jdbc/BankDB</res-ref-name>
```

```
          <res-type>javax.sql.DataSource</res-type>
          <res-auth>Container</res-auth>
          <res-sharing-scope>Shareable</res-sharing-scope>
        </resource-ref>
      </session>
      <entity>
        <description>no description</description>
        <display-name>CustomerEJB</display-name>
        <ejb-name>CustomerEJB</ejb-name>
        <home>CustomerHome</home>
        <remote>Customer</remote>
        <ejb-class>CustomerBean</ejb-class>
        <persistence-type>Bean</persistence-type>
        <prim-key-class>java.lang.String</prim-key-class>
        <reentrant>False</reentrant>
        ...
        <resource-ref>
          <res-ref-name>jdbc/BankDB</res-ref-name>
          <res-type>javax.sql.DataSource</res-type>
          <res-auth>Container</res-auth>
          <res-sharing-scope>Shareable</res-sharing-scope>
        </resource-ref>
      </entity>
    </enterprise-beans>
```

The assembly-descriptor section defines security roles and then details of the restrictions that apply. The methods of the entity bean are unrestricted (they can only be accessed via session beans). Some methods of the customer controller are generally available, while others are restricted to users in the Admin role:

```
    <assembly-descriptor>
      <security-role>
        <role-name>BankCustomer</role-name>
      </security-role>
      <security-role>
        <role-name>BankAdmin</role-name>
      </security-role>
      <method-permission>
        <unchecked />
        ...
        <method>
          <ejb-name>CustomerControllerEJB</ejb-name>
          <method-intf>Remote</method-intf>
          <method-name>getDetails</method-name>
          <method-params>
```

```
              <method-param>java.lang.String</method-param>
            </method-params>
          </method>
          ...
      </method-permission>
      <method-permission>
        <role-name>BankAdmin</role-name>
        <method>
          <ejb-name>CustomerControllerEJB</ejb-name>
          <method-intf>Remote</method-intf>
          <method-name>getCustomersOfAccount</method-name>
          <method-params>
            <method-param>java.lang.String</method-param>
          </method-params>
        </method>
        ...
      </method-permission>
      <method-permission>
        <unchecked />
        <method>
          <ejb-name>CustomerEJB</ejb-name>
          <method-intf>Remote</method-intf>
          <method-name>getPrimaryKey</method-name>
          <method-params />
        </method>
        ...
      </method-permission>
```

The next section of the deployment file specifies all methods of both beans to have container-managed transactions (with transactional controls required):

```
      <container-transaction>
        <method>
          <ejb-name>CustomerControllerEJB</ejb-name>
          <method-intf>Remote</method-intf>
          <method-name>getCustomersOfAccount</method-name>
          <method-params>
            <method-param>java.lang.String</method-param>
          </method-params>
        </method>
        <trans-attribute>Required</trans-attribute>
      </container-transaction>
      ...
      <container-transaction>
        <method>
```

```
            <ejb-name>CustomerEJB</ejb-name>
            <method-intf>Remote</method-intf>
            <method-name>setCity</method-name>
            <method-params>
               <method-param>java.lang.String</method-param>
            </method-params>
         </method>
         <trans-attribute>Required</trans-attribute>
      </container-transaction>
   </assembly-descriptor>
</ejb-jar>
```

With this elaborate system deployed, both bank administrators and web-based customers will be able to access and update the banking records. Both can share a reasonably high degree of confidence in the reliability of the system.

Exercises

Practical

The practical for this chapter is to download the Java Enterprise development kit from http://java.sun.com/, install the system, and implement the sequence of examples associated with Sun's EJB tutorial.

Short answer questions

(1) Explain the role of a 'Home' interface and of the corresponding EJB system-generated HomeImplementation object.

(2) Explain the conceptual programming models underlying 'stateful' and 'stateless' session beans; explain the life cycles of such beans.

(3) Explain how 'Local' interfaces represent an optimization of 'remote' interfaces; what limitations apply?

(4) Explain why 'coarse-grained' object models are appropriate for remotely accessed objects.

(5) Explain the role of an EJB container.

(6) Outline reasons why an application might be better designed with a session bean acting as an intermediary that manipulates entity beans rather than having the client application code access the entity beans directly.

Explorations

(1) Sun's EJB implementation is the 'reference' implementation and is the most up-to-date and complete. However, there are a number of other free implementations available

through the Internet, and the commercial systems from IBM and from Inprise can both be obtained on free limited period trial licenses. Research and report on the available alternatives.

(2) Pick one of the free implementations (e.g. JBoss from `http://www.jboss.org/`), and download, install and reimplement the first two or three examples from Sun's tutorial. Write a report comparing the ease of use of the EJB reference implementation and the JBoss implementation.

Your school may have a license for an academic version of a commercial product, such as IBM's WebSphere, that allows you to install a version with restricted capabilities on your own computer (with no limited time usage restriction). If such a system is available, you should also investigate it. (Limited term free licenses of commercial products are not usually practical, they expire just about the time you understand how the system works.)

(3) Research and write a report on the similarities and differences between the Enterprise Java and the Microsoft .NET models for enterprise computing.

(4) Sun's introduction of EJB caused some conflict with the Object Management Group (the consortium that controls, and slows, the development of CORBA). EJBs overlapped with the proposed 'CORBA Component Model'. The conflict has been resolved by some reworking of EJBs and their acceptance as a limited form of the full standard CORBA Component Model (CCM).

Research and report on proposals for the CORBA CCM. Your report should outline some of the additional functionality that OMG would like in a full (level 2) implementation of the CCM. Try to find out about any non-EJB implementations of CCM (there has been some work; for example the C++ MICO CORBA has some CCM development and EJCCM have a partial Java: see `http://www.mico.org/` and `http://www.ejccm.org/`).

11

Future technologies?

This chapter is an eclectic mix of technologies that have attracted attention recently. The first section looks at a recent success story – a well-understood problem, a fairly obvious solution, and a company that made that solution work (and made its owners rich). The next two sections pick on a few topics where it is clear that there are interesting potential applications and some appropriate technologies, but where no one has yet found quite the right match of application and technology. If you can come up with the right mix, you will achieve the kind of success described in the first section. The final section takes a brief look at some technologies that are being heavily promoted by companies such as IBM, and Microsoft; despite the heavy promotion of these technologies, not everyone is convinced of their utility.

11.1 (Lack of) Speed kills

In the e-commerce world, it's performance, performance, performance. The speed of your site is directly equated to sales.

Kevin Ertrell, Internet Technologies Manager, Tower Records

Suppose you have a web site that takes millions of hits daily, and you want to deliver images, sounds and streaming video. How are you going to get the server capacity and communications capacity to handle the resulting load?

You could install an IBM mainframe that emulates a thousand PCs running Linux (with a disk transfer throughput another couple of orders of magnitude larger, and a mean time between failures that is also one or two orders of magnitude larger). You could then connect your mainframe to the Internet via a 600 Mbit per second link. The only result would be that you would be deeply in debt and still unable to handle the traffic.

There is an obvious solution. The client connects to and downloads a main web page from your home site, but the links to multimedia content reference other sites on the Internet where this content is replicated. Clients get slightly different versions of a download page; the versions differ in the replication sites for the multimedia data. Ideally, these other sites will be close (in Internet space) to the requesting client so that the data have to travel across the minimum number of network links. With the load from different clients distributed over different replication sites, and with the network transmission times reduced by Internet proximity, you can provide your clients with a better service at a lower cost.

The solution is fairly obvious, but does require a lot of work. You have to have multi-media content servers distributed around the continent, or even around the world. These must be kept consistent with respect to the content data. All your pages have to be dynamic, generated by a program that chooses the content server that will be referenced in the links incorporated in returned pages. This content server can be chosen on the basis of the client's IP address; you just need a 'geographic' database that maps IP addresses to geographic regions, and regions to content servers.

It is not hard to build a crude database mapping IP addresses to physical locations (after all, a simple lookup converts the IP address to a domain name, and some domain names incorporate country codes as the top-level domains, while the '.us' domain has state and postal subdivisions as its sub-domains). DNS can also provide some supplementary information about the system administrator that may include a snail mail address. Other data regarding domains may be available from domain name registries. Using these retrieved data, you can create records for an IP/location data table. There are a few examples constructed in this way that are available through the Internet (one is hosted by http://www.networldmap.com/); these services can resolve most US-based IP addresses to the nearest city, but for much of the rest of the world they limit location information to the country (as identified from the last element of domain names). One of these mapping systems used to have a feature that allowed you to contribute information to their database – so if they didn't guess where you were, you could tell them.

The Akamai corporation did a little more work when it constructed a more sophisticated version of such a database. Akamai also established several server farms in different locations, where they could host multimedia data belonging to their clients. Finally, Akamai created the support software that would run on their clients' own servers – the software that would distributed an updated version of web content to Akamai's servers, and the components that would handle the IP/location mapping via a data table and then substitute appropriate servers in all the links in returned pages.

Companies that have 'Akamaized' have found it made a big difference to the performance of their web sites:

On Monday our traffic doubled, so we added two new servers with no effect. Tuesday afternoon we called Akamai. Tuesday night we were Akamaized and instantly six to ten times faster.

Craig Macubbin, Chief Technology Officer, BET.com

If we had to scale to support this level of business by adding hardware, we'd need to add significant infrastructure. By distributing our content with Akamai, we are saving up to $1 million in infrastructure enhancements.

Dan Smith, Director, LimitedTechnology services, the technology arm of
Victoria's Secret

Once you can differentiate customers by location, you can use potentially more effective sales targeting. Many sites incorporate banner advertising. You can change the source used for the banner advertising, subcontracting the space to an agency based in the region or country of the client. The advertisements that then appear are those that have been placed by local companies that are more likely to attract customer interest.

11.2 Personal internet presence

The guys at Akamai (and rival companies) have got rich by exploiting the geographical distribution of the network. Where might you get rich?

Provision of a 'personal internet presence' is an application area that has hardly started to be exploited. The first attempts are there. Some of the main portals, like Yahoo and Excite use persistent cookies that identify clients and permit provision of personalized portals as with 'My Excite', 'My Yahoo' and 'My MSN'. Amazon uses persistent cookies that permit it to recognize returning customers who are greeted with a personal welcome and a list of new Amazon offerings that, based on past purchases, might be of interest to the client.

An approach that relies on cookies works for clients who always use the same workstation. But many Internet users will work on different machines at different times. Such users can login to different web sites and have the login information saved in a temporary cookie. A site can again offer each client a 'personalized' environment once the login is complete. 'Login' systems can support services other than simple e-commerce; for example, instant messaging is becoming increasingly popular. Once logged in to a messaging service, users are informed about the login status of nominated 'friends' and can exchange messages with chosen correspondents, or with all members of impromptu user groups, or with members of regular discussion groups. The disadvantage of 'login' systems for users is that they have to invent, and later remember, their chosen names and passwords at each of the sites that they use.

Microsoft's 'net passport' attempts to provide a unifying service for sites that need logged-in customers. Passports hold data like a person's name, address and credit card information (though this may move to Microsoft Wallet eventually). These data can be viewed and edited by a user; they are maintained on a supposedly secure passport server. A single login at the Microsoft passport site sets up session data on the passport server that identifies the client. When the client moves to a participating passport site, a single-click login operation will result in that site obtaining the client identification data from the passport server. The passport can support services other than standard e-commerce; for example, it can also hold data for a service like Microsoft's GameZone – data like player aliases and preferences. (The passport mechanism works by using a carefully choreographed sequence of HTTP redirects with data passed in query strings. It requires no server-to-server contact and since it is built entirely using standard HTTP it will work with all browsers.)

There are other aspects to your 'Internet presence'. For example, if you often buy or sell at eBay, those with whom you conduct commercial transactions will eventually accord you a rating. This rating reflects how reliable and prompt you are with payment, or with provision of goods.

Passports and 'peer ratings' are the beginnings of a personal Internet presence. However, they are probably just the beginnings of something much more sophisticated that will eventually emerge. One possible extension might be simple scriptable web avatars that can conduct some transactions automatically. These could for example run on those workstations that are permanently connected to the Internet via DSL; they could perform tasks like accepting and filtering advertising email, and selecting news items from a news feed. When a user returns to their workstation, they will find a review of the day's material already prepared as a display document. But these are all things for the future, a future that you can help create.

11.3 Peer-to-peer

Obviously, there is lots of raw computing power out there in Net-world. Think of all those Pentium 4 PCs with 256 Mbyte of memory, 40 Gbyte of disk storage and a clock speed of 2.5 GHz or more, permanently attached to the Internet via DSL modems. Part of the day these machines are 'busy' being used for Net games, 'perving the Pornnet', conducting discussions on chat servers, and so forth. Most of the day, these machines are idle. The idle machines represent a huge potential resource of computational power. This distributed computational power represents a technical solution – the right problem just needs to be found.

The conventional Internet style is 'thin client displays data from big server'. This style does not attempt to exploit the computational power of the client. 'Peer'-style approaches treat the partners in a network more equally; each can contribute to an overall system, though maybe in different ways. DNS represents a successful if rather specialized peer-to-peer system; each of the zone name servers handles a small part of the work, and all work together to solve the problem of mapping domain names to IP addresses. Akamai's groups of content servers, which duplicate the multimedia content of web sites, can also be thought of as a proven application of another specialized form of peer-style computing. 'Peer-to-peer' technologies attempt to find other more general applications for the distributed computing power.

There are many different 'peer-to-peer' technologies. Their common element is a move away from the thin client/power server web model. They may involve sharing of CPU power, sharing of disk space for temporary data, or sharing of disk space for long-term replication of data. Their architectures vary. DNS has a strict hierarchical structure, with its root servers and servers in each domain and sub-domain. There is a well-defined distribution of responsibility: each server handles requests for names and addresses in its zone and may delegate responsibility to other name servers handling sub-domains. Other peer-to-peer systems have a central authority – a server that delegates tasks to worker machines, or which acts as a contact point where potential collaborators may identify one another. Other systems are more amorphous; these systems have multiple contact points; from these, collaborators pick up the IP addresses of some arbitrary set of machines that happen to be working at the same time. This arbitrary set of machines becomes the collaboration group for the new participant.

The SETI@Home project represents one of the longest running examples of peer-to-peer systems that use a centralized architecture. This 'Search for Extraterrestrial Intelligence' involves the processing of data recorded on radio telescopes. The recorded data is random noise in the radio spectrum; the searchers hope that somewhere in all the recordings there will be a trace of a weak but regular signal. Regular signals would indicate deliberate radio transmissions; these would imply the existence of an intelligent life form controlling their source. Participants in the SETI@Home project must first download an analysis program; this program can run instead of a screensaver when a computer is idle. When running, this program asks the main SETI@Home server for another block of radio data; the data block gets downloaded and processed. The client returns a summary that is then checked by the SETI@Home server for any significant signal.

The SETI@Home model has been adopted in a number of other systems that involve a large computational task that can be broken into regular sub-tasks. An example use was the cracking of one of RSA's encryption challenges. RSA had published some encrypted messages; the challenge was to decrypt one to reveal a secret. The encryption algorithm was known, there was just a rather large number of possible encryption keys, so a brute force method was applicable. The code was cracked using a SETI@Home-like mechanism for distributing subsets of the range of keys to each of the thousands of participating computers. An example of a more useful application of this technology is the Stanford Alzheimer and Amyloidogenic Disease Research Program; this requires studies of how proteins fold to into a specific three-dimensional shapes. This project is one of several sponsored in part by Intel (`http://www.intel.com/cure/`); Intel's aim is to increase the number of applications for this form of collaborative computation.

The Napster file-sharing system raised the prominence of peer-to-peer systems. Napster again had a central node. Napster clients would connect to this node, registering their IP addresses and providing details of resources (mostly pirated audio recordings) that they were making available. The central server also handled search requests. A client seeking a particular named resource could run a search request at Napster's server; the result would be a list of IP addresses of those other clients who were offering copies of that resource. The client seeking a resource would then open a peer connection to a chosen one of the clients offering that resource. With its thirty million clients, Napster established that there was a potential market for an alternate, lower cost mechanism for distributing audio recordings.

The technically sophisticated users of the old Napster system have moved on to a more truly peer-to-peer distributed system known as Gnutella (along with others such as KaZaA). Like Napster, Gnutella is in the 'business' of 'file sharing'. However, there is no single point of vulnerability (not even to attacks by lawyers). There are published lists of IP addresses for machines that will normally be operational and participating in the Gnutella network, but these machines may not actually offer any shared resources. Would-be participants in the Gnutella network try connecting to these known sites until one responds. The new participant registers its current IP address (usually a transient IP address as allocated by an ISP for a dial-in session) and downloads the IP addresses of a collection of currently registered participants. The collection of IP addresses represents the new participant's community with whom files can be shared. Of course, these communities overlap and the entire world of Gnutella can be reached by a message that traverses the necessary number of hops. A Gnutella member can 'broadcast' a request for a resource to those other participants for whom it has IP addresses. The recipients of this request may be able to respond directly; otherwise, they can rebroadcast the request to the members of their own view of the Gnutella community. The hard part is to prevent the same request being replicated and repeatedly being exchanged between machines; there are limits on how many hops a request may take, and other limits on propagation.

There are other file sharing systems that proclaim aims nobler than the sharing of compressed audio files. Both Freenet and Publius are concerned with publication of information in a form that will resist censorship. Members provide permanent storage for files; these maybe encrypted and signed with digests to guarantee their authenticity. Persons seeking a particular document will be able to find its decrypt key and then find a copy of the document somewhere on the network.

There are already companies seeking to find ways of commercially exploiting the CPU-sharing and file-sharing facets of the peer-to-peer systems. Other companies are exploring the use of peer-to-peer architectures to support various models for collaborative groupwork or workflow systems. These companies include United Devices (which is collaborating with Intel on the SETI@Home-derived 'distributed supercomputer' approach), and Endeavours Technology and Ikimbo, who are exploring ways of combining Napster-like file sharing and instant messaging to build systems for *ad hoc* collaborative work groups.

11.4 ... and on to 'Web Services'

A client's order, entered via a form in an HTML page and recorded by a script, a servlet, or maybe even an EJB, is just the start of a chain of activities. In the server company, the order must be processed further. It may be possible to fulfill the order from stock, but it may be necessary to purchase parts from one or more suppliers. When the ordered items are complete, delivery by a courier must be arranged. The ordering of parts and the arrangements with couriers and so forth, all involve exchanges of data between the computer systems of the various companies that are involved in the overall commercial transaction.

Obviously, it is attractive to automate these data exchanges among companies. It seems quite inappropriate for a clerk to have to read a printout of an e-commerce order and re-enter much of the same data in a web form generated by a supplier's computer system. It would be more efficient if the computer systems involved could communicate directly.

This section takes a brief look at existing technologies and newer 'web service' technologies that can help in the further automation of web commerce.

11.4.1 The existing world of distributed objects

In the last decade, such collaboration among computer systems has generally involved the use of distributed object technology with implementations based on CORBA (Common Object Request Broker Architecture) or Microsoft's evolving COM/COM+/DCOM/DNA/... systems, or Java RMI, or more recently Java EJB systems. While these implementation technologies have many similarities, CORBA is the most complete and sophisticated. CORBA/RMI/EJB/DCOM systems all involve client–server relationships among objects that exist in programs running on the computer systems of the companies participating in collaborative commercial activities.

If you were developing a system that could deal with a customer's order and place any orders for additional parts from one of your suppliers, you would start by getting the interface for the CORBA object that your parts supplier uses to handle business-to-business orders. This interface would specify the operations (i.e. methods or member functions) that the object supported along with details of their arguments, data types used and exceptions thrown. This interface would be defined in the CORBA Interface Definition Language (IDL). You would choose your implementation language (say C++ for example), and you would then pass the IDL describing the supplier's server object through an IDL-to-C++ compiler. This process would generate a class defining the client-side stubs (proxy objects) that you could use in your C++ CORBA client program.

Your program would create an instance of this stub class and arrange for it to bind through the network to the supplier's actual order-handling object; then your code would treat this stub object as if it were the real order-handling object. Your supplier would provide information on how to do the binding (most likely, the supplier would give you the URL of its CORBA name server and the name of the object that you needed to contact). Ultimately, the supplier's information and name server process would yield some kind of object identifier with the TCP/IP address of a host process and an internal identifier for the server object. (If both you and your supplier were using a sophisticated CORBA implementation, the object identifier might include additional data such as the identifiers of replicated server processes that handle load balancing or failure rollover, along with data on security constraints that could automate the exchange of client and server authentication certificates.) The identifier gets embedded in an instance of the client-side stub object in your program, and is used to open a TCP/IP connection when a server operation is first requested.

When you ran your program, the requests that your code made to your stub object would be converted into messages that would invoke actions by the real order-handler object running in your supplier's computer. Your code could be in C++; your supplier's version might be in Cobol, Ada, C++, Java or any of the other languages that has a defined IDL-to-language mapping. Data exchange is efficient; complex data structures are easily transferred. For example the CORBA system supports things like iterators that allow large collections of results to be obtained a group at a time. The client–server TCP/IP connection is normally kept open, allowing the sequences of requests and responses that make up a typical commercial transaction. The connection is closed when the client no longer needs the service.

If you were considerably more ambitious, you could make use of CORBA's 'dynamic invocation'. This allows your client program to obtain details of a server interface at run time. Once your program has details of the operations supported by the server object, it can construct request objects that name the method and incorporate argument values. It is a bit like using Java reflection to invoke methods of a Java object, but the CORBA standards define how these dynamic calls can be made irrespective of the implementation languages used in the client and server processes. Obviously, it is much harder to write a program that can generate requests to a server, or servers, whose functionality is potentially changeable. Dynamic CORBA has always been a rarity.

CORBA's strength is in the standardized services that it provides to supplement the basics of a remote object invocation. These services include support for distributed transactions, events, and naming services. The CORBA transaction service allows a client to define a transactional context that then can be applied to a sequence of operations on different servers and databases; the transaction service handles all the complexities of coordinating a distributed transaction. An events or 'notifications' service allows a client to register with an event channel expressing an interest in certain types of data message; for example, a client might register with a 'stock ticker' event channel expressing a desire to be informed when prices of certain stocks change by more than a specified amount. The event channel receives a stream of messages such as stock prices, handles the message filtering tasks for each client, and invokes callbacks on a client when data of interest appear.

CORBA has a conventional naming service that returns an object reference for a known object; the naming service is like the phonebook white pages: you look up the name of a known service agency or trade person and you get their number. CORBA also has a 'trader service' that is analogous to the phonebook 'yellow pages'. You use the phonebook yellow pages by looking at the advertisements placed by various service providers or trade persons in a particular category, and pick the service you wish to contact. A CORBA trader process has a repository where service suppliers ('exporters') can publish details of the services that they offer. A service is characterized by its interface (the operations that are supported) and by a set of properties. The properties used to characterize a service have to be agreed by service providers; they are typically 'quality of service'-style properties, or charging rates for services. A particular service provider exports a service to the trader by supplying values for these property fields.

A client seeking a service provider can contact a CORBA trader, specifying the service required. The client can submit constraints; these are defined in a reasonably complete language for manipulating boolean-valued expressions. The constraints define combinations of tests that are to be applied to the property values of the different exporters of a service; a client seeks only those exporters whose offers satisfy the specified constraints. The trader applies these constraints to check the suitability of services published by different exporters. Traders can be federated; a trader can forward a client's request to other traders who might have more suitable services registered. Eventually, the client receives a set of data records identifying the possible servers. Client code can then select and bind to a chosen server.

Traders are a standard part of the CORBA world and are available with most CORBA implementations. Interestingly, the success stories for CORBA as published by suppliers like Iona and Inprise very rarely include any story praising the success of a trader-based system (transactions, events and other services all figure prominently, but traders don't seem popular). Most use of traders has been for internal company applications. There was never much progress toward having competing companies agree to standard IDL service interfaces, and associated quality of service properties, that could be published in federated traders and accessed by clients working across the Internet.

The main disadvantages of CORBA (and comparable technologies) are the perceived complexity of programming and difficulties with interoperability. Programming for the client side is usually quite simple, but on the server side the programmer must deal with many resource management issues in addition to application coding.

There are really two aspects to the interoperability problems: Microsoft, and inconsistent implementations of the evolving CORBA standard. While more than eight hundred companies worldwide have cooperated within the Object Management Group to develop the CORBA technologies for heavy duty systems integration and legacy system maintenance, Microsoft has insisted on the creation of its proprietary COM, COM+, DCOM, DNA product group. There are bridging mechanisms – CORBA programs can invoke operations on Microsoft COM objects – but these mechanisms for interoperation are limited and clumsy. The other problem is that CORBA implementations do vary. At any particular time, CORBA implementations from different vendors may match versions from CORBA 2.2 through to the latest 2.6 or whatever. The implementations will only be partly interoperable; basic invocations on objects in the other system will work, but more advanced capabilities (like security elements in object references) may not be supported, or a particular implementation might not support the current notification (event) service etc.

There are other problems with systems that communicate using TCP/IP. Many companies use firewalls that restrict access to a few ports – such as the HTTP port 80. These firewalls block communications to other ports, such as the ports that are dynamically allocated for CORBA clients and servers. The developers of Java RMI ran into this problem when first creating the RMI network protocol and so provided an alternative communications protocol based on HTTP. This RMI/HTTP protocol is costly. Clients outside the firewall package their requests as HTTP post requests. The HTTP daemon uses CGI; each request gets handled by a server-side CGI program that reads the posted request and reconstructs the original RMI request that is then sent to the RMI server within the firewall protected zone. The response is picked up by the CGI program, packaged as an HTTP response and returned to the client. This is hideously clumsy, but it works. There is a serious anomaly here. Systems administrators block ports because they worry that request traffic to arbitrary ports may involve operations being run on their machines; then they permit operation traffic to tunnel through HTTP (so losing the security they thought they had gained and adding a substantial bottleneck to the traffic flow).

Despite its faults, CORBA is a mature product with many implementations and much support. But now it is to be replaced by the new 'Web Services' technologies.

11.4.2 Steps towards a future world of distributed objects

The term 'Web Services' covers a group of interrelated technologies. The components include a service directory system that is considerably more ambitious than the CORBA trader scheme, a service description system that will replace CORBA IDL style descriptions, and a remote procedure call mechanism that relies on message traffic tunneling through HTTP or SMTP (the mail protocol). There are many claims advanced for Web Services, but one of the most emphatic is that this technology group will realize the potential for dynamic creation of integrated applications that was promised but never really achieved with CORBA trader and CORBA dynamic invocation schemes.

Web Services originated with a much less ambitious system. In the late 1990s, a system was defined that allowed remote procedure calls (RPC) to be made in a technology-neutral manner. All conventional RPC mechanisms are technology-specific. The original RPC mechanisms were defined for C programs and depend on client stubs generated through programs like rpcgen; these stubs communicated with server-side infrastructure using a standardized but RPC-specific protocol. Java RMI again has its client stubs and server components, and another quite different wire protocol for communication. CORBA, as described in the previous section, has its Internet InterOrb Protocol for communication between its client stubs and its server infrastructure. The Microsoft world had another scheme for COM and its derivatives. The XML-RPC proposal (originally from the UserLand company) avoided these technology specific communications protocols, and so allowed the client and server implementation technologies to be completely separated.

All remote calls are ultimately similar. They involve a request message that identifies the method to be executed, the argument data for the method and the server where the operation will run (i.e. 'server process' as IP address and port, and where appropriate a 'server object' as identified by some opaque identifier interpreted only in the server process). A response is invariably some form of data structure that packages either an exception or a function result along with any 'out' argument values. With XML-RPC, these request and response messages became plain text messages. Such messages have complex but regular structures; naturally, XML emerges as the appropriate mechanism for defining the structures of these text messages. An XML DTD or Schema can define the forms for the messages, specifying the structure in terms of elements that represent a method call. A method call element would obviously contain an attribute or nested element with the method name, and a number of nested elements each characterized by type and value for the arguments. A client using XML-RPC can use a textual template and substitute in strings that represent the values of the actual arguments for a call.

An XML-RPC request was posted via HTTP to a URL that represented a web server script (ASP or similar) or a CGI program. This script or CGI program had to parse the incoming XML document and extract details of the actual server object, method and arguments. Then the CGI program would act as a proxy client invoking the real server. At this point, it is again technology-specific; a COM service would be invoked using COM mechanisms, and a Java RMI service would be invoked using RMI technology (you can't avoid the technology-specific programming, you can merely move it out of the actual client and into a proxy client). The server's response (encoded in a technology-specific manner) would be retrieved by the CGI program or web server script and converted into textual form. At this stage, the intermediary code could again use a simple text template for the response and slot the returned data into the appropriate fields. The web server then returns the XML response document as the result of the original HTTP post request. The client would need to parse the XML document and extract the returned data values.

This is another example of the adage that 'all problems in computer science are solved by using another level of indirection'. Here, the problem of technology-specific client-side coding and communications protocols has been solved by indirection through the additional server-side intermediary. Everything technology-specific is confined to the server realm; client and communications are technology neutral. Of course, you always pay in terms of performance costs when you add a level of indirection. Here, the costs are noticeable.

Conventional RPC mechanisms aim for efficiency. TCP/IP connections are established and maintained open for the duration of a sequence of requests and responses; data representations of requests and responses are designed for efficiency of data transfer and encoding/decoding at communications endpoints; and state can be maintained in server-side objects. A CORBA Iterator is an example where server state is useful and complex structures can be transferred. Iterators are returned when a client requests a large number of data records. A CORBA iterator allows these to be transferred a group at a time compactly represented in network-friendly sized packages.

In contrast to the conventional wire-efficient RPC mechanisms, XML-RPC is costly. Each request and response requires the establishment of a new TCP/IP connection to a web server. This is going to matter when the client–server interaction involves long sequences of requests. Each interaction involves XML parsing; firstly the server must interpret the request, and subsequently the client must parse the response document. XML-RPC favors stateless servers with single-shot requests–responses. Instead of something like the stateful CORBA iterator that returns data in parts, an XML-RPC server for the same data access role would return a gigantic XML text document containing a full set of results. These performance problems did not figure too highly in early XML-RPC applications, many of which were proof of concept applications where the service was a low-use, stateless server with methods that involved minimal data transfer (e.g. a weather service that gives the forecast for a specified city).

A revised version of XML-RPC was submitted to the W3C (the body that standardizes everything to do with the web); the proposal was sponsored by Microsoft, IBM and Ariba, along with UserLand and other smaller companies. This revision became SOAP: the Simple Object Access Protocol. (Subsequent revisions dropped the 'Simple Object Access' interpretation because SOAP servers can be procedural programs! SOAP is now merely an uninterpreted name for a protocol.)

Of course, an XML-RPC or SOAP client program must possess details of the server and the methods that it offers. With Java RMI and EJB, such details took the form of the definition of a 'Remote' interface; with CORBA, the details were defined using the Interface Definition Language. Essentially, an interface defines a class, listing its methods. Each method is characterized by a return type and by a list of parameters that are also characterized by their data types. Obviously, such an interface declaration can be represented as a structured textual document. Once again, XML has a role: it can be used to define these interface documents.

Defining the interfaces of servers is the role of the Web Services Description Language (WSDL) component of Web Services. WSDL documents define the location of a server (its URI), individual message formats and operations (request and response message combinations).

The Universal Discovery, Description, and Integration component of Web Services is the enhanced replacement of the CORBA trader system. The intent of UDDI is to have a number of registries where service suppliers can publish details of their services. Both Microsoft and IBM run production and prototyping UDDI registries to encourage the adoption of these technologies. Companies offering network-accessible computational services will advertise these services in major registries.

A UDDI directory entry has a number of subsections. The 'business entity' data include company name, address, description (which often reads like a corporate 'vision statement'!), and so forth, along with codes from standard classifications (e.g. North

American Industry Classification System) that characterize a business's activities (e.g. Microsoft Corporation has an entry that records it as an instance of the NAICS 'Software Publisher' category). The 'business services' data contain descriptions of services offered along with 'binding templates' that specify these services. Services are not limited to HTTP-based web services; a company may list things like fax contacts, phone lines for 'help desks', and mail and ftp servers. Even if an entry is given for a 'uddi-org:http' binding, this may simply represent the URL of one of the company's web pages. A 'business service' entry for an actual web service will include a reference to a 'tmodel' record; among other data, this tmodel record will include a link to the WSDL interface definition for the service. (There is no direct analog of the CORBA trader 'properties' section that allowed quality of service parameters to accompany an advertised interface.)

11.4.3 UDDI, WSDL and SOAP

This section contains a few small illustrations that may help make more concrete the various Web Services components.

A UDDI directory, such as that available at `http://uddi.microsoft.com/`, can be searched for service providers using a number of criteria including NAICS classification code and geographic location. For example, a geographic search for service providers in Menlo Park and in Palo Alto California (location of the Stanford Research Institute, Stanford University etc. – the very heart of e-World) revealed just two providers: Glenbrook Systems Incorporated, which has its company home page online, and RDC Interactive, which has listed the names and contact details of three senior executives; neither company defined any other service. Another search using NAICS categories (Information/Data Processing Services) was more successful, resulting in 28 providers, some of whom defined actual web services.

Examples of web services include those of digipot.com, Calc and IBM. Digipot supports online lotto services on `http://contest.eraserver.net/`; its services include facilities for logging in, getting details of results and game statistics and so forth, and all are defined via WSDL documents linked to the UDDI records. The Calc services proved to be dead links; they purportedly included a four-function calculator accessible via SOAP, and a more intriguing service that claimed it would find MP3 recordings. IBM naturally defines many services (IBM and Microsoft are collaborating on Web Services, hence the IBM entry in the Microsoft UDDI). IBM's service entries include references to web pages (e.g. `http://www.ibm.com/PartnerWorld/`) and telephone and email contact points. A SOAP-based web service for publishing UDDI entries to IBM's prototyping registry was listed, but access to the WSDL definition was blocked by a server security setting. (Another of the web service providers will have had no responses to his offerings; he had registered his access address as `http://localhost`.)

The `http://www.xmethods.org/` server is a location where rather more WSDL-defined services can be easily located. A part of the xmethods listing of recently introduced web services is shown in Table 11.1. The majority of these services are best described as 'proof of concept' exercises. In these, the server has only a single function, or group of similar functions, with a string argument for a number, zip code, ISBN or similar, and returns a single string result. The concept of a remote procedure call is sufficiently well established

Table 11.1 Some of the Web Services published at `http://www.xmethods.com/` (highlighted entries are discussed in the text).

Service name	Description
Airline Carrier Codes	Provides two-letter codes for all known commercial airline carriers
ApniUrdu Urdu Translator	Translates English Sentences into Urdu
BibleWebservice	Retrieves Biblical text
Periodic Table	*Get atomic weight, symbol and atomic number for all elements*
Amazon.com Web Services	*Access Amazon.com using SOAP*
MapPoint	*Comprehensive mapping and geographical information service*
ImageConversion	Converts images between bitmap, JPEG, and GIF file formats.
HK Weather Forecast	Get 5 days Hong Kong weather forecast
Currency Convertor	Get conversion rate from one currency to another currency
UPS Online Tracking Web Service	Retrieve UPS online tracking information
great circle distance	Great circle distance between two points of longitude, latitude
Convert Number to Words in Spanish	Convert number to words in Spanish
InfosVille	Returns longitude, latitude and height from a given city; only for France
UPC Database Lookup	Look up grocery items by UPC number
Country – Population Lookup Service	Gives the population for a given country
BorlandBabel	A 'babel fish' that speaks Swedish Chefish, Jive, Drawl, Eleet and other dialects
Monthly Car Payment	Calculates your monthly car payment
Captain Haddock's Curser	*Generates random curses from Captain Haddock in various languages*
Belgium Cities	Search on postal codes and cities in Belgium.
GetLocalTime	Returns the local time in South Africa
Temperature Conversion Service	Converts Fahrenheit to Centigrade and vice versa
Calculator	*Simple math calculations*
Agni Find MP3	Finds MP3 files on the Internet
Inch ↔ Millimeter Converter	Converts inches ↔ mm

now that further proofs are unnecessary. Instead, examples are needed that illustrate servers that can support transaction-aware, multi-step processes involving a client and multiple cooperating servers.

The xmethods examples include a calculator. If this were defined in IDL, its interface would be something like the following:

```
interface Calculator {
   float Add(in float x, in float y);
   float Multiply(in float x, in float y);
   float Divide(in float numerator, in float denominator);
   float Subtract(in float x, in float y);
   float Log10(in float x);
   float LogE(in float x);
   float sqrt(in float y);
   long Abs(in long ix);
   float Tangent(in float arcradians);
   ...
}
```

As a proper web service, the calculator's interface is defined in WSDL (much praised by the proponents of Web Services as providing a 'machine and person readable' definition of how to interact with a service). The complete WSDL definition is long (approximately 1500 lines); it is in part as shown in the following annotated listing:

```
Naturally, there are various "header" files to include that
specify the schema used in this XML document
<?xml version="1.0" encoding="utf-8"?>
<definitions xmlns:http="http://schemas.xmlsoap.org/wsdl/http/"
xmlns:soap="http://schemas.xmlsoap.org/wsdl/soap/" xmlns:s="http://
www.w3.org/2001/XMLSchema"
xmlns:s0="http://www.xml-webservices.net/services/maths"
xmlns:soapenc="http://schemas.xmlsoap.org/soap/encoding/"
xmlns:tm="http://microsoft.com/wsdl/mime/textMatching/"
xmlns:mime="http://schemas.xmlsoap.org/wsdl/mime/"
targetNamespace="http://www.xml-webservices.net/services/maths"
xmlns="http://schemas.xmlsoap.org/wsdl/">
Type definitions are used to specify the arguments and results
of the server operations.
   <types>
      <s:schema elementFormDefault="qualified"
         targetNamespace="http://www.xml-webservices.net/services/maths">
         <s:element name="Add">
            <s:complexType>
               <s:sequence>
```

```
            <s:element minOccurs="1" maxOccurs="1" name="a"
                type="s:float" />
            <s:element minOccurs="1" maxOccurs="1" name="b"
                type="s:float" />
        </s:sequence>
      </s:complexType>
    </s:element>
    <s:element name="AddResponse">
      <s:complexType>
        <s:sequence>
          <s:element minOccurs="1" maxOccurs="1"
            name="AddResult" type="s:float" />
        </s:sequence>
      </s:complexType>
    </s:element>
```
*Similar definitions that specify the argument and return types
for each of the defined operations.*
```
    <s:element name="Subtract">
    ...
    </s:element>
    <s:element name="SubtractResponse">
    ...
    </s:element>
    ...
  </types>
```
*The next section has "message definitions" that make use of defined
data types.*
The first group define SOAP messages.
```
  <message name="AddSoapIn">
    <part name="parameters" element="s0:Add" />
  </message>
  <message name="AddSoapOut">
    <part name="parameters" element="s0:AddResponse" />
  </message>
  ...
  ...
```
*The same services can be invoked with a simple HTTP Get request
that passes data in a query string, e.g. Add?a=3.5&b=4.7*
```
  <message name="AddHttpGetIn">
    <part name="a" type="s:string" />
    <part name="b" type="s:string" />
  </message>
  <message name="AddHttpGetOut">
    <part name="Body" element="s0:float" />
  </message>
```

```
...
...
```

*The server can also be invoked using HTTP Post requests
with the parameter data defined as name, value
pairs in the body of a request message.*

```
<message name="AddHttpPostIn">
  <part name="a" type="s:string" />
  <part name="b" type="s:string" />
</message>
<message name="AddHttpPostOut">
  <part name="Body" element="s0:float" />
</message>
```

```
...
```

*The "portType" section of the document defines the actual
service operations in terms of the request and response messages.
These definitions are given for SOAP, HTTP-Get, and HTTP-Post
protocols.*

```
<portType name="SimpleCalcSoap">
  <operation name="Add">
    <documentation>Add two numbers</documentation>
    <input message="s0:AddSoapIn" />
    <output message="s0:AddSoapOut" />
  </operation>
  <operation name="Subtract">
    ...
  </operation>
  ...
</portType>
<portType name="SimpleCalcHttpGet">
...
</portType>
<portType name="SimpleCalcHttpPost">
  ...
</portType>
```

*The next section has definitions of "bindings"; these complete
the specification of the various requests and responses that
must be handled in the client.*

```
<binding name="SimpleCalcSoap" type="s0:SimpleCalcSoap">
  <soap:binding
    transport="http://schemas.xmlsoap.org/soap/http"
    style="document" />
```

*The binding has sections for each of the operations along
with the appropriate target URL.*

```
    <operation name="Add">
      <soap:operation
```

```
                soapAction="http://www.xml-webservices.net/services/maths/Add"
                style="document" />
            <input>
                <soap:body use="literal" />
            </input>
            <output>
                <soap:body use="literal" />
            </output>
        </operation>
        <operation name="Subtract">
            ...
        </operation>
    ...
    </binding>
```

Similar binding definitions are needed for the other protocols.

```
    <binding name="SimpleCalcHttpGet" type="s0:SimpleCalcHttpGet">
        <http:binding verb="GET" />
        ...
        </operation>
    </binding>
    <binding name="SimpleCalcHttpPost" type="s0:SimpleCalcHttpPost">
        <http:binding verb="POST" />
        ...
    </binding>
```

*Finally the service (actually three services, SOAP, HTTP-Get,
And HTTP-post) are defined with their server's URLs and their
Communications bindings.*

```
    <service name="SimpleCalc">
        <documentation>This Web Service mimics a calculator.</documentation>
        <port name="SimpleCalcSoap" binding="s0:SimpleCalcSoap">
            <soap:address location="http://www.xml-webservices.net/services/
                maths/calculator.asmx" />
        </port>
        <port name="SimpleCalcHttpGet" binding="s0:SimpleCalcHttpGet">
            <http:address location="http://www.xml-webservices.net/services/
                maths/calculator.asmx" />
        </port>
        <port name="SimpleCalcHttpPost" binding="s0:SimpleCalcHttpPost">
            ...
        </port>
    </service>
</definitions>
```

It is an adage that 'beauty is in the eye of the beholder'; similar subjectivity rules in assessments of the relative readabilities of IDL and WSDL service definitions.

While a WSDL service definition may be human readable, it is scarcely writeable. Fortunately, if the server-side developer uses an appropriate development environment, the generation of WSDL can be automated. Appendix C contains a small illustration of the use of Microsoft's Visual Studio .NET system. Visual Studio .NET provides excellent support for the service developer. The developer defines the server class in C#, Visual Basic or one of the other Microsoft-approved languages; the main server class is defined just like any other class that will be used in the server program. The developer then simply tags those methods that are to be accessible as part of a Web Service, and Visual Studio .NET does the rest of the work needed to create a WSDL service definition document.

A client will typically have to compose a SOAP XML packet with a request. The SOAP request is implicitly defined by the WSDL document. A SOAP request invoking the Calculator's Add function would take the following form:

```
POST /services/maths/calculator.asmx HTTP/1.1
Host: www.xml-webservices.net
Content-Type: text/xml; charset=utf-8
Content-Length: length
SOAPAction: "http://www.xml-webservices.net/services/maths/Add"

<?xml version="1.0" encoding="utf-8"?>
<soap:Envelope xmlns:xsi="http://www.w3.org/2001/XMLSchema-instance"
xmlns:xsd="http://www.w3.org/2001/XMLSchema" xmlns:soap="http://
schemas.xmlsoap.org/soap/envelope/">
  <soap:Body>
    <Add xmlns="http://www.xml-webservices.net/services/maths">
      <a>float</a>
      <b>float</b>
    </Add>
  </soap:Body>
</soap:Envelope>
```

(The requestor would substitute the stringified values for the float arguments into the `<a>float</a>` and `<b>float</b>` elements of this template, and then compute the actual content length for the complete message.) The expected form of the XML document with the response would be

```
HTTP/1.1 200 OK
Content-Type: text/xml; charset=utf-8
Content-Length: length

<?xml version="1.0" encoding="utf-8"?>
<soap:Envelope xmlns:xsi="http://www.w3.org/2001/XMLSchema-instance"
xmlns:xsd="http://www.w3.org/2001/XMLSchema" xmlns:soap="http://
schemas.xmlsoap.org/soap/envelope/">
  <soap:Body>
```

```
<AddResponse xmlns="http://www.xml-webservices.net/services/maths">
    <AddResult>float</AddResult>
</AddResponse>
</soap:Body>
</soap:Envelope>
```

There are various ways that such requests can be constructed. Some client-side toolkits offer something like a 'soap request' class that has methods to set the server's address and the name of the remote method, and to define the arguments; an 'invoke' method of this class will result in the generation of the actual SOAP XML document and its dispatch to the server. Microsoft's .NET system uses a different (and really rather better) approach, having a client-side proxy class whose public methods mimic those of the remote server. This proxy class is generated automatically from the WSDL document in much the same way as a CORBA client-side proxy is generated from IDL by an IDL compiler or a Java RMI client proxy is generated using rmic.

The Microsoft server-side infrastructure allows for requests to be received as simple HTTP get and post-style messages with name/value pairs defining the arguments. Such requests are resolved in the same way as those submitted using SOAP documents. This facility may simplify the implementation of clients (which merely need to generate a HTTP get); more importantly, it also allows for simple testing of the service before real clients have written. Visual Studio .NET generates a suite of Web pages that document a new service and which allow HTTP get-style invocations. Many of the web services published at http://www.xmethods.com/ include these test pages, so allowing immediate experimentation with the service.

The Calculator Web Service includes these test pages; one is illustrated in Figure 11.1. Submission of these inputs naturally results in an XML response document that Internet Explorer can display:

```
<?xml version="1.0" encoding="utf-8" ?>
<float
xmlns="http://www.xml-webservices.net/services/maths">
210</float>
```

Figure 11.1 A test page for invoking a Web Service via the HTTP get protocol.

(Unfortunately, it doesn't work quite correctly; the decimal points in the inputs are invariably lost, so instead of 7.6 + 13.4 the system treats this as 76 + 134.)

There are some more sophisticated examples in the xmethods listing. For instance, the group that prepares tutorials for IBM's Alphaworks development site has a Web Service that converts image files. Its WSDL definition defines methods such as bmp2gif (in: a BMP image; out: the corresponding GIF-formatted image); the input and output data types are defined as arrays of binary data. Naturally, this service does not have HTTP get and put interfaces; it can only be accessed via the SOAP protocol. This IBM example has a downloadable client that can be used to invoke the operations on user-supplied images.

The Amazon offering moves slightly closer to commercial reality for Web Services. Amazon has defined a set of Web Services with methods that include searches for books by a given author, for DVD/VHS products featuring a particular actor/actress, or for products identified by product code. The WSDL port operation definition for an 'actor' search operation is:

```
<operation name="ActorSearchRequest">
  <input message="typens:ActorSearchRequest" />
  <output message="typens:ActorSearchResponse" />
</operation>
```

The message types are

```
<message name="ActorSearchRequest">
  <part name="ActorSearchRequest" type="typens:ActorRequest" />
</message>
<message name="ActorSearchResponse">
  <part name="return" type="typens:ProductInfo" />
</message>
```

with data types that define the arguments for an ActorRequest:

```
<xsd:complexType name="ActorRequest">
  <xsd:all>
    <xsd:element name="actor" type="xsd:string" />
    ...
    <xsd:element name="devtag" type="xsd:string" />
    <xsd:element name="version" type="xsd:string" />
  </xsd:all>
</xsd:complexType>
```

and that define a response as being an array of 'Product Details' that contain many possible fields (the same Details records are used for all searches; only the relevant fields are used in a response):

```
<xsd:complexType name="ProductInfo">
  <xsd:all>
```

```
          <xsd:element name="Details" type="typens:DetailsArray" />
        </xsd:all>
      </xsd:complexType>
      <xsd:complexType name="Details">
        <xsd:all>
          <xsd:element name="Url" type="xsd:string" />
          ...
          <xsd:element name="Artists" type="typens:ArtistArray" />
          ...
          <xsd:element name="Directors" type="typens:DirectorArray" />
          <xsd:element name="TheatricalReleaseDate" type="xsd:string" />
          ...
        </xsd:all>
      </xsd:complexType>
```

Amazon hosts these Web Services on its own site. Developers of client programs can obtain a kit that has Java and Perl components for accessing these services. For example, the ActorSoap class builds and submits an appropriate SOAP request with the necessary parameters (these have to be set via setParameter method calls as defined in Amazon's AbstractSoapQuery base class). The result of a query is returned in a hashtable structure with the individual data elements, as specified in the WSDL ProductInfo declaration, being accessible by name:

```
public class ActorSoap extends AbstractSoapQuery
{
  public ActorSoap()
  {
    super();
    this.parameters.put("Host","http://soap.amazon.com/onca/soap");
    this.parameters.put("Actor","");
    ...
  }

  public Object issueRequest() throws MalformedURLException,
    ServiceException, RemoteException
  {
    com.amazon.soap.axis.AmazonSearchService service =
      new com.amazon.soap.axis.AmazonSearchServiceLocator();
    com.amazon.soap.axis.AmazonSearchPort port =
      service.getAmazonSearchPort(
        new URL((String)this.parameters.get("Host")));
    com.amazon.soap.axis.ActorRequest request =
      new com.amazon.soap.axis.ActorRequest();

    request.setActor((String)this.parameters.get("Actor"));
```

```
    ...

    this.result = port.actorSearchRequest(request);
    return this.result;
  }
}
```

These classes allow client-side developers to obtain data from Amazon and manipulate these data according to the needs of their own applications. The development of supplementary web portals feeding traffic to Amazon should not be a major imperative for other companies; any use of these Amazon Web Services must support a company's own core activities. Of course, from Amazon's perspective there will be no justification for maintaining these Web Services if their use by client companies simply places a load on Amazon's server machines and databases that is not compensated by an increase in customer purchases.

There is one real Web Service among the xmethods examples listed in Table 11.1. This is the MapPoint service from Microsoft. MapPoint supports location aware services: it can compute distances, find routes and render maps. Its services allow client applications to use Microsoft-hosted applications and geographic databases that can perform tasks such as:

- Obtaining country or region name, entity ID, latitude and longitude coordinates, codes and language for a specified entity.

- Calculating great circle distances between specified points.

- Finding elements of interest (chosen from specified types) near to a selected point.

- Returning an area map image.

- Computing a route between specified points, returning route details superimposed on a map image.

A client of these services will typically be a company that requires a sophisticated web site that presents web pages that are customized according to client location; examples might be a real estate agency or a motorist support group. The location-specific pages generated by the company may be HTML browser pages or pages suitable for a mobile platform such a radio and GPS equipped PDA. Client location data may be obtained from HTML textfield inputs, or possibly from client-side GPS inputs. The company generates these pages using its own server applications, with these applications invoking Microsoft MapPoint web services as needed. Of course, such a company could also use MapPoint services from within purely in-house Windows and Java applications that need map data.

A MapPoint application requires use of the Microsoft-hosted services with their databases, and of an application (MapPoint Server) that must run on one of the company's own servers. This application acts as a proxy through which the Microsoft-hosted components are accessed. Microsoft can also supply software for wireless GPS clients; demonstration services include instant messaging for groups of mobile users who happen to be in the same area. The MapPoint service has to be purchased, and usage paid for in accord with the number of queries made on Microsoft's web servers.

The final word in this section is left to Captain Haddock at his residence at `http://www.tankebolaget.se/` (the WSDL service definition for Captain Haddock's Curser is `http://www.tankebolaget.se/scripts/Haddock.exe/wsdl/IHaddock/`). When asked to comment on the human readability of WSDL service definitions, the Captain responded '*huggormsavföda*'.

11.4.4 Web service promises

Existing web services are information services based on stateless servers. Each request is independent; no state memory is needed, no transactional boundaries need be honored, nothing gets changed in the server-side databases. Web Services don't have to be so limited. For example, services can access 'Session' and 'Application' objects in much the same way as PHP, ASP or servlet/JSP applications; HTTP cookies are again used as session keys. But even with some server-side state data, there is a long way to go before really sophisticated distributed applications can be built. The mechanisms that will be used are still at little more than proposal state; the 'Business Processing Language for Web Services, WS Transactions and WS Coordination' specification was only released in mid-2002. Web Services have to develop further before they can claim to be a true replacement to CORBA for the creation of distributed applications that are interoperable over systems developed using 801 companies' products (the 800 in OMG, plus Microsoft).

A service like MapPoint is useful. But many companies would prefer to purchase similar software together with a suitable geographic database and run an equivalent service locally. Remote access to information is best restricted to cases where the information is rapidly changing, or where the data are truly proprietary to the service provider. Where the data are fixed (atomic weights, topographic maps) or slowly changing (street maps), then local copies will be more convenient. Remote access to computations, like image conversions, is even less justifiable; few developers would choose a Web Service version over use of a local link library with the same algorithms. Remote access obviously incurs delays from network latency; we are expected to ignore these, for we are assured that bandwidth on the net is rapidly increasing. More seriously, if you contract out an essential part of your web site generation processes, you become dependent on quality of service elements over which you have no control. Some developers remember the day early in 2001 when a misconfigured DNS table took `microsoft.com` off the web for almost a day; 'mafia boy' hit a number of major sites with a very effective distributed denial of service attack in early 2000; and then there was that earlier incident when Microsoft forgot to renew its payment for its `microsoft.com` domain name.

Some proponents of Web Services argue that this technology will lead to more open architectures for programs. Instead of monolithic, fully featured applications, the future model is to have a shell with externally supplied services. Examples are given of word processors that subcontract spell checking to a web service, or a web commerce program that subcontracts its user login mechanism to one web service, its credit card checking to another, its inventory management to a third, and so forth. With the benefits of UDDI and WSDL, it has been suggested that the applications (possibly with a little assistance from their users) could negotiate service terms with different suppliers of services such as the spell checker or the credit card checker.

These proposals for dynamic extension and integration of applications vary in their plausibility. It is virtually certain that a future release of Microsoft Office will include links to a somewhat limited version of the MapPoint Web Service. This feature will allow a user who has funds in his or her Microsoft Wallet to click a button and add a map to a Word document. Future desktop share portfolio management applications will have Web Service-style links to feeds that, at an agreed subscription price, will provide updated share prices. Such programs will come pre-configured with selections of possible service providers who offer compatible 'share price' Web Services in much the same way as Windows systems come with pre-configured lists of potential Internet Service Providers.

The 'openness' of such applications is not that great. The word processor with a sub-contracted spelling checker cannot be marketed until Web Service spell checking is available. Naturally, the developer of the word processor will be in the best position to offer a subscription-based spell checking service (guaranteeing itself a steady income flow). Of course it is not a monopoly. The Web Service interface will be published, and other companies can develop rival products and offer these via UDDI. The commercial feasibility of such endeavors is, however, questionable. Penetration of the market will be very hard because few users of word processors will wish to go to the UDDI registries to search for rival offerings of the spell checking and other subcontracted services. Certain companies will of course be able to promote their own offerings aggressively, somewhat in the style whereby Windows XP convinces neophyte users that they must get themselves issued with a Microsoft Passport before they will be allowed to use the Internet.

Currently, the 'Discovery and Integration' aspects of Web Services are not that dynamic. You discover a service like MapPoint, or the Amazon client services, possibly through UDDI but much more plausibly from promotional advertising or from a news item somewhere on idg.net. You download the executive summary, the white papers and the technical overview documents. You negotiate with project team, project supervisor and management. You download the development kit and get your company to pay for a trial subscription. You generate stub classes from the WSDL definition, or obtain these classes as part of the development kit. You install any necessary helper applications and authentication certificates. You run your demonstrator applications and convince the project team, supervisor and management that this is the way to go. Your company pays for a full license and you have finally integrated an external Web Service into your application.

Web Service proponents foresee a quite different, much more dynamic scenario where an application can itself discover and integrate external services. The APIs for clients that want to interrogate a UDDI service are defined, so it is quite feasible for an application to obtain data structures that hold details of offered services. The WSDL service specifications are linked from these UDDI entries and can be downloaded and parsed with a DOM parser to produce – well, an elaborate tree structure with lots of nodes. It is at this point that the exercise of automated integration becomes *interesting*. For example, the xmethods listing has two services that provide details of atomic weights. The Web Service that is hosted at http://soap.fmui.de/webservices.php offers the methods:

- `getNameBySymbol`

- `getMassBySymbol`

- `getNumberBySymbol`

- `getElementBySymbol`

along with others like `getNameByNumber` and `getMeltingPointByNumber`,

The rival service hosted at `http://www.webservicex.net/` has a more limited range of methods:

- `getAtomicWeight`

- `getAtomicNumber`

- `getElementSymbol`

- `getAtoms`

The program that is automatically integrating its Web Service supplier of chemical data now confronts some interesting problems. How will a program determine the essential equivalence of methods such as `getAtomicNumber` and `getNumberBySymbol`? How can it determine what the returned values will be? (The webservicex version is used in an example in Appendix C; the returned data were not quite what was expected.) These methods take a string argument identifying the element; should the client use 'Fe' or 'Iron' (or 'Eisen', when it is a German service)? Obviously, a program that is resolving these issues must possess a high degree of intelligence. Such programs are not yet available. However, if you are prepared to wait just a little while longer, they will emerge triumphantly from the laboratories of the Artificial Intelligentsia.

Of course, agreed standards for services will reduce such problems. You can expect major business processing areas to be covered by standards that define the signatures of service methods (the Open Applications Group is working on this issue; see `http://www.openapplications.org/`). So eventually all credit card checkers may use the same method signature in their web servers, with standardized arguments for card number, expiry date, name and other data. Standardization of the interfaces will make it slightly more feasible to have applications that integrate their Web Service suppliers at run time. However, there are still problems.

How should your application select a chosen service from among the alternatives that it has discovered? The choice will have to take into account quality of service issues and costs. As yet, there are no standards in this area (at the moment there is no replacement for the 'properties' data that CORBA traders used to characterize functionally equivalent CORBA services). With most existing services, there is no pricing mechanism that can be discovered on the Internet (if you want to use MapPoint, you phone Microsoft and negotiate a deal).

Further, most services involve long-term contractual obligations. If you want Microsoft to handle your client login via the Passport service, you need a contract with Microsoft. You will need a contract with your credit card agency that has been agreed between their lawyers and your lawyers; this agreement will commit you to pay them so much for each request that you submit. You will have a preferred courier for delivery, again with some degree of contractual binding. These business service connections are not really things that should be dynamically reassigned by a program that is using some scoring algorithm to rank and select amongst UDDI-advertised services.

There are some interesting possible scenarios for a world where you do let your programs renegotiate their web service contracts. You could have your program select among UDDI-advertised credit card checkers, each day picking the service that has the lowest charge for each card checked; this might save you money. But one day, you could find that your program decides to integrate with the 'Dodgy Brothers Credit Card Agency' (`http://www.dbcredit.bv/`) that is charging US$ −0.25 for each card (that's right: they promise to pay you for each credit card that you ask them to verify).

Exercises

Explorations

(**1**) Research and report on the systems available for mapping IP addresses to geographic locations.

(**2**) Research and report on suggestions for how knowledge of a client's geographic location potentially can be, and currently is being, exploited by e-commerce systems.

(**3**) Write a short report that clarifies the sequence of message exchanges needed for a client to login to a Microsoft Passport site, and the subsequent message traffic that avoids the need for a further login when the same client moves to another Passport site.

(**4**) Research and report on work by the 'Liberty Alliance' that seeks to create an alternative to Microsoft Passport.

(**5**) AOL and other companies launched litigation in the US contending that Microsoft was exploiting its monopoly position with regard to Passport. What is their case? How has this progressed?

(**6**) Microsoft Passport first appeared in 1999. It is used in MSN sites, and there are a few other major sites such as eBay that utilize Passport, but the growth of use has not been that marked. Research the penetration of Passport into commercial web sites and write a report on current usage and on the factors that have resulted in slower than expected growth.

(**7**) Research and report on recent developments of the Intel-sponsored 'SETI@Home-like' distributed computing systems.

(**8**) There are a number of 'toolkits' for building peer-to-peer systems, for example Sun's JXTA system. Research these tool kits and write a report that identifies the type of peer-to-peer application that they support and the facilities that they provide.

(**9**) It is reported that the audio recording companies are seeking permission from US legal authorities to deploy software systems that will attack peer-to-peer computing networks that they contend are trafficking in pirated audio recordings. Research the current state of these developments and write a report on their current status and on the ethics of US corporations launching denial of service attacks on individual computer systems.

(10) Winners, losers and also rans – write a report on the current applications of peer-to-peer technologies.

(11) Explore the arguments that contend that the 'Web Services' architecture will allow future applications to be created by combining numerous Web Service-based micro-applications. Write a report identifying the strengths and weaknesses of these arguments and reporting on current illustrative examples.

(12) If the 'Web Services' model succeeds, software companies will no longer sell complete but complex shrink-wrapped software products; instead, they will sell simple low-cost 'shell' products that rely on subscription-based or fee for service-based web components. Explore and write a report how such a change will affect software development, marketing and revenue. Your report should consider the actual feasibility of small third party developers successfully creating and marketing alternatives to the web service components that are marketed by the primary software developer.

(13) Review the latest 'Web Services' as reported at `http://www.xmethods.com/`; how will these change the world for the software developer?

Appendix **A**
Minimalist guide to HTML and JavaScript

Your web sites will naturally contain a large number of static HTML pages. These will include informational pages with many pictures, cross-links and small amounts of styled text; they will also include static form pages. You, or more likely a web designer colleague, will produce these pages using one of the popular software packages such as DreamWeaver or FrontPage. No knowledge of HTML is needed to produce these pages.

However, some limited knowledge of HTML is required because you must write programs that will generate HTML response pages. Most readers will have experience with HTML coding; for those that haven't, there are several good guides on the web (try http://www.wdvl.com/Authoring/HTML/). The following notes simply review the most essential features required in form pages and simple response pages.

Client-side scripting (JavaScript) has two roles. Firstly, it allows you to perform some simple verification tests on form data before these data are submitted. The checks cannot do very much more than verify that all form fields contain data. You cannot rely on such checks; many users disable JavaScript in their browsers (and there is always the possibility of a hacker submitting data that purport to have been collected and checked in a form that you displayed but are really carefully hand-edited data that are intended to disrupt your server). JavaScript checks must always be repeated in your server-side programs. Their role is simply to avoid time-wastage associated with innocent errors. There is no point in sending form data to a server and invoking a CGI program if a simple check will reveal that the data would be rejected. Some of the packages used to prepare web pages include macros that can add standard JavaScript checks for data in form fields – so you don't necessarily have to write any JavaScript yourself.

The second role for client-side scripting is to achieve all those dynamic effects with multi-layered documents, popup menus, rollover images that change and so forth. These are definitely best handled with the aid of a web page preparation program, but can be coded manually.

The treatment of JavaScript here is again very cursory. It is intended simply to highlight the most important features (once again, there are many tutorials on the web, a good selection of links is in http://www.wdvl.com/Authoring/JavaScript/).

A.1   HTML essentials

HTML (HyperText Markup Language) documents contain content text and HTML tags. The tags are interpreted by a browser program. Some tags define the overall structure of a document; others, like link tags and the input tags used in forms, provide 'functionality'; most tags define formatting requests that the browser uses to control the appearance of the content text that is displayed to the user.

Markup tags are differentiated from content text by typographic conventions; with HTML the characters '<' and '>' delimit a tag (if you need a 'less than sign' in content text, you have to enter the escape character combination <, while the 'greater than' sign is coded as >). A tag will contain a tag name and usually attribute data. A tag, such as an 'input text' tag in a form or a 'horizontal rule' formatting tag, may be a complete entity in itself. For these tags, the browser processes the tag and its attributes and produces an appropriate representation in the displayed document. The majority of tags set some property of the following content text; for these, the structure consists of a 'start tag' with attributes, a block of content text and finally an 'end tag'. A strict markup language (one that complies with the dictates of the Standard Generalized Markup Language) always has clearly defined 'start tag' and 'end tag' elements. XML is an example; it allows structures like:

```
<example_body_tag attributes>body of tag with content text
</example_body_tag>
```

and

```
<example_simple_tag attributes />
```

HTML is a little sloppy in this regard; in many cases it is possible to omit the 'end' tag. Fortunately, browsers care little about letter case; the tags <html>, <HTML>, <Html> etc. are all equally acceptable.

HTML was originally conceived as a markup language for text documents, with the 'hypertext' features being realized through special markup tags for the inter- and intra-document links. The HTML tag language has a limited repertoire of text formatting tags, such as a variety of different 'headings' that can serve as chapter titles, section titles and subsection labels. A browser will have defaults for the fonts, styles and colors used for such headings. These defaults can be overridden by supplementary style data that are either specified in the HTML document, or are defined in some supplementary style definition document. Other formatting tags define differing paragraph formats, such as standard content text paragraphs and list-style paragraphs. Still other text formatting tags can change the font, style or color of a particular group of words. HTML is not intended to define completely the layout of a document as you can do in a word processor. A browser adjusts the layout of a document to fit into an available window; for example, the browser changes the length of lines to suit the window width. A browser may allow a user to specify overrides, so text may not actually appear in the font or the color specified in the document.

Structural tags were added to the HTML tag set as pages became more elaborate. An HTML document should have distinct 'head' and 'body' sections. Information in the 'head' section is not displayed by the browser; instead it serves primarily as meta-data, providing information about the content. For example, the head section of a static HTML page will often contain a list of keywords that should be used when characterizing that page in a web index, such as that used by the Google search engine. Other structural elements include frames, tables and subwindows reserved for images or applets. Table tags provided the first detailed control over the layout of elements within a page. Images, and later applet subwindows, added further structural control; the page author can specify the size of a subwindow that is reserved for such a component. The browser's text layout engine arranges for the content text to flow around the reserved subwindow areas. Image maps added navigational mechanisms that were more attractive to users than long lists of hypertext links. Frameset and frame tags provide the page designer with additional structural control; these tags allow a page designer to split the browser window into separate regions that are used to display different HTML pages. Further structural extensions lead to the idea of multi-layer documents; the base layer that displays the normal content text can be overlaid with other layers that contain special graphic elements. The visibility of the layers is controlled by scripted code running in the client.

Initially, the only functional elements in an HTML page were the hypertext links and the 'anchors' that defined the positions of text sections referenced through intra-page links. The web ceased to be a vanity publishing medium and became an interactive tool when forms were added; forms could employ many special tags that defined different types of input field. The introduction of client-side scripting and event-handling mechanisms added more functionality to the pages. The script code can check data in input fields, display simple dialogs and alerts, and even change the appearance of items in the page.

Server-side scripting elements add yet more complexity to an HTML source document. A browser should never receive a page containing any server-side scripts; instead, the web server should have processed them prior to sending the page to the client. Server-side script elements are replaced by automatically generated fragments of content text and HTML formatting tags; this generated content text will typically contain data extracted from a server-side database.

A fully featured HTML source document can be very complex. It may contain server-side scripting elements that are interpreted on the web server. There can be script code that is being returned to the client for execution in the browser. There will be structural tags defining major sections in the HTML document and controlling the placement of images and tables. There will be style directives setting policies for the display of content text. Finally, there will be the content text and associated formatting tags.

The pages that must be generated by web servers should be simpler. Your web site will need pages that attract the interest of potential customers; these pages will need to use all the features like multi-layered documents, multiple images and elaborate layouts. But the pages that ultimately matter most are the forms used to get the customers' credit card details and the response pages returning an order tracking number. These vital pages should be kept simple to avoid distracting the user.

A1.1   HTML document structure

A typical HTML document will have the form:

```
<html>
<head>
  meta data, function definitions for client side scripting,
  title, ...
</head>
<body>
  Content text and associated format tags
  Embedded hypertext links
  Possibly forms with input tags
</body>
</html>
```

The main static pages in your web site will have meta directives that define data for indexing engines, such as the Google search engine:

```
<meta name="keywords" content="Java, HTML, Javascript PHP, ...">
```

or directives that provide information to caching systems in proxy servers or in client browsers:

```
<meta http-equiv="expires" content="1 Apr 2005">
```

or directives that specify a 'stylesheet' that is used to set consistent display styles for standard HTML components in all documents forming part of a web site:

```
<link rel=stylesheet type="text/css" href="mystyle.css">
```

Generated pages will sometimes need to include expires directives and/or links to stylesheets.

Function definitions and variable declarations for client-side scripting should be placed in the head section. These are illustrated later in the JavaScript section. The 'customer interest' pages in your web site may well include JavaScript for dynamic effects like popup menus; these should be avoided in form pages and response pages. The only JavaScript that should be included in generated pages should be standardized code used to check input values in form pages.

All pages should have a title tag:

```
<title>Order form for books from Acme</title>
<title>Your order has been processed</title>
```

You may need to use framesets. These will allow you to have simple forms and response pages and yet keep something of a decorative style if this is required on all pages in your company site. The following defines a simple layout with two columns: one for company information and the second for the order form:

```
<html><head><title>XYX Corporation</title></head>
<frameset cols="25%,75%">
   <frame src="CompanyInfo.html" name="LeftMargin">
   <frame src="OrderForm.html" name="MainPart">
<noframes>If your browser doesn't handler frames,
<a href="noframe.html">alternative source</a> is available.</noframes>
</frameset> </html>
```

(HTML pages embedded in frames do not define their own titles.) A slightly more elaborate arrangement results in a column down the left side of the browser window, a company logo document in the top right and the form occupying the largest area. This is achieved with a frameset page with a subordinate frameset page in one of the frames. The main frameset page is:

```
<html><head><title>XYX Corporation</title></head>
<frameset cols="25%,75%">
   <frame src="CompanyInfo.html" name="LeftMargin">
   <frame src="Frame2.html">
<noframes>If your browser doesn't handler frames,
<a href="noframe.html">alternative source</a> is available.</noframes>
</frameset> </html>
```

The subordinate frameset page is:

```
<frameset row="25%,75%">
   <frame src="CompanyLogo.html">
   <frame src="OrderForm.html" name="MainPart">
</frameset> </html>
```

You could utilize this frameset with the company logo and other data displayed all the time while you show a sequence of forms in the main display area.

A1.2 Basic formatting for the 'body' of an informational page

HTML has a set of 'heading' tags for section and subsection titles contained within a page:

```
<h1>Welcome to our cyber shop</h1>
<h2>Special offers</h2>
```

The heading types are h1...h6 (with h6 being very small). The browser will have default fonts, sizes and styles defined for each heading type.

Normal content text paragraphs start with a `<p>` tag (the ending tag, `</p>`, is usually omitted). The browser will use a small amount of vertical space to separate paragraphs. In the source document, the text forming a paragraph can be free form, with random amounts of whitespace characters. The browser will tidy the text so as to best fill the line width available in its window. If you need to insert line breaks at specific points in a paragraph, you must use break tags (`<br>`).

There are a variety of list paragraph formats. An 'unordered list' is delimited by the start `<ul>` and end `</ul>` tags, with each list item starting with an `<li>` tag (the `</li>` end tag is again usually omitted). A browser will display an unordered list using some form of bullet character to mark the start of each list item; the text of a list item will be indented to some degree. Ordered lists are similar, except they use numbers rather than bullet marks to identify list items. (There is another more elaborate definition list format; definition lists are used for example in the 'Javadoc' HTML documentation for Java classes, these Javadoc HTML documents name the methods of a class together with definitions of their operation.)

Occasionally, you need to override the browser's text engine and have a text paragraph displayed with line breaks as defined in the document source. Examples appear in all web pages that must display fragments of program code. For these, you can use the `<pre>...</pre>` tags. Text between these tags is not run together in the normal way, instead being left with its original whitespace and line breaks. It would be unusual to have such paragraphs in a commercial site.

An `<hr>` tag can be used to place a horizontal rule (line) between paragraphs.

Specific styles can be requested for groups of words. HTML defines tags for both 'logical' and 'physical' styles. Logical styles are meant to express something about the nature of the stylized text; these tags include `<cite>...</cite>` (for a citation), `<quote>...</quote>` (for a quotation), `<code>...</code>` (for a fragment of program text within a text paragraph) and `<del>...</del>` (marks text deleted since previous version of a document). Browsers have defaults defined for how such styled text is displayed; for example, both citations and quotations might simply be presented in italic text, while a code fragment might temporarily switch to a fixed pitch font such as Courier. The physical tags include `<b>...</b>` (the embedded text is displayed in a bold style), `<i>...</i>` (italic style), `<strike>...</strike>` and `<blink>...</blink>` (a style to annoy your readers). There really isn't much difference between the logical style tags and the physical tags; cited text may appear the same as italicized text, while deleted text appears just like strike-thru text. (Netscape understands the `strike` physical tag but not the `del` logical tag.) The logic tags were really an early attempt at marking the content of a document in such a way that it could be interpreted by a program ('find all citations in these pages'). Later, XML was developed to handle such semantic structuring of content.

Most tags take attributes that modify their behavior. For example, the 'heading' tags can have an alignment attribute (`align="center"` etc.); the horizontal rule tag can have alignment, width (fraction of page) and size (thickness) attributes. Most attributes are specified in *name=value* form; a few are just flags that can be included when needed. Details of the attributes available for tags are available online (links from `http://www.wdvl.com/Authoring/HTML/` or the `http://www.w3c.org/`); they are also covered in HTML encyclopedias such as *Using HTML 4* by M. E. Holzschlag (QUE Publishers). (The values for attributes should be given in quotes, but browsers tolerate the omission of quote marks.)

As an example, the following source file:

```
<head>
<title>This is a demonstration HTML page</title></head><body>
<h1 align=center>HTML, you will <em>love</em>it (<small>maybe</small>)</
h1>
<p>This document contains some text
that illustrates various features of <strong>HTML</strong>.
<small><em>Most readers should be familiar with basic HTML tags
but the publishers felt that some example materials should be
included.</em>
</small>
<p align=right>You have some limited control over the layout of your
text. You
can <code>change the style</code> of small text segments. Basic style
controls include <small>size changes</small>, <b>switch to bold
<em>and italic</em></b>
styles. <del>Strike thru text is also
possible</del>
<br>
Note how you keep the last alignment set when you simply insert a break
in your paragraph.
<p>You can have horizontal rules:
<br>
<hr>
of varying lengths
<br>
<hr align=center width="50%">
and thicknesses
<hr size=10 noshade>
<p>There are a number of list formats.
<uL>
<li>first bullet point
<li>second bullet point
</Ul>
A type attribute in the &lt;ul&gt; tag allows you to specify the form
of the bullet (though
you should expect variations among browsers as to actual appearance).
<p>
Numbered lists take attributes that specify numbering style and first
value:
<ol type="I" start=8>
<li>a roman 8
<li>a roman 9
<li>a roman 10
```

```
<li>a roman 11
<li>imagine the fun of doing long division with roman style numbers.
</ol>
<hr width=80% size=4>
<p>You can include preformatted text:
<pre>
&lt;table border&gt;
&lt;caption&gt;Results for Sorcery 121&lt;/caption&gt;
&lt;tr&gt;
  &lt;td colspan=2 rowspan=2&gt;
  &lt;/td&gt;
  &lt;th colspan=2 align=center&gt;Examination&lt;/th&gt;
&lt;/tr&gt;
&lt;tr&gt;
  &lt;th&gt;Fail&lt;/th&gt;
  &lt;th&gt;Pass&lt;/th&gt;
&lt;/tr&gt;
&lt;tr align=center&gt;
  &lt;th rowspan=2&gt;Practical&lt;/th&gt;
  &lt;th>Fail&lt;/th&gt;
  &lt;td>35&lt;/td&gt;
  &lt;td>3&lt;/td&gt;
&lt;/tr&gt;
&lt;tr align=center&gt;
  &lt;th>Pass&lt;/th&gt;
  &lt;td>29&lt;/td&gt;
  &lt;td>163&lt;/td&gt;
&lt;/tr&gt;
&lt;/table&gt;

</pre>
</body></html>
```

would appear something like the following when displayed in a browser with a narrow window:

HTML, you will *love* it (maybe)

This document contains some text that illustrates various features of **HTML**. *Most readers should be familiar with basic HTML tags but the publishers felt that some example materials should be included.*

You have some limited control over the layout of your text. You can change the style of small text segments. Basic style controls include size changes, **switch to bold** *and italic* styles. ~~Strike thru text is also possible~~
Note how you keep the last alignment set when you simply insert a break in your paragraph.

You can have horizontal rules:
_____

of varying lengths   _____

and thicknesses
_____

There are a number of list formats.

* first bullet point

* second bullet point

A type attribute in the <ul> tag allows you to specify the form of the bullet (though you should expect variations among browsers as to actual appearance).

Numbered lists take attributes that specify numbering style and first value:

```
 VIII  a roman 8
   IX  a roman 9
    X  a roman 10
   XI  a roman 11
  XII  imagine the fun of doing long division with roman style numbers.
```

You can include preformatted text:

```
<table border>
<caption>Results for Sorcery 121</caption>
<tr>
        <td colspan=2 rowspan=2>
        </td>
        <th colspan=2 align=center>Examination</th>
</tr>
<tr>
        <th>Fail</th>
        <th>Pass</th>
</tr>
<tr align=center>
        <th rowspan=2>Practical</th>
        <th>Fail</th>
```

```
        <td>35</td>
        <td>3</td>
</tr>
<tr align=center>
        <th>Pass</th>
        <td>29</td>
        <td>163</td>
</tr>
</table>
```

A1.3   Including images

Browsers can display images in GIF, JPG and PNG formats (and maybe others). Images are included using an `<img>` tag. The attributes for this tag include:

- `src` URI for image
- `alt` Some text to display in lieu of image if browser settings prevent loading of images
- `align` (Optional) Specifies alignment relative to surrounding text
- `hspace, vspace` (Optional) Specify extra padding space around image (values given in pixels);
- `width, height` (Optional) If not specified, the image is displayed using its natural dimensions; it is best to specify image sizes (even if these are just the natural dimensions) for this allows the browser to continue working on page layout while the image is downloaded.

An example of an img link is:

```
<img src=CompanyLogo.gif alt="Our logo" width=100 height=100>
```

An 'image map' is a hypertext navigation device that uses an image and associated 'map' data to define a set of links. A user viewing the image on a browser window can click a point in the image; the browser checks to determine which of the map regions contains the point. If the point was in a region, the browser follows the link. An image map is defined by adding an extra `usemap` tag in the image and providing the map data structure in the page:

```
<img src="images/campus_map.gif" usemap="mapA">
<map name="mapA">
```

```
    <area shape=rect coords="30,50, 80,110"
      href="#Unibar.html" >
    <area shape=poly coords="20,120,70,120,..."
      href="#Library">
  ...
  </map>
```

A1.4   Links

Inter-page and intra-page links are specified using `<a href=...>...`*content*`...</a>`
tags. The `<a>...</a>` combination should bracket a displayed element; usually, this element will be a fragment of text, but an image may be used. It is this displayable element
that acts as the link that a user may click.

The attributes of the link tag include `href` and `target`. The `href` attribute will define the
URI of the location of the linked resource. If this is an intra-page link (within the page),
the URI will identify an anchor point defined in the same page. If this is an inter-page link
(between pages), the URI will identify the other page, and optionally an anchor point
within that page.

The `target` attribute is optional. Normally, when a browser follows a link it replaces the
contents of its window with the contents of the referenced resource; however, the page
author can instead specify the use of a new window or, in a frameset context, can identify a
target frame. (Options for `target` include `_blank`, `_top` and `_self`, and an application-
specified window/frame name. The `_blank` option opens a new window where the linked
document will be displayed. Options `_top` and `_self` are mainly useful in framesets and
mean replace the complete frameset or replace the current frame contents. If a specific
name is used, an existing frame or window with that name will be used or, if necessary, a
new window with that name will be opened.)

Some examples of links are:

```
<a href="JobsPage.html">Want to work for us?</a>
<a href="CDSales.html"><img src=CD.gif width=40 height=40></a>
<a href="#TOP">Go back to top of page</a>
<a href="LegalStuf.html#RETURNS">Policy on return of goods</a>
<a href="/cgi-bin/Holiday?Dest=Canada" target="_blank">Holiday in
Canada</a>
```

As illustrated by the last example, links are not limited to static entities. A link can specify
the URI of a program that generates pages dynamically. In such a case, the link may
include a query string that passes parameters for a get request to that CGI program or
server-side script.

Anchor points have to be set for any intra-page links. An anchor point is defined using
an `<a>` tag with a `name` attribute: An example fragment of a page using intra links is:

```
<a name="TOP"><H1>Welcome to Acme Corporation</H1></a>
<ul>
```

```
<li><a href="#ABOUT">About Acme</a>
<li><a href="#INVEST">Information for potential investors
...
</ul>
<a name="ABOUT"><h2>About Acme</h2></a>
...
<a href="#TOP">Go to top</a>
...
```

The URIs used in inter-page links can be absolute or relative. An absolute URI will include the protocol (http of course), the hostname and port, and the path to a resource. A relative URI may simply be a page name (the referenced page is in the same directory as the page containing the <a> link); but it may consist of a pathname (same host and port, different part of filespace) or a relative pathname, e.g. ../otherbranch/thefile.html (go up one directory and look for a subdirectory called otherbranch; there we should find the file called thefile.html).

A1.5   Styles

The browser defines defaults for the display of text and the general appearance of a page. However, you can override these defaults and specify detailed aspects of how text should appear, you can also control aspects like background colors for the page and for tables (or specify the use of a tiled image background for a page).

These overrides of default styles can be specified in a number of ways. One approach is to include extra attribute data within the tags that appear in the page. For example, you can set general properties of a page through attributes in the <body> tag:

- background   specifies the URI for an image that will be used to tile the window area.

- bgcolor   alternative to background, sets the background color for the window.

- link, vlink, alink sets the colors for links, previously followed links, and activated links.

- text   sets the color for text displayed on the page.

Colors are specified either by entering a hex digit string that has the values for the red, green and blue components, or by naming a standard color. (It is best to stick to the 'standard' colors. The standard palette has more than 130 colors, with romantic names like 'cornflower', 'rose' and 'goldenrod'; details may still be available from http://www.brobstsystems.com/colors1.htm.) If you want to specify a color, you enter a hex string with a form like #DD30AA – strong red (DD), weak green (30), fairly strong blue (AA) – which means that this is a rather unattractive light mauve color.

The <font> tag can be used to change the appearance of subsequent text (up to the </font> tag). The font tag's attributes include:

- `size`   specified in the range 1..7 (normal font is size 3) or as an increment change relative to current size.

- `color`   name or rgb string.

An example is:

```
<font color=red size=+2>Important note</font>
```

Instead of using the `font` tag, you can simply add a style attribute to a paragraph or heading tag:

```
<h1 style="color:red; font-family:Courier">
<p style="font-size:14pt; color:blue">
```

It is unwise to change styles in random ways for particular elements in a page; the result is generally a messy appearance that distracts your readers. If you want to use special styles, it is best to use them consistently within a page. This can be achieved by adding 'style' definitions in the head section of the page, and then referencing these in the body.

A style directive for the page heading could be something like the following:

```
<style>
h1 {
  font-size :16pt;
  font-family: helvetica, sans-serif;
  color: #11EE33
}
h2 {
  font-size:14pt;
  test-align: right;
}
</style>
```

Such a style directive redefines the form of all h1 and h2 headings used in the document. You can define special paragraph classes:

```
P.note { font-size: 6pt;
  left-margin: 0.5cm; right-margin: 1.0cm;
  color: rgb(177, 202, 89)
}
```

This defines a new 'note'-type paragraph that uses small lettering. You would use it in your document by specifying the class name in the paragraph tag:

```
<p class="note">You should note the following ...
```

If styles are used seriously, they should be applied uniformly across an entire web site. This is achieved by moving the style definitions into a separate stylesheet file, and having a link to this file in the header of all pages. A fragment of such a stylesheet file is:

```
BODY {
   background-color: #FFFFFF;
   background-image: none;
   text: #000000
}
P.Subject1 {
   font-size:24pt;
   font-family: Arial, Helvetica, Sans-Serif;
   text-weight:bold;
   color:#ff0000;
   text-align:center
}
P.Subject2 {
   font-size:20pt;
   font-family: Arial, Helvetica, Sans-Serif;
   text-weight:bold;
   color:#cc0000;
   text-align:center
}

P EM { background: #aaffaa }
```

This stylesheet sets the background to white and default text to black for all pages. Two specialized heading-like paragraph styles are defined. The 'emphasis' tag is redefined so that <em> text has a green background.

Stylesheets should be left to a web designer. This isn't really the province of a programmer whose primary task is the development of serious server-side applications.

A1.6   Tables

Tables are extensively used in commercial sites. You will often need to display things like the contents of shopping cart; the normal flowing text presentation used by the browser is obviously inappropriate for such data.

Tables are not hard to define; they are just a little tiresome. A typical table definition has:

- A table tag with options like overall alignment, background color and a specification for any border lines to be drawn around table entries.

- A caption.

- A row with column headers for the columns in a table.

- Many rows with table data.
- An end table tag.

An example table definition is:

```
<table border=2 align=center>
<caption>Your shopping cart</caption>
<tr>
  <th>Product</th>
  <th>Quantity</th>
  <th>Unit cost</th>
</tr>
<tr>
  <td>Toothpaste</td>
  <td>1</td>
  <td>$3.45</td>
</tr>
<tr>
  <td>Soap 4-pack</td>
  <td>1</td>
  <td>$4.20</td>
</tr>
<tr>
  <td>Shampoo - extra body</td>
  <td>1</td>
  <td>$9.90</td>
</tr>
</table>
```

This will be displayed in a style something like the following:

Your shopping cart

Product	Quantity	Unit cost
Toothpaste	1	$3.45
Soap 4-pack	1	$4.20
Shampoo	1	$9.20

Table layouts can become quite a lot more elaborate because you can define table cells that span multiple rows and/or multiple columns. The table definitions illustrated earlier:

```
<table border>
<caption> Results for Sorcery 121</caption>
```

```
<tr>
  <td colspan=2 rowspan=2> </td>
  <th colspan=2 align=center> Examination</th>
</tr>
<tr>
  <th> Fail</th>
  <th> Pass</th>
</tr>
<tr align=center>
  <th rowspan=2> Practical</th>
  <th> Fail</th>
  <td> 35</td>
  <td> 3</td>
</tr>
<tr align=center>
  <th> Pass</th>
  <td> 29</td>
  <td> 163</td>
</tr>
</table>
```

will be displayed something like:

Results for Sorcery 121

		Examination	
		Fail	**Pass**
Practical	**Fail**	35	3
	Pass	29	163

A1.7   Forms

Forms are essential to commercial sites. A form groups a set of input fields through which a user can submit data for processing on your server. The form tag itself identifies the program that will process the submitted data; in addition, it specifies details of how the data are transferred and, optionally, can specify a target window or frame wherein the program's response is to be displayed. A form will contain a 'submit' action button; when this is activated, the browser collects all the form data and sends these data to a web server, and thence on to the designated server program.

Each input field in a form is named. The browser picks up the data value from the input field, and packages this value (as a string) along with the name into a name=value string. These strings are joined together, with ampersand (&) separator characters to form a string containing all the input form data. This string is incorporated in the request that the browser sends. There are restrictions on allowed characters; these restrictions are defined by the HTTP protocol used to submit the requests. The `name=value` data pairs can contain letters and digits, all other characters (space, commas, dollar signs etc.) must be encoded. A simple encoding scheme is applied; this converts spaces to plus signs, and all other characters to escape sequences that have a % sign followed by two hex digits. The browser performs the encoding when data are submitted; the program that processes the data must first reverse the encoding.

When forms were introduced, there was an attempt to make them familiar to people who had experience with dialogs as used in Windows and Macintosh systems. There are various types of input field, including simple text entry fields, checkboxes, radio button clusters (for mutually exclusive selections of options), various forms of popup or scrolling selection menus supporting single and/or multiple selections, and action buttons, such as the button that triggers the actual submission of the data. All these elements resemble the standard components in Windows/Macintosh dialogs.

The following form illustrates a variety of input components:

```
<h1>Fred's Pizzas, Order Form</h1>
Pizza size
<p>
<form action="http://www.dontdeliverpizzas.com/pizzaorder.cgi"
  name=pizzaform method=POST >
Regular <input type=radio name=p_size value=reg>
Family <input type=radio name=p_size value=fam>
Popular <input type=radio checked name=p_size value=pop>
<p>
Toppings
<select name=tops size=3 multiple>
  <option>Cheese
  <option>Pepperoni
  ...
  <option>Sun dried tomatoes
</select>
Extras
<select name=xtra size=1 multiple>
  <option selected>Coke
  <option>Ice cream
  ...
  <option>Salad
</select>
Delivery
<select name=deliv size=1 >
  <option selected>Express
  <option>Gorrila
  <option>Fat lady who sings
  <option>Female stripper
  ...
```

```
</select><br>
<hr>
<em>You MUST fill in the following fields:</em>
<p>
Your name
<input type=text size=20 maxlength=50 name=customer >
<p>
Address
<textarea name=address cols=40 rows =3>
</textarea>
<p>
email <input type=text size=20 maxlength=50 name=email>
<p>
phone <input type=text size=20 maxlength=20 name=phone>
<hr>
<input type=submit value="Place Order">
</form>
```

The form tag itself must contain an action attribute with the URI for the processing program and a method attribute. The method determines whether the request uses an HTTP get request or an HTTP post request. If a get is used, the form data are appended to the URI as a query string; if a post is used, the data form the body of a HTTP message.

The example uses:

- radio

A 'radio button' data entry field; the buttons in a radio button group all have the same name. In the example this is p_size (for pizza size). Each radio button must specify the value that is to be returned if it is selected ('reg', 'fam', 'pop'). One member of a radio button group should be specified as being preselected ('checked').

- select

There are three select input fields. Each select input field has a <select> start tag, a body with a group of option inputs, and a </select> tag. The <select> tag will contain a name, a size specification that controls its display, and an optional multiple attribute.

The first selection, named tops, permits multiple selections and is displayed as a scrollable text pane with three options shown. The second selection, xtras, is similar, but is displayed as a single button that can be activated to produce a popup menu showing its options. The third selection, the one defining delivery service, only permits a single selection.

Each option simply specifies the data displayed (the </option> tag is normally omitted). If an option is selected, its text element is returned as part of the input data. It is possible to specify an alternate value; for example, you could have <option value=1>Cheese<option value=2>Pepperoni etc. and get back the numeric values rather than the name strings.

A selection that has been used to make multiple choices will result in multiple entries in the generated input string, e.g. tops=Cheese&tops=Pepperoni&top=Sun+dried+tomatoes.

- `textfield`

A `textfield` is an input element for entry of a small amount of text. Other attributes in an input `type=text` field include `size` (number of characters displayed in browser window), `maxlength` (input truncated to this length if too long), and a name for the field. You can optionally specify an initial default value (`value=...`).

- `textarea`

A `textarea` is used for entry of larger amounts of text. The attributes in the tag specify the number of rows and the number of characters per row. A `TextArea` is displayed as a scrollable text box.

A `textarea` is specified using start and end tags; any content text between these tags acts as the initial content of this input field.

- `submit`

An input `type=submit` is displayed as an action button with the value string defining the button name.

When displaying a form, a browser will continue to use its default text flow layout mechanism and embed the input elements in with the continuing text. So normal content text can be used to define labels next to input fields. The example form would appear something like the following:

Fred's Pizzas, Order Form

Pizza size

Regular ○ Family ○ Popular ◉

Toppings | Cheese / Pepperoni / Ground beef | ▾ Extras Coke ▴▾ Delivery Express ▾

You MUST fill in the following fields:

Your name [   ]

Address [   ]

email [   ]

phone [   ]

[Place Order]

Have a good day.

The form displays produced using this default flow layout mechanism are rather amateurish looking. You will typically have to use tables to help lay out the labels and input fields in your forms. For example, the following table-structured form definition:

```
<p>
Please supply details so that we can select appropriate items
from our great range of products.
<form action="/cgi-bin/Select.cgi" method=post>
```

```
<table align=center border=2>
<tr>
  <th align=left>Your name</th>
  <td><input type=text name=Name size=20></td>
</tr>
<tr>
  <th align=left>Your address</th>
  <td><textarea cols=20 rows=2 name=Address></textarea></td>
</tr>
<tr><th align=left>Your age</th>
  <td><select name=age size=1>
    <option value=kid>Less than 14
    <option value=teenager>14-19
    ...
    </select>
  </td>
</tr>

<tr>
  <td>Male<input type=radio name=sex checked value=Male></td>
  <td>Female<input type=radio name=sex value=Female></td>
</tr>
<tr><td colspan=2 align=center><input type=submit value="Submit
details"></td></tr>
</table>
</form>
```

results in a better looking form display:

e-Mart New Customer Page

Please supply details so that we can select appropriate items from our great range of products.

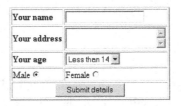

A.2 JavaScript essentials

JavaScript has essentially nothing to do with Java. It started as 'Livescript' and changed its name when the Java craze set in strongly in 1995. JavaScript has aliases JScript and ECMAScript (there are small differences among these scripting languages, but they are really just dialects of the same language).

It is a traditional scripting language, which means that it is typeless and a little sloppy about variable declarations. Scripts typically start with declarations of global variables, but these are not essential. If a script interpreter encounters a variable that you forgot to declare, it will obligingly introduce a global for you. This makes it easy to whip up code quickly (and easy to create buggy JavaScript programs). Variables don't have defined data types. A variable can hold values of different types (string, integer, real number, Boolean) at different stages of a function's execution. The interpreter will automatically convert data as required. A variable may start holding a string extracted from an input field in a form; when this is used in a numeric expression, the interpreter automatically converts the string to number (a zero value is obtained if no conversion is possible).

JavaScript's syntactic structures place it in the overall Algol/Pascal/C/Java group (opinions vary; I see an Object Pascal dialect as being the most likely parent language). You can define functions and even simple classes with public data members and public member functions (it is quite rare to have to define your own JavaScript classes). Functions use sequence, selection, and iterative structures that will be familiar to any who has programmed in Pascal, Java or even Visual Basic. Like other imperative languages, calculations are expressed as sequences of assignment statements. Expressions combine data values with operators. JavaScript has a repertoire of operators (+, -, /, *) similar to those in C, Java etc.; the operators have the usual precedence rules.

There are a few built-in functions. More importantly, there are a number of provided classes. Many of these are singletons (only one instance of the class exists). These classes allow scripts to access details of the browser, to modify windows, to access documents in windows, and to read data from forms embedded in the documents. The classes that provide access to browser features inevitably vary. The consequence is that JavaScript code is browser-dependent. If you want to achieve elaborate visual effects that are portable across browsers, you will have to incorporate runtime conditional tests to identify the browser together with code fragments that are then specific to each common browser. (The simple code needed to check data in input fields is fortunately independent of browser type.)

Browsers incorporate interpreters for JavaScript. Script interpreters are always fairly slow, but this hardly matters. JavaScript is not intended for elaborate calculations; instead its roles are simple data checking and the production of pretty visual effects. Performance is not an issue.

JavaScript code is incorporated in an HTML page as:

- Global variable declarations (included in the page header section).

- Function declarations (also included in the page header section).

- 'Main line code' fragments that are executed when the browser's page formatting engine encounters JavaScript statements embedded in the content text.

- Code fragments, mostly calls to functions, which are embedded in HTML tags.

- Code fragments that are embedded the header or among the content text. Sometimes such code is necessary to initialize data and perform tasks like preloading images. Such fragments could be assembled into a function that is invoked as the page is loaded.

The interesting use of JavaScript is to give your page some interactive functionality. This is achieved via the fragments incorporated as attributes in HTML tags.

User interaction with any graphical user interface (GUI) is invariably handled through an event-handling mechanism. The user moves the mouse cursor across GUI elements, thereby generating events that represent its entry and exit from each element. The user selects items from lists, generating item selection events. The user clicks the mouse button while the cursor is over a button visual component, and thereby generates an action event.

This general event model has been specialized for use with page displays in browsers. The browser has the code that handles the users actions. It generates 'events' that are sent to GUI elements defined by specific HTML tags in the document. Most events relate to input elements in forms or to links, and the browser can identify the appropriate element positioned under the cursor.

Different HTML tags are associated with specific types of events. For example, links (`<a href=...>...</a>` tags) respond to 'mouse over' and 'click' events. Text input fields (`<input type=text ...>` and textarea) allow the user to select text; the action of selecting text can be used to generate a 'selection' event that may be used to trigger some processing. Almost all input fields in a form can sense 'click' events. Text input fields and selections for multiple choices can detect when they are initially picked (by a mousedown button action) for data entry, and when they cease to be the selected input element. Other notable events in the life of a page are the acts of loading and unloading the body; these too can be detected and used to trigger the execution of a JavaScript function.

For example, a page author might want extra information displayed whenever the user moves the cursor over the links in a page. This could be achieved by arranging for JavaScript functions to be called whenever 'mouse over' events are sent by the browser to display elements corresponding to a link (text fragment or image). The extra information displayed might be as simple as a string shown in the browser's status box (bottom line of the browser window). This arrangement is achieved by having onclick attributes in each link, with the value for the attribute being a fragment of JavaScript code asking the browser to display a specific message in the status bar.

A2.1   JavaScript coding constructs

The main sections of JavaScript code will consist of global variable and function declarations. These should occur within a `<script>...</script>` tag element in the header part of the HTML page. The script tag takes an attribute specifying the scripting language (only common choice is JavaScript). The following example illustrates the script tag:

```
<script language="javascript">
<!--
var pizzasize;
function emptyField(textObj)
{
  if(textObj.value.length == 0) return true;

  for(var i=0; i<textObj.value.length;i++) {
```

```
        ch = textObj.value.charAt(i);
        if(ch != ' ' && ch != '\t') return false;
        }
    return true;
    }

    ...
    -->
</script>
```

Conventionally, the actual script is enclosed within HTML comment tags (`<-- ... -->`). Archaic browsers that don't understand script tags can then ignore the script elements.

Variables have names that start with letters and contain letters, underscores and digits. Variables should be declared using the `var` keyword. A declaration outside of a function body is a global. Local variables may be declared within functions, or within inner blocks, or even in loop constructs. A `var` declaration simply names a variable or a set of variables; type data are not required (and cannot be specified).

Assignment statements take the usual form: *variable* = *expression*. JavaScript has C's additional assignment operators such as +=, *= etc. Expressions are built up from constants and variables combined with operators. JavaScript has the arithmetic operators (+, -, /, *, %), a string concatenation operator (+), comparison operators (==, !=, >=, <=), logical operators (&&, ||, !), and for completion it even has bit operators (operating on 32 bit values, <<, >>, &, |, ^).

Functions are built in the normal way as a sequence of assignment statements, selection statements and iterative statements. Semicolons may be used as statement separators, but interpreters happily tolerate their omission. JavaScript does not possess a `case` statement, but does have the usual conditional statements: `if(condition)action` and `if(condition)action1 else action2`. There is a `while` iterative construct, and a C-style for loop (`for(initialization; termination test; repeat action)`). C-style `break` and `continue` statements may be used in loop constructs. JavaScript has preserved the Pascal `with` clause; this can simplify code that must set many elements of a struct (class instance). There is a specialized `foreach` iterative construct that allows access to each data member in a struct.

Function declarations take the form:

```
function name(arg1, arg2, ...) { body }
```

(Again, the only unusual feature is the lack of type data). Comments use C++/Java style with the `//` escape sequence introducing a line comment and block comments taking the form `/*... */`.

Objects have public data members and member functions. The '.' member access operator is used. The code fragment shown above is working with a 'text object' that holds text data entered in an `<input type=text ...>` form element or a `textarea`. Such a text object has a `value` data member (`textObj.value`) which is a string (character array). The `charAt()` member function can be used to obtain the character at a specific point in a string (so we get the expression: `textObj.value.charAt(i)`).

A2.2   System-supplied classes and objects

You can write complex programs in JavaScript. The language supports arrays, and user-defined classes. There are function libraries, including the whole set of mathematics functions like `sqrt` and `atan`. But the vast majority of JavaScript code is intended simply to apply checks to data or adjust the appearance of elements in the GUI display. Such code works largely in terms of instances of system-supplied classes.

The system-supplied classes include:

- **Navigator**

Naturally a singleton class, the only instance of class `navigator` will contain data members and member functions that relate to the browser running the script.

Its data members include `appName` and `appVersion`; both are strings, and they contain name and version data characterizing the browser.

- **Window**

The main `window` object contains data members and member functions relating to the window in which the HTML document with the script is being displayed. A script may create additional windows.

A window includes data members for its name, an array of frames if it is a frameset window, a history object, and a location object. Its member functions include functions for putting up alert boxes and simple dialogs, and for displaying text in a status bar.

- **History, Location** and **Frame**

These objects are owned by a window. The `history` object offers member functions that cause the browser to move 'back' or 'forward' in the history list, so changing the currently displayed page. A `location` object provides access to details of the current document – the name of the host from which it was obtained, the port, the pathname to the file etc.

- **Document**

A document object has numerous data members including members defining colors for links, background color and text color. (You can do silly things like have code that changes these colors in response to a user's mouse actions on the page.) Other data members include an array of data-defining forms contained within a document, another containing all the links, and a third with all the anchor point definitions. Member functions include an open function that lets code open new windows.

- **Form**

A `form` object's data members include the strings `action`, `method` and `target`. There is also an array data member, `elements`, that contains all the components in the form – its various input controls such as checkboxes, buttons and text inputs. These are listed in the order in which they occur in a form, so if your form (`theForm`) has two input text fields and a submit button these could be accessed as `theForm.elements[0]`, `theForm.elements[1]` and `theForm.elements[2]`.

• Button, Submit, Reset, Text, Textarea, Password, Select, Checkbox and Radio
The instances of these classes represent input elements as found in forms. Their data members include strings for the name and value of the input element. Other data vary. For example, a checkbox has data members that specify whether it is currently checked and whether it is checked by default. A select object has a data member defining the number of options it contains, and an array of options objects.

The methods for these objects vary. They correspond to the events that can be associated with an object of that type. Thus, button objects and submit objects have a click member function (there is no need to wait for a user, you can write JavaScript code to click the submit button as soon as some data have been entered in a form). A text object has methods focus (set it to accept keyed input from the user), blur (stop accepting input) and select (pick some part of the text).

• String
A string object will contain an array of characters (not directly accessible). Its only public data member is a length value. The class defines simple functions for accessing characters, and case shifting the string (e.g. to lower case). Other string member functions create new strings (e.g. the italics member function returns a string consisting of the original string embedded between <i> and </i> tags.

There is a natural ownership relationship among objects that reflects the basic structure of a displayed HTML page. A window holds a document; the document contains a named form; the form has several named input fields. Code in the document can explicitly reference a specific input field via a path name (e.g. window.document.form_name. inputfield_name).

Member functions should obviously be invoked on objects. So, if you want to display a warning message in a little alert box, you need to invoke window.alert(message). However, JavaScript interpreters are very understanding, and it is sufficient to invoke alert(message): the interpreter will work out which object should handle the alert request!

A2.3   Events

Events start as user actions with the mouse or keyboard. The browser interprets these and will forward events to function elements within a page that have registered interest in the events. For example, the browser can detect mouse clicks when the cursor is over a button, checkbox, radio button, link, text input or select input. The various forms of buttons and checkboxes can elect to receive 'click' events. If the mouse click did occur in such an input element, the browser will invoke the 'onclick' code associated with the input element. Mousedown events in text input fields and select input fields represent the user starting to input data into such fields; the input field is becoming the 'focus' for subsequent inputs. Again, if the input element has registered an interest, the browser will invoke its 'onfocus' code.

The event types and possible listeners are:

- Click

Used by button, reset, submit, radio and checkbox input fields, and by links. The code invoked can produce some immediate response to the user's action.

- MouseOver

Used by links; the code invoked typically does something that provides the user with more detail about the linked resource (e.g. by writing a message in the browser's status bar).

- Submit

Used by forms. The invoked code typically checks the form data. If problems are found with the data, the code will display some explanation in a dialog box and abort the actual data submission step.

- Change, Focus, Blur

These are used by text, textarea and select input fields. A focus event is generated when the input field acquires input focus; a blur event is sent when focus is transferred to some other input. A change event occurs every time text is added to a text field or the option selection is varied in a select input field. (It would be an unusual form processing application to need to monitor changes at this level of detail.)

- Select

Select events can be passed to text and textarea input fields whenever the user does a text selection action.

- Load, Unload

These events are handled by the window object. Interest in such events is registered via the body tag. A load event allows code to be executed as soon as the page has been loaded. An unload event occurs when the user tries to move on to another page. Many pernicious web sites have code that picks up unload events and responds by opening additional windows that continue to try to advertise the web site's services.

Event handlers appear as extra attributes in the appropriate HTML tags. The attribute name will identify the event type of interest (some tags can handle several types of event); the attribute value will be a fragment of inline JavaScript code. In most cases this inline code will be a call to one of the JavaScript functions defined in the <script>...</script> section in the page header. For example:

```
<body bgcolor=#ffffff onunload="displayMoreTiresomeAdvertising()">
<form action="/cgi-bin/ProcessOrder.pl" method="post"
  onsubmit="return validateOrder()">
<a href="OnSpecial.htm"
  onMouseOver="{ window.status='Check out todays specials!!!'; }">
```

A2.4 JavaScript for data validation

The pizza form illustrated earlier can be enhanced with JavaScript for data validation. Obviously, the pizza supplier cannot fulfill an order that fails to provide contact details such as name, address and phone number (you cannot verify that the details are correct, or even plausible; all you can do is check that all essential fields contain some input data). Processing can be a little more elaborate; in this example, the script code calculates the cost of the pizza order and displays this cost in a dialog that asks the purchaser to confirm that the order should be submitted. Other minor uses of scripting involve text displays in the status bar that are shown whenever the user selects a text input field.

These additions require very minor changes to the HTML page shown earlier. Some event handlers must be added as 'on-X' attributes in specific HTML tags:

```
<h1>Fred's Pizzas, Order Form</h1>
Pizza size
<p>
<form action="http://www.dontdeliverpizzas.com/pizzaorder.cgi"
  name=pizzaform
  onSubmit= "return confirmPizza(pizzaform)"
  method=POST >
Regular <input type=radio name=p_size value=reg>
...
Delivery
<select name=deliv size=1
  onfocus="{ window.status='Choose among delivery options!';}" >
<option selected>Express
...
</select><br>
<hr>
<em>You MUST fill in the following fields:</em>
<p>
Your name
<input type=text size=20 maxlength=50 name=customer
  onfocus="{ window.status='remember to tell us your name';}">
<p>
...
```

The onSubmit code, in the form tag, invokes the confirmPizza function, passing a reference to the form as an argument (this is done by have a name specified for the form, and then using this name as the argument).

The code for confirming the order will first check that there are data in the input fields for the name, address etc. Then a price is calculated and displayed in an 'OK or Cancel'-style dialog. This code involves a number of separate JavaScript functions:

```
<script language="javascript">
<!--
var pizzasize;
function emptyField(textObj) { ... }
```

```
function basecost(radioObj) { ... }

function toppingscost(selectObj) { ... }

function extrascost(selectObj) { ... }

function deliverycost(selectObj) { ... }

function confirmPizza(formObj)
{
  if(emptyField(formObj.customer) ) {
    // Use window.alert() to inform user of error
    alert("You forgot to enter your name");
    return false;
    }

  // Similar checks on address, email, and phone fields
  ...
  if(emptyField(formObj.phone) ) {
    alert("We need your phone");
    return false;
    }

  // work out cost
  total = basecost(formObj.p_size);
  total +=toppingscost(formObj.tops);
  total +=extrascost(formObj.xtra);
  total +=deliverycost(formObj.deliv);

  // use confirm method (in class window) to put up a
  // dialog with "OK" and "Cancel" options; dialog returns true
  // if OK selected
  return confirm("The cost is " + total + ", place order?");

}

// -->
</script>
```

A reference to the pizza form will be passed as an argument to the confirmpizza function; the form argument is treated as a data structure in the body of the code. The names of the input fields in this form are known; they are treated as field names within the formObj data structure. First, a reference to the input field 'customer' is passed to the emptyField function.

This function is defined as:

```
      function emptyField(textObj)
      {
        if(textObj.value.length == 0) return true;
        for(var i=0; i<textObj.value.length;i++) {
          ch = textObj.value.charAt(i);
          if(ch != ' ' && ch != '\t') return false;
        }
        return true;
      }
```

This function is passed a reference to an object that will be a text input field (either and `<input type=text ...>` or a `TextArea` object). The `value` member of a text object contains the input text. The `emptyfield` function returns true if the length of the content text is zero. If there is some content text, the loop checks for a character other than space or tab; any non-whitespace character is accepted as being sufficient to make this a valid input. (More restrictive tests could be applied, such as checks for alphabetic character strings.)

If all input fields contain acceptable input text, the `confirmpizza` function continues by calculating the cost of the pizza. The total cost is obtained by subsidiary functions that determine base cost, cost of extras and toppings, and delivery cost; these costs are determined by the data selections in the radio button cluster and the selection boxes. First, the base cost is derived from the pizza size collection in the radio button cluster. A reference to the cluster (`formObj.p_size`) is passed to the `basecost` function:

```
      function basecost(radioObj)
      {
        pizzasize = 1;
        if(radioObj[0].checked) cost = 7.00; // regular
        if(radioObj[1].checked) {
          cost = 11.00; // family
          pizzasize = 2;
        }
        if(radioObj[2].checked) {
          cost = 15.00; // popular
          pizzasize = 3;
        }
        return cost;
      }
```

A radio cluster object like p_size has an array representing the individual choices; these may be checked to determine the selection made. The `basecost` function sets a global variable `pizzasize`; the value of this variable is used in the `toppingscost` function. This function is given a reference to the `tops` selection element in the form; it loops through the options, incrementing the cost for each option chosen:

```
function toppingscost(selectObj)
{
  tcost = 0.0;
  for(var i=0;i<selectObj.length;i++)
    if(selectObj[i].selected) tcost += 0.50*pizzasize;
  return tcost;
}
```

The other functions, extrascost and deliverycost, again work with selections and calculate costs depending on the choices made:

```
function extrascost(selectObj)
{
  ecost = 0;
  if(selectObj[0].selected) ecost += 1.70; // Coke
  ...
  return ecost;
}

function deliverycost(selectObj)
{
  if(selectObj[0].selected) Dcost = 1.50; // Express
  else if(selectObj[1].selected) Dcost = 15.0; // Gorrila
  ...
  return Dcost;
}
```

A2.5   JavaScript for visual effects

The other use of JavaScript is the creation of visual effects. Such effects should not be used on the order form and response pages of a commercial site, but can be valuable in other parts of a web site. JavaScript can be used to provide popup menus that assist navigation, rollover effects on tables and other elements, and even elaborate animations. All such effects have costs, like bulkier pages and slower downloading; they should be used with discretion.

The example here illustrates 'rollover' effects with tables. The table purports to be part of a web page for a specialist supplier of antiques. The table is made up of picture elements, some of which also function as links. These links listen for mouse events, specifically mouseover and mouseout events. When a user moves the cursor over a picture, the associated link gets a mouseover event; this is handled by changing the display so that it shows extra information in another portion of the table. The display is reset to its initial state when the link receives a mouseout event.

The HTML for the table definition is:

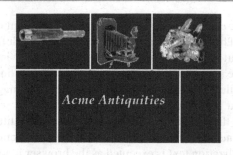 

```
<table border=0 cellpadding=0 cellspacing=0 width=600>
<tr>
  <td valign=bottom align=center>
  <a href="#Sci"
    ONMOUSEOUT="resetText()"
    ONMOUSEOVER="chooseText(1)">
  <img src=science.gif border="0"
    width="180" height="140"
    Alt="Science">
  </a>
  <a href="#Photo"
    ONMOUSEOUT="resetText()"
    ONMOUSEOVER="chooseText(2)">
  <img src=photo.gif border="0"
    width="150" height="140"
    Alt="Photo">
  </a>
  <a href="#Rocks"
    ONMOUSEOUT="resetText()"
    ONMOUSEOVER="chooseText(3)">
  <img src=rock.gif border="0"
    width="170" height="140"
    Alt="Rocks">
  </a>
  </td>

</tr>
<tr>
  <td valign=bottom align=center>
  <img src=side.gif width="100" height="180">
  <img src=home.gif width="300" height="180" name="text">
  <img src=side.gif width="100" height="180">
  </td>
</tr>
...
</table>
```

The first row comprises three links, each using an image as the link element (the example uses intra-page links , e.g. href="#Photo"). The links have attributes that define code that handles mouseover and mouseout events. The event-handling code is defined in JavaScript functions declared at the start of the HTML page. These functions change the picture that is displayed in the middle of the second row in the table. The image tag for the changeable picture is named so that it can be referenced from the code.

The JavaScript code that performs the dynamic visual trickery consists of a little bit of code to set up a collection of images, and the chooseText and resetText functions called in response to mouse events. The initialization text is executed as the browser loads the page. It defines a new ImageArray class (the function ImageArray serves as both a class definition and a constructor). An ImageArray holds three Image objects (image objects are provided in JavaScript; such objects represent the attributes of an <img> tag). The three entries in the ImageArray are pictures that contain differing advertising messages for display in the middle row of the table. The rest of the initialization code specifies the source files with the images.

```
<script>
<!--
// Create an image array
   choices = new ImageArray(3);
   // Specify the source images
   choices[1].src = "sciwords.gif"
   choices[2].src = "photowords.gif"
   choices[3].src = "rockwords.gif"
   // Define "class" ImageArray as something that owns an array of Images
   function ImageArray(n) {
     this.length = n
     for (var i = 1; i<=n; i++) {
       this[i] = new Image()
     }
     return this
   }
   // Switch named image to use select image from choices ImageArray
   function chooseText(num) {
     document.images.text.src = choices[num].src
   }
   // Rset original image
   function resetText() {
     document.images.text.src = "home.gif"
   }
}
// -->
</script>
```

The chooseText and resetText functions simply change the source specified for the image that makes up the main part of the middle row in the table.

The above example is a little unusual for visual gimmickry code in that it is not browser-dependent. Popup menus probably constitute the most common use of JavaScript; these work by controlling the visibility of elements placed in different 'layers' of a page. A menu's visibility can be controlled through mouseover and mouseout events for an image link in the main document layer (such a link doesn't have to go anywhere, it is simply acting as an event handler). Browsers vary in the document structures that they provide and in the functions that are used to manipulate the visibility of elements. However, the code is fairly standardized, consisting of separate segments for different browser types. If you view the source code of a page that uses popup menus, you will get a version of this code. You can adapt any of the better-written versions of the popup menu code for use in your own pages; the code can be made completely generic, with menu entries and corresponding URL links being defined simply as names in initialized JavaScript string arrays.

Popup menus have some valid uses, as do simple rollover effects. More elaborate JavaScript code for animations can amuse, but really such coding is a waste of time. Your web designer colleague will be a lot more productive using multimedia tools, such as Shockwave.

Appendix B

Active Server Pages: ASP (scripting)

Microsoft's Active Server Page (ASP) technology and the Internet Information Server application together represent an alternative basis for server-side development in Windows environments; one that may be attractive for organizations that prefer to use standard Microsoft products. The style of ASP server coding is somewhere between PHP and scriptlet-style JSP. ASP pages contain script code embedded in HTML text, and the code makes heavy use of a few predefined objects such as 'request', 'response', 'session' and 'application' objects. ASP is almost a simple to use as PHP, and so competes for all those lightweight sites where PHP is appropriate. Microsoft's newer ASP.NET, reviewed briefly in Appendix C, offers a more complex, richer development environment; it is suitable for the more challenging web sites and for creating XML-based Web Services.

Windows systems incorporate a web server. Modern variants such as Windows 2000 contain Microsoft's Internet Information Server (IIS), while earlier systems may have the more limited Personal Web Server (PWS). In the typical 'out of the box' configuration, the web server component is disabled. It can be enabled through the Add Programs control in the Control Panel (you will need your Windows installation CD available); the site http://www.w3schools.com/asp/asp_install.asp has instructions in its ASP section on how to install IIS or PWS on all possible varieties of Windows operating systems. One caution: after installation on a Windows 2000 or similar system, the IIS server, a file transfer (ftp) server and a mail handler (SMTP) server become automatically started services. This means that whenever you are connected to the Internet, these services are active. This may violate your contract with your local Internet Service Provider (ISP); ISPs often have different charging mechanisms for home users and for commercial organizations that host web services. Furthermore, it increases your exposure to attack by hackers who will exploit any weaknesses that exist in IIS versions that do not incorporate the latest security patches. You should use the Services control in the Control Panel to change the setting so that IIS and the others are manually launched, and so will only be active when you are experimenting with web applications.

The default installation script results in the creation of an Inetpub folder on your main disk; this contains directories used by the file transfer, mail server and web server programs. Its wwwroot subdirectory contains initial sample pages. For simple learning exercises, it is sufficient to place all materials (static HTML pages, ASP script pages for dynamic content, images etc.) in the wwwroot directory and its subdirectories.

Once you have IIS installed, you can aim your Internet Explorer browser at http:// localhost. You will see pages that document the administrative controls for your IIS server, and that describe how to implement ASP pages. This online reference material contains terse but quite complete documentation on all aspects of server side programming with ASP.

The most commonly used 'scripting' language for ASP pages is a simplified dialect of Microsoft's Visual Basic. Several alternatives are supported, including a server-side variation of JavaScript and Perl. (Support for VBScript and JavaScript is built in; other languages require installation of add on components and DLL libraries). As noted, VBScripts utilize the system-supplied session, response and other objects; these can be supplemented by additional COM (Component Object Model) objects that are instances of classes implemented in languages such as C++. Such extensions add power, but organization is somewhat complicated. Again, the newer .NET technologies are superior; server-side components are written using programming languages that are richer than VBScript (the choices include a much extended Basic, and C# – a kind of safe subset of C++); development environments like VisualStudio.NET assist with deployment.

B.1 ASP basics: 'request' and 'response' objects

Simple ASP web sites can be built with scripting code that utilizes the supplied request and response objects. The request object holds the incoming data; the response object is associated with the buffers where the response message is assembled from predefined HTML tags, content text, and text that is generated by the script. Inevitably, these objects have some similarities to the request and response objects that you encounter in the Java servlet/JSP models. These objects support operations and have data attributes. They also own 'collections'; for example, a request object has collections for holding data from cookies, name/ value data from a form, and data defining server properties. These collections act a bit like Perl associative arrays: a name (e.g. name of a form field, or name of a server variable) can be used as an index into the collection, and the result is the value associated with the name.

The Request object:

- Owns
  - Collections for cookie, form, query string, and server variables.
  - A 'total bytes' attribute that holds the number of bytes in the body of a HTTP request message.

- Does
  - BinaryRead: function that can be used to read content data of request message (for applications that upload files etc.).

Similarly, the Response object:

- Owns
  - A cookies collection.
  - A large set of properties including those used to set the content type of the response (text/html, text/plain etc.), the expiry date, charset details and so on.

- Does
  - AddHeader, Redirect, Write, BinaryWrite, ...

The following example, illustrating basic ASP programming, is a reprise of the 'Hunger' example from the PHP section (see Figure 6.1). This little web application helps hungry web surfers determine the location of the nearest McDonald's restaurant. This example requires that an HTTP get operation display a simple form with a map picture that is used as an <input type=image ...> field in the form. Such an input field acts as a submit button; when a user clicks the image, the coordinates of the click point are returned as part of the next HTTP request. This is a post request to the same ASP page; in the code that handles a post request, the input coordinates are compared with the coordinates of known restaurants.

The page, Hunger.asp, contains:

- The declaration of a function that finds the closest of a set of points to a point defined by (*x*, *y*) argument data; the function prints a label associated with the chosen point.

- Scripting code that:
  - Determines the request type.
  - If it is a get request, the generated response is the predefined HTML code defining the simple form.
  - If it is a post request, the generated response contains some predefined HTML and the address data obtained from the auxiliary function.

The VBScript code for this example is:

```
<%@ LANGUAGE = VBScript %>
<%
' VBScript code within <% ... %> tags
' VBScript comments start with single quote
' Definition of subroutine and data table that are
' used to define locations of local McDonald's Restaurants
' sub name(arguments) ... end sub
sub findMac(x, y)
    dim xcoord(5), ycoord(5), address(5)
' Data defining the location of McDonald's Restaurants within the
' area associated with display map
' (Coordinates are the pixel cords of image points corresponding
' to restaurant locations)
' (VBScript uses () for array subscripting, not [])
'subscripts in VBScript are 0...n so this array has six elements
```

```vbscript
          xcoord(0) = 130
          ycoord(0) = 310
          address(0) = "Crown Street Mall, Wollongong"

          ...

          xcoord(5) = 145
          ycoord(5) = 383
          address(5) = "266 Cowper, Warrawong"

' Simple VBScript to find reference point closest to (x,y) arguments
' (sqr function is VBScript's square root, the full list of VBScript
' functions is not included in the local ASP documentation, but the
' documentation does include a link to a part of the Microsoft Developer
' Network site that does include a table of VBScript functions)
          dim ndx
          dim choice
          dim mindist
          mindist = 1.0E+6
' for index = start to end do ... next : standard VBScript counting loop
          for ndx = 0 to 5
            dim dx, dy, val, dist
            dx = x - xcoord(ndx)
            dy = y - ycoord(ndx)
            val = dx*dx + dy*dy
            dist = sqr( val)
' if ... then ... end if : standard VBScript conditional construct
            if dist < mindist then
              choice = ndx
              mindist = dist
            end if
          next
' write text into the buffer used to build response
          response.write(address(choice))
        end sub
%>
<%
' Main part of ASP page starts here!
' Determine request method
' If get, display page with clickable map
' If post, accept selected x,y coords and work out location
' of nearest McDonald's.
' If anything else, well complain unknown request method (put, options, ...)

          dim   req_method
```

```
' Lookup request method in the "servervariables" associative array
    req_method = request.servervariables("REQUEST_METHOD")
    if req_method = "GET" then
' Canned text defining submit form with its map input button
%>
<html><head><title>Hunger!</title></head>
<body bgcolor=white>
<form action=hunger.asp method=post>
<table frame=border rules=all align=center>
<caption>Desperate for a Big Mac?</caption>
<tr>
<td rowspan=2><input type=image src=iwol.jpg name=map></td>
<td><img src=mac.jpg></td>
</tr>
<tr><th>Click on map</th></tr>
</table>
</form></body></html>
<%
' Pick up with next part of scripting code, now test for "Post" method
' note the form of the equality test within the conditional
    elseif req_method = "POST" then
' If it is a post method, then output standard response text with a
' little dynamically generated insert obtained by invoking the findMac
' subroutine
%>
<html><head><title>Your nearest MacDonalds ... </title></head>
<body>
<h1 align=center>Your nearest MacDonalds</h1>
<p align=center>
<img src=mac.jpg>
<p align=center style="font-size:24pt; color:blue">
<%
    dim x, y
' Pick up the map.x, map.y input data (the data take the image name
' with .x, and .y appended)
    x = request.form("map.x")
    y = request.form("map.y")
' Invoke the findMac function, it adds a line to the response
    call findMac(x,y)
%>
<p align=center>
<img src=mac.jpg>
<p>
</body></html>
<%
```

```
    else
' It is some unusual request method like Options, Head, Put,
' Ignore it
%>
<html><head><title>Error!</title></head>
<body bgcolor=white>
<p>
Cannot handle requests of type <%= req_method %>.
</body></html>
<%
    end if
' Terminating if ... then .. elseif ... else construct that tests
' request method
%>
```

The example code shown, together with two image files (the map, `iwol.jpg`, and a McDonald's arches decorative image, `mac.jpg`), could be deployed in a subdirectory `Examples` of the `C:\Inetpub\wwwroot` directory. The page can be accessed by pointing a browser at `http://localhost/Examples/Hunger.asp`.

B.2 Adding 'session state'

Real web applications invariably need to maintain client data. It is the same old HTTP protocol underneath, so the same old hacks emerge for handling client state. If you have a limited and predefined set of users who will be accessing a site, you can use HTTP authentication to control a login sequence, and then in your ASP scripts you can access the `REMOTE_USER` server variable. The user identity can then serve as a filename, or a key for a temporary database table where state data can be maintained. (With IIS, this form of authentication integrates with the Windows NT user database; the accounts used by clients must be Windows accounts defined by the administrator.) The login mechanism is fairly limited in its range of applications; but the alternative of hidden fields in forms is always possible. Hidden fields have their limits; they only work when your state data are acquired through a sequence of forms that must be completed in succession, and the supposedly hidden data are actually quite open to view and modification. Where web site exploration is freer and hidden fields are inappropriate, application-specific cookies, whose values hold session data, may be used; but these have the same disadvantages of exposure and susceptibility to modification.

The preferred solution is to use session variables in the server and cookies for user identification. The ASP reference manual from Microsoft states:

*ASP provides a **unique** solution for the problem of managing session information. Using the ASP Session object and a special user ID generated by your server, you can create clever applications that identify each visiting user and collect information that your application can then use to track user preferences or selections.*

Sessions, maintained in association with an automatically set user identification cookie, are enabled by default with ASP. When the first access is made to an ASP page in the site, the ASP interpreter in IIS will create a user identification cookie and a 'session' object associated with this cookie (the mechanism is identical to that used in servlet/JSP systems). A session object can hold a collection of name/value pairs set by ASP scripts (much like a servlet session object's 'attribute' collection). The automatically generated cookie is set to expire when the browser terminates; the associated IIS resident data structure is automatically garbage collected if left unused for a long period of time (default is about 30 minutes). An ASP script can discard the data structure as soon as the data processing is complete.

The Session object:

● Owns:
  – Collections for 'contents' and 'static objects' (the 'static objects' collection might contain something like a database connection used on a per-session basis; 'contents' are name/value pairs set by application code).
  – Attributes for session identifier, timeout and 'location' (data similar to Java internationalization information).

● Does:
  – 'Abandon': releases all session data at end of current script (rather than wait for timeout).
  – `Contents.Remove`, `Contents.RemoveAll` (clear specified item or all items in the contents collection).

One ASP page can place data into the contents collection of its associated session object; these data can then be picked up later by some other ASP page that gets accessed later.

The following example is a reworking of the e-mart example used in Chapter 6 (see Figure 6.2). The PHP version illustrated the use of hidden form fields to hold name and address data; here, these data will be held in the session object.

This web application consists of an `Emart.asp` page and a `Page2.asp` page. The `Emart.asp` page handles a get request by displaying a form that allows users to enter their name, address, age group and sex. The data are posted back to the same `Emart.asp` page; the post request is handled by saving the name and address data (in the associated session's contents collection) and the generation of a form with multiple checkboxes that allow selection of purchases. The data selected in this second form are posted to the `Page2.asp` page. The code on this page simply lists the selected purchase items, along with name and address data retrieved from the session object. The form's appearance is essentially the same as the versions shown in Figure 6.2.

Although conceptually the `Emart.asp` page represents a single unit, its code is split among several files. The actual Emart.asp pages is:

```
<%
' Determine request method
    dim   req_method
```

```
    req_method = request.servervariables("REQUEST_METHOD")
    if req_method = "GET" then
%>
<!-- #include file ="GetEMart.inc" -->
<%
    else
%>
<!-- #include file ="PostEMart.inc" -->
<%
    end if
%>
```

The page is essentially a simple structure: '*if get request then generate first form else process input*'. The details would obscure this structure, so they have been moved into separate include files.

The GetEMart.inc include file contains simply static HTML:

```
<html><head><title>e-Mart New Customer Page</title></head>
<body>
<h1 align=center>e-Mart New Customer Page</h1>
<p>
Please supply details so that we can select appropriate items
from our great range of products.
<form action=EMart.asp method=post>
<table align=center border=2>
<tr>
  <th align=left>Your name</th>
  <td><input type=text name=Name size=20></td>
</tr>
<tr>
  <th align=left>Your address</th>
  <td><textarea cols=20 rows=2 name=Address></textarea></td>
</tr>
<tr><th align=left>Your age</th>
  <td><select name=age size=1>
    <option value=kid>Less than 14
    <option value=teenager>14-19
    ...
    </select>
  </td>
</tr>
<tr>
  <td>Male<input type=radio name=sex checked value=Male></td>
  <td>Female<input type=radio name=sex value=Female></td>
</tr>
```

```
<tr><td colspan=2 align=center><input type=submit value="Submit
details"></td></tr>
</table></form></body>
```

The `PostEmart.inc` include file contains a mix of static HTML and VBScript code to generate a form with selected items. It relies on a further include file, `EmartProducts.inc`; it is this file that contains the data defining the products that are available and provides a function that determines whether a product might suit a customer of a specific age group and sex.

```
<!-- #include file ="EMartProducts.inc" -->
<html><head><title>Our products for you</title>
</head><body>
<h1 align=center>
Products specially selected to appeal to you
</h1>
<%
' Check data from form

Name = request.form("Name")
Address= request.form("Address")
Age= request.form("age")
Sex= request.form("sex")

if Name = "" then
  response.redirect("baddata.html")
end if
if Address = "" then
  response.redirect("baddata.html")
end if
' Save data in session
session.contents("Name") = Name
session.contents("Address") = Address

%>

<form action=page2.asp method=post>
<table align=center border=2>
<caption>Some items of interest</caption>

<%
dim ndx
for ndx=1 to numproducts
  dim ok
  ok = suits(ndx, Age, Sex)
```

```
   if ok then
%>
<tr>
<td><input type=checkbox name=purchase value="<%= title(ndx) %>" </td>
<td align=left><%= title(ndx) %> </td>
</tr>
<%
   end if
next
%>
<tr><td colspan=2 align=center><input type=submit value="Order now!">
</td></tr>
</table></form></body></html>
```

Input data are obtained from the request's 'form' collection. If a user fails to enter data in a required field, the VBScript code arranges for redirection to a simple error report page. If data were entered, the name and address information are saved in the session.contents collection. Then a loop is used to add table entries for suitable items to the purchase form that is displayed.

The details of products, and the function that checks their suitability for a client, are held in another include file:

```
<%
' Arrays defining Emarts products
' (as in PHP example, this is just a simple exercise,
' a real application would get its data from a database)
dim    title(18)
dim    agegroup(18)
dim    gender(18)

dim    numproducts

numproducts = 18

title(1) = "Playstation"
agegroup(1) = "kid"
gender(1) = "Either"

title(2) = "Barbie doll"
agegroup(2) = "kid"
gender(2) = "Female"

...

function suits(item, age, sex)
```

```
' VBScript is similar to Pascal, the return value of a function
' is assigned to a variable with same name as function
suits = (age = agegroup(item)) and ((gender(item) = "Either") or
   (gender(item) = sex))
end function
%>
```

Pages that involve lots of code and static HTML can be simplified through the use of include files (commonly these are given the file extension .inc, but this is not mandatory). If you do use .inc files, you should be careful to set your web server so that these are not available for download; smart hackers can guess filenames and simply submit download requests for script files and thereby gain details of your code (and hence identify vulnerabilities).

The final Page2.asp page has code that retrieves the session variables and lists the chosen purchases. The purchases are multi-choice items. The entry request.contents("purchase") becomes an array that can be accessed by the analysis code. The Count property of the array returns the number of elements defined; standard array subscripting can be used to access the individual purchase choices:

```
<html><head><title>Listing input</title></head>
<body>
<h1 align=center>Listing all data received in form</h1>
<%
   dim itemschosen
   itemschosen = request.form("purchase").Count
   if itemschosen = 0 then
%>
<p>Go back and buy something!
<%
   else
%>
<ol>
<%
   dim ndx
   for ndx = 1 to itemschosen
%>
   <li><%= request.form("purchase")(ndx) %>
<%
   next
%>
</ol>
<%
end if
%>
<p>
```

```
Data received from:
<br>Name : <%= session.contents("Name") %>
<br>Address : <%= session.contents("Address") %>
</body>
</html>
```

B.3 Database access

The e-mart example in the last section is of course a toy. Its data are predefined in arrays, and all it does is list the items chosen. A real web application would obtain the products data from a database, and store the user's submitted order in some other database table. ASP naturally provides database access via ODBC and OLE DB (OLE DB is an extension of ODBC that can handle additional data sources apart from standard relational databases). ASP scripts can obtain a connection to an ODBC or OLE DB data source; a source that is a conventional relational database will handle the usual select, update, insert and delete SQL requests. Connections, and other components, can be obtained from the predefined Server object.

The ASP Server object has a few properties and helper methods (e.g. a timeout value for a script, which helps avoid problems with buggy ASP script pages that have infinite loops, and methods for generating escaped HTML strings etc.). The Server's main role is to act as a factory that can create additional components. Components include:

- A file access component (for reading and writing data files).

- A 'browser capabilities' component (holds details about the browser as obtained from the HTTP request headers; this may be useful if you need to generate complex dynamic HTML pages containing client-side JavaScript code that must be configured for different browsers).

- A logging utility (accesses the IIS server logs).

- PageCounter, Counters, 'Advertisement Rotator' and 'Content Rotator': assorted utilities that help display changing advertisements and so forth.

- Database access component.

The database access component is the most important. It combines parts of the roles that JDBC allocates to java.sql.Connection and java.sql.Statement objects. A database connection can be obtained to a chosen database, and can then be used to submit SQL query and update requests.

Prototypical ODBC style code illustrating the acquisition and use of a database connection is as follows:

```
<%
'Ask for a database connection
' (Basic's "Let" keyword can be omitted from assignments like
```

```
' "x = 3" - rather than "Let x= 3", but the keyword "Set"
' is required when assigning to pointer-like reference
' variables.)
set db = Server.CreateObject("ADODB.Connection")
' Connect to database, the name - MyDatabase - is matched
' to the actual database via the ODBC Data Sources resource
' in the Control Panel
Call db.Open("MyDatabase")
' Define query, standard sql constructs
sql = "Select * from MyTable"
' Create object to store results
Set resultset = Server.CreateObject("ADODB.Recordset")
' Run query on database
Call resultset.Open(sql, db)
' Loop through result set generating rows of an HTML
' table from rows in resultset
resultset.MoveFirst()
while Not resultset.EOF
%>
' Field names match column names in database table
<tr>
    <th><%= resultset.Fields("Name").Value %></th>
    <th><%= resultset.Fields("Address").Value %></th>
    <th><%= resultset.Fields("City").Value %></th>
    <th><%= resultset.Fields("Postcode").Value %></th>
</tr>
<%
Call resultset.MoveNext()
WEND
%>
...
<%
resultset.close
db.close
%>
```

A database connection is created with the createObject request essentially specifying the class of the object that is to be created. The actual connection to the database is made with the open call; the name in this call is the name of a 'System DSN' created using the ODBC Data Sources control in the Windows Control Panel. The example below uses Microsoft Access, which does not require account names and passwords. Account name and password data, as necessary for more sophisticated databases, can be included in the open call in the script or specified in the ODBC Data Sources record.

The SQL request is defined as a string. Since this is a 'select' request, a RecordSet must be created to hold the response data; the Server object is again used to create the additional component. Once the query string, the database connection and the RecordSet for the response have all been created, the request can be run. The retrieved results can then be accessed as illustrated with the while loop structure.

The following example is an ASP version of the E-Pal (email pen friend system) used as an illustration for database access with Perl. The database consists of a single table that holds records on people participating in the scheme; the table can be created directly in Microsoft Access's design view, but conceptually it is defined by the following SQL:

```
CREATE TABLE EPAL
   (email    varchar(32)      NOT NULL,
    type     varchar(8)       NOT NULL,
    want     varchar(8)       NOT NULL,
    interest1   number(4),
    interest2   number(4),
    interest3   number(4),
    interest4   number(4),
    interest5   number(4)
);
```

Participants provide an email contact address, details of their own sex (male, female or 'eperson' for those who prefer not to reveal personal details too early), any requirements for gender of correspondent (male, female, eperson or any), and five interest numbers. These numbers represent interests picked from a fixed list.

The database can be created, as epals.mdb, in the Examples directory within your wwwroot directory. The Data Sources tool in the Control Panel should then be used to create an ODBC entry that references this database (e.g. 'EpalDB' – a 'system DSN' linked to the epals.mdb file). Note that a database set up like this can be downloaded by visitors to your web site (try asking for http://localhost/Examples/epals.mdb!). As noted below, the administration tools used with IIS allow the setting of access restrictions on files; it is not a good idea to allow your database to be quite that readily accessed.

A get operation on the EPAL.asp page results in the display of an application form (opposite); the form allows new members to join or existing members (and non-members) to run searches.

The post operation returns the submitted data to the same EPAL.asp page. If the data represent a request to be added to the database, a new record is created. Otherwise a search is run against the data table that finds existing members with interests that overlap those of the suitor.

Once again, the actual EPAL.asp page is made up from a number of separate include files, each file handling a particular aspect of the task. There is also a supporting Errors.asp page used to report problems like a user entering an email address that already exists as the key for an entry in the database table. The main EPAL.asp page is:

```
<!-- #include file ="EPALInterests.inc" -->
<!-- #include file ="DoAdd.inc" -->
<!-- #include file ="DoSearch.inc" -->
```

Finding an email-friend with common interests

What do you want to do:
○ Add your details to e-pal database
◉ Search the database for contacts

You are
○ Male ○ Female ◉ EPerson

You want to contact
○ Male ○ Female ○ EPerson ◉ Any

Your email address : Emma@hotmail.com

Pick EXACTLY FIVE (5) interests from the following list:

AmateurDramatics
Archery
ArmyReserve
Astronomy
Athletics
AFL
Ballet
Baseball

[Submit Query]

```
<%
' Main part of page starts here!
' Determine request method
    dim   req_method
    req_method = request.servervariables("REQUEST_METHOD")
    if req_method = "GET" then
%>
<!-- #include file ="GetEPAL.inc" -->
<%
  else
%>
<!-- #include file ="PostEPAL.inc" -->
<%
  end if
%>
```

The EPALInterests file contains simply the declaration of an array with the names of the interests; this array is used to populate the HTML selection control. The files DoAdd and DoSearch have the code that accesses the database, performing the logic needed to verify and add a new record and to find existing records that match a request. The GetEPAL file contains the code needed to build the request form, and the POSTEPAL file has the functions needed to resolve a submission and invoke either addition of search operations.

The GetEPAL file is largely static HTML with just a little scripting where the selection list is built from entries in the interests array defined in the EpalInterests file:

```
<html>
<head>
<title>EPals 'R' Us</title>
</head>
<body>
```

```
<h1>Finding an email-friend with common interests</h1>
<form method=post action=EPAL.asp>
What do you want to do:
<br>
<input type=radio name=act value=add>Add your details to E-Pal database
<br>
<input type=radio name=act value=search checked>Search the database for
contacts
<br>
<hr>
You are<br>
<input type=radio name=self value=MALE>Male
<input type=radio name=self value=FEMALE>Female
<input type=radio name=self value=EPERSON checked>EPerson
<br>
<hr>
You want to contact<br>
<input type=radio name=other value=MALE>Male
<input type=radio name=other value=FEMALE>Female
<input type=radio name=other value=EPERSON>EPerson
<input type=radio name=other value=ANY checked>Any
<br>
<hr>
Your email address :
<input type=text size=20 name=email>
<br>
<hr>
Pick EXACTLY FIVE (5) interests from the following list:
<br>
<select name=interests size=8 multiple>
<%
  dim ndx
  for ndx = 1 to numinterests
%>
    <option value="<%= ndx %>"><%= interests(ndx) %>
<%
  next
%>
</select>
<br><hr>
<input type=submit>
<hr>
</form></body></html>
```

The PostEPAL code checks the action selected and invokes the appropriate processing function. The code incorporates a few data validation checks. For example, an 'addition' operation is only valid if an email address of the would-be user is included. The check on the email data is simple; this fragment of code is really intended to illustrate redirection to another error-handling page. An error message is passed through to this page (the message is placed in the session object, from where it can be retrieved by the code in the Errors.asp script).

```
<%
' Check form data
  dim email
  dim action
  dim numinterest

  action = request.form("act")
  email = request.form("email")

  if (action = "add") and (email = "") then
    ' Note lines that are too long are split in this list
    session.contents("EPALERROR") =
", because you didn't give your email address!"
    response.redirect("Errors.asp")
  end if

  numinterest = request.form("interests").count

  if numinterest <> 5 then
    session.contents("EPALERROR") =
", because you did not specify exactly five interests"
    response.redirect("Errors.asp")
  end if

  if action = "add" then
    call doAddRecord()
  elseif action = "search" then
    doSearch
  else
    session.contents("EPALERROR") =
", because didn't understand request!"
    response.redirect("Errors.asp")
  end if
%>
```

The Errors.asp page generates an error response with a specific message taken from the session object:

```
<html><head><title>EPAL System: Error report page</title></head>
<body>
<h1 align=center>Sorry</h1>
<p>
Sorry, but we were unable to handle your request
<%
  dim reason
  reason = session.contents("EPALERROR")
  if reason <> "" then
    response.write(reason)
  end if
%>
.</body></html>
```

The DoAdd file has the code for opening a database connection, creating the SQL statement that will insert data, and then invoking the update operation. The SQL statement is
built up by appending static text and data elements taken from the request form.

```
<%
sub doAddRecord
  set dbw = Server.CreateObject("ADODB.Connection")
  Call dbw.Open("EPalDB")
  sql = "insert into Table1 values ('"
  sql = sql + request.form("email")
  sql = sql + "', '"
  sql = sql + request.form("self")
  sql = sql + "', '"
  sql = sql + request.form("other")
  sql = sql + "', "

  dim ndx
  for ndx = 1 to 5
    sql = sql + request.form("interests")(ndx)
    if ndx < 5 then
      sql = sql + ", "
    end if
  next

  sql = sql + ")"
  dbw.Execute(sql)
  dbw.close
  dim msg
  msg = "<html><head><title>Thank you for joining E-Pals</title></head>"
  msg = msg + "<body><h1>New member</h1>"
  msg = msg +
```

```
"<p>Your details are in the E-Pals database; hope you meet lots of
friends"
  msg = msg + "</body></html>"
  response.write(msg)
end sub
%>
```

The search function is fairly lengthy. The matching criteria are not readily expressed in SQL, so the program must work by retrieving all records and evaluating the match procedurally. A couple of auxiliary functions are used to check gender requirements and to determine whether a particular interest is included in those accompanying the search request. The main structure is, however, quite simple; it is simply connect to the database, submit a query of the form select * from table, and then iterate through the results using a while loop. (Most of the static HTML and content text needed to format a response page are omitted from this listing.)

```
<%

function checkinterest(ival)
  ' check whether interest ival from database record is among interests
  ' listed in request
  dim ok
  dim ndx
  ok = false
  for ndx = 1 to 5
    dim tmp
    tmp = request.form("interests")(ndx)
    tmp = int(tmp)
    ok = ok or (ival = tmp)
  next
  checkinterest = ok
end function

function gendermatch(otherSelf, otherWant)
  dim self
  dim want
  self = request.form("self")
  want = request.form("other")

  dim ok
  ' is requestor of interest to person with record in database
  ok = (self = otherWant) or (otherWant = "ANY")
  ' is person in database of interest to requestor
  ok = ok and (otherSelf = want) or (want = "ANY")
  gendermatch = ok
```

```
end function
sub doSearch
  set db = Server.CreateObject("ADODB.Connection")
  Call db.Open("EPal2")
  sql = "Select * from Table1"
  Set resultset = Server.CreateObject("ADODB.Recordset")
  Call resultset.Open(sql, db)
  resultset.MoveFirst()
  response.write("<html><head><title>E-Pals for you</title></head><body>")
  dim pals
  pals = 0
  while Not resultset.EOF
    dim otherSelf
    dim otherWant
    dim ndx
    dim ival

    otherSelf = resultset.Fields("type")
    otherWant = resultset.Fields("want")

    if genderMatch(otherSelf, otherWant) then
      dim count
      dim interest
      count = 0
      interest = resultset.Fields("interest1")
      interest = int(interest)
      if checkinterest(interest) then
        count = count+1
      end if
' Similar code checking others ...
...
      if count > 2 then
        response.write("<li>")
        response.write(resultset.Fields("Email"))
        pals = pals + 1
      end if

    end if

    Call resultset.MoveNext()
  WEND
  if pals = 0 then
    response.write("Sorry, no matches yet; try again tomorrow")
  else
    response.write("</ul>")
```

```
      end if
      response.write("</body></html>")
      resultset.close
      db.close
   end sub
   %>
```

With Unix and an Apache server one has to consider both Unix file permissions and the access controls that the Apache configuration script sets on directories. The situation with IIS, running on an NT-based system, is somewhat similar. Files have file system 'security' properties that can be set (right click on the file's icon in Windows Explorer, or an ordinary display of a folder, to bring up a menu, then pick 'Properties' to get a dialog where you can set security controls). These security controls employ the user and group names defined for the users of the NT computer; there is an 'Everyone' user to allow general access. The Internet web services components have an additional set of file control properties (accessed via the Internet Information Services tool in Administrator tools). An Explorer-like view allows the subdirectories in the wwwroot directory to be viewed, files selected and permissions set. The web server will use whatever is the more restrictive setting when determining the kind of access that a client may have to a file. You can use the Internet Information Services tool to remove actual read access from the database file and script fragments like the .inc files; this prevents them from being downloaded by inquisitive clients. You will need to set quite open file system access to the directory that contains your database (Microsoft Access may need to create temporary files, so it requires directory modification and write permissions for everyone). If your file system access controls are too restrictive, you will get an error from the ASP interpreter whenever you run a script that tries to perform database operations.

B.4 A touch of class

The .NET version of Visual Basic is a fully fledged object-oriented language; the old Visual Basic 6 language is object-based (you can define classes and instantiate objects, but you cannot utilize inheritance), and VBScript – well, it has some slight pretensions to being classy. Anything elaborate requires the definition of a class in C++ (or Visual Basic), creation of COM component from this code, registration of this component with the operating system, and creation of instances of this class via the Server object's createObject method. It is a long and overly complex process. But even simple classes, such as are supported by VBScript, are useful in improving the quality of ASP code.

The 'hunger' example shown above is crying out for the use of a simple class. Each McDonald's restaurant is characterized by three data elements (address and x and y coordinates); these intrinsically belong together and should not be scattered over three arrays as shown in that code. A McDonald's restaurant should also be responsible for determining how far it is from your given location. The code reworked to use a VBScript class is as follows:

```
<%@ LANGUAGE = VBScript %>
<%
dim myCollection(10)

class MacD
  private m_address
  private m_x
  private m_y

  property get Address()
    Address = m_address
  end property

  property let Address(anAddress)
    m_address = anAddress
  End property

  property let X(xval)
    m_x = xval
  end property

  property let Y(yval)
    m_y = yval
  end property

  public function distance(xcoord, ycoord)
    dim dx
    dim dy
    dx = m_x - xcoord
    dy = m_y -ycoord
    distance = sqr(dx*dx + dy*dy)
  end function
end class

set myCollection(0) = new MacD
myCollection(0).Address = "Crown Street Mall, Wollongong"
myCollection(0).X = 130
myCollection(0).Y = 310


...

set myCollection(5) = new MacD
myCollection(5).Address = "266 Cowper, Warrawong"
myCollection(5).X = 145
myCollection(5).Y = 383
```

```
    dim macCount
    macCount = 5

    ' subroutine and data table
    ' used to define locations of local MacDonalds Restaurants
    sub findMac(x, y)

      dim ndx
      dim choice
      dim mindist
      mindist = 1.0E+6
      for ndx = 0 to macCount
        dist = myCollection(ndx).distance(x,y)
        if dist < mindist then
          choice = ndx
          mindist = dist
        end if
      next
      response.write(myCollection(choice).Address)
    end sub
%>
```

A class is defined by the class <name> ... end class element; it declares data members and member functions with access controls. This class has three private data members; accessor and mutator functions are defined through the property get and property let methods shown. The class also defines a public function distance that computes the distance from a specified point. (You can have a no-argument 'constructor'-like function, which must be named class_Initialize, but you cannot override this with constructors that take arguments.)

Visual Basic 6 supports the concept of a 'collection class', and has a number of such classes predefined; all have to support the same interface with foreach loops etc. Only a few of these classes, like the RecordSet collection associated with a database, are available by default for VBScripts (others can be used if you have suitable classes implemented as COM components). Here a simple array is used to store instances of the MacD class. These are created using the new operator and assigned to elements of the myCollection array (since this is essentially a pointer assignment, the set keyword must be used). Once created, the mutator property methods are used to initialize the data members. Class instances are used in the conventional way, as illustrated by the call to a MacD's distance function from inside the loop in the findMac function.

B.5 More advanced uses of ASP and ASP's future

As tens of thousands of programmers will attest, ASP is widely deployed, being used in a major fraction of current web servers. Many scripts and classes can be purchased to supplement the standard ASP components. For example, you will find that there are several dozen 'shopping cart' components that you can obtain via the WWW that are either free or which can be purchased at relatively low cost. Applications that involve 'roles' and allow different access according to role, like that illustrated with servlets in Section 7.6, can be constructed (though with ASP, constraint definition is more programmatic and less declarative).

With ASP easy to use, and essentially free, it is still worthwhile using in small experiments. However, Microsoft has moved on. Support for the old-style ASP and Visual Basic 6 will be phased out over the next few years. The replacement .NET technology is more ambitious and complex, which may make it somewhat harder when starting; but .NET has numerous advantages. The most obvious for developers is a better model for the interaction between client browser and web server, a model that allows for a consistent and systematic use of objects throughout the code. The consistent object model is coupled with a much improved scheme for separating display text and components from processing code. The revised .NET dialect of Visual Basic is sufficiently different from the Version 6 dialect that if you don't know VB6 it isn't worth learning, and if you do know VB6 you had better forget it. The new server-side languages are more powerful and come with an enhanced library of classes and components (and it is a library which is easier to work with than the older COM extensions for earlier Microsoft systems). The web server is no longer 'scripted' (running a slow interpreter); instead code is compiled into an intermediate form that can be loaded, and then, at run time, there is a final conversion step to actual instructions; the result is faster execution on the server.

Appendix C

.NET

With .NET, Microsoft is working to establish a position of control over Internet-based commercial services and software development similar to that which it already has over desktop computing. The .NET initiative is ambitious. It includes:

- Sophisticated development tools.

- Mechanisms for closer integration of client-side interaction with browser forms and the corresponding server-side processing.

- Support for a variety of languages for server-side programming.

- Emphasis on the concept of integrated web services along with the provision of some frequently used components of a web service.

- An enterprise computing architecture comparable to that introduced in the chapter on EJBs.

The .NET technology is aimed more at enterprise-level web applications than at the simple applications, with a client-side data entry form plus server-side processing and database access, that have been illustrated in the main chapters in this text. But even with lightweight applications, its new features will facilitate development.

The .NET technology is proprietary, platform-specific, closely integrated with Microsoft's OS and Intel machine architectures. (There are suggestions of versions for Linux, even one purportedly from Microsoft, but these are likely to be as elusive and ultimately incomplete as were earlier supposed ports of COM and DCOM to Unix.) Developers from the Unix/Linux communities will have to switch both hardware and software platforms to utilize .NET. Even developers who have traditionally utilized Microsoft products will find some challenges in .NET (for example, the dialect of Basic has evolved substantially, making much existing ASP code incompatible with ASP.NET, while another aspect of change leaves ActiveX controls and similar components partially orphaned, as these have only restricted capability for integration with .NET systems). However, given the resources that Microsoft is able to put into the development and marketing of .NET, it is inevitable that this product group will establish a significant if not dominant position in the market.

There are similarities between some aspects of .NET and the Java technologies. This is more a consequence of 'convergent evolution' of software than it is copying. In the world of software, it is relatively easy for developers to pick up a good idea and adapt and enhance it in some new context. As an example, Microsoft's original ODBC was a smart way of providing database-neutral source code, a concept that reappears in later offerings like JDBC (and it is almost certain that Microsoft's .NET model for web client/web server interaction will be mimicked in future Java offerings). With .NET, 'Java-like' features include:

- 'Managed code' (where a major aspect is support for automatic garbage collection).

- Use of an intermediate code form in compilation and execution (where Java compiles to byte codes that are interpreted, and in limited cases, converted to machine code by hot-spot compilers, .NET languages compile to an intermediate language that is then converted to machine code at run time).

- Mechanisms for deploying components through systems that have declarative style configuration files (like the web.xml files for servlets and the more elaborate deployment files for EJBs).

- Automated support for transactions (as with EJBs).

- Security features similar to those provided by Java's security managers and their permissions lists, these control the access to system resources that is allowed to components.

- Namespace management.

C.1 Visual Studio .NET

You should forget crude development methods like editing code in Notepad and compiling it with a simple javac command at a Command Prompt. To develop for .NET, you really need a costly edition of Visual Studio .NET. Of course, in return for their cost, integrated development environments like Visual Studio do give you a lot of powerful productivity aids.

The .NET version of Visual Studio is a single integrated development environment for all aspects of web application development and all supported languages. Its design draws upon Microsoft's substantial experience with earlier visual integrated environments, such as the Visual Basic and Visual C++ programming environments, the Visual Interdev web application environment and Visual FoxPro database development environment. Typical of a high-end development environment, Visual Studio .NET includes components for:

- Graphical tools for creating both forms and the 'boiler plate' code that is needed to handle the routine aspects of data processing for these forms.

- Sophisticated code editors that are syntax-aware; these incorporate features like automatic font face and font style changes that highlight methods, comments, reserved words and other programming elements, and that can also close and re-open blocks of code (allowing suppression of detail).

- XML editors (with support for the latest XML features such as schemas in preference to DTDs).

- Context-sensitive menus, toolbars and help systems.

- Access to documentation on system-supplied classes.

- Debuggers that allow inspection of the contents of variables at breakpoints or errors (somewhat preferable to the odd `System.out.println` statement); the debugger allows views of the different parts of a multi-tier application.

- Source code version management.

- Tools for database integration.

- Test tools that run scripts that exercise components.

- Prototyping facilities, in the development environment, that allow a preliminary view of the operation of a web site.

- Deployment tools.

- UML design documentation tools.

- Tools for performance analysis of working web applications.

(Some of these components are only available in the higher end "enterprise" editions of the Studio.) Different programming languages are supported through add-in modules, some of which come from third-party suppliers (e.g. ActiveState supplies the modules for Perl and Python).

The studio supports the development of different types of application. It can create simple old-fashioned text-based 'console' applications that run in a Command Prompt window. It incorporates a Winforms component that is used to develop Windows desktop client applications. Winforms applications can make greater usage of the GUI facilities in a Windows system, but obviously are more difficult to deploy on a large scale than are applications that use standard web browsers as clients. Winforms applications may be appropriate for use on local intranets, but most developments will utilize the Webforms and Webservices features of the studio.

The Web forms and services components of the studio automatically generate a substantial amount of 'boiler plate' code and XML deployment specifications that are needed for .NET applications. For example, code generated by Web forms can automate the preservation of state for form-based controls, while the setting of an extra tag on a server method is sufficient to allow the web services component to generate the XML documents needed to describe the service and also generate simple test pages that allow the service to be invoked.

C.2   A new model for web serving

You cannot change HTTP; it is still basically a stateless protocol and all you that you can get from a client is a collection of name/value pairs when the client submits a completed form. So it might seem that you are stuck with a primitive model. The client fills in all the fields of a form. Limited JavaScript checking takes place on each field; if these checks are satisfied, all the data from the form are converted to name/value pairs that are sent to the server. A server script, or process even, is started. This script or program will be essentially procedural code that uses submitted data to populate the fields of some structure and then calls further validation and processing functions that eventually lead to the generation of a response page. While the processing code may make use of objects rather than simple structs, it is at best hybrid (a mix of the OO model and a procedural mainline). (A single instance servlet running a doGet() method that steps through the data unpacking, checking, processing and response writing steps really isn't embodying an object model). The entire mechanism is kludgy, with differing computational models jarring against one another.

A web browser user's experience in terms of interaction is also limited and clumsy. Winforms-style applications in Visual Basic have long provided much more dynamic graphical user interfaces, with the code needed to handle the interface being generated largely automatically. The elements that appear in a form displayed by a Visual Basic program are representations of objects in the underlying program. User actions involving the interface, like button clicks and item selections, are converted to events that are routed to these objects. The object that handles the event can store data entered by the user, and can cause an immediate graphical response that shows the effects of the user's action. Thus a button can handle a click event and get a grid display to update itself with new data taken from some data source. Much of the coding of such connections can be accomplished within a GUI development environment that shows the objects and allows for the establishment of links representing method invocations.

Are we stuck with a clumsy programming model and limited user interaction in our web systems? Not necessarily. All problems in computer science can be solved with one more level of indirection (through a pointer, or an extra layer of interpretive code). With ASP.NET, Microsoft is supplying an extra level of interpretive overhead that provides for a more uniform object-based programming style and potentially a more interactive interface for the user. (It does have costs: each interactive element in a browser-displayed form becomes responsive at the cost of an extra HTTP post request to the server, so server machines are going to be hit with an increased request load. Network delays mean that the interfaces will never be as responsive as Winforms-style applications.)

The new model for web serving is really the old Visual Basic Windows programming model. User controls in HTML pages are visual representations of objects that exist in the server. User actions involving the controls are mapped to events that are passed to server-side objects. These server objects handle the events and create an updated form that is displayed to the user. Programmers write the event-handling code and no longer need be concerned with mechanical details such as the extraction of the name/value pairs. (The request, request.form and response objects used in ASP are all still there, but they only get used for manipulating cookies, finding server parameters and other specialized tasks.)

Of course, all these new mechanisms must still work with old browsers and the limited HTTP request model. A conventional browser cannot be expected to be able to do more than render standard HTML tags and run JavaScript code fragments, so changes on the client side are limited to what can be done with these features. All fancy interactive controls defined in an ASP.NET application will ultimately have to be rendered as HTML controls. HTML controls can have associated 'on-X' events that can be used to trigger JavaScript. The JavaScript associated with an event for a generated HTML button, list or checkbox can fake a form submission request with a chosen set of name/value argument data.

The server-side code will receive these HTTP requests. The name/value pairs submitted can identify the control, the method (the type of 'on-X' event in the browser), and the argument(s) (data in selection boxes, list, text fields etc.). A specialized page class (derived from a system supplied class) will have been defined with methods that handle the events associated with each control displayed in that type of page. The server process will hold an instance of this class and will have to invoke the appropriate method on this instance. The dispatch code needed to read the name/value data and convert these to a method invocation on a server object is totally regular in structure (it is similar to the code used in dispatch functions in RPC-based systems, RMI or CORBA). In addition to the page object, there are other server-side objects that are instances of standard system supplied classes that represent buttons, lists, grids and so forth.

The JavaScript needed in the client and the dispatch code needed in the server may both get quite involved. Such coding is error-prone if done manually, but its regular structure is such that it can all be generated automatically. The compilers in the Visual Studio environment handle this automatic generation.

The source pages for ASP.NET web pages (.aspx pages) are generated using the graphical editors in the studio. They are basically XML-compliant HTML pages (all HTML tags properly closed etc.), but they contain mostly ASP-XML defined tags rather than standard HTML. These ASP-XML tags identify the specialized controls that appear in the displayed browser page. The IIS server must read .aspx pages and generate vanilla HTML pages for display in the client. Details of the client's browser are available at this HTML generation step, so the HTML code generated can take account of differing capabilities. The client-side JavaScript code that will be needed to work with the controls is generated at the same time as the marked up HTML document. (There is a caching mechanism that avoids the repeated translation of pages that will not have changed.)

The code that is to process events involving the controls may be included in the .aspx source page (the result is something like an ordinary ASP page with a script section declaring methods, and then the HTML tags, content text and specialized tags). This is fine for simple examples, but, as evident from the examples on PHP and ASP scripting, it becomes unattractive once the scripts become elaborate. The recommended practice for ASP.NET is to separate concerns. An .aspx file contains HTML tags, content text and specialized ASP-XML tags. The code for handling page events is in a separate 'code behind' file (the file type of this file depends on the implementation language chosen: a Visual Basic file would be .aspx.vb, while a C# implementation would use a .aspx.cs file). The programmer who writes the code must define a class that is derived from Microsoft's System.Web.UI.Page class (e.g. MyNetPageClass). The .aspx file declares that it is defining a subclass of this class, and contains a link to the source file with the programmer's class definition.

C.3   An example of the 'new world order' for web servers

The following example illustrates something of the style of this new web browser to web server relationship. The application involves an imaginary college of higher education. This college has a number of faculties, each of which specifies unit courses on offer to students. The need is for a web-based system where a potential student can pick a faculty, see a list of titles of courses (subjects) on offer, and possibly select a course and get additional data displayed. Course details are to be obtained from database tables.

For this simple example, imagine that the database contains two tables, CodeTable and SubjectTable, with definitions like:

```
Create table CodeTable {
   Code    varchar(10),
   Faculty varchar(10),
   Title   varchar(127)
);

create table SubjectTable (
   Code        varchar(10),
   Description varchar(255),
   Schedule    varchar(127),
   Coordinator varchar(63)
);
```

The conventional solution would probably have a welcome HTML page with a form that has an HTML selection element whose options name the faculties. Submission of this form would result in a CGI program/PHP script/ASP script/servlet extracting the name of the chosen faculty from among the name/value pairs received, running a database select query (select * from CodeTable where Faculty=?) to generate data that are returned in an HTML table that constitutes a part of the returned page. This table of course titles would also include check boxes, and would be part of a form that could be submitted to obtain supplementary details about a chosen course. If this form is submitted, it gets handled by another server-side script or program; this script picks up the name/value pair identifying the selected checkbox and generates a response page with the additional subject details (select * from SubjectTable where Code=?).

A .NET style solution is simpler, and can be made more 'user friendly'. Further, the .NET code generators handle much of the server-side coding. The .NET solution will have a single web page with an interactive listbox that allows a potential student to select from among the faculties, a table (grid) that shows the subjects on offer (by default, showing the subjects offered by the Arts faculty), and a second grid that appears when a particular course (subject) is selected from the table of offers. The main table display listing subjects

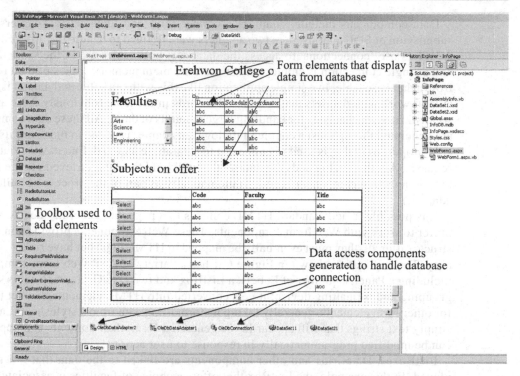

Figure C.1 Visual Studio .NET development.

is set to 'page' through the large collection of subjects on offer, showing them a few at a time. The application is to be fully interactive; a button click on the faculties listbox changes the subjects display table and a click on a selection button in the display table is to result in the appearance of the additional data. The .NET solution involves two main files. One is an XML document defining the appearance of the page, and the second is the 'code behind' document with Visual Basic (.NET dialect) handling the events and the interactions with the database.

Figure C.1 shows a prototype for the .NET page as it is developed within the Visual Studio environment. The development environment is reminiscent of Visual Basic Windows Forms development. The main window shows the structure of the eventual web page; this page is going to be laid out in the browser with form elements placed at defined (x, y) coordinate positions, rather than in accord with the typical flow layout of HTML pages (this is achieved using stylesheets etc.). The toolbox window offers a set of components for the developer; there are 'data components', 'web form' components, 'HTML' components and others. When a component like an ASP listbox has been added to the form, an additional dialog window can be opened; this dialog allows the developer to select options that control the display style for the listbox and provide a link to data that define the elements that will appear in the list. Another window allows for viewing and editing of the code that is being generated in the 'code behind' file associated with the form window.

Data components include 'adapters', 'connections' and 'data sets'. Adapters handle submission of SQL queries; here two adapters were defined to handle the different tables. Adapters use 'connections' to access the database; both tables are in the same database and a single connection is employed. Datasets are main memory copies of data retrieved from a database table. In a simple application like this with fairly limited data, it is reasonable to work with datasets that contain all records in the table (obviously there are more sophisticated mechanisms for handling large amounts of data). All these data components are generated through just a couple of dialogs; an adapter is added to the form, its associated properties dialog is used to connect it to a database and to define its associated SQL requests. Another dialog adds the dataset that will hold the data retrieved via the adapter. (The connection component is added automatically as part of the process of building the adapter.)

It is possible to add standard HTML controls to a page, but generally developers will prefer to work with Web form components. These Web components provide similar constructs (after all, they must eventually be mapped to HTML tags) but have richer functionality. The application shown in Figure C.1 has a variety of ASP Web form components, including a Panel, a number of Labels, a ListBox and two DataGrids. A Panel is simply a grouping and formatting device; it gets converted into HTML elements that set the style for other form elements, generally taking its formatting data from a stylesheet. Labels are simply text strings that will appear in the generated form; their contents and appearance can be modified programmatically in response to user actions.

ListBoxes, DataGrids and other components are linked to the data that must be displayed. In this example, the ListBox that offers a choice of faculties is associated with a list of faculty names; these names were entered via a Visual Studio dialog. The ListBox is set in 'single selection' mode and is an 'auto post back' element, i.e. the browser will automatically post back a request whenever a selection is made in the faculties list. The two datagrids are 'bound' to the datasets that will hold data retrieved from the database. The 'Subjects on Offer' datagrid, which is used to display course code, faculty and title data also has selection action buttons associated with each row. These can activate retrieval of specific subject data. The subject details data grid can be hidden until there are data available for it to display. All these construction details are handled via Visual Studio dialogs.

The page can be switched from 'design' view to 'HTML' view:

```
<%@ Page Language="vb" AutoEventWireup="false"
Codebehind="Erehwon1.aspx.vb" Inherits="InfoPage.Erehwon1"%>
<!DOCTYPE HTML PUBLIC "-//W3C//DTD HTML 4.0 Transitional//EN">
<HTML>
  <HEAD>
...
  </HEAD>
  <body MS_POSITIONING="GridLayout">
    <form id="Form1" method="post" runat="server">
      <asp:listbox id="ListBox1" style="Z-INDEX: 101;
        LEFT: 73px; POSITION: absolute; TOP: 138px"
        runat="server" AutoPostBack="True" Width="151px">
```

```
        <asp:ListItem Value="Arts">Arts</asp:ListItem>
        ...
        <asp:ListItem Value="Law">Law</asp:ListItem>
        ...
    </asp:listbox>
    <asp:label id="Label1" style="Z-INDEX: 102; LEFT: 73px;
        POSITION: absolute; TOP: 82px" runat="server"
        Width="143px" Height="52px"
        Font-Size="XLarge">
        Faculties
    </asp:label>
    ...
    <asp:datagrid id=DataGrid1 ...
        DataSource="<%# DataSet11 %>"
        ... >
        ...
        <Columns>
          <asp:ButtonColumn Text="Select"
            ButtonType="PushButton"
            CommandName="Select">
          </asp:ButtonColumn>
        </Columns>
        ...
    </asp:datagrid>
    ...
  </form>
 </body>
</HTML>
```

At this stage, it is just an XML 'markup document' using mainly Microsoft's ASP tag set. It is also rather like a JSP! The page declares itself as a subclass of the class that Visual Studio and the developer create in the 'code behind' file; the body of the page becomes the body of an output function in this derived class. Just as a compiled JSP is a servlet that runs and writes to its response object, so a .NET page is eventually an instance of .NET managed class that runs and writes to its response object.

When a browser requests the page, the IIS web server will apply the XML transforms and convert these ASP tags into code that writes HTML tags (along with some autogenerated JavaScript code). This code is then run. The resulting vanilla HTML page can be displayed in any reasonably modern web browser, as illustrated in Figure C.2.

The HTML and JavaScript code that resulted from IIS's translation of those ASP tags is:

```
<!DOCTYPE HTML PUBLIC "-//W3C//DTD HTML 4.0 Transitional//EN">
<HTML>
Lots of includes on stylesheets etc
```

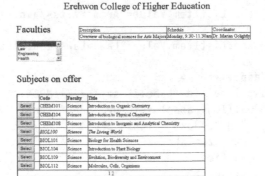

Figure C.2 The page displayed in a browser.

```
<HEAD>
  <title>Erehwon College</title>
  ...
</HEAD>
```
Set page in grid rather than flow mode
```
<body MS_POSITIONING="GridLayout">
```
Define the form, hidden fields for session state identifiers etc.
```
<form name="Form1" method="post" action="Erehwon1.aspx" id="Form1">
  <input type="hidden" name="__EVENTTARGET" value="" />
  <input type="hidden" name="__EVENTARGUMENT" value="" />
  <input type="hidden" name="__VIEWSTATE" value="dDwt...Kq68" />
```

Define JavaScript helper function that posts back form when necessary
```
<script language="javascript">
<!--
  function __doPostBack(eventTarget, eventArgument) {
    var theform = document.Form1;
    theform.__EVENTTARGET.value = eventTarget;
    theform.__EVENTARGUMENT.value = eventArgument;
    theform.submit();
  }
// -->
</script>
```
Declaration of HTML selection and options that correspond to ASP.ListBox with the list of faculties; onchange event invokes a postback.

```
    <select name="ListBox1" id="ListBox1" size="4"
    onchange="__doPostBack('ListBox1','')" language="javascript"
    style="width:151px;Z-INDEX: 101; LEFT: 73px; POSITION:
    absolute; TOP: 138px">
```

```
        <option value="Arts">Arts</option>
        <option selected="selected" value="Science">
          Science</option>
        ...
      </select>
        ...
```

Definition of main HTML table that corresponds to main ASP.DataGrid;
it shows a subset of subjects in the selected faculty, has post-back
selection buttons that get details of selected subject, and has controls
for paging through the full set of subject in the faculty.

```
      <table cellspacing="0" rules="all" bordercolor="Black" ... >
        <tr style="font-weight:bold;">
          <td> </td>
          <td>Code</td>
          <td>Faculty</td>
          <td>Title</td>
        </tr>
```

Entry for a single subject

```
        <tr>
          <td><input type="submit"
            name="DataGrid1:_ctl2:_ctl0"
            value="Select" />
          </td>
          <td>CHEM101</td>
          <td>Science</td>
          <td>Introduction to Organic Chemistry</td>
        </tr>
        <tr>
          ...
        </tr>
        ...
```

Current selection highlighted with italcs

```
        <tr style="font-style:italic;">
          <td>
            <input type="submit"
            name="DataGrid1:_ctl6:_ctl0"
            value="Select" />
          </td>
          <td>BIOL100</td>
          <td>Science</td>
          <td>The Living WOrld</td>
        </tr>
        ...
```

Postback control that "pages" through subjects (there are too
many to show all on one Web page)

```
        <tr align="Center">
          <td colspan="4"><span>1</span> 
            <a href="javascript:__doPostBack
              ('DataGrid1:_ctl12:_ctl1','')">2</a></td>
        </tr>
      </table>
```
Second HTML table, this corresponds to second ASP.DataGrid
```
      <table cellspacing="0" ...
        id="DataGrid2" ...
        <tr>
          <td>Description</td>
          <td>Schedule</td>
          <td>Coordinator</td>
        </tr>
        <tr>
          <td>Overview of biological sciences for
            Arts Majors</td>
          <td>Monday, 9.30-11.30am</td>
          <td>Dr. Marian Golightly</td>
        </tr>
      </table>
    </form>
   </body>
  </HTML>
```

The translated form is all in standard HTML. There is a small JavaScript function that does a form post back whenever there is an 'on change' event in the HTML selection list of faculties, or when the page fields in the main table are used. The buttons in the table are submit buttons with names that identify the table row selected. (The _VIEWSTATE hidden field is an exceedingly long session key; ASP.NET pages can keep persistent data in Session and Application collections, either in memory or in database tables.)

Of course, there does have to be some *real* code associated with the application, and the developer does have to write parts of this code, even if much is handled by the development environment. The code is in the 'code behind' file and is as follows (some extra line breaks have been added to allow the code to fit on the printed page):

```
Public Class Erehwon1
  Inherits System.Web.UI.Page
  'This Basic dialect has real class, complete with inheritance!
  'Here define an application specific subclass of stand Page class

  'An instance of Erehwon1 owns a ListBox, two DataGrids, two labels, some
  'Adapters, DataSets, and Connections
  Protected WithEvents ListBox1 As System.Web.UI.WebControls.ListBox
  Protected WithEvents Label1 As System.Web.UI.WebControls.Label
```

```
    Protected WithEvents Label2 As System.Web.UI.WebControls.Label
    Protected WithEvents OleDbDataAdapter1 As
      System.Data.OleDb.OleDbDataAdapter
    Protected WithEvents OleDbSelectCommand1 As
      System.Data.OleDb.OleDbCommand
    Protected WithEvents OleDbConnection1 As
      System.Data.OleDb.OleDbConnection
    Protected WithEvents DataSet11 As InfoPage.DataSet1
    Protected WithEvents DataGrid1 As System.Web.UI.WebControls.DataGrid
    Protected WithEvents OleDbDataAdapter2 As
      System.Data.OleDb.OleDbDataAdapter
    Protected WithEvents OleDbSelectCommand2 As
      System.Data.OleDb.OleDbCommand
    Protected WithEvents DataGrid2 As System.Web.UI.WebControls.DataGrid
    Protected WithEvents DataSet21 As InfoPage.DataSet2
    Protected WithEvents Panel1 As System.Web.UI.WebControls.Panel

#Region " Web Form Designer Generated Code "
' Big chunk of code created by Visual Studio, much of it code to
' support debugging.
' Standard code for a Page class defined in superclass
...

#End Region
Code to handle "events" for the various web page elements.
There will be a 'load page' event whenever page resumes;
a listbox selection index change event when user picks a
faculty, and datagrid page change and item selection events.
Page object gets called to handle these events, and operates
on objects that represent the controls.

    Private Sub Page_Load(ByVal sender As System.Object,
        ByVal e As System.EventArgs) Handles MyBase.Load
      If Not IsPostBack Then
        loadSubjectData("Arts")
      End If
    End Sub

How should page handle a listbox selection index change?
Well, it should ask the listbox what item (faculty) is currently selected,
and arrange to load the relevant data into main datagrid
    Private Sub ListBox1_SelectedIndexChanged(ByVal sender As System.Object,
        ByVal e As System.EventArgs)
        Handles ListBox1.SelectedIndexChanged
      Dim which As String
```

```
            which = ListBox1.SelectedItem.Value
            loadSubjectData(which)
        End Sub
```

Helper function for loading data (about the only part of the code that is really entirely the responsibility of developer!)

*Database adapter is working with a 'prepared statement' of form "select * from CodeTable where Faculty=?"; set the parameter. Then get the adapter to run the query and refill the in-memory data set.*
Then tell DataGrid to reload its data from this dataset.
(Since no subject selected yet, hide the second grid.)

```
        Private Sub loadSubjectData(ByVal whichFaculty As String)
            OleDbDataAdapter1.SelectCommand.Parameters("Faculty").Value =
                        whichFaculty
            DataSet11.Clear()

            OleDbDataAdapter1.Fill(DataSet11)
            DataGrid1.DataBind()
            DataGrid1.SelectedIndex = -1
            DataGrid2.Visible = False

        End Sub
```

How should the page handle a selection in main grid?
It should ask the grid object for code number of selected subject, then it should again get a data adapter to set its SQL parameters, run a query and load an in-memory data set.
Finally, it should tell the other grid object to display the retrieved data.

```
        Private Sub DataGrid1_ItemCommand(ByVal source As Object,
            ByVal e As System.Web.UI.WebControls.DataGridCommandEventArgs)
                Handles DataGrid1.ItemCommand

        If e.CommandName = "Select" Then
            Dim subjectCode As String
            subjectCode = e.Item.Cells(1).Text
            OleDbDataAdapter2.SelectCommand.Parameters("Code").Value =
                subjectCode
            DataSet21.Clear()

            OleDbDataAdapter2.Fill(DataSet21)
            DataGrid2.DataBind()
            DataGrid2.Visible = True
```

```
        End If
    End Sub
```

How should the page handle a user's request to display a
different page from the list of all subjects offered by a
Faculty?
It should find which page is required (by asking the event
Object that holds these data), it should confirm which faculty
is selected (by asking the listbox with the faculty list), and
then it should again invoke the data adapter loading mechanism.

```
    Private Sub DataGrid1_PageIndexChanged(ByVal source As Object,
        ByVal e As System.Web.UI.WebControls.DataGridPageChangedEventArgs)
            Handles DataGrid1.PageIndexChanged
    Dim currentFaculty As String
    If (ListBox1.SelectedIndex > -1) Then
        currentFaculty = ListBox1.SelectedItem.Value
    Else
        currentFaculty = "Arts"
    End If
    DataGrid1.CurrentPageIndex = e.NewPageIndex
    loadSubjectData(currentFaculty)
    End Sub
End Class
```

The code style is quite different from any other web server model illustrated in this text. Instead of largely procedural code to rummage through a collection of name/value pairs and writing HTML text line by line, we now have a specialized Page object that owns some components like ListBoxes and which handles events (commands) affecting the components that it owns.

In this example, four functions had to be defined by the developer; three are overrides for default 'do nothing' functions provided in the framework, and the fourth is an application-specific auxiliary function. The page_load function is invoked each time the page is accessed (which will be the first get from a browser and all subsequent post requests). The first invocation sets up the default contents of the main data grid.

The other two 'event handling' functions deal with user selections in the listbox or in the main subjects table. Note the code style: it is all a matter of asking other objects for values in data members or asking other objects to perform functions. The ListBox1 object is asked for the string with the name of the faculty that was selected; the DataGridCommandEventArgs object that represents the selection action on the HTML table is asked for the contents of a particular column in the selected table row. DataAdapters are requested to rerun parameterized queries and to fill datasets.

At no point are there statements actually writing text to the response page. HTML page generation is automatic and is performed once all grids, listboxes etc. have been updated with rebound data.

This new model does involve overheads. However, it is so convincingly better for the developer that it is inevitable that similar component libraries and runtime support functions will appear in the Java world and possibly in association with future versions of Perl and PHP systems.

C.4 Programming languages

Microsoft has several objectives in this part of the .NET initiative. First, Microsoft expanded the range of languages that could be used for development and invented a couple of new ones. Second, the 'Common Type System' guarantees that components developed in different languages will interoperate. The Common Type System also includes a large class hierarchy of system-supplied classes. It is a language neutral class hierarchy; a particular class might be implemented in C#; a VB or C++ programmer can use instances of that class, and can even define new derived classes. All will interoperate, so allowing separate parts of an application to be implemented in differing languages. A third aspect of this facet of .NET is the common Microsoft Intermediate Language (MSIL or IL). It is IL that makes it possible to support multilingual development; at the IL level, all languages become the same. A class defined in particular programming languages gets compiled to IL to produce structures with meta-data describing the class and its methods, and code data with the IL code implementing the methods (much like a Java .class file). Fourthly, there is the Common Runtime system. This is responsible for processing IL code; it deals with conversion to real instruction code sequences, security controls, memory management and so forth.

Earlier generations of developers using Microsoft software overwhelmingly chose VBScript in their ASP pages, but there were always alternatives such as Perl scripting. With .NET, the server side has been opened up to many more languages (there are claims for around twenty, including Fortran, Cobol, Perl, Python and Microsoft's J# dialect of Java). Microsoft's favorite is C#. For a long time, Microsoft restricted its own developers to a 'sane subset of C++'; C# is kind of a realization of this concept in a distinct language. C++ can work in its unfettered, full capability mode, but this produces 'unmanaged' executables that do not fully integrate with the .NET framework; if restrictions are complied with, C++ can generate 'managed' IL code.

A new web-based development should not seek to employ multiple languages, for such usage will lead to maintenance problems. The ability to use multiple languages is more a benefit during migration to the .NET system and eventual standardization (presumably on C# if Microsoft continues its current line). Meanwhile, developers can utilize their existing expertise in particular languages and learn to use the .NET system and to exploit its class libraries.

The Common Type System defines standard IL data types. In earlier Microsoft implementations of distributed computing (DCOM etc.) there were always problems with things like very different representations of strings in Visual Basic and C++. Such differences complicated the development of interoperable COM components. In future, all languages will use the same data types.

The Common Type System starts (in a very Java-ish manner) by distinguishing value types, like integers, and reference types. Simple value types now all have the same representation irrespective of language, with defined sizes for integer, long and other built-in types. Instances of reference types will contain 'pointers to objects in the heap'. Objects are naturally instances of classes; the CTS model for its class system is quite similar to that of Java, with one extension to partially accommodate 'unmanaged code' (with real C++ classes and pointers) within the overall type framework. Like Java, the CTS model for classes envisages a single inheritance tree with a root class (System.object). Of course, single inheritance is too limiting, but it is not wise to follow C++ and take on the full complexities inherent in a multiple inheritance scheme. Instead, a class can implement more than one interface, but can only inherit from one parent class.

A CTS 'reference' is an abstraction. Reference types can be pointers (this is where real hard core C++ hackers can fit in), interfaces, or 'self-describing types'. Self-describing types can be arrays of other types (arrays all derive from a System.Array class), or classes (echoes of Java once again). (There are a few more exotic types, for example 'delegates'; these happen to be something like a function pointer as used in C/C++.)

Unmanaged code (typically, C++) can create objects in the C++ heap and access these via pointers. However, most code will be managed code that creates instances of managed classes; these are created in the heap area controlled by the common language runtime system and and which are reference counted and garbage collected. These classes:

- Can implement multiple interfaces but have a single parent class (and are ultimately derived from System.Object).

- Use private, protected and public access control qualifiers on members.

- Can have:
  - Fields (data members).
  - Properties (somewhat like CORBA attributes, these appear as readable or read/write data members but may be implemented as functions).
  - Methods.
  - Events; something akin to making a Java class implement one of the Listener interfaces; event handling allows an object to be passed 'events' that ultimately derive from user actions on a GUI interface.

Self-describing types have meta-data associated with them (just like the instance of the Class class in Java that holds the meta-data that describe the methods of a Java class). There is a hierarchical naming system that resembles that used for packages in Java. The System namespace groups system supplied functionality into separate namespace units that contain definitions of appropriate classes; for example it contains:

- System.Collections: (arraylist, sortedlist, hashtable, comparer)

- System.Text (classes for encoding strings e.g. a Unicode encoder)

- System.Security (security manager and similar classes)

- System.Security.Cryptography (classes for DES encryption, MD5 digests and so forth)

- `System.Runtime.Remoting` (classes for a part of .NET that is generally comparable with Java Remote Method Invocation; it also includes classes needed for SOAP)

- `System.Data` (classes needed to tie applications to databases)

- `System.Threading`

- `System.Reflection`

While some parts are new, many of these services were available in earlier Windows environments. The reworking is, however, a major improvement, as it changes the Windows system interface from a collection of five thousand arbitrary functions into a well-structured and documented hierarchy.

Classes created by .NET developers should be created in namespaces defined using the company name as a root name (once again, this is similar to the Java package conventions).

A .NET application will require a specific set of classes that must be correctly deployed into a working directory. Here, the .NET framework introduces the concept of 'assemblies'; an assembly has a manifest file that specifies the files that comprise the application (the files include `.aspx` web files and `.cs` or `.vb` 'code behind' files, along with XML files and schema and other configuration files). (There is no really good Java analogue to an assembly; an assembly's manifest contains some of the deployment data that might appear in a 'web application archive' (`.war`) file, or an 'enterprise application archive' (`.ear`) file.) Earlier Windows object models like COM emphasized the sharing of component code among applications, and had rather complex mechanisms for registering shareable components with the operating system. The new system is much simpler, but still makes provision for shareable components if these are desired. In addition to listing the components in its manifest, an assembly can also contain security constraints controlling the use of components. An assembly's name becomes a part of the fully qualified names of those classes that are defined within it. Assemblies also support versioning. If a web-based project is undergoing rapid development, you may have client applications that expect to link with different versions of the components; these will get to work with the appropriate versioned assemblies. (Limits on sharing of component code, and proper versioning, will reduce the occurrence of a peculiar Windows malady, known as 'DLL hell', that occurs when one application replaces a shared component with a new improved version that is not appreciated by those other applications that previously shared the original.)

The actual runtime files in an assembly are MSIL executables. MSIL is officially an 'open standard' (having received an imprimatur from a European standards committee). Its form defines a kind of high-level assembly language for an idealized stack machine (there is a disassembler somewhere in the .NET toolchest so you can view the code generated by a .NET compiler). MSIL loaders perform a verification step similar to that used in Java class loaders; this checking verifies that the code is type-secure and is not manipulating objects in inappropriate ways; nor is it performing tricks with reference values or stack frames. (Of course code that comes through .NET compilers doesn't do any of those awful things, but you do have to allow for carefully hand-coded MSIL assembly source created by a hacker of evil intent.)

MSIL is converted to machine instructions for a specific architecture and runtime operating system by a 'Just In Time' compiler (or Jitter). Some interpretive overhead will remain even in Jitted code. As in Java, operations that involve operating system resources must be checked against the security constraints defined for a component, so method invocations will often involve lengthy checking prior to an actual 'jump to subroutine' instruction.

The common language runtime system is responsible for loading, verifying, interpreting, Jitting and applying declarative access constraints when running MSIL code. It is also responsible for thread management and garbage collection. Its Java analogue is the Java Virtual Machine. The runtime provides for more security in running downloaded code than was possible with the earlier ActiveX controls (for these had full access to a host machine once downloaded and started).

C.5   Web services

The Microsoft company is one of the true believers in the future importance of web services. A web service is typically defined in terms like 'programmable application logic accessible via the Internet'. Web services are fundamentally just remotely accessed functions (or invocations of methods of remote objects in an object world). Although many examples given for web services imply use by human users via web browsers or fat client applications, web services are intended more for the context of program-to-program communication. A particular client application program invokes remote services offered by other server applications.

Once again, Visual Studio .NET (together with some auxiliary programs) offers a substantial amount of support for web service development, and a well conceived object style of programming. There are two aspects to be covered – being a client of a web service, and being a service provider.

A program that is to be a client of an existing web service will have to invoke operations that are described in the published WSDL document that defines the service. From the client's perspective, the web service is just another object that has public methods; obviously, the best approach is to have a little stub object that mimics the remote interface. Client code invokes operations on the stub; these result in requests that pass across the network to the server. The result, in the form of an XML response document, will be parsed by the stub, which will return the data to the calling code. The .NET environment supports this proxy object model. (It isn't the only possible model. The Apache Java client and the Perl client both involve code that has the client instantiating some form of 'SOAP Request' object and invoking methods to set the name of the remote method, and to define names and values of parameters.)

With .NET, you take the WSDL document that defines the remote service and run it through a stub generator (very similar to rmic for Java RMI or an IDL 'compiler' for CORBA IDL). For example, the www.xmethods.com site recently listed a newly published 'Web Service' that allows a program to invoke a service that can return the atomic weight, chemical symbol and atomic number for all elements. (In the past, one would never have considered anything other than a static initialized data array for such data; but no matter, this is the Internet age, so let us exploit the web.) This useful service, implemented using Microsoft .NET, is hosted by www.webservicex.net. A part of the WSDL document that defines the service is:

```xml
<?xml version="1.0" encoding="utf-8"?>
<definitions xmlns:http="http://schemas.xmlsoap.org/wsdl/http/"
xmlns:soap="http://schemas.xmlsoap.org/wsdl/soap/"
...
targetNamespace="http://www.webservicex.net" xmlns="http://
schemas.xmlsoap.org/wsdl/">
  <types>
    <s:schema elementFormDefault="qualified"
        targetNamespace="http://www.webservicex.net">
      <s:element name="GetAtoms">
        <s:complexType />
      </s:element>
      <s:element name="GetAtomsResponse">
        <s:complexType>
          <s:sequence>
            <s:element minOccurs="0" maxOccurs="1"
              name="GetAtomsResult" type="s:string" />
          </s:sequence>
        </s:complexType>
      </s:element>
      <s:element name="GetAtomicWeight">
        <s:complexType>
          <s:sequence>
            <s:element minOccurs="0" maxOccurs="1" name="ElementName"
              type="s:string" />
          </s:sequence>
        </s:complexType>
      </s:element>
      <s:element name="GetAtomicWeightResponse">
        <s:complexType>
          <s:sequence>
            <s:element minOccurs="0" maxOccurs="1"
              name="GetAtomicWeightResult" type="s:string" />
          </s:sequence>
        </s:complexType>
      </s:element>
...
      <s:element name="string" nillable="true" type="s:string" />
    </s:schema>
  </types>
  <message name="GetAtomsSoapIn">
```

```
        <part name="parameters" element="s0:GetAtoms" />
    </message>
...
    <message name="GetElementSymbolHttpPostOut">
      <part name="Body" element="s0:string" />
    </message>
    <portType name="PeriodicTableSoap">
      <operation name="GetAtoms">
        <documentation>Get element list</documentation>
        <input message="s0:GetAtomsSoapIn" />
        <output message="s0:GetAtomsSoapOut" />
      </operation>
      <operation name="GetAtomicWeight">
        <documentation>Get atomic wieght by element name</documentation>
        <input message="s0:GetAtomicWeightSoapIn" />
        <output message="s0:GetAtomicWeightSoapOut" />
      </operation>
      <operation name="GetAtomicNumber">
        <documentation>Get atomic Number by element name</documentation>
        <input message="s0:GetAtomicNumberSoapIn" />
        <output message="s0:GetAtomicNumberSoapOut" />
      </operation>
...
    </portType>
    <portType name="PeriodicTableHttpGet">
      <operation name="GetAtoms">
        <documentation>Get element list</documentation>
        <input message="s0:GetAtomsHttpGetIn" />
        <output message="s0:GetAtomsHttpGetOut" />
      </operation>
...
    </portType>
...
    <binding name="PeriodicTableSoap" type="s0:PeriodicTableSoap">
      <soap:binding transport="http://schemas.xmlsoap.org/soap/http"
        style="document" />
      <operation name="GetAtoms">
        <soap:operation soapAction="http://www.webservicex.net/GetAtoms"
          style="document" />
        <input>
          <soap:body use="literal" />
        </input>
        <output>
          <soap:body use="literal" />
        </output>
```

```
    </operation>
    <operation name="GetAtomicWeight">
...
    </operation>
...
  </binding>
  <binding name="PeriodicTableHttpGet" type="s0:PeriodicTableHttpGet">
...
  </binding>
...
  <service name="PeriodicTable">
    <port name="PeriodicTableSoap" binding="s0:PeriodicTableSoap">
      <soap:address
        location="http://www.webservicex.net/periodictable.asmx" />
    </port>
...
  </service>
</definitions>
```

This service can return a string with a list of the element names (the no argument function
GetAtoms), and can return the weight, atomic number and symbol of an element specified
by name.

The .NET system can read such a WSDL file and will produce a client proxy class with
the following definition:

```
Imports System
...
Imports System.Web.Services
Imports System.Web.Services.Protocols
Imports System.Xml.Serialization

Public Class PeriodicTable
  Inherits System.Web.Services.Protocols.SoapHttpClientProtocol

  Public Sub New()
    MyBase.New
    Me.Url = "http://www.webservicex.net/periodictable.asmx"
  End Sub

  '<remarks/>
<System.Web.Services.Protocols.SoapDocumentMethodAttribute("http://
www.webservicex.net/GetAtoms", RequestNamespace:="http://
www.webservicex.net", ResponseNamespace:="http://www.webservicex.net",
Use:=System.Web.Services.Description.SoapBindingUse.Literal,
```

```
      ParameterStyle:=System.Web.Services.Proto-
    cols.SoapParameterStyle.Wrapped)> _
    Public Function GetAtoms() As String
       Dim results() As Object = Me.Invoke("GetAtoms", New Object(-1) {})
       Return CType(results(0),String)
    End Function

    Public Function BeginGetAtoms(ByVal callback As System.AsyncCallback,
       ByVal asyncState As Object) As System.IAsyncResult
       Return Me.BeginInvoke("GetAtoms", New Object(-1) {},
          callback, asyncState)
    End Function

    Public Function EndGetAtoms(ByVal asyncResult As System.IAsyncResult)
       As String
       Dim results() As Object = Me.EndInvoke(asyncResult)
       Return CType(results(0),String)
    End Function

    '<remarks/>
    <System.Web.Services.Protocols.SoapDocumentMethodAttribute("http://
    www.webservicex.net/GetAtomicWeight", RequestNamespace:="http://
    www.webservicex.net", ResponseNamespace:="http://www.webservicex.net",
    Use:=System.Web.Services.Description.SoapBindingUse.Literal,
    ParameterStyle:=System.Web.Services.Proto-
    cols.SoapParameterStyle.Wrapped)> _
    Public Function GetAtomicWeight(ByVal ElementName As String) As String
       ...
    End Function

    ...
End Class
```

(The default is to generate C# code; here a Visual Basic client stub was explicitly requested.)

Each of the public functions defined via the server WSDL document becomes a set of three methods in the generated class. Functions like GetAtoms() are normal synchronized functions; they block the calling thread until a response is received from the Web Service. SOAP systems also support an asynchronous call, return mechanism. A program could invoke the BeginGetAtoms() function which would dispatch the SOAP request packet and then return. The program could continue with other work until it needed the response, at which point it would call EndGetAtoms(); this call would block until the response was received.

An instance of this PeriodicTable class could be created in any program that needed this service. When operations were invoked on the PeriodicTable object, it would get out onto the Internet and communicate with the server at www.webservicex.net. For this example, the client program is an aspx.vb program that uses the PeriodicTable web service to place data in a web page (this is purely for illustration; a web service client does not itself have to be involved with web-style processing).

The example program displays a web page with the list of elements in one asp:label field, an asp:textbox for input of a chosen element name, and three more label fields for the data retrieved for the chosen element. The textbox is set to cause a post operation whenever its contents are changed.

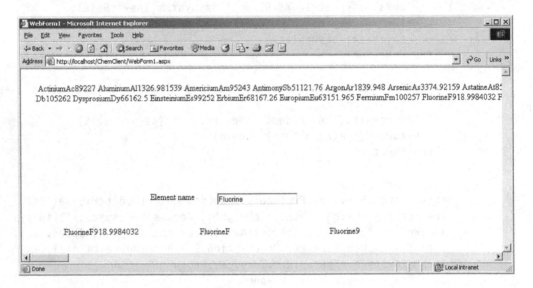

Figure C.3 Client page for Atomic Weight Web Service.

The 'code behind' is:

```
Public Class Chem1
  Inherits System.Web.UI.Page
  Protected WithEvents TextBox1 As System.Web.UI.WebControls.TextBox
  Protected WithEvents Weight As System.Web.UI.WebControls.Label
...
  Protected WithEvents AtomicNumbe As System.Web.UI.WebControls.Label
  Private myTable As PeriodicTable = New PeriodicTable()

  Private Sub Page_Load(ByVal sender As System.Object,
    ByVal e As System.EventArgs) Handles MyBase.Load
      TheElements.Text = myTable.GetAtoms
  End Sub

  Private Sub TextBox1_TextChanged(ByVal sender As Object,
    ByVal e As System.EventArgs) Handles TextBox1.TextChanged
```

```
            Dim element As String
            element = TextBox1.Text
            Weight.Text = myTable.GetAtomicWeight(element)
            Weight.Visible = True
            Symbol.Text = myTable.GetElementSymbol(element)
            Symbol.Visible = True
            AtomicNumbe.Text = myTable.GetAtomicNumber(element)
            AtomicNumbe.Visible = True
        End Sub
    End Class
```

As is quite common, this Web Service did not operate as expected; the returned values for weight, atomic number and symbol all have these data appended to strings with the element name.

Creating your own Web Service is just as easy. Given the other services that have been published via the registries, an 'enlightenment' service, similar to that offered by the JSP Guru example, should prove a winner. Visual Studio has an ASP.NET Web Service option that allows such services to be built and tested. The service is defined as a simple class with one method, EnlightenMe. The code is

```
Imports System.Web.Services

<WebService(Namespace := "http://tempuri.org/")> _
Public Class Guru
    Inherits System.Web.Services.WebService

    ...

    <WebMethod()> Public Function EnlightenMe() As String
        Randomize()
        Dim choice As Integer
        Dim str As String
        choice = 500 * Rnd()
        Select Case choice
        Case 0
            str = "Those whom the gods love grow young."
        Case 1
            str = "Alas, I am dying beyond my means."
        ...
        ...
        End Select
        Return str
    End Function
End Class
```

All that the programmer need do is tag the appropriate methods with the `WebMethod()` tag. Visual Studio .NET generates the associated WSDL document, and a test infrastructure that allows the operations defined by the service to be invoked. The generated web pages that form part of this testing infrastructure illustrate the appropriate forms for HTTP-style access to the Enlightenment web service as well as the SOAP packages that would have to be exchanged. This page also incorporates an HTTP get invocation on the service, thus allowing for actual testing; it results in the display of the XML response with a chosen aphorism.

When the service had been fully tested, it could be deployed onto a web server machine and then be registered with one of the UDDI servers. Its registration would define a URL for the `asmx` file. When IIS receives a request for this resource, it would instantiate and run a Guru Web Service object.

C.6 Microsoft infrastructure and Web Services

Microsoft already provides support services, some of which use the Web Service-style invocations. These include Passport, Wallet, an Alert service and the MapPoint Web Service.

Microsoft Passport is currently the most important. At least twenty million Internet citizens already hold Microsoft Passports. The service provides a single login account that can be shared by numerous independent commercial sites. It is implemented using purely standard HTTP.

Passport works using browser session cookies. When you start your browser (on your own machine or on some Internet café machine), there are no cookies set. You go to the `www.cheapcds.com` site and choose to 'login' so that the CheapCDs company can recognize you as a regular customer with special discount privileges etc. The 'login' button on `www.cheapcds.com` is actually a redirect back to a machine in Microsoft's `passport.com` site; the link has a query string that supplies data identifying the CheapCDs page, to which you will return when login has been completed. When your browser switches to go to the passport site, it remembers to send any `passport.com` cookies, but there aren't any yet. Login is handled by the Microsoft site (the web page used for login is either the Microsoft standard, or a co-branded page contributed by CheapCDs). The Microsoft site returns a redirection page to the browser; this page has some `passport.com` cookies. These redirection data reference the appropriate CheapCDs page, and have a query string that contains your passport identity in encrypted form (the encryption key is unique to each participating company). The CheapCDs site now has your details and their page encodes these in their own 'passport session cookies' that are returned with their personalized welcome page. All subsequent interactions between you and the CheapCDds site use these `cheapcds.com` cookies, allowing the site to track you and maintain session state.

If you now jump to another Passport site, CheapBooks, you will get first the general public entry page with a login button. When you try to login to CheapBooks, your browser is again redirected to the Microsoft Passport site; of course, your browser attaches its `passport.com` cookies when it goes to this site. The Microsoft site recognizes you as logged in, and does not redisplay a login page. Instead, it encrypts your Passport details (this time with the key agreed with CheapBooks) and bounces you back to the CheapBooks site with your details hidden in a query string.

The Wallet system is currently a holder for data like your credit card number and expiry date. Sites that participate in Wallet can obtain these data from Microsoft servers for a logged in Passport user who has selected to use the additional Wallet services. This avoids re-entry of credit information.

The Alert system illustrates how Microsoft (and other companies; Microsoft is just quicker starting) hope to get a 'service' role handling routine web tasks for other companies. Alerts are public notices from companies to customers, useful for special offers, announcements of new products or product recalls, and similar activities. Microsoft Alerts will work for combinations of companies that wish to use this service, and customers who elect to be Alert aware. Conventionally, a company would simply maintain its own list of registered customers and send emails. With Microsoft Alert, customers establish profiles that identify the companies from which they wish to receive alerts and supply additional data specifying the preferred form of alert (for example, the system can send an alert as an SMS message to a mobile phone rather than as an SMTP mail message). Companies that wish to send information to their customers give it instead to Microsoft. Microsoft then distributes the information for a small charge (such as US$0.75 per message per customer). Such services are attractive to Microsoft as they establish a nice degree of dependency amongst client companies (who no longer have lists of those of their own customers who wish to receive product information).

The MapPoint service, described briefly in Chapter 11, is Microsoft's Web Service for geographical data.

C.7 Enterprise architecture

There are significant similarities between the overall .NET architecture and the J2EE Enterprise Java architecture. In both systems, interaction with clients is handled by server objects that are instantiated on demand in some form of 'container'. The code for these objects is 'managed', which basically means that the system handles most aspects of resource management (garbage collection, thread pools, database connections etc.) and that there is some interpretive aspect to code execution that allows for security controls to be applied to all operating system-related functionality. Both systems provide a substantial degree of automation for database access, allow applications to involve objects instantiated in different containers on different machines, have declarative support for transactions, have users with roles and role constraints on functionality, and use XML deployment descriptors.

In the Java world, the front-end objects are servlets that are instantiated in a Web container. These servlets may be organizational servlets that handle the receipt of the request and invocations on other objects (beans or EJB objects), and forward results to other servlets for final formatting of response pages. Other servlets will be Web Service servlets (with the common Apache SOAP system, Web Services are implemented as classes whose methods will be invoked by a more-or-less generic servlet that handles receipt of SOAP requests and composition of SOAP responses). The final group of servlets will be those generated from JSPs. In the .NET world, the main client interaction components are the objects that are generated for .aspx pages and which are instantiated in 'common language runtime' environments accessible from IIS. In both systems, these objects are typically stateless (any state data being kept in separate Session or Application objects), instantiated on demand, reused as appropriate, and garbage collected when necessary. Related XML files contain deployment data with any access control requirements.

The front-end objects are limited to control flow, extraction of input data, and generation of the final 'pretty page' response. Any real work will be done by other objects, which are instantiated and used by these front-end objects. These other objects will include instances of application-specific classes that embody business rules, and instances of system supplied or auto-generated classes that handle database access. In a simple servlet system, these other objects will be instantiated in the same virtual machine. In an EJB-based system, these other objects are in 'containers' other than the web server container; typically, these containers will be hosted on other machines. The .NET architecture has similar provision for object distribution. With .NET, objects can be 'remoted'. If an object is remoted, the front-end code ends up with a stub object from some auto-generated class, while the real implementation object exists in another CLR environment, again most likely running on some other machine.

The .NET 'data sets' correspond to collections of entity beans. The code for these datasets is auto-generated, and so compares with container-managed persistence schemes for EJBs. In simple cases, a dataset is a read-only, in-memory copy of data taken from a database; in more complex applications, the datasets are more like SQL-obtained data collections with a moveable cursor and update attributes.

The Java systems have the advantages of greater maturity, multiple vendors and a degree of systems independence. The .NET system is entirely new; Microsoft has had to create a class library comparable to that which evolved for Java over seven years. The .NET advantages include a better web client/web server model, better product focus from a company with a very clear mission, an ability to gain some leverage from a near monopoly control of the client environment, and marketing that eclipses Sun's Java efforts.

Index